FRENCH INTERNATIONAL POLICY UNDER DE GAULLE AND POMPIDOU

The Politics of Grandeur

By the Same Author

The Uncommon Defense and Congress, 1945–1963

FRENCH INTERNATIONAL POLICY UNDER DE GAULLE AND POMPIDOU

The Politics of Grandeur

EDWARD A. KOLODZIEJ

Copyright © 1974 by Cornell University.

All rights reserved. Except for brief quotations in a review, this book, or parts thereof, must not be reproduced in any form without permission in writing from the publisher. For information, address Cornell University Press, 124 Roberts Place, Ithaca, New York 14850.

First published 1974 by Cornell University Press.
Published in the United Kingdom by Cornell University Press Ltd., 2-4 Brook Street, London W1Y 1AA.

Cornell University Press

ITHACA AND LONDON

First published 1974 by Cornell University Press.
Published in the United Kingdom by Cornell University Press Ltd., 2-4 Brook Street, London W1Y 1AA.

International Standard Book Number 0–8014–0829–6
Library of Congress Catalog Card Number 73–20791

Printed in the United States of America by The Colonial Press, Inc.

To A. A. A.

THREE MUSES

Contents

Tables

8

Preface

"This war is not limited to the territory of our unfortunate country," said an obscure French general in a London radio message to his beleaguered countrymen on June 18, 1940. "The war has not been decided by the battle of France. This is a world war. . . . There still exist all the means we need to crush our enemies someday."[1] General Charles de Gaulle's hopes for France—"her independence, security, and greatness"[2]—depended on how well she enlisted the resources of the world in her favor. De Gaulle resumed the task of calling the world into France's employ when, after twelve years of self-imposed exile, he returned to power in 1958 to establish the Fifth Republic.

The immediate cause of de Gaulle's resumption of power was the Algerian War, which had brought France to the brink of civil war and destroyed the Fourth Republic. By ending the war, de Gaulle had the chance to resurrect his proposal, first elaborated at Bayeux in 1946, of a republic under strong presidential leadership. The resolution of the Algerian dispute also gave France an opportunity to re-emerge as an independent force in world politics. Once the costly struggle was settled, de Gaulle proclaimed that France would no longer pit itself against the tide of history in the Third World. Rather, it would champion the principle of national self-determination as a means to transform the bipolarity inherited from World War II into a multipolar international order in which France would again find itself in the first rank. No longer would France conform to the bloc politics of the superpowers and, specifically, to the hegemonic dictates of the United States. No longer would France be supposedly weakened by submission to its Atlantic and European partners; it would contribute,

1. Charles de Gaulle, *Discours et messages,* 5 vols. (Paris: Plon, 1970), I, 4. Hereafter cited *Discours*. Translations are those of the author unless otherwise indicated.
2. *Ibid.,* I, 204.

precisely through the *assertion* of its own national interests, to the creation of a Europe strong enough to arbitrate the end of the Cold War.

This study examines key parts of French global policy under the Fifth Republic from 1958 to 1974. It covers the administrations of President Charles de Gaulle (1958–1969) and the five years of his successor, Georges Pompidou (1969–1974). Within the framework of specific French strategic, economic, and diplomatic policy areas, it reviews some of the principal proposals advanced and the steps taken to revise international relations. From this perspective, France's attempt to change the alignment patterns and the distribution of power between and among states is viewed as an object of French foreign policy; its concrete strategic, economic, and diplomatic policies are seen as means in the service of larger global aims. Conversely, the discussion also treats France's global policy as a means of achieving its narrower national foreign policy goals.

This approach to French foreign policy is from the point of view of France's bilateral relations with other states and international organizations as they are reflected in the decisions and actions of the French government and leadership. Interstate and intergovernmental relations are stressed as distinguished from transnational relations between persons, groups, or corporations. Relevant domestic constraints on policy are noted, but there is no attempt to explore fully the linkages between domestic and foreign policy as they bear on French behavior abroad. Emphasis is on the limits posed by other states on French behavior and on the political and ideological imperatives which the governments of the Fifth Republic imposed on France by articulating a global policy responsive to the particular needs of France and of other states.

The specific policy areas that are discussed exemplify general tendencies in French foreign policy and behavior. I hope this study will provide a useful framework of analysis for these and other facets of French policy. It characterizes rather than exhausts what might be said of French efforts to reconstruct relations between industrialized states and between developed and underdeveloped nations—that is, the East-West and North-South axes on which international relations turn. Whether these findings are applicable to other areas that can only be touched upon here will depend on additional research. These include, for example, France's policy toward foreign investment, labor, and technological development as well as its aims and pursuits in Black Africa and Latin America.

The analysis revolves around two paradoxical themes. On the one hand, Gaullist France contributed significantly to the transformation of international politics from a bipolar to a modified multipolar system. This change opened the way for important and salutary developments in world politics. Nationalism and national interest diluted many of the inflexible demands of competing superpower ideologies, relaxed the restraints of bloc politics, and created new avenues for East-West negotiation beyond the Cold War. These shifts in orientation facilitated a process of détente between the superpowers on a global scale. The states of East and West Europe enjoyed more freedom to develop bilateral ties across the security barriers of the NATO and Warsaw pacts, and a new diplomatic framework was created within which a final European settlement might be reached. New participants, most notably Communist China, were also drawn into international politics, and their claims were afforded opportunities for nonviolent expression and remedy.

On the other hand, French efforts on behalf of a multipolar international system largely did not produce the results expected by the Gaullists of increasing France's influence, status, or independence vis-à-vis the superpowers, its European partners, or Third World states to which it attached special importance. France remains dependent on the United States for its security even as French criticism of NATO reinforces a trend in American defense policy, given impetus by the Vietnam War, of constricting France's (and Europe's) access to American military power. France's economic and social well-being is also in great part a function of the policies of the United States and its European collaborators, including Great Britain, within the European Economic Community. France's capacity to shape Europe's political future lies more in its ties with the United States, the Soviet Union, and its European allies, especially Germany, than in its own hands. Finally, its ability to influence the behavior of Third World states, as its experience in Algeria suggests, is seriously circumscribed.

France's limited resources and the constraints posed by other states account more for its dependency and the narrow range of its maneuverability in foreign policy than do the defects of its leadership. Yet an analysis of the security, economic, and diplomatic strategies pursued by the de Gaulle regime suggests that Gaullist policies aided beneficial systemic change but gradually weakened France's global posture and its regional positions in Europe and the Mediterranean. If the nationalist course of the de Gaulle government prompted other states to assert themselves before the superpowers, it also encouraged them to do likewise in their dealings with France, and it hampered France and other states in Europe and the Third World in their attempts to combine their will and resources to resist the encroachments of the United States and the Soviet Union. France's lead rather than its leadership appealed to other states bent on promoting their own parochial concerns even at French expense.

The lasting legacy of the de Gaulle regime is the voice and vitality that it lent to a new world politics beyond superpower control. Notwithstanding the brilliant liquidation of the Algerian War and the remnants of French empire, its work was, ironically, incomplete in adjusting France to a multipolar world of its own construction. To President Georges Pompidou, de Gaulle's successor, fell the task of fashioning global and regional strategies more in keeping with the modesty of France's means and opportunities for initiative than with Gaullist rhetoric and aspirations.

Several considerations prompt a study of French foreign policy from the dual perspectives of the international system and of specific French foreign interests and objectives. First, the two are so fused in French thinking and practice that neither France's global policy nor its concrete geographic and functional initiatives can be understood or evaluated apart from each other. A dual thread runs throughout French foreign policy. One thread rationalizes France's global policy to support its specific demands on other states; the other shapes, partly and sometimes decisively, its pronouncements and behavior in particular policy areas to promote its global conceptions.

The French act on the assumption that the international system is the product of the myriad transactions between states, involving both acts of commission and omission. Under the regimes of de Gaulle and (to a lesser extent) Pompidou, the Paris government understood, more than most other regimes appreciated, that states shape the international environment and their role within it through their unilateral initiatives and through the alignments (or dealignments) they pursue with other states, implicitly and explicitly, in working toward their goals. The patterns of cooperation, competition, conflict, and conciliation characterizing interstate relations at any point in time influence profoundly how a nation will participate in the international arena, what it can expect from its efforts, and whether it will achieve its objectives. These patterns form an international system of relations whether the leadership of a state perceives the effect of its state's action or not. They are like the ordered utterances of M. Jourdain, Molière's Bourgeois Gentilhomme, who only belatedly learned that his manner of speaking was prose. Analysis of the structural elements of interstate behavior suggests that over time they form a grammar of power relations, rules, and expectations through which are mediated the nation's policies and actions abroad. In the very pursuit of narrow political aims, each national actor, through its words and deeds, contributes its own idiom to the evolving international grammar of power. This study supplies some of the Gallicisms that shed light on France's foreign policy behavior and on its role in shaping the international system to suit policy objectives. It offers evidence that, under the Fifth Republic, France attempted to work its will simultaneously at micro- and macro-levels of global politics, seeking, through mutual reinforcement, to advance its influence and interests in both realms.

The French case also illustrates the difficulties facing middle-range powers when they attempt to make basic changes in international relations through their own separate efforts. Gaullist France was determined to free its foreign policy as much as possible from exterior controls and to maximize its influence and prestige. Its modest success (some would say apparent failure) throws light on the narrow limits within which a middle-range power must work to shape its relations with the superpowers, with other middle-range powers like itself, and even with weaker states in the Third World. The French experience exposes, too, the enormous problem now facing statesmen who, like Charles de Gaulle, try to advance the particular interests and objectives of their states and also to develop recognized and enforceable rules to regulate the relations of an expanding universe of divergent and heterogeneous states around the globe.

Finally, in pursuing a doubtful *grandeur* for France, de Gaulle articulated a critique of contemporary interstate relations that deserves more attention than it has received from students and practitioners of international politics. Many have tended to dismiss the Gaullist arguments as more politically self-serving than conceptually illuminating. Closer study of Gaullist charges—that the postwar system was unstable (tending to war) and illegitimate (undermining the nation-state)—exposes some of their deeper intellectual roots. Also meriting more sympathetic evaluation is the Gaullist alternative, outlined in Chapter 1, of an oligarchical system, composed of hierarchies of states, which might have different members according to whether the security, economic, diplomatic, or even cultural policy sector is under examination.

In the Introduction, de Gaulle's concept of international relations is presented along with his vision of a new international system in which France would play a more significant role. The succeeding chapters develop the major themes of the analysis, trace French policies in specific functional and geographic areas, and analyze them as means of altering the existing international system and of achieving narrower national objectives. Stress is placed on French relations in the Atlantic area and in Europe because they are critical to the realization of French foreign policy objectives. Part I reviews French military and monetary policies within the Atlantic bloc and, specifically, toward the United States. Part II focuses on French policy toward the economic and political integration of Western Europe and toward East-West relations. These questions are approached largely from the perspective of France's bilateral relations with Britain and Germany, on the one hand, and with the Soviet Union, on the other. French policy toward the European Economic Community is developed in French terms, that is, as the residual product, by and large, of the bilateral relations between the member states. Part III studies French policy toward North Africa, especially Algeria, and toward the Middle East within the context of the Arab-Israeli conflict. The discussion of French policy in the Mediterranean area illustrates, not fully explicates, France's understanding of and approach to the Third World. The concluding chapter evaluates the Gaullist critique of the international system as well as French efforts, including those of the

Pompidou regime, to make fundamental changes in the alignments between states.

I have relied principally on original sources supplemented by extensive personal interviews with experts, government officials, and political leaders in the United States and Europe. The statements, declarations, communiqués, and news conferences of French officials and of government bodies responsible for foreign affairs have been examined and compared to France's actual behavior in foreign policy. Documents issuing from international bodies, including the European communities, the United Nations, the International Monetary Fund, NATO, and the Organization for Economic Cooperation and Development, were reviewed. I also examined the pronouncements of the major states with which France has had dealings. These original sources are supplemented by extensive secondary sources, including materials from the impressive newspaper and article files of the Fondation Nationale des Sciences Politiques in Paris as well as the literature, newspapers, and articles to be found in the United States.

I conducted more than one hundred interviews on both sides of the Atlantic. Most of them took place in Paris and Brussels during my stay in Europe from February 1970 through August 1971. For purposes of verifying and enlarging my conclusions, I conducted further interviews during a return visit to Europe for two weeks at the end of September 1972.

This work owes a great deal to a large number of people, without whose generous help it could not have been undertaken or completed. A Rockefeller Foundation Fellowship in International Relations launched me on the study in the fall of 1965–1966, permitting me to spend time in Paris to collect materials and conduct interviews. A Ford Foundation Social Science Fellowship allowed me to return for a year and a half from February 1970 to August 1971. The Center for the Study of Science and Technology and Public Policy under the direction of Mason Willrich assisted my research in its closing stages in France, particularly as it relates to the French civil and military nuclear program and to French policy toward science and technology. Additional supplementary grants from the Wilson Gee Committee of the University of Virginia and the University Research

Board of the University of Illinois facilitated work in preparing the manuscript for publication. I am grateful to Professors Enno Kraehe and H. R. Snyder, the respective chairmen of these groups.

I should especially like to thank those colleagues who commented extensively on the manuscript at its various stages. Jean Klein and Walter Schutze of the Centre d'Etudes de Politique Etrangère read the entire manuscript and provided invaluable advice on how to improve it. Both possess an enviable grasp of the historical evolution and current complexities of French foreign policy. William Andrews merits special gratitude for his incisive remarks about the general argument and organization of the study. Also helpful on parts of the manuscript were Pierre Hassner, Donald Hodgman, Stanley Hoffmann, W. W. Kulski, Robert Legvold, and I. Wiliam Zartman. The anonymous readers engaged by Cornell University Press to review the manuscript also deserve my appreciation for their detailed and informed criticism. My former colleagues at the University of Virginia —Paul T. David, Dante Germino, Laurin Henry, Paul Shoup, Ralph Eisenberg, Robert Wood, and Leland Yaeger—also were encouraging. The criticisms of these readers strengthened the conceptual framework of the study and clarified obscure points. They also freed the manuscript of countless errors of fact and opinion. What flaws remain are of my own doing.

Always dependable was Adele Hall, who patiently typed the numerous versions of the manuscript over a five-year span. Cora Pitts lent secretarial assistance, and my secretaries at the University of Illinois, Ruth Gartner and Ida Noll, were always attentive to my ceaseless demands on their time. May I single out, too, for special commendation the Centre Universitaire International and its able staff under the direction of Françoise Sudre.

I am also indebted to Jean Touchard, Secretary General of the Fondation Nationale des Sciences Politiques, for granting me permission to use the excellent library facilities of the center, where Clotilde Ferrand rendered valuable help. I also extensively used the libraries of the Atlantic Institute (Paris), the European Economic Commission (Paris, Brussels, and Washington), and the Centre d'Etudes de Politique Etrangère. Madeleine Ledevilec at the Brussels EEC library deserves special mention for her assistance. Jean Moreau of the EEC press and information section was instrumental in making contacts for interviews. My thanks also extend to Alexandre Marc, of the Centre International de Formation Européenne, who generously provided me with office space and facilities to compose my research findings. The University of Virginia library staff and its director, Ray Frantz, gave attentive and supportive assistance. The completion of the manuscript would have been seriously retarded except for the kind help of Richard Austin and his staff at Alderman Library. Robert Lamson of the National Science Foundation was also a constant source of support.

Some of my analyses originally appeared in different form in journals: "Revolt and Revisionism in the Gaullist Global Vision: An Analysis of French Strategic Policy," *Journal of Politics,* XXXIII (May 1971), 422–447; © by the Southern Political Science Association; "French Mediterranean Policy: The Politics of Weakness," *International Relations* (England), XLVII (July 1971), 503–517; "France and the Atlantic Alliance: Alliance with a De-aligning Power," *Polity,* II (Spring 1970), 241–266; "France Ensnared: French Strategic Policy and Bloc Politics after 1968," *Orbis,* XV (Winter 1972), 1085–1108; and "French Monetary Diplomacy in the Sixties: Background Notes to the Current Monetary Crisis," *World Affairs,* CXXXV (Summer 1972), 5–39. I acknowledge the gracious permission of the editors to draw on this material.

My wife, Antje, and our four children have been a constant source of encouragement. The push and pull of daily family life and the clatter of unexpected noises and unpredictable crises accompanying it are not recommended as necessary conditions to foster research and writing, but without my family the research and writing would not have been as worth while—or even possible.

EDWARD A. KOLODZIEJ

Champaign-Urbana, Illinois

1

Introduction: The Gaullist Fifth Republic and International Relations

Charles de Gaulle's conception of international relations and of France's global role heavily influenced France's foreign policy during and after his tenure in office. Building his presidency on the support of the French people, expressed through national referenda and presidential and parliamentary elections, de Gaulle dominated the French government and determined its foreign policy initiatives abroad. From the inception of the Fifth Republic in May 1958, de Gaulle indelibly stamped its institutions with his personality. Succeeding a confusing parade of prime ministers, cabinet heads, and legislators under the Fourth and Third Republics, de Gaulle as President of the Republic spoke for France. As his successive prime ministers—Michel Debré, Georges Pompidou, and Couve de Murville—discovered, their personal discretion and maneuverability were sharply defined by what he would tolerate. During the Fourth Republic, or after his resignation from the presidency, Gaullism could exist without de Gaulle. Between May 1958 and April 1969, the two were inseparable;[1] for over a decade, the Fifth Republic was the de Gaulle republic.[2]

Rationalizing de Gaulle's views is not easy. While few would dispute his great influence on French foreign policy, there is considerably less accord on the intent of his words and deeds or the specific political objectives that he was pursuing at any given moment.[3] Dis-

---

1. Two attempts at defining "Gaullism" are Jacques de Montalais, editor of the Gaullist newspaper *La Nation*, in his *Qu'est-ce que le Gaullisme?* (Paris: Maison Mame, 1969); and Jean Charlot, *Le Gaullisme* (Paris: Armand Colin, 1970).

2. See, for example, Roy C. Macridis and Bernard E. Brown, *The De Gaulle Republic* (Homewood, Ill.: Dorsey Press, 1960), and Supplement, 1963.

3. Three useful, though divergent, interpretations of Gaullist foreign policy are Guy de Carmoy, *The Foreign Policies of France: 1944–1968*, trans. Elaine

tance in relations with others was an inherent feature of de Gaulle's political style. "The man of character . . . ," he wrote during the formative years of his political and military development, "is inevitably aloof, for there can be no authority without prestige, nor prestige unless he keep his distance." [4] For him, words were as important to describe an event or to analyze a problem as they were to create the political reality that influences and directs the behavior of states and men. The political art, de Gaulle is quoted as saying, consists in "crystallizing in words that which the future is going to demonstrate." [5] His war memoirs suggest an extraordinary hindsight in predicting the outcome of World War II.[6] Also, his staged news conferences with their planted queries, rhetorical questions, and the stylized use of the third person appeared calculated to produce preconceived political effects.[7] Audacious and even insulting language, designed to attract attention, signal policy changes to underlings and foreign governments, command respect, or simply to outrage, served higher political purposes as de Gaulle illustrated in his stormy relations with President Franklin Roosevelt and Prime Minister Winston Churchill during World War II.[8] Even silence helped to confound enemies and to enhance personal authority.[9]

No consensus exists on how to distinguish between candor and dis-

---

P. Halperin (Chicago: University of Chicago Press, 1970); Alfred Grosser, *French Foreign Policy under de Gaulle*, trans. Lois Ames Pattison (Boston: Little, Brown, 1965); and W. W. Kulski, *De Gaulle and the World* (Syracuse: Syracuse University Press, 1966). The essays of Stanley Hoffmann, cited throughout, are indispensable.

4. Charles de Gaulle, *The Edge of the Sword*, trans. Gerard Hopkins (New York: Criterion Books, 1960).

5. Herbert Lüthy, "De Gaulle: Pose and Policy," *Foreign Affairs*, XLIII (July 1965), 561.

6. Charles de Gaulle, *Mémoires de guerre* (Paris: Plon, 1954–1958), I–III, Livres de Poche. Hereafter cited *Mémoires*.

7. See, for example, Ambassade de France, Service de Presse et d'Information, *Major Addresses, Statements, and Press Conferences of General Charles de Gaulle, 1958–64* (New York, 1964), *passim*. Hereafter cited *Major Addresses*.

8. See, for example, Milton Viorst, *Hostile Allies—FDR and de Gaulle* (New York: Macmillan, 1965); and Dorothy S. White, *Seeds of Discord* (Syracuse: Syracuse University Press, 1964).

9. De Gaulle, *Edge of the Sword*, p. 58. See, for example, André Passeron, *De Gaulle parle: 1962–1966* (Paris: Fayard, 1966), p. 187; *Major Addresses*, pp. 45, 179.

simulation in Gaullist prose. It is wrapped in such elusive phrases as a "European Europe" or an "Algerian Algeria." Ambiguity creates personal mystery which, in de Gaulle's view, is the culminating virtue of the leader. Political maneuverability derives from both. "If one is to influence men's minds," de Gaulle said over forty years ago, "one must observe them carefully and make it clear that each has been marked out from among his fellows, but only on condition that this goes with a determination to give nothing away, to hold in reserve some piece of secret knowledge which may at any moment intervene and the more effectively from being in the nature of a surprise." [10]

Contradictions, lapses, and confusions in Gaullist rhetoric have their parallel in French foreign policy—more precisely policies—of the Fifth Republic. If President de Gaulle's long-range designs remained constant, his tactics changed often, and logically incompatible but not necessarily politically incoherent strategies were frequently pursued. The Fifth Republic, created to assure French control of Algeria, became the vehicle for Algerian independence. France ostensibly placed the *force de frappe* at the disposal of European security, yet insisted on national autonomy in the use of nuclear weapons. It claimed to lead the economic integration of Europe, yet sought, as the crisis of 1965 revealed, to limit European union and to assert its ascendancy over its EEC partners. It purported to be the only state truly committed to European political union, yet it proposed a European confederal structure that would have slowed, if not frustrated, the development of common political institutions within the Six. It championed self-determination in the Third World, yet offered big-power rule by the five nuclear powers, including France, as the principal international mechanism to assure global order. It advocated world disarmament and denuclearization of the superpowers, yet refused to attend the Geneva arms control talks or sign accords that aimed at slowing the arms race and diminishing the probability of global nuclear conflict.

Under the Fifth Republic, Gaullist views about international politics supplied much of the conceptual basis for what appeared to be conflicting policies. An analysis, however provisional, of Gaullist assumptions and perceptions suggests some of the sources of French

10. De Gaulle, *Edge of the Sword*, p. 42.

policies. Many explanatory factors lie beyond the scope of this work.[11] Reviewing de Gaulle's political thought, however, reveals some of his contribution to the political, if not always logical, rationale underlying the seemingly endless shifts in posture and policies of the Fifth Republic in foreign affairs.

Underlying Assumptions of Gaullist Political Thought and Action

The Meaning of the Nation-State

The nation-state is fundamental to de Gaulle's political thinking.[12] The precise meanings of the terms "nation" and "state" are, however, unclear. "Nation" refers principally to a given people, with their own language, customs, mores, and traditions, usually identified with a specific geographical area.[13] A people becomes a nation, more than a mere grouping or aggregate of individuals or even a tribe, when they consciously recognize their common history and accept a collective destiny, apart from the specific desires and circumstances of their individual lives. The ties binding a nation, while less tangible than the blood ties of a tribe or enlarged family grouping, are no less compelling. The nation owes its existence as much to human creativity as to biological necessity. For de Gaulle, as for his intellectual parents, the subtle Henri Bergson and the nationalists Charles Maurras and Maurice Barrès, the nation is fundamentally organic and developmental, not mechanical and static. It lives and dies like a person. The self-identity of a people develops slowly, requiring centuries of mutual regard to manifest itself in joint enterprises, before they are able con-

11. Two useful works that probe French domestic politics and the internal basis for French foreign policy are Philip M. Williams, *French Politicians and Elections: 1951–69* (Cambridge: Cambridge University Press, 1970); and Pierre Viansson-Ponté, *Histoire de la république gaullienne* (Paris: Fayard, 1970). The latter is a first installment of a history of the Gaullist years.

12. Grosser, *op. cit.*, pp. 13–28; useful, too, is Godfried van Benthem van den Bergh, "Contemporary Nationalism in the Western World," *Daedalus,* XCV (Summer 1966), 828–861; also relevant and well conceived is Stanley Hoffmann's article, appearing in the same issue, "Obstinate or Obsolete? The Fate of the Nation-State and the Case of Western Europe," pp. 862–915.

13. See, for example, Passeron, *De Gaulle parle* (Paris: Plon, 1962), pp. 403–404, 424–425, 426–432, 469, 474; Passeron, *De Gaulle parle: 1962–1966,* pp. 261, 265, 274, 305, 317.

sciously to differentiate themselves.[14] Self-identity reaches its most heightened form when a people consciously acts together, as in war. Within the Gaullist myth, the Gauls, forebears of the French nation, became a separate people in resisting their Roman conquerors. A product of human history, the nation needs no justification beyond the recognition of its reality. The notion of humanity itself cannot be understood apart from the existence of differentiated peoples. Man exists as a plurality of peoples; a man's identity derives as much from the people of whom he is a part and from the state to which he is bound, legally and morally, as from his own personal striving.

The idea of nation or people assumes an importance in Gaullist thought comparable to that of "class" in the Marxist interpretation of history, in which class is the political embodiment and vehicle of historical reality. Gaullism insists instead that the nation and those who direct its affairs define political reality, which determines economic and cultural values; material factors are fundamentally subordinate to the acts of political will that impose themselves on the behavior of men. Humanity is experienced, not as a whole, but as a plurality, divided into nations or peoples and resolvable into multiple sources of political authority. Each people represents a separate and identifiable collective will. Gaullism rejects the Marxist claims for the Communist party and the proletariat that it purports to lead; there can be no appeal beyond the nation as the final arbiter of human values and the political leaders, however chosen, guiding its destiny.

Where Marxism foresees the elimination of classes as the end of history, Gaullism projects the continued emergence of new nations and the demise or readaptation of older ones to new conditions of international life. For de Gaulle, there is no clear end to the historical process; that would be tantamount to the termination of human creativity. Where Marxism portrays history as the struggle of classes, Gaullism speaks of the rise and fall of nations. Where Marxism envisions final peace in a classless world order, Gaullism remains at-

14. William Pickles, "Making Sense of de Gaulle," *International Affairs,* XLII (July 1966), 412. Students of de Gaulle differ on the question of his intellectual parenthood. In a letter to the author, Stanley Hoffmann throws doubt on Marras' influence on de Gaulle. Jean Lacouture states the conventional view in his *De Gaulle,* trans. Francis K. Price (London: Hutchinson, 1970), pp. 181–196, especially pp. 182–183.

tached to the probability that continued conflict, not cooperation, will animate relations among men owing allegiance to separate nations.[15] Where Marxism treats the state as a coercive instrument of capitalist rule and announces its eventual elimination in a classless world, Gaullism extols the state as the highest representation of a people's genius and historical development and proclaims its continued vitality and relevance in human affairs.[16]

Determining de Gaulle's definition of the state is also difficult and poses a number of intractable problems about his understanding of the relation of the nation to the state. He appeared to define the state in terms of its purposes. For France these are threefold: domestic order, external security, and, unique to France, *grandeur*. To establish order, the state must assure the personal security of each citizen and lay down laws to govern the relations of citizens to each other and to the state. The preservation of internal order constitutes the initial basis of the state's claim to moral and legal legitimacy and its right to command the outward behavior of its people and to expect their inner loyalty.

The state's capacity to provide external security against what de Gaulle believed are the almost inevitable encroachments of other states further strengthens its claim of authority over its citizenry; in fact, as de Gaulle affirmed on numerous occasions, it is tantamount to a definition of the state itself. In 1959, before a closed group of French military officers, de Gaulle said, "If France's defense were long allowed to remain outside the national framework or to become an integral part of, or mingled with, something else, then it would not be possible for us to maintain a State. In any period of history, the government's *raison d'être* is to defend the independence and the integrity of the territory. It arises from this necessity. Especially in France, all our regimes have been based on their ability to do so." [17] Because the state's claim to the citizen's allegiance lies in the discharge of its minimal responsibilities for assuring internal order and external security, to the degree that the state abdicates these obligations or assigns their execution to other states or political bodies, it

15. Passeron, *De Gaulle parle: 1962–1966,* pp. 174, 185–191.
16. Passeron, *De Gaulle parle,* pp. 451–483.
17. Roy C. Macridis, ed., *De Gaulle: Implacable Ally* (New York: Harper and Row, 1966), p. 133.

impairs its legitimacy and, accordingly, compromises its authority. This line of argument is especially important to the French brief defending France's critique of superpower hegemony and, specifically, its withdrawal from NATO in 1966.

De Gaulle's condemnation of the Vichy regime sheds light on his conception of the sources of the state's authority and the legitimacy of the government charged to execute its responsibilities for defense and foreign policy. In surrendering to Germany, the Vichy government could no longer claim to represent France. Its incompetence declared it illegitimate. The Vichy regime forfeited its agency as the legal representative of France when it prematurely capitulated to Germany although France's empire and many of its military units remained intact and France's allies were prepared to assist in the liberation struggle. No French regime had the right to surrender French independence as long as there were individuals and groups ready to assume France's defense. "Nothing is lost," de Gaulle affirmed after the collapse of the Third Republic. "It is necessary that France . . . be present at the victory. Then, she will rediscover her liberty and her *grandeur*." [18]

De Gaulle's Free French movement, although outside the institutional framework of the Third Republic, acted, unlike Vichy, in defense of France's higher and more compelling responsibilities. In assuming the obligation for national security, the Free French could claim to be the legitimate representative of France. According to de Gaulle, whatever the Anglo-American powers may have otherwise believed, France did not perish in the disaster of spring 1940. Its sovereignty was temporarily transported to England in the person of de Gaulle and was embodied in the elite that, as de Gaulle described at Bayeux in 1946, sprung spontaneously from the nation's human reserves, transcending class and party, to redeem its independence and greatness. This revival was admittedly accomplished outside the discredited Third Republic, but inside the legitimate framework of the French state. [19] In supplanting Vichy, the Free French under de Gaulle

18. Quoted in Général de Gaulle, *La France n'a pas perdu la guerre* (New York: Didier, 1944), p. xi.
19. The notion of natural leaders springing from among the people in times of crisis is still strong in French strategic thought. See Général d'Armée Aérienne, M. Fourquet, "Emploi des différents systèmes de forces dans le cadre de la stratégie de dissuasion," *Revue de défense nationale,* XXV (May 1969), 767.

claimed to link, legally and morally, the Third and Fourth Republics. De Gaulle's government in exile could assert its authority over all Frenchmen since it still executed France's sovereign duties of security and *grandeur*. "The [French] government," said de Gaulle in response to the belated recognition of the Provisional Government of the French Republic by its allies, "is satisfied that one may well wish to call it by its name." [20]

De Gaulle's claim to legitimacy rested partly on his idealistic conception of the French people on whose behalf his government acted. The French (*français et françaises*) of all ages, not just those living in a given historical period, were the repository of political authority. According to de Gaulle, no leadership could validly interpret and wield the national authority of the hexagon unless it acted in trust to this legacy and possessed the support of the French of the moment. This suggested that a twofold condition for legitimacy existed in de Gaulle's mind: the freely expressed approbation of the French people, provisionally registered in periodic referenda called by an elected head of state, and the faithful discharge by the government of France's traditional state functions. Owing its existence to an occupying power, Vichy did not meet either condition. Even conceding that it commanded the temporary acquiescence of the populace, it would still have forfeited its right to rule. Momentary consent was a necessary, but not a sufficient, condition for legitimacy. Keeping the covenant with the French who were dead and yet to be born was equally important. Vichy may have provided an uneasy domestic order based on foreign arms, but it failed on the scores of security and *grandeur*. In de Gaulle's terms, Petain's Vichy failed the French. During his campaign for the presidency in 1965, de Gaulle presented perhaps the most revealing statement of his understanding of the distinction between the people or nation and the state and the proper relation that should obtain between them:

And the French? Well! It is they who make France. It is they who are responsible for it, from generation to generation. France, it is more than the French of the moment, France comes from afar, it is what it is now, and thus it has a future; in other words, France embraces all French generations and, first of all, of course, the living generations. These living

20. De Gaulle, *Discours*, I, 410.

generations are responsible for France and it is in this manner, it is true, that I consider, in their totality, the French, and it is in this manner that I wish that the French, in their totality, consider themselves. There is in that respect among them . . . a solidarity that I say to be national, for lack of which France risks not to be what it is for all time, and consequently . . . to no longer, properly speaking, exist.[21]

Living generations were important to de Gaulle as a guide for governmental action and a source of immediate authority for the state. Periodic referenda and electoral consultations resolve nettling political questions in "an irremediable way," renew confidence in governmental leadership, and check the influence of party and parliamentary maneuvering.[22] Ultimate political authority, however, derives from the historical reality of the French nation-state. Historical France is superior to the contingent majorities that can be marshaled to express their consent to a particular regime or its policies.

Grandeur and the French Mission

How can France simultaneously transcend time, history, and even the geographical space to which a people and nation are bound, and yet depend on the resources of a people and their leadership for the achievement of its purposes? What links the history of a people to the destiny of the state and to its leadership of the moment? De Gaulle's illusive notion of *grandeur* suggests a tenuous explanation of his understanding of the connection between the actions of a people through history and the achievement of the state's purposes in time. His celebrated exposition of *grandeur,* in the opening paragraph of his war memoirs, distinguished a providentially created France from Frenchmen of the moment. He attributed to the latter whatever mediocrity may appear in France's "acts and deeds." De Gaulle asserted the proposition as self-evident that "France is not really herself unless she is in the first rank; that only vast enterprises are capable of counterbalancing the ferments of disintegration inherent in her people. . . . In short . . . France cannot be France without *grandeur*." [23]

Grandeur carries important implications for French foreign policy.

21. Passeron, *De Gaulle parle: 1962–1966,* p. 134.
22. Williams, *op. cit.,* p. 127.
23. De Gaulle, *Mémoires,* I, 5.

On the international plane, it designates a big-power role for France, much like that understood and acted upon by those responsible for French foreign policy under the Third and Fourth Republics.[24] Along with a small number of other chosen states, France has the responsibility to define the hierarchical structure of international relations and the role to be played by lesser units, to determine and assure basic security arrangements, and to regulate the economic and diplomatic processes by which relations are to be conducted. As a great power, France's actions are an example and its policies a guide for other states, both large and small. *Grandeur* derives from the execution of this ambitious international role. In defining the conditions of international political life for other states, France necessarily enjoys a higher status than those states which accept rather than shape the international framework in which they act.[25] They are lesser bodies because their security, solvency, and status are ultimately consigned to the policies and preferences of other states.

The goal of *grandeur* assumes equal importance in French domestic political life. First, it allegedly compensates for persistent domestic ills and division. Pursuing *grandeur* harnesses the energies of Frenchmen, distracting them from petty personal concerns and mutual animosities. It cautions France's political leaders against absorption, as under the Third and Fourth Republics, in the play of party politics with its innumerable special pleadings, endless bids for seamy favors, consuming recriminations, and chronic instability. Domestic policy is subordinated to foreign affairs. Gaullism, as one acute observer of Gaullist thought notes, regards the nation "as a human entity which acts in a world made up of other such entities. In this perspective, foreign policy is the only true policy. The sole aim of internal policy is to assure order and unity, and to develop an influence to be used abroad." [26]

Social change, for example, is justified less on its own merits than in light of its functional utility in advancing French international

24. See the discussion by Anton W. DePorte, *De Gaulle's Foreign Policy: 1944–1946* (Cambridge: Harvard University Press, 1968), pp. 1–15. These themes are developed at length in de Gaulle's *Mémoires*.

25. For a perspective analysis, see Stanley Hoffmann, "De Gaulle's Mémoires: The Hero as History," *World Politics*, XIII (Oct. 1960), 140–154.

26. Remark of Alfred Grosser, quoted in Bergh, *op. cit.*, p. 835.

status. On numerous occasions, de Gaulle governments proposed more far-reaching social legislation than the Socialist party. The reforms of the Provisional Government from 1944 to 1946 on tenant farming, health, and social security were critical in re-establishing stability in France and confidence in its political institutions after the enormous dislocations of the war. De Gaulle's intent in promoting these changes was not keyed primarily to improving the quality of French life. In working for internal reform with French officials of different political persuasions, including Communists, de Gaulle notes: "Once again I remarked that if the goal guiding them was perhaps the same for them as for myself, the motives guiding them were not identical with my own. . . . I perceived that they were scarcely aware of the motive inspiring me, which was the power of France." [27]

The effort of the French state to stimulate economic production, promote efficiency, and expand markets is also tied to the goal of enlarging France's influence and prestige abroad. "This conception of a government armed to act powerfully in the economic domain," de Gaulle candidly observed, "was directly linked to my conception of the state itself. I regarded the state not as it was yesterday and as the parties wished it to become once more, a juxtaposition of private interests which could never produce anything but weak compromise, but instead an institution of decision, action, and ambition, expressing and serving the national interest alone." [28]

Grandeur and Popular Government

But how are the energies of the nation to be marshaled to realize the state's responsibilities for order, security, and *grandeur*? For de Gaulle, only some form of presidential government, democratically based, would be equal to his purpose for France. At Bayeux in 1946, de Gaulle declared: "The Greeks once asked Solon 'What is the best Constitution?' He answered 'Tell me first for which country and for what time?' . . . Let us take ourselves for what we are. Let us take the century for what it is. We have to bring about . . . a drastic reconstruction that will make it possible for each man and woman to lead a life of greater ease, security, and happiness, and that ought to

27. Quoted in Grosser, *op. cit.,* p. 16.
28. Macridis, ed., *op. cit.,* p. 70.

increase our numbers and make us more powerful and united. We must preserve the freedom that we have safeguarded with so much effort. We must assure the destiny of France in the midst of so many obstacles that confront us and endanger peace. We must show ourselves to all other peoples for what we are to aid this poor and old mother of ours—the Earth." [29] The conditions of another age might have recommended a different form of government. Strong, monarchical rule suited France during the seventeenth and eighteenth centuries; Bonapartist regimes, the nineteenth century; popular government, the present age. It was to be de Gaulle's special task to forge an alliance between the partisans of democratic rule and *grandeur*.

For de Gaulle, democratic practices were indispensable means with which to organize the internal human and material resources of the French nation and to apply them to the ambitious missions of the French state. Personal dictatorship would have discouraged mass participation in the undertakings of the state; popular rule demands it. A return to democratic government was seen as the more reliable and effective way to revive the French nation after the war. An authoritarian regime, aside from possibly provoking civil strife, could neither rally popular support to speed recovery at home nor assure an independent policy abroad. De Gaulle's social and political reforms after World War II sought to regain the confidence of the French people in their government and in themselves and to build a solid domestic foundation for France's resumption of its international responsibilities.

The contrast with Woodrow Wilson is instructive. Wilson worked tirelessly to enlist American nationalism in the service of popular government. His new nationalism was more than an appeal to popular sentiment. It sought to widen participation in government as an end in itself and to extend hope and protection to a larger number of people. De Gaulle reversed priorities. Democracy, too, was in the service of France.

De Gaulle likewise rejected the Wilsonian inclination to accept democratic rule as universally valid for all peoples. For de Gaulle, the establishment of democratic government depended upon a large number of factors, including a people's character and experience as

29. *Ibid.,* p. 43.

well as the special internal and external conditions defining their political life. It was neither logically necessary nor historically accurate to link the notion of liberal democracy to national self-determination. Popular rule was too narrow a principle on which to base global order. Self-determination had a broader meaning and was coterminous with the national expression of a people, only one part of which was reflected in its governmental forms.

De Gaulle neither identified self-determination with popular government nor insisted on their simultaneity in dealing with foreign states. He could deplore the Communist regimes in China and the Soviet Union, yet resign himself to the *de facto* domestic power that these authoritarian regimes exercised. De Gaulle and Wilson would have doubtless agreed that peace is likely to be fostered in an international system based on national self-determination, but de Gaulle would have rejected Wilson's restrictive understanding of that term. De Gaulle professed to see little significant difference between the international behavior of democratic and nondemocratic states. All were assumed to be motivated by the same desire to promote their own interests, even at the expense of other states. For de Gaulle, international peace was a function of a balance of power among rival states, whatever their forms of government; for Wilson, peace depended on a new concert of like-minded states by and large inspired by democratic rule.[30]

A presidentially based government alone met de Gaulle's tests of popular consent, internal cohesion, and external strength. Only such a government had sufficient political power and authority to pursue vigorously a policy of *grandeur*. As early as 1946, at Bayeux, de Gaulle visualized presidential rule as the key to national unity and *grandeur*. He appealed to the French people to adopt a new constitution: "Let us be lucid and strong and give to ourselves the rule of national life that will unite us even when all the time we are prone to divide against ourselves! In our whole history, great misfortunes of a

30. This view of Woodrow Wilson is drawn from Wilson's own writing. For a perceptive analysis of Wilson's views on international relations, see Robert E. Osgood, *Ideals and Self-Interest in American Foreign Relations* (Chicago: University of Chicago Press, 1953). Inis L. Claude, Jr., *Power and International Relations* (New York: Random House, 1964), pp. 94–106, provides a contrasting view.

divided people alternate with inspiring feats of a free nation grouped together under the aegis of a strong state." [31] His ideas rose out of the ashes of the Fourth Republic to give birth to strong presidential rule under the Fifth Republic.

The crowning achievement came in 1962 when de Gaulle, overriding the objections of the traditional parties, moved boldly to amend the French Constitution to provide for the direct election of the president. In his mind only such a procedure could verify conclusively the French president's claim to represent France as a whole and assure the national support which he would need to substantiate his position as the guarantor (le garant) of French independence and integrity in periods of calm and crisis. The absence of such a national voice in January 1940 had left a deep impression on de Gaulle. The parliamentary institutions of the Third and Fourth Republics might have served France in peacetime, but they obviously could not withstand great internal or external stress. Foreign military force destroyed the Third Republic; civil strife, engendered by colonial wars, dealt a death blow to the Fourth Republic. No party or individual could assume legitimate responsibility for the conduct of the state, least of all could the prime minister, the indentured servant of rival parliamentary parties, whose conditional support he enjoyed only so long as the expediencies of the moment suited their rapidly shifting fortunes. The prime ministers, as the events of 1940 and 1958 demonstrated, proved to be institutionally weakest, whatever their estimable personal qualities, when strong, central leadership was demanded to forestall imminent national disaster. The institutions of the Fifth Republic were to be able to withstand such shocks.

The Constitution of the Fifth Republic reflects Gaullist thinking. A popularly elected president enjoys formidable legal powers to fulfill his responsibilities. He designates his ministers of government, convenes and presides over the Council of Ministers, announces state decisions in the form of decrees or ordinances, appoints all principal civil servants, officers, and judges, negotiates treaties, and is commander in chief of the armed forces. Unlike his predecessor of the Fourth Republic, the president of the Fifth Republic also has the power to dissolve the National Assembly, and he has recourse to

31. Macridis, ed., op. cit., p. 43.

national referenda to test public sentiment on issues of moment. In cases of grave crisis, whether from foreign or domestic sources, he exercises, as de Gaulle did during the Algerian War, such emergency powers as are necessary to protect the institutions, laws, and independence of the Republic.[32]

De Gaulle's repudiation of parliamentary democracy, based largely on divided party rule, was unceasing from his unsuccessful attempt to establish a new French government after World War II until his resignation in 1969. Restricted to a narrow electoral base, the parties were unable to represent the views of the French people as a whole or to promote the interests of France abroad. The domestic and foreign ills of the Fourth Republic—financial deficits, economic instability, a weakened franc, incipient civil war, external humiliation, and debilitating colonial conflicts—were attributed to the weakness of France's governing institutions. Neither the parties nor the National Assembly, viewed by de Gaulle as politically animated by delicate, necessarily tenuous, and inherently contradictory compromises, could deal decisively or coherently with these problems.

De Gaulle believed that the institutions of the Fourth Republic prevented men of talent and virtue from addressing themselves to France's multiple problems. Referring to Guy Mollet at his first news conference on May 19, 1958, de Gaulle expressed esteem for his long-time rival, but added that "in the regime in its present form, no man of merit can succeed." [33] The institutions of the Fifth Republic would presumably draw the talents of statesmen toward larger, national goals, providing a larger stage on which personal ambitions could find expression; alternatively, the institutions would be sturdy enough so that, for short periods of time, they could survive men of lesser capacity, modest vision, or weaker wills than de Gaulle's. Building his support on mass appeal, the French president would tie the government more closely to the French people, overcoming the traditional dichotomy between electoral sentiment and government coalitions so characteristic of the Third and Fourth Republics.[34] The destruction of the old parties in favor of mass groupings (there will only be us and the Communists, as de Gaulle and his supporters

32. *Ibid.*, p. 52.
33. *Major Addresses*, p. 5.
34. Williams, *op. cit., passim.*

often said) would mute, if not resolve, the petty clashes of personality and party to which traditional French parliamentary democracy appeared particularly vulnerable.

Charismatic Leadership and Popular Consent

A review of de Gaulle's conception of *grandeur* still begs the question of his understanding of the fundamental relation of the French state to its people. The lack of clarity and articulation in his writings and speeches is all the more regrettable since his reliance on notions like "the people" or "the nation" and "the state" are central to his philosophy of history and of politics. On the one hand, de Gaulle theoretically viewed history as essentially shaped and informed by the acts of a glorious France, humanity's most advanced civilizing agency. This vision bears some of the marks of Hegel's characterization of the Prussian state over a century ago. France's destiny is described in terms of necessity, retrospectively revealed in its history or, as de Gaulle suggests, in his own experience as it crystallized in his memoirs. An unidentified source, greater than the French people, ordains France's mission and presumably acts as muse for de Gaulle's pen. On the other hand, the French state's realization of its purposes depends on the French people in whom de Gaulle expresses little confidence or regard. They dissipate their energies in internal conflict and devote themselves more to personal than to ennobling national pursuits.

De Gaulle remained skeptical, however, of the durability of his alliance of democratic rule and national glory. His disdain of French public opinion is well documented. To his mind, most Frenchmen betrayed a marked preference for their domestic hearths over foreign adventure, for the bargaining of the market place over subtle diplomatic maneuver, for the perfection of a comfortable personal life over the display of martial virtues or the acquisition of ascetic habits of self-denial and civil discipline.[35] "So long as a country is not immediately threatened," de Gaulle noted in an early and influential writing, "public opinion will be strongly opposed to increasing the

35. Read, for example, Jean-Baptiste Duroselle's essay, "Changes in French Foreign Policy since 1945," in Stanley Hoffmann, ed., *In Search of France* (New York: Harper and Row, 1963), pp. 305–358.

burden of armaments, and to accepting the need for additional man-power." [36] These views were reconfirmed in de Gaulle's mind shortly before his death. In a final interview with André Malraux, de Gaulle complained that "the French people no longer have any national ambition. They no longer wish to do anything for France." [37]

De Gaulle's extrication from his self-created dilemma was perhaps more personally and psychologically satisfying than politically rele-vant in an age demanding complex organization to rule mass popu-lations and respond to their demands. For him it lay in the charis-matic leader who personally forges the link between the transcendental purposes of the French national state and the transient support of a volatile and distracted populace. The bond between leader, people, and state develops out of the attraction of the leader's personality and vision and of the people's need for a strong chief of state capable of guiding them through the inevitable crises endemic to their political life. Unless France and its people are devoted to great enterprise abroad, they find themselves, according to de Gaulle's mournful pre-diction, always in "mortal danger," susceptible to internal collapse or foreign domination. The resolute leader elicits heroic efforts from the French people, making them worthy of an already ascribed virtue inhering in them and in their state. The people and the state are mysteriously personified in the charismatic leader.[38] In expressing his will, he embodies the general will.

Yet no amount of institutional manipulation can assure the tenuous and necessarily personal alliance between the masses, the state, and the governing elite. If the alliance is broken, according to de Gaulle, the French people are ultimately at fault. In resigning after the April 1969 electoral defeat of his proposal to reform the Senate and de-centralize French administration, de Gaulle accepted the result as a sign that the French electorate no longer wished to follow him, not that his proposals or personal authority were impaired. De Gaulle's

36. De Gaulle, *Edge of the Sword*, p. 109.
37. André Malraux, *Les Chênes qu'on abat* (Paris: Gallimard, 1971), p. 23.
38. Hoffmann, *World Politics*, 1960, pp. 140–155. See also the probing psy-chological analysis of de Gaulle written by Inge and Stanley Hoffmann, "The Will to Grandeur: De Gaulle as Political Artist," *Daedalus*, XCVII (Summer 1968), 829–887.

contract, as he told Malraux in their last meeting, was with France, not with his contemporaries. "This contract was capital because it did not have any form; it never had. It is without hereditary right, without referendum, without anything, but I was led to take charge of France's defense and its destiny. I responded to this categorical and silent appeal." [39]

De Gaulle's distinction between the French nation and state, on the one hand, and Frenchmen of the moment, on the other, strikes resonant notes in the writings of Latin writers who contrasted Rome and the Romans. His conception of the French nation and state assumed many of the transcendental qualities attributed by Roman authors, like Cicero, to Rome. Rome was eternal while the Romans lived and died. A Roman earned a higher moral worth in serving Rome. So Frenchmen, too, gain an enhanced personal value in serving France. While each French citizen has a free choice whether to devote his talents to the higher purposes of the nation and state and, by that token, to larger humanitarian purposes, his moral, if not physical, obligation is, in the Gaullist view, restricted. His individual merit is morally dependent on the achievement of the animating goals of the nation and state. The ideological dispositions and private successes of a citizen do not measure his true value as a person. The sole standard is the significance of his service to France. In this sense de Gaulle could welcome both Communists and monarchists in the struggle against Vichy France and Nazi Germany. " 'Is it simply political tactics?' he asked. 'The answer is not for me to unravel. For it is enough that France is served.' " [40] He could praise individual Communists, including Maurice Thorez,[41] yet repudiate the Communist party and, playing on the fears of the Right and Center, use it as a foil to advance himself and his political allies in successive electoral campaigns. The interests of France, defined by the charismatic leader whose own fate is inextricably tied to his self-projected

39. Malraux, *op. cit.*, p. 22.
40. Lüthy, *op. cit.*, pp. 564–565.
41. DePorte, *op. cit.*, p. 301, n. 10. DePorte quotes de Gaulle on the occasion of Thorez' death in 1964: "For my part, I do not forget that at a decisive moment for France, president Maurice Thorez—whatever his action may have been before and after—contributed, in answer to my call and as a member of my government, to the maintenance of national unity."

conception of France, are superior to the interests of the individual Frenchman whatever the expense that the latter might suffer.[42]

Superpower Dominance: Unstable and Illegitimate

According to the Gaullist analysis, *grandeur* could be realized only if the international system and France's role within it were transformed. First, as discussed in Chapter 9, a new North-South relation between developed and underdeveloped states would have to be built out of the wreckage of the European colonial empires, including France's. The Algerian War would be liquidated, and Algeria and the remaining parts of France's colonial holdings in Black Africa would be granted independence. Second, as Chapters 2 to 8 sketch, an East-West relation would have to be created that would simultaneously weaken the American and Russian empires consecrated at Yalta and rally Europe, with France as its western focus, to reassume its traditional leadership in world politics. The Gaullist vision of a reconstituted international order within which a revived France would play a principal role may become clearer if de Gaulle's conception and critique of contemporary international relations is understood.

The Primacy of the Nation-State

For de Gaulle and his supporters, the nation-state has paramount historical and moral worth. Durability validates it in the experience of those states which rest on the support of a nation or people whose histories extend over centuries. Men have died for these entities. For de Gaulle, such sacrifice is proof of their existence and determining influence. Conflicts over political philosophies or between rival governmental regimes are necessarily provisional and ephemeral, but below the surface of these tempests remain the states and the nations or peoples on which the merit of regimes and ideologies depends. At Blois in spring 1959, de Gaulle declared that "pretensions, ambitions, regimes, come to nothing." [43] The following September, he affirmed at Dunkirk that "regimes . . . pass, but the people will not pass." [44]

---

42. De Gaulle, *Mémoires,* III, 36.
43. Passeron, *De Gaulle parle,* p. 386.
44. *Ibid.,* p. 387

China and Russia, for example, existed before communism. They would persist as nation-states even after the passing of the ideological fashions to which their leaders are presently committed.[45]

The Gaullist government's condemnation of the Russian invasion of Czechoslovakia, discussed in Part II, was characteristic. International ideological movements could not replace the nation-state as the basic international unit. Their very novelty and lack of roots in the experience of the peoples of the globe are fatal defects. For de Gaulle, the nation-state commanded the broader communal loyalties of the vast majority of men over the past half millennium; it alone possesses the attractive power to sustain those loyalties in the foreseeable future. It has proved more lasting and compelling than any other rival political persuasion. No international government can survive unless it is based on the several and separate existences of nation-states. According to de Gaulle, history remains the product of interstate, not class, relations.

An increase in the number of participating nation-states after World War II did not, according to Gaullist thinking, change the fundamental nature of state behavior as much as it affected the modalities of international politics. The intrinsic opposition of states, whatever the seeming durability of the cooperative arrangements to which they might be party, was rooted in their separateness,[46] and these states would strive ceaselessly to improve their power and prestige relative to others. There was no respite to the struggle, nor, in Gaullist terms of reference, was there any feasible or desirable alternative to it. "International life, like life in general, is a battle," de Gaulle often observed.[47]

In the context of a national history that stretched over a thousand years of wars and battles, most Frenchmen, like de Gaulle, did not find this struggle extraordinary. The national call to *grandeur* laid bare French ambitions. Like other French leaders, including those among his opposition, de Gaulle assumed that the United States would work to preserve and expand its postwar ascendant position.

45. Passeron, *De Gaulle parle: 1962–1966,* pp. 154–155.

46. The long history of these views in political thought is discussed in Kenneth Waltz, *Man, the State and War* (New York: Columbia University Press, 1959).

47. *Major Addresses,* p. 78.

"The French, faced with American acts, waste little time deploring their impact," as one perceptive analyst observes, "because they expect great powers to act that way, i.e., to try to preserve their privileged position by rewarding the most docile and by opposing the most rebellious of their allies, to try to reach agreements with each other behind the backs of weaker partners, to use force in the defense of threatened positions." [48] The French journalist André Fontaine well described de Gaulle's attitude: "Ideologies are . . . transitory while the fact of nations endures—and with it the fundamental rivalries, born of geography and nourished by history." [49] The advent of new states did not change history; it presented, rather, new possibilities for rivalry and provided novel opportunities for a diplomatically skilled France to benefit from the quarrels of others.

Doubtful Triumph of the Nation-State System

The triumph of the nation-state, as the political unit around which the peoples of the world are organized, occurred at the very moment in history when its practical utility and its intrinsic moral worth were most open to question. The very scientific, technical, social, and economic forces which facilitated the extension of the nation-state also endangered its future. The French recognized that many of the constraints that had hitherto prevented global conflict had been overcome. Advances in military technology opened all states to swift destruction or invasion. The fall of France in 1940 was the precursor of the devastating effects of modern warfare.

Where internal control measures were absent, moreover, progress in communications, transportation, and trade exposed the people of all states to foreign influence. Regional political-military conflict that formerly could have been insulated from other areas of the globe now posed a strategic threat to all states. No longer could political developments in North America and in Europe, for example, proceed, as during the nineteenth century, independently of each other, largely in terms of the balance of forces on each continent. The rise of two

48. Stanley Hoffmann, "Perceptions, Reality, and the Franco-American Conflict," *Journal of International Affairs,* XXI, No. 1 (1967), 63. Also Malraux, *op. cit.,* pp. 136ff.

49. André Fontaine, "What Is French Policy?" *Foreign Affairs,* XLV (Oct. 1966), 59.

superpowers and the globalization of the nation-state system, with its varied expressions of national and parochial interest, created the conditions for an expanded spectrum of possible threats to a state's existence, its independence, its goals—or to all three. The larger number of states diverse in language, regime, economy, and culture generated the occasion for an increase in the number and form of state conflicts. Local balances of power, while still characterized by unique diplomatic and strategic elements, increasingly depended on the bipolar struggle between the superpowers.

All states were seen by de Gaulle to be embraced in a global grid of interwoven conflict relations. Tension at any local point encouraged the spread of interstate conflict through the world-wide network. As the number of parties to a conflict grew, the possibility arose that the intensity, duration, scope, and objectives of the original conflict would expand. Each activated fusion point threatened to initiate a chain reaction of increasing force throughout the interlaced system of conflict patterns. An acceleration of the arms race, for example, could conceivably trigger greater economic and technological rivalry which itself might lead to an enlargement of the goals initially sought by competing states. Or, the diplomatic goals pursued by a state might prompt an increase of military pressure that would have an offsetting and even deleterious effect on that state's relations not only with its immediate competitor but also with other states that perceived a threat to their positions.

Nation A might oppose nation B over goals N and M and employ means X and Y, but not Z—say, a rupture of diplomatic relations—to assert its claims. The political or diplomatic confrontation (A and B over N and M) can be viewed as a horizontal level of conflict that potentially embraces other states, C and D. What means are employed, whether X, Y, or Z, or some combination, represent varied and multidimensional forms of vertical confrontation. Conflicts may escalate along either scale and become reciprocally reinforcing across scale lines. This feedback effect might spread to other states with the result that the parties to the conflict would encompass wider geographical areas, larger numbers of diverse peoples, and progressively greater human and material resources. Bilateral state conflict increasingly resists self-containment and tends to expand beyond the initial disputants and to implicate peripheral states, regional groupings

(NATO and Warsaw pacts), and international agencies (United Nations). States associated with A and B, through security pacts, trade ties, cultural and technological accords, become implicit and even direct parties to the quarrel between A and B. All elements of the international community of states are potentially activated to include all states and the means at their disposal—as if World War I was revisited with vastly more disastrous implications for international order. If allowed to proceed unregulated (hence the need for France to have a great power role), interstate conflict would soon exceed the capacity of the contending states to manage, and it would threaten the freedom of all states to stand apart from contests that adversely affected their interests.

The Gaullist analysis conceded the increased dangers of globalized state conflict. These, Gaullists believed, could be managed at tolerable cost. Indeed, as outlined below, a plural international system, if allowed to develop free of the refracted influence of the superpowers, was potentially more stable because the greater number and geographically extended nature of interstate conflicts would tend, in effect, to be self-regulating, as one offset the other; states would also find themselves crosspressured, aligned with other states in some areas and opposed in others. What James Madison had hoped would occur in American politics with the creation of a large republic with a great number of diverse interests—a more perfect balance between internal order and individual liberty—could be realized in a sense at the international level under contemporary conditions.

Paradoxically, the greater incidence of interstate conflict, arising from the multiplicity of national interests, strengthened the possibility of realizing a more acceptable harmony between the competing objectives of international order and national independence than could be achieved through superpower bipolarity. In any event, the risks and costs run by states, like France, in promoting a pluralistic international order were alleged to be less than those already incurred in a duopolistic international system. Moreover, only a pluralistic international system, encouraging larger bilateral ties between states in all their spheres of activity, could advance Gaullist aspirations on behalf of France for increased global influence, enhanced international status, and national glory. France's fate was viewed as inextricably bound to the destiny of the nation-state as a political tool and source of ethical norms within a more decentralized system than that which arose out of World War II.

Critique of Superpower Rule

According to the analysis of the French president, the superpowers would conduct their bilateral relations in ways that could only be detrimental to other states. Managing the tensions would become increasingly difficult since no state or combination of states could perform the moderating role of balancer as Britain did during the nineteenth century. Unchecked by another powerful state or a group of states, the United States and the Soviet Union were being drawn simultaneously in two contradictory directions: toward war or toward mutual accord and subsequent condominial rule of the international system.[50] Global war would destroy third states; superpower rule would erode the *raison d'être* of each state to provide for the security and solvency of its populace and, concomitantly, would weaken its intrinsic legal and moral authority which depended ultimately on its discharge of these functions.[51] Since the French defined the stability and legitimacy of the international system in terms of the preservation of the nation-state, they rejected either proclivity as an intolerable menace to the interests and status of the weaker states. The inclination to war was destabilizing, for it loosened the restraints on global nuclear hostilities; the tendency toward hegemonic rule was illegitimate, for it robbed the nation-state of its *raison d'être.*

On the one hand, Gaullist doctrine foresaw that superpower discord nurtured systemic instability. Under these circumstances, the prospect grew that their conflict would spread around the globe, menacing the existence and interests of all states. When locked in struggle, with world-wide interests, each superpower would seek hegemonic status; each would attempt to impose its will on its antagonist; each would be driven by the fear that, unless it exploited opportunities to expand its power, its antagonist would gain an advantage. The struggle would gradually approach total proportions as each would act reciprocally on the other, forcing the struggle to ex-

50. *Major Addresses*, pp. 58–59, 75–78; Ambassade de France, Service de Presse et d'Information (New York), Speeches and Press Conferences, No. 208, July 23, 1964, pp. 7–9. Hereafter cited S&PC.
51. Macridis, ed., *op. cit.,* p. 133.

pand and intensify. Neither would feel that it could afford to lose a client to the other nor permit a neutral to fall into the other's camp. The superpower conflict would tend to assume the aspect of double-entry accounting: an asset of one would be counted as a liability for the other. As each state would act to increase its power, its move would tend to be counterbalanced by its opponent.

President de Gaulle predicted that, if unhindered, the superpower conflict would envelop all of the states. The weaker states would be the objects, not the subjects, of the competition. Where the balance of terror inhibited or precluded superpower intervention, either directly or through proxy powers, the superpowers would shift their efforts from the traditional quest for possession goals (territory, resources, commercial privilege) to what Arnold Wolfers has termed milieu goals (influencing political and economic systems abroad, cultural exchanges, or technological feats).[52] They would manipulate lesser states internally for superpower advantage; subversion and revolutionary warfare would gradually replace conventional and nuclear forms of military conflict.

The absence of alternative sources of support gave a small state incentive to appeal to a superpower to support its claims against its local opponents. The wars in the Middle East and Vietnam confirmed the de Gaulle regime in these assumptions. The reluctance of France's European partners to assume a greater responsibility for their own defense added fuel to the Gaullist fire and fed de Gaulle's criticism of the corroding effects of the American protectorate. The profligate use of military force to which the Gaullists believed the superpowers were prone, given their material wealth and superior military capability, would encourage smaller states to resolve their differences through force rather than through political accommodation. The use of violence by a great power would relax restraints on violence. An official statement of the French government, issued on June 21, 1967, two weeks after the initiation of the Six Day War, most pointedly reflected the extreme statement of the Gaullist view: "The war unleashed in Vietnam by American intervention, the destruction of lives and property that it entails, the fundamental sterility that stamps it,

52. Stanley Hoffmann, *Gulliver's Troubles* (New York: McGraw-Hill, 1968), pp. 57–66, usefully employs Arnold Wolfers' concept to contemporary international politics.

however powerful may be the means employed and however terrible be their effects, cannot fail to spread the trouble, not only locally but at a distance. Hence, the attitude of China and the haste of its armaments. Hence, on the other hand, the psychological and political process that resulted in the struggle in the Middle East." [53] These effects were likely to be reproduced in other areas of state interchange although perhaps with immediately less convulsive impact on global peace than military escalation between the superpowers.

On the other hand, French strategic thinking projected the possibility of growing superpower strategic equilibrium and diplomatic alignment on global policy, developments that would eventually subject third states to Soviet-American direction. According to the French analysis, the superpowers had incentive to coordinate their foreign and strategic policies and organize the global community into an international condominium.[54] Building on their respective blocs, the superpowers were inclined, as the Yalta conference was supposed to have demonstrated, to divide the globe into two spheres of influence. Within each sphere there could be only one center of strategic power and diplomatic initiative. Each sphere would be under the control and management of the major-bloc state. A Soviet-American duopoly would further infringe upon, and conceivably extinguish in some instances, the political independence of other states. To a greater or lesser degree, states would gradually lose their capacity to pursue an independent diplomacy; or their security functions, which sustain their claims of sovereignty, would be entrusted to (or assumed by) a big power. "A government which . . . did not assure national defense," de Gaulle told President Kennedy, "could have only an *apparent* legitimacy." [55]

53. Ambassade de France, Service de Presse et d'Information (New York), *French Foreign Policy,* Jan.–June 1967, p. 103. Hereafter cited *FFP,* with appropriate date.

54. *Washington Post,* June 22, 1967, pp. A1, A17. The theme of superpower incentives for cooperation is treated, for example, in Raymond Aron's *Peace and War,* trans. Richard Howard and Annette Baker Fox (Garden City: Doubleday, 1966), especially pp. 536–572. Aron writes in the introduction to the American edition: "We have reached the state where she [the Soviet Union] conceals, under the veil of invective, an implicit accord with the United States" (p. xvi).

55. Malraux, *op. cit.,* p. 133.

The Gaullist case against the superpowers was outlined in France's justification of its withdrawal from the NATO military organization in 1966 and in its announced determination to proceed with the construction of its own nuclear force. De Gaulle formulated the French argument in this way:

The world situation in which two super-states would alone have the weapons capable of annihilating every other country; would alone possess, through deterrence, the means for ensuring their own security; would alone hold, under their obedience, each its camp of committed people—this situation, over the long run, could only paralyze and sterilize the rest of the world by placing it either under the blow of crushing competition, or under the yolk [sic], of a double hegemony that would be agreed upon between the two rivals.

In these conditions, how could Europe unite, Latin America emerge, Africa follow its own path, China find its place, and the United Nations become an effective reality? As America and the Soviet Union failed to destroy their absolute weapons, the spell has to be broken. We are doing so, insofar as we are concerned, with our resources alone.[56]

The Cold War froze what otherwise would have been a fluid system of interstate relations. It hindered shifts in alignment among states on what potentially could have been an ever-increasing number of separate issues, ranging from cultural exchange to monetary and trade policies. For the Gaullist analysis, such a condition was contrary to the expected and French-preferred tendencies of nation-states. It unduly constrained them from striking among themselves a varying set of bilateral relations of varying duration that best served their interests as they defined them over time under changing internal and external circumstances. Cold War bipolarity was alleged to be insensitive to these nuances of state interest and perspective and to the variable effectiveness of different forms of state strategic power, military and nonmilitary, depending on the contestants in conflict and the period under examination. The superpower conflict impeded the processes of political accommodation among states. It frustrated the satisfaction of small-state demands, and ignored, at the peril of international stability, their determination to assert their rival claims. Thus, de Gaulle hailed the need for a revolution in international

56. S&PC, No. 253A, Oct. 28, 1966, p. 6.

government: "Since this division of the world between two great powers, and therefore into two camps, clearly does not benefit the liberty, equality, and fraternity of peoples, a different order, a different equilibrium are necessary for peace." [57]

National Interest and Universal Mission

If the construction of a more stable and legitimate international order was the long-run objective, the reconstitution of France as a global power was the immediate goal. In President de Gaulle's view, there could be no lasting peace unless France participated in global politics.[58] Its weight and voice were needed as balancer, broker, arbiter, and critic of international relations. Yalta had established an unfortunate precedent, resulting in the division of Europe and the superpower struggle. What contributed to France's security, solvency, and status simultaneously bolstered France's pursuit of its transnational goals and contributed to a more stable and legitimate international order.

Gaullist France spoke not just for itself, but for Europe and for the emerging nations of the Third World. Unlike the superpowers it allegedly made no claims on other states. France's promotion of its own self-interests benefited other states, including the superpowers whose conflict threatened to overwhelm them unless checked by a revived France at the head of similarly motivated and disinterested states. France's rehabilitation as a global power would promote more stable and legitimate relations between states. Its self-interest and universal mission were one. Assisting France's quest for *grandeur* was in the interest of other states, too.

If the immediate objective was France's restoration, then the operational Gaullist ideal was independence. France must always be free to act on its own views of its best interests and on behalf of other states, indeed, of humanity as a whole. Restrictions on its freedom of maneuver *ipso facto* would diminish its greatness and hamper the execution of its international responsibilities. Given the changing for-

57. Ambassade de France, Service de Presse et d'Information (New York), *Foreign Affairs*, No. 175, April 27, 1965, pp. 3–4. Hereafter cited *FA*.

58. Charles de Gaulle, *Mémoires d'espoir: Le renouveau, 1958–62* (Paris: Plon, 1970), and the fragment of volume two, *L'Effort, 1962* (Paris: Plon, 1971).

tunes of international life, France must be prepared, according to Gaullist doctrine, to seize opportunities as they arose to enhance its stature, in order ultimately to exert more influence on international relations and, most importantly, on the superpower relationship. Independence, as André Fontaine has recognized, is also an end in itself. To the degree that it can be realized, however fleeting the experience and whatever the specific locus of state action, it fulfills one of the indispensable conditions for national *grandeur*.[59]

Alignments and Alliances in Gaullist Thought

To de Gaulle, all alignments, whether tacitly struck or formalized in alliance, were conditional. Each arrangement was but one more means at the state's disposal. No one alignment could satisfy all its interests. In a private letter, President de Gaulle chided a Gaullist historian for having painted too pessimistic a picture of the rejection of the Fouchet plan in 1962 and of the growing quarrel between France and the United States and its West European partners. He explained that these conflicts were but means to larger ends. Since these alignments had lost some of their usefulness, others would have to be sought.[60]

French standards alone, not those of other states, would measure the utility of an alignment or alliance. The Atlantic Alliance, for example, was only one of a number of tools of French diplomacy, and as the 1960's wore on, its value diminished, given the French perception of a fundamental redistribution of global power in favor of the United States. If the Franco-American alliance were broadened by the unilateral action of the United States, as effectively occurred in the Lebanese landings of 1958 or in the Vietnam War, it would have to be revised with the mutual consent of the parties. If international conditions changed, commitments would have to be re-evaluated. How could it be otherwise in de Gaulle's view? What is lasting is the state, not its accords. Alliances bind only as they respond to the differential interests of the alliance partners. They extend the state. For the Atlantic Alliance to be viable, it must enlarge French power. Through the treaty, allied power is at France's disposal. If

59. Fontaine, *op. cit.*, pp. 58–76.
60. Interview with Paul Marie de la Gorce, Paris, June 1970.

an alliance conflicts with French national policy, the former must
yield. Each state decision to submit itself to alliance policy is calculated and evaluated in terms of its utility. If differences develop between alliance and national policies or over the framework within
which joint decisions are reached and executed, either the alliance
and its commitments must be amended to suit state needs or the state
is obliged to reduce its support and reliance on the alliance, and even
contemplate its abandonment. International politics should not submit to a higher law of consistency than would be expected of the
temporary alignments between factions and parties in domestic politics. Within Gaullist thought, the states were even less morally obliged
to keep, indeed they had a duty under some circumstances to break,
commitments. The fate of the domestic regime and even its internal
political divisions depend on the preservation of the state as an independent actor.

The Gaullist position was orthodox. The maintenance of the state
and the augmentation of its influence are overriding objectives of
balance-of-power politics. The administration of George Washington
had assumed the same stance almost two hundred years ago in announcing American neutrality in the war between Royalist England
and Republican France. Alexander Hamilton, ably arguing the Gaullist case, saw no reason to honor the Franco-American Friendship
Treaty of 1778 if its execution involved the United States in Europe's
quarrels, of little concern to a distant America, and impaired its political independence. Washington felt treaty pledges were void when
they risked the vital interests and even existence of the state that
made them. Their validity depended on the contracting states, not
the reverse. With the turnabout in power between the Old and New
World, Gaullist France reverted to classical international dogma. The
alliance partners had exchanged places in the hierarchy of states, but
the rationale for limited mutual cooperation remained largely the
same.[61]

From the Gaullist perspective, international relations were the

61. Felix Gilbert reviews the Hamilton argument in *The Beginnings of
American Foreign Policy* (New York: Harpers, 1961), pp. 320–322. For paral-
lel French thinking of recent vintage see Michel Debré, "France's Global
Strategy," *Foreign Affairs*, LXIX (April 1971), 395–406.

total bilateral relations struck between states at any given time, whether implicitly or explicitly agreed upon, and included any subject of mutual interest. These relations structure international relations and set out the expected conduct by which states will carry out joint activities, compete, or conflict. Included among these structures are international organizations. Whatever the complexity of their internal organization or the size, expertise, and extent of their operations, they are responsible to the individual states that created them. Although they may enter into international contracts or act apart from the states that established them, or even, at times, act contrary to the views of one or more of the member states, such assertions of independent activity are viewed either as usurpations or, more generally, as responses to the pressures and interests of a state or clique within the organization. For the Gaullists, such was the case in the 1965–1966 EEC crisis and the United Nations Congo action in the early 1960's. The EEC Commission and the United Nations Secretariat, acting partly on their own initiative, partly in accord with France's partners in these agencies, transgressed their legal and moral competence. The affairs evidenced, too, the pretensions of their leadership—Walter Hallstein in the EEC and Dag Hammarskjold in the United Nations —to challenge national authorities; for the French president, these national and personal affronts were inadmissible and were resisted.

International organizations are additional arenas of state interaction and stakes in the pre-existing struggle between states for their particular objectives. As objects and instruments of state conflict they are, themselves, incompetent to make binding rules on the members. France rejected both UN attempts to assess it financially for the Congo operation of the early 1960's and the EEC Commission proposals in 1965 that would have increasingly placed the European community's budget under the supervision of the European Parliament instead of the member states. The French case before the International Court in the Congo crisis is revealing. The French government argued that the financial obligations assessed against a state are valid only to the extent that the state accepts them. "Any other conception would lead to granting the United Nations powers that the states have never granted to any organization, even the most integrated. Such an abuse of the international personality of the United

Nations would make of it a super state." [62] To be sure, new expectations of state conduct constantly arise from the workings of the international organization, but their ultimate validity depends on their mutual acceptance by the members. States, especially those whose histories extend over centuries, are of permanent value; international instrumentalities are, by their origin, expedients, subject to transformation and abolition when they no longer serve national purposes.

The Nature of Foreign Policy

Foreign policy reduces itself essentially to the task of developing alignment and dealignment strategies with other states to meet needs at all levels from security and solvency to cultural enrichment. The number of French attempts to establish new alignments within the Atlantic Alliance, Europe, and the Third World that would advance France's interests and influence are impressive. These are discussed in greater detail in the chapters that follow, but a brief review of some highlights may illustrate the larger global objectives underlying each new French initiative to redefine its foreign ties and the instrumental character of its exterior alignments.

The directorate scheme for the Atlantic Alliance and the proposal for a revision of the international monetary system, if implemented, would have placed France on a par with the United States in the making of Western military strategy and financial policy. France's continuation of the policy of reconciliation with Germany after 1958, leading to the treaty of 1963, the Fouchet plan of the early 1960's, and the rejection of Britain's entry into the Common Market of 1963 aimed partially at insulating the little Europe of the Six from Anglo-American influence and at asserting French leadership. Moreover, successful development of the Gaullist political plan for Europe would have effectively outflanked efforts to achieve political integration through the EEC. The opening of the East European campaign around the search for privileged ties with the Soviet Union, beginning approximately in 1964, sought to make France the spokesman of the non-Communist world in Western Europe. After 1968, however, France slowly drifted back into the American orbit of in-

62. International Court of Justice, Pleadings, Oral Arguments, Documents, "Lettre du gouvernement de la république française au greffier de la cour," Feb. 15, 1962, p. 134.

fluence and even suggested a grouping of France, Great Britain, West Germany, and Italy as the core of a new political structure for Western Europe.

Similarly, the Third World promised gains. In ending the Algerian War, France sought to establish a privileged relation with the Algerian government based on economic, technical, and cultural aid and cooperation. The recognition of Red China (1964) and well-publicized visits to Mexico and Latin America (1964) and Cambodia (1966) were designed to strengthen French ties with the states of these regions and to widen French influence in the underdeveloped world. Meanwhile, traditional relations with Black Francophone Africa were sustained. After the Six-Day War, France responded quickly to fill the vacuum left by the Anglo-American powers among the Arab states and multiplied its efforts to improve its relations with the Arab peoples. In the closing months of de Gaulle's rule, France's much-publicized Mediterranean policy was launched. It sought to strengthen France's bilateral ties with all of the states of the Mediterranean region, especially in the Maghreb, where France's interests were traditionally rooted, and with the seaboard states of Europe, including Spain, Italy, and Greece, despite their divergent governing regimes.

As these ties were being knit, actions were taken to cut or reduce other relations whose utility had diminished. France gradually withdrew from the NATO organization from 1959 to 1966, although it remained within the Atlantic Alliance as a hedge against a possibly expansionist Soviet Union or a revived Germany. The development of the *force de frappe* accelerated this dealignment process as France increasingly claimed an independent strategic posture that would both remain beyond American influence and fulfill French and European security needs. Commitments under the Rome Treaty of 1957, principally dealing with majority voting, were revised unilaterally in the 1965–1966 crisis with the European Community. French-German relations were strained in placing Germany in a position to have not only to choose repeatedly between Paris and Washington, but also to accept France's lead in normalizing relations with the Soviet Union and reducing American influence in Europe. The French-Israeli entente was liquidated when its retention proved embarrassing and costly for French efforts among the Arab states. In the middle

1960's, partly out of personal and national pique, partly out of calculation, the Gaullist regime allowed its relations with Tunisia and Morocco, its former protectorates, to lapse. These ties were repaired as part of the regenerated Mediterranean policy after 1968.

Tactics of Alignment and Dealignment

Gaullist dealignment strategy was closely linked to two characteristic methods of diplomacy. The first tactic was to attack the strongest, yet most politically vulnerable ally; this had been done during World War II. The ploy can be executed at minimum cost and with low risk since a counterattack by the more powerful partner is not likely, considering the larger convergence of interest against the common enemy; if it should occur, the self-fulfilling prophecy can be employed as proof of the major ally's imperial proclivities. Furthermore, for a weaker power, opposition is a desired goal in itself. It clearly manifests an independent will, presses the stronger ally to make concessions, and provides, at the very least, some psychic income for the embattled leadership and people of the weaker partner who feel the discouraging weight of their own impotency.[63]

Under conditions of waning Cold War and nuclear stability, attacking the United States served a number of specific Gaullist purposes. It created an interest with the common antagonist, the Soviet Union, to have France at the bargaining table between East and West. It could be used as an advertisement to all states that France genuinely pursued an independent policy and was the only state to resist American economic, technological, and even cultural expansion in Europe. It provided an example for the European states to follow in defense, international trade, monetary policy, and technological development. The Santo Domingo affair of 1965 provided an occasion to attack American hegemonic tendencies in Latin America. Criticism of American policy in Vietnam was similarly helpful in attracting Communist and neutralist support. French objections to alleged American inculpation in the Six-Day War ingratiated France

63. To oppose and resist is a distinct Gaullist trait. "Refusal is the supreme value," says Malraux of de Gaulle. "Perhaps his definition of character is not only to say: 'No,' but he is at ease only when he says: 'No'" (*op. cit.*, pp. 81–82)

among the Arab states, particularly those under revolutionary regimes. Moreover, attack on the closest ally had the presumed salutary effect of re-establishing the lost global balance between the United States and the Soviet Union after the 1962 missile crisis. The dissolution of the specific relation with Israel, whatever the particular profit to France's account among the Arab regimes, had the parallel effect, according to French apologists, of re-establishing the regional equilibrium upset in Israel's favor after the Six-Day War.

Second, Gaullist France applied the tactic of the empty chair in multilateral negotiations not to its liking. The ploy was used against the NATO organization, SEATO, the EEC, the WEU, the IMF, and the eighteen-nation disarmament conference meeting in Geneva. Beyond the assertion of its position respecting the issues in dispute between itself and its partners within these organizations, France's absence served general instrumental purposes. First, its nonparticipation threw a pall of illegitimacy over the proceedings; these groups, implied Gaullist leaders, could not make binding decisions for France without its consent. The repeated assertion of this tactic implicitly reaffirmed, if only retrospectively, de Gaulle's condemnation of the Yalta conference to which France had not been invited. Europe's division, which according to Gaullist doctrine was confirmed at Yalta by the Big Three, was not valid. In Gaullist eyes, France had indeed something to offer in bargaining with the victorious powers of World War II and a revived Germany over questions of existing frontiers and security arrangements. France's recognition of the Oder-Neisse line between Germany and Poland was more than an acceptance of the inevitable. It consecrated the frontier.

The same mental set animated the belief of the Gaullist government that France's approval was necessary to reach an accord for Southeast Asia and the Middle East. In Vietnam, France recognized the special dispensing power of the nuclear states and the legitimate interests of the Soviet Union and China in the region. In the Middle East, France accepted not only the *de facto* presence of the Soviet Union, but its legitimate right to be there. Alternatively, withdrawal from the NATO organization and SEATO proceedings in effect were meant to dilute the moral and legal capacity of the United States to use these bodies to make authoritative decisions for geographical areas falling within France's sphere of interest. This point was made more directly and positively in de Gaulle's directorate proposal to reorganize Western alliance arrangements.

The practice of the empty chair is tantamount to the claim for a partial or full veto power in the decisions of the international bodies to which France is a party. Assertion of the right advanced the view that France has a special role in international relations. Again, refusing to be present at international deliberations not of its choosing dramatically, if not always effectively, manifests France's foreign policy independence. It is a particularly useful device in executing a dealignment maneuver against an ally for the benefit of an alignment gain with the common adversary. Gaullist France's loudly proclaimed silence in the councils of international bodies communicated its intent to remain apart from the international arrangements contemplated there. As long as these forums responded to superpower control, French participation and submission to their rules tended to frustrate the Gaullist aim of weakening, not reinforcing, the Cold War structure of international politics. Its withdrawal from NATO in 1966 and the quarrel with its EEC partners in 1965–1966 simultaneously drew France closer to the Soviet Union, whose opposition to a strong Atlantic Alliance and European Economic Community was of long standing, and relaxed its ties with its Western allies. Like the tactic of frontal assault against the major ally, the policy of the empty chair also applied pressure on France's European and North American allies to make concessions to elicit its cooperation and, in effect, to inflect their policies toward its lead. Finally, by absenting itself from distasteful negotiations, France could avoid the role of *demandeur*. In French diplomatic practice, the stance of suppliant is bad form, an object of reproach, and inevitably a weak negotiating position, opposed to *grandeur* and good bargaining sense. In placing its proposals on a take-it-or-leave-it basis, it can hope to escape the psychic burdens of the *demandeur* but still retain influence.

The Gaullist Alternative: Oligarchy for Duopoly

In attempting to rationalize French global policy under the Fifth Republic, one must realize that it did not spring full-blown from a detailed blueprint that de Gaulle brought with him into office. It was articulated largely as a response to the specific circumstances and problems confronting the Gaullist government. A slogan, like "Europe from the Atlantic to the Urals," often attributed, not fully accurately,[64] to de Gaulle, suggests little of the scope, flexibility, and suppleness of Gaullist activity and the countless conceivable combinations of states and levels of action which might be contemplated to serve state ends.[65] Within this linear representation are uncomfortably crowded the bewildering stops and starts, offensive thrusts and defensive retreats, and the curious lapses and anomolous commissions of Gaullist policy. Greater malevolence is also often attributed to de Gaulle and French foreign policy than evidence or a detached examination of Gaullist words and acts might justify. Certainly de Gaulle's anti-American bias can be exaggerated.[66] Gaullist global conceptions, like its conceptions of alliance and alignments, remain disciplined to state needs for security, status, and solvency, whether applied by Presidents Charles de Gaulle or Georges Pompidou. The elegance of its rhetoric masks more than reveals the opportunistic aspects of French foreign policy. Gaullist capacity to suggest attractive visionary futures, beyond the superpower struggle and the Cold War, obscures the hesitancy underlying its foreign policy, especially before the questions of reconciling European unity and French national independence. The dramatic initiative of Gaullist foreign policy hide, too, a pronounced tendency to "muddle through" in the hope that stalling tactics will gain time when a more propitious future, more sympathetic to French aspirations, will arrive.

The ceaseless search for new alignments for calculated gain exposed a fundamental dualism, more inbred than learned, more instinctively accepted than consciously articulated, which underlies French foreign policy behavior. It is rooted in the tension, already noted, between national interest and universal mission. Each new shift in policy marks a re-evaluation of France's over-all consensual

64. For a complex presentation of the "Atlantic to the Urals" formula, see Edmond Jouve, *Le Général de Gaulle et la construction de l'Europe, 1940–1966*, 2 vols. (Paris: Librairie Général de Droit et de Jurisprudence, 1967), I, 536ff. For a contrasting view, consult René Courtin, *L'Europe de l'Atlantique à Oural* (Paris: Editions l'Esprit Nouveau, 1963).

65. Lüthy, *op. cit.*, pp. 561–573.

66. John Newhouse, *De Gaulle and the Anglo-Saxons* (London: Deutsch, 1970), presents the common view. Malraux, *op. cit.*, pp. 127–138, suggests that de Gaulle admired the United States, but feared its power and dynamism.

and conflict relations with other states, yet each shift is justified as selfless, not self-serving. If French foreign policy appears opportunistic in mode and means, it remains, in its own image, steadfast in its commitments to effect a more legitimate and stable international order. It can play off enemy and ally, yet claim to be a reliable partner. It can insist on strict compliance to treaty obligations, as with the accord on agriculture in the EEC, and still refuse to adhere to other provisions of the Rome Treaty that constrain its freedom of maneuver. Its short-run practices for marginal political profit are viewed as theoretically consistent with its long-run commitment to the construction of a more equitable and peaceful world. Its global goals are at once revisionist, in seeking to rehabilitate France's lost *grandeur* and rank as a first-rate power, and revolutionary, in seeking to undo superpower rule and fashion a world order based on the multiplicity of nation-states and responsive to their individual needs.

Within the Gaullist exegesis, it makes little sense to criticize French foreign policy as narrowly nationalistic. It makes no more sense to Gaullist supporters to condemn French foreign policy as destructive of international stability. According to this view, the superpowers have proved more mischievous. In pressing its views, France not only asserts the obvious—that states act on their own interests—but proposes to build international relations on the universal expression of particular state interests. That the superpowers act on their own interests is not so odious or unexpected as their refusal to allow other states to assert their demands. The nation-state is not only the sole feasible unit on which to rest global government, but it also should be. The "is" and "ought" are one. State behavior and state morals are different aspects of the same phenomenon. How could it be otherwise since there is no other vantage point beyond the nation-state from which to criticize its actions? Its actions, as it were, are self-justifying.

Presumptions of Participation

The Gaullist position distinguishes between what might be termed apparent and real authority in international relations. Apparent legitimacy inheres in the nation-state as an organized and internationally recognized political entity. Real legitimacy, however, derives from the actual capacity of a state to enforce binding rules—from its ability to influence or compel the behavior of other states as well as its own citizens. Apparent authority refers to the inherent moral and legal equality of states; real authority, to their inequality of power. Until a state can carry out its foreign and domestic responsibilities and create the means for independent action, its international authority remains impaired, and to that degree its right to demand allegiance from its nationals is defective.

Similarly, groups or *ensembles* of states, like those in Europe, can become political entities with international stature only if they establish a capacity and will to act together, free from outside influence, and to develop capabilities, including military force under central political direction, to enforce their will. As one perceptive Gaullist observer has remarked, "Not all the countries that are treated (often necessarily) as states by other countries and by international organizations are states in the proper sense of that term. Those that do qualify, . . . for the title, do so because they are historical facts and exercise real power." [67] To the degree that states permit their principal duties to be executed by other states, they compromise their claims to sovereignty and limit their diplomatic maneuverability and political independence. The proclamation of statehood does not automatically confer the right to participate in the shaping of international accords bearing on the state's behavior. This right is earned in its exercise, in the state's effective projection of its will abroad whether through economic strength, moral suasion, or, especially, military force.

According to Gaullist views, international transactions depend on the strongest states; only they have the material strength to achieve their objectives. States are, therefore, divided into two principal categories—great powers and dependencies—with subtle gradations within each set. The dictates and demands of weaker states have force only when accepted or supported by a larger state. Their international pronouncements are viewed more as petitions to be heard or rejected, according to the dispensations of the stronger states, than as absolute claims with intrinsic merit because of their source. A rule of expected state behavior becomes universally valid as soon as it enjoys the support of the major states which are willing to en-

67. Pickles, *International Affairs*, 1966, p. 412.

force it. Laws that cannot be executed are not ultimately binding. Yet those accords and prescriptions that are collectively decided upon by the most powerful states are subject to continual revision and reversal in response to the evolving perceptions of their interests and mutual power status.

Within this vision, a small number of global powers would be charged with the responsibility for world stability, which would be founded on their anticipated determination to conserve and expand their power and status within the international system. The regulatory activity of the great powers would assure regional stability. Their material superiority and presumably unchallenged political authority within their spheres of interest would manage regional conflict relations. The accommodation of small-power interests would be consigned to the dispensing power of the great states to which they would bear fealty. Small-state appeals beyond their zones of influence would presumably be discouraged both by the protector power and by other major states fearing open conflict or reprisal in the form of a political attack against the vulnerable parts of a big state's sphere of influence or the eruption of costly and possibly uncontrollable military hostilities involving nuclear weapons.

Stability between geographical zones would rest on a mixture of political and strategic conflict, competition, and cooperation among the major states. Political stability would partly depend on the willingness of the great powers to recognize their respective areas of concern and to develop (as envisioned in de Gaulle's directorate scheme for NATO or his special relation with Germany within the EEC) consultative mechanisms for great-power global policy and action. Where intersecting interests conflicted, as in the Middle East or Vietnam, a common accord among the major powers was the advisable solution. Failing agreement, conflict and competition between the major states would then keep international order. The big states could be expected to defend their interests.

The Congress of Vienna, and not Versailles, inspired this Gaullist mode of international relations. Membership would be provisionally placed at five, including the United States, the Soviet Union, Communist China, England, and France. These powers assumed responsibility for international stability the moment they developed their own nuclear striking forces. These peoples have long and distinguished histories, and not completely by accident, they are the permanent members of the UN Security Council.[68] War would be discouraged because the great powers would check each other more effectively than the United States and the Soviet Union could alone and because they would regulate and police interstate relations within their areas of principal regional concern. Greater global stability would then presumably result.

Incentives for Smaller States

Critics of Gaullist global views are quick to point out the seeming contradiction between France's criticism of superpower hegemony and its claim to big-power status.[69] Fixation on logical inconsistencies overlooks the political attractiveness of the French position for other states. The de Gaulle government did little to hide its contempt for weaker states or its determination to impose France's will on them, if the opportunity arose. Other states would do likewise in similar circumstances. On the other hand, Gaullist France could reasonably assume that other states, whatever the feelings of their leaders or sentiments of their peoples, had incentive to join with France to manipulate the superpower conflict to their respective advantages, to avoid the risks and costs inherent in being drawn into the Soviet-American struggle and to resist too close a tie to one or the other of the superstates in their dealings with each other. French policies and actions could then be justified, at least partially, as a contribution to these systemic objectives, however otherwise France's particular self-interests might be served at the expense of the other great states.

The Gaullist regime could hope that other states would either align their policies as marked out by France or would develop among themselves closer and more direct ties to establish "zonal relations" outside superpower control or influence. Either development served French global strategy, which was aimed at weakening, if not breaking, the hold of the superpower conflict and potential consensus on the freedom of action of other states. The multiplication of bilateral ties between a great number of heterogeneous states, with or without

68. S&PC, No. 228, Sept. 9, 1965, p. 10.
69. Carmoy, op. cit., and Kulski, op. cit., are representative.

France but outside the orbits of the United States and the Soviet Union, could generate incentives for all states to maintain an active interest in the preservation of peace, even though the particular relations struck between them over different time periods on behalf of contingent political ends would be provisional and subject to rapid and unpredictable rupture and revision.

First, the determination of each state to maintain its own identity would be harnessed to the preservation of the international order. Since war anywhere on the globe threatened to spread to other states, peace would be considered a universal value and a vital interest of all states. Giving free rein to national self-determination would become the basis for continuing, if not necessarily cooperative, relations among states. In this sense, the Versailles Treaty, which sought global stability through the creation of new states and the redrawing of state boundaries consistent with national feelings, partially served Gaullist designs. The revolutionary force of nationalism would become a conservative force by giving vent to its expression in the form of an enlarging universe of nation-states. Gaullist doctrine anticipated that those states would be disposed to play, and would be progressively capable of playing, a role, however small initially, in defining those security relations of the international system that affected their aims and independence rather than leave these tasks to one or the other of the superpowers, or both, to determine for them. Within Gaullist thought, nationalism was counted upon to prompt states, almost as a reflex, to join in opposition to any other state or group of states that might appear to seek hegemonic status. On the other hand, states were expected to resist too close an association, even in combining against a common enemy of the moment, out of fear that in avoiding one threat to their independence another might be inadvertently created.

Second, within an enlarged and universalized system of states, increasingly more states might perceive that a greater number and variety of interests and perspectives would be accommodated than under superpower direction. Even the superpowers would be brought to the view that they should not only tolerate greater diversity but also reduce their efforts to control all segments of the international scene to suit their particular political conceptions. Each state would strive to strike those relations—military, economic, cultural—that appeared to maximize its interests and objectives. Each state would be encouraged to calculate how it could improve its position vis-à-vis others. Advantages to one state at the expense of another would tend to cancel themselves out. Damage to a set of security or economic relations, because of the expansionist tendencies of a particular state, for example, should be self-correcting over time as adversely affected states reassessed their relations and aligned with similarly threatened states to meet the new challenge.

No state would achieve all of its goals, but each would tend to receive—or would perceive itself receiving—some compensation for its efforts. Given shifting alignments and the ever-present possibility of change and opportunity to make new bargains, the hope of remedy for unrequited personal, group, and state demands would be sustained. The future would remain open and expectant for all states. Out of such a selfish pursuit of interests, a web of interlocking global relations, fundamentally bilateral in nature, though multilateral in appearance, gradually would be woven, ensnaring all of the states within a closely knit pattern of self-generated relations that presumably would be responsive to state needs and aspirations. States would still have incentive and opportunity to make demands on each other, but short of threatening the system of international relations as a whole on which their capacity to pursue their interests depended and to which they were tied by their own contradictory alignments.

The stable operation of international relations would depend on the freedom of states to shift their allegiances, within any given set of defined relations over time. It is expedient for global stability that interstate relations be permeable and uncertain. In limiting the continuous realignment of states on specific international issues, bloc politics, argued de Gaulle, hardened state relations, intensified conflict, and encouraged the outbreak of hostilities. Moreover, if the groupings of states were transitory and contingent, individual states would be given little incentive to undertake large enterprises or run great risks that would threaten other states since they could not depend on their allies of the moment. The distinction between enemy and ally would gradually disappear. State ambitions to dominate would thus be pitted against each other. The possibility of global domination hopefully would also be checked by the relative weakness of any one state in comparison to the total number of states and resources available to the international community to oppose the expansionist power.

In managing its conflict-cooperative relations, each state would be encouraged to be conservative in breaking or exchanging its relations with others, fearing loss, through thoughtless ventures, of its laboriously accumulated wealth of satisfactory interests and relations. The stability of international politics would not depend solely on one over-all balance of power, as previously conceived, but on a series of shifting equilibria among states varying with the activity in question. Thus the military powers of a state might conceivably be offset not only by the military forces of other states but also by vulnerability, say, to economic pressures. This was the situation with which the United States, for example, found itself confronted during the middle 1960's. Its military power was increasingly offset by rising Soviet capabilities, and its economic pre-eminence was progressively challenged by its European allies.

A complex network of hierarchies among states would be established, corresponding to the comparative advantage of each. The most important would still be the military hierarchy dominated by the nuclear states whose strategic prowess essentially defined the global security system. Within this security framework would be developed other state hierarchies based on other forms of influence. The nuclear powers need not be among the leaders of these alternative economic, cultural, or diplomatic groupings, but might even be forced to share international status with smaller states. These other hierarchical formations, by themselves, could not revise the global security framework. De Gaulle thought nuclear weapons had changed the rules of strategic balance too fundamentally. State competition in other than military policy could still pose serious challenges for the great powers, especially the United States and the Soviet Union. Each hierarchy was itself a specific functional balance of power. Each was in a manner superimposed upon a geographical distribution of strategic power that roughly reflected the sphere of influence of the nuclear states.

The strivings of states for international influence would be translated into continuing and subtle changes, functional and geographical, in their relative bilateral standing. This very instability in relative stature and status would tend to be stabilizing as a greater number of states would find outlets for their particular creative possibilities. Superpower efforts to achieve international order by stifling the particular national drives of other states was an invitation to disorder. The superpower formula was self-defeating since smaller states would continue to assert their independence in whatever forms of influence were available to them, individually or collectively. The French nuclear program gave point to the argument. The wiser course was to harness the expression of national independence to the stability of the international system. According to the Gaullist analysis, while shifts within specific balances of power and the relative status of the states within each balance register changes in state behavior, interest, and power, over-all international relations would remain stable with respect to the propensity of states to avoid war in resolving their differences.

It was sufficient for the French case that greater divergency and variety in state relations result, not that superpower dominance be replaced by a democratic form of international decision making centered, for example, in the General Assembly of the United Nations. Oligarchy was still more preferable to small states than duopoly. The multiplication of independent and competing centers of political authority and influence corresponded in greater measure to a stable and legitimate vision of international transactions even if it did not promise to produce a perfect harmony between apparent and real authority. The Gaullist objective of redistributing global power to France's advantage would also strengthen the conditions necessary for small-power initiative, consistent with their means and genius, in world politics.

An oligarchical system, composed of distinct hierarchical orders defined by different forms of state influence would encourage a greater harmony between the *de facto* distribution of material power among nation-states and their *de jure* political authority. The nation-state—and France's example was offered as proof—could still act as the protector of its public domain and the guarantor of the personal safety and welfare of its citizens. "With respect to the problems in the world," President de Gaulle observed, "our [France's] independence leads us to act in accordance with our present concept . . . : that no hegemony exercised by anyone, no foreign intervention in the internal affairs of a State, no prohibition made to any country on maintaining peaceful relations with any other is justifiable. On the contrary, in our view, the supreme interest of mankind dictates that each nation be responsible for itself, free from encroachments, aided in its progress without conditions of allegiance." [70] Rejected was the notion that global peace could be preserved only through the continued military monopoly and interventionist schemes of the superstates or through collective security arrangements—NATO, the Warsaw Pact, or the United Nations—that in the Gaullist view obscured the particularistic drives of the United States or the Soviet Union.

French global policy under the Gaullist Fifth Republic may be conceived in terms of four overlapping circles or groups of states. These include the Atlantic Alliance under the leadership of the Anglo-American powers, and especially the United States, the little Europe of the European Economic Community, Eastern Europe under Soviet influence, and the Third World. By playing off one or the other of these circles and by maintaining subbalances among the states within each, as in the Middle East, France becomes within the Gaullist analysis a pivotal world state—the center of each circle. The structural lines of international relations would then intersect at Paris. The French weight, while small, could still be potentially influential in resolving or diminishing conflicts, particularly in situations where the contending forces neutralized themselves. From its central location, France's weight could be shifted from one circle to another or within a group or *ensemble*. The result would be a complex balance within and between them that would be an additional guarantee of world peace.

In any event, whatever the measure of France's influence, it could still judge from its independent position the merit of the claims of the contesting parties, suggesting possible solutions along the way, or it could simply make its good offices available, as in the Paris peace talks over Vietnam, to resolve quarrels between states with whom it could be on good terms. It would be a part of each circle, but not of any one. In playing these alternative roles—as balancer, broker, arbiter, and critic—France's national interests and international status would be advanced. A by-product would presumably be greater sta-

70. *FA*, No. 175, April 27, 1965, p. 2.

bility and the enlargement of state opportunities to participate in the shaping of their future relations with each other.

The Gaullist multipolar vision, as an alternative to threatened superpower dominance, would presumably be stabler because, as the next chapter details, it would rely on multilateral, not bilateral, nuclear deterrence; more legitimate, because it would favor the freedom of action and independence of a greater number of states whose power and position would be enhanced relative to the United States and the Soviet Union; more attractive, because it would promise more states a more fluid international politics, freeing them to pursue and satisfy more effectively their special interests as they saw fit; feasible, because more states, not just two, would have a stake in international stability; and realistic, because it would adjust the structure and processes of international relations to the inevitability of greater national diversity evidenced in the spread of the nation-state as the primary unit of global politics.

The following chapters examine whether France has been able under the Fifth Republic to inch the international system toward its notions of stability and legitimacy and, simultaneously, to maximize its national independence, influence, and global status. The discussion below of selected, but critical, areas of French foreign policy toward the Atlantic community, Europe, and the Third World analyzes the foreign policy record of the de Gaulle and Pompidou administrations from these national and systemic perspectives. The concluding chapter evaluates both administrations from these two viewpoints.

PART I

FRENCH INTERNATIONAL POLICY IN THE WESTERN BLOC

2
Security within NATO

Security, Independence, and Grandeur

The Gaullist understanding of national security matched the breadth and complexity of the Gaullist conception of international politics. It surpassed the narrower concerns of the Third Republic which, after World War I, was contented with demanding diplomatic guarantees and disarmament accords that would assure France's military superiority in Europe against future German aggression. It exceeded, too, the aspirations of the Fourth Republic, which, after the Communist *coup d'état* in Czechoslovakia of February 1948 focused on international security accords to meet the danger of Soviet global expansionism. Early in World War II, de Gaulle had already defined the search for French security in larger terms than the defeat of the Nazi regime and the subsequent erection of barriers to future German militarism. In the darkest days of the war, de Gaulle joined France, which he alone claimed to represent, to the allied effort against the Axis powers only on the condition that its cooperation be understood, not as subordination, but as the freely granted consent of a sovereign state possessed of the same rights and status as the wartime Big Three.[1]

The Gaullist provisional government of 1944–1946 and the Gaullist Fifth Republic of 1958–1969 were in essential harmony on the basic point that France's independence in military strategy and diplomacy must be won against ally and enemy. In each case—against Germany in World War II and the Soviet Union in the Cold War—the ally-adversary remained the Anglo-American powers. Resisting the demands and entreaties of France's strongest and most dependable allies, even while cooperating with them against a common foe, was not a novel characteristic of French foreign policy. Anglo-French

1. De Gaulle, *Mémoires*, II, 5–6; J. R. Tournoux, *La Tragédie du général* (Paris: Plon, 1967), pp. 460–461.

relations during the Crimean War and World War I, for example, were similarly marked by discord and disillusionment. De Gaulle could claim a respected place in this tradition of French diplomacy.

Under de Gaulle, the Fifth Republic strove to fashion a strategic policy and military posture that would both serve French interests and be French. The passive defense doctrine of the Third Republic, symbolized in the Maginot Line and embodied in the policy of appeasement, proved disastrous. The Third Republic followed an independent course, but its policies did not serve France. On the other hand, the Fourth Republic, in subordinating France to the United States, served French interests in the immediate aftermath of World War II when France was weak, but its policies were not French. The Fifth Republic proposed to do both.

Being French and in the French interest were defined by the Gaullist regime as being equally opposed to the encroachments of enemies and to the presumptions of allies. Both usurped the functions of security and solvency that properly attached to the French state. The Soviet Union would subjugate France and the rest of Europe to the Red Army as Germany had subjugated them before; the United States would erode France's authority, confirmed in the daily discharge of its responsibility to represent and defend the French people and to arbitrate their internal disputes. Moreover, if France acceded to allied blandishments or enemy extortion, it would forfeit its claim to big-power status. Within the Gaullist view, French national security, independence, and *grandeur* merged. Over time, there were neither permanent allies nor enemies but persistent threats, altering ceaselessly in shape and substance, to the independence of France and to the expansion of its global power and prestige.

The security policies of the Gaullist government fall roughly into three periods. From 1958 to 1962, France pursued its security policies largely within the Atlantic Alliance. Its temporary acquiescence was largely determined by continued Soviet pressures in Western Europe, signs of Soviet progress in strategic weaponry that signaled the possibility of its growing global superiority in the Cold War, and, most importantly, the burdensome and internally divisive war in Algeria. When these conditions changed, so did Gaullist support for an international framework within which French power and prestige might be maximized.

From 1962 to 1968, France sought to free itself from American strategic and diplomatic policies within the Atlantic Alliance. As Chapters 5 through 7 detail, it attempted to wean West Germany from American tutelage and, failing in that attempt, to align its diplomatic policies increasingly with those of Soviet Russia. As for its strategic policies, with which this chapter is primarily concerned, the French government fought, on the one hand, to block American attempts to constrain its strategic and diplomatic maneuvering and, on the other hand, to sustain its criticisms of both superpowers and the alleged instability and illegitimacy of the present international system.

The final period in French strategic policies may be dated from the spring of 1968. The May revolt of students and workers, the succeeding financial crisis, the growing assertion of German economic power and diplomatic independence, and the Russian invasion of Czechoslovakia forced a constriction of Gaullist diplomatic activity and of French attempts to reshape the international environment. The lower international profile, adopted by the Pompidou government, had already been sketched for France by the de Gaulle regime in its final year in power.

Big Power Status through Cooperation and Cooptation, 1958–1962

The De Gaulle Directorate

Early in the de Gaulle administration, France pressed for equality with the United States and Great Britain in making policy for the Atlantic Alliance. It based its claim on its global interests and on its long history of exercising international responsibilites, and not, as later, on the respective military capabilities available to the Western Big Three.[2] The importance which the Gaullist government attached

2. Tournoux, *op. cit.*, pp. 314–342; André Fontaine, *Le Monde*, Nov. 11, 13, 1968; David Schoenbrun, *The Three Lives of Charles de Gaulle* (New York: Atheneum, 1966), pp. 286–317; James Reston, *New York Times*, May 1, 1964, p. 34, May 3, 1964, p. 10E; U.S., Congress, Senate, Committee on Government Operations, *Hearings, Atlantic Alliance*, Part 7, 89th Cong., 2d sess., 1966, pp. 228–231, hereafter cited *Hearings, Atlantic Alliance*; John Newhouse, *De Gaulle and the Anglo-Saxons*, pp. 53–84. Special attention is drawn to Wilfred L. Kohl, *French Nuclear Diplomacy* (Princeton: Princeton University Press, 1971), pp. 70–81. Kohl's study is the most comprehensive review of French defense policies under the de Gaulle administration.

to French status within the alliance is suggested by the timing of de Gaulle's celebrated (although never officially published) memorandum of September 17, 1958, which was sent to President Eisenhower and Britain's Prime Minister Harold Macmillan. In the midst of preparations for the submission of a new constitution to the French electorate and of efforts to bring the army in Algeria under government control, de Gaulle chose to raise the delicate and controversial points that NATO should be global, not confined to Europe, and that there should be Western big-power accord on world-wide diplomacy and on the contingencies in which nuclear weapons would be employed.[3]

De Gaulle confirmed these views in his news conference of September 5, 1960. He found fault "with the limitation of the Alliance to a single area of Europe." [4] "We feel that, at least among the *world powers* of the West," de Gaulle observed, "there must be something organized—where the Alliance is concerned—as to their political conduct and, should the occasion arise, their strategic conduct outside Europe, especially in the Middle East, and in Africa, where these three [the United States, Britain, and France] are constantly involved. . . . If there is no agreement among the principal members of the Atlantic Alliance on matters other than Europe, how can the Alliance be indefinitely maintained in Europe?" French interests around the globe precluded France's submission to an exclusively European alliance. American monopoly of strategic policy also came under attack. NATO's integrated arrangements, according to de Gaulle, placed "everything . . . under the command of the Americans" and assured that only they would "decide on the use of . . . atomic weapons. . . . Given the nature of these weapons, and the possible consequences of their use, France obviously cannot leave her own destiny and even her own life to the direction of others." [5]

De Gaulle reportedly proposed "an arrangement whereby the Washington-Paris-London governments would agree on common policies—each having a veto on the others—on what to do in Asia, Africa, and elsewhere outside the North American area." [6] The de Gaulle memorandum had analyzed the grave risks France ran in

3. *Major Addresses,* p. 96.
4. *Ibid.* Emphasis added.
5. *Ibid.*
6. *New York Times,* May 1, 1964, p. 34, May 3, 1964, p. 10E.

maintaining an alliance with the United States which pledged its members to collective security. Crises, such as the American landings in Lebanon in July 1958, were cited, and complaints were raised that France was not properly consulted on such decisions, although the de Gaulle government had been alerted about the impending American landing.[7]

Through the formal establishment of a "tripartite organization to take joint decisions on global problems," Western accord could be expected on a common diplomatic and strategic policy. Such an organization "would be authorized to 'draw up strategic plans' and also be empowered to 'put them into effect' with specific application . . . to 'the use of nuclear weapons anywhere in the world.' " [8] An exception would be made in the obvious case of a direct attack against the homeland of any of the members of the triumvirate. Theaters of operation would presumably be marked out. One of the Big Three would be principally responsible for each sphere. This view is suggested in de Gaulle's reported remark to Secretary of State John Foster Dulles that "of course, a common policy in North Africa would necessarily be a French policy." [9] The coordination of theater policies would be tantamount to the outline for a world-wide security plan to protect Western interests. In any event, whether the Anglo-American powers adopted the directorate scheme or not, de Gaulle indicated "that henceforth France would 'subordinate' her participation in NATO to the 'recognition of French worldwide interests' and 'equal participation' by France in global strategy." [10]

President Eisenhower's reply of October 20, 1958, indicated that the United States, like France, had adopted a number of approaches to meet the world Communist threat. The Atlantic Alliance was only one, albeit important, means to meet this common danger. France and the United States would cooperate to meet this menace through NATO, not by reduction of American global strategic and diplomatic maneuverability and its commitments around the world to one or-

7. Schoenbrun, *op. cit.,* p. 298.

8. *Ibid.* Quoted by Schoenbrun, who claims to have had access to the de Gaulle memorandum.

9. *Ibid.,* p. 303. The same olympian views are expressed in the Tournoux presentation of de Gaulle's off-the-cuff views about the validity of French claims to equality. Tournoux, *op. cit.,* pp. 314–342.

10. Schoenbrun, *op. cit.,* p. 299.

ganizational framework, however significant. President Eisenhower vaguely hinted at "very serious problems" arising within and outside the NATO pact if it were extended beyond Europe and the Mediterranean. The sole problem specifically identified was the anticipated opposition of the other NATO allies to the creation of a select club within the alliance whose decisions would affect their vital interests but from which they would be excluded.[11] No rebuttal was made to the Gaullist criticism of exclusive American control over NATO's nuclear policies. President Eisenhower's policy largely defined the responses of the Democratic administrations of John F. Kennedy and Lyndon B. Johnson to the Gaullist scheme.[12]

United States assessment of allied reaction to de Gaulle's proposal was basically correct, although it is not clear to what degree, if any, American expectations influenced the formation of European opposition. Italy's Prime Minister Fanfani announced on October 29, 1958, a week after President Eisenhower's reply to the de Gaulle proposal, that Italy would not accept an inferior position within the alliance. German Chancellor Konrad Adenauer was equally cool. He found de Gaulle's views in conflict with the concept of French-German equality to which the French president had reportedly subscribed in talks with him. To this chorus of protests were joined those of Canada, Norway, and Holland. After de Gaulle's September 5 news conference, Belgian Prime Minister Henri Spaak observed that a tripartite directorate was not acceptable to the majority of NATO states. On November 10, 1960, Adenauer reaffirmed his confidence in United States leadership and rejected the notion that any other nation should have a privileged position in the alliance.[13] The European states preferred to be equally unequal rather than accord to any

11. *Ibid.* See also Tournoux, *op. cit.,* p. 342; *Hearings, Atlantic Alliance, passim.*

12. See *New York Times,* May 3, 1964, p. 10E. Also illuminating are the pertinent pages on French-American relations found in Arthur Schlesinger, Jr., *A Thousand Days* (Boston: Houghton Mifflin, 1965), and Theodore Sorenson, *Kennedy* (New York: Harper and Row, 1965).

13. Kulski, *De Gaulle and the World,* p. 166. See especially *L'Année politique, 1958,* pp. 452–454. Adenauer's position represents somewhat of a turnabout from his joint statement with de Gaulle after their first meeting on September 14, three days before de Gaulle sent his memorandum to Eisenhower. Schoenbrun, *op. cit.,* p. 297.

one of their number the privileged status enjoyed by the United States within the Atlantic Alliance.

Algeria and Anglo-American Support

Barely hidden below the surface of the directorate scheme were two issues of immediate import—the Algerian War and the French construction of an atomic bomb—over which the wartime Western Big Three were sharply split. Part of Anglo-American coolness to the French directorate proposal was attributable to their opposition to, and growing embarrassment over, France's Algerian policy. They had little sympathy for France's determination to keep its Algerian colony. The United States saw Arab-Western relations, already severely damaged by the Suez invasion of 1956, being impaired, perhaps irreparably. Maintenance of the untenable French position weakened the Western position in the Cold War struggle in the Third World. The decision of the Nasser government to turn to Czechoslovakia for arms in 1955 had signaled a major step in the increasing penetration of the Soviet Union in the Middle East. American policy circles were concerned, too, that the 400,000 French troops earmarked for European defense were stationed in Algeria. From the American perspective, European defense was being sacrificed for peripheral alliance concerns. During the Eisenhower and Kennedy administrations, the United States strove to avoid a choice between its European ally and the Arab states. It provided hesitant support to the French or abstained on United Nations resolutions condemning France's North African policy. France was isolated within the Atlantic Alliance and discreetly admonished to extend independence to its North Africa possessions.

The reaction of the de Gaulle government to the reluctant British and American attitude toward France's Algerian problem is expressed in a speech of Prime Minister Michel Debré on August 16, 1959: "It belongs to a renewed France," he said, "to make its allies understand that it is in the right to demand from all of them the support for a cause [Algeria] which is much greater than one people or one generation." [14] In contrast to London and Washington, Paris linked the

14. *L'Année politique, 1959,* pp. 479–480. See also the interviews of C. L. Sulzberger with de Gaulle and important French officials, in C. L. Sulzberger, *The Last of the Giants* (New York: Macmillan, 1970), p. 624.

alliance in Europe to Algeria and North Africa. American and British insistence on limiting the Atlantic Alliance to Europe inevitably devalued the importance of the alliance for the Gaullist government which, following a policy line congenial to French army thinking, portrayed its efforts in Algeria as a major contribution to Communist containment. For de Gaulle, Algeria was a more immediate political problem than the Soviet threat to Western Europe.

Lukewarm Anglo-American support not only abandoned France to face its adversaries alone, but forsook de Gaulle personally, who was already under heavy attack, including assassination attempts on his life, for his Algerian policy.[15] Moreover, as the Lebanese landings of July 1958 suggested, France's allies threatened further to disrupt France's internal order and tenuous international position by drawing it into unsought conflicts. It was understandable in Gaullist terms that the United States and Britain should act to minimize their involvement in the entangling web of the Algerian War. They had their own interests to defend. Nevertheless, Gaullist logic found it inexcusable that they should do so at the expense of an ally, even though France might have behaved likewise in similar circumstances. Given their conception of international relations, Gaullists were bound to question the value of an alliance that could not respond to their perception of the immediate dangers to France's vital interests.

The Anglo-Americans and the French Nuclear Program

The Atlantic Alliance was also found wanting when measured against the French decision to pursue an independent nuclear weapons program, including the construction of a strategic strike force. The French charged that the United States failed to assist an ally in building its military resources to meet the common foreign danger from the East—the basis for the Atlantic security pact—and to accord France equal status which, at a minimum, required its acquisition of the same access rights to United States nuclear information and material as Great Britain.

The United States opposed the development of an independent French nuclear weapons capability. It had largely resisted requests to furnish raw materials, instrumentation, and information to assist

15. Passeron, *De Gaulle parle, 1962–1966*, pp. 435–436, lists the attempts on de Gaulle's life.

the French nuclear program. It had similarly brought pressure on its NATO allies to discourage their contribution to the French nuclear effort, for both civilian and military purposes.

The troubled history of French-American nuclear relations began in World War II when the French sent a team of nuclear scientists to participate in the construction of the first atomic bomb. Whatever the merit of their claims, the French felt strongly that they deserved more recognition for their contribution to the Anglo-American success. After the war, the French pursued a vigorous nuclear program. Despite chronic governmental instability, work was initiated on basic atomic research and on the applicability of atomic energy to industrial uses. After 1950, these efforts were gradually subordinated to a progressively enlarging program of weapons development. When the de Gaulle administration assumed office in May 1958, preparations were well advanced and a formal government decision had been taken to explode an atomic device.

There is little basis for the Gaullist charge that the Fourth Republic had conceded leadership to the United States in civilian and military nuclear policy. In launching a national program, however, the Fourth Republic had counted upon the cooperation of its strongest ally to speed its program to completion, especially for the supply of vital raw materials and information which were already available to the Soviet Union. Fourth Republic governments vainly hoped that France would be eligible for the special assistance received by Great Britain after the amendment of the McMahon Act in 1954 and 1958.[16] Against this background of unrequited expectations, latent French hostility to United States nuclear dominance under the Fourth Republic and open opposition to American leadership in the Atlantic Alliance under the Fifth Republic can be more clearly understood.

Although the French pleaded the case for American nuclear assistance to meet Soviet pressures, the Fourth Republic's atomic weapons program sought principally to influence allied, not enemy, opinion. The elaboration of French nuclear strategic doctrine, discussed

16. Four indispensable studies of French nuclear policy include Bertrand Goldschmidt, *L'Aventure atomique* (Paris: Fayard, 1962); *idem, Les Rivalités atomiques: 1939–1966* (Paris: Fayard, 1967); Wolf Mendl, *Deterrence and Persuasion* (London: Faber and Faber, 1970); and Lawrence Scheinman, *Atomic Energy Policy in France under the Fourth Republic* (Princeton: Princeton University Press, 1965).

below, developed later, in the 1960's, and only after the decision had already been taken by the de Gaulle government to build a *force de frappe*. "French nuclear weapons," as one close observer of French atomic policy notes, "were thought of not so much as a 'force de dissuasion' than as a 'force de persuasion.' " [17] In this view, and with the exception of the Communist Left, Gaullist and anti-Gaullist were largely in accord in the 1950's. René Pleven, a principal author of the European Defense Community Treaty (EDC) and later a critic of French withdrawal from the NATO organization in 1966, advocated a nuclear weapons program as early as 1954. The Mendès-France government, which was charged with the responsibility of submitting the EDC document to the National Assembly, was similarly persuaded that France would have to develop a nuclear weapons program.

Pleven and the supporters of European union, unlike Mendès-France, argued that a European security framework would be responsive to United States pressures for European rearmament and would at the same time satisfy French anxieties over the remilitarization of Germany. In the absence of European guarantees, the French position would be weakened within the Western alliance. A rearmed Germany, outside of the EDC, would allegedly have a direct relation with the United States. Its security and foreign policy claims would not have to be mediated first through the European security system. In the long run, EDC would resolve remaining French fears of a resurgent Germany by fusing French and German security interests, as the Coal and Steel Community had joined the economic development of both states.

Majority sentiment within the Mendès-France government was skeptical of such institutional guarantees. It focused more on preserving French independence in military policy, including the development of nuclear energy for peaceful uses. Among the suggested amendments to the EDC treaty that the Mendès-France regime submitted to France's European partners was a provision to exempt the French from the nuclear restrictions, inserted in the treaty to meet German objections of discrimination. France's European allies rejected its suggested revision of EDC. A short time later, after a

17. Mendl, *op. cit.*, p. 18.

heated and tumultuous debate in which Gaullists and Communists, although motivated by conflicting interests, found themselves temporary allies, the National Assembly defeated EDC.[18] The Gaullists sought to retain national control over France's military forces; the Communists hoped to weaken France's contribution to Western defense; both opposed German rearmament and worked to reduce American influence over French foreign policy.

The Gaullists opposed any international controls on France's armed forces and on its nuclear program, even at the risk of encouraging German rearmament outside an international framework. They objected to the European Defense Community and Euratom, which would obstruct development of the French nuclear effort. Some of the more extreme Gaullist elements preferred to view Euratom as an American-sponsored attempt to hobble France's military and diplomatic independence. Even European-leaning Socialists, like Guy Mollet, whose investiture speech as prime minister on January 31, 1956, committed his government to the peaceful development of the French atom within Euratom, gradually moved from opposition to support of a French nuclear weapons program in the late 1950's. The major cause of his change of mind was the Suez disaster of 1956, which exposed the weakness of the French position vis-à-vis the superpowers, especially the United States.[19]

Gaullists believed that a nuclear force under national control would bridge the strategic and diplomatic gap between France and the other nuclear powers. Under the Fourth Republic, the French were more agreed on the continued support of a military nuclear research and development program than on the international framework within which it should be placed—whether the Atlantic Alliance, Euratom, the European Defense Community, or, after the defeat of EDC, the Western European Union. The Fifth Republic never wavered in its course to keep the *force de frappe* exclusively in national hands.

A major problem facing the French nuclear program after World War II was access to uranium stores. These were largely under the control of the United States and the United Kingdom. Through contract with the Belgian government, the United States had also secured

18. *Ibid.*, pp. 27–28.
19. Scheinman, *op. cit.*, pp. 139ff; Goldschmidt, *Rivalités atomiques*, pp. 215–223.

exclusive rights to Congolese uranium reserves. These rights were renewed just before Belgium's entry into Euratom, a move to protect its national interests that did not escape French criticism—or later emulation. A 1955 accord precluded Belgian sale of uranium to third parties without consulting the United States. French attempts to buy Belgian uranium failed over a disagreement on price. French overtures to buy Canadian uranium were similarly stifled by previous contractual agreements with the United States. The French refused to pay the same price for uranium as the Americans and English if they were obliged to restrict the use of the metal to civilian purposes. They publicly bridled at the discrimination although it is doubtful that the French could have met the peaceful use provisions even if they had swallowed their pride. To these difficulties was added the abortive French proposal to join with Great Britain in the construction of an isotope separation plant. The United States objected that the project would violate Anglo-American atomic accords. This was the first time, according to one authoritative French source, that the United States directly "manifested their opposition to French atomic armament." [20] Nevertheless, a series of decisions taken in the 1950's progressively expanded the military component of the French nuclear program.

French-American nuclear relations were further strained in the last days of the Fourth Republic and throughout the Fifth. In response to the Sputnik scare of October 1957, the United States proposed to its NATO allies to stockpile atomic weapons in Europe, to place IRBM's under joint two-key controls with the host states, and to provide information and even material for the construction of atomic submarines. The McMahon Atomic Energy Act was subsequently amended to permit the transfer of information and materials concerning atomic arms and submarines on the condition that the receiving state had made substantial progress in nuclear armament.

In July 1959, Secretary of State John Foster Dulles reiterated the United States submarine offer to the French during an official visit. The French delegation sent to Washington in February 1959, however, discovered that only U235 could be furnished. French re-

20. Goldschmidt, *Rivalités atomiques,* pp. 225–227. The entire section, pp. 199–234, should be read carefully for a first-hand report of French feeling within the Commissariat de l'Energie Atomique.

quests for the purchase of an atomic motor and technical data relating to the submarine were denied because Congress refused to share United States atomic know-how with France. The embittered reaction of one French scientist, who has been a major figure within the nuclear program since its inception in the late 1930's, suggests the depth of national chagrin: "The American government refused to treat France as a true partner, not only at the highest organizational level of the alliance, as General de Gaulle had proposed, but also within the very framework of an offer solemnly made by President Eisenhower." [21] Only the British met the test of substantial progress. The French had to content themselves with 440 grams of enriched uranium as a balm for another American-inflicted slight that reminded them again of their second-class status within the alliance.[22]

Several other abortive attempts to secure allied support added to French frustration. Canada again refused to sell uranium to France for other than peaceful uses and added the condition, as a consequence of its signature of the Test Ban Treaty, that the material sold could not be used for open testing, whatever the eventual purpose.[23] The French sensed American pressure behind the Canadian refusal. The reluctance of the United States to authorize the sale of large computers to France for nuclear research and instrumentation to measure atomic tests reinforced these suspicions. The sale of computers was finally permitted in 1966, but only after France agreed again to the restriction that they be used for peaceful purposes.[24] French missile development for the *force de frappe* was arrested an estimated three to five years when the United States intervened to forbid Aerojet General Corporation to supply solid rocket fuel information to two French groups charged with the responsibility for missile development.[25] The nuclear plant at Pierrelatte was constructed to pro-

21. *Ibid.*, p. 242. See also Goldschmidt, *L'Aventure atomique*, pp. 200–204; Goldschmidt's account of alleged American deviousness may be misleading in light of the clear intention of Congress and the White House, expressed in the hearings on amending the McMahon Act, to discourage, except for Britain, nuclear assistance to allies. See William A. Bader, *The United States and the Spread of Nuclear Weapons* (New York: Pegasus, 1968), pp. 15–130.
22. Bader, *op. cit.*, pp. 59–62; Goldschmidt, *Rivalités atomiques*, pp. 241–242.
23. Goldschmidt, *Rivalités atomiques*, pp. 262, 278.
24. *Ibid.*, p. 263.
25. *Ibid.;* Mendl, *op. cit.*, p. 60.

duce a fully controlled French supply of enriched uranium since the United States-Euratom accord again restricted the European purchases of American U235 to peaceful uses.[26]

The United States did make a number of concessions to its alliance partner that have been conveniently ignored by successive French governments. Franco-American bilateral agreements supplied useful, if modest, amounts of raw materials for the French nuclear program. French scientists were invited to American atomic proving grounds and profited from personal ties with their American counterparts. Trips to the United States and international conferences, such as those on atomic energy held in Geneva in 1955 and 1958, furnished useful information to the French. Moreover, early in the Kennedy administration, the French received authorization to buy twelve KC-135 air-to-air fuel tankers for their fleet of sixty-two Mirage atomic attack bombers. Without them, the Mirage force would have been doomed to one-way suicide flights to the Soviet Union.

President Kennedy probably was correct in concluding that additional assistance to Gaullist France, as his special envoy General Maxwell Taylor was said to have advised, would not have appeased France's nuclear appetite, nor, short of complete equality with the United States on political and military matters, would the French government have been willing to bend to American policies.[27] General de Gaulle's directorate proposal and Gaullist France's conception of alliance, reflected in its expectations of American support for its Algerian policy and nuclear aspirations, supported the President's assessment.

The Global Implications of the Directorate Scheme

An implemented directorate would have had important implications for the structure of international politics. It projected the evolution of a multipolar strategic and diplomatic system within which the nuclear powers would play a determinative role both in shaping East-West alliance policy and in organizing world order. A dual system of bloc politics would crystallize—at first within the alliance, on two

26. Goldschmidt, *Rivalités atomiques,* pp. 237–309, is revealing regarding American use of international accords to discourage nuclear proliferation.
27. *L'Année politique, 1962,* pp. 608–609.

levels between nuclear and nonnuclear states, and, subsequently, between alliances, specifically the NATO and Warsaw blocs. Discrimination between alliance powers, based on their nuclear capabilities
and their historical claims to world leadership, would be institutionalized. Only the three Western nuclear states would be equal; the
other NATO powers would be subordinated. Despite its economic
strength, Germany would be relegated to a formally defined secondary level. Divided politically and forbidden to develop nuclear weapons under the Treaty of Paris of 1954, it could not be considered by
the French as a fully reinstated sovereign state. Its future depended
on preceding accord of the wartime Western Big Three and the Soviet
Union. Directorate decisions would be tantamount to *faits accomplis*
for the remaining twelve members of the alliance since they would
have little recourse to defy their protectors alone or in combination.
Lacking nuclear weapons, their political interests would be indentured
to their security requirements, which would remain at the disposal
of the Franco-Anglo-American *supraalliance* within NATO.

The directorate would have transformed the logic and the incentives of alliance diplomacy. The twelve nonnuclear states of the alliance would be induced to lobby not only in Washington, but in London and Paris. Gaining the ear of one of the three nuclear powers
would assure that their views would be heard in the counsels of the
other two since solidarity among the Big Three would be a prerequisite for alliance cohesion. The alliance would tend to break into three
groupings of client and protector states. The East-West balance would
not be initially affected, but would remain stable while new alignments
and coalitions would presumably be formed between the nuclear
three and the nonnuclear twelve within the Atlantic grouping. Such a
framework would have advantages for smaller states since the expanded leadership would make alliance policy more fluid and increase
their access to policy circles.

Compensating for the policy limitations that each nuclear state
would place on its partners within the triumvirate would be the assurance that each could count on the other once common objectives
had been decided upon. The coordinated power and authority of the
alliance would, indeed, be difficult to resist. The "position of strength"
argument advanced by former Secretary of State Dean Acheson to

deal with the Communist world would have been realized, but only through a pre-established system of shared decision and responsibilities within the alliance among the Western nuclear powers.[28]

A NATO directorate had obvious benefits for France. France would tolerate the imposition of a coordinating mechanism within the nuclear tier of the Western states because its national power would be increased through its access to the power of the fourteen other states. Moreover, its influence over the United States could be enlarged. The directorate would extend, not limit, French statecraft, as NATO had allegedly done in Algeria. France would gain a veto over United States global policies and privileged access to American decision-making channels. France would be placed on a par with the superpowers—the realization of the elusive goal of *grandeur* so persistently pursued by de Gaulle. France would become a great power, if not initially through its material strength, then through its special alliance with a superstate. Internal alliance solidarity would mean unlimited allied support; consultation would imply eventual unanimity.[29]

Gaullists believed the possession of nuclear weapons would equalize the influence and political authority of small and larger nuclear allies due to the revolutionary destructive power of these weapons. Their use by one ally would inevitably affect the vital interest of all others. Political conflict with the alliance antagonist, involving an ally directly or through proxies, would seriously increase the prospect of escalation to nuclear levels and pose the possibility of allied involvement. If an alliance were to serve state objectives, including survival itself, it would have to embrace all allied political and strategic interests. On the other hand, a small nuclear power could effectively widen the protective scope of an alliance by assertion of a nuclear threat to protect its interests, thus creating a vital interest for the major nuclear powers. None could safely ignore the threat—allies or enemies. The military power and political objectives of the third

28. For a review and critique of the "position of strength" argument, see Cora Bell, *Negotiations from Strength: A Study in the Politics of Power* (New York: Knopf, 1963).

29. For a terse, but useful, discussion of the flaws of limited and total alliances, see George Liska, *Nations in Alliance* (Baltimore: Johns Hopkins Press, 1962), pp. 76–78.

nuclear state would be conceptually integrated into the strategic and diplomatic calculations of the other alliance powers.[30] The alliance leader, specifically, would have to consider any interest defined as vital by an ally as equally vital to him since nuclear weapons would presumably be relied upon by the smaller state to protect its claims.

One French strategist carried this Gaullist view of alliance through to its logical conclusion, going beyond what official policy statements were willing to claim. The bonding of interests between nuclear alliance partners would prevail, according to General André Beaufre, whether the common opponent was stronger, weaker, or on an equal plane with the major protector. In the first instance, the initially stronger foe would fear retaliation against his depleted arsenal in the wake of his preventive or pre-emptive attack against the middle power of the rival alliance. In the latter cases, the stronger and weaker nuclear allies would still be induced to align their stances. The opponent would fear attacking the stronger alliance partner over a peripheral interest and would also fear attacking the smaller power, which would open the way to a reprisal from the alliance protector. The stronger alliance partner would act on these assumptions of opponent behavior and support its weaker ally. Its political objectives, even if divergent from those of its ally, would be subordinated to its strategic calculations. The intermediate case of strategic balance between protector powers yielded the same response. In each group of possibilities, *"everything will take place as if the interests of the third party had become those of his ally."* [31]

The de Gaulle government posed a dilemma for the United States. France would have accepted United States leadership if French strategic and foreign policy views could have ultimately prevailed within the alliance. In the absence of their acceptance and ratification within a formally established directorate that was both the highest authoritative voice of the alliance and a symbol of French greatness, de Gaulle served notice that France was free to pursue its own policies without the previous consultation and consent of its allies. Whether de Gaulle seriously thought that his proposal would be accepted, a

30. "French Defense Policy," *Survival,* X (Jan. 1968), 12–16.
31. André Beaufre, *Deterrence and Strategy,* trans. R. H. Barry (New York: Praeger, 1966).

question of considerable disagreement among observers,[32] is some-what beside the point.[33] More important were the limitless dimensions of Gaullist ambitions and the world-wide political and strategic terrain on which he proposed to act. The directorate scheme either would succeed in bending American will to French purposes or, in the probable event of its rejection or only partial acceptance, it would place the onus for the gradual and enlarging division between French and American policies on the United States government. The audacity of de Gaulle's diplomatic offensive perhaps can be suggested in the representations of the French government to the United States for nuclear assistance, including the *force de frappe,* in order to better influence and shape American global policy. In this ambition, de Gaulle was not completely alone, for the shifting government cabinets of the Fourth Republic harbored similar hopes. Seen from Paris, through the Gaullist perspective on alliances, these hopes were politically reasonable, despite their logical inconsistencies.

Security Policies in the Aftermath of the Algerian War

Strategic Threat: Re-evaluation and Response

As the failure of the Gaullist government to secure a privileged position for France within the Atlantic Alliance became more evident—a repulse that was expected, according to some sources—[34] the Gaullist regime devoted increasing attention to a revision of the official view of the strategic threats facing France and its quest for big-power status. The reorientation of French global perceptions and policy was given impetus by the resolution of the Algerian War, which freed French resources and political and moral energies for a greater range of global strategic and diplomatic moves. Moreover, while the Gaullists charged that the present international system was illegitimate and unstable, they further asserted, especially after the

32. See Tournoux, *op. cit.,* and Newhouse, *op. cit.,* for skeptical views of Gaullist sincerity dealing with the directorate scheme.

33. Sulzberger, *op. cit., passim,* offers a more sympathetic view of the de Gaulle proposal for a NATO triumvirate. Interviews conducted in Washington and Paris support Sulzberger's presentation.

34. Tournoux, *op. cit.,* pp. 320–322. See n. 2 above which reviews the literature on the de Gaulle proposal for a directorate.

Cuban missile crisis, that the superpower balance itself was in danger of being upset by the apparently growing strategic superiority of the United States. The response of Gaullists to their own perception of the changing strategic threats to France may be seen in three lines of closely associated activity: (1) the reinterpretation of the Soviet-American balance of terror; (2) the development of the *force de frappe* as a response to the enlarged conception of the global threats pressing on France; and (3) Gaullist resistance to the Kennedy administration's flexible response strategy and multilateral nuclear force proposals (MLF), which were viewed, with some validity, by the de Gaulle government as strategic and diplomatic moves, respectively, to discipline or isolate an intransigent France.

The preceding chapter has discussed the French perception of systemic threat, deriving from superpower conflict or accommodation. Less obvious, according to French strategists, was the difference in the nature and immediacy of the threats posed by each superstate. Until the Russian invasion of Czechoslovakia in August 1968, Gaullist France argued that the external Soviet threat had diminished in the 1960's and had been gradually replaced by a more pervasive American strategic threat that eroded the independence and sapped the authority of smaller states.

The French depreciation of the Soviet military threat rested on a number of factors. First, the balance of terror between the superpowers sharply reduced the probability of war. Both sides were assumed to fear the ravages of nuclear war that would be beyond their control. Each would suffer certain destruction out of all proportion to the political stakes at issue. The threat of mutual destruction encouraged the Soviet Union and the United States to avoid a direct confrontation and to move toward tacit accord on a policy of peaceful coexistence, even at the expense of client and neutral state interests, rather than toward war.[35] The test ban and nonproliferation treaties promoted so intensively by the United States and the Soviet

35. The significance of the balance of terror and its paralytic effect on superpower strategy and diplomacy is a persistent theme in French thought. See *Major Addresses*, pp. 61, 219, 226; and S&PC, No. 19, Oct. 22, 1963, p. 5; No. 203, Feb. 24, 1964, p. 3; No. 166, April 16, 1964, p. 4; No. 206, April 28, 1964, p. 3; No. 212, Nov. 22, 1964, pp. 3–4; No. 169, Dec. 2, 1964, pp. 2–3; No. 219, Feb. 4, 1965, p. 3; No. 243, April 3, 1966, p. 3; No. 245, April 4, 1966, p. 2; *FA*, No. 192, April 1966, p. 2.

Union lent credence to this belief, held more widely than simply in Gaullist circles.[36] "The balance of terror between Soviet and American nuclear forces leads both of them necessarily," as the late Gaullist Armed Forces Chief of Staff, General Ailleret argued, "to renounce . . . total war to promote their policy." [37]

Second, the French pointed to the internal economic and political problems confronting the Soviet Union and the constraints that lagging economic and social progress placed on the ambitions of the Soviet leadership. The latter was itself internally divided and, since Stalin, hampered in mounting large-scale foreign adventures except when its security and imperial rule in Eastern Europe were felt to be directly threatened, as in Hungary or Czechoslovakia. Faced by rising consumer demands at home, it seemed to have grown increasingly prudent and conservative abroad, assuming a nationalist posture in its foreign dealings and striking a less responsive attitude toward the revolutionary tenets of Communist ideology.[38] Its cautious policy in Vietnam and its more assertive, but still circumscribed, probings in the Middle East sustained the French analysis. These were positions that a Czarist government might well have assumed.

Third, political developments in Eastern Europe indicated the lessening capacity of the Soviet Union to control its satellites except through overt and costly coercion. In October 1966, President de Gaulle declared the Cold War over between France and Russia's client states in Eastern Europe: "Everyone is aware that we are in the process of renewing, deeply and positively, our relations with Poland, Rumania, Yugoslavia, Czechoslovakia, Bulgaria, and Hungary. Today, between all these peoples and ours, the cold war appears silly when growing and friendly cooperation is being organized." [39] The French found evidence for optimism in the pattern of visits between French and East European ministers and heads of state. With perhaps the sole exception of President de Gaulle's visit to Poland in September 1967, French urgings to Eastern bloc countries to develop

36. Aron, *Peace and War*, pp. 369–572.
37. Général Ailleret, "Défense 'dirigée' défense 'tous azimuts,' " *Revue de défense nationale*, XXIII (Dec. 1967), 1923–1932.
38. *Major Addresses*, pp. 100, 234; *FA*, No. 163, Oct. 29, 1963; S&PC, No. 208, July 23, 1964, p. 5; No. 212, Nov. 22, 1964, p. 3; No. 243, April 13, 1966, p. 3.
39. S&PC, No. 253A, Oct. 28, 1966, p. 6.

greater independence from the Soviet Union appeared to have fallen on receptive ears.[40] In May 1968, during a state visit to Rumania, de Gaulle became the first Western head of state to speak before a Communist national legislature. The deviating course set by Rumania and, until August, Czechoslovakia, reinforced France's confidence in the slow erosion of the Eastern bloc of European states.[41]

The French preferred to see the desire for national self-determination as the long-term deciding factor in Eastern Europe. The brief Czech experiment with a nationally defined Communist state ostensibly strengthened French convictions that national, not ideological, political trends would eventually prove determinative in the Communist bloc.[42] "It is too late for nations to be won over by foreign domination [and] occupation," observed President de Gaulle in the wake of the Russian invasion of Czechoslovakia, "and it is too late for any ideology, especially Communism, to convert a nation." [43] The Russian invasion was viewed mainly as a conservative move to maintain the Eastern bloc intact and to throttle liberalizing forces within the Warsaw Pact and within the domestic affairs of the bloc powers, including elements within the Soviet Union itself. The military occupation of Czechoslovakia did, however, seriously change the Gaullist timetable for the evolution of a looser Warsaw Pact and greater Russian disposition to reach a final political settlement acceptable to the West in Europe. Russian political avarice could not be completely discounted, nor could the possibility of superpower conflict, a temporarily muted view in French thought, revived after the second Czechoslovakian crisis.[44]

Fourth, Western Europe's rising strength was conceived as a powerful counter to Soviet or United States expansionism, whether military, economic, or political.[45] Although the confrontation between

40. De Gaulle's independence message may have impressed some minority segments of the Polish leadership. See A. Ross Johnson, "Franco-Polish Relations," *Survival,* IX (Dec. 1967), 387–392.

41. *Washington Post,* Feb. 27, 1968, p. A1. President Richard Nixon's visit to Rumania in summer 1969 suggests the validity of the Gaullist thesis.

42. *New York Times,* Sept. 10, 1968, p. 14.

43. *Ibid.;* see also Aug. 31, 1968, pp. 1ff.

44. See Chapter 3 for further discussion.

45. *Major Addresses,* pp. 96, 208; S&PC, No. 197, Oct. 18, 1966, p. 4; *FA,* No. 163, Oct. 29, 1963, p. 6; S&PC, No. 202, Feb. 24, 1964, p. 3; No. 206, April 30, 1964, p. 2; No. 208, July 23, 1964, pp. 4–5; No. 209, Feb. 5, 1965, p. 3; No. 243, April 13, 1966, p. 3; *FA,* No. 192, April 1966, pp. 1–2; *Le Monde,* Jan. 3, 1965, p. 3; *New York Times,* Aug. 11, 1967, p. 13.

the United States and the Soviet Union in Europe was still considered the major threat to global peace, Asia, Africa, Latin America, and the Middle East were increasingly portrayed as focal points for the struggle between the superpowers. The causes of this gradual shift were perceived as multiple, including national rivalries, modernization, and overpopulation. These factors stirred already deep social and political unrest and perpetuated the misery of the underdeveloped states.[46] The French expected the rising power of China in Asia to deflect the Soviet Union from violence in Europe to expand its domain. Official French views considered the rupture between these Communist giants complete and permanent. The differences were perceived as basically national, even racial, and only incidentally ideological. Confronted by ascending Chinese power in the East, the Soviet Union, in the French view, was encouraged to reduce tensions on its western borders to secure its European flank; Russia was still Western and white. An emerging China, although presently torn by internal division and retarded by slow economic and technological development, was assigned an eventually dominant role in Asia.[47] These expectations were reflected in France's recognition of the Chinese Communist regime and in its neutralist policy toward South Vietnam.[48]

The Cuban missile crisis catalyzed French strategic fears of rising American global supremacy. Until the Czechoslovakian invasion, the United States, not the Soviet Union, was increasingly pictured as the primary object of concern. President de Gaulle and his followers were convinced, as a close observer of European-American relations recognized, that, after the Soviet-American confrontation in Cuba, the United States had become the dominant world power and that the Soviet Union had temporarily accepted its strategic inferiority. A new era had appeared in which "the struggle against the ally" constituted the "principal objective." [49]

The delicate task facing the French government in attempting to

46. Ailleret, *Revue de défense nationale,* 1967, p. 1928.

47. *Major Addresses,* pp. 234–235; *FA,* No. 163, Oct. 29, 1963, p. 3; S&PC, No. 203, Feb. 24, 1964, p. 3; No. 206, April 28, 1964, p. 3; No. 208, July 23, 1964, p. 5; No. 243, April 13, 1966, p. 3; No. 244, April 14, 1966, p. 2.

48. U.N., General Assembly, *L'Intervention de Couve de Murville,* 20th sess., Sept. 29, 1965, pp. 4–5.

49. *Le Monde,* Sélection hebdomadaire, July 27–Aug. 2, 1965, p. 2.

expand France's influence was simultaneously to re-establish the supposed lost balance between the superpowers and to contest superpower dominance as illegitimate and unstable. As a matter of strategic priority, the perceived pre-eminence of the United States within the international system elicited a French counterreaction. Stripped of ideological differences and historical circumstances, the Fifth Republic's resistance to American hegemony in Europe was of a piece with the Third Republic's lifelong opposition to Germany's threatening presence and to the Fourth Republic's response to menacing Russian moves after World War II. Gaullist France accepted the necessity to contest American power *as* power. French strategic doctrine was revised accordingly to take account of the rising American threat.[50] Expanding United States power threatened to menace the international balance by pulling more and more states within its orbit of attraction. In the closing years of Gaullist rule, the possible development of a unipolar system became one of the major concerns of the French government. Many Gaullist critics in France shared the same view. The United States was portrayed as the sole superpower.[51] The de Gaulle regime assumed, moreover, that the United States would seek to preserve and extend its dominant position. "The United States," asserted President de Gaulle, "has become the greatest power and it is automatically led to extend its power . . . to exercise a preponderant weight, that is to say, a hegemony over others." [52]

French emphasis on the obstacles posed by the United States to the realization of France's security objectives was based on the assumption (as Chapter 1 suggests) that unless the state fully controlled the weaponry and strategy upon which its security depended, including the decision to go to war, it would gradually forfeit its security function and its political authority. To the extent that another state performed that role, it implicitly assumed the authority of the client state. The decision of war or peace flowed from the hands of the

50. Two government efforts in this respect are Ailleret, *Revue de défense nationale*, 1967, pp. 1923–1932; and Notes and Etudes Documentaires, No. 3343, Dec. 6, 1966, reprinted as "French Defense Policy," *Survival*, Jan. 1968, pp. 12–16.

51. Maurice Duverger, "America the Superpower," *Interplay*, I (Oct. 1967), 12–14. See also *Le Monde*, Oct. 27, 1965, p. 1, Nov. 7–8, 1965, p. 1.

52. *Le Monde*, July 15, 1967, p. 7. See also in this connection, Stanley Hoffmann, *Journal of International Affairs*, 1967, p. 63.

client to the protector. As the state's security role shrank, its political independence and, ultimately, its sovereignty would be gravely weakened. Moreover, psychically and legally, a people's allegiance to a particular state was conceived as rooted in their willingness and capacity to defend themselves. In that commitment they identified themselves as a separate people or nation. If a state desired to remain a political entity, the execution of a security role was essential. The French consistently relied on the logic of these propositions to justify their withdrawal from the NATO organization in 1966. French Foreign Minister Couve de Murville summarized their position shortly after the announcement of France's departure: "The French people no longer have the feeling that they are responsible for defense. They rely on these international commands, and, from that time on, in a way losing [sic] their military personality, losing the sense of their responsibilities, we have started down a road on which we risk next losing our independence, because a country that is not concerned with its defense is not an independent country." [53]

Gaullists alternately feared that too great a dependence on the United States for security would either incapacitate France to meet its external requirements or weaken the determination of the French people to develop a nationally controlled military system. The fear of overdependence expressed itself in the conflicting anxieties of being drawn by allies into foreign wars or of being abandoned by them when their help was most needed, as after World War I. The French government chose to believe that the Cuban incident of 1962, when the United States acted before consulting its NATO allies, simultaneously raised both possibilities.[54] "The Americans, finding themselves exposed to a direct atomic attack from the Caribbean, acted to rid themselves of that menace," observed de Gaulle in 1963. "The means which they immediately decided to employ in order to counter a direct attack were automatically set aside from something other than the defense of Europe, even if Europe had been attacked. No one in the world can say if, where, when, how, to what extent the American nuclear weapons would be employed to defend Europe. American nuclear power does not necessarily and immediately meet all the

53. S&PC, No. 242, April 7, 1966, pp. 1–2.
54. Major Addresses, pp. 216–219.

eventualities concerning Europe and France." [55] The French also voiced fear that rigid alliance policies might result in strategies and operational orders that might neither possess their approval nor conform to their national policy. Allied powers might use French territory or air space for purposes adverse to France's foreign policy objectives.[56]

Science and technology were seen to play two increasingly indispensable and reciprocally reinforcing roles in the development of independent national security forces. First, scientific and technological progress was the basis for modern weapons development. Failure to organize such a base condemned a state to dependency on more advanced nations. As the possibility of war between the superpowers receded, the contest of the laboratories became of greater significance than the potential forms of battlefield warfare. Moreover, science and technology were understood as a new factor of production. They spawned growth industries, spurred the development of new products in electronics, computers, aeronautics, and precision goods, and created market opportunities abroad.[57] These enterprises were unique, for they devoted themselves to the rapid transformation of new scientific and technological discoveries into industrially profitable products and processes. They were also key industries in the national effort to maintain a competitive position in the global arms race.

The notion of pioneer and follower enterprises circulated through the government. The former were founded on knowledge and new technology; the latter depended on more traditional factors such as labor and capital. Followers were tied to techniques and methods that owed their development largely to the first half of the twentieth century. Competition among these industries was a function of price and efficiency in production. New industries, however, battled over product discrimination and the creation of new markets based on innovations. Traditional industries would gradually succumb to the new internationally organized combines since they would not be able to afford the rising costs of research and development per unit of out-

---

55. *Ibid.,* p. 217.
56. Ailleret, *Revue de défense nationale,* 1967, pp. 1923–1932.
57. An indispensable study for an understanding of French science policy is Robert Gilpin, *France in the Age of the Scientific State* (Princeton: Princeton University Press, 1968).

put, foreign patents and licenses, or the infrastructure and prerequisites for the retention of skilled personnel. The enterprise "that has at its disposal the superior technique is master," concluded one influential report. "It is the ultimate rationale in competition." [58]

United States industry, motored by massive government aid for research and development, was viewed by the French as a formidable challenge to a French-based technology and science and to France's capacity to develop a separate and viable military defense system. De Gaulle warned the French in 1964 "that it is necessary . . . to push relentlessly our technical and scientific research, in order to avoid sinking into a bitter mediocrity and being colonized by the activities, inventions, and capacities of other countries." [59] French concern turned on the growing disparity between American research and development support and economic expansion in Europe. One French report estimated American research and development expenditures at $16 billion in 1962–1963. This sum was five times more than the comparable expenditures of the EEC or EFTA states considered separately and two and a half times larger than those of the OECD countries.[60] A more thorough and authoritative OECD report essentially confirmed these statistics. With comparable populations, the United States was spending $93.70 per capita for scientific and technological exploration compared to $24.80 for the European Six and Great Britain.

The distance between pioneers and followers appeared to be widening, for the United States, with a GNP twice as large as that of the Common Market and England, was devoting approximately 3.1 percent of its productive resources to scientific and technological exploration as compared with less than 2 percent for the Europeans.[61] The French identified American government support for research and development, which flowed through large-scale and long-term military and space programs, as the principal factor explaining the United States advance. That three quarters of the research and development effort in the United States, both private and public, was financed by

58. *Le Progrès scientifique*, No. 76, Sept. 1, 1964, p. 12. The article is attributed by Gilpin to Pierre Cognard. It should be read in its entirety.

59. Quoted in Gilpin, *op. cit.*, p. 39.

60. Cognard, *op. cit.*, p. 15.

61. Gilpin, *op. cit.*, pp. 27–28.

the federal government did not escape French notice. The most capitalistic nation in the world, concluded the French, rested on a socialized science.[62]

Manpower figures for those engaged in science and technology heavily favored the United States, too. In the early 1960's, the United States had 435,600 scientists and engineers and 723,900 personnel in supporting capacities or a total of 1,159,500 persons connected with research and development. The European states of the EEC and the United Kingdom could only count on 147,000 engineers and scientists, and 370,000 in supporting roles, a total half as large as that of the United States. Per capita figures reveal more sharply the heavy concentration of American resources in newer modes of industrial and military activity. The United States used 6.2 personnel per thousand in research and development contrasted with 2.9 for Europe. For each 1,000 in the work force, the United States engaged 10.4 in science and technology; the Europeans, 4.6.[63] The brain drain was also tilted toward the American pole. Between 1956 and 1961, 4,868 engineers and scientists migrated to the United States, including 1,304 from the EEC countries and Great Britain. A sharp Gaullist critic, who shared the government's anxiety over the American challenge, argued further that France was not keeping pace with the United States in economic competition because it was falling behind in the training of scientists and engineers and refused to cooperate with its European partners.[64] The Fifth Five-Year Plan called for 12,500 to 17,500 scientists and engineers. This figure was half the number needed to support a research effort in France that would be proportionate to that of the United States in terms of the GNP of each country.

Closely tied to France's fears concerning American technological superiority was its reaction to the rising economic power of the United States in Europe. The increasing dependence of Europe on American technology was signaled by an enlarging unfavorable commercial balance of payments, the expanding influence of American firms in

62. *Ibid.,* p. 132; Cognard, *op. cit.,* pp. 8, 15.
63. Gilpin, *op. cit.,* p. 28.
64. Jean-Jacques Servan Schreiber, *The American Challenge,* trans. Ronald Steel (New York: Atheneum, 1967), pp. 146–148. A similar criticism of Gaullist policy may be found in Gaston Deferre, "De Gaulle and After," *Foreign Affairs,* LXIV (April 1966), 440ff.

the European Common Market, and the rising American investment in military-space programs on which the development of a state's global strategic position was seen to depend.

In 1962, for example, the French suffered an unfavorable technological balance of payments of $67 million while the United States enjoyed a net balance of $514 million. Two thirds of the French debt was owed to the United States. By 1964, the French deficit rose to between $80 and $100 million and gave no indication of declining. The lag in French patent filings was also disturbing to the government. Between 1957 and 1963, American patents averaged approximately 17 percent of Western European patents while only 10 percent of American patents were held by the European states. The imbalance between the United States and France was even more striking. In 1961, United States patents were equal to 45 percent of all French patents. The French could claim only 2 percent of American domestic patents. The trend lines also pointed downward for the French. In 1930, France stood second only to the United States in the export of patents. In the postwar period it became a net importer.[65] One careful student of French science notes that the number of registered American patents in France increased by 80 percent during the middle 1950's and in the first three full years of Gaullist rule. The number of foreign patents per hundred of French patents had increased several times that of any other European nation.[66]

The French Strategic Response: Force de Frappe

The central importance of the *force de frappe* to the Gaullist conception of strategic threat cannot easily be exaggerated. It was intended to be responsive to internal and external strategic threats, both national and systemic, projected by the de Gaulle government. It was to be a tool of French diplomacy and *grandeur*. It was to foster internal cohesion and economic and social progress. It was, ultimately, a challenge to superpower rule. It was essential to the Gaullist critique of the instability and illegitimacy of the present international system. Its creation was not only evidence that France was a great power but proof that the nation-state was still a viable

65. Gilpin, *op. cit.*, p. 35
66. *Ibid.*, p. 36.

human agency, materially capable of defending its citizens and, therefore, morally competent to claim their final allegiance. With the stakes so high, there is little wonder that Gaullist France should have developed an elaborate rationale for the *force de frappe,* built on military, diplomatic, psychological, economic, technological, and scientific grounds.

The *force de frappe* was presented as the instrument of global stability and national independence. Any increase of the latter was felt to enhance the prospect of a more legitimate international system. French nuclear doctrine insisted on the relevance of the *force de frappe*—and implicitly on the nuclear forces of other states—to the development of a more stable security system. The bipolar nuclear superiority of the United States and the Soviet Union vis-à-vis France was conceded, but considered of lesser strategic import than the dialectical tension between the superpowers. For the French, the balance of terror greatly neutralized the effective military power of the two giants and provided a middle-range power the conditions for the successful pursuit of an independent nuclear strategy and diplomacy. The superpowers were trapped in a strategic dilemma of their own creation. They had to threaten to use nuclear weapons to protect their respective interests while striving to avoid a direct confrontation that could only be mutually suicidal. For the French, a superstate's material capacity was important in discouraging an adversary's untoward behavior, but less significant than its ability to manifest a steadfast will to use what military means it had to support its political demands. French doctrine considered the viability of a nation's deterrent posture to be largely the function of the certainty that nuclear weapons would be employed. It was precisely because that certainty was not fully calculable that neither superstate could be sure when a confrontation would reach the point of "instant zero" and a nuclear war could be initiated. The uncertainty that each shared limited the present and future strategic maneuverability of both sides.

Since uncertainty could be overcome only at the risk of a nuclear war, each side was induced to elaborate a complex *notional* system of anticipatory nuclear wars. The moves and countermoves of the other were projected progressively in time and space; every conflict situation harbored the possibility of escalation. French strategists saw nuclear deterrence between the superpowers being inevitably extended in logic, through the pervasive threat of escalation, to cover every major conflict between them and to anticipate the actions and reactions of the opponent. "The strategy of deterrence," according to an official French government publication, "is finally a strategy of anticipation." [67] Conscious of their massive nuclear power and aware of the escalatory possibilities of conflict anywhere around the globe, the United States and the Soviet Union had incentive to be extremely cautious. The very existence of nuclear weapons in their arsenals logically led them to the notion of virtual nuclear warfare as a substitute for open hostilities. Karl von Clausewitz's view of war as diplomacy by other means became diplomacy by pretended nuclear war. War assumed progressively the trappings of eighteenth-century formal maneuvers without a clash of arms. The ideal of Maurice Compte de Saxe—of fighting wars without pitched battles—returned in the garb of nuclear weapons in which psychic stress and manipulation substituted for the clash of arms. The prudence of the superpowers, argued French strategists, provided middle-range powers who possessed nuclear weapons a measure of liberty to pursue an independent nuclear strategy in support of their political designs.

A middle power's nuclear arms would be grafted (*se greffer*) onto the dialectic of virtual nuclear war being ceaselessly enacted by the superpowers. Its effective strategic influence was shaped largely by the dramatic global struggle between the nuclear protagonists of the international system. Consequently, the range of a small nuclear power's freedom of strategic and diplomatic action and its capacity to assert its political claims hinged, according to French logic, on how well it could influence this fundamental systemic conflict through its participation in anticipatory nuclear warfare. The balance of terror placed an increased premium on diplomacy since the actual appeal to war among nuclear powers was presumed to be precluded except under the most dire circumstances. Nuclear weapons became the indispensable props for a diplomatic drama, with endlessly evolving scenarios, fashioned by the state actors. War was still the final arbiter of state differences forming, as it were, the climax of each scene, but it assumed progressively more a notional or virtual form than a direct, physical clash of arms. Deterrence was the object of

67. "French Defense Policy," *Survival,* Jan. 1968, p. 13.

nuclear weapons. French doctrine insisted, in addition, that virtual nuclear war was the new ultimate arbiter of the political claims between disputing states.[68]

Official French doctrine implicitly argued that multilateral deterrence theoretically increased global stability. The sharing of mutual risks and the interdependence of nuclear strategies of all nuclear powers decreased the maneuverability of all antagonists. A wider range of interests among nuclear armed states was raised to higher levels of mutual and vital concern. The geographical areas over which big-power conflict was engaged were narrowed. Nuclear deterrence penetrated conventional military conflicts and served to stabilize them. It remained endemic to all political conflicts. Multilateral deterrence forced nuclear opponents to calculate the military responses, not only of the major foe, but also of a third and even fourth nuclear power. This more complex situation derived from the increased uncertainty of state responses to nuclear threats.[69] The behavior of the third nuclear power had to be anticipated and its nuclear capacity, however small, covered.[70] These calculations were relevant whether a strike was contemplated or not. Moreover, they had to be projected into the future to determine the evolving nuclear strength of the third power. Future potential and present capabilities were manipulable factors in the multilateral deterrent struggle.[71] The third power assumed a role of varying importance depending on the perception of its interests in the projected virtual nuclear wars threatened by the superpowers in support of their security and foreign policy objectives.

The problems of strategic calculation became equally difficult for ally and enemy with respect to the anticipated responses of the smaller nuclear power. Stability was viewed less as a function of soli-

68. For additional relevant commentary, see Beaufre, *Deterrence and Strategy*, pp. 93–94; *Major Addresses*, pp. 179–181, 216–219.

69. For a perceptive discussion of instability at conventional levels in the absence of a nuclear threat, consult Beaufre, *Deterrence and Strategy*, pp. 50–60.

70. Other sympathetic proponents of multilateral deterrence, besides Beaufre and French doctrinal interpreters, include George Liska, *Imperial America* (Baltimore: Johns Hopkins Press, 1966), pp. 269–284; *idem, Europe Ascendant* (Baltimore: Johns Hopkins Press, 1962), pp. 103–119, 142–170; and Roger Masters, *The Nation Is Burdened* (New York: Knopf, 1967), pp. 44–83.

71. S&PC, No. 208, July 23, 1964, p. 9.

darity of the NATO organization and Atlantic Alliance, as Beaufre argued,[72] than as the direct outgrowth of multilateral deterrence operative among the nuclear states and the conscious blurring of the enemy-ally distinction in the strategic conflict. The third and smaller nuclear power employed its striking force to influence simultaneously its temporary alliance partner and its enemy. Among nuclear states— and nonnuclear powers—alignment and dealignment would respond increasingly to a wider range of political purposes and strategic needs. "The aggressor's certainty that he would sustain intolerable losses is the only guarantee that we can have against aggression," argued Georges Pompidou in defense of the French withdrawal from NATO. "That is what justified our own deterrent force. That is what leads us to remain in the Atlantic Alliance. You [Gaullist critics] tell us NATO has guaranteed peace in Europe for 15 years. What an error if you are referring to the integrated organization. What has guaranteed peace is the alliance, in so far as it brought to bear the threat of the Strategic Air Command." [73] Pompidou's barbed comments, although aimed principally at domestic critics, had a strategic point. As discussed further below, France's nuclear forces could presumably deter an opponent from attacking it directly, and retaining national control could influence American policy more effectively than submission to a European or Atlantic framework.

The de Gaulle government supported these global claims with the additional argument that a *force de frappe* indirectly served European defense. Since France, unlike the United States, was a part of the continent, its national defense was indistinguishable from that of Western Europe; it was no island unto itself. In creating an independent national force, France kept Europe's political future open. "By defending our own independence," Prime Minister Georges Pompidou maintained before the National Assembly in 1966, "we are defending most of Europe to which we belong, and we are the real Europeans." [74] Under French leadership, in possession of nuclear strike

72. André Beaufre, "Le Problème du partage des responsabilités nucléaires," *Stratégie*, No. 5 (July–Aug.–Sept. 1965), 7–20.

73. *New York Times*, April 21, 1966, Section 4. Compare S&PC, No. 243, April 13, 1966, and the more revealingly critical nature of M. Pompidou's remarks regarding United States strategy in *Le Monde*, April 27, 1966, p. 2.

74. S&PC, No. 224, June 17, 1966, p. 3.

forces, a new European security equilibrium would supposedly arise that would break the superpower control over Europe and would rest on the solid footing of preceding accord among the European states.[75]

In any event, a *force de frappe* was asserted to provide an adequate national defense. The first-generation French nuclear force was composed of sixty-two Mirage IV bombers, each capable of carrying a nuclear payload of approximately 60 kilotons, or three times the blast effect at Hiroshima.[76] The second generation was planned as a surface-to-surface missile (SSBS) force with a range between 1,800 and 2,000 miles. These missiles were to be hardened in concrete silos in the Albion Plateau of Haute Provence.[77] Each missile would be armed with a charge of about 240 kilotons, or about four times the explosive power of the Mirage IV bomb. The IRBM force would be an intermediary phase before the introduction of a seagoing nuclear submarine force in the 1970's.[78] A fleet of five nuclear-powered submarines, each carrying sixteen missiles, was planned for deployment by 1980. The first two submarines joined the fleet in 1972. These missiles have a range of approximately 1,500 miles and are armed with 500-kiloton atomic weapons. The third and succeeding submarines were to have missiles with a strike range of about 2,000 miles and were expected to be armed with thermonuclear weapons.[79]

75. Michel Debré, "Contre la force multilatérale," *Notre république*, Jan. 1, 1965.

76. Ambassade de France, Service de Presse et d'Information, *France and Its Armed Forces,* New York, Dec. 1964; Pierre Messmer, "L'Armement nucléaire français," *Le Républicain indépendant,* July 1967. See also M. Messmer's presentation of the French military program on December 1, 1964, before the National Assembly, *FA,* No. 171, Jan. 1965, pp. 1–12. Kohl, *op. cit.,* pp. 178–204, presents a detailed description of the three generations of the French nuclear program. Also useful as an updated official source is the White Paper issued by the defense ministry under Michel Debré in June 1972, *Livre blanc sur la défense nationale,* 1972, I, 11–19. Hereafter cited *Livre blanc.*

77. Judith H. Young, "The French Strategic Missile Programme," Adelphi Paper No. 38, Institute of Strategic Studies, July 1967, p. 5.

78. *Le Monde,* Sélection hebdomadaire, Dec. 7–13, 1967, p. 1.

79. Ambassade de France, Service de Presse et d'Information, "'The Redoubtable,' France's First Nuclear-Powered Submarine," April 1967. *Livre blanc,* p. 12, and *Le Monde,* Dec. 5–6, 1971, p. 24, offer additional information on the French missile and nuclear warhead program.

These strike capacities contrasted with American and Soviet strategic forces already developed in 1970. The United States had 1,656 land and sea-based ICBM's and 520 SAC bombers capable of delivering a total of over 5,300 warheads with a deliverable explosive power of 5,600 megatons. The Soviet Union possessed 1,790 land and sea-launched ICBM's and 145 long-range bombers. Even with SALT I, increases in delivery vehicles and especially warheads and deliverable megatonnage were expected throughout the 1970's. Add to these approximately 700 Soviet IRBM's and MRBM's aimed at Western Europe.[80]

French military theorists conceded the modest size of their projected forces. They contended, however, that they could deter other states, even superpowers, because they possessed a destructive capability that would offset any gain envisioned by a potential aggressor. The French force was alleged to be proportional in strategic capacity to France's political interests. Sufficient striking power to destroy only so much of the enemy's vital centers that he would be deterred from attacking a smaller nuclear power was necessary, not annihilation of the enemy homeland. France might be destroyed in the nuclear exchange, but the aggressor would presumably absorb more damage than could be reasonably offset by the anticipated benefits of his attack on France.[81] The logic of proportional national deterrence applied with greater force to nonnuclear states and, by implication, granted France a critical security hedge against a possibly emergent Germany, as some German strategic writers recognized.[82]

The key importance of the *force de frappe* was (and is) diplomatic. On the one hand, it was to afford France the right to protect its interests in the counsels of the great powers and, as the French claimed, to support the interests of smaller states threatened by the

80. See Joseph I. Coffey, *Strategic Power and National Policy* (Pittsburgh: University of Pittsburgh Press, 1971), pp. 3–20; also Institute for Strategic Studies, *The Military Balance, 1970–1971,* pp. 2–10.

81. *FA,* No. 169, Dec. 2, 1964. The idea of proportional deterrence is elaborated in the writings of Pierre Gallois which appeared in such influential journals as *Politique étrangère.* For a general review of his earlier and later positions regarding nuclear deterrence, see, respectively, his *Balance of Terror,* trans. Richard Howard (Boston: Houghton Mifflin, 1961), and *Paradoxes de la paix* (Paris: Presses du Temps Présent, 1967).

82. See, for example, Georg Picht, *et al., Die Force de frappe* (Freiburg/ Breisgau: Walter-Verlag, 1965).

superpower condominium. The interests of European and African states which would be joined to France's could be protected.[83] The basis for a new strategic-diplomatic system would thus be laid. Its nuclear weapons were viewed as a *"jeton de présence"* at the bargaining table.[84] Without them France's voice would presumably not be heard nor would its views be accorded much weight. Even critics of the Gaullist policies accepted the necessity of a nuclear weapons program to influence American policy and to provide some insurance for national defense against the unlikely, but still possible, contingency of an American withdrawal.[85] The de Gaulle government could reason that its influence over the United States was minimal within the alliance, like that of Great Britain, and it might exert a greater impact on American views by placing the *force de frappe* beyond the Atlantic Alliance. On the other hand, a strike force solely in the hands of the French state might blunt attempts at diplomatic blackmail that so effectively operated in the Suez crisis of 1956. The French were certain that, unlike England, they would not bow to American pressures or be intimidated by Soviet threats.[86]

The French emphasized deterrence rather than defense to underscore their determination to underwrite their political interests with nuclear weapons. In contrast to United States stress on second-strike forces, "pauses" in retaliating against an enemy nuclear attack, selected nuclear destruction, or tit-for-tat warfare, French strategists played on the horrors of nuclear exchanges and insisted on the maintenance of a credible first-strike force. Credibility, as suggested above, was conceived more in terms of the resolve of French leader-

83. See the views of Arthur Sulzberger, Feb. 2, 1960, *New York Times,* International edition, p. 6; also *Combat,* Oct. 22, 1959, p. 1.
84. "French Defense Policy," *Survival,* Jan. 1968, pp. 15–16.
85. Raymond Aron, *The Great Debate,* trans. Ernst Pawel (Garden City: Doubleday, 1965), p. 261. Also examine the following French works which support an independent nuclear deterrent and striking force: Alexandre Sanguinetti, *La France et l'arme atomique* (Paris: Juillard, 1964); Louis Vallon, *Le grand dessein national* (Paris: Calmann-Lévy, 1964), pp. 171–190; Club de Grenelle, *Siècle de Damoclès: La force de frappe stratégique* (Paris: Pierre Couderc, 1964); for a critical review of the *force de frappe,* see Jules Moch, *Non, à la force de frappe* (Paris: Laffont, 1963); Club Jean Moulin, *La Force de frappe et le citoyen* (Paris: Editions du Seuil, 1963), and *Pour ou contre la force de frappe* (Paris: John Didier, 1963), *passim.*
86. Goldschmidt, *Rivalités atomiques, passim.*

ship to use nuclear weapons than of the material conditions of their effective employment.[87] De Gaulle's audacious assertion of his personal will buttressed French credibility.[88] France's nuclear forces were designed to support its bargaining position by transforming strategic military confrontations into diplomatic conflicts. Its influence would increase as its differences with the larger nuclear states were converted from strategic to diplomatic quarrels. Nuclear weapons were to assure the operation of this transformation process.[89]

The psychological significance of the *force de frappe* should not be overlooked. It had at least three important psychic dimensions. First, it was designed initially as a means of bridging the gap between the army and the nation.[90] The French army had suffered successive defeats in World War II and political setbacks in Indochina and Algeria. De Gaulle's decision to terminate the Algerian conflict and to withdraw from the last outposts of the French empire came as a traumatic shock to the army. Much of the professional officer corps, shamed by defeat and by failure to keep its bond with those Muslims who had sided with France, again felt abandoned by the Metropole. De Gaulle understood that his tenure in office depended on ending the army's alienation, a task very much in his mind during conversations with President Kennedy and other world leaders.[91] The *force de frappe* offered a ready tool. It promised a new basis for France's defense that would remain under the tight political control of the president of the Republic and would not depend on colonial possessions, so much a part of France's military posture for over a century.

Second, the French nation needed to renew confidence in its ability to defend itself and to regain the sense of identity that results from making common cause against a foe. A national nuclear force

87. *FA*, No. 169, Dec. 2, 1964. The widely accepted views of Albert Wohlstetter in American strategic circles were given short shrift by the French; see his "The Delicate Balance of Terror," *Foreign Affairs*, XXXVII (Jan. 1959), 211–234; also his "Nuclear Sharing: NATO and the N + 1 Country Problem," *ibid.*, XXXIX (April 1961), 355–387.

88. Beaufre, *Deterrence and Strategy*, especially pp. 78–103.

89. Michel Debré, *Courrier de la nouvelle république*, Sept. 1962, p. 6.

90. This is the principal thesis of Edgar S. Furniss, Jr., *De Gaulle and the French Army* (New York: Twentieth Century Fund, 1964).

91. Schlesinger, Jr., *op. cit.*, p. 353.

was supposed to strengthen France's ambition to restore its continental military pre-eminence, lost in the War of 1870, and to revive pride in the French people.[92]

Finally, France sought in nuclear weapons the material sanction for its efforts to assert its right to a privileged international position that derived from France's long history of involvement in world politics, its alleged superior cultural status, and its presumed intelligence and demonstrated success in arranging the affairs of states. Like efficient land armies and battle fleets before, nuclear weapons were to be the great equalizer among the major states. France would gain equality with the superpowers because it had its own nuclear weapons, beyond the reach of any other state's control.

The domestic component of the *force de frappe* extended to include scientific, technological, and economic goals. The *force de frappe* was incorporated within the Gaullist efforts to reform French society and to adapt it to all levels of international competition with the great powers. Through the *force de frappe* the French state would use its military modernization program to stimulate innovative industries and secure for France a primary place in world markets and in the continued struggle among states for technological supremacy. It was deemed the only way by which expensive modernization programs could be politically supported and basic reforms in the society, including the expansion and democratization of all levels of education, could be undertaken. "For the de Gaulle Government," concludes one thorough study of French science, "the lesson to be drawn from the American and Russian experiences is that the route to modernization is through massive armament and space programs. Such programs enable the Government to build up underdeveloped sections of the country and provide support for those areas of the economy in which scientific research and technology meet, for example, electronics, aviation, and nuclear energy. These areas are the most vivid ones in determining the standing of a nation in the world today."[93] In this connection, the French undertook a nuclear-space program larger than that of all of its partners in the EEC combined.

92. Mendl, *op. cit.*, p. 63.
93. Gilpin, *op. cit.*, p. 290.

American Challenge to the Force de Frappe

Flexible Response. The Kennedy administration's flexible response strategy and its campaign for an Atlantic multilateral nuclear force posed two challenges to the French *force de frappe*. The first attacked the French force on strategic grounds; the second sought either to harness French nuclear power to American control or to isolate France diplomatically within the alliance, and even beyond. Other attacks stemmed from domestic sources which either supported the American proposals or preferred to see the French nuclear program housed within the European Economic Community and Euratom or within the Western European Union and based on close Anglo-French cooperation. De Gaulle skillfully repulsed each of these frontal and flanking attacks.

Flexible response conceived the defense of the Western alliance as a geographic whole, from the shores of the Pacific to West Berlin in the heart of the Warsaw bloc. Geographic boundaries and national sensitivities were considered subordinate to a collective Western response to the Soviet threat.[94] Shortly after assuming office in 1961, the Kennedy administration proposed the rapid development of Western military forces to meet Soviet aggression at all anticipated levels of military conflict, covering a range from strategic nuclear weapons to conventional and irregular warfare. Within the alliance a division of labor was envisioned. The United States would provide the bulk of the alliance's nuclear forces, which would remain under American direction to minimize the possibility of nuclear war erupting from misunderstanding, miscalculation, or inadvertence. If war should arise, centralized nuclear control would supposedly limit damage to the West, for it would assure the destruction of Soviet atomic forces and would end the war more rapidly on terms most beneficial to Western interests.[95]

Europe would be expected to furnish most of the conventional

94. Two indispensable works for an understanding of the Kennedy administration's flexible response strategy are Maxwell Taylor, *The Uncertain Trumpet* (New York: Harper and Row, 1959), and William Kaufmann, *The McNamara Strategy* (New York: Harper and Row, 1964).

95. Alain C. Enthoven, "American Deterrent Policy," in Henry A. Kissinger, ed., *Problems of National Strategy* (New York: Praeger, 1965), pp. 120–134.

forces of the alliance and undertake increased defense expenditures. Former Secretary of State Dean Acheson unofficially supplied a summary of the Kennedy-Johnson conception of European-American burden sharing in the alliance. He and the administration believed the soundest defense plan for the West was one in which "Europe would furnish the bulk of the conventional power and the United States the nuclear power, as well as very substantial conventional forces." [96] Kennedy planners no longer felt that the West had to concede conventional superiority in Europe to the Soviet Union,[97] but could meet the threat through a better division of labor within the alliance. The Europeans were urged to believe that their greater effort in building conventional forces would expand their influence over American military strategy and diplomacy in Europe and even perhaps in the Third World, where the United States increasingly held their interests in its charge.[98]

United States strategists saw the *force de frappe* as a threat to the execution of a flexible response strategy and to American nuclear dominance within the Atlantic Alliance. Flexible response was designed to give the American president the option between holocaust and surrender. Accordingly, ground troops in Central Europe of participating NATO countries were to be rationalized under American direction and even increased, including a French contribution, to maintain the conventional level of hostilities as long as possible. The French nuclear program and the war in Algeria stood as obstacles to the realization of a flexible response posture.

The *force de frappe,* or any independently controlled allied nuclear force, also posed serious difficulties for the execution of the American-inspired proposal for a nuclear counterforce strategy for NATO. President Kennedy announced the American campaign against all forms of nuclear proliferation, particularly the French program, in his news conference of April 18, 1962. Secretary of Defense Robert S. McNamara, however, assumed responsibility for the attack on the French system. At the NATO spring meeting in Athens in 1962, he exposed to allied view the enormous nuclear striking power of the

96. Dean Acheson, "The Practice of Partnership," *Foreign Affairs,* XLI (Jan. 1963), 258.
97. Kaufmann, *op. cit.,* pp. 102–167.
98. Acheson, *op. cit.,* p. 258.

United States in order to emphasize that the United States possessed enough nuclear might for the Western alliance. In June at the University of Michigan, he argued that the target system for NATO countries was "indivisible." "If, despite all our efforts," said the defense secretary, "nuclear war should occur, our best hope lies in conducting a centrally controlled campaign against all of the enemy's vital nuclear capabilities, while retaining reserve forces, all centrally controlled." [99] The *force de frappe* would allegedly add little to Western material strength not already possessed in abundance by the United States. Its possible independent use and vulnerability tempted an enemy to strike pre-emptively. These possibilities undermined centralized use of Western nuclear might and necessarily weakened the United States' capacity alone to define Atlantic military policy. Secretary McNamara dismissed the French force as "dangerous, expensive, prone to obsolescence, and lacking in credibility as a deterrent." [100] In further pronouncements against French deviationism, the Kennedy administration added the arguments that the French system divided the alliance by implying distrust of America's announced intentions to defend Europe, diverted resources from the more immediate task of building European conventional forces, promoted global nuclear proliferation, and ran undue risks for the West since its use would precipitate attacks on population centers rather than on enemy strategic capabilities.[101]

The de Gaulle regime pointedly rejected flexible response. The debate was largely fought on grounds of military doctrine, but these exchanges were over larger political stakes than military policy. American pressure for flexible response attacked France's right and capacity to develop an independent military strategy and diplomacy and its claim to big-power status which, once re-established, would serve as the basis for a gradual transformation of the international system, leading to greater decentralization of global strategic power and diplomatic initiative.

99. Kaufmann, *op. cit.*, p. 117. Andrew J. Pierre, *Nuclear Politics* (New York: Oxford University Press, 1972), pp. 259–262, ably distinguishes various aspects of Defense Secretary McNamara's controlled central war concepts and flexible response.

100. Kaufmann, *op. cit.*, p. 117.

101. Henry A. Kissinger, *The Troubled Partnership* (Garden City: Doubleday, 1965), p. 121.

Flexible response was rejected as inapplicable to Europe. The central geographical position of Russian ground forces, sustained by superior tactical air cover, permitted the Soviet Union to concentrate its military power quickly against weak points in Western defense. Moreover, large amounts of European territory would have to be yielded before defensible lines of resistance could be established. Europe would meanwhile be largely destroyed. The same logic applied to tactical nuclear warfare proposals for Europe. According to influential French strategists, the bombardment of troop centers and the Soviet logistics infrastructure, foreseen in tactical nuclear battle plans, "would wipe out Europe over a depth of eighteen hundred miles from the Atlantic to the Soviet frontier." [102] The French chose to see no essential difference between postattack environments of conventional, tactical nuclear, or strategic warfare in Europe.

The French distinguished, however, among defense postures with respect to their utility for over-all Western nuclear deterrence of Soviet aggression. Preparations for conventional and tactical nuclear warfare merely weakened nuclear deterrence at the decisive strategic level and encouraged the very Soviet aggressive designs that deterrence was supposed to preclude by narrowing the differential between punishment and political gain.[103] Soviet leaders might be tempted to strike Europe with conventional forces on the strength of the increased possibility, engendered by a flexible response posture, that the Soviet homeland might still be spared. France intended, as General Charles Ailleret argued, to destroy "the root of . . . aggression and its chances of drawing strength, by dropping strategic nuclear bombs on the war potential of the country unleashing the aggression, and thus causing that country to give up its aggression." [104]

The French also faced the problem of determining when a strategic nuclear strike should be initiated. General Ailleret distinguished between apparent and real aggression. A variety of involuntary and unauthorized incursions were classed as apparent aggressions that did not warrant a strategic nuclear response. Real aggression, however, was defined as "penetration, involving the use of force against

---

102. General Ailleret, "Flexible Response: A French View," *Survival,* VI (Nov.–Dec. 1964), 258–265.

103. Beaufre, *Deterrence and Strategy,* pp. 31–77.

104. Ailleret, *Survival,* Nov.–Dec. 1964, p. 263.

such defense elements as may be met, reaching a depth of territory defined according to the nature of the region concerned and employing such a volume of forces that the latter can only be considered to be acting in accordance with the will of their country to conquer a part of Western Europe." [105] Such a real aggression would be determined by units positioned as close to the enemy lines as possible. If these units were overrun, it would be assumed that an all-out attack had been launched. The breaking of the line would trigger the French nuclear forces, and presumably those of the Western alliance. Such a defense posture, observed the French, not only enhanced the deterrent effect of nuclear weapons but also permitted the West to decrease its men under arms while increasing simultaneously the efficiency of these smaller forces to meet enemy attacks in other areas of Europe and the globe. The French favored the Eisenhower administration's massive retaliation strategy and its reliance on trip-wire forces along the East-West frontier which, if overrun, would signal a NATO nuclear attack.

The execution of the Kennedy flexible response strategy for NATO would have effectively diluted the strategic independence and political utility of the *force de frappe*. Given its limited resources, France could not afford to meet the anticipated rise in force level requirements of flexible response and still sustain a major nuclear effort of its own. The de Gaulle regime had decided to maintain defense spending in the 1960's at approximately 5 percent of a slowly mounting gross national product. To compensate for the increase in spending for nuclear arms, while holding over-all military expenditures constant, force levels were cut and the modernization of conventional forces, sought by elements in the army, was stretched out. Between 1960 and 1967, the total number of French effectives fell from one million to five hundred thousand along with the reduction in the length of military service from 28 to 12 to 15 months.[106] In the early 1960's the de Gaulle regime projected an armed force of "five or six mechanized divisions and one or two airborne divisions." [107] These were to be organized into so-called forces of maneuver and interven-

---

105. *Ibid.*, p. 264.
106. Institute for Strategic Studies, *The Military Balance: 1960–1968, passim.*
107. Pierre Messmer, "The French Military Establishment of Tomorrow," *Orbis,* VI (Summer 1962), 210.

tion. A third grouping of forces, besides nuclear and nonnuclear components, was to be organized into an operational defense of the territory (DOT). These were to be reserve units which would expand forces of maneuver or, if France were overrun, would break into guerrilla bands to harass an occupying power. The 1967 defense budget, published before the disruption of May 1968, indicated a cut relative to previous projections of almost one billion francs for conventional equipment, 760 million francs for air training and support, and 240 million francs for tactical atomic arms.[108] Expenditures for DOT forces appeared to be little more than the total of civilian security forces already available for internal purposes.

If for no other reason than resource limitations, French and American nuclear strategies were bound to be different. Whereas the superpowers, with their superior resources and continental size, could segment their strategic and political policies and could generate separate sets of options within each sphere—hence the Kennedy flexible response proposals—France could not. Commanding fewer resources, it had to rely on the *force de frappe* both for its strategic posture and for its maneuverability in global diplomacy. A gain in military strategic options for the United States, as one keen observer of European politics notes, would have led to a reduction in French political choices.[109] Joining the *force de frappe* to the Atlantic Alliance or to a European framework would have contradicted the Gaullist rationale for building a separate national nuclear weapons system at great expense. It would have ensnared France in the very web of dependency relations and restraints which the *force de frappe* was supposed to preclude.

The French readily conceded the higher risks involved in their strategic posture compared to Pentagon recommendations. Unlike American strategists, the French gave little attention to the problems of conducting a central nuclear war, such as maintenance of communications with the state's military forces and with the enemy, control over the amount of force to be employed, limits on damage to civilian population centers, and the swift termination of hostilities. The French offered the Western alliance little alternative between ineffectual dip-

108. *Le Monde,* Oct. 15–16, 1967, p. 7. See also *Livre blanc,* I, for a summary of the latest French military planning goals.
109. Kissinger, *Troubled Partnership,* pp. 31–184.

lomatic reaction and nuclear war. But the higher risks of devastating war were tolerated and even encouraged because the very manipulation of the risk of atomic war enhanced France's bargaining position relative to its allies and present and potential enemies. The French rationalized that the risk, while potentially high, was of low probability in light of superpower aversion to nuclear war and, in particular, of a perceived diminishing Soviet threat. As long as the Atlantic Alliance remained intact and most of its members participated in NATO, the possibility of France being abandoned by the alliance or the United States was not very likely. France could count on its European partners to retain the American commitment, let NATO strategists exercise themselves over military problems, and free itself to pursue its own interests largely through patient diplomacy.

President de Gaulle's exaggerated claim that there can be no Atlantic Alliance without France was in practice given a reverse interpretation: that France could enjoy United States protection without formally conceding dependency. The American global system of security pacts could be turned to the French advantage, for France found itself covered by the American protectorate whether it wished to be or not.[110] Whatever the degree of France's recalcitrance, the United States, argued the French, had little choice but to defend Europe and, by that token, France, because it was in America's minimal interests to deprive the Soviet Union of Europe's resources and to protect the bonds that had been forged across the ocean by history, culture, and economic interests. De Gaulle's foreign minister, Couve de Murville, underlined these French estimates in his address to the National Assembly defending the French government's departure from NATO:

People will object . . . [that] our unilateral action risks jeopardizing everything by leading the United States to take its protection away from a dissenting France, if not to abandon all of Europe.

Strange questions . . . not only because they depict the Atlantic Alliance as a one-way commitment—that of the United States toward Europe —but also because of the lack of consideration they imply for Washington's policy, as if Washington were committed to this Europe-American partnership only because the Europeans are docile allies. Were there not

110. *Major Addresses*, p. 42.

on this side of the Atlantic essential interests for the other side, which it wanted and still wants to watch over?[111]

France could have its nuclear cake and eat it, too. It could claim big-power status without facing the larger problem of maintaining alliance cohesion to meet the Soviet threat or to organize for war which it dismissed as improbable. Considering the overwhelming nuclear superiority of the United States and the Soviet Union and their ability to take defensive measures against smaller nuclear states, such as pre-emptive strikes or the deployment of ABMs, the strategic value of the *force de frappe* might well be questioned. But, as Gaullist critics have long recognized, the diplomatic, prestige, and technological benefits of the program were of overriding importance for de Gaulle, even if cast in a rationale of strategic military need. The United States might chafe under the logic of nuclear deterrence and security interests outlined by the French and manifest reluctance to extend its protective umbrella over ungrateful allies, but its options were limited. To permit these areas to fall to an expansionist opponent would be a prohibitive loss. United States nuclear protection had already been extended to areas of lesser importance, if measured against repeated American pronouncements of unreserved support of European security. The United States had run the risk of nuclear war over Cuba, Formosa, Israel, and Vietnam. French strategists felt sure that the United States would value Europe as highly in a crisis where American and allied military and economic investments were so great and where complementary strategic and political interests were so compelling.

The possible return of the United States to isolationism was ruled out. The French, nevertheless, played on the fears of their European allies by casting doubts on the United States defense commitment to Europe. Flexible response gave point to the French critique. The United States was accused of attempting to use Europe as a nuclear battleground while its territory would remain a sanctuary in a war with the Soviet Union. In an argument that the French were to employ with greater regularity in justifying their departure from NATO,

111. S&PC, No. 242, April 7, 1966, pp. 1–2. See also the address by former Prime Minister Georges Pompidou before the National Assembly, S&PC, No. 244A, April 15, 1966.

they charged the United States with having unilaterally revised alliance strategy without previous allied accord. The French portrayed flexible response as an implicit lowering of United States resolution to defend Europe. This attitude played on already widely circulating European fears, especially in West Germany, of a basic change in the American willingness to protect Europe against Soviet blackmail and possible military incursions.

The specter of United States liberation of a devastated Europe loomed large in allied thinking. The French cleverly emphasized the increased cost to Europeans of the Kennedy design. Some of de Gaulle's bitterest European critics agreed on this assessment of the American defense changes.[112] France's strategic position was also much closer to Germany's. Its massive retaliation doctrine reinforced its claim to be the true European power. Finally, the division of labor within the alliance was a source of great concern to the Europeans; the French insisted that it promised to reduce the European states to technological vassalage and to mortgage their futures irremediably to American economic and technological prowess.[113]

Multilateral Nuclear Force. The second most significant American challenge to French nuclear independence was the proposal for a multilateral nuclear force (MLF) for NATO. The history of the MLF is long and tortuous and cannot be easily reviewed here.[114] Its roots lie in the Eisenhower administration's offer to assign five Polaris submarines to NATO in an effort to meet European apprehensions about the American nuclear commitment to Europe, to afford Europeans some insight into the problem of controlling and using nuclear weapons, and to provide the rudimentary elements of an allied consulting process on nuclear strategy. The French rejected successive versions of American nuclear sharing schemes.[115] The cul-

112. Interview, Dirk Stikker, former Secretary-General of NATO, March 1965.
113. See, for example, Ailleret, *Survival*, Nov.–Dec. 1964, pp. 258–265; *idem, Revue de défense nationale*, 1967, pp. 1923–1932; and Gallois, *Paradoxes de la paix.*
114. Richard E. Neustadt, *Alliance Politics* (New York: Columbia University Press, 1970), presents an interesting and readable account of the background politics in Washington and Whitehall leading to the MLF proposal.
115. Robert E. Osgood, *NATO, The Entangling Alliance* (Chicago: University of Chicago Press, 1962), *passim.*

mination of these proposals occurred at Nassau in December 1962, when the United States agreed to supply Polaris missiles to Britain in partial compensation for the Pentagon decision to scrap the Skybolt air-to-ground missile that was to extend the life of Britain's V-Bomber force. Britain agreed to construct the submarines and warheads for the missiles and pledged to place its nuclear forces under a NATO multilateral command, but insisted on the right to use submarine forces without international restriction in the event that supreme national interests were at stake.

Notice of the Nassau accord was sent to President de Gaulle after it had been announced to the press. The United States extended the same terms to France as it had to Britain. As de Gaulle's reply demonstrated, however, the personal slight of failing to inform him beforehand, an Anglo-American tactic applied to de Gaulle during World War II, whether consciously or inadvertently, would be paid in kind. At the same time, the more important national and systemic differences between French and Anglo-American strategic policy would be clearly articulated.

De Gaulle's public reaction to Nassau took the form of a news conference on January 14, 1963. De Gaulle saw little use in the MLF proposal. France had neither nuclear submarines nor thermonuclear warheads. Unlike England, it did not have privileged access to vital technical information and materials in these areas. By the time French technology would be able to employ the Polaris, France expected to be capable of producing its own delivery vehicles. In any event, the MLF entailed a "web of liaisons, transmissions, and interferences" that violated French defense doctrine of independent use of nuclear weapons.[116] The *force de frappe,* if integrated, would not be responsive to France's needs, and its withdrawal during a crisis, de Gaulle observed, would jeopardize the MLF at the very time that its swift and effective use was most urgently needed.[117]

De Gaulle pursued the central point that the integration of nuclear weapons could not be reconciled with national use. In his exposition, he questioned the viability of the Western alliance under American direction and concluded that American unilateral action in the Cuban

116. *Major Addresses,* p. 219.
117. *Ibid.*

missile crisis had compromised European defense. He stressed that the United States, in placing its security interests above those of Europe, had acted without having consulted or received the consent of its alliance partners. "Thus the immediate defense, and one can say privileged defense of Europe and the military participation of the Europeans which were once basic factors of their [United States] strategy," de Gaulle said, "moved by the force of circumstance into second place." [118]

Playing further on European fears, de Gaulle questioned whether the United States would aid Europe in time of crisis. "No one in the world—particularly no one in America—can say if, where, when, how and to what extent the American nuclear weapons would be employed to defend Europe." [119] That Europe would have been gravely threatened, as President Kennedy had observed,[120] if the United States had not responded to the Russian challenge in Cuba appeared beside the point to de Gaulle. He remained silent, too, about his solid support of the American president's action after he had been informed of the American response by a special White House emissary. In the wake of Nassau and the smashing American victory in the test of wills with the Soviet Union, de Gaulle thought more of rationalizing his determination to furnish France with nuclear weapons than of bolstering the American position in NATO or of reinforcing its strategic superiority over the Soviet Union. The market value of the alliance had been *ipso facto* discounted in the very success of the alliance leader. The Cuban affair demonstrated to de Gaulle the decisive strategic and diplomatic significance of nuclear weapons. He was not prepared to surrender this instrument to the United States. "If one spontaneously loses . . . the free disposition of oneself," he continued, "there is a strong risk of never regaining it." [121] The power to dispose belonged only to the nuclear nations.

De Gaulle's news conference made a shambles of the Kennedy administration's Grand Design for Europe. It exposed the fundamental contradiction between American support for European unity (including England) and equality with the United States and con-

118. *Ibid.*, p. 217.
119. *Ibid.*
120. Sorenson, *op. cit.*, p. 642.
121. *Major Addresses*, p. 216.

tinued American monopoly of Europe's defense.[122] De Gaulle denied the possibility of achieving unity in Europe or equality with the United States in the absence of an indigenous European defense system. An Atlantic Europe would be weak internally since it would lack a capacity and will to protect itself. It would fall prey to American pressures as the European states would be played off against each other, each valuing its relationship with the United States more than possible cooperative relationships with its immediate neighbors. Great Britain's decision to go along with the United States on strategic lines fatally impaired, in Gaullist eyes, its ability to contribute to Europe's separate development. Tied to the United States and under Pentagon tutelage, it would not likely be disposed to support French policy and prestige goals.

In vetoing Britain's bid to enter the Common Market in 1963, de Gaulle raised a different standard for American-European cooperation. Military inequality could not be the basis for political and economic equality across the Atlantic. The compartmentalization of alliance policy could produce little more than rhetorical obeisance to the principle of equality while the substance of the principle would be emptied of effective import. For Gaullist France, an alliance among sovereign equals that tolerated a separate policy domain in defense, insulated from allied influence and criticism, was inherently unequal. The Gaullist rebuff strengthened the resolution of MLF enthusiasts in Washington to press the program upon Europe. The campaign raged in fits and starts from 1963 until the winter of 1965, when President Johnson abruptly tabled the MLF proposal and ordered a "cease-fire" between the United States and France.

The American rationale for the MLF, like its history, is long, and it changed in focus and announced intent depending on shifting political alignments and international circumstances.[123] Even its composition was revised from that of a submarine fleet to a proposal to build twenty-five surface vessels carrying Polaris missiles with a range of 2,500 miles. The crews of the ships were to be of mixed nationality, and commands were to be assigned according to financial contribution with the proviso that no nation could furnish more than 40 per-

122. *Department of State Bulletin*, XLVII (July 23, 1962), 131–133.
123. See n. 114 above.

cent of the total. The shift to surface vessels, despite their increased vulnerability, was in response to Congressional refusal to accept nuclear sharing schemes involving American atomic submarines. The MLF controversy has been described in other sources. For our purposes, it is more important to examine its impact on France's global aspirations.

An implemented flexible response strategy would have outflanked French military efforts since France's limited resources would have been diverted from atomic to conventional arms and its attention would have been deflected from national to alliance (and therefore American) nuclear concerns. The MLF posed not only a threat to France's strategic independence but also to its freedom to maneuver politically. British and German participation within the MLF would have increased their respective positions in Washington without necessarily enhancing France's, and all three would have been drawn deeper into the American orbit of influence. Britain already menaced France's continental pre-eminence in its application to join the Common Market. Tied to the United States in a special nuclear accord, it would be viewed, as Gaullists were eager to point out, as an American Trojan Horse in Europe. It was no accident, as many observed, that President de Gaulle linked his veto of Britain's request to enter the EEC to the MLF in his news conference rejecting the Nassau accord. In addition, Germany stood to enlarge its hold over American policy at France's expense. Its leverage within the alliance was already perceived to be greater than France's. Its security was entrusted to the alliance and its contributions of territory, logistical support, money, and manpower were larger than those of any other NATO state. The MLF would have given Germany access to American nuclear strategic policy and, perhaps worse, reactivated a latent security threat for France, which the *force de frappe* was partly, if only implicitly, constructed to prevent. The bonding of German-American relations within the MLF ring would have inevitably devalued the strategic and diplomatic utility of an independent French nuclear force. German access to nuclear weapons would have destroyed what remained of the Franco-German friendship treaty of 1963. The possible German-French basis, however slight, for an eventual European nuclear force would also have been undermined.

According to the French, the MLF would have forestalled the creation of an independent European nuclear force either because the Europeans would never have been able to agree on a common authority—Germany would be tied to the United States—or because the United States would never have relinquished its veto power.[124] In the midst of the MLF debate, President de Gaulle advanced the tentative hope that the *force de frappe* could become the kernel of an all-European deterrent. At Strasbourg he voiced support for a Six which would "put into practice among themselves in the political domain—which is first that of defense—an organization . . . which would truly be theirs, with its objectives, its resources, and its obligations." [125] An independent French nuclear force was to prepare the ground for the second liberation of Europe.[126]

Finally, the MLF was criticized as a brake on efforts to promote a détente with the Eastern bloc and, specifically, with the Soviet Union. German participation in nuclear planning and operations was viewed as an insurmountable obstacle to accord with the Soviet Union over the political fate of Europe.[127] British and Scandinavian concern similarly advised abandonment of the multilateral scheme.[128] The American response to the political problem was deemed characteristic. While the United States sought to expand its strategic options through the MLF and, concomitantly, attempted to offer a partial solution to the German question, Gaullist France saw its po-

124. Kissinger, *Troubled Partnership*, p. 52. There was reason for French concern if Arthur Schlesinger's account of the MLF negotiations offer an indication of American intent. Schlesinger, Jr., *op. cit.*, especially pp. 842–888. Also, Stanley Hoffmann, *Gulliver's Troubles*, p. 518. It should be noted that the British had little use for the MLF. See Pierre, *op. cit.*, pp. 217–300. Pierre's thorough discussion of the British nuclear program provides many useful parallels with the French effort.
125. S&PC, No. 212, Nov. 22, 1964, p. 3.
126. How such a European force might be oganized politically is suggested in an anonymous article, "Faut-il réformer l'alliance atlantique," *Politique étrangère*, XXX, No. 3 (1965), 230–244.
127. Remarks of Gaullist Deputy General Billote before NATO parliamentarians, *Le Monde*, Nov. 20, 1964, p. 2; *Combat*, Dec. 2, 1965, p. 1. See also the discussion of Charles Planck, *The Changing Status of German Reunification in Western Diplomacy, 1955–1966* (Baltimore: Johns Hopkins Press, 1967), pp. 51–54.
128. *L'Année politique, 1964*, p. 301.

litical options narrowing through the creation of what it considered to be a strike force of dubious strategic value and political relevance for its systemic designs.[129]

Ineffective Domestic Opposition to the Force de Frappe

The remaining challenges to Gaullist nuclear and security policies were domestic. Ineffectual and divided, de Gaulle's opponents contested official policy on a number of conflicting grounds. Some critics objected to the higher expenditures for the *force de frappe* because they would detract from the prosecution of the Algerian War. Others, especially within army circles which were tied to conventional weapons systems, correctly felt that the nuclear weapons program would mean the neglect of the nonnuclear elements of the armed forces.[130] Still others, like General Valluy, worried about the viability of a national defense outside the NATO framework. Influential political writers, like Raymond Aron, feared a chauvinistic base for the French weapons program would weaken the American commitment to Europe. Finally, the most sustained attacks came from those, including representatives from the camps above, who hoped to build a united Europe on the French nuclear deterrent because they felt, like de Gaulle, the need to be independent from the United States or were compelled to opt for the European solution because of the high costs of such a credible nuclear force in the face of the nuclear strength of the superpowers.

De Gaulle dealt systematically with each of these groups, dividing his enemies and increasingly forcing them into retreat. In 1960, the de Gaulle regime handily defeated two censure motions over the *force de frappe*.[131] Another and more serious attempt to sidetrack the program developed two years later over the government's request for an additional 200 million francs for the nuclear separation plant at Pierrelatte which was essential for the construction of a hydrogen

129. This is one of the useful insights to be found in Henry Kissinger's *Troubled Partnership, passim.*

130. See the army's semiofficial objection to the emphasis placed on the *force de frappe* in "L'Armée de terre et l'armement atomique tactique," *L'Armée,* Jan. 1965. Kohl, *op. cit.,* pp. 169–177, discusses the domestic opposition to de Gaulle's nuclear policies ably and efficiently.

131. *L'Année politique, 1960,* pp. 102–122.

bomb. Initial government estimates had seriously underestimated the cost of the plant. Scientific Research Minister Gaston Palewski set the cost of the plant over five years at 4,500 million francs, about four times the original estimates. After the French Senate rejected the supplemental appropriation, Prime Minister Georges Pompidou placed the question before the National Assembly for its vote of confidence. Refusing to accept amendments to the government's proposals, he recalled parliamentary support for the nuclear program that preceded the Gaullist government's accession to power. He advanced the argument that de Gaulle used effectively two years later in his counterattack on the MLF. Anticipating Centrist critics, Pompidou stressed that the French effort was in the service of European unity: "The day can be very near wherein the political union of Europe will be constructed. It will extend, of course, to defense. . . . The possession by France of a nuclear arm . . . will be an essential element of this [European] defense." [132] The motion to censure received 206 votes, 35 short of the 241 required for passage.

The heart, if not the head, of Gaullism was more pointedly expressed by Prime Minister Michel Debré's exposition in the debate on censure. "There does not exist, and I can tell you there will not exist for a long time, anything other than national atomic forces, corresponding to the efforts of some nations. It ought to be understood that these forces should cooperate. But integration does not exist for the good reason that no one desires it." [133] Certainly Gaullist France wished no part of it. The stock Gaullist argument that no thought could be given to the transfer of French nuclear weapons to Europe since there existed no legitimate and competent political authority to receive them sterilized much of Pompidou's argument over European union. Only the French nation-state possessed such competence, and it could relinquish its control only at the cost of its political legitimacy. If nuclear weapons were a symbol of national independence and could not be integrated into a supranational body, how could the French *force de frappe* ever be the kernel of a European nuclear force? The French assumed the curious stance of wanting Europe, yet refusing to contemplate the assignment of their nu-

132. *Ibid., 1962,* p. 90.
133. *Ibid., 1960,* p. 562.

clear weapons, an indispensable condition, to the construction of Europe. Ardent Gaullists—and there were many of them—saw nothing strange about the paradox posed by Gaullist strategic conceptions.

After de Gaulle's smashing referendum and legislative victory of November 1962, on the question of the popular election of the French president, his parliamentary opposition was never again able to mount a serious threat to his nuclear policies. The 1965 presidential election forced de Gaulle into a ballotage, but his opponents garnered their support either among the Left that objected to the government's economic and social policies (constrained partially by its ambitious nuclear program) or among Centrist and Conservative groups that supported the French nuclear effort, but objected to France's boycott of the EEC and its opposition to European union. Having to face only weak and divided opposition at home, the Gaullist government was indifferent to proposals for active French participation in Euratom, preferring national to European-based nuclear programs,[134] and expressed contempt, especially after Nassau, for any notion that France might use the WEU framework to build a European defense system with England. French Defense Minister Pierre Messmer no longer felt his agency need abide by the terms of the Paris Treaty of 1954, which provided the basis for German rearmament, to report France's nuclear stockpiles. This requirement, according to Messmer, did not envision French acquisition of an independent nuclear system. It did not apply to England, so it should not apply to France either. It required the wrenching disruption of 1968 to compel the de Gaulle regime and its parliamentary majority to revise government priorities in favor of domestic social and economic reform and to encourage French strategists to rethink France's isolation within the Atlantic Alliance.

134. Lawrence Scheinman, *Euratom: Nuclear Integration in Europe, International Conciliation,* No. 563 (May 1967).

3

Security outside NATO

Clash of Grand Designs

By the end of the Algerian War and the American victory in Cuba, Gaullist security policy faced three overriding questions of successive sequential importance: (1) to prevent either a possible superpower war or a more probable superpower accord that would jeopardize European interests and French aspirations for greater world power and prestige; (2) to offset American military superiority by righting, largely through diplomacy favoring the Soviet Union, what appeared to be the temporarily tilted superpower balance; and (3) to work toward a reconstruction of the international system that would retain most, if not all, of the advantages of uneasy stability currently existing and promise greater political autonomy and maneuverability for all states. De Gaulle expected a new world politics, based on his principles, to normalize state relations, distorted by the Cold War, and to enhance French status and influence.

A partial answer to these security problems was the *force de frappe*. A fuller answer was French withdrawal from NATO's integrated command in 1966 and refusal to support Soviet-American efforts to define common rules to control the spiraling strategic arms race. This negative or denial strategy drew its rationale from an alternative image of global order and cooperation, specifically of American-European relations, to that sketched by President Kennedy. In a deeper historical sense, the Kennedy Grand Design served as foil for de Gaulle's conception of global relations which was significantly shaped by his wartime experience when the Anglo-American states initially refused to accept France as an equal.[1] The larger significance of France's with-

1. For sympathetic treatments of Kennedy policy toward Europe, see Arthur Schlesinger, Jr., *A Thousand Days*, pp. 842–923; Theodore Sorenson, *Kennedy*, and Joseph Kraft, *The Grand Design* (New York: Harper, 1962). For critiques of Kennedy policy toward Europe, see Henry A. Kissinger, *The Troubled Partnership*, and Seyom Brown, "An Alternative to the Grand Design," *World Politics*, XVII (Jan. 1965), 232–242.

drawal from NATO and its intransigence on questions of global and, in particular, European military stabilization can be illuminated by a review of the Gaullist alternative to the Kennedy image. Like de Gaulle's other formulations of global policy, this counterpoise to American hopes was discernible in its broader outlines, but vague in its concrete details, particularly on such crucial points as the membership, status, and relative material power of the major participants, yet it suggests still another form of interstate organization compatible with the realization and expression of France's *grandeur*.

The Kennedy administration rested its security policies on the clear and present danger of the Soviet Union to Europe and the Third World and on the emerging threat to Asia of Communist China. To meet these Communist threats, a flexible response strategy was prepared that would divide the military duties of Atlantic Alliance members who would share in shaping Western global policy roughly according to their contributions. While a military arms build-up was promoted to implement the American strategy, attempts were simultaneously launched to establish more visible and formal ground rules for arms competition between the Western and Eastern blocs. Nuclear proliferation was specifically attacked. This assault included attempts to discourage national nuclear systems within the Atlantic Alliance and to encourage superpower cooperation in halting global proliferation in the form of the Test Ban Treaty of 1963 and the Non-Proliferation Treaty. The framework for both military preparations against, and negotiations with, the Communist states was to be the Atlantic Alliance.

Within the Western alliance equality between the United States and its European allies was envisioned, but it could occur only when Europe was sufficiently united to deal as an equal with the United States. The nation-state was considered obsolete in Europe although it was still considered appropriate for the United States. Its day was over in Europe because of the past miseries of war to which nation-state struggles had given rise and because of the limited size of the European states in relation to the United States. The Kennedy administration gave new impetus to the notion of a united Europe that successive Washington administrations had supported. It would be a union of Western states, including Great Britain. Its inclusion was essential to the American scheme to assure continental Europe a nation of unflagging commitment to democratic rule, centuries of experience in global leadership, and the close cultural, commercial, and financial bonds that the British people would presumably retain with the United States. Once Europe was united on a federal model a new era of American-European strategic, diplomatic, and economic interdependence would be initiated.

The United States identified the Atlantic Alliance as the appropriate framework within which to resolve the division of Europe and Germany. The military expansion of the early 1960's carried forward an idea, first promoted during the Truman administration, that only from a situation of strength could the West successfully negotiate with a malevolent Soviet Union. Relations with the Eastern Communist bloc would be bilateral, between it and the alliance under United States leadership, not between individual European states and the Soviet Union and its satellites. It was assumed that West Germany would be firmly tied to the Western alliance, its external security dependent on the United States commitment. The presence of American troops in Europe was an implicit assurance to allied states and the Eastern bloc that German militarism would not again arise in Central Europe.

The Atlantic Alliance would be the foundation on which the West would erect a global security system. The plan was already outlined in the American network of security pacts that had been largely completed by the late 1940's and early 1950's. Once Europe united and assumed a strength equal to the United States within the alliance, it would be accorded broader and ultimately equitable responsibilities for concerting alliance security policies.

The Atlantic Alliance would also serve as the basis for a new economic relationship between Europe and America. Trade would be liberalized. Barriers to the flow of capital, technology, and even labor would be diminished. To foster this development the Trade Expansion Act of 1962 was passed. The European Economic Community would expand, including Great Britain, and European economic policies would be framed within a larger alliance context. These policies, in turn, would be elaborated within the Organization for Economic Cooperation and Development (OECD). The creation of this organization in the closing days of the Eisenhower administration out of the Organization for European Economic Cooperation bespoke Europe's rising economic strength. The OECD would be outward looking and would serve, as its new name signified, as a vehicle for greater West European investment in the underdeveloped states. Through its military strength the Atlantic Alliance would combat the East-West split; through its combined economic, scientific, and technological power, it would mend the North-South division between rich and poor states. As Europe demonstrated a capacity to regulate its own affairs in co-operation with the United States, the latter would gradually be permitted to expand its global role without losing its European base.

The Gaullist image of the Atlantic Alliance and its place in France's global policy conflicted with the Kennedy design on almost every critical point. After 1962, the United States was considered the principal strategic threat to French and European autonomy. Its menace to internal European independence eclipsed in importance the residual external military threat posed by the Soviet Union. The perception of Communist China as an immediate danger to European interests was totally rejected. For de Gaulle, Western military strategy could not be principally built upon a notion of a division of labor among allied states because that would contradict the moral and political basis of the alliance. No state could long survive as a separate entity if it left "its destiny up to the decisions and actions of another state however friendly it might be." [2] Nuclear weapons were indispensable to preserve a state's political independence. Alliance strategic policy would therefore have to be a function of the accords reached among the nuclear powers of the alliance. The directorate plan would be realized whether the United States formally approved its establishment or not. By creating nuclear weapons, the United States, Britain, and France—so French strategists argued—assumed the major responsibility for the defense of the West. Nuclear proliferation was not a stumbling block to peace since the impulse for the creation of national nuclear forces arose from the pre-existing political divisions among states. Nor could arms limitation accords reached by the superpowers possess universal validity or applicability since the legitimacy of such arrangements would have to be determined solely by the states affected by them.

European unity was considered impossible by de Gaulle unless Europe assumed primary responsibility for its own defense. Atlantic

2. *Major Addresses,* p. 124.

military integration and European political unity were incompatible principles, which has been conceded by some American apologists.[3] Britain's failure to recognize the contradiction, according to Gaullist leaders, weakened its credentials for membership in the EEC. A Europe incapable of defending itself—or of willing first to be European—would inevitably be exposed to Soviet external pressures and, consequently, would be compelled to accede to the American protectorate. America's Europe would be "governed . . . by anonymous, technocratic and stateless committees; in other words, a Europe without political reality, without economic drive, and therefore doomed, in the face of the Soviet bloc, to being nothing more than a dependent of that great Western power, which itself had a policy, an economy and a defense—the United States of America."[4] The nation-state, however, was still alive in Europe and thriving from the vantage point of Elysée Palace. De Gaulle was closer to the historical significance of President Kennedy's July 4, 1962, Atlantic interdependence speech in Constitution Hall than was the American chief executive. France had no relish for increased defense taxation for the Kennedy administration's flexible response strategy when it could not be assured of enlarged representation in Washington where its political future was to be held in trust to the American nuclear guarantee.

The French identified the principle of integration within the Atlantic Alliance as an obstacle to lasting peace in Europe. The Soviet Union was assumed to be irrevocably opposed to the unification of Germany as long as West Germany remained inextricably bound to the Western defense system. Whatever the position of strength of the West, a Western-oriented and armed Germany was viewed as a nonnegotiable point. The East European states could not be assured against potential German expansionism that could conceivably engage American military might. Yet the French insisted on the indispensability of a European settlement for global peace.

The French believed the threat of war in Europe would persist as long as the "German anomalies" existed. Resolution of this long-term threat was of greater importance than the short-run benefits of continued alliance security that was concluded to be inherently unstable. French doctrine attributed instability to the subordinate position of the

3. Schlesinger, Jr., *op. cit.*, pp. 842–923.
4. *Major Addresses*, pp. 233–234.

European states within the NATO and Warsaw pacts, the uncertainty surrounding Germany's future, and the uneasy confrontation between the military forces of the two alliances in the center of Europe.[5] The United States and the Soviet Union preferred short-run military security to the risk of dismantling either military alliance for the sake of what they perceived as a dubious basis for long-run political stability.

A new equilibrium of strategic forces in Europe was deemed more relevant to the triple problem facing French global policy than continued cooperation within the NATO framework. Gaullist France claimed to be the authentic representative of European interests in negotiations with the Soviet Union. A French-Russian entente was suggested as the basis upon which Europe's security interests and political goals could be assured. Russia would be tempted to align itself with French initiatives toward a European peace accord that promised both to guarantee German tutelage within a larger European security framework and to weaken United States presence on the continent. The states of East and West Europe could conceivably be brought gradually into a common security framework that would resolve the fears of German rearmament by absorbing German energies and ambitions in the construction of a loose, but definable, third force in Europe and presumably in world politics. Germany would be tempted into cooperation for the sake of its own unity. The American guarantee for Europe would be retained in a diluted form either through formal redefinition of alliance commitments or through the anticipated workings of mutual self-interest between the United States and Europe. The United States would still have an interest in keeping Western Europe from falling under the Russian yoke. France's repeated condemnation of both superpowers underscored its determination that, though willing to cooperate more closely with the Soviet Union, it did not wish to trade the dominance of capitalist America for that of Communist Russia. As the French perceived the equilibrium of world forces in the 1960's, a globally superior America would be partially offset by an ascendant Soviet Union, held at bay by a strong and nationally based Europe under forceful French leadership, armed with a minimum deterrent force. France would not be reversing alliances,

5. S&PC, No. 216, Feb. 4, 1965, pp. 10–12.

as some Gaullist critics intimated; it would be shifting the center of influence of the alliance blocs on European policy. Its policy of peaceful engagement in Eastern Europe, its strategic and diplomatic disengagement, but not rupture, with the Atlantic Alliance, and its independent course in arms control and disarmament policy suggest the subtle balances that the Fifth Republic was attempting to strike.

The first practical task facing Gaullist France in the 1960's was to weaken the American hold over the Atlantic Alliance, but short of annulling France's alliance obligations. This objective culminated in the French memorandum of March 10–11, 1966, sent to all allied powers. It outlined France's plans to withdraw its units from NATO, to expel all foreign troops from French territory, and to void certain bilateral accords with the United States, Canada, and West Germany that largely dealt with their installations on French soil.[6] The French justified their actions on previously articulated grounds: (1) the diminution of the Soviet threat; (2) the depreciation of the United States nuclear guarantee; (3) the unwillingness of the de Gaulle government to integrate France's nuclear forces into NATO; (4) the resurgence of a politically and economically strong Europe; (5) the reconstitution of France's sovereignty that had been impaired not only by the presence of foreign bases on French territory but also by dependence upon the United States for its defense; (6) the need to thaw East-West relations frozen by monolithic blocs under the control of the superpowers; and (7) the increasing influence of the Third World, especially of China, in world politics which occasioned the re-evaluation of alliance ties. France also countered American criticism that it had unilaterally changed its alliance obligations by asserting that the NATO organization was never meant to be an indispensable condition for the operation of the 1949 alliance. Indeed, the United States

6. Ambassade de France, Service de Presse et d'Information, *French Foreign Policy, 1966: Official Statements, Speeches and Communiqués*, pp. 25–27. Hereafter cited *FFP* with appropriate semiannual date. (Only the 1966 issue, the first of the series, was published as one volume.) These documents are translations of the French publication, titled La Documentation Française, *La Politique étrangère de la france, textes et documents*, which is issued twice a year. Hereafter cited *PEF*, when the French text is used. The French translations are approximately two years behind the French edition and are not always complete or accurate.

was said to have been the more serious offender in having revamped its strategic policies and posture without having first consulted its European allies.[7]

The timing of the March memorandum was unexpected, but not its issuance. It was foreshadowed in a series of French actions following the launching of the directorate scheme in September 1958. Shortly after the final unsuccessful meeting of United States and French officers concerning the implementation of de Gaulle's Atlantic troika proposal, the French government withdrew all naval units in the Mediterranean from NATO control and placed them under national command in time of war. French Foreign Minister Couve de Murville stressed the need to protect lines of communication between the French community in North Africa and France. In an ensuing news conference, President de Gaulle suggested the real basis for the action, that the alliance would be "more vital and strong as the great powers unite on the basis of . . . cooperation . . . rather than on the basis of integration in which peoples and governments find themselves more or less deprived of their roles and responsibilities in the domain of their own defense." [8] During this period the de Gaulle government also refused to permit the emplacement of IRBMs in France under joint-control arrangements and the stockpiling of nuclear weapons on French territory. French recalcitrance eventually led to an impasse on the IRBM question and to the transfer of American fighter-bombers, dependent on nuclear stockpiles, to Germany where the control problem had been resolved.[9]

The French disengagement from NATO moved along other fronts, too. Already discussed was the refusal of the Gaullist government to entertain any American nuclear sharing proposals for the alliance. France equally dismissed the interallied tactical force that had been suggested at the Nassau meeting. Two French divisions returning from Algeria, and earmarked for NATO, were not assigned to SACEUR although France lagged in meeting its quotas under previous NATO

7. *FFP*, pp. 24–28.

8. *Major Addresses*, p. 49. Consult Kohl, *French Nuclear Diplomacy*, pp. 207–266, for a useful review of French-United States relations in the Atlantic Alliance during the de Gaulle era.

9. *L'Année politique, 1959*, pp. 564–569.

accords. On June 21, 1963, the French Atlantic fleet was withdrawn from NATO, followed ten months later by the withdrawal of French naval staff officers. In September 1964, French surface vessels refused to participate in NATO naval war games. In the following year, France failed to take part in the "Fallex" exercise, refused to adopt a rifle calibre similar to that used by United States units, and rejected the 1963 Athens guidelines on the use of atomic weapons. To this list, as former NATO Secretary General Dirk Stikker indicated, "should be added details on French positions in the NATO Council on split communiques after ministerial meetings, and France's hostile attitude towards the International Secretariat and the Secretary General on basic questions of procedure and administration." [10]

In withdrawing from NATO, the French government made it abundantly clear that the Atlantic Alliance was still relevant to European security. "Barring events that in the coming years might change East-West relations in a fundamental way," the March memorandum noted, the French government foreswore any intent to terminate its membership in the alliance and considered "that the alliance should continue so long as it appears necessary." [11] The NATO organization served little strategic use other than to promote American interests by undermining France's efforts to develop a national defense and by hampering its ability to make independent diplomatic initiatives, especially toward Eastern Europe where its credibility was in question as long as it acted as a subaltern of the United States. The costs of NATO were unnecessary. Since the American nuclear deterrent was, for the foreseeable future, the basis for Western defense, it could be retained through alliance. Even the alliance, understood as a mutual guarantee pact, need not have been considered, according to a revised French view, as automatically applicable to all conflict situations involving the United States and Europe with the East.

The French government made some attempts to qualify its understanding of the Atlantic charter. In President de Gaulle's letter of

10. Dirk Stikker, "The Role of the Secretary General of NATO," in *The Western Alliance,* ed. Edgar S. Furniss, Jr. (Columbus: Ohio State Press, 1965), p. 15

11. *FFP,* 1966, p. 25.

March 7, 1966, to President Johnson, French assistance to a NATO ally was confined to *"unprovoked* aggression." [12] Georges Pompidou, prime minister under de Gaulle at the time, used the phrase again in his remarks before the National Assembly on April 13: "We wish to maintain the Alliance concluded in 1949 that makes us united in the face of possible *unprovoked* aggression." [13] In a radio interview a week later, then Foreign Minister Couve de Murville reasserted the condition: "The alliance is a treaty that joins all the member countries—there are 15 of us present—and that binds us to go to the aid of any one of our allies who is the object of an attack, of an *unprovoked* attack." [14]

France's attempt to restrict its alliance commitments to its interpretation of "unprovoked attack" was part of a larger diplomatic effort to differentiate French and American policies in almost every significant area. Besides those already mentioned, it included policies toward the Third World, especially toward the conflicts in the Middle East, Latin America, and Asia, international monetary regulation, and trade and investment opportunities within Europe and France. Between 1962 and 1968, France strove to become a diplomatically unaligned state within what it conceived to be a progressively more narrowly defined security alliance.

The Continued Objection to Superpower Rule: Arms Control and Disarmament

France's nonalignment with the United States paralleled an increasing diplomatic alignment with Soviet policies, especially toward the Third World. But this outward show of accord obscured a more profound break with superpower security policies in the field of arms control and disarmament. After the Cuban crisis, both superstates renewed efforts to stabilize their arms race and to cooperate in arresting the military progress of potential competitors, like France and China, which had launched ambitious nuclear weapons programs.

In attacking superpower arms control and disarmament policies, France posed as the defender of small-state interests. France condemned the test-ban and nonproliferation treaties as strategically de-

12. *L'Année politique, 1966,* p. 411. Emphasis added.
13. S&PC, No. 243, April 13, 1966, p. 3. Emphasis added.
14. S&PC, No. 242, April 7, 1966, p. 2. Emphasis added.

stabilizing and politically discriminatory. According to former Defense Minister Pierre Messmer, a comprehensive nonproliferation treaty would "lead to new tensions and create new and dangerous situations for world peace." [15] The superpowers, not France, were blamed for encouraging proliferation and its attendant dangers. President de Gaulle stressed that the treaties in no way altered "the terrible threat the nuclear weapons of the two rivals bring to bear on the world, and above all on the people who do not possess them." [16] The United States and the Soviet Union were the *causus primus* of a globally destabilized security system. They insisted, through their nuclear arms control proposals, on protecting their monopoly of strategic striking power. French critics, both Gaullist supporters and opponents, viewed arms control measures as falsely parading under the banner of disarmament and as hampering authentic arms reduction steps.[17] In the French view, disarmament included limitations on the production of fissile material and nuclear weaponry, the reduction of existing nuclear stocks under international control procedures, and the elimination of long-range delivery vehicles.[18] French military strategists asserted that the implementation of these measures would reduce superpower strategic capabilities and, correspondingly, enhance the relative strategic strength of the smaller powers, thus generally equalizing bargaining positions. Global execution of the test-ban treaty and the verification and market control features of the nonproliferation pact would, on the contrary, further weaken the military strength of nonnuclear states and smaller nuclear powers, like France. Only the

15. *Washington Post*, Jan. 23, 1968, p. A10.

16. U.S., Arms Control and Disarmament Agency, *Documents on Disarmament*, 1963, pp. 267–268. The most succinct, yet probing, review of French policy toward disarmament and arms control is Jean Klein, "Désarmement ou 'arms control': La position française sous le Ve république," *Etudes internationales*, III (Sept. 1972), 356–389; see also Kohl, *French Nuclear Diplomacy*, pp. 164–168.

17. See comments of Jules Moch in *Arms Control, Disarmament, and National Security*, ed. Donald G. Brennan (New York: Braziller, 1961), pp. 446–450; see also Wolf Mendl, "French Attitudes in Disarmament," *Survival*, IX (Dec. 1967), 393–397; Civis, "La France et le désarmement en 1965," *Revue de défense nationale*, XXI (April 1965), 513–517; Marc E. Geneste, "A French View," in *Arms Control for the Late Sixties*, eds. James E. Dougherty and J. F. Lehman, Jr. (Princeton: D. Van Nostrand, 1967), pp. 45–51.

18. See n. 16 above and *Documents on Disarmament*, 1965, pp. 461–462; *FA*, No. 106, July 2, 1960, pp. 1–2.

nontransfer provisions of the nondissemination treaty escaped serious criticism. The French dismissed them as utopian since they assumed that nuclear states would "never consent to share their nuclear arms with others." [19]

French strategists judged nuclear arms control treaties as means to reduce the political leverage of smaller states without making compensating progress toward global peace. The French insisted on vertical disarmament of the superpowers before accepting the arms control measures aimed at reducing horizontal proliferation. Disarmament, moreover, was made contingent upon progress toward détente. The Fifth Republic consistently subordinated disarmament and arms control proposals to the achievement of political accords among states. The major stumbling block to peace, according to the French, remained the division of Europe and the future status of Germany, not simply the rising stocks of nuclear weapons in national arsenals. For France, disarmament proceeded first through détente; for the superpowers, détente developed initially through arms control followed perhaps at some distant period by disarmament.[20] "Disarmament can be a factor in bringing about a détente," de Gaulle's Foreign Minister Couve de Murville suggested. "But without the détente itself, it is inconceivable. . . . There must be a first step, which can only be made in the political field. . . . We would all try together to settle the political conflicts that arise, whether in Europe, Asia, or elsewhere. . . . Then everything would become possible, starting with effective disarmament." [21] Arms control was rejected; disarmament was tolerated only as a negotiating point. Both depended on a movement toward détente as defined by the French themselves and, presumably, by each state whose interests were at stake.

French arms control and disarmament policies under de Gaulle

19. *Intervention de Couve de Murville,* p. 9.
20. See remarks of President Richard Nixon at his first news conference: "What I want to do is to see to it that we have strategic arms talks in a way and at a time that will promote, if possible, progress on outstanding political problems at the same time—for example, on the problem of the Mid-East and on other outstanding problems in which the United States and the Soviet Union, acting together, can serve the cause of peace" (*Washington Post,* Jan. 28, 1969, p. A8).
21. S&PC, No. 144, April 30, 1959, p. 6.

were designed to advance revisionist objectives. They would have structured global politics within a security framework fashioned through preceding political accord among the five nuclear powers. Shortly after President de Gaulle's return to power, France objected to Big Three nuclear negotiations without France. It reluctantly consented to the ten-nation disarmament conference in which its position within the Western camp was weakened with the addition of Italy and Canada to the discussion and further diluted by the presence of the Soviet satellites of Poland, Bulgaria, Rumania, and Czechoslovakia.[22] Its reservations about participating were softened somewhat when the Geneva meeting was held under the auspices of the Big Four, not the United Nations. France's claim to major-power status was preserved although its arms control and disarmament views were submitted to the scrutiny of nine states rather than limited to the nuclear powers. This was as far as the French would go in expanding disarmament negotiations. The Soviet proposal for an eighty-one-member United Nations committee on disarmament to study the Soviet demand for complete and general disarmament was rejected out of hand.[23] After the dissolution of the ten-member Geneva group, following disruption of the scheduled Big Four meeting in Paris in May 1960, France continued to resist proposals for expanded United Nations discussion on disarmament. It subsequently boycotted the eighteen-nation disarmament meeting under United Nations auspices which arose out of bilateral talks between the United States and the Soviet Union in 1961.[24]

The grounds for France's empty-chair policy were substantive and, more importantly, systemic. Fifth Republic policy rejected the complete and general disarmament schemes of the Soviets as well as the willingness of the United States to discuss such proposals. President de Gaulle's exchanges with former Premier Nikita Khrushchev on disarmament stressed France's primary interest in nuclear disarmament and, specifically, in the control of nuclear delivery vehicles. French interest in the control of fissile materials and nuclear arms production receded not only because such limitations, if instituted, might have restricted French development of the *force de frappe*, but

22. *L'Année politique, 1958*, pp. 462ff; *ibid., 1959*, pp. 502–503, 532.
23. *Ibid., 1959*, pp. 472–473.
24. *Ibid., 1961*, p. 548.

also because effective verification and inspection mechanisms were not felt to be readily available.[25]

The systemic grounds underlying French open-chair policy toward the Geneva disarmament talks were almost exclusively political. Primary importance was attached to France's unique responsibility for global security, a duty presumed to be sanctioned by history and geography and implicit in France's possession of nuclear weapons. France's willingness to cooperate in disarmament discussions depended upon preceding political agreement on outstanding differences among the nuclear powers. French policy under the Fifth Republic insisted on the special obligation of the nuclear powers for global order, including arms control and disarmament accords, and for the settlement of interstate conflicts that threatened global peace, whether involving nuclear powers directly or not. The French did not envision the active participation of other states in disarmament discussions and, by implication, in the processes of conflict management and resolution. If the major powers were in accord, strategically and diplomatically, no other state or set of states could withstand their collective will. The presence of nonnuclear states created incentives for the nuclear powers to compete for their political favor. In its turn, France suggested that small states were induced to complicate big-power accords with special interest pleadings, yet they were unable to support effectively their claims with adequate material strength. Without nuclear weapons, they forfeited their right to determine their political fate and foreswore whatever influence they might have had over nuclear states regarding their vital interests. These matters would remain in the hands of the strong powers, including a nuclearized France. In justifying France's open-chair policy at Geneva, President de Gaulle observed:

We . . . do not see any reason to increase the size of the honorable assembly that is being held there, which intends to present irreconcilable plans and can do nothing but moan a little, like the chorus of old men and women in ancient tragedy: "Insoluble difficulty! How to find a way out?". . . .

So long as . . . disarmament is not being carried out . . . we have, with regard to ourselves, the obligation and the necessity of . . . our own

25. *Ibid.*, 1960, p. 497

atomic deterrent force. Consequently, we shall continue our tests in any case until the goal is reached, unless . . . the others rid themselves of their means of destruction. From this point of view . . . , we do not see why we should be at Geneva. Of course, if there should one day be a meeting of States that truly want to organize disarmament—and such meeting should, in our mind, be composed of the four atomic powers—France would participate in it wholeheartedly. Until such time, she does not see the need for taking part in proceedings whose inevitable outcome is . . . disillusion.[26]

Meanwhile, the French dismissed the Geneva gathering as self-defeating since France's views were ignored there. The nonnuclear states who participated had little or no means to effect global security; and the approach preferred by the French of preceding agreements on genuine disarmament measures or on political differences among the nuclear powers was improperly subordinated to military arms accords.

France arrogated big-power status to itself whether other states, especially the superpowers, were formally willing to concede that status or not. France's nonparticipation at Geneva was premised on the conviction that refusal to cooperate was tantamount to the nullification of effective arms control and disarmament measures. France's nuclear prowess was deemed sufficiently impressive, diplomatically if not strategically, to block the execution of global arms accords. Its relative strategic position would improve as the *force de frappe* progressed from a vulnerable system of Mirage bombers to an invulnerable striking force of nuclear submarines.

The implications of the French design were clear enough. Capitulation by the other nuclear powers to the French position would have constituted the effective implementation of the NATO directorate scheme on a global basis. The NATO directorate would have been expanded to include all nuclear powers, and the two-tier decisional process envisioned for NATO would have been globalized. Arms control and disarmament discussions would have been indistinguishable from negotiations on political conflicts affecting the interests of the nuclear powers and the strategic and political conditions for worldwide security. Within this revisionist French perspective of a re-structured global security and diplomatic system, the discussion of

26. *Major Addresses*, pp. 181–182.

political détente would have tended to be simultaneous with the realization of arms control and disarmament agreements. In the French view, the latter would have been superfluous since they would have been derived from previously accepted political arrangements among the nuclear powers. The nuclear states alone would have collectively commanded the necessary military means to enforce their will on other states while balancing each other strategically through the operation of a multilateral deterrent system.

French proposals for four-power settlement of the Middle East conflict[27] and for five-power talks, including China,[28] to resolve the Southeast Asian struggle were logical components of France's elitist design for the international system. The nuclear powers were ascribed special responsibility for global security. Their nuclear capabilities were presumed to constitute sufficient material power to assure a global security system, if they could agree among themselves on the political preconditions of such a system. Moreover, their physical strength could regulate regional balances of power such as those which were in flux in the Middle East and in Vietnam. Smaller powers contesting for regional dominance were considered incapable of realizing their objectives without big-power cooperation or acquiescence. The French embargo of military aircraft to Israel illustrated the de Gaulle government's conviction that the Middle East conflict depended on the nuclear powers for material and political support. Lacking such aid, the regional powers would be capable only of limited military operations. Hostilities could then be contained regionally. The mobility and firepower of military forces operating in the area would be reduced and the area diplomatically isolated from effective outside support.

The overwhelming strategic power of the nuclear states would structure international relations and define the range of small-power strategic and diplomatic initiatives. President de Gaulle posed his condition of previous nuclear power accord for global peace within a revisionist framework in his September 1965 news conference:

It happens, actually, that the five States on which the destiny of Southeast Asia depends, in the final analysis, and which, moreover, are those

27. Ambassade de France, Service de Presse et d'Information, *Official Statements*, No. 134, June 2, 1967; *Washington Post*, Jan. 16, 1969, p. A23.
28. S&PC, No. 228, Sept. 9, 1965, p. 10.

that possess atomic weapons, together founded twenty years ago the United Nations Organization and are the permanent members of the Security Council. They could tomorrow—if they so desired and naturally once they come together—see to it that this institution, instead of being a theatre of the main rivalry of two hegemonies, becomes the framework in which the development of the world would be considered and in which the conscience of the human community would thereby grow stronger.[29]

Since the de Gaulle regime was skeptical about the prospects for nuclear power entente and cooperation, it remained committed to independent nuclear policies and nationally based systemic views. These remained immune to change until 1968 when their domestic political support and exterior economic and military effectiveness were unexpectedly tested.

French Strategic Policy and Bloc Politics after 1968

The Russian invasion of Czechoslovakia in August 1968 underlined how much France depended on the American security guarantee. The Russian action diluted the political unity (not to mention the domestic financial claims) of an independent *force de frappe*. The French nuclear system had been advanced as the indispensable ingredient of a new security framework for Europe in the postbloc period, marked by the diminishing importance of the NATO and Warsaw organizations and the decreasing presence of American and Soviet forces in Central Europe. Continued polycentrism in Eastern Europe and the gradual liberalization of the totalitarian regime in the Soviet Union were to be the political prerequisites of such a security system. The Czech incident dashed French hopes that these conditions could be soon realized in Europe.

On the surface, the French government refused to concede that its détente policy and underlying assumptions about Soviet behavior had been seriously damaged by the Czech affair. The Soviet invasion was characterized by Defense Minister Michel Debré as "an accident along the route" toward détente, as a move to re-establish Soviet authority in the East European states, and not as a preliminary step to Soviet military expansion. The French under the de Gaulle and Pompidou administrations, as Chapters 7 and 8 below describe, were willing to accept, for the short run at least, that large military forces

29. *Ibid.*

were likely to be maintained by the Soviet Union to preserve its rule in Eastern Europe. But the possibility that the Soviet Union's ambitions might not be limited to the reassertion of control over its Eastern satellites could not be fully discounted. There was the derivative anxiety that, even if the Brezhnev regime did not contemplate any aggressive move against the West European states—a point repeatedly affirmed by French officials to assure Moscow of Paris' confidence in their mutual regard for progress in détente—the Soviet Union's political influence would still grow in West European capitals unless its military ascendancy were matched by a firm Western response. Efforts were quietly set in motion to repair France's sagging alliance fences with its Western allies and, specifically, the United States.[30] Attacking the United States was profitable so long as the Russian threat was not immediate. As the possibilities of Russian military and diplomatic expansion suddenly became real again and as American attention turned from Europe (partly because of engagements elsewhere, partly because of growing impatience with the size of its global burdens), the dilemma facing French strategists became more sharply focused. The need to cut back military expenditures, a heightened perception of threats abroad, and an Atlantic partner itself suffering from bloc fatigue, in part brought on by repeated Gaullist attacks, forced French strategists to pose a security question they had conveniently slighted during the heyday of France's détente policy toward the Soviet Union between 1963 and 1968: How could France reduce or escape dependency on the United States without reducing the dependability of the United States? In other words, how could France "get away closer" from the American colossus?

Realignment à la Carte

If the events of 1968 did not change France's announced foreign policy objectives, major operational shifts were soon discernible as France worked to harmonize its strategic imperatives with its political needs and aspirations. Changes could be detected in France's strategic doctrine, its alliance diplomacy, the size and distribution of expenditures for force levels and weapon systems, and the greater attention devoted to the relation of military spending to economic

30. *Herald Tribune*, International edition, Nov. 11, 1970, pp. 1, 4.

growth and foreign trade. This reordering began in the final year of the de Gaulle administration and continued into the Pompidou presidency, culminating in the third military five-year plan under the Fifth Republic passed by the National Assembly in November 1970.

As early as November 1968, less than a year after the announcement of the Ailleret doctrine of an all-horizon defense, criticism of Gaullist policy began circulating discreetly within French military circles.[31] The November 1968 number of the prestigious *Revue de défense nationale* featured General Edmond Combaux's critique of Ailleret's *"défense tous azimut."* Combaux attacked Ailleret's strategic recommendations for warping military spending at the expense of conventional forces, for weakening the tie between the nation and national defense in assigning the state's military functions to a professional elite (just the reverse of what the *force de frappe* was supposed to do), and, worse, for actually increasing France's dependency on the United States. The latter charge was crucial for it disarmed Ailleret's argument.

Combaux posited the rule that "the range of the arms always determines the radius of the fortresses or the size of the fortified areas." [32] Thus, the superpowers, acting implicitly on this principle of military logic, created a global alliance network in order to establish their primary defenses as far from their shores as possible. According to Combaux's analysis, Ailleret's strategic notions also implied a defense that would be far from population centers and as large and secure a terrain on which to maneuver as possible. But Ailleret was unable to accept the conclusion of his own thinking, for it would have led to the recommendation of closer, not looser, alliance ties—precisely what he sought to avoid. Yet only allies could afford France the geographic scope and material possibility of executing Ailleret's strategic notions of national independence. "It is not sufficient for France to possess rockets of intercontinental range," concluded Combaux. "It is essential to recognize the environment in which these weapons operate and the limitations of their use. They

31. Edmond Combaux, "Défense tous azimut? oui, mais . . ." *Revue de défense nationale,* XXIV (Nov. 1968), 1600–1618. See also the useful analysis of Combaux's thought in *Combat,* Nov. 4, 1968, p. 2.

32. Edmond Combaux, "French Military Policy and European Federalism," *Orbis,* XIII (Spring 1969), 151.

will have value only if they are part of a coherent defense system. Because the dimensions of the system greatly exceed the capabilities of our nation, the need for a permanent defense association with France and her neighbors is inescapable." [33]

For Combaux, if Atlantic ties were ruled out by Gaullist fiat, the only feasible alternative to salvage Ailleret's (and France's official) doctrine was, ironically, a global alliance framework based on France's cooperation with its European partners. Ailleret's (and de Gaulle's) globalism was not so much questioned as was its operational effectiveness if based solely on France's limited striking power and territory.

The confirming signal that France had amended its strategic doctrine was given in May 1969, in the *Revue de défense nationale* article under the signature of General Fourquet, Ailleret's successor as French commander in chief. First, Ailleret's notion of a strategic threat arising from any point in the globe was revised in favor of the traditional view of "an enemy coming from the east." [34] Second, a modified version of NATO's graduated response strategy was substituted for Ailleret's largely all-or-nothing doctrine. Barring a direct enemy strike against France, the first encounter with enemy forces was portrayed at the conventional level. Once breached, the second clash would be a tactical nuclear one. The employment of these weapons would test the intentions of the adversary in order to prevent a premature launching of strategic forces and would manifest France's will to resist. Fourquet also narrowed previous French conceptions of the autonomous use of tactical and even strategic nuclear weapons. Although their independent employment was not ruled out, emphasis was placed on their utilization in coordination with France's Western allies, but with more an Atlantic thrust than the European direction indicated by Combaux. If the French conception of an escalation ladder had very few rungs, a function partly of the limited nuclear means disposed by France, Fourquet's formulation was still more in accord with announced NATO strategy. Troop reductions in NATO in the late 1960's induced NATO planners to rely on earlier use of nuclear weapons than had initially been envisioned when the Ameri-

33. *Ibid.*, p. 152.
34. Général Fourquet, "Emploi des différents systèmes de forces dans le cadre de la stratégie de dissuasion," *Revue de défense nationale,* XXV (May 1969), 762.

can shift to graduated response was first proclaimed. These changes had the effect of drawing French and American-inspired NATO views closer together although for different reasons.[35]

These doctrinal alignments between NATO and French strategy also found practical, albeit limited, expression in what Michel Debré, as defense minister in the Chaban-Delmas cabinet, termed a policy of selective cooperation between France and its alliance partners.[36] Even after France's 1966 withdrawal from NATO, it continued to play a part in several NATO agencies. It participated in the technical weapons development group at the Hague. French experts increased their membership on NATO technical committees. Ties to the NADGE, an early warning system, indispensable for the protection of France's Mirage forces, were retained. French companies built radar components for the network, and a French general assisted in installing the warning system in Turkey.[37] Progress was recorded, too, in coordinating French-NATO air defenses. France similarly took steps to join in the construction of a new NATO communications network and cooperated in running the NATO oil pipelines across France and in conducting NATO antisubmarine warfare research at the La Speiza Center in Italy. French-NATO contacts were also multiplied in joint training exercises to improve the efficiency of French conventional forces. As early as fall 1968, French naval and air units participated in NATO maneuvers in the Mediterranean, in which French admirals actually commanded joint NATO exercises, and assumed surveillance functions over Russian operations in the area. In 1971, the French air force "defended" against the combined elements of six NATO countries. It was reported, too, that French troops in Germany had conducted joint exercises with American troops.[38]

French authorities insisted, nevertheless, that these activities in no way contradicted the decision to quit NATO's integrated command structure, nor suggested any desire to return to the fold.[39] These assertions of Gaullist creed did not square easily with some forms of allied

35. *Le Monde,* April 5, 1969, p. 5.
36. Michel Debré, "France's Global Strategy," *Foreign Affairs,* LXIX (April 1971), 395–406.
37. *Le Nouvel observateur,* Jan. 1, 1971, p. 26.
38. *Economist,* June 24, 1972, p. 45, usefully summarizes the instances of French-NATO cooperation.
39. Interviews, Paris, January–May 1971; Brussels, March 1971.

military cooperation in which the French had shown an interest. Participation in the NATO communications network or aerial defense, for example, implied prior French acceptance of alliance priorities under certain defined operating conditions. What passed for integration within the Brussels group had largely been the product of such consent arrangements among alliance states. The French argument over the loss of independence was always overstated. NATO never achieved the hopes of its public pronouncements in integrating the military capabilities of the member states within a single command structure. The French were not unaware of the difference, but preferred, often solely for reasons of domestic and foreign diplomatic consumption, to beat the NATO horse when political opportunity beckoned.

On the other hand, French disposition to cooperate with alliance military efforts can be exaggerated. The Pompidou administration's military nuclear program discussed below showed no sign of relaxing national control of such forces. France, moreover, remained silent on two key strategic questions: its declared and operational commitment to join NATO in a European war and its willingness to employ French troops to strengthen NATO's front-line defenses.[40] The French president was to answer these critical questions and, more importantly, to decide when French nuclear weapons would be used. On the question of cooperating with NATO, a fundamental ambiguity underlay French military doctrine and behavior. What perhaps can be confidently said is that, after 1968, the French manifested more reluctance than before to close off their strategic options in calling on allies to meet commonly perceived exterior threats.

The inadmissibility of France's return to NATO, or its hesitancy to cooperate more closely with the organization, did not preclude gestures of loyalty to the Atlantic Alliance. It was part of the French hedge against an uncertain future. Doubts that France would leave the Atlantic Alliance after 1969, when member states had the right to renounce unilaterally their treaty obligations, were laid to rest. Indeed, new oaths were taken of France's commitment to the Western alliance, its special security ties with the United States, and its interest in retaining substantial numbers of American troops in Europe. President

40. *Economist*, June 24, 1972, p. 45.

Pompidou brought this message to the United States in his visit of February 1970. He thought it "normal that there be an American presence in Europe." [41] In a speech before the Ecole Militaire in July 1970, Michel Debré acknowledged the critical defense role played by American military power. "We ought to be aware," said Debré, "that there exists around us a circle of nations to which we belong and which have in common a cultural and moral treasure as well as a conception of social life. The security of this grouping, in many ways, makes a whole whose principal pillar remains the United States. *It is normal to give a privileged place to Franco-American relations.*" [42] In welcoming Leonid Brezhnev to France for an official visit on October 25, 1971, President Pompidou emphasized France's economic and social links "to the Western world" and "its alliances" as "an integral part of her policy." [43] After 1968, the French security problem was posed less as one of blocking American penetration into Europe than of assuring the availability of American military power as a deterrent to Soviet military or diplomatic expansion in Europe.

The Search for Independence

In temporarily acceding to American financial and strategic power, post-1968 France did not abandon the pursuit of independence. Defense Minister Michel Debré left little doubt of his ministry's determination, within the means available, to fashion an independent military program. Submitting to exterior control "would be" in Debré's estimation, "the end of France, the end of our nation, the end of our country, with its personality and pride, and its liberty." [44] In keeping with this reaffirmation of Gaullist doctrine, French defense policy

41. *U.S. News and World Report*, LXVII (March 2, 1970), 44.
42. *Le Monde*, July 3, 1970, p. 5. Emphasis added. See also the review of French defense policy by Jacques Tatu in *Le Monde*, Oct. 17, 1972, pp. 1, 3; the remarks of Foreign Minister Maurice Schumann at the NATO ministers meeting, *ibid.*, Dec. 9, 1972, p. 1; and the news conference of Michel Debré, *ibid.*, Feb. 17, 1972, p. 8.
43. Ambassade de France, Service de Presse et d'Information, *Address Delivered by Georges Pompidou*, Grand Trianon, Oct. 25, 1971.
44. *Le Monde*, Oct. 2, 1971, p. 10. This sentiment is reaffirmed in Debré's "Défense de l'Europe et sécurité en Europe," *Revue de défense nationale*, XXVII (Dec. 1972), 1779–1804. Also relevant are Debré's remarks on the defense budget for 1973 before the French Senate, *Le Monde*, Dec. 6, 1972, p. 10.

diverged, at different rates of change and intensity, from that of its Atlantic allies in at least five areas: (1) the development of national military forces; (2) East-West security negotiations; (3) bilateral security ties in the Third World; (4) arms control and disarmament, with special reference to arms sales; and (5) bilateral security ties in Western Europe.

First, the French strategic and tactical nuclear program continued under tight national control. The third five-year plan for military expenditures, passed by the National Assembly in November 1970, called for the maintenance of the Mirage nuclear forces until 1976, the emplacement of eighteen IRBMs in concrete silos (instead of the twenty-seven first projected), and the completion of three Polaris-type submarines by 1974–1975. France expected to have deliverable thermonuclear weapons by the end of the 1970's, and atmospheric tests proceeded in the Pacific despite strong protests, including a boycott of French products, by Australia and New Zealand.[45]

After a decade of relative neglect, new impetus was given to the development of tactical nuclear forces. In 1974, expenditures were set at 618 million francs, five times more than a year before. By the end of the year, air and ground units, possessing a total stock of 120 warheads, each of 10 to 15 kiloton strength, were expected to be operational.[46] These forces were to remain under strict national control. No effort was made to coordinate them with NATO forces, although informal contacts between French and American officers were reported.[47] Along with France's conventional forces, these units were counted upon to meet an initial enemy thrust, to test its size and the opponent's determination, and to lay the groundwork for a strategic nuclear strike. Tactical nuclear units were seen principally as battlefield elements. To a lesser degree, some sentiment favored considering them as a means to communicate serious French government intent—a kind of "shot across the bow"—to use strategic atomic weapons against the homeland of an aggressor unless it terminated its attack.[48] Home forces, so-called DOT units (Défense Operation-

45. *Le Monde*, June 23, 1972, p. 5, presents a review of the French testing program.

46. *Livre blanc*, pp. 20–21; *Le Monde*, Sept. 27, 1973, pp. 1, 16.

47. Interviews, Paris, Brussels, March, May 1971.

48. *Livre blanc*, pp. 20–21, and examine Lucien Poirier, "Dissuasion et puissance moyenne," *Revue de défense nationale*, XXVII (March 1972), 377.

nelle du Territoire), were designed primarily to defend nuclear sites and, should France's military units fail to prevent enemy occupation, to become the nucleus of guerrilla resistance.[49]

Though the French realized their nuclear forces were vulnerable, the Pompidou regime's political objections to bloc politics or superpower condominium sustained the strategic propositions that France could act separately in a nuclear war, even in Europe, and that joint nuclear planning inherently weakened over-all deterrence between East and West. Maximum national control was needed to test enemy aggressive motives and to afford as much strategic and diplomatic maneuverability as possible to the French president in reacting with French forces, including the *force de frappe,* against an enemy attack. The French remained skeptical of NATO interest in maintaining a high threshold before using nuclear weapons. If there was to be any nuclear "pause" in NATO planning and operations, the French intended to influence allied responses during that period through their own threat to use nuclear weapons independently and make their strategic views prevail over those of their stronger allies, especially the United States. "Because the nuclear risk is not divisible," wrote Defense Minister Michel Debré in the April 1971 issue of *Foreign Affairs,* "any nuclear cooperation which might have a strategic character is simply not possible. The decision to employ nuclear forces can be made only by a single nation, which is to say that any regulations laid down in advance, which set forth the conditions for employment, diminish the deterrent's credibility." [50] The indivisibility of the nuclear risk partially underlay the rationale for French refusal to participate in NATO's Nuclear Planning Group or its so-called Eurogroup.

These assertions of independence were less impressive, however, when the French military expenditure program was examined. President Pompidou's five-year military plan reinforced the downward trend in such expenditures, relative to over-all government spending and to GNP, that had been established in the two previous five-year plans of his predecessor. Military spending relative to these two fac-

49. *Livre blanc,* p. 1617.
50. Debré, *Foreign Affairs,* April 1971, p. 401. Also of interest is his "Les Principes de notre politique de défense," *Revue de défense nationale,* XXVI (Aug.–Sept. 1970), 1245–1258.

tors steadily and consistently declined between 1960 and 1970. In 1960, military spending composed 28 percent of the government's budget and 5.5 percent of France's GNP. Fourteen years later, in 1974, the respective figures were projected at 17.4 percent and 3.35 percent. The events of 1968, as the Defense Ministry admitted, accelerated this downward slide. While the rate of increase in government spending jumped from 9.4 in 1968 to 16.4 percent a year later, reflecting increases in social spending, the rate of growth in military expenditures actually declined in the same period from 6.1 to 3.9 percent. In 1970 and 1971, more funds were for the first time devoted to national education than to defense. Higher absolute spending on defense ($4.2 billion in 1965 against $5.2 billion in 1971) was further offset by inflation, the 12.5 percent devaluation of the franc in August 1969, and larger expenditures on military personnel to retain and attract experienced cadres. Consequently, program objectives, as suggested above, were stretched out and the combat effectiveness of units, especially among conventional forces, was permitted to lag. Arms purchases and development was also reoriented to respond as much to the economic demands of foreign arms competition as to strategic imperatives.[51]

Second, France strove to distinguish its views on East-West negotiations from those of its Western allies. These centered on the American-sponsored NATO proposal for mutual and balanced force reduction (MBFR), Soviet-American strategic arms limitation talks (SALT), the renewed Soviet call of March 1969 for a European security conference, and Big Four talks over Berlin. France showed least enthusiasm for MBFR. On not altogether consistent grounds it refused to associate itself with the June 1968 NATO resolution proposing force reductions between the Western and Communist military pacts. The proposal was condemned as a reinforcement of bloc politics, since states were likely to negotiate within the framework established by the alliance leaders of the two rival military groupings. The French argued that the Soviet Union was not interested in MBFR

---

51. The relevant documents are published by the Comité Interministériel pour l'Information: *Le Budget de la défense nationale en 1970* (Dec. 1970); *Le Budget de la défense nationale* (Jan. 1970); and *La troisième loi de programme militaire* (Nov. 1970). See also *Le Monde,* Sept. 27, 1973, p. 16, and Nov. 10, 1973, pp. 5–7.

anyway, a view later contradicted by the Soviets in their offer of May 1971 to put East-West talks on such a basis.[52] More plausibly, the French suggested that if the Soviet Union should accept the NATO proposal, there was a serious risk that European security would be compromised since the geographic and military positions of the two superpowers were asymmetrical in Europe. A uniform formula for force reductions applied to both camps would necessarily weaken the Western alliance.[53]

There was evidence to suggest that, at the military-strategic level, France was not interested in any change in the European East-West balance, however much it pressed for greater diplomatic, cultural, economic, scientific, and technical exchanges between all European states.[54] The argument against American or allied troop withdrawal before tangible gains had been realized in negotiations with the Soviet Union was instead strengthened. In his news conference of September 23, 1971, President Pompidou implicitly drew a distinction between détente through increased nonmilitary cooperation between European states and détente through changes in the military disposition of member states. Concern for nonmilitary progress was not to interfere with the maintenance of the West's defense capabilities. There was a shift away from the Gaullist stress on détente over defense.[55] On the other hand, French Foreign Minister Maurice Schumann objected before the National Assembly on November 3, 1971, that MBFR was an obstacle to the calling of the European security conference.[56] The French believed that any tampering with the European military balance must await a deepening political détente. Military accord between the rival blocs was to be the final, not initial, stage of European détente. The conflicting posturings of the Pompidou administration were tantamount to a French call for an armed détente: "Yes" to any nonmilitary moves that would lessen East-West tensions, "No" to any weakening of the West's bargaining position,

52. *Herald Tribune,* International edition, May 15–16, 1971, pp. 1, 2.
53. Interviews, Paris and Brussels, January–May 1971.
54. See, for example, Ambassade de France, Service de Presse et d'Information, *Statement of the Principles of Cooperation between France and the Union of Soviet Socialist Republics,* Oct. 30, 1971.
55. *Le Monde,* Sept. 25, 1971, p. 3.
56. Ambassade de France, Service de Presse et d'Information, *Address by Maurice Schumann before the National Assembly,* Nov. 3, 1971.

stemming from a diminution of American troop strength or Western military capabilities.

These considerations partly explained France's decision to demur on those parts of the NATO foreign ministers' communiqué of June 4, 1971, which dealt with the decision to explore talks with the Soviet Union on MBFR and to designate representatives to undertake such contacts. They explain, too, French refusal to be associated with Chancellor Willy Brandt's proposal, made during his visit to Washington in June 1971, of a symbolic reduction of NATO and Warsaw pact states. President Pompidou in his scheduled visit to Bonn under the Franco-German treaty expressed concern that the Bonn suggestion, aimed at American critics of existing United States force levels in Europe, might accelerate a dangerous disintegration of European defense.[57] However, as the prospects grew that the Vienna meetings would be held despite French "empty chair" tactics, the Pompidou government took a more active role in defining the West's negotiating stance. Foreign Minister Maurice Schumann encouraged his NATO counterparts at their meeting in December 1972 to stress the reduction of foreign, not European, troops. If American troops were to be withdrawn, it did not mean that Europe, or France, had to follow suit.[58] Moreover, President Pompidou acknowledged in Moscow during his January 1973 visit that France would consider the possibility of participating at some point in the MBFR talks,[59] temporarily softening a harder position, stated earlier, that refused to contemplate French participation in MBFR or to link these discussions with those of the European Conference on Security and Cooperation.[60] However, by the close of 1973, as discussed below, there were signs of a return to a more inflexible position on MBFR and of an increased reticence to see the ECSC move too far toward solidifying the Soviet position in Europe or toward encouraging American troop withdrawals from the Continent.

The French also took a dim view of SALT, although the official

57. *Le Monde,* June 6–7, 1971, p. 2, and July 8, 1971, p. 2.
58. *Ibid.,* Dec. 9, 1972, p. 1.
59. *Ibid.,* Jan. 14–15, 1973, p. 1.
60. *Herald Tribune,* International edition, Sept. 25, 1972, p. 1. See also the probing articles of Jacques Tatu, *Manchester Guardian,* Oct. 28, 1972, p. 14, and Nov. 4, 1972, p. 15.

line was to claim that it was only a concern of the United States and the Soviet Union and to encourage such negotiations.[61] Both MBFR and SALT ran counter to the French preference for political accords between East and West states in lieu of arms control arrangements that the French felt would probably respond more to the internal economic needs and global security imperatives of the superpowers than to those of the small and middle powers of Europe. De Gaulle had repeatedly warned against a superpower agreement over the heads of the European states whose protection depended upon one of these continental powers. This theme continued in the counsels of the Pompidou regime.

Defense Minister Michel Debré pressed the point even further than de Gaulle that a Soviet-American settlement on weapons and military expenditures might actually increase political and military instability in Europe. The French could not escape their own logic, which dictated that the nuclear balance between the superpowers inevitably made Europe an area of secondary value for them in the event of a nuclear exchange and disposed them to compromise their differences at the expense of the European states.[62] In the absence of a European political solution, responsive to the views of all affected parties and specifically approved by France, there was the risk that the states whose demands were not satisfied would have an incentive to upset the Soviet-American agreement. Precedent could be found in the aerial hijackings undertaken by the Palestinian Arabs to assert their interests after having been excluded from the Rogers plan for the Middle East.[63]

Soviet interest in disarmament and military disengagement was also perceived as considerably less than that of the United States. SALT or MBFR or both might leave Europe militarily exposed. After Czechoslovakia, the Gaullist prophecy that the United States could not be trusted to defend Europe began to haunt French policymakers as much as the possibility that an American-Soviet accord, in the form of a strategic arms agreement, might compromise France's security and political interests. Some, like Michel Debré, clung to the

61. Klein, *Etudes internationales,* Sept. 1972, pp. 378–379.
62. Debré, *Foreign Affairs,* July 1971, p. 403.
63. *Le Monde,* Sept. 26, 1971, p. 1.

notion that America's commitment to defend Europe depended "on the strategic superiority of the United States." [64] The passing of such superiority, due more to technological change rather than to diminished resolve, heightened doubts about the reliability of American security guarantees.[65]

The residual hope that a strictly defined military accord between the superpowers to slow the arms race might increase the marginal strategic value of the *force de frappe* further complicated the French calculus.[66] But in the renewed realism after 1968, this expectation was given less weight than before in announced and operational French strategic maneuvering. French officials no longer pretended that their nuclear force could soon substitute fully for the American guarantee. They hoped that an enhanced *force de frappe* would strengthen, however slightly, the French bargaining position over a European political settlement.[67] Nuclear weapons were the entry fee for a prominent place at the world disarmament conference table, a mark of France's status as a regional power in Europe, the Mediterranean, and Africa, and a support for its legal position as a member of the Big Four (and an arbiter of Germany's fate) and as a permanent member of the UN Security Council. Nuclear weapons played a less prominent role in French diplomacy under the Pompidou administration than under its predecessor. Their eclipse as diplomatic instruments did not mean, however, their abandonment.

Not surprisingly, the French initially displayed more interest in a European security conference. Despite its possible snares—especially the reinforcement of bloc politics and superpower dominance—it potentially offered greater room for diplomatic maneuver than did military accords. France's strength lay, if anywhere, in its finely calibrated

64. Debré, *Foreign Affairs,* July 1971, p. 397.

65. *Le Monde,* Oct. 2, 1971, p. 10. Michel Jobert, Schumann's successor as foreign minister, reiterated this theme before the United Nations, *Le Monde,* Oct. 11, 1973, p. 10.

66. Klein, *Etudes internationales,* Sept. 1972, p. 378, refers to this factor in his excellent review of French arms control and disarmament policy. See also his "Les SALT et la sécurité en Europe," *Revue française de science politique,* XXIII (Aug. 1973), 849–853.

67. Interviews, Paris and Brussels, January–May 1971. See also the remarks of French Foreign Minister Michel Jobert before the National Assembly. Journal Officiel, *Débats parlementaires, Assemblée Nationale,* June 19, 1973, pp. 2258–2264. Hereafter cited *Débats parlementaires.*

diplomacy, not in military power plays where its record since 1940 had not been markedly distinguished. Political, not strategic, understandings with adversary states was the preferred French method.

President Pompidou, like his predecessor, nurtured the Franco-Soviet détente begun in the middle 1960's. The vigor of German Chancellor Willy Brandt's *Ostpolitik* gave new impetus to French efforts to remain the favored European interlocutor of the Soviet Union. The French president staked out the diplomatic terrain in his first speech at the Kremlin during his eight-day visit to the Soviet Union in October 1970. Expressing optimism that a security conference could promote the independence of European states, the president of the French Republic called for active preparation for such a meeting.[68] He reiterated his desire for an early convening of a security conference in his January and September news conferences in 1971 and in his meeting with Brezhnev in October.[69] The French position was also aimed at the sentiment of the East European states which looked upon the conference as a means of stabilizing European security and as a diplomatic lever on the Soviet Union, impeding its resort to the Brezhnev Doctrine.

While President Pompidou conciliated the Soviet Union and the East European states, his ministers were more qualified in their pronouncements concerning a European security conference. Within a month of the Soviet proposal, Defense Minister Michel Debré, attending NATO anniversary celebrations in Washington, observed unofficially that the Soviet suggestion might bolster the superpower hold over Europe. French officials privately expressed the same view, emphasizing that a conference could be held only after very careful preparations and with the consent of all affected parties.[70] These temporizings were given greater weight in French pronouncements that suggested that a Berlin settlement was a prerequisite for the convening of a European security meeting. In November 1970, Prime Minister Jacques Chaban-Delmas stated during his official visit to

68. Comité Interministériel pour l'Information, *Visite officielle du président de la république en U.R.S.S.,* Oct. 6–13, 1970, No. 69, Oct. 1970, p. 8.

69. *Le Figaro,* Jan. 22, 1971, p. 6.

70. Interviews, Paris and Brussels, January–May 1971. See also Defense Minister Michel Debré's remarks at the Washington NATO meeting of April 1969. *Le Monde,* April 11, 1969, p. 2.

Poland that France could neither agree to the convocation of a security meeting nor engage in preparatory multilateral contacts for such a conference in the absence of a Berlin accord.[71] A month later, Foreign Minister Maurice Schumann supported a strong NATO resolution citing a Berlin settlement, in effect, as a prior condition for the Soviet-sponsored conference. President Pompidou attempted to reconcile the divergent views issuing from the Elysée Palace, the National Assembly, the Quai d'Orsay, and the Defense Ministry in his January 1971 news conference. He drew a careful distinction between a juridic prerequisite, which France had not invoked over Berlin, and political prudence which suggested that success in reaching an accord on European security was not likely unless the Berlin question had first been resolved.[72]

The reported remarks of Foreign Minister Maurice Schumann at the NATO meeting in Portugal of June 1971 lent additional weight to the view that a Berlin accord was the French (and allied) price for a European security conference. By then, the major Western powers of the Atlantic Alliance agreed that sufficient progress had been made in Big Four talks over Berlin to soften NATO resistance to the Soviet proposal.[73] While refusing to participate in bloc-to-bloc discussions on arms limitations, the French were, however, careful to eliminate language from the June 4 communiqué that might engender frictions with the Soviet Union. At French insistence reference to Soviet reinforcement of its Mediterranean fleet was dropped in favor of ministerial "preoccupation" with developments in the region. Also canceled at French behest was language calling attention to the expansion of Soviet naval power in other regions of the world. Joining with many of its European partners, the Elysée rejected proposals that might have been construed as adding more conditions, beyond Berlin, to the convening of a European security conference.[74]

Fall 1971 brought further implied conditions. These included, partly in deference to German wishes, final settlement of the Big Four Berlin accord signed on September 3, mutual ratification of the Moscow and Warsaw treaties, and the successful conclusion of intra-

71. *Le Monde,* Nov. 28, 1970, p. 7.
72. *Le Figaro,* Jan. 22, 1971, p. 6.
73. *Herald Tribune,* International edition, June 4, 1971, pp. 1, 2.
74. *Le Monde,* June 6–7, 1971, p. 2.

German talks. The French also elaborated on the Finnish suggestion of multilateral discussions to be held in Helsinki preparatory to the convening of the security conference. France preferred, as Foreign Minister Maurice Schumann observed, "a conference meeting alternately at two levels: at the level of foreign affairs ministers . . . and . . . at the level of three committees charged with . . . the areas of security, exchange of goods, and also exchanges of ideas or people. . . . It goes without saying that—if the results so justify—a meeting at the highest level could crown the undertaking." [75]

Accordingly, the French, like some of their NATO allies, referred to the Soviet proposal as the "Conference on Security and Cooperation in Europe," a broader heading than that first advanced by Moscow.[76] The conference might legitimate the Soviet Union's eastern empire, but the French expected that it would also elicit Soviet concessions, permitting greater contacts between East and West European states. The Soviet Union might even allow itself to be drawn into an institutional framework aimed at encouraging European ties in all nonmilitary sectors and at containing Soviet maneuverability in Europe as much by diplomacy as by military threats. Judged by the communiqués that were issued, institutionalizing the process of East-West cooperation in Europe as an outcome of the conference appeared to be the thrust of Foreign Minister Maurice Schumann's visits to Hungary and Bulgaria in September 1971.[77]

In French eyes, the government's oscillations and reservations on a European security conference made political sense. On the one hand, France could assert in principle to be in the vanguard of efforts to reconcile East and West. On the other hand, its reservations served in practice as a brake on the precipitate convening of a security meeting and, later, on hasty and ill-considered deliberation of critical security issues once state representatives met in Helsinki. The conflicting French reactions to the security conference, SALT, MBFR, and Berlin were all of a piece. They evidenced the growing hesitancy of the French government to entertain new military proposals for European security. A higher premium was placed on preserving existing defense arrangements, however unstable, than on initiatives, like MBFR,

75. *Address by Maurice Schumann, op. cit.,* p. 6.
76. *Ibid.,* p. 7. Italics added.
77. *Le Monde,* Sept. 10, 1971, p. 4; Sept. 12–13, 1971, pp. 1, 3.

whose consequences were necessarily uncertain. After 1968, initiatives for defense changes arose elsewhere than Paris, which lagged behind, where it had once led, its Atlantic and European partners in the search for cheaper, more durable, and politically viable security arrangements.

Even the Brandt government's *Ostpolitik* was questioned increasingly in French ruling circles although France could justly claim to have been in the forefront of the détente race to win Soviet favor.[78] France had always considered itself as the appropriate interlocutor for Germany with the Soviet Union. The Brandt government, acting on its own advisement in normalizing its relations with its Eastern neighbors, offered little opportunity for the French to play their self-conceived intermediary role. However much the French might applaud Germany's efforts to improve its relations with Eastern Europe as a confirmation of their own Eastern policy, Chancellor Brandt's independent brand of *Ostpolitik* could only reinforce the image of an emergent Germany, progressively beyond French influence, and raise anxieties about the possibly adverse strategic, political, and economic implications of the German-Soviet *rapprochement*.

There was little left to the French government than to second the German effort, as President Pompidou did at the Kremlin in October 1970[79] and to sign a new protocol with the Soviet Union that attempted to match in importance, without ensnaring legal ties, the treaty, signed by Germany the preceding August, that recognized the frontiers established by World War II and that promised economic and technological concessions to the Soviet Union.[80] Rather than define new areas of agreement, the Franco-Soviet accord reaffirmed the privileged diplomatic relations between the two countries, their special global security responsibilities, especially within the UN Security Council, and their determination to enlarge their economic ties.[81]

78. Useful for a review of French official thinking is the publication of the Comité Interministeriel pour l'Information that summarizes President Pompidou's visit to the Soviet Union, *op. cit.* An annex is included that presents Foreign Minister Maurice Schumann's analysis of the German-Soviet treaty of August 12, 1970, that seeks to quiet French fears of another Repallo, pp. 37–40.

79. *Ibid.*, pp. 7–9.

80. *L'Express,* Aug. 7–23, 1970, pp. 14–17.

81. *Visite officielle du président de la république, op. cit.,* pp. 3–5, 36. France's dubious favor in Soviet circles is raised further into question if one

The diplomatic tit-for-tat between Germany and France continued into fall 1971 when, partly to counter the German-Soviet communiqué of September 1971 that raised the possibility of two Germanies in the United Nations, the French signed not only another economic, technical, and industrial accord with the Soviet Union but a "Statement" of Franco-Soviet principles of cooperation and a "Declaration" of their points of agreement on world issues. At the same time, the Pompidou regime demurred to Soviet feelers for a French-Soviet treaty during Brezhnev's visit. Increasing concern about Soviet intentions in Western Europe and a more conservative domestic orientation disposed Paris to stress the differences between the two states. France's alliance ties in Western Europe and the Atlantic and its liberal and capitalist economic and political institutions, as President Pompidou suggested in his remarks at a dinner in honor of Brezhnev, made a formal friendship treaty between the two states untimely.[82]

French concern about retaining an independent position in East-West security negotiations became more pronounced in the second half of 1973. The Pompidou government increasingly linked MBFR and SALT to the ECSC negotiations as separate, but reinforcing parts, of an adverse trend in European security developments.[83] Objections to MBFR grew sharper. Establishment of a special military zone in

---

observes the close parallel in language between the protocols signed by the Soviet Union with France and later with Canada in May 1971. Privileged relations have now been reduced to little more than an intent on the part of the consenting states to engage in regular political consultations at fixed intervals. Whereas French-Soviet officials will confer twice a year, Canadian-Soviet representatives will meet only once. Le Monde, May 21, 1971, p. 5.

82. PEF, July–Dec. 1971, p. 159. See also issues of Le Monde during Brezhnev's visit from October 26 through November 1, 1971. Soviet commentators reflecting the official government's line stressed the historic and continuing national interests between the two states. Illustrative are Y. Borisov, "USSR-France: Forty-Five Years of Diplomatic Relations," International Affairs (Moscow), XV (Oct. 1969), 71–77; T. Vladimirov, "USSR-France: Important Step in the Development of Relations," ibid., XVI (Dec. 1970), 57–58; and idem, "Soviet-French Cooperation: A Steady Progress," ibid., XVII (Aug. 1971), 69–71.

83. Débats parlementaires, pp. 2260–2264. See also his speech at the first meeting of the ECSC at Helsinki, Le Monde, July 5, 1973, pp. 1–2, his address to the United Nations, Le Monde, Oct. 11, 1973, p. 10, and his presentation to the National Assembly, Ambassade de France, Service de Presse et d'Information, "Highlights from the Statement of Michel Jobert before the National Assembly," Nov. 12, 1973.

central Europe as a consequence of an MBFR accord was perceived as a move toward promoting Germany's military neutralization under American or Soviet or joint superpower auspices. The first possibility, the least unpalatable of the three, was also considered the most unlikely as a result of MBFR and SALT. A special zone in central Europe not only called into question Germany's attachment to the West including its role in a European union, but NATO's forward base system resting on American nuclear weapons. The French viewed MBFR as a convenient diplomatic instrument for Washington to decrease the American burden and commitment to defend Europe in return for Soviet political accommodations, conceivably detrimental to European security interests, and to diminish domestic criticism of Nixon administration policy, already under fire over the Watergate scandal and rising inflation. SALT I and II and the Nixon-Brezhnev accord of June 22 on the prevention of nuclear war were interpreted as additional steps toward American withdrawal from the Continent.

The second and third possibilities regarding Germany's future and European security interests appeared more likely and also more repugnant to Paris. Decreasing American military support tempted Germany to seek its future in the East and strengthen neutralist sentiment in Europe, disposed to granting political and economic concessions to the Soviet Union under the aegis of the European Conference on Security and Cooperation. These developments were seen to have at least three unfortunate results: security interests of the individual European states would be damaged; the possibility of European union, based on a common defense policy and resting on French confederal notions would be reduced; and increased East-West European exchanges as a way of weakening the Soviet hold over its clients would be foreclosed. The United States still held the key to Germany's defense; the Soviet Union, to its unification presumably through neutralization. Under these circumstances, the current defense needs of the long-run political aspirations of the German people for unification might prove more attractive to Bonn than the possibilities of European union. The four-power Berlin accord and Brandt's *Ostpolitik,* however much they decreased the likelihood of a military confrontation between the NATO and Warsaw blocs, also threatened to weaken the capacity of the West European states, including France, to define their own security arrangements and the terms of their union.

These considerations apparently underlay two new developments in French security policy in the second half of 1973: the first within East-West negotiations; the second in interallied talks within the Atlantic Alliance. French interest in the ECSC declined as Soviet-American cooperation in arms limitation and in diplomatic crisis management, exemplified by the Yom Kippur War, progressed. The articulated condition for French engagement of Soviet power in negotiations within the ECSC was the maintenance of armed détente, defined by President Pompidou in his trip to China in September 1973 as "détente plus defense equals security." [84] Since the French perceived the West's military strength to be eroding, they acted on the assumption that its bargaining position with the Soviet Union was also weakening. At the opening of the first meeting of the ECSC at Helsinki in July 1973, French Foreign Minister Michel Jobert warned against optimism about the likely positive results of the gathering: "It is crucial . . . that public opinion know that a conference as prestigious, as awaited as this one may be, can—contrary to expectations—mislead people by false assurances." [85] Security was still a product of national effort, and not the fabrication of multilateral accords: "The resolution of each nation to defend itself is indispensable. The nation that forsakes itself will be forsaken. The nation which has the courage to confront [its security problems] will be respected. Here are a few simple principles that should accompany our reflections, as those of the public, which wishes to believe in a great world event. Security is earned; it is not won in a game of chance." [86]

At the United Nations on October 10, ECSC was recognized as an important international happening (from which France could withdraw without great expense to its policy aims) whose success or failure was not to be taken as the final test of détente: "This conference is not the paradise of détente, the alpha and omega of conciliation." [87]

84. *Le Monde*, Sept. 16–17, 1973, p. 6. Pompidou's formulation was adopted from a characterization of détente by Chancellor Willy Brandt.
85. *Ibid.*, July 5, 1973, p. 2.
86. *Ibid.*
87. *Ibid.*, Oct. 11, 1973, p. 10.

A superpower-determined détente was of questionable value in meeting European security needs defined beyond physical protection to include national independence and the free circulation of goods, men, and ideas. Jobert compared such a détente to the habit of a celebrated actress who dressed herself only in perfume. "I fear," he said, "that we may risk shivering if we are as scantily dressed by détente." [88] Within the ECSC the French pressed for concrete Soviet adherence to the principle of the sovereign equality of states, limits on interfering in their domestic affairs, and greater opportunities for transactions between states of different social and political systems.[89] If initial French hopes for the ECSC could not be realized, Paris resisted its use to solidify Soviet hegemony in Eastern Europe, to gain increased access to Western economic and technological assistance without compensating political concessions, or to confer on Moscow an enhanced say over West Europe's future, leading conceivably to the accelerated departure of United States troops and the diminution of its nuclear guarantee, as well as Germany's neutralization and its withdrawal from the process of constructing a united Europe as a counterweight to the superpowers.[90]

The second set of French reactions to East-West negotiations, catalyzed by the Yom Kippur War, which saw, as discussed in Chapter 10, further evidence of superpower cooperation, revolved around French-American relations within the Atlantic Alliance. On July 19, while Brezhnev and Nixon were meeting in Washington to sign an accord on preventing nuclear war, Jobert exposed the American call of April 1973 for a re-examination of Atlantic relations as an additional threat to European security:

When the United States proposes to the . . . Nine . . . a dialogue on the goals . . . of the alliance, on the conditions of its reorganization, on those of a new organization, whatever the factors placed on the scale, it is essentially those of defense that are and will be determinant.

When the United States asks about the cost of its presence in Europe, I hear military presence, when it asks its partners to share more equitably the burden of which it assumes, it says, the largest part, when it desires

88. *Ibid.*
89. *Ibid.*, Oct. 22, 1973, p. 6.
90. A perceptive editorial in *Le Monde*, July 6, 1973, p. 1, sketches these possibilities.

that concessions here be compensated elsewhere, I mean on a commercial level, the European states well know that the true debate, the true question, are those of their security.[91]

Subsequently, as the French attacked the development of an American-Soviet condominium and spread doubts about Washington's reliability, they also sought public pledges of American support of European security interests. The most publicized confrontation occurred during the NATO foreign ministers meeting of December 1973. French Foreign Minister Michel Jobert's criticism of Soviet-American military and diplomatic cooperation drew a retort from Secretary of Defense Henry Kissinger who, in defending Washington's actions, necessarily reaffirmed its determination to defend Europe.[92] Meanwhile, French assertions of loyalty to NATO and to the Paris-Washington security tie were multiplied and a more conciliatory French posture on monetary differences between the two states was assumed at the IMF meeting in Nairobi of September 1973.[93] Holding a stronger ally to its treaty obligations, used effectively by Paris against its European partners within the EEC over agriculture, was called into service again as the nexus of interests between the United States and Europe appeared to be dissolving in the superpower *rapprochement,* spurred ironically by the French example in withdrawing from NATO, which diminished its usefulness as a vehicle for East-West accord.

The French felt themselves being ensnared against their better judgment and to some degree their wills in a web of relations principally spun by the United States, the Soviet Union, and West Germany. In the early 1970's France seemed to prefer often the part of Penelope, unraveling rather than binding the tapestry of military security relations being woven by these states. Toward the United States, Pompidou's France saw utility in developing limited, concrete forms of cooperation with NATO, while eliciting public pronouncements from Washington of continued fidelity to its guardian role for Europe's security. On the other hand, while it also shared some United States doubts about a European security conference, it remained skep-

---

91. *Débats parlementaires,* June 19, 1973, pp. 2260–2264.
92. *New York Times,* Dec. 11, 1973, pp. 1, 5.
93. *Le Monde,* Sélection hebdomadaire, Oct. 4–10, 1973, pp. 1, 10–11.

tical principally over SALT and MBFR and deplored American failure to consult with its European partners during the Middle East crisis. Toward the Soviet Union, French diplomacy hesitated over the convening of a European security conference while, in tacit accord with Germany and its other Western allies, citing an expanding series of conditions as a test of Soviet intentions. As soon as the conference convened, it depreciated the importance of the gathering while holding the Soviet Union to accountability on the granting of mutual concessions and insisting throughout to be the Soviet Union's privileged partner in détente, recognized under the Moscow and Paris accords of 1970 and 1971. Toward Germany, maintaining war-won rights still controlled French strategic thinking. The Pompidou regime, like its predecessor,[94] was alert to any move by another power that might dilute France's privileged right to participate with the superpowers on equal terms in settling Germany's future.

After the weakness of France became apparent in the final year of de Gaulle's rule, the French government preferred to hold on to the legal and political gains already secured as in Berlin and Germany rather than to gamble for more influence on security in Europe through new initiatives that might change the existing military balance. If France had any remaining capacity to influence events bearing on its security interests, it was more in frustrating the designs of other states than in imposing its will on them. French influence rested more on its juridic claims and agile diplomatic maneuvering than on its strategic striking power or economic strength.

French presence in the underdeveloped world represented the third major element of the search for independence after 1968 and was linked closely to the sale of arms abroad. The Pompidou government's stress on regionalism over Gaullist globalism, symbolized in France's much-heralded Mediterranean policy, became the guideline for military planning.[95] "Our zone of privileged action," explained

94. De Gaulle was clear on this point in his revealing talk with Sulzberger, n. 30, above: "The real sovereignty of Berlin was awarded to the victors of World War I. . . . The allies—you [the Americans], we, and the British— have the responsibility of sovereignty."

95. See Chapter 10 for an elaboration of the Pompidou regime's accent on regionalism and for the sources cited therein. Relevant is Louis Legendre, "Méditerranée et problèmes de défense," *Revue de défense nationale*, XXVII (Oct. 1972), 4175–4187

General Mitterand to a group of distinguished defense specialists, "remains . . . the Mediterranean, the Atlantic façade of Brest to Dakar, and Northern equatorial Africa." [96] France was linked to most of the states of this region in a series of bilateral military assistance accords. Except for Niger, the Popular Republic of the Congo, and Mauritania, which indicated an interest in revising their relations with France, the network of security and economic ties with the Black Africans remained essentially intact under the Pompidou government.[97] In 1970, approximately twenty technical military assistance groups were operating in Africa and Asia and about twelve thousand French troops were stationed in various parts of Africa. A small, highly mobile force, capable of intervening abroad in limited engagements to support French interests and treaty obligations, was already established under the second military *loi-programme*. Direct military support for the government of Chad since August 1968 suggested the kind of intervention contemplated by the French government.[98] It followed the Gabon example of February 1964 when French paratroopers reinstated the deposed president of Gabon.[99] French military planning was oriented more toward responding rapidly to prevent the subversion of friendly governments than to carrying on a war of attrition, like Vietnam or Algeria, that would quickly sap France's limited conventional capabilities, not to mention domestic political will.

The fourth significant element of France's search for an independent strategic posture in the post–de Gaulle period was arms control

96. Général J. Mitterand, "La Place de l'action militaire extérieure dans la stratégie française," *ibid.,* XXVI (June 1970), 901.

97. *Le Monde,* July 22, 1972, p. 1.

98. Reports on the French participation in the fighting in Chad are somewhat difficult to find in French or foreign newspapers. For bits of information about the French effort, estimated to have involved 1,500 troops, see *West Africa,* Sept. 5, 1970; *Herald Tribune,* International edition, March 31, 1970; *Observer,* Oct. 26, 1969; and *West Africa,* Oct. 18, 1969. *The Military Balance, 1970–1971* of the Institute for Strategic Studies listed 2,500 troops in Chad, as of June 1970, and 12,500 in Africa. The Chad figures appear high. France's military access to Chad was highly tenuous in light of mass demonstrations, led by the president of Chad, against French interference in Chad's affairs. See *Le Monde,* Sélection hebdomadaire, July 26–Aug. 1, 1973, pp. 1ff.

99. Useful newspaper accounts of the Gabon expedition are found in the *Manchester Guardian,* Feb. 20, 1964, Feb. 24, 1964; and the *Sunday Times* (London), Feb. 24, 1964.

and disarmament. Continuity, not change, was the dominant theme. Gaullist strictures against arms control accords that did not represent authentic disarmament or that had as their object or effect to reinforce the military, and especially the nuclear, dominance of the superpowers and bloc politics were observed. The Pompidou administration resisted any attempts by the superstates or the world community, particularly within the United Nations, to compromise the realization of its military program. France's opposition to MBFR or to the test ban and nonproliferation treaties was rooted in these reservations.

For these reasons, too, the Pompidou regime continued de Gaulle's "empty-chair" policy toward the eighteen-member Geneva disarmament group, the sole important vestige of this Gaullist tactic. The French, like the Chinese, objected to the organization of the Geneva conference in which the United States and the Soviet Union shared the chairmanship of the meeting. The Pompidou administration, like its predecessor, doubted that so large a negotiating body could move effectively toward disarmament. Paris still remained attached to the notion that the nuclear powers had a privileged and priority status in discussing such questions. The absence of China bolstered the French case, since little could be expected from the Geneva assembly without China's consent. Further weakening the credibility of the Geneva group was Pekin's reaffirmation before the United Nations in November 1971 of its previously stated view that it would deal with disarmament only in the context "of a world conference to discuss the question of the complete prohibition and thorough destruction of nuclear weapons." [100]

The French arms control and disarmament stance, however, faced increasingly difficult tests in the 1970's as changed international conditions raised into question many of the political assumptions on which its policy rested. The rival policies pursued by the Soviet Union and China complicated France's ability to negotiate between the two Communist giants. On the one hand, Pompidou's France readily assented to China's condemnation of superpower efforts to retain their nuclear monopoly. The remarks of the chairman of the Chinese delegation to the United Nations in fall 1971 might well have been voiced by the French representative: "Since the 1960's the two nuclear

100. "Chinese Views on Disarmament," *Survival*, XIV (March–April 1972), 88.

powers have concocted the Partial Nuclear Test Ban Treaty, the Treaty on Non-Proliferation of Nuclear Weapons, etc. These agreements . . . are . . . means for consolidating the nuclear monopoly of the two super-powers and carrying out nuclear threats and nuclear blackmail. . . . In the absence of complete prohibition and thorough destruction of nuclear weapons, it is impossible to expect the other countries, which are subjected to the threat of the two nuclear powers, not to develop nuclear weapons for the purpose of self-defence." [101] On the other hand, France was flattered and attracted by the Soviet proposal made by Leonid Brezhnev on March 30, 1971, at the 24th Communist Party Congress in Moscow for a meeting of the five nuclear powers to discuss disarmament. Chinese opposition dampened further interest in the proposal although France was most disposed of the nuclear states to explore the suggestion. Politically challenging the Soviet Union (and logically rejecting France's elitist accent in disarmament discussions), Pekin took the position that " 'the prevention of nuclear war, the elimination of the nuclear threat as well as the complete prohibition and total destruction of nuclear arms' are problems which touch the peace and security of all the countries of the world, and nuclear nations cannot arrogate to themselves the right to arbitrarily decide them within the framework of a conference cut to their own measure." [102] The Chinese similarly rejected the Soviet counterproposal to convene a world disarmament conference because it did not clarify the object of such a meeting, nor define "effective measures to eliminate nuclear arms from the arsenals of states." [103]

The French also had trouble maintaining a viable, differentiated position on most of the principal arms control and disarmament measures on the agenda of the international community. Not only were pressures intense, such as those of the superpowers on France to conform to the test ban and nonproliferation treaties, but there was also the danger, as the MBFR discussions suggest, that France might be isolated or excluded from world forums making decisions that would affect its security interests. It denounced the Soviet-American compromise treaty forbidding nuclear devices on the floor of the

101. *Ibid.,* p. 87.
102. Klein, *Etudes internationales,* Sept. 1972, p. 365.
103. *Ibid.,* p. 366.

oceans within twelve miles of a nation's shore as a discriminatory move weakening the capacity of smaller states to defend themselves, since the superpowers were already armed with long-range sea- and land-based missiles that were beyond the reaches of coastal defenses. In the same vein, France declined to support either the Anglo-American proposal prohibiting biological weapons or the wider Soviet view of banning both biological and chemical weapons. The former was too narrow; the latter provided no effective control measures. It also initially abstained from signing, then under Latin American entreaties later agreed to, the Treaty of Tlatelolco, defining Latin America as a nonnuclear zone within which signatories would be obliged to refrain from threatening or using nuclear weapons.[104]

The gathering number of arms control proposals placed France in an increasingly awkward diplomatic position. Their popularity among Third World states hampered French diplomacy among the developing states. The confrontations with New Zealand, Australia, and Peru over open nuclear testing were embarrassing. It was also difficult to remain on good terms with the other nuclear powers. France wished to inhibit the proliferation of nuclear devices even while proceeding toward the manufacture of its own thermonuclear weapons. In response to these conflicting considerations, Pompidou's France made greater use of the tactic first employed by de Gaulle in his latter months in office. In January 1968, Armand Bérard, the French delegate to the United Nations, announced that "France . . . which will not sign the non-proliferation treaty will behave, in the future, exactly like the States which would decide to adhere to it." [105] France under Pompidou adopted much the same position in discussions dealing with the banning of biological and chemical weapons and with the Latin American denuclear zone proposal.

However potentially important these areas of arms control and disarmament may have been, they could not match in immediacy or significance France's policy toward the sale of arms abroad. This represented perhaps the most striking advance in France's relative strategic standing.[106] In 1970, France's arms shipments tripled in

104. *Ibid.*, pp. 373ff, and *Le Monde,* Sélection hebdomadaire, July 19–25, 1973, p. 9.
105. Klein, *Etudes internationales,* Sept. 1972, p. 371.
106. The annual issue of *The Military Balance* provides a running account

value over those of the previous year, jumping from $456 million to $1.3 billion. France replaced Britain as the third most important exporter of arms, exceeded only by the United States and the Soviet Union, which exported $2.7 billion and $2.0 billion worth of arms, respectively. In 1970, military sales totaled 8 percent of all French exports and 25 percent of the industrial shipments abroad. The bulk of the French success was in aerospace where Mirage sales in 1970 alone posted contracts valued at $650 million. The spectacular performance of the Mirage in the Six-Day War helped expand sales to fifteen states around the globe. Approximately two out of three Mirages were destined for foreign consumption. By the close of 1972, 763 Mirage III's and V's were sold abroad, and 480 were purchased by the French air force.[107] Helicopters, tanks, missiles, and missile-launching patrol boats were the other attractive sellers.

The French merchandised these military products much like soap chips or automobiles. Easy credit, weak political restrictions, and service contracts were parts of each package deal. Even arms fairs were organized to attract customers.[108] The French were particularly successful in penetrating American arms markets. These included industrial states like Germany (an order for over $200 million in patrol boats was placed in 1970)[109] and less-developed states, like Colombia, Brazil, Argentina, and Peru, which bought Mirages. The latter two South American states also bought other arms, including AMX tanks. The expansion of French arms sales to Latin America threatened the previous American monopoly.

Franco-American competition had grown so intense by the spring of 1971 that it elicited presidential notice on both sides of the Atlantic. In a May 1971 report to Congress, President Nixon recommended

of French arms deals. Useful summaries of French arms policy are found in the following: Jean Klein, "Commerce des armes et désarmement," *Politique étrangère*, XXXIII (1968), 351–360; *idem*, "Les Aspects actuels de la réglementation du commerce des armes," *ibid.*, XXXIV (1969), 161–190; Jacques Isnard, "French Arms Exports," *Survival*, XIII (April 1971), 134–135. Also helpful are these articles: C. L. Sulzberger, *Herald Tribune*, International edition, Feb. 22, 1971, p. 4; Josette Alia, *Le Nouvel observateur*, Nov. 1, 1971, pp. 24–25; Richard Booth, *Le Monde diplomatique*, April 1970, p. 10; and Georges Chafford, *Com'at*, Feb. 5, 1969, p. 7.

107. *Le Monde*, May 6–7, 1973, p. 8.
108. *Ibid.*, Sept. 17, 1970, p. 14.
109. *Ibid.*, Oct. 26, 1970, pp. 1, 2.

that military assistance to Latin America double from its base of $75 million a year. Arms manufacturers were advised to boost sales abroad.[110] On May 23, President Pompidou was reported to have advised the French military to develop simple, cheap, and *exportable* arms.[111] While motivation for the French marketing effort in arms was varied, its principal root remained the desire for an independent strategic and diplomatic policy, however much economic considerations predominated on the surface. Military sales maintained France's delicate balance of payments, created jobs, and spurred industrial expansion (a high priority of the Pompidou-inspired French Sixth Plan).

In 1970, the number of defense workers engaged in foreign exports doubled over the previous year, reaching a peak of 100,000 or more than one-third of the entire defense work force of 270,000. It was hoped, too, that these initial commercial successes would lead to greater military and even civilian sales of French products.[112] One close observer of French arms policy, drawing on budget debates in the National Assembly, ably summarized the complex considerations underlying the French position: "The exportation of war materials was presented as an essential element of France's policy of independence because it contributes to the financing of the nuclear force, assures an autonomous supply of material to the armed forces, guarantees social stability and economic progress, and maintains the balance of payments in equilibrium." [113]

There was some expectation that increasing arms sales abroad would enlarge French political influence in recipient states, but gains were difficult to assess. The de Gaulle and Pompidou regimes had to weather serious internal political storms over their arms policies. Pro-Israeli elements in France sharply attacked the Gaullist embargo on arms to Israel. Their criticisms intensified as French arms sales in-

110. *Herald Tribune*, International edition, May 22–23, 1971, p. 3; *Le Monde*, May 19, 1971, p. 32.
111. *Le Monde*, May 23–24, 1971, p. 32.
112. A revealing analysis of French thinking regarding arms sales to Arab states is found in two articles by Paul Balta, Middle East correspondent for *Le Monde*: "La France et le monde arabe: Les réalités économiques," I, *Revue de défense nationale*, XXVI (May 1970), 813–835; and "La France et le monde arabe: Les réalités politiques," II, *ibid.*, XXVI (June 1970), 924–934.
113. Klein, *Etudes internationales*, Sept. 1972, p. 384.

creased to Arab countries, capped by a contract for 110 Mirages to Libya in early 1970.[114]

Black African states also criticized France for arms sales to South Africa and Portugal. These admonitions had little success in applying pressure on the Pompidou regime. Paris introduced the distinction that the sale of arms for exterior defensive purposes was legitimate, but that objections could be validly raised against the shipment of arms destined for internal repression. The Elysée promised to restrict its sales to the former category.[115] To this end, there was some interruption in the sale of helicopters to South Africa after the visit of Kenneth Kaunda, the president of Zambia, who, in fall 1970, toured European capitals on behalf of several Black African states to discourage military assistance to the white governments of Rhodesia and South Africa or to the Portuguese colony of Angola.[116] Experience with France's leaky embargo of arms to Israel,[117] the persistence of strong economic, military, and diplomatic incentives to keep arms sales high, and the inherent and obvious difficulties of applying, coherently and consistently, the French distinction between interior and exterior use of arms threw considerable doubt on the serious intentions and feasibility of French cooperation with international efforts to restrict the sale of arms abroad. On the other side of the ledger, and acting unilaterally, France reportedly refused to let arms contracts with approximately twenty countries because of their insolvency, aggressive foreign policies, or suspected duplicity in acting as agents for states with which France would not deal directly.[118]

Finally, there were signs of renewed French interest in developing

114. The Israeli case is summarized in Uri Dan, *et al., De Gaulle contre Israel: Documents sur l'embargo* (Paris: Jacques Lanzmann, 1970). The French defense is found in the presentation of Prime Minister Jacques Chaban-Delmas, Comité Interministériel pour l'Information, *La Politique de la France en Méditerranée*, Feb. 1970. See Chapter 10 below for a discussion of the political dimensions of the Mirage sale to Libya. Latest reports indicated that France expected to fill the complete order for Mirages to Libya despite Tripoli's announced intention to transfer these to Egypt, one of the members, along with Syria and Libya, of a newly created federation of Arab states. *Le Monde*, May 6–7, 1973, p. 8. At this writing the federation appeared defunct.

115. *Herald Tribune*, International edition, Oct. 22, 1970, p. 1.

116. Klein, *Etudes internationales*, Sept. 1972, p. 385.

117. See Chapter 10 below.

118. *Le Monde*, May 22–23, 1970, p. 32.

security ties with other West European states. However, expectation easily outdistanced realization in French exercise of their European options. The negligible progress made in Anglo-French nuclear co-operation despite its tempting prospects and enlarging superpower arms accords was a rough index of the hesitancy of the Pompidou regime to develop closer West European defense ties. Greater mutual understanding between the two states, signified by Britain's entry into the Common Market, was a necessary, but by no means a sufficient, condition for military cooperation, especially in nuclear affairs. With Britain entering the EEC, France could presumably draw to some degree on Anglo-American defense ties to underwrite its security objectives in Europe without being forced into more formally binding relations with the United States within NATO. France's relative strategic standing would seem to have been enhanced vis-à-vis Germany and Russia although it was too early at the time of Britain's entry into the EEC to say what concrete benefits, if any, France would be able to derive from what President Pompidou indirectly called a new *entente cordiale* during his appearance on BBC in May 1970.

On the other hand, specific examples of progress in French-British nuclear cooperation were difficult to find. Suggestions were floated as early as May 1969 by Georges Pompidou, during his campaign for the French presidency, that he would be "ready to talk to the United Kingdom about an agreement" on nuclear defense policy that would be the basis for an independent West European effort. Prime Minister Chaban-Delmas a month later echoed President Pompidou's views.[119] These probes, which never materialized in concrete proposals, were consistent with the vague hints of President de Gaulle to the newly arrived British ambassador, Christopher Soames, in February 1969, that France and Britain form the nucleus of a European grouping that would coordinate its foreign and defense policies.[120] That little actually occurred in defense talks between the two states was sug-

119. Quoted in Ian Smart, *Future Conditional: The Prospect for Anglo-French Nuclear Cooperation,* Adelphi Paper No. 78 (London: Institute for Strategic Studies, 1971), p. 28.

120. For commentary on the Soames affair, see André Fontaine, *Le Monde,* Feb. 20–21, 1969; Roger Massip, "Complot contre le marché commun," *Revue politique et parlementaire,* No. 797 (March 1969), pp. 5–8; and extracts from the British Parliamentary debates, *Times* (London), Feb. 25–26, 1969.

gested by the reported French (and British) reluctance to raise defense issues during the May Paris summit, opening the way for Britain's entry into the Common Market, between Prime Minister Edward Heath and President Georges Pompidou.[121]

On the surface, compelling economic and technical arguments would appear to dispose France to favor joint efforts with the British on nuclear policy.[122] The British were far ahead in nuclear weapons development, including multiple warhead technology, penetration devices, and hardening techniques. They were especially advanced in the design, manufacture, propulsion, and operation of nuclear-powered submarines. France experienced considerable difficulty in these areas. The nuclear propulsion program got off to a false start, for example, when the French attempt to use natural uranium as a fuel proved abortive after much money and time were spent on the project. The nuclear program was plagued throughout the 1960's by high and continually mounting costs and slow technological development. In the seven-year period of 1965–1971 an average of 25.5 percent of the French defense budget was devoted to nuclear weapons; approximately half of the expenditures for heavy equipment was spent on the nuclear program. Furthermore, to speed deployment and increase effectiveness of the French nuclear fleet, Britain had much to offer in computer technology, intelligence and satellite systems, navigational equipment, logistics support, management techniques, and command and control data. For its part, France had made appreciable strides in missile technology where Britain was weak. This included both long-range and tactical nuclear missiles, like *Pluton*. A common problem facing both states was to begin planning for a new generation of weapons for the 1980's. Neither country could easily bear the technological and economic costs of this enterprise alone.

121. Interviews, Paris, May 1971; *Herald Tribune,* International edition, May 22–23, 1971, p. 2.

122. See Smart, *op. cit.,* for a searching analysis of the prospects of Anglo-French nuclear policy. Most of the technical and economic data of this discussion is drawn from Smart's work. Another useful appraisal, more optimistic in forecast, is Andrew J. Pierre, "Nuclear Diplomacy: Britain, France, and America," *Foreign Affairs,* XLIX (Jan. 1971), 283–301. See also the proposal of two British MP's, Eldon Griffiths and Michael Niblock, "Anglo-French Nuclear Deterrent," *Atlantic Community Quarterly,* VIII (Summer 1970), 196–209.

The French had a particularly acute short-term problem of strategic vulnerability. The retarded development of a fully operational submarine-launched ballistic missile system saddled the French with a highly vulnerable nuclear striking force until the late 1970's. The 36 Mirage IVA bombers in operational status (the remainder of the 62 Mirages was held in reserve) and the 18 IRBM silos in Haute-Provence were relatively easy targets for Soviet strike forces. And even if the French met their scheduled projection of three nuclear submarines by 1974–1975, they were not likely to be able to maintain one submarine always on station. Here, too, coordination with the British fleet of four boats would appear advisable. Between the two states, they could maintain as many as four ships at sea at peak periods. The greater range of British missiles and the longer operational experience of the British fleet encouraged the French to re-examine their nuclear policies in search of possible areas of cooperation.

Working out cooperative technical accords, however attractive the incentives, was easier to envision than to realize. If experience was any guide, the French record in developing successful arrangements with its allies in aircraft and civil nuclear energy programs did not offer great room for hope.[123] There was little assurance that France would not run into even more difficulties in the politically more sensitive area of national defense. By the close of 1972, France's inclination to "go it alone" in weapons production threatened permanently to exclude it from the efforts of its West European allies to clarify United States policy on making the Lance, a tactical nuclear missile, available to European states and the decision of Britain, Germany, and Italy to produce a replacement for American Phantom and Starfighter jets.[124] Declining arms sales in 1971—about 15 percent below 1970—[125] added to pressures for France to join in multilateral ventures with its European partners to meet the technological and economic requirements of modern weapons production and to keep pace with superpower competition for military markets.

Looking initially only at the French side of the equation of Anglo-French cooperation dampened optimism. Most of the already voiced antipathies to NATO integration applied. Opposition to bilateral or

123. René Foch, *Europe and Technology* (Paris: Atlantic Institute, 1970).
124. *Le Monde,* Dec. 23, 1972, p. 8.
125. *Ibid.,* March 11, 1972, p. 28.

multilateral control arrangements that might constrict France's nuclear independence was still strong in the Pompidou government. In October 1971, Defense Minister Michel Debré reaffirmed his hostility to any transnational controls on French armed forces, including purely European schemes.[126] On the other hand, Debré cited European political unity as the precondition for military integration, a stricture reaffirmed by his successor, Defense Minister Robert Galley, in presenting the 1974 military budget to the National Assembly.[127] Prospects for union remained slim. There was little reason for President Pompidou to change the view he expressed shortly before his trip to the United States in 1970 "that it's more difficult to unify seven than six, eight than seven, or 10 than nine" states.[128]

Sharp differences among the Six, and particularly between France and Germany, over monetary, trade, and agricultural policy gave scant support to the thesis of growing convergence in the foreign and economic policies of the EEC states, as discussed in Chapters 7 and 8. Germany also preferred to bolster the Eurogroup within NATO rather than to explore French hints of increasing military cooperation on defense planning and weapons production within the Western European Union. This previously scorned multilateral mechanism looked more attractive as United States pressures for European conformity to Washington's views grew and as the possibility of a common market in weapons production among Britain, Germany, and Italy within the NATO Eurogroup became more real, challenging the competitiveness of the French arms industry.[129]

Barriers on the British side were equally impressive. Control problems were sticky. Working outside the NATO and Nuclear Planning Group was not possible in the immediate future. The Conservative government of Prime Minister Edward Heath was intent on reconciling Britain's new commitment to Europe with continued support for NATO. Britain participated in the decision of most NATO states at the close of 1971 to increase their defense spending for alliance

126. *Ibid.*, Oct. 2, 1971, p. 10.
127. Smart, *op. cit.*, p. 26. Also *Le Monde*, Nov. 10, 1973, p. 5.
128. *U.S. News and World Report*, March 2, 1970, p. 45.
129. Foreign Minister Michel Jobert alluded to these possibilities in his presentation to the WEU Assembly on November 21. This was the first time in eleven years that a French foreign minister appeared before this group. *Le Monde*, Nov. 24, 1973, p. 9.

purposes by more than $1 billion. Moreover, restrictions arising out of Anglo-American accords limited what nuclear information could be passed to the French without United States consent. These included the 1963 sale accord on Polaris missiles and the 1955 and 1958 agreements on nuclear weapons and nuclear propulsion.

The American and British governments were also of one mind that some place must be found for Germany in any nuclear relation between France and Britain. France, however, was not prepared to entertain proposals that might increase German access to nuclear weapons. "What would become of peace," Debré publicly stated, "if in the name of Europe, Germany had access to nuclear force? That is presently to state the immediate limit of any political coordination." [130] And even if France could vault these apprehensions, closer German collaboration in nuclear affairs could not be easily reconciled with its diplomatic effort in Eastern Europe.

The limits of European defense cooperation appeared clearer in the early 1970's than the opportunities for their enlargement. It would be too much to argue that France would abandon its efforts with its European allies to reconcile the competing demands for lower defense spending, maximal security, increased political influence abroad, and national independence. Rather, the French government, following a line made clear in 1968, saw little chance of reconciling these imperatives in the immediate future and was reluctant to advance specific proposals, beyond rhetorical pleas for a greater European defense effort, that would pool human, material, and technological resources within institutional arrangements capable of executing common policies of the Nine. The French government was hemmed in on all sides. It was torn between making gestures to assure the retention of the American security guarantee at low strategic, political, and economic cost and preparing for the day when the American commitment would be reduced and troops withdrawn. Yet it was reluctant to make too obvious and precipitate an adjustment for fear of accelerating the American disengagement before an adequate European security framework—a dim future prospect—could be substituted. Significant segments of public opinion, centered in old-line Gaullist elements, still objected to any notion of European defense in which French con-

130. Debré, *Revue de défense nationale*, 1970, p. 1249.

trol over its nuclear forces might be weakened although the government's urging of a European defense policy, elaborated most clearly by Foreign Minister Michel Jobert,[131] implied some restrictions on national policy. On the other hand, the Pompidou regime did not wish to arouse the Soviet Union and slow political détente in Europe, nor, in giving too much head to talk of European defense, to stimulate German military appetites as the MLF, for example, had done a decade earlier.

As much by default as by desire, the Pompidou government focused on strengthening its domestic political and economic base and on encouraging closer economic and political cooperation with its European partners rather than on promoting rapid changes on defense questions at home or abroad. It bided its time for the day when France might again attempt to dominate the world—or at least the European—stage on questions of peace and war. Hamlet, not Henry IV, was now playing. Oratorical bombast gave way to reflective soliloquy and self-conscious ambiguity

131. See n. 83 above.

4
Search for Solvency

For over a decade, from the inception of the Fifth Republic in 1958, Charles de Gaulle's France made telling points in the debate over bloc politics and American imperial proclivities. The rhetorical brilliance and dramatic posturing of the French president obscured the fundamental dependence of France on its Atlantic and European allies, especially the United States, and, in economic affairs, Germany. It required the successive shocks of the May events, with their attendant economic upheaval, and the August invasion of Czechoslovakia to reveal, even to the most devoted Gaullist and to de Gaulle himself, how much the French offensive against superpower rule had been seriously checked. These events, however, were more symptomatic than determining. They exposed more than undermined the pre-existing weak and shaky material foundation on which the Gaullist critique of bloc politics rested and robbed it of much of its practical, if not all of its theoretical, force.

The difficulties faced by Gaullist France in attempting to free itself from American military strategic influence can be understood better if its inability to end the dollar's dominance and to reform the international monetary system is first analyzed. This campaign complemented France's efforts to revise the security system within which it was ensnared. Neither attack can be fully evaluated in isolation, but must be seen in reference to the other.

Although it would be misleading to reduce France's economic weakness and dependence to its monetary policies and position, this feature of Atlantic relations is a fruitful area of study. The impact of American economic influence on France and Europe, while varied in its forms and modalities, including trade, investment, and research and development, was most immediately felt in the organization and operation of the international monetary system. In many ways, it encapsulized the American economic challenge to Europe. The framework of economic relations between the United States and the Euro-

176

pean states depended critically on the dollar. A revision of power relations between both sides of the Atlantic could hardly be imagined
in the absence of a fundamental change in the dollar's international
role.

An examination of franc diplomacy under the de Gaulle and
Pompidou regimes is instructive for several reasons. First, it throws
additional light on the Gaullist attack on bloc politics and, specifically,
on what French diplomacy perceived were the hegemonic tendencies
of the United States. To promote France's interests, the de Gaulle
government sought reform of the international monetary system and
reduction in the dollar's central role. The franc was to be upgraded,
if not raised to the status of the dollar, and the position of Paris as
an international financial capital was to be advanced. The distance
between Wall Street and the Place de la Bourse would be shortened.

Second, against this background, French monetary policy under the
Fifth Republic appears as the reciprocal of the American position. As
American policy progressively de-emphasized gold and even the
dollar in favor of a negotiated paper standard, so de Gaulle's France
gradually abandoned its campaign for a return to a pre–World War
II gold standard in favor of maintaining a tie between gold and the
creation of international monetary reserves (Special Drawing Rights).
Moreover, as United States policy under the Nixon administration
moved away from support of fixed exchange rates in favor of other
states floating their currencies against each other and against the dollar, France under the Pompidou regime quietly dropped Gaullist revisionist schemes of the international monetary system and insisted
instead on adherence to the Bretton Woods accords. The failure of
franc diplomacy to accomplish its announced goals under the de
Gaulle regime affords a crude measure of the success of American
dollar diplomacy.

Third, the French critique of American monetary policy, despite
its meager practical results from the perspective of Gaullist global
aspirations, did have one outcome of potentially long-run effect. It
publicly exposed more clearly than other states might have wished the
weaknesses of the postwar international system. It focused early on
the problems raised, by no means resolved, in basing international
monetary transactions on the dollar—a national currency. The system is particularly sensitive to the pressures of American foreign

policy needs that go beyond economic factors and to the vicissitudes of American domestic economic and political imperatives. The interests and objectives of other states whose currencies are tied to the dollar are thus inevitably raised into question.

Fourth, the continuing importance of the dollar and the difficulties encountered in redefining its role and status suggest the narrow options that were open to French policymakers under the de Gaulle and Pompidou governments. Gaullist France was torn between two unpalatable choices: to acquiesce in American monetary leadership or to promote a common European economic policy capable of marshaling sufficient resources and pressure to influence American policy. For orthodox Gaullists the first choice had always been intolerable, the second fraught with the danger of drawing France into unwanted European community commitments whose supranational make-up, objectionable in principle, served in practice as a device progressively to attract France into Germany's sphere of economic influence. The national strategy adopted by the de Gaulle regime neither extricated France from its dilemma nor noticeably increased its political or economic independence within either the Atlantic or the European communities. The Pompidou government displayed more reserve in its public criticism of American monetary policies and more diplomatic finesse in striking bargains with its European or Atlantic partners. Yet France under President Pompidou had still not escaped the choice of acceding to United States financial power or of building a countervailing European grouping capable of matching United States influence in the operations of the international monetary system.

Background to the Franc Challenge

The foundation of the postwar international monetary system was laid in 1944 at Bretton Woods, which created the International Monetary Fund (IMF). The system was based on the fixed parities of currencies defined by reference to gold at thirty-five dollars an ounce. Members contributed stated amounts of their national currencies and gold to the Fund in order to facilitate international transactions. Currencies were to be fully convertible although a transition period was anticipated for those states devastated by war. Convertibility referred to transactions only on current account. National authorities retained control over capital transfers and could presumably follow domestic credit policies adapted to their own needs, insulated to some degree from the effects of policies pursued elsewhere. The system provided means to foster freer trade among states. It also established procedures for international negotiation and decision to forestall the beggar-thy-neighbor policies of competitive devaluations, trade restrictions, and dumping that characterized economic relations during the 1930's. It was generally agreed at the time of the IMF's formation that these policies accelerated the economic collapse of the Western democracies and paved the way for the rise of fascist governments in Europe.

The International Monetary Fund disposed only modest credit facilities to assist member states in temporary balance-of-payments difficulties. Neither mechanisms for centralized credit control nor for the development of new sources of international credit were contemplated. Periodic adjustment in currency exchange ratios that, once fixed, were not to vary more than approximately 1 percent of the official rate, would correct for serious disequilibria. Under IMF surveillance, members who ran chronic deficits were expected to devalue to encourage exports and slow imports; surplus states, to appreciate their currencies to produce the reverse results.

The postwar monetary system, international in form, but largely dependent on a national currency for its operation, effectively responded to the requirements of European recovery and the rising global demand for trade and economic development. Only massive injections of American dollars could make it work. Only the enormous productive power of the United States could fill the void caused by six years of war. American economic leadership flowed naturally from its billions of dollars of assistance to Europe, under the Marshall Plan and the mutual security program, and to the Third World. Rising expenditures for security, as the Cold War developed, reinforced American economic dominance. The logical, if not always intended, effect of these policies was increasingly to make the dollar the basis for credit, reserve creation, and long-term capital supply in international monetary transactions. By September 1968, for example, gold accounted for only 53 percent of free world–reserves against 91 percent before World War II. Dollars and sterling, as international reserves, rose from 9 to 38 percent. Centralized credit reserves, which rose from zero to 9 percent, completed the balance.[1] One keen observer of Atlantic relations well summarizes the principal factors accounting for the emergence of the rule of the dollar in international monetary affairs: "Because the American economy is so large, because prices . . . have been stable, because foreign aid and military dollars by the tens of billions were poured into Europe, because the United States is the only major international source of investment capital and short-term funds, because the American capital and money markets are so large and efficient, and because the supply of monetary gold was growing much more slowly than the world's need for reserves, it was well-nigh inevitable that the dollar would become the principal vehicle currency and reserve asset for most of the non-Communist world." [2]

As long as the European states concentrated on reconstructing their destroyed economies, they had little difficulty acknowledging their dependence on the United States. Until the late 1950's, Europeans needed all the dollars they could procure to finance their recoveries, expand their capital markets, facilitate trade expansion, and reconstitute their own monetary systems. Thanks to a unilateral decision of the American government, which held three-quarters of the world's gold supply after World War II, the dollar was made fully convertible into gold. With the dollar assured to be as good as gold, European central banks often preferred to hold American currency which they could then place on American capital markets at interest. Capital funds moved with increasing ease across national boundaries, and many of the controls on capital movements envisioned at Bretton Woods, while still applicable to some degree, were considerably weakened. Capital transfers were conveyed by financial vehicles under American control and fueled by American dollars. The insulation of capital flows in order to attain particular national political and economic objectives was gradually worn away with the uniting of national capital and money markets among the non-Communist states. Moreover, accounts between states were as often as not settled in dollars rather than gold. Thus, more by practice initially than by con-

1. Robert Triffin, "The Thrust of History in International Monetary Reform," *Foreign Affairs,* XLVII (April 1969), 480.
2. Harold van B. Cleveland, *The Atlantic Idea and Its European Rivals* (New York: McGraw-Hill, 1966), p. 72.

scious design, the dollar was accepted without question as the principal international monetary reserve for the states of Western Europe and North and South America.

American deficits were considered beneficial. They supplied needed dollars and, more than gold, were the major source of new international liquidity, essential to the expansion of world trade. Dollar dominance also tied the United States to Europe as a barrier against American return to isolationism. For commercial, capital, and reserve purposes, the dollar rapidly became indispensable. The gold exchange standard adopted at Bretton Woods gradually became a dollar exchange system after the end of World War II.[3]

But the economic disparities between the United States and Europe gradually disappeared. By 1958, in what proved to be a fortuitous conjuncture with the establishment of the Fifth Republic, exchange controls were finally ended. The Common Market was already showing signs after only a year of new *relance* of the European states toward unity. As the rate of American economic growth declined in the recession of the late 1950's, Europe's economic expansion accelerated. While the economies of the United States and Britain stagnated, the European Six registered increasingly higher average growth rates. Europe was also slowly developing its own sources of capital although the creation of a European Common Market was a great spur to American investment in Europe.

Meanwhile, American deficits mounted. Except for 1957, immediately following the Suez crisis, the United States ran annual deficits between 1950 and 1971. In the middle period between 1959 and 1966, the American balance-of-payment deficits from all sources equaled $21.4 billion compared with a EEC surplus of $12.9 billion during the same period. Of this deficit only one-third or $7.4 billion was settled in gold. The remaining $14 billion was regulated in dollars, which largely became part of the official short-term dollar assets of the European states. By September 30, 1967, private dollar holdings abroad totaled $15 billion; those in the hands of monetary authorities in non-Communist countries were $14.4 billion. These claims, com-

3. Harold van B. Cleveland, "Monetary Problems of the Atlantic Community," *Proceedings of the Academy of Political Science,* XXIX (1968), 111–127; Victor Volcouve, *La Crise du franc* (Paris: Editions du Seuil, 1969), pp. 58–64.

bined with United States debts to international organizations, brought the total of United States liabilities to $31.2 billion.

During the same period, United States gold supplies dwindled as private and public holders of dollars cashed them for gold. Between 1950 and March 1968, the United States gold stock dropped from $22.8 billion to $10.5 billion. As each year passed, the ability of the United States to cover dollar claims abroad with gold diminished. The European states were the largest gainers in gold. By 1964, European gold reserves had exceeded those of the United States, amounting respectively to $18.9 billion and $15.5 billion. Germany and France were in the lead among the European states in reducing the foreign-exchange portion of their monetary reserves. Germany reduced its foreign-exchange holdings from $3.3 billion to $1.7 billion between 1963 and 1965. France did likewise during the same period; its foreign-exchange holdings, principally in dollars, fell from $1.4 billion to $800 million. Its gold reserves increased from $3.7 billion at the end of 1964 to over $5 billion at the end of 1966.[4]

As long as the European states were preoccupied with reconstructing their devastated economies, they accepted American monetary leadership. Their dire circumstances constrained them to tie the realization of their domestic economic objectives to American economic policies. Differences between Europe and America over national economic objectives—price levels, growth rates, employment, investment, interest differentials—were subordinated to the tasks of rehabilitation. But as the European states grew economically stronger and self-reliant, it was only to be expected that they would wish to assume greater control over their economies. A necessary condition toward these objectives was the exercise of greater influence over American economic and, specifically, monetary policies. This newly manifested European desire had its parallel in security affairs where to gain greater control over their national security the European states pressed to influence American defense doctrine and behavior. If con-

4. Fritz Machlup, *Remaking the International Monetary System: The Rio Agreement and Beyond* (Baltimore: Johns Hopkins Press, 1968), pp. 96–103; Volcouve, *op. cit.,* p. 80; Georges Plescoff, "International Liquidity: The Case of the Common Market," *American Economic Review,* LVIII (May 1968), 608–619

fidence in the American nuclear deterrent was central to European security concerns, so confidence in the American dollar was at the root of their economic worries. The focus of their anxieties was on the American balance-of-payments deficits that gave no sign of solution. The French government under President Charles de Gaulle was particularly alert to the American embarrassment and, as the 1960's unfolded, exploited its temporary advantage.

The Diplomacy of the Franc

The French campaign against the prevailing international monetary system and the dominating role of the dollar had two dimensions: oral and operational. In retrospect, it seems clear that the French were far more successful in exposing, through precise analysis and elegant prose, the weaknesses of the Western monetary system and the vulnerability of the dollar as a reserve currency than in convincing either the United States to adopt their proposals or their European partners to follow their lead in reforming the system. In addition, while the rhetorical attack was largely economic in its mode of presentation, the operational side of French franc diplomacy strongly suggests that the attack on the dollar and the international monetary system was part and parcel of the Gaullist assault on the privileged American position in Western Europe and one more effort in the quest to maximize France's national independence and global influence in an international order dominated by two superpowers.

The French Critique of the Monetary Order

Throughout the 1960's, the French government developed its case against the hegemony of the dollar and international monetary practices. Its brief responded to the new economic and political conditions prevailing between the United States and Europe. Only the major structural features of the French argument can be presented here, but enough can perhaps be distilled from the heated exchanges between France and its Atlantic and European allies to characterize, reasonably accurately, the general French position. The most dramatic statement of some of the principal elements of the French critique appears in President de Gaulle's news conference of February 4,

1965.[5] It reiterates arguments presented by French officials[6] as early as 1962 at international monetary conferences.

American deficits were attacked on several grounds. Foreign acceptance of dollars permitted the United States to shift the burden of its indebtedness to others and encouraged the United States to run even larger deficits. Unlike other states, it was not obliged, given the dollar's reserve role, to settle its accounts in gold. Revaluating European currencies upward was ruled out as a perhaps economically feasible, but politically untenable, move to offset an overvalued dollar. The dollar's pivotal position, argued the French, left Washington to define the rules for the international monetary system to suit the convenience of the American economy. Sustained deficits, moreover, were seen to have significant, adverse effects on the national economies of the European states. They allegedly exported inflation through capital creation in the form of dollar loans to states and individuals by increasing the total amount of currency and credit within a national economic system. In addition, they facilitated American takeover of European enterprises.[7] American companies could draw upon European credits furnished them through the recyclage of dollars held by Europeans on the American capital market or through the London-based Euro-dollar market.[8] Accumulating American deficits

5. De Gaulle, *Discours,* IV, 330–334.

6. Indispensable for an understanding of French franc diplomacy are the scholarly articles of Jacques Wolff in three numbers of the *Revue de science financière,* No. 4 (Oct.–Dec. 1968), 782–829; No. 1 (Jan.–March 1969), 5–76; No. 2 (April–June 1969), pp. 205–234.

7. The problems posed by American investment go beyond this discussion of the French critique of the monetary system although they are intimately linked to the economic relations between the United States and Europe. Some of the complexities of the problem are presented in Charles P. Kindleberger, *American Business Abroad* (New Haven: Yale University Press, 1969); and Richard N. Cooper, *The Economics of Interdependence* (New York: McGraw-Hill, 1968). Two shorter works of note are Allan Johnstone, *United States Direct Investments in France* (Cambridge: MIT Press, 1965), and Christopher Layton, *Trans-Atlantic Investments* (Paris: Atlantic Institute, 1966).

8. By summer, 1971, the Euro-dollar market was estimated at $57 billion. *Le Monde,* June 22, 1971, p. 15. The Euro-dollar constitutes a market for deposits of dollars and increasingly for other currencies held in Europe and centered in London. Begun in 1958 with the re-establishment of convertibility it has grown from $3 billion in 1959 to its present size. This capital market escapes national control and by the late 1960's constituted a major destabilizing element in monetary transactions. "The Euro-dollar money and bond

introduced a fundamental disequilibrium or instability to international monetary transactions. As confidence in the dollar weakened, a function in part of its lessened capacity to be redeemed in gold, strong incentives arose among dollar holders to shift massive sums, often overnight, to gold or to sounder European currencies, like the mark or the Swiss franc.

De Gaulle's ministers elaborated upon these themes in later conferences. They considered the monetary system basically inequitable since the cost of holding the American debt was unequally shared by the member states of the IMF. Moreover, the present system unfairly discriminated, economically and politically, between Anglo-American and European currencies. European monies, and especially the franc, were supposed to be of equal proportional strength to the dollar, based on the relative capacities of these states to produce goods and services and to compete in world markets. They deserved reciprocal consideration, if not perhaps as a reserve currency—that solution was ruled out for *any* national currency—then as an acceptable vehicle for commercial and capital transactions. This implied that Paris, like New York and London, should be recognized as a world financial center.[9]

These economic considerations were logically linked to broader political values that were in keeping with Gaullist conceptions of international relations as based solely on the authority of nation-states. The international monetary system was condemned *ipso facto* because it rested on a national currency, the dollar. The French were certain the United States would act on its own interests in preserving the dollar and in protecting and promoting its economic goals. This line of reasoning was analogous to French criticism of the American nuclear monopoly. Granting French assumptions (to be proven quite accurate in later dollar crises) the United States would always choose its own interests over those of the European states even at the expense

---

markets," notes one distinguished international economist, "are equivalent of a free port; or a Tangiers where no regulations apply, but on such a scale that they limit the national independence of the major financial powers." Charles P. Kindleberger, *Power and Money* (New York: Basic Books, 1970), p. 175.

9. *FFP*, Jan.–June 1968, p. 64. There is no substitute for following the French criticism through these official publications that began in 1966. Representative are the statements of Michel Debré, in *ibid.*, 1966, pp. 118–122; *ibid.*, Jan.–June 1967, pp. 72–74; *ibid.*, July–Dec., 1967, pp. 51–54, 146–148.

of the security or monetary system on which the Europeans relied to protect their interests. This threat of loss or abandonment was related to Europe's dependence on American military and economic power. As long as the monetary system turned on the dollar, Washington could be expected to use its privileged position to promote American economic needs ahead of those of member states in the monetary grouping. It would pass the cost of maintaining the dollar's uniquely influential status along to the other members of the system which would be forced, lacking effective alternatives, to carry an increasingly greater financial burden. Their own dependency would be reinforced. Their very solvency, which permitted them to accept dollars, was an invitation to the United States to tie them closer to its economic will. "It is a question of understanding," said Michel Debré, finance minister in the Pompidou cabinet in 1968, "that the political equality of nations, like the economic independence of nations, is tied to the fact that their currencies are not attached to another national currency on which they would be dependent." [10]

Since the creation of currency was an inherent act of sovereignty, no nation was competent to act as the guarantor of the international monetary system, nor could other states, even if they were disposed to accede to American economic prowess, have confidence that their economic objectives would be respected by the United States. Indeed, their foreign policy views were already being overridden, according to the French, in the Vietnam War, which was supported indirectly by European credit in the form of excess dollar holdings.[11] The liberty permitted the United States in international economic and financial transactions freed them, the French believed, to pursue foreign policy goals that were inimical to European interests.

The French accepted the American retort, plausible until 1971, that its commercial balances were generally in excess, but that its deficits arose from other external factors, such as military security, foreign investment, and foreign aid. Of these three factors, the French would only tolerate excesses on the side of Third World aid, an area of

10. *Ibid.*, 1966, pp. 121–122.
11. President Kennedy recognized the constraints on American foreign policy posed by the nation's growing deficits. The Gaullist attack struck "gold," so to speak, although American policymakers were careful not to admit publicly to these limitations. See Sorenson, *Kennedy, passim.*

diminishing interest to the United States. The French case against American military presence in Europe and in Asia aimed, before 1968, at reducing American military spending. The French ejection of foreign troops from their soil cost them millions of dollars in foreign exchange; the loss was justified on political, not economic, grounds. The French attitude toward American investments was bearish though on dubious economic grounds. The loss to French investment accounts and the holding of large gold reserves were not only parts of French economic policy, still mercantilist and conservative in its assumptions about international monetary policy, but also integral parts of French global policy. The American explanation of its deficits, as contributions to Western defense and European economic welfare, were hardly persuasive. Constricting American military and monetary influence in Europe was precisely what Gaullist France hoped to do.[12]

Operational Phase of Franc Diplomacy

French arguments may have struck responsive chords in the financial circles of Europe but the Gaullist recommendations for changing the international monetary system were less enthusiastically received. President de Gaulle's February 4 address was the starting point for the French call for an international monetary system based on standards independent of the fluctuations of another state's national currency and economic behavior. The only answer, following a thesis stated tirelessly and repeatedly by French economist Jacques Rueff, was gold:

We hold as necessary that international exchange be established . . . on an indisputable monetary base that does not carry the mark of any particular country.

What base? In truth, one does not see how in this respect it can have any criterion, any standard, other than gold. Eh! Yes, gold, which does not change in nature, which is made indifferently into bars, ingots, and coins, which does not have any nationality, which is held eternally and

12. A brief for the French position by a sympathetic American journalist is found in Waverly Root, "De Gaulle and the Dollar," *American Scholar,* XXXVII (Summer 1968), 469–481. A more strictly economic presentation is given in Fritz Machlup, "World Monetary Debate—Bases for Agreement," *The Banker,* CXVI (Sept. 1966).

universally. . . . No money counts . . . except in direct or indirect relation to gold. Doubtless, one does not think to impose on each country
the manner in which it should conduct itself domestically. But the supreme
law, the golden rule . . . that must be placed in operation and honored
in international economic relations is the obligation to bring into equilibrium between monetary zones, through transfers of the precious metal,
the balance of payments resulting from their exchanges.[13]

A week after de Gaulle's pronouncements on gold, Finance Minister Giscard d'Estaing outlined a plan for the creation of international
reserves and for the management of the monetary system by the major
financial centers of the Western world. Although addressed to the
economic circumstances of 1965, it embodied most of the monetary
principles underlying Gaullist official thinking before and after and is
worth examining in some detail. Raising the economic criticisms mentioned above, d'Estaing proposed that states henceforward settle their
deficits only in gold, not in the currency of another state (the dollar
or the pound). Excessive reserves based on the currencies of other
states were to be gradually eliminated. Those "monies invested with
international responsibility" (presumably including the franc with its
zone franc obligations) would then become fully convertible into gold
and would be used in the transactions of central banks according to
agreed-upon procedures.

New international reserves could be created, but only through
common accord, and only if linked to gold. Such an instrument would
be appropriately called CRU ("believed" in French, but Collective
Reserve Unit in more skeptical, professional financial circles). The
CRU's would be distributed among the Group of Ten within the
International Monetary Fund.[14] These leading industrial states, forming a closed club, would allocate them among themselves in proportion to their gold stocks.[15] According to the French, the virtue of the

13. De Gaulle, *Discours,* IV, 333. In his *Le Péché monétaire de l'occident*
(Paris: Plon, 1971), Reuff exposes his views on gold again and provides useful documentary material on his relations with the de Gaulle government.
14. The Group of Ten is composed of the original six EEC states (except
Luxembourg), the United States, Great Britain, Canada, Sweden, and Japan.
15. The plan presented by Giscard d'Estaing is found in Wolff, *Revue de
science financière,* 1968, pp. 795–796; see also *Les Echos,* Feb. 12, 1965, p. 177;
Economist, Feb. 6, 1965, pp. 567–569; *Le Monde,* June 15, 1965, p. 1ff; *Le
Capital,* Feb. 16, 1965.

plan was its reinforcement of gold in international monetary transactions and the alleged automaticity and impartiality of an exchange system built on a commodity rather than a national currency, like the dollar, or, what Robert Triffin has called, "a negotiated credit-reserves standard." [16]

New reserves created to assist states in balance-of-payments difficulties or to facilitate international trade would be the product of an accord among the principal Western industrial and financial powers (the Group of Ten) and would be treated more as a credit extended to recipient states than as a reserve which could be counted as a real asset. The dollar would be placed on a par with other state currencies and would enjoy neither special economic benefits nor political status. American influence in the IMF, where it held more votes than any other state and controlled the votes of many of the smaller states, particularly among the Latin American countries, would be correspondingly diluted since it would have to submit to the regime agreed to by other central monetary authorities.

The plan would presumably be attractive to European states which made up a majority of the Group of Ten. Since the inception of the Group of Ten in 1961, due partly to French enterprise, France enjoyed some support from EEC central banks in its efforts to expand the influence of the Ten at the expense of the IMF and, implicitly, the United States, which still dominated the organization. States within the Group of Ten would have increased leverage, through control of mechanisms for the creation, use, and deposit of CRU's, over American economic policies that influenced, often adversely, the achievement of their particular economic objectives. In other words, the international financing of the American debt would be subject to some form of French influence. Under this scheme, France would gain in at least two ways. A new and formidable barrier would be raised against foreign economic penetration not to the liking of French monetary authorities; control of interior economic policies would thus be enhanced. France's capacity to influence international monetary policies and, correspondingly, Atlantic security and diplomatic goals—much as the United States was able to do through its financial leverage—would be improved.

16. Triffin, *Foreign Affairs*, 1968, pp. 486–487.

Basing the new monetary system on gold played to France's strong gold position in the middle 1960's. It stood to gain, financially, from an appreciation of the price of gold and, politically, in the expansion of its international economic role. An increase in international reserves tied to gold would have tended to push the price of gold upward. This would have had the effect of devaluating the American dollar at what was viewed as an acceptable cost to France's trade position. The political, economic, and prestige gains in diminishing the power of the dollar were just compensation in Gaullist eyes.

Few states took the French plan seriously. There was little sentiment to return to a gold standard that never really functioned as automatically or as impartially as the French would have had others believe. Before World War I, its operation depended on British financial power. As the pound experienced increased difficulties, leading to the devaluation of 1931, the American dollar gradually assumed the financial responsibilities for the operation of the monetary system, such as it was. The Bretton Woods conference did not officially consecrate the dollar's central role, but paved the way for its ascendancy. If other Europeans, like the French, feared the inflationary pressures of enlarging dollar holdings in their central reserves, they also worried about provoking a strong deflationary economic policy in the United States that would draw them along or about encouraging American isolationist sentiment, fed already by the increasing burdens of the war in Vietnam.[17]

The French proposals went against the grain of historical practice among states in their international monetary dealings. Gaullist aspirations for French *grandeur* in world economic affairs blinded Gaullist realism about prevailing conditions of interstate monetary relations. Gold could not provide adequate liquidity for expanding world trade, and the French plan, with its accent on erecting obstacles to credit creation, did not offer an attractive solution for financing and facilitating commerce. Nor did it make much sense to many central bankers and government officials to permit reserve creation to be so heavily influenced by the uncertainties and hazards of gold production and prospecting or by the fluctuations of gold and dollars (or pounds)

17. Plesoff, *American Economic Review*, 1968, 612–613, suggests the economic cross-pressures experienced in Europe over dollar fluctuations.

held by central banks. It seemed to be even less reasonable to give a premium to gold-producing countries, like the Soviet Union and the Union of South Africa, and permit these states and their suspect political regimes to affect Western monetary practices.

The United States could hardly have been less disposed to the French plan. If implemented, it would have undercut American attempts to discourage the use of gold in monetary transactions and weakened pressures encouraging states to hold their dollars in lieu of converting them into gold. Nor could the probable inflationary effects of an increase in the price of gold be discounted. More significant was the American determination to retain the dollar's dominant position. A revaluation of gold would weaken American economic influence and monetary leadership; it would strike a blow at American global prestige not only in the Atlantic area, between North America and Western Europe, but in the Third World where the superpowers were increasingly engaged.

Even if the French wish to return to the gold standard is viewed more as a negotiating stance than as a statement of minimal Gaullist objectives for the reform of the monetary system, there is evidence that France's relentless criticism of the United States diluted rather than reinforced its influence on the evolutionary course of international monetary policy in the 1960's. Few, if any, states had any illusions that France's position was solely dictated by economic considerations. The stakes were ultimately political and were so recognized by American negotiators.

American policy responded more to the collective will and economic pressures marshaled by the European states as a group than to the intransigence of any one member. Indeed, the American negotiating position hardened vis-à-vis France as the Gaullist offensive against American hegemonic rule gathered momentum after 1965. American policy was more sensitive to the real economic leverage of Germany than to the diplomatic moves and military strategic ploys of France. Gaullist bombast and unimpressive French GNP figures were no substitutes for concerted European pressures in inflecting American monetary policy.

French diplomacy also unwittingly enlisted "in the service of the Prussian king." An unintended effect of French franc maneuvering was to thrust Germany again into the role of intermediary between

France and the United States. France's determination to impress its monetary views on its Atlantic and European partners did more to accelerate Germany's emancipation from French influence than to force it to choose between Paris and Washington. Despite the French-German treaty of 1963, Germany generally preferred, when pressed to decide, the American over the French monetary option.

The questionable results of franc diplomacy under the de Gaulle government may be seen by examining the two general lines along which international monetary policy moved in the 1960's. These included the creation of international liquidity in the form of so-called Special Drawing Rights within the IMF and the formulation of international accords to protect the international monetary system against speculative pressures in the form of massive and precipitate shifts from the dollar to gold or from one currency to another.[18]

International Liquidity and Special Drawing Rights

In terms of the intensity and gravity of the Franco-American monetary clash, French franc diplomacy may be divided into four periods. From 1958 to 1962, French efforts focused on strengthening the franc. These centered on a 17.5 percent devaluation in December 1958 that was linked to a major economic stabilization plan. The success of the devaluation and subsequent austerity measures that discouraged imports and promoted exports permitted France to institute the first set of accords on lowering internal tariffs among the EEC countries on January 1, 1959. A strong franc was to be the economic foundation of France's increasing independence in foreign affairs.[19]

The second phase, from 1962 to 1965, culminated in President de Gaulle's February 4 news conference. This period represents a departure from the relative passivity of franc diplomacy of the first four years of Gaullist rule, although it was restrained in comparison to what followed. It was largely restricted to verbal assaults on United States deficits and did not overtly attempt to hinder American efforts to gain European cooperation for its proposals to protect the dollar.

The principal skirmish during this second phase of the Franco-American monetary conflict developed over the American proposal

18. Cleveland, *Proceedings of the Academy of Political Science*, 1968, p. 110.
19. De Gaulle, *Mémoires d' espoir*, pp. 139–171.

at the Tokyo IMF meeting in September 1964 to increase IMF capital quotas by 50 percent. Finance Minister Giscard d'Estaing accused the United States of fostering world inflation through its deficits. The French minister also opposed the American recommendation for greater IMF quotas for member states.[20] For the French, an increase in IMF quotas merely facilitated the access of debtor states to increased international credits that would further reinforce global inflationary pressures. The French minister insisted that, if supplementary contributions were decided upon despite his government's reservations, one-quarter of them should be in gold. Such a rule would discourage debtors from subscribing to IMF increases in order to be eligible for complementary credits. Britain and America were hostile to the French recommendation that would have forced gold purchases, weakening the dollar and pound, which the increased IMF credits were designed to strengthen.[21] A compromise was reached on a 25 percent increase with France voting against the proposal and abstaining on a resolution to increase quotas for sixteen other states.

The height of the Franco-American monetary conflict occurred, not surprisingly, in the period between February 1965 and May 1968, when differences between the two states were sharpest over alliance policy and a European settlement between East and West. From all outward appearances the franc was on the offensive, a "gold war" in the view of one observer.[22] But appearances were deceiving. French and American announced and operational policies tended to move in inverse relation to each other. As Gaullist rhetoric intensified the attack on the American dollar, so the effective force of French diplomatic pressures seemed to diminish. The opposite was true for the United States. Outwardly unperturbed by French verbal assaults, it quietly applied its economic and military leverage on France's partners, prodding them to piecemeal amendment of the international monetary system that was more suited to the circumstances of a weakened dollar in the 1970's than to the "situation of strength" enjoyed by the dollar in the postwar period. The American offensive to bolster

20. Interviews, Paris, January–May 1971.
21. L'Année politique, 1965, p. 284; Wolff, Revue de science financière, 1968, p. 793.
22. For a less sympathetic analysis of French monetary policy, see Carmoy, Foreign Policies of France, pp. 440–450.

the dollar offset the French attack to weaken it as the foundation of the international monetary system. The analytic and oratorical skills of French negotiators, backed only by France's modest economic and military means, offered no balance to the material weight of the United States. The American purse was, to quote Beaumarchais' Don Bazile, "full of irresistible arguments."

The American monetary position in the middle 1960's was based on two optimistic assumptions: the eventual rectification of the United States balance-of-payments position and the equivalence of the dollar to gold. Since American deficits were the principal means of creating new international liquidity, the United States pressed for the creation of a new international reserve. It would be tied neither to gold nor the dollar, but rest on the strength of the domestic economies of IMF members who would be responsible for its creation. It would replace the anticipated shortage of dollars once the American balance of payments was brought into line. The United States also wished that these reserves be automatic (open to all participants in the scheme), transferable between central banks, and nonreimbursable. They would not be considered credits extended to a debtor state in balance-of-payments difficulties, but real assets resting on the acceptance of foreign monetary authorities rather than on a commodity of intrinsic market value, like gold.[23]

French diplomacy concentrated more on the economic problems of adjustment (balance of payments) and confidence than on liquidity.[24] The CRU proposal was in some sense a French defensive move to deflect IMF and EEC attention from the more liberal reserve creation recommendations of the United States. The amounts to be defined would be limited and related to the existing distribution of gold stocks among the Group of Ten. The IMF, where American strength was great, would be by-passed in favor of the smaller grouping where the French erroneously believed that they would have more influence. To their monetary case they added the argument that international liquidity was adequate and that it should be subordinated as an issue on the international monetary agenda to the structural reform of the

23. *Le Figaro,* May 6, 1971, p. 8.
24. Machlup, *The Banker,* 1966.

system. In no case were international reserves of any kind, even CRU, to be considered, much less approved, until the United States balance-of-payments deficits were remedied. And when the CRU began to be taken seriously by reserve states, the French lost interest in their own suggestion.[25]

The French also objected to the creation of international reserves through the chance operation of American deficits rather than through the conscious deliberation and consent of states in accordance with their particular liquidity needs. There was no logical connection between United States deficits and international liquidity needs except historical practices arising out of the abnormal conditions of World War II. The creation of new reserves even by the common consent of IMF members would not deal with the American problem and would actually exacerbate the existing deficiencies of the international monetary system. Creating more reserves would reinforce the vicious circle whereby debtor states, like the United States, could finance their indebtedness only to incur even greater liabilities. Debtor states would be tempted to dig themselves in deeper and deeper beyond a point which creditors would find possible to fill. As the debtors faulted on their obligations, they threatened to bring down the monetary system with them.[26]

Meanwhile, French diplomacy took the field on several fronts. France clashed openly with IMF authorities who believed that the IMF, not the Group of Ten, was the proper framework for monetary negotiations and reserve creation. The IMF leadership, following American views, also resisted French suggestions that the monetary system should increase its reliance on gold as its principal pillar of support. France gained some slight satisfaction when the Group of Ten asked that the Six be given increased weight in these negotiations.[27] In January 1965, the Bank of France announced that it would begin converting its dollar reserves into gold. It would maintain its dollar balances equal to its foreign debt of approximately $1 billion. (It had been $3 billion in 1958.) Finance Minister Giscard d'Estaing's insistence that the action was technical, not political, lost

25. Machlup, *Remaking the International Monetary System*, p. 9.
26. *FFP*, 1966, pp. 118–121; *ibid.*, July–Dec. 1967, pp. 52–54.
27. *L'Année politique, 1965*, pp. 262–263.

much of its credibility, for it was soon followed by President de Gaulle's open challenge to dollar hegemony.[28]

In his news conference of September 9, 1965, President de Gaulle reaffirmed France's desire for a monetary system compatible with an international political system beyond superpower dominance. It could not recognize, therefore, that the money of any state had any "automatic or privileged value in relation to gold, which is, which remains, which ought to remain . . . the sole real standard." [29] By the close of 1965, French franc diplomacy, drawing principally on European support, implanted the need for reform on the international monetary agenda. (The United States did not object so long as liquidity topped the list.) The French campaign also increased and magnified doubts about American optimism regarding the end of dollar deficits and the importance of finding new sources of international liquidity. Finally, the Group of Ten, not the IMF, was charged with the study of these problems.[30]

For a time, the French position appeared to be gaining ground. The German government, with greater dollar balances than its EEC partners, proposed a plan to compromise the Franco-American conflict. The Federal Republic, like France, favored the creation of new reserves by a restrained group, not the entire membership of the IMF. Voting would be partly by majority, partly by unanimity. New reserves, while not derived from gold, as the French would have liked, would be tied to the metal in its utilization. In July 1966, the Group of Ten, seeming to side with the French, affirmed the adequacy of international liquidity and the desirability of regulating the American balance of payments before creating new liquidity. If the French had had their way, no new forms of international liquidity would have been used to finance the deficits of reserve states.[31]

Those reserves that might be created, suggested the French, were to be the product of joint decision of that "group of major states with a key role in the functioning of the international monetary system." [32] Attempting to block discussion of international liquidity, France de-

28. *Ibid.*, pp. 209–210.
29. De Gaulle, *Discours*, IV, 384.
30. Wolff, *Revue de science financière*, 1968, pp. 782–829.
31. *Ibid.*, Jan.–March 1969, pp. 5–76.
32. *FFP*, 1966, p. 102.

murred on those propositions calling for a study of the problem and continued meetings on the subject.[33] France's decision to remain partially isolated within the Group of Ten seemed to be justified a few months later when a joint communiqué of the Six, issued shortly before the IMF conference in September 1966, adopted language paralleling French recommendations: (1) the end of balance-of-payments deficits was to be the precondition of new international liquidity; (2) industrial states, and especially the EEC countries, had special responsibility for determining new reserves if they were to be created at all; and (3) an increase in liquidity was, whatever the United States might argue to the contrary, no answer to Third World economic needs.[34] These were to be met by assured purchases and higher world prices for primary commodities.[35]

By January 1967, as franc diplomacy seemed to be making headway, French hesitancy to recommend openly an increase in the price of gold slackened. Finance Minister Michel Debré, who had replaced Giscard d'Estaing, suggested study of an increase in the price of gold as an alternative to Anglo-American proposals for monetary change.[36] But the French preferred an attack strategy to a blocking posture. The question of the price of gold was to be subordinated, too, to the development of "a comprehensive world financial policy" that would define the "mechanism and volume of international credit, remuneration of the central banks' foreign currency holdings [dollar, gold, or other acceptable reserves], settlement of international debts, even an increase in the European quotas, that is, their gold payments to the IMF." [37]

On January 17, Debré formally advocated at a meeting of the Six that a study be initiated to revise IMF quotas for member states. It was a move aimed at increasing European voting power. Previous French insistence that the Group of Ten be the center for monetary reform was tempered. If the IMF could be revised along the new line in French thinking, it would better serve France's interests than the smaller body which was increasingly spurning French overtures.

33. *Ibid.*, pp. 102–103.
34. Wolff, *Revue de science financière*, Jan.–March 1969, pp. 20–27.
35. *FFP*, 1966, pp. 38–39.
36. *Ibid.*, Jan.–June 1967, p. 7.
37. *Ibid.*, p. 8.

Within the IMF, France would assume the leadership of the European states and reinforce its hold on franc zone countries. Thus, the reform of the monetary system was added to preceding French conditions for reserve creation—the formal pronouncement by monetary authorities of a penury of reserves and the end of American deficits. The United States would pay a high price for more international liquidity. On still another front, Michel Debré, citing the end of exchange controls in France in January 1967, heralded Paris as a new international monetary and financial center. A year earlier, he had created the Banque de Paris, with $6 billion in deposits, the largest in Europe.[38]

Throughout 1967, the French continued to score what later proved to be paper victories in their campaign to increase the importance of the franc in Western financial circles. In meetings of the Six in the first seven months of 1967, particularly at the Hague in January and Munich in April, French negotiators could take passing comfort from the fact that their preconditions were receiving increased notice. The potential veto right of the Six on new reserve creations was firmly established. Sentiment outside the United States seemed inclined toward treating such "reserves" as credit facilities, not money. While automatic among participants, restrictions would be placed on their transferability, reimbursability, duration of issue, and volume. Reserve states in deficit were to be obliged to balance their accounts before drawing rights would be extended to them, according to their IMF quotas, but not before there was common accord that a shortage of global liquidity existed. Finally, these drawing rights would be linked to gold in some fashion.[39]

Responding to Washington's insistence, however, France's European partners, while sharing many of its doubts about the monetary system and American liquidity preferences, felt obliged to examine American proposals. France found itself making concessions on an issue which it did not even wish to recognize as valid. It could be encouraged, nonetheless, by the outcome of the Group of Ten meeting in July 1967, where American negotiators accepted the term "Special Drawing Rights" (SDR) rather than "reserve instrument." The

38. *Ibid.*, pp. 72–74; also Paul Ferris, *Money Men in Europe* (New York: Macmillan, 1968), pp. 103–125, for a review of Debré's policies.
39. Wolff, *Revue de science financière*, Jan.–March 1969, pp. 5–76.

preferred European term permitted the French to consider the new monetary facility as a credit extended by one state to another rather than as an acceptable international currency as good as gold. Also, a reconstituted IMF would be the framework for the creation of SDR's.

The IMF meeting at Rio de Janeiro in September 1967 approved an Outline for SDR's. Through artful and ambiguous diplomatic language, Franco-American differences were papered over. Each state could leave the conference firm in the belief that its position had been accepted. The Outline envisioned a closed payments system between participating central banks. As a concession to French sentiment, a member state of the IMF was not obliged to participate. Allocations were to be made by a majority vote of 85 percent. The EEC states, with 17 percent of the IMF vote, would, if united, have enough strength to block the creation or expansion of SDR balances. SDR's were to be created in proportion to IMF quotas already existing. Their use was to be restricted to balance of payments or total reserve needs, both very liberally defined. A state was obliged to accept SDR's in the amount of three times its accumulated allocation, say, $300 million if it were eligible for a drawing of $100 million. A state using the new right was expected to stay within 70 percent of its "average net cumulative allocation." In other words, the funds were technically reimbursable, as a credit might be, only up to 30 percent of a state's over-all average drawing. What constituted an overdraft, however, was difficult to define.

While complicated rules governed transferability of SDR's, they were flexible enough to permit a state, for example Belgium, to use its SDR's in transactions with another state, like Italy, for dollars or other mutually acceptable currencies than lira. A state might also use its SDR's to buy its own currency. The United States could use its SDR's to buy dollars to protect its gold supply and to sterilize excess and potentially unstable dollar balances. Finally, SDR's were defined in terms of a fixed amount of gold that, not accidentally, corresponded to the value of the dollar at $35 an ounce.[40]

As long as the SDR's appeared to be a credit (that would have to

40. Machlup, *Remaking the International Monetary System*, contains an extended discussion of the SDR scheme.

be paid back), and not an international currency, Gaullist France could consent to the Rio Outline. But the United States persisted in its view that the SDR's were new money. They would be an addition to American reserves that other states would, by common consent, be obliged to accept like dollars or gold. They could be used, as financial analysts explained, as a sponge to absorb dollars that might threaten the American gold supply. The dollar remained officially convertible into gold although the United States had reached understandings in the late 1960's with some central banks to slow down the conversion rate and to maintain higher dollar balances over gold than they might have wished. Despite the subtle verbal distinctions of the Outline, the American view prevailed. The SDR, as one international authority concluded, was an "international money accepted by the participating monetary authorities in payment for various convertible national currencies." [41] Unlike previous international accords, including the Bretton Woods agreement, the plan identified no central source or "debtor" whose liabilities were the reserve assets of national monetary authorities. The willingness of participating states to accept SDR's was the basis for confidence in the new financial instrument. Notwithstanding its "funny money" rules of use, it constituted a liquid asset available to any state. States were required to make their currencies available to others on demand, restricted only by the rules agreed upon by the participating states.[42]

Cutting the Tie between Gold and the Dollar

Even as a third form of international currency was being created, confidence in the dollar and the monetary system was gravely shaken in the rush of dollar holders to redeem them into gold in the period between November 1967 and March 1968. The immediate cause of the gold rush was the British devaluation of November 1967, which threw an increased burden on the dollar and accentuated the instability of the international monetary system, resting on the theoretical equality of dollars and gold. (SDR's were first added in 1970.) Immediately after the pound devaluation, the open gold market centered in London came under heavy pressure. The seven active mem-

41. *Ibid.*, p. 34.
42. *Ibid.*, pp. 33–34.

bers of the gold pool, formed in 1961, sold gold on the market to keep its price from rising above $35 an ounce.[43] The cost of keeping the dollar-gold relation stable was estimated at $1.6 billion for 1967.[44] In four weeks, American gold reserves were depleted by $900 million.[45]

The gold drain continued despite these efforts. A second, more serious rush developed in March 1968. Between December 1967 and March 1968, the United States lost $2.4 billion in gold and its over-all stocks diminished to $10.7 billion.[46] The price of gold rose at one point to $50 an ounce.[47] To end the lesion, the London gold exchange was again temporarily closed. Gold pool members agreed in Washington to stop selling gold to the private market. They would transfer gold only among themselves and at the official price of $35 an ounce. In the open market, outside the "club," the price of gold would be determined by supply and demand among speculators, industrial users, hoarders, or whoever else might wish to enter the market. In sum, gold would be traded on two markets.[48]

France's interpretation of the pound and dollar crises conformed to its perception of the international monetary system. It was the occasion for renewed French calls for reform. On the one hand, the French government answered Anglo-American criticism that its Cassandra-like predictions and its alleged failure to assist both currencies were major causes for the lack of confidence in the two reserve currencies. The French countered erroneous reports that they had failed to contribute to the $1.4 billion IMF loan as well as to the $3 billion in central bank grants accorded the United Kingdom in late 1967 to bolster the pound.[49] Nor was it true that France used Algerian funds to redeem dollars for gold, although newspaper accusations

43. The active members were the United States, Britain, Germany, Netherlands, Belgium, Switzerland, and Italy.

44. Volcouve, *op. cit.*, p. 77, and *Problèmes économiques*, No. 1067 (Aug. 1968), pp. 8–11.

45. Machlup, *Remaking the International Monetary System*, p. 105.

46. *Ibid.*, p. 106.

47. Volcouve, *op. cit.*, p. 80.

48. Kindleberger, *Power and Money*, pp. 220–223.

49. Volcouve, *op. cit.*, pp. 69–70; *FFP*, July–Dec. 1967, p. 131. Even the usually authoritative *L'Année politique* reported that the French government had failed to cooperate with the central banks' loan to Britain, *L'Année politique, 1967*, pp. 247–249.

were psychologically and economically destabilizing for monetary transactions before they were proved false.[50] On March 15, 1968, in the midst of one of the most concentrated speculative attacks on the dollar, Finance Minister Michel Debré granted an interview in which he stressed the steps taken by France to support international monetary stability. France had accelerated its debt payments to the United States in the early 1960's, maintained low interest rates to discourage capital flights, and actually purchased gold from the United States after August 1966 to meet its balance-of-payments commitments. The long-standing French criticism of American policies was also noted to demonstrate that France was taking advantage of a crisis to press its case for reform.[51]

On the other hand, the Gaullist regime stepped up its attack on the dollar and pound by a number of concrete moves. In May 1967, when there were increasing signs of British economic trade difficulties, President de Gaulle cited the uncertainty surrounding the pound and its reserve responsibilities as additional obstacles to British entry into the Common Market.[52] Foreign Minister Couve de Murville reaffirmed these criticisms in a policy statement before the National Assembly on November 7.[53] At his November 22 news conference, President de Gaulle, going beyond EEC recommendations, drew evidence from the pound's devaluation and Britain's special request for additional loans to justify his second veto of negotiations with Britain over its application to join the EEC.[54] In the same address, French technological achievements were lauded while United States economic progress in pioneer technological industries was deemed attributable by the French president, "not so much to the organic superiority of the United States as to the dollar inflation that it is exporting to others under the cover of the gold exchange standard. It is rather remarkable that the total of annual deficits in the American balance of payments over the past eight years is exactly the total of American in-

50. See Root, *American Scholar,* 1968, pp. 469–481. Interviews in Paris, January–May 1971, confirmed the view that the Bank of France was not responsible for the Algerian sale.

51. *FFP*, Jan.–June 1968, pp. 47–48.

52. *Ibid.,* Jan.–June 1967, p. 68.

53. *Ibid.,* July–Dec. 1967, pp. 104–106.

54. *Ibid.,* p. 141.

vestments in the countries of Western Europe." [55] The French used
the OECD conference of November 30 once more to parade their
case against using national currencies as international reserves. Un-
derstandably, they were not sympathetic to the American argument,
heard with increasing frequency thereafter, that surplus states had a
responsibility along with debtors for international equilibrium.[56]

In February 1968, Michel Debré broadened the attack. "In no
way," he said, "should a national currency be substituted for gold
because that would result in imposing on the world the consequences
and risks of a national monetary policy." [57] Meanwhile, France kept
its gold exchange open during the six-month gold rush. Added to the
dollar's burdens was the public disclosure during the November crisis
that France had withdrawn from the gold pool the previous June.[58]
Debré's observation that Canada, Sweden, and Japan had also
dropped out of the pool was a debator's point,[59] more logically than
politically satisfying to American policymakers. They felt confronted
with yet another example of France's mischievous moves to undermine confidence in the dollar. The French departure also had the
effect of increasing the American contribution to the gold pool from
50 to 59 percent.

President de Gaulle used the March 20 meeting of his Council of
Ministers to intensify the war of nerves. The statement is worth quoting in its entirety because it marks, first, a departure from the usual
form of such Council pronouncements that rarely attribute personal
views directly and, second, because it affords a glimpse of the colored
French perception of the monetary crisis and of the seemingly impending demise of the dollar and pound. The monetary system arising
out of World War II appeared to be bankrupt, and the hegemony of
the dollar, supported by an uncertain pound, seemed to be at its end:

55. *Ibid.*, p. 135.
56. *Ibid.*, pp. 146–148.
57. Wolff, *Revue de science financière*, April–June 1969, p. 228.
58. Interviews, Paris, January–May 1971, support the thesis that *Le Monde*
financial expert, Paul Fabra, discovered, through his own enterprise and in-
genuity, rather than through official French channels, that France was no longer
participating in the gold pool. See also John Hess, *The Case for De Gaulle*
(New York: Morrow, 1968), p. 44.
59. *FFP*, Jan.–June 1968, p. 48.

The life of the world at present calls for a growing economic activity and, consequently, ever widening trade. It therefore requires an international monetary system worthy of the world's confidence.

Now, the crisis of the dollar and the pound that is currently developing illustrates that the present system, based on privileged reserve currencies, is not only inequitable but from now on inapplicable. To seek to impose it any longer would be to condemn the world to serious economic and social trials.

A monetary system based on gold which alone is immutable, impartial and universal must therefore be implemented. This reform would naturally include an organization of international credit consistent with the far-reaching, mobile and rapid nature of trade in our times.

It goes without saying that a real and complete righting of the American and British balance of payments would be desirable in any case. France is ready to take part in such an international monetary renovation and hopes to see the European Economic Community play its rightful role in it. Meanwhile, France reserves her freedom of action with respect to any arrangement that would tend to delay the renovation.[60]

On March 30, France and the franc zone states demurred on key points of the Group of Ten's communiqué at Stockholm that approved the Rio Outline. And while the IMF was publicly presenting the new SDR plan on April 22, Michel Debré was concluding a franc zone conference in Paris that affirmed the French rejection of the Stockholm agreement.[61] To these counterdollar moves must be added the refusal of France at the March 25 conference of EEC finance ministers to accept German suggestions that the implementation of Kennedy Round tariff accords be accelerated to ease United States balance-of-payments deficits.[62]

The Collapse of the Franc Offensive: The Fourth Phase

Paris saw the dollar doomed as well as its free convertibility into gold. The decision to create two gold markets confirmed the French analysis. For the French the SDR proposal was reduced to an ineffective palliative to repair a shattered system and fortify what appeared to be the already rapidly deteriorating dollar and pound. The Gaullist regime was blinded by its own hopes for the franc. It took the May

60. *Ibid.*, p. 50.
61. *Ibid.*, p. 75.
62. *Ibid.*, pp. 53–54.

events in France to bring home the lesson that the dollar had scored a victory on the issue of SDR's and, more importantly, in the duel with gold.

The French made a capital political miscalculation based on a plausible economic assumption drawn from the unfortunate experience of the European states with paper currencies and rampant inflation:[63] that in the struggle between gold and the dollar, gold would win. France's policy of holding large gold reserves at the expense of internal economic growth was partly based on its confidence in gold. When forced to choose between the two international monies, France's European partners chose to support the dollar and the existing monetary system, whatever the uncertainties surrounding the dollar's future and the American economy. France's gold standard proposals responded neither to the commercial nor to the capital needs of other states.[64] Nor did they take account of Europe's dependency on the dollar or, particularly in the case of Germany, on American security guarantees. These levers were decisive in the dollar-franc conflict.

The French overestimated the influence of the franc to challenge the dollar and underestimated European fears that France's example, if followed, would pose too risky a threat to monetary and economic stability. As suspect as they might be, there was no readily available alternative to American monetary and military assurances. None of the European states shared France's confidence in its solutions, nor were they prepared to accept French leadership in matters of national solvency and security, as the EEC crisis of 1965–1966 and the NATO crisis of 1966 demonstrated. It was also becoming clearer, at least to economic analysts, that after the summer of 1966 the franc, not the dollar, was the more vulnerable currency. Indeed, Finance Minister Michel Debré had hedged his fight against the dollar in relaxing his predecessor's restrictions on the entry of American capital into France. Debré encouraged the entry of foreign capital to stimulate economic growth, create jobs, and offset France's declining trade losses. French industry increasingly found itself priced out of world markets. Unable to rely either on its economic base for support or on its potential allies in Europe, French diplomacy lost the "gold war"

63. *New York Times,* Feb. 23, 1965, p. 17.
64. Interviews, Paris, January–May 1971.

even before the May events revealed the shaky foundation on which the French monetary offensive rested.

The May events triggered an economic and financial crisis in France that opened the fourth phase of franc diplomacy. The first casualty of the spring upheaval was the franc. At the beginning of May 1968, the Bank of France held $7 billion in gold and foreign currency reserves. The serious disruption in French production for most of May and June, followed by the normal vacation slowdown in July and August, seriously damaged France's commercial position, already under strain for almost two years. Between May 1 and July 4, French reserves dropped $1.8 billion.[65] Foreign competitors replaced French firms unable to fill orders. Rising labor costs as a result of the Grenelle accords to end national strikes set a pattern that cut profit margins and decreased further the competitiveness of French exports. Adding to these trade losses was the normal propensity of importers to accelerate payments for goods and for exporters to do the reverse as a hedge against a possible devaluation. Most significant was the flight of private capital, seeking haven in dollars and especially German marks. France's social turmoil, receding commercial balances and reserves, and government proposals to increase the tax on inheritance and excess profits contributed to the panic. At least part of the $600 million purchase of stocks by holders of francs in 1968 on the New York stock market was motivated by a desire to find protection against these adverse trends.[66] By the close of 1968, French balance-of-payments deficits soared to more than $3 billion, the highest figure since World War II.[67]

To halt the rise in foreign deficits, France instituted selected import quotas and advanced aid to exporters. These actions, while contravening France's obligations to remove all remaining barriers to the creation of a full customs union on July 1, 1968, presented the EEC with a *fait accompli* that could not be easily repudiated. A $400 million cutback in government spending, even for such favored programs as nuclear weapons and missile development, was made. November nuclear tests in the Pacific were canceled and fewer funds were allocated to the nuclear submarine program. On May 30, the French govern-

65. *L'Année politique, 1968,* p. 263.
66. Volcouve, *op. cit.,* p. 86.
67. *L'Année politique, 1968,* p. 263.

ment established exchange controls. Approximately a month later the Bank of France increased the discount rate from 3.5 percent, set in 1965, to 5 percent in order to brake the movement of capital out of the country, to slow down speculation, and to encourage foreign investors to leave or increase their deposits.[68] A $1.3 billion swap was negotiated between France and European central banks and the Federal Reserve of New York. France marshaled its IMF credits of $985 million and asked to be relieved of its share of $230 million of the $1.4 billion loan made to Britain in the wash of the pound crisis less than a year before. To hold the line on the franc, requiring large sales of gold, the government rejoined the gold pool and accepted the March rules largely set down by the United States. French ministers still insisted, with lessening credibility, that France's monetary views had not changed.[69] Doctrinal revision would catch up later with modifications in France's behavior.

Losses in reserves continued to mount through the summer into the fall. In July, reserves fell $666.8 million, approximately $250 million each in August and September, about $135 million in October, only to decline steeply again in November by $280 million.[70] Gold sold in Paris 12 percent higher and French currency 10 percent lower in value than abroad. Foreign stocks on the Paris Bourse jumped 12 to 15 percent in worth.[71] Successive increases in interest rates which normally would have slowed the flight of capital abroad ended by fanning fears of an imminent devaluation. Trust in the French government's ability to protect the franc was shaken. The unfortunate conjuncture of a general rise in world interest rates also contributed to undo French moves. At the height of the November crisis, interest rates in the open market climbed to 9 percent.[72]

The franc, moreover, became a foil to the German mark. As confidence in the franc declined, rumors grew that the mark would be revalued upward. Speculators thus had a dual incentive: to rid themselves of doubtful currency in order to acquire a strong one—and at a

68. Kindleberger, *Power and Money*, p. 222.
69. On French official policy, see *PEF*, 1968, pp. 95, 134, 172–173; *Le Monde*, Nov. 21, 1968, p. 1, reviews the budget cuts.
70. Volcouve, *op. cit.*, p. 14.
71. *L'Année politique, 1968*, p. 177.
72. Volcouve, *op. cit.*, p. 21.

profit. The assurances of the French president on November 13 and his prime minister a week later that the franc would not be devalued fell on deaf ears. A devaluation which, according to President de Gaulle, "would be the worst of absurdities" appeared inevitable.[73] The French government faulted an undervalued mark, not an over-valued franc, as the immediate cause of the crisis. The Gaullist leadership was being forced to employ, not without some irony and perhaps personal embarrassment, the American argument that surplus states had a greater responsibility for international equilibrium than debtors because of their wealth. Being thrust into the role of *demandeur* also had its unsettling effects, not the least of which was the bad diplomatic form it struck.

The hastily called meeting of the finance ministers of the Group of Ten held in Bonn on November 20 failed to extricate the French from their predicament. The Bonn government would not go beyond its earlier decision to tax exports by 4 percent and relieve charges on imports by a similar amount. This action had the effect of a hidden re-evaluation. The ruling German coalition of Christian Democrats and Socialists under Chancellor Kurt Kiesinger did assume the largest share—$600 million—of the $2 billion in credit extended by the Group of Ten to France to buttress its reserve position. Bonn also blocked short-term capital received by private banks and instituted authorization procedures on new foreign commercial accounts.[74] But it would not revalue.

Pressures from industrialists, worried about the loss of markets, and farmers, concerned about lower revenues, weighed heavily on the co-alition government in Bonn. The Christian Democrats, facing presidential and legislative elections in March and September 1969, respectively, were sensitive to these groups on which their support rested. The change in American administrations assured that pressures from Washington on the Bonn regime to revalue would be weak. The problem would be part of a larger package of negotiation with the new Nixon government that would also necessarily deal with American security guarantees, all the more important after the Russian invasion of Czechoslovakia in August 1968. The German government had

73. *PEF*, July–Dec. 1968, pp. 172–173, 273.
74. *Ibid.*, p. 26.

ample reason, despite the strong French demand for a mark re-evaluation, to await the devaluation of the franc. But political grace seemed absent when it was most needed in Germany's novel assertion of its economic and political power. At the close of the Group of Ten meeting, German Finance Minister Joseph Strauss, not his French counterpart, told reporters that a devaluation of the franc was imminent; only its "modalities" were "left to the discretion of the French government." [75]

The French president answered the German challenge in a brief communiqué on November 23, stating briefly that the parity of the franc would be maintained.[76] On national television the next day, President de Gaulle explained his actions in the face of growing speculation: production was increasing along with exports and French access to its own reserves and foreign credits exceeded $7 billion. Devaluation would also require greater austerity and credit losses.[77] A few days later, exchange controls were reinstituted.

The Johnson administration eased the French government's resignation to American financial dependence. Minimum public notice was taken of the dollar's support of the franc. Messages of encouragement were quietly dispatched during the financial crisis, including a personal cable from President Johnson congratulating the French president on his stand to hold the franc at parity. The halting of bombing on North Vietnam and the request to establish peace negotiations in Paris, begun in May 1968, nursed a cordiality that might otherwise have been absent from the normalization of relations between the two states forced as much by domestic unrest in both countries as by the conscious desire of the two governments.

The irritations over German defiance were not so easily assuaged. Bonn's offer of credits and trade controls, while positive gestures, were not sufficient to quell French fears that Germany's assertion of its own economic interests forewarned of future demonstrations of German political independence. For the first time since World War II, Germany had refused to comply with a French demand on an issue of capital importance that touched the stability of the French

75. *Ibid.*
76. *Ibid.*, p. 177.
77. *Ibid.*, pp. 179–180.

government and the personal authority and prestige of the French president. Germany had passed from passive partner to alliance broker between Paris and Washington, and then to national state, with its own interests to preserve and promote. Anxieties over a revived Germany, capable of exerting weighty economic and diplomatic influence in the service of German national goals, were, by his own accounting, uppermost in President de Gaulle's thinking in his last months in office.[78] It was characteristic of de Gaulle to have focused on the external political implications of French monetary policy and to have depreciated their internal economic effects despite widespread social and political unrest in France.

French Monetary Policy under Pompidou: "More Now"

Uninterrupted upheaval in the international monetary system, with the erosion of the Bretton Woods system of fixed parities after 1968, makes comparison difficult between the monetary policies of the de Gaulle and Pompidou administrations. The problems faced and the responses given by each were shaped by different internal economic and political considerations. If these basic dissimilarities are kept in mind, some provisional contrasts can be discerned.

First, under Pompidou, French monetary policy placed greater importance on domestic economic goals than on foreign policy objectives. Rapid economic growth and a larger, if not always more equitable, distribution of economic benefits to a greater number of the working population were viewed as prerequisites of government policy to avoid a recurrence of the May events.[79] The Pompidou Sixth Plan focused on a growth rate of approximately 6 percent a year, full employment, higher productivity through plant modernization and more efficient use of labor (excess farm labor was to be diverted to industrialization), checks on inflation, and increased trade competitiveness for French products abroad. These immediate, and not fully compatible, economic goals (full employment and inflationary controls) were not so alien to de Gaulle's calculations—witness the stabilization

78. See the final interview of C. L. Sulzberger with President de Gaulle of February 1969, although first published November 11, 1970, at the time of de Gaulle's death, in *Herald Tribune,* International edition, pp. 1, 4.

79. See Chapter 8 below for a more extensive discussion of the orientation of the Pompidou administration to foreign policy.

programs of the late 1950's and early 1960's—as they were subordinated in the final years of his regime to foreign policy priorities. Conditioned by experience, as a former banker, to what de Gaulle dismissed as "quartermaster" concerns, Pompidou was more alert than his predecessor to the weaknesses of the French economy. Having fashioned the electoral strategies for the Gaullist party in the 1967 and 1968 legislative elections, he was also more mindful than the waning de Gaulle of the economic requirements of social and political stability. The pursuit of French power and prestige abroad were perceived as functions of a strong domestic economy resting on a stable internal order. The institutions of the Fifth Republic and the fate of the Pompidou regime, after the trauma of 1968 had passed, were tied to these objectives.

Second, French dependence on its European allies and on the United States was acknowledged. Pompidou assumed that exterior alignments in monetary affairs, as in other nonsecurity areas, must preserve and promote France's internal economic development. For de Gaulle, domestic welfare was important for what weight it afforded in advancing France's international stature. Holding the franc line was intrinsic to the politics of independence, but this policy made increasingly less economic sense after the challenge to the franc in fall 1968. Reserve losses mounted to an average rate of $300 million per quarter in the first half of 1969.[80] The newly installed Pompidou government devalued the franc 12.5 percent on August 8. Easing France's economic plight further was the upward revaluation of the mark shortly thereafter by 9.3 percent, one of the first decisions of the newly elected Brandt regime. The Pompidou government acted to bolster its ties with France's principal financial and trading partners. France joined the SDR scheme and requested an enlargement of its IMF quota from $985 million to $1.5 billion. By these moves French Finance Minister Giscard d'Estaing, while still holding gold to be the proper basis for monetary transactions, acceded to a *fait accompli* (the SDR) and strengthened France's voice in IMF affairs (the end of the empty chair).[81] Meanwhile, the Pompidou government prepared for the Paris summit, opening the way to completion of the

80. *L'Année politique, 1969*, p. 130.
81. *Ibid.*, p. 138. *PEF*, July–Dec. 1969, pp. 87–92.

financial regulation of agriculture and of the final phase of the Common Market among the Six.

In his February 1970 visit to the United States, President Pompidou conceded the primacy of the dollar: "At the present time, by a certain number of decisions, of measures adopted within the framework of the [Group of] Ten or within the framework of the International Monetary Fund or directly with South Africa,[82] the Government of the United States has organized a system in which gold has ceased to be the reference of the international monetary system and in which, in fact, the dollar has replaced gold." For the first time, a French president publicly recognized the dollar as "the basis of the international monetary system." [83]

Third, the Pompidou administration chose to work within the international monetary system and to extract what benefits it offered rather than to press for monetary reform, as such, or to use the issue as an instrument to discipline or embarrass the United States for political purposes. De Gaulle had opted to an appreciable degree for the latter objectives. Monetary reform was another way to weaken the dollar's role in international relations. Gains for France were measured by the perceived erosion of the dollar's international prestige and the diminishing influence of the United States in world affairs. Of lesser importance to the de Gaulle government were the material rewards to be drawn from selective and self-interested cooperation with the dollar (an unpalatable client role) or from striking the necessary compromises with France's European partners to organize a competitive front against the dollar. The de Gaulle regime placed itself in the curious position of having correctly identified the shaky foundations of the international monetary system, resting on a weakening dollar, only to have failed to draw much benefit from its prescience.

Protecting the franc from outside pressures and promoting its competitive position in foreign markets were the Pompidou government's immediate monetary objectives. Its posture in the international debate

82. *L'Année politique, 1969,* p. 135.

83. The statements of President Pompidou during his trip to the United States are grouped in Comité Interministériel pour l'Information, *Visite officielle du président de la république aux etats-unis,* May 1970, pp. 7–8.

over monetary reform, given impetus by the end of dollar convertibility in August 1971, was dictated more by these specific aims than
by a desire to transform world politics, partially through a restructuring of interstate monetary relations. Opportunities for short-run
gain were valued over long-run benefits whose realization depended
on a reform of the monetary process, but whose final outcome could
not be predicted with accuracy. A low-risk policy yielding small, but
sure, profits was judged a better investment than the high-risk monetary enterprises preferred by the de Gaulle government. Neither the
dubious prestige of France's monetary isolation nor the psychic comfort of grudging acknowledgment by European capitals that de
Gaulle's criticisms of the dollar's infirmities were telling could by
themselves do much to strengthen the franc. In contrast to his predecessor, President Pompidou preferred to exploit economic rather than
psychic and diplomatic opportunities to advance the conjunctural
needs of the French economy and the franc either by cooperating
(and compromising differences) with the United States and with
France's European partners or by playing them off against each other.
For Pompidou, the final test of a reform proposal (and the utility
of different monetary alignments) was the marginal gain that ac-
crued to France. To be sure this was Gaullist orthodoxy, but a principle recognized more in the breach than in the observance during de
Gaulle's final years. The Pompidou government traded off Gaullist
grand designs in world politics—whose systemic impact was not without effect—for tangible material benefits. Paris under Pompidou
wanted "more now."

Until January 1974, when the franc was floated, French monetary
policy revolved around several principles. These amounted more to a
set of tools useful in interstate monetary bargaining on France's behalf than to a comprehensive formula for reform. Fixed parities between currencies, to be revalued only under multilateral auspices—
preferably through a strengthened IMF—were central to the Pompidou brief. Wider margins between currencies could be tolerated, but
only as a concession to American political and economic weight, and
not as an application of what the French purported to believe was
sound economic dogma. The base of the system was to be tied in some
way to gold. Increasing the price of gold and reinstituting, however

provisionally or partially, dollar convertibility, were set pieces of the French case.[84]

The importance attached by French officials to one or the other of these components varied roughly with the position adopted by the United States in monetary negotiations and the sentiments of its European colleagues. The French posture was essentially defensive. The United States, not France or the other European states, set the agenda for discussion. The French tended to move in muted counterpoint to the recommendations issuing from Washington and Bonn. Gaullist criticisms of American policies were reiterated, but more to chide Washington to adopt self-disciplinary measures to bring American balance of payments into equilibrium than to challenge the dollar as the West's principal currency and, indeed, the pivot around which the franc turned. Not surprisingly, French criticisms responded to the relative fortunes of the franc and the dollar. As the former strengthened and the latter weakened, French criticisms tended to rise. By late 1970, when the French economy was entering one of the most dramatic periods of expansion in this century, French complaints about the laxity of American domestic controls grew.[85] At the OECD meeting in December 1970, President Pompidou charged that American deficits were a major cause of world inflation and were endangering France's effort to stabilize prices, which increased by more than 5 percent in 1970.[86]

While France was moving to bolster its position within the Bretton Woods system, United States officials were advancing increasingly more pervasive proposals to modify it. By February 1973, with the second devaluation of the dollar, American thinking within the Treasury (if not the Federal Reserve) had evolved to a point that was close to a total abandonment of the postwar monetary system. The double market for gold, created in 1968, had slowed, but did not entirely arrest, the steady loss of American gold reserves (and was abandoned by fall 1973). Continued balance-of-payments problems,

84. For representative samplings of the French case, see the following citations covering statements of Finance Minister Giscard d'Estaing and President Pompidou: *PEF,* July–Dec. 1970, pp. 70–74, 131–132; and especially *ibid.,* July–Dec. 1971, pp. 115–120.

85. Interviews, Paris and Brussels, 1971–1972.

86. *L'Année politique, 1970,* pp. 161–162.

affecting both goods and services and short-term capital flows, made the prospect of renewed dollar convertibility increasingly tenuous. The decreasing competitiveness of American goods in world markets, partly attributable to the dollar's overvaluation, were a high price to pay for the dollar's reserve role in international monetary transactions.

The Nixon administration struggled to manage a number of contradictory pressures: to preserve the dollar's centrality, to maximize American economic maneuverability—free of multilateral controls— and yet to shift a larger burden of the monetary system to Europe's (and Japan's) shoulders. The Bretton Woods system no longer served these conflicting purposes. Proposals to widen margins between currencies gave way gradually to bolder suggestions in favor of flexible rates—ideas long current in academic circles.[87] The market would decide the dollar's relative value. Subtle daily shifts in exchange parities would replace the crude guesses taken by monetary authorities under crisis conditions to accurately peg currencies. Successive, unpredictable, up-and-down revaluations of the West's major currencies from the late 1960's onward provided Washington with accumulating evidence of the sluggish responsiveness of the fixed-rate system to rapidly changing market conditions and to the relative shifts in the dollar's value to other currencies, especially the mark and the yen. Under flexible exchanges, moreover, speculators would run greater risks in pressuring a weak currency. Market interventions by state central banks to keep currencies within agreed margins would be rendered superfluous. Avoided, therefore, would be the hundreds of millions of dollars in losses suffered, for example, by the central banks of Japan and Germany, which spent their reserves in vain attempts to maintain their undervalued currencies in the open market.[88]

The vacillating French position on gold and SDR's illustrated the cautious stance of the Pompidou administration in responding to United States proposals for changes in monetary practices. It appeared

87. The following works are pertinent: Milton Friedman, *Essays in Positive Economics* (Chicago: University of Chicago Press, 1953), especially Part II, pp. 117–273; Egon Sohmen, *Flexible Exchange Rates* (Chicago: University of Chicago Press, 1961); Milton Friedman and Walter Heller, *Monetary vs. Fiscal Policy* (New York: W. W. Norton, 1969).

88. The Bundesbank reportedly lost $600 million in early 1973 in making dollar purchases. *International Currency Review*, V (Jan.–Feb. 1973), 64.

calibrated more to improve French standing in Washington and in European financial centers than to effect a major change in interstate monetary relations. The critical questions were how much support could any proposal for change generate for the franc or, negatively, how much insulation would be provided to protect the French economy from the adverse effects of dollar dominance, European competitiveness, or the periodic disruptions of money markets by sudden speculative flows. Qualifications gradually crept into hitherto unreserved French support for gold as the *numéraire* of the international system. In step with evolving majority sentiment among the Western financial powers, Giscard d'Estaing tempered the French view of gold. In his September 1972 address to the International Monetary Fund Board of Governors the French minister backed away from an exclusive gold standard—a respectful bow to international thinking and American influence—while reaffirming, on grounds of principle, that gold was still the best impartial indicator of value. A year later at the IMF meeting in Nairobi, the French, fearing speculation against the franc that would be adverse to their commercial interests, moved closer to the American position in demoting gold's role in the reserves of states and as the basis for international transactions. President Pompidou's explanation for the shift reveals the sensitivity of his administration to the franc's weakness and the need for Atlantic and European support to maintain its competitive position:

It is evident that . . . reserves ought to comprise . . . other things than money. . . . *I do not believe that it can be only gold.* I do not believe so for theoretical reasons. . . . I do not believe so either for practical reasons because there are a certain number of important countries [the United States] which will not accept it, and consequently we do not have any chance, even if we wished, to impose it because, I repeat, we cannot isolate ourselves monetarily. It is too easy for a money like the franc to be vulnerable, and we do not wish to be so, and we do not wish to be subject to attacks. . . . We have seen it in 1968. We could see it again. . . . We well know that a money . . . like the franc is fragile and that, consequently, it must be part of a grouping accepted by everyone.[89]

89. *Le Monde,* Sept. 29, 1973, p. 3. Emphasis added. Giscard d'Estaing's remarks are found in IMF, Board of Governors, *Statement of Hon. Valéry Giscard d'Estaing,* Press Release No. 36, Sept. 27, 1972, p. 6.

This flexibility in striking a balance between the ideal and possible in international negotiations was a characteristic of the French approach to monetary policy under Pompidou's direction. Gold was not to be completely abandoned, but France was prepared to swell the trend toward gold's demonetization when such a shift appeared politic.

Similarly, Paris switched to a strong defense of the SDR as a model in defining a new international monetary system. Whereas France had initially opposed this American initiative to the point of de Gaulle's application of a partial empty chair tactic to the IMF, the unilateral American protective moves announced by President Nixon in August 1971 prompted a renewed French interest in SDR's. They had the virtue of having been created through multilateral procedures within the IMF. Carrying conditions for their issuance and use, they afforded some modest means to discipline heavy users, like the United States. In pushing SDR's in the late 1960's, the United States under the Johnson administration acknowledged American responsibility for reaching international monetary decisions within a multilateral setting. It was Gaullist France, ironically, which demurred although, as a weaker power, it had incentive to bind the United States to legal obligations favoring its and Europe's economic position.

As the Nixon administration acted with increasing regularity before consulting the European states on its monetary moves—the August 15, 1971, announcement being only the most dramatic, not the sole, instance—SDR's assumed a new importance, ultimately to replace the dollar as the principal international currency.[90] They represented one of the few international sanctioned means to combat the Nixon administration's inclination to define American monetary practices more by internal standards—domestic prices, jobs, and income—than by the claims of other states. Secretary of the Treasury John Connally, doubtless aiming part of his remarks at a home audience, also put foreign capitals on notice of a change in American financial thinking: "No longer can considerations of friendship or need or capacity justify the United States carrying so heavy a share of the common burdens. And, to be perfectly frank, no longer will the American people permit

90. Interviews, Paris, Brussels, and Washington, 1971–1972. See also observations of President Pompidou and d'Estaing, respectively, in Le Monde, Sept. 29, 1973, p. 1, and Oct. 4, 1973, pp. 44–45.

their Government to engage in international actions in which the true long-run interests of the United States are not just as clearly recognized as those of the nations with which we deal." [91] Connally's successor, George Shultz, was equally firm in defending American interest rates against European pressures to increase them. National needs would be the controlling factor in interest rate determination.[92]

French temporizings on gold and SDR's were calculated to salvage, not sink, the Bretton Woods system. After the successive crises of 1968, the Pompidou regime resisted any rapid change in an international monetary environment to which it had keyed its domestic objectives. Economic expansion and political stability were stressed. Until 1973 this inclination translated itself into a vested interest in maintaining the essential features of the postwar system and, specifically, in preserving France's generally favorable exchange-rate position vis-à-vis other currencies. There was also the Common Market's agricultural program whose smooth functioning would be facilitated by fixed exchange rates. A favorable parity position, tied to a fixed, if flexibly defined, exchange system, was relied upon to stimulate French economic growth, raise the level and encourage a more equitable distribution of national income, reduce unemployment, and, as a political by-product, foster Gaullist party rule. These economic indicators were measures of the regime's political health.

Supporting the objective of European monetary and economic union also marked a significant departure from Gaullist practice. The Pompidou administration moved in this direction for several reasons. The franc's enfeeblement during the crisis of fall 1968 made urgent the need for greater and easier access to external reserves to support France's monetary position. The franc's international standing was intimately related to the policies of France's European and Atlantic partners; Gaullist pronouncements could not stem the loss of confidence in the franc nor stay the tide of speculation mounted against it.

Second, European monetary union promised to buttress the common agricultural policy. Tying Germany more closely to monetary cooperation, presumably in French terms, would reinforce the agri-

91. John B. Connally, "Mutual Responsibility for Maintaining a Stable Monetary System," *Department of State Bulletin*, LXV (July 12, 1971), 42–46. See also Connally's statements in the *New York Times*, Sept. 15, 1971, p. 1.
92. *Le Monde*, Sélection hebdomadaire, March 15–21, 1973, p. 8.

cultural program threatened by floating currencies. Encouraging British participation in European monetary union would likely loosen its ties with the United States while binding it to the Brussels agricultural support system. These were critical aspects of the Pompidou administration's strategy to strengthen the EEC as an extension of French economic and political influence.

Third, a common European stance on monetary policy, much like the successful cooperative effort organized during the Kennedy Round trade negotiations in the late 1960's, was a potentially formidable lever over United States monetary behavior.[93] The SDR negotiations, even in the face of France's reluctance to join its European partners, led to a strong European voice in IMF affairs, a result accepted by the United States more with resignation than enthusiasm.

Progress toward European monetary and economic union was modest in the first four years of Pompidou government. The summit meeting of December 1969 authorized forward movement.[94] The consent dovetailed with the French interest in the common agricultural policy; the financial regulation for agriculture was the most important outcome of the meeting.[95] Monetary harmony was requisite for the effective implementation of the Common Market's agricultural program that depended as much on its financial arrangements as on production and marketing controls for its success.[96] The EEC committee authorized by the summit and headed by Luxembourg Prime Minister Pierre Werner reported its recommendations in fall 1970.[97]

93. Even the friends on Atlantic monetary cooperation concede the increased stature of the European states in monetary and economic bargaining with the United States; see Cleveland, *Atlantic Idea,* pp. 65–95.

94. *PEF,* July–Dec. 1969, pp. 137–139.

95. See below, Chapter 8, pp. 405–406.

96. Pierre Uri, *The Future of European Agriculture* (Paris: Atlantic Institute, n.d.).

97. The "Barre Report" of February 12, 1969, prompted the summit go-ahead on union. EEC, *Commission Memorandum to the Council on the Co-ordination of Economic Policies and Monetary Co-operation within the Community,* Supplement to Bulletin No. 3, 1969. The principal findings of the Werner Committee appear in EEC, *Interim Report on the Establishment by Stages of Economic and Monetary Union;* "Werner Report," Supplement to Bulletin No. 7, 1970. The Commission's response is found in EEC, Commission, *Memorandum and Proposals to the Council on the Establishment by Stages of Economic and Monetary Union,* October 30, 1970.

These subsequently assumed the form, after amendment by the member states, of an EEC resolution adopted by the Council of Ministers on March 22, 1971.[98] The meeting of President Pompidou and Chancellor Brandt in January 1971, to compromise the serious differences of approach and interest toward union of France and Germany, paved the way to the Council accord.[99]

The EEC agreement of March 1971 is not easy to summarize. It was less a plan for monetary and economic union than a partial list of some modest steps toward union on which accord could be reached. Theoretical coherence and completeness were sacrificed for a provisional accord—not without relevance for domestic political consumption—that held open the hope of wider agreement in the future as experience in working together accumulated. The mutual obligations assumed by the contracting parties were minimal. The Six agreed to a phased evolution toward economic and monetary union over a ten-year span, beginning January 1, 1971. In the first phase (1971–1973), several joint actions were contemplated. First, cooperation between central banks was to be reinforced. They were invited to coordinate their monetary and credit policies and to write guidelines for determining bank liquidity, credit allocations, and interest rates. Second, procedures were established to coordinate short-term economic policies. The Council of Ministers was to meet three times a year on the community's economic situation and to adopt quantitative measures to direct short-term economic policies. These were to assist the development of common approaches among the member states toward incomes, credit, and investment policies. Third, the Council created machinery for medium-term financial aid to help members in balance-of-payments difficulties with an initial subscription of $2 billion. Conditions were defined for the partial or total reimbursement, transfer, and mobilization of debts. At German insistence a so-called "prudence clause" was adopted. It permitted abandonment of the monetary accord, particularly its binding financial commitments, after five years if sufficient progress toward union had not been reached after

98. *PEF,* Jan.–June 1971, pp. 94–95. The text of the resolution, while written in early 1971, was not formally approved until March 22.

99. *Le Monde,* Jan. 27, 1971, pp. 1, 5; *Gazette de Lausanne,* Jan. 27, 1971, p. 1F.; and *Journal de Genève,* Jan. 25, 28, 1971.

three years to warrant moving to the second phase. Each state would effectively decide what constituted adequate progress.[100]

The Council resolution of March 21, 1972, expanded upon these accords. Common Market countries, with Britain, Ireland, and Denmark participating, pledged themselves to reduce the maximum margin between the official exchange rates of EEC currencies to 2.25 by July 1, 1972. The Group of Ten agreement at the Smithsonian Institution in December 1971 permitted fluctuations between the dollar and other currencies up to 4.5 percent before intervention was to be required. The European margins would form a so-called "snake in the tunnel" within the IMF agreed-upon limits. A coordinating committee was organized to bring together the views of already established committees concerned with monetary affairs, including the short-term economic policy, the monetary, and the budgetary policy committees. Some gesture was made to insulate the Common Market states from destabilizing capital flows. Government and banking authorities were to be granted power to regulate some investments, commercial transactions, reserve requirements, and the lending discretion of credit institutions. Deadlines for reports from the EEC Commission and the enlarging constellation of committees were also set.[101]

These efforts were nudged forward at the October 1972 European summit held under the instigation of the Pompidou regime. A European Monetary Fund was to be established by April 1973 under central bank direction, to concert action on narrowing margin fluctuations, to expand convertibility of European currencies, to agree on a European unit of account (previously defined in terms of the dollar's official weight in gold), and to facilitate short-term monetary support among member states. Pledges for parallel progress in economic cooperation were again taken to appease German and Dutch sentiment. Finally, principles that were to inform international monetary reform were set out: "fixed but adjustable parities; the general convertibility of currencies; effective international regulation of the world supply of liquidities; a reduction in the role of national currencies as reserve instruments; the effective and equitable functioning of the adjustment

100. European Community Press Release, Sept. 25, 1971, provides a useful summary of the monetary accord.
101. European Community Press Release No. 9, March 29, 1972.

process; equal rights and duties for all participants in the system; the need to lessen the unstabilizing efforts of short-term capital movements; [and] the taking into account of the interests of the developing countries." [102]

What was perhaps most striking about these efforts toward cooperation was their tenuous effect on the actual evolution of the international monetary system since the Hague summit of 1969. The March 1971 accord, representing over a year of deliberations and bargaining among the Six, fell apart less than three months later when Germany floated the mark in May to stem a massive inflow of speculative capital. Vigorous French and commission objections proved unavailing. French Finance Minister Giscard d'Estaing rejected the proposal of his German counterpart, Karl Schiller, for a joint float. The Pompidou regime favored the Commission plan, largely inspired by Raymond Barre, the French vice-president of the EEC, to place controls on short-term capital and to establish a double market for commercial and financial transactions.[103] The breakdown of the hurried EEC conference to deal with the May crisis on a common basis led to piecemeal measures taken by each state to protect itself against such exterior pressures and rising inflation. The joint communiqué acknowledged the disarray.[104]

Further confusion was thrown into the European monetary camp when President Nixon ended dollar convertibility and placed a 10 percent surtax on foreign imports in August 1971. The reaction of the European states was mixed. The Pompidou government called for a European summit to discuss what common measures to take to meet the monetary crisis.[105] Meanwhile, Paris created a double market for dollars. Commercial transactions continued to be based on the rate of approximately 5.5 francs to the dollar. Financial transactions, including long-term investment and tourism, were to be carried out at the floating rate for the dollar. Bonn remained committed to a floating mark.

102. Ambassade de France, Service de Presse et d'Information, *European Summit Conference*, Oct. 21, 1972, pp. 3–5.

103. Interviews, Brussels, May 1971.

104. *PEF*, Jan.–June 1971, pp. 159, 161–162, and remarks of Giscard d'Estaing, pp. 162–167.

105. *Ibid.*, July–Dec. 1971, pp. 76–77.

If the European Nine opposed the United States surtax, they differed on their approach to lowering EEC tariff barriers to facilitate United States trade with Europe and the Third World. Germany, still preoccupied with its security and *Ostpolitik,* was open to trade concessions for the United States on which its foreign policy goals still significantly hinged. France turned a deaf ear to such appeals.

At the Smithsonian meeting to redefine parities among Western currencies, the European states were unable to organize a common front in bargaining with the United States. American monetary diplomacy, guided by the not always gentle or experienced hands of Treasury Secretary John Connally, played on the incentives of cooperating with the United States and on the internal divisions of the Europeans themselves. Hints were dropped that the surtax might be modified in Germany's favor because Bonn, unlike its partners, was cooperative.[106] On France's behalf, President Nixon met with President Pompidou in the Azores to announce the impending devaluation of the dollar. The prestige showered on the French to be the first to know publicly of the United States decision was paid in kind by President Pompidou's consent to trade talks between the Common Market and the United States.[107] At the Washington meeting, each of the European states worked to maintain its relative position to the dollar and to its partners' currencies. One observer remarked that "in the run up to the Smithsonian realignment it . . . looked as though the French were primarily interested in negotiating against the Germans rather than against the Americans and the Japanese."[108]

The European states experienced continued difficulties in 1972 in harnessing their collective power to influence the evolution of the international monetary system. In June, Britain abandoned the March 1972 agreement to narrow margins and floated the pound. Italy selectively applied Common Market rules, departing from their letter when its interests might otherwise be adversely affected. Denmark abandoned the "snake" altogether. The European states soon discovered that the $2 billion in short-term credits established under the March 1971 accord was too small to prevent, or ride out, a major

106. *Ibid.*
107. *Ibid.*, pp. 279–283.
108. Ian Davidson, "Monetary Union: The Emperor's Clothes," *International Currency Review,* IV (July–Aug. 1972), 29.

speculative wave. The Europeans stopped far short of pooling their exchange reserves. Meanwhile, speculations were fueled by a Eurodollar market estimated at approximately $70 billion in 1972. During the week preceding the pound's flotation, $2.6 billion flowed out of London.[109] The mark (and dollar) crisis of early 1973 was of such a magnitude that the Europeans were helpless, with the tools at hand, to stem the flow of speculative capital. The resulting common float of six of the nine EEC states (France, Germany, Denmark, and the Benelux), and the separate floats of Ireland, Britain, and Italy, were crude measures of how far the Nine had still to go before the faint outline of monetary and economic union would be seen. (Norway and Sweden also joined the common float.)

Why was progress toward monetary and economic union so slow and halting? Why was its impact on the evolution of the international monetary system so irregular and inconclusive? A full answer to these questions would require a discussion of the economic and monetary policies of each European state, a task that goes beyond the terms of this analysis. Understanding how French monetary diplomacy bore on the others may perhaps clarify the situation.

As noted already, the critical factors influencing the Pompidou administration's monetary policies, and its interest in pursuing European union, were its dedication to domestic economic growth and full employment. Economic doctrine (to float or not to float) or political ideology (to increase or decrease France's participation in the European community) were less ends in themselves, than handy tools to assist France's economic expansion and to realize the anticipated benefits of rapid economic growth—a higher standard of living, more jobs, and widening social and political stability.[110] In the mind of the Minister of the Economy and Finance [Giscard d'Estaing], as one observer of French monetary policy noted, "the principle of French monetary policy is neither the gold standard, . . . nor fixed parities, nor the dollar standard . . . but . . . the 'standard' of [economic] growth and full employment." [111]

The tergiversations of French behavior toward European economic and monetary union and the changes in France's monetary position

109. *Ibid.,* p. 27.
110. "The French Franc," *ibid.,* IV (March–April 1972), 45.
111. *Le Monde,* Sélection hebdomadaire, March 15–22, 1973, p. 8.

were largely explicable in terms of the Pompidou regime's domestic economic objectives. European economic and monetary union would have to be French-inspired, responsive to interests defined by Paris. Strengthening European monetary cooperation, the principal substantive thrust of the Pompidou government's triptych of "completion, enlargement, and strengthening" for the European community,[112] would have to conform to French needs and perspectives.

Gaullist strictures against exterior international controls could not be fully discounted, of course, as factors conditioning French behavior. The Pompidou regime successfully resisted German demands for stronger community institutions to regulate national economic and monetary policies. As long as the franc was weak, the French economy fragile, and domestic political and social life susceptible to abrupt and unpredictable upheaval on the model of 1968, Bonn sought some way to minimize its financial obligations to defend other European currencies, like the franc, with its own reserves and to exercise some influence over the national policies of its EEC partners. The "prudence clause" of the March 1971 Council of Ministers was the necessary *quid pro quo* to reassure Germany. In bending to French opposition to institutionalized Common Market monetary controls, to be administered in Brussels, it would not be giving a blank check to Paris to underwrite the franc.

On the other hand, the Pompidou regime placed itself in the seemingly paradoxical position of resisting community institutional controls over French monetary practices while pressing for stronger "community" authority to deal with the dollar crisis and the rapid dissolution of the old international monetary system. Proposals to control foreign capital and develop a double market, recommendations compatible with the impressive government controls over the French economy, countered German hopes, linked to more liberal economic doctrine than French thinking, for a common European float against third currencies. If the measures proposed by France were applied at the community level, they would have tended to short-circuit the Brussels bureaucracy, except for technical assistance, in favor of increased coordination among central banking institutions. Their work would have been tied closely to that of the Council of Ministers. A

112. These points are elaborated in Chapter 8.

common community policy would in reality have been the product of parallel actions taken by the cooperating states rather than of concerted action taken by community officials.

The economic debate between France and Germany over which should come first—monetary or economic union—was similarly viewed in French circles in pragmatic terms. French preference for confining the first steps toward union largely to monetary coordination contrasted with the German focus on harmonizing the economic and budgetary policies of the European states from which monetary union was seen to derive as a logical consequence. Pompidou's France had no appetite for involved haggling over the merits of national and community economic controls versus a free market or over the virtues of coordinating national economic activities versus developing community institutions to be invested with adequate authority to direct national policies toward commonly defined ends. Paris opposed any notion of community institutions that might interfere with the unhindered pursuit of its domestic economic aims. A strengthened institutional framework at the community level might foster European union, but, conceivably, at the expense of French economic prosperity and political independence. There was also the unstated fear—understood, but never publicly mentioned—that stronger community institutions, given German economic strength, would inevitably come under Bonn's influence.[113]

Whatever the number and solemnity of Paris' pronouncements in favor of European monetary union, the Pompidou government preferred often to strike an advantageous bargain with the United States without the intervening influence of its European partners. Pursuing a double strategy, Pompidou's France looked to its European partners or to the United States for benefits; and it searched relentlessly for whatever bargaining levers were available to play one side of the Atlantic off against the other for its advantage. Despite its show of support for a West European monetary grouping to balance the dollar's influence and to achieve some measure of European independence, the Pompidou government adopted monetary and investment policies that tied the franc to the dollar's fate. Between the franc devaluation of August 1971 and the decision to float of March 1973,

113. Interviews, Brussels and Paris, September 1972.

the Pompidou regime followed a strategy alternately of soliciting United States support for its position while seeking means, national and European, either to minimize the adverse effects of unilateral American behavior or to gain some influence over American economic decisions. The parallel with French military policy, discussed in Chapter 3, was obvious. Until the franc regained its strength, policies favoring fixed parities, commitments to multilateral decision-making within the IMF, a double market for the franc, and community controls over speculative capital were aimed at advancing France's trade position. The Elysée and the editors of *Humanité* shared the same interest in keeping French products competitive. As a close student of French monetary diplomacy observed: "The sole concern which inspired the [French] chief of state . . . appeared to be that of re-affirming at any cost the penetration of French exports and to do nothing which might . . . favor imports to the detriment of national production . . . : no revaluation of the franc through floating exchanges . . . because such a move could place [full] employment in peril and increase the pressure of foreign competition in French markets." [114] Considerations of parity advantage led the Pompidou regime to tie the franc to the dollar by creating a double market for the franc. The commercial market was keyed to the official rate of 5.5 francs to the dollar. Government pronouncements justifying the double market as a way of escaping American dominance barely hid the umbilical cord uniting the two currencies. Paris had no wish to give too great a trade advantage to the United States (or its other partners) or to permit market forces to push the franc to levels that would decrease the competitiveness of French goods in world trade. At the Smithsonian meeting, France had to accept, like its partners, the roughly 8 percent devaluation of the dollar. (Its call for an increase in the price of gold amounted to much the same outcome.) [115] France was, nevertheless, notably more successful in maintaining the franc's parity to the dollar than were its European partners in preserving the parities of their currencies to the American standard. How well the franc has fared relative to the mark in holding its peg to the dollar was suggested by the fact that the franc increased in value about

114. *Le Monde,* Sélection hebdomadaire, March 15–22, 1973, p. 8.
115. *International Currency Review,* IV (Jan.–Feb. 1972), pp. 28–29.

17 percent from its devaluation in August 1969, while the mark increased 43 percent in the same period.[116] The franc revaluation after the Smithsonian meeting was less than the weighted average of the revaluations of the other European states. The significance of this advantage perhaps can be better appreciated if it is remembered that 38 percent of France's trade was with its European partners. Toward the mark, the franc was slightly devalued, gaining a further advantage for French exports to Germany, its principal trading partner.

The French decision to join the European float of March 1973 can also be understood in light of the conjunctural needs of the franc and the French economy in early 1973. By late 1972, the franc had temporarily become one of the strongest currencies in the West. Since 1970, French balance of payments were in surplus, rising to approximately $700 million in 1972. The French economy was expanding at a rate of over 5 percent a year, faster than any other Western state, and even Japan. Productivity increases reached a dramatic 8 percent in 1971 within a stable labor force. This rise offset average wage increases of 11 percent. Export prices, while up 2.7 percent in 1971, were still below the 6 percent increase in the consumer index and the 6 to 8 percent increase in import prices.[117]

The vigor of French monetary diplomacy in pressing, and largely achieving, a favorable exchange rate position, was a crucial part of the French government's strategy to improve France's export position and, in turn, to increase the size and rate of growth of its GNP. By early 1973, however, when still another dollar crisis erupted, France could no longer plead franc weakness and expect other states to carry the dollar burden. Incentives were at play to make a franc float a reasonable course despite the political and psychological inconveniences in having to do a public about-face.

If France had stood alone and the other European states had floated —Britain had been floating since June 1972—it risked becoming the next target for speculative flows. France's double market, while useful

116. *Le Monde,* Sélection hebdomadaire, March 15–22, 1973, p. 8, has a useful table displaying the fluctuating values of principal European currencies to the dollar between 1967 and March 1973.

117. The issues of the *International Currency Review,* published every two months, should be consulted. Each issue contains a useful sketch of the French economy's doings and prospects as well as a health report on the franc.

during the early climb to stability, was beginning to hemorrhage badly. In 1972, the Bank of France had to absorb $1.5 billion. The failure of the Left to win the March 1973 legislative elections, the relative docility of French labor unions since 1968, and the anti-inflationary campaigns of August and December 1972 reinforced foreign confidence in the franc.

Second, in floating the franc, French officials were able to bring their announced and operational monetary policies—ostensibly aimed at European independence from the United States—into closer harmony. With some paradoxical truth, they could plausibly argue that, through floating, they enhanced the freedom of maneuver of the franc and other European currencies relative to the dollar. Before March 1973, this claim had a hollow ring that did not escape the notice of government critics.[118] In adopting American proposals to float the franc, Paris was relieved of supporting the dollar, and Washington was spared another formal devaluation if its guess of a 10 percent reduction in the dollar's value was proved wrong by market forces.

Third, the utility of hanging on to fixed parities in support of French trade was reaching a point of diminishing returns. Other factors, like galloping inflation, were becoming more a barrier to expanded trade than was a change in exchange rates.

Fourth, Bonn's 3 percent upward revaluation of the mark in March made the franc float easier since French products became more attractive on the German market. The float was "dirty" enough—six of the Common Market Nine floated jointly—to provide some protection for the administration of the common agricultural program. The six jointly floating currencies were to stay within a margin of 2.25 percent of each other. United States willingness to assist the support of the dollar further assured Paris about floating the franc. These included Washington's acceptance of larger swap arrangements and expanded controls on Euro-dollars, agreement to slow the end of restrictions on long-term capital until American trade balances improved, and consent to study ways to consolidate the American debt.

Pressures on the franc in late 1973 prompted further departures from the Pompidou administration's announced commitments to fixed

118. See the trenchant analyses of Paul Fabra and Philippe Simonnot in *Le Monde*, Sélection hebdomadaire, March 15–22, 1973, p. 8.

exchange rates and to European monetary union as central elements of international monetary reform. A trade deficit estimated at $4 billion in 1973 induced the Paris regime on January 19, 1974, to float the franc free of the European joint float. The aim of this *de facto* devaluation was to stem speculation, gain temporary trade advantages, and protect French reserves, which were being depleted at a rate of $50 million a day to keep the franc within the 2.25 percent margin of the European "snake." The franc, whose value had reached a high of 3.18 francs to the dollar in summer 1973, fell to 5.45 in the wake of the float. The dramatic turnabout in France's economic fortunes arose principally from the Arab oil embargo of fall 1973. The price of oil quadrupled, accelerating the downward trend in France's previously favorable balance of trade.[119]

The franc float dramatized the flexibility and pragmatism of French monetary diplomacy under the Pompidou government. Consistency in objectives, not policies, was the guiding principle. The float of January 1974 was tantamount to an abandonment of preceding Pompidou regime pronouncements on international monetary policy. It moved France closer to the American view of floating exchange rates, threw the role of the International Monetary Fund further into question, and diminished the prospects of European economic and monetary cooperation spearheaded by the French as late as December 1973 at the EEC summit conference in Copenhagen. French Finance Minister Giscard d'Estaing's characterization of the six-month float as a "parenthesis" in French support for European monetary union did little to hide the principal priorities guiding the shifting twists and turns of French monetary policy. Neither economic doctrine nor reformist sentiment was permitted to hinder achievement of the regime's domestic economic goals, centering on trade, employment, and growth. Even the common agricultural program would have to be adjusted to the changing imperatives of the French economy and the political needs of the Paris government.

The Pompidou regime, no less than its predecessor, recognized

119. Background discussion of the French float may be found in Paul Fabra's article in *Le Monde*, Sélection hebdomadaire, Jan. 17–23, 1974, p. 1. See also the following issues of the *New York Times*: Jan. 21, 1974, pp. 1, 18; Jan. 21, 1974, pp. 37–38; Jan. 22, 1974, pp. 1, 51; Jan. 23, 1974, pp. 45, 50; and Jan. 24, 1974, p. 45.

France's economic dependence on its European and Atlantic partners, but it was more resourceful and less bothered by economic or political orthodoxy in pursuing its domestic economic goals. In floating the franc, as in insisting before on cooperation among major currency nations and on fixed rates, the object was to maximize France's advantage and maneuverability within a framework of interdependence. France's unilateral moves were taken with some calibrated expectation of the likely response of France's commercial and monetary associates. In asserting an independent monetary course, reminiscent of de Gaulle's refusal to devalue the franc in fall 1968, the Pompidou government was attempting to define an acceptable level of interdependence. There was a parallel between France's security and monetary policies: in remaining outside NATO, France still relied on American military protection; in breaking with its European partners on monetary coordination, it counted on them to provide outlets for its products and to support its agricultural program. Whether France's economic health in the long run could be preserved in the absence of a basic reform of the international monetary system, including European monetary cooperation, was a question gone begging in Pompidou's France.

PART II

FRENCH INTERNATIONAL POLICY IN EUROPE: WEST AND EAST

5
Rebuilding Western Europe in the Gaullist Image

Europe and the International System

"Rightly to be great," Charles de Gaulle once wrote, quoting Hamlet, "is not to stir without great argument." [1] De Gaulle's quarrels with the superpowers easily and often assumed these dramatic proportions. His unflagging criticisms and attacks were consistent, too, with the succeeding line of Hamlet's soliloquy, counseling "quarrel in a straw, when honour is at the stake." For, in resisting the United States and the Soviet Union, the expression of Gaullist defiance was often of greater importance than the issue in question. But, if an unexpected and eloquently pronounced "No" caught public notice, it held little promise of significantly influencing the outcome of the superpower struggle. Being an impediment and making a purposeful impact were distinguishable effects. France's intervention might inspire other states to follow its example without necessarily adopting its prescriptions for a reconstituted international system in which France would enjoy enhanced status and say. Increased diversity and deviation would probably complicate more than dissolve Soviet-American domination of international relations. There was also the double and conflicting risk either of destabilizing global conflict relations past the point of great power management or of merely isolating France in its singularity.

There was perhaps some psychic compensation for Gaullist France in remaining apart, and hence different, or in manipulating the risks run by the superpowers in their attempt to maintain their hegemonic positions. Gaullist strategic and foreign policy, as French nuclear strategy suggested, was willing to run both dangers if gains for French influence and prestige could be achieved. But neither isolation, however splendid, nor the role of the sorcerer's apprentice were substi-

1. De Gaulle, *Edge of the Sword*, p. 1.

tutes for original, or, through pliable allies, derivative power formidable enough to impress France's will on global politics and to set in motion the construction of a more stable and legitimate order within which it would play a leading part. Indispensable to this larger design, as de Gaulle outlined, was a strong national French state, resting on a solvent economy, enlarging industrial capacity, and advancing technology; moreover, France's resources would have to be subject to the will of its chief executive who alone would be the guarantor of the state's independence and the principal architect of its quest for *grandeur*.[2] Second, given France's modest size, even if modernization should succeed it would still need the assistance of other states sharing its vision of a new international order. Under French leadership, these states would be formed into new groups or *ensembles* that would enhance France's power and reflect its *grandeur*. The formation of such a global equilibrium within which the European states would enjoy a central position became an imperative of Gaullist foreign policy.

De Gaulle and his close collaborators identified four loosely defined *ensembles* or groups of states that would compose the principal parts of a transformed global equilibrium of power to incorporate and go beyond the Soviet-American duopoly. First, there were the states under United States influence in the Americas and in the Atlantic area, particularly Canada and Great Britain. Gaullist efforts to change the internal balance of power of this grouping in France's favor through the directorate scheme had proved abortive by 1959. Containing this *ensemble* from without rather than transforming it from within became the recommended course for most of the Gaullist years.

The second component of a multipolar state system was Western Europe. In various formulations of this grouping, the peoples of the Rhine, Alps, and Pyrenees were almost invariably mentioned. Sometimes Britain and the states of the Mediterranean, principally Greece, were included. The kernel was usually defined as the little Europe of the Common Market.[3] The critical axis was Paris and Bonn around which the Benelux states and Italy were expected to revolve. Later

2. *Major Addresses*, p. 73.
3. De Gaulle, *Discours*, IV, 4–5.

Spain and perhaps Portugal would be added as their authoritarian regimes evolved along Western liberal lines. The neutralist states of Austria, Switzerland, and even Communist Yugoslavia, at the outer peripheries of West and East Europe, would also be gradually drawn to the Western *ensemble*.[4]

Great Britain's membership, while not excluded out of hand, depended finally on its accepting the conditions laid down in Paris. Not only were France's primacy and interests within the European community to be acknowledged, but Britain's "special relation" with the United States, particularly in nuclear and monetary policy, would have to be terminated. Otherwise, the Anglo-American weight was estimated to be too great to resist either by France or by a French-led Western Europe. France's attack on American economic security and diplomatic policies were to be the guiding signals for West European unity. Europe would define itself in resistance to the American colossus.[5]

An independent Europe would serve three systemic purposes. First, an economically strong and politically cohesive Western Europe was the precondition for the revision of, and eventual European disengagement from, the Atlantic system under American domination. During the transition from dependence to independence, especially in security affairs, the American nuclear guarantee would be retained as an expedient. The de Gaulle government dismissed the argument, voiced in opposition circles, that the American security pledge might be withdrawn if Europe (and France) advanced independent interests and policies too rapidly which were in basic conflict with Washington.[6] According to Gaullist reasoning, the United States had little alternative other than to provide a nuclear umbrella since it could ill afford the loss of Western Europe to the Soviet Union. "American troops . . . in Germany," as one very highly placed Gaullist official observed, "are not there to please the Germans, but are part of the American Cold War strategy." [7] "To contribute to building Western Europe into a political, economic, cultural and human group,

4. Lord Gladwyn, *Europe after de Gaulle* (New York: Taplinger, 1969), pp. 32, 52–54.
5. This is the message of John Newhouse, *De Gaulle and the Anglo-Saxons*.
6. Raymond Aron, *Great Debate, passim.*
7. Interview, Paris, May 1971.

organized for action, progress and defense," as de Gaulle announced on May 31, 1960, "[was] what France wanted to work toward." [8] France's *grandeur* would then be transformed into Europe's glory:

But if the Atlantic Alliance is necessary at present for the security of France and of the other free peoples of our continent, they must, behind this shield, organize to achieve their joint power and development. . . . Neither the Rhine, nor the Low Countries, nor the Alps, nor the Pyrenees, nor the English Channel, nor the Mediterranean, for which they fought so long and so bitterly, any longer set them one against the other. . . . The nostalgia inspired in each of these lands by its relative downfall in relation to the great new empires has drawn them closer in the feeling that together they would regain this grandeur for which past centuries had given them the talent and the habit. To this must be added the fact they constitute an incomparable whole, precisely when our time, which abolishes distances and obstacles, demands large ensembles.[9]

Second, Western Europe, once disengaged from the United States and organized under French auspices, could be a counterweight to the East European *ensemble* under Soviet domination and an arbiter between the Washington and Moscow blocs. In his war memoirs, written in the latter 1950's, de Gaulle signaled this second aim of West European union. France would cooperate with the states of the East and West to rebuild its strength while attempting simultaneously to persuade the West European neighbors along the Rhine, the Alps, and the Pyrenees to form a political, economic, and strategic bloc: "to make this organization one of three world powers and, if it be necessary one day, as the arbiter between the Soviet and Anglo-Saxon camps." [10] In this formulation the states of the English Channel and the Mediterranean were not included, but by 1960, at the beginning of France's offensive for European political union, the tendency was

8. *Major Addresses,* p. 78.

9. *Ibid.,* pp. 78–79. In light of Edmond Jouve's painstaking study, *Le Général de Gaulle,* of de Gaulle's understanding of Europe, it may appear presumptuous to be so assertive regarding Gaullist views of Europe. A summary statement of de Gaulle's conception of Europe's role in world politics is presented here for purposes of analysis. Jouve's exhaustive study should be consulted for more thorough examination of the shifts, contradictions, and subtleties of Gaullist prose and political moves.

10. De Gaulle, *Mémoires,* III, 211.

to be inclusive; none would be excluded at the peripheries of the Six unless it excluded itself in refusing France's leadership.

Third, a loose West European grouping under French direction was but a means to the achievement of yet another equilibrium between East and West Europe that would go beyond détente and entente between the two European groupings to cooperation between the individual states across bloc lines. The creation of this *ensemble,* however, was seen more as a distant possibility than an imminent probability. It awaited the dissolution of the Soviet empire. Meanwhile, West and East Europe would remain apart. The process of interweaving the two *ensembles* would begin with the harmonization of French and Russian foreign policies in the Third World and eventually in Europe. The success of this venture would, in the Gaullist analysis, be tantamount to the end of the Cold War. According to the French president, Europe's (and Germany's) division was the product of the superpower confrontation institutionalized in the military structures of the Warsaw and the NATO pacts. A united Western Europe, with its own defense and foreign policy, would be sufficiently independent from Washington to be credible in Moscow. Western Europe appeared potentially powerful enough, too, if united under French direction, to negotiate with the Soviet Union from a position of strength and to attract the East European states, additional leverage that itself could be applied on the Kremlin. Such an independent group would be less threatening to Russia than the Atlantic Alliance under American domination. The hoped-for French-Soviet entente would make Russia a member of the European *ensemble,* not its rival. Germany would be harnessed to a European political framework more responsive to French than American suggestion. Bereft of empire and expansionist aspirations, and, unlike Germany, with no claims on the Soviet Union, France was, for de Gaulle,[11] the logical interlocutor between Western Europe and Russia. Under its auspices, Germany and Russia would conceivably be reconciled. The privileged relation between France and Germany, while retained, would be tied to a larger, more encompassing French-Russian entente. Once France's leadership in Western Europe was assured and a better balance between East and West Europe was

11. *Major Addresses,* p. 44.

achieved, Europe's and Germany's division could be addressed. In French eyes, Russia, not the West, was the court of final appeal on German unification. So long as Germany remained in NATO, it was considered a threat to Russia. Yet it was no answer to free Germany from a multilateral system within which its security could be guaranteed and its national ambitions and energies absorbed. Encouraging neutralist notions in Germany invited West European submission to its giant Slavic neighbor. Soviet leaders were not expected to take very seriously proposals for German unification unless they were assured that Russia would not again be subject to attack from Central Europe. A united Western Europe would substitute an acceptable multilateral framework for the Atlantic arrangement which the French argued was unacceptable to Russian rulers.

The development of cooperative bilateral relations among all European states from the Atlantic to the Urals would be the precondition for the construction of a new North-South balance. A revived relation between industrial and nonindustrial states would thus constitute the fourth component of a new global equilibrium that would be the basis of a world political system which would be viewed as less dangerous and more legitimate to most states of the globe. As de Gaulle explained:

Now, in the last analysis and as always, it is only in equilibrium that the world will find peace. On our old continent, the organization of a western group, at the very least equivalent to that which exists in the east, may one day, without risk to the independence and freedom of each nation and taking into account the probable evolution of political regimes, establish a European entente from the Atlantic to the Urals. Then Europe, no longer split in two by ambitions and ideologies that would become out-of-date, would again be the heart of civilization. The accession to progress of the masses of Asia, Africa and Latin America would certainly be hastened and facilitated. But also, the cohesion of this great and strong European community would lead vast countries in other continents, which are advancing toward power, also to take the way of cooperation, rather than to yield to the temptation of war.[12]

Among the states "advancing toward power" China was central to the Gaullist analysis. With its influence in Asia, China's pressure on

12. *Ibid.,* p. 78, pp. 44–45.

the eastern borders of the Soviet Union would be a compelling reason for Russian willingness to make peace with its Western neighbors.

United Europe: The Gaullist Dream

De Gaulle's opposition to the European communities during the 1950's, including the European Coal and Steel Community (ECSC), the European Defense Community (EDC), the European Economic Community (EEC), and Euratom, worried Europeans devoted to unity. He temporarily laid many, if not all, of these anxieties to rest when in an early news conference, he observed that "France . . . has recognized the necessity of this Western Europe which in former times was the dream of the wise and the ambition of the powerful." [13] But in contrast to the institutional integration sought by Europeans of a federalist persuasion, like Jean Monnet, de Gaulle paradoxically proposed to build European union, not by gradually transcending the nation-state, but by making it the foundation of an expanding confederation of like-minded and interested states.[14] As an abstract goal, union could have no content in the Gaullist exegesis. Its institutionalized forms and announced purposes depended on what meaning the European states, each with its own interests and perspectives, were prepared to attach jointly to the concept. For de Gaulle, the rise of two empires, the Third World, and the subsequent decline of the West European states as the pivot of world politics and human history created the revolutionary conditions that counseled, if not compelled, the West European states to contemplate some kind of unified response. These conditions advised them to subordinate their differences and bury the memories of their historical struggles in the effort to define themselves in relation to the non-European world. The principal reference points were, on the one hand, the United States, Europe's daughter in de Gaulle's condescending and romantic characterization, and the black and yellow races of the underdeveloped world, on the other.[15] Russia, for all its deviationist ideology, authoritarian regime, and expansionist pretentions, remained European and ultimately could be assimilated, de Gaulle felt, within his

13. *Ibid.*, p. 78.
14. Stanley Hoffmann, *Daedalus*, 1966, pp. 862–915.
15. *Major Addresses*, p. 44.

world view. Geography, history, and race tied it to Europe. In the absence of an internal federator after the classic pattern, followed by Prussia in uniting Germany during the nineteenth century, outside pressures would be relied upon to achieve European unity on confederal lines in the twentieth century without the submission of the confederation to any one of its parts, whether Germanic or Slavic in origin.

States were the only realities on which to construct Europe for two, not fully compatible, Gaullist reasons: only a Europe built on states "would be effective for action" and "would be approved by the peoples outside and above the states." Other routes to union, such as the European communities, were dreams.[16] The contradiction noted in Chapter 1 between popular consent and a state's authority, resting on the discharge of its functional responsibilities, principally for security and foreign policy, was now transported to the European level in the debate over unity. Moreover, the titanic conflict between a righteous de Gaulle and a tarnished Vichy government, tacitly but only temporarily supported by a majority of Frenchmen, was reenacted twenty years later on a European stage. Now Gaullist France assumed the role of keeper of international morality and champion of a united Europe capable of resisting both the exterior encroachments of the superpowers and the internally demeaning inclinations of European governments ready to renounce a global role for Europe and, by extension, for France. This self-ennobling stand obscured still another fundamental contradiction, exposed more in Gaullist France's actions than in its words, between the French president's conception of state authority and the refusal of successive Fifth Republic governments either to advance proposals leading to a transfer of the French state's responsibilities for defense or monetary policy or to welcome such a gradual transformation of the functional basis of international authority.

This conflict between thought and action led to still another contradiction. For, if de Gaulle and his supporters professed to believe that the peoples of the several European states, if consulted, would not approve the transfer of state authority to supranational bodies, their conception of state authority implicitly denied that a people

16. *Ibid.*, p. 93.

could assign the defense and exterior obligations of their state to another state or to a supranational body. Even if universal suffrage were instituted to elect a European parliament, as many European federalists hoped, such a body was declared to be intrinsically incompetent to assume the French state's most important functions. The authority of the French state was original and ultimately separate from the people living at any historical period. They might be consulted on the creation of a new constitutional order or on selected questions of high policy (such as Algerian independence) in order to generate popular support, but neither their government nor they could cede the state's principal functions, and hence its authority, to some other agency. Neither could endow such a body with the authority that neither possessed.

Yet Gaullists insisted that the way to European union was through the governments of the member states. Appeal to the European masses was rejected as a mirage. Such a mass body did not exist, historically or politically, despite Marxist doctrine; only differentiated peoples existed, each "with its own spirit, its own history, its own language, its own misfortunes, glories, and ambitions." [17] And these peoples had assigned, seemingly irretrievably, the question of unity to the discharge of their separate governments. "I believe very profoundly," stated Prime Minister Michel Debré, "that the responsibility of Governments to their electorates is that it is very difficult— in international cooperation—for the Government to abandon to independent authorities the power of undertaking work for which in the last resort they are responsible to their countries." [18] The circularity was thus complete. Only states had legitimate political and moral authority to command, and it was not transferable; only the people could confer legitimacy on governmental actions, but they would not be asked.[19]

The charismatic leader again squared these circular arguments. De Gaulle spoke for France "by virtue of the mandate that the people

17. *Ibid.*, pp. 92–93.
18. Quoted in Susanne J. Bodenheimer, *Political Union: A Microcosm of European Politics, 1960–1966* (Leiden: A. W. Sijthoff, 1967), p. 134.
19. See Edward A. Kolodziej, "On De Gaulle and Gaullism," *Review of Politics,* XXXIII (October 1971), 568–572, for a review of some key Gaullist notions of authority

have given me and of the national legitimacy that I have embodied for twenty years." [20] It was inconceivable for de Gaulle to transfer to a supranational body the authority and responsibilities of the French state for which he was charged (and which he personally defined) only to have that European directorship pursue lesser goals than did France. A united Europe would have to assume not only the functions of a national state, but, like France, would have to seek *grandeur* as its natural destiny. The condition for more perfect union was the joining of Europe's and France's objectives. The only union worth having would align the security, diplomatic, economic, cultural, and even technological policies of France and its European neighbors toward third states. The test of union, after the bargaining, negotiating, and compromising were completed, was how well the alignment outcomes promoted France's specific interests, status, and global goals.

Consistent with his understanding of international relations and of France's universal mission, transnational ideals, and national interests, de Gaulle's notion of European unity was defined at any point in time as the residual product of intermeshing bilateral state accords and behavior between European states. In other words, these bilateral agreements, if superimposed on each other, would reveal layers of multilateral alignment that for all practical political purposes would be tantamount to the "state" of European union. European union was therefore an illusive and ambiguous Gaullist term, more easily adapted to propagandistic and ideological purposes than to accurate description.

However elastic and illusive European union may have been in de Gaulle's mind, it had some definable characteristics. On the strength of the Fifth Republic's announced and operational policies, the Gaullist conception of union tended to have the following traits. First, a European political union would be composed of differing groups of states, depending on the harmony of their external perspectives and interests. Second, the multilateral alignments would vary in substantive content, depending on whether economic, security, or diplomatic stakes were involved, yet each set of accords within a policy area would presumably respond to the over-all political needs of the individual cooperating states. Third, the alignment structures would

20. De Gaulle, *Discours,* III, 116

be of varying duration and the union provisionally achieved, while presumably held together by common, irreducible interests, would not necessarily be perpetual, but contingent on responsiveness to these interests and the larger, evolving international and domestic conditions upon which they rested. Fourth, it would be a union of states, not regimes, open to all European states, not just those in Western Europe committed to a liberal political philosophy.[21]

Fifth, it would assume multiple forms. Gaullists placed minimal stress on constructing institutions before foreign policies were harmonized. The French president in his brief campaign in favor of European confederation was aware of the need for procedural mechanisms beyond those available to the individual states or endemic to traditional bilateral diplomacy, but these were neither to be permitted to supersede a state's authority, particularly for those nations invested by circumstance or desire with global responsibilities, nor to hamper its maneuverability toward the achievement of other desired political objectives.

The Gaullist confederation had some properties that were distinguishable from the states comprising it. The confederation, projected in the Fouchet negotiations, would have created a novel legal and political instrumentality in international relations. Withdrawal was not an act to be taken lightly, nor were states outside the grouping to be placed on an equal plane with those within it. Still the confederation would be sensitive to the differences in size, power, will, and aspirations of the participants. Interstate bargaining within the confederation would not so much be suspended as disciplined to the search for a common position among the European states relative to third parties.

Gaullist France reserved the right, however, to decide whether the confederation would be compatible with France's privileged relations with non-European states and special global status. It could not be conceived apart from these pursuits and was ultimately an instrument for their realization. Bilateral ties across *ensemble* lines would neither be excluded, nor necessarily mediated through the confederal structure, nor would a higher value always be placed on them than others that might be struck with outside powers. For a West Euro-

21. William Pickles, "Making Sense of de Gaulle," *International Affairs*, XLII (July 1966), 410–420.

pean confederation would be no blind alley. It would lead to wider political vistas of global dimensions, or be abandoned. As one sensitive Gaullist interpreter has pointed out, de Gaulle preferred a France weakened in its own isolation to a relatively stronger France which, while party to an uneasy union with other European states, was still dependent on one or the other of the superpowers; it would be compromised inevitably in its commitment to a more ambitious future as a global power.[22]

Such flexible notions of union accommodated themselves, more easily than many uninitiated to Gaullist dialectics might have expected, to the existence of the European communities established under the Fourth Republic in the Paris and Rome treaties. The socioeconomic benefits of the communities, particularly the Common Market, were too important to ignore. The EEC, the most important of the three communities, established a Commission whose authority derived directly from the Rome Treaty, and not from the individual states.

The Commission's independent status, in potential conflict with Gaullist preconceptions, facilitated the discharge of three significant community functions. First, the Commission could initiate proposals and act as honest broker for the Six in compromising differences. Second, it could function as the executive organ of the community, implementing policies reached in the Council of Ministers, composed of the permanent representatives of the signatory powers. Third, it could serve as the "watchdog or custodian of the Treaty, entrusted with ensuring that the basic text and all subsequent legislation are correctly observed." [23] The willingness of the member states to make national sacrifices for the sake of commonly enjoyed benefits that none could individually achieve was the so-called community spirit that animated the negotiations of the Six, especially at the inception of the community enterprise. The community method was expressed in the relation between the Commission and the Council of Ministers. An active Commission, endowed with expertise and initiative, was

22. Stanley Hoffmann, "America and France: Minimum Feasible Misunderstanding—I," *New Republic,* April 5, 1969, pp. 7–21, and *ibid.* April 12, 1969, pp. 20–23.
23. Michael Palmer, *et al., European Unity* (London: George Allen and Unwin, 1968), p. 174.

expected to propose to a passive and manipulatable Council of Ministers ways and means of perfecting European economic and political union.[24]

De Gaulle accommodated France to these supranational institutions, as the discussion below reveals, either by emptying or redefining the original meaning and aims of the community charter to suit his views or by disregarding or dismissing as expedient the many instances of day-to-day supranational decision making within the community that Gaullist France tacitly accepted, actively demanded, as in agriculture, or was impelled by its partners to acknowledge.

The Community Alternative to de Gaulle's Political Union[25]

It might be helpful to sketch briefly the doctrinal difficulties experienced by European community supporters—and not without reason—in adjusting to de Gaulle's Europe. The latter threatened to undo not only the personal ambitions and political dreams of the Europeans who had constructed the communities, but the accomplishments that had indeed been achieved. For European federalists, like Jean Monnet and Walter Hallstein, the traditional West European nation-state was obsolete. Exhausted by wars and social and economic upheaval and overtaken by states of continental size, the political structures of middle and small states were incapable, according to the federalist thesis, to assure their traditional goals. Said Walter Hallstein, head of the Common Market Commission: "To yesteryear belongs the political concept of national sovereignty, the idea that the national unit, relying on itself, its own strength and skills, should be the final and the only valid yardstick of the historical process." [26]

24. The best discussion of the early beginning of European political and economic integration within the European communities remains Leon Lindberg, *The Political Dynamics of European Economic Integration* (Stanford: Stanford University Press, 1963).

25. Many comparisons have already been made between the Gaullist and federalist positions. Three useful treatments among many others are J. B. Duroselle, "General de Gaulle's Europe and Jean Monnet's Europe," *World Today*, XXII (Jan. 1966), 1–13; Bodenheimer, *op. cit.*, pp. 28–52, 131–151; David Calleo, *Europe's Future* (New York: Horizon, 1965), pp. 45–133; and John Lambert, *Britain in a Federal Europe* (London: Chatto and Windus, 1968), pp. 113–143.

26. Bodenheimer, *op. cit.*, p. 132.

In contrast to Gaullist doctrine, the European federalists defined the internal development of the European states as the immediate task for union. Foreign and security policy questions could be addressed once progress had been achieved in economic and social policy. The community spirit and method would impel the states forward, almost automatically, toward these responsibilities. Each new accord was seen to carry with itself a "spillover" effect. "Spillover" allegedly resulted when "a given action, [say, a new financial regulation] related to a specific goal [an integrated agricultural policy] creates a situation in which the original goal can be assured only by taking further actions [an increase in the discretionary power of the Commission], which in turn create a further condition and a need for more action" [more sweeping financial regulations and forms of control].[27] Political integration would evolve out of economic union; the supranational institutions of the latter would be the model for the former. The communities would be merged and a single commission would be charged with ever-enlarging political functions and correspondingly invested with greater authority.

The central root of the Gaullist-federalist argument was their radically different understandings of political authority and legitimacy. Whereas de Gaulle rejected the notion that the communities were, or even could be made, competent in security and foreign affairs, many federalists believed that the establishment of a community will, embodied in the Paris and Rome treaties, had already created adequate community authority, even in these sensitive areas of external relations. For the federalist, membership in the economic communities implied more than the granting and gaining of material benefits along the lines of the Organization for Economic Cooperation and Development (OECD) or the General Agreement on Tariffs and Trade (GATT). It carried the obligation to work toward political union through economic integration of all major aspects of national economic life.[28] It was sufficient to justify the absorption of larger state responsibilities as the economic and social relations among the

27. Lindberg, *op. cit.,* p. 10. Lindberg offers the negotiations over the free trade area, the acceleration decision, and the incorporation of agriculture into the Common Market as examples of the "spillover" effect. See text, *passim.*
28. *Ibid., passim.* See also Lindberg's "The European Community as a Political System," *Journal of Common Market Studies,* V (June 1967), 344–387.

Six developed. For Gaullists and federalists, political authority was functionally related, but the former distinguished between economic and social policy—low politics—and defense and foreign affairs—high politics. A state could delegate the first group to a supranational body without compromising itself, and its authority could be reassumed; the latter could not be assigned without threatening the independence and existence of the state.

For the federalists, a definitive delegation of authority had already taken place in the Paris and Rome treaties and could not be reclaimed. Union had been theoretically, if not practically, realized in the creation of a process of decision making tied conceptually to only thinly disguised assumptions of economic determinism. An integrated economic community would grow beyond that of arbiter and broker to absorb the principal responsibilities of the constituent states. It would develop into a single, cohesive political order. The community was understood to have replaced bilateral state relations with a mechanism for joint decision and action. The community method more than the matter of accord was the innovating idea. "European unity is the most important event in the West since the war," wrote Jean Monnet, "not because it is a new great power, but because the new institutional method it introduces is permanently modifying relations between nations and men." [29]

The communities were supposed to circumvent the perils of traditional diplomacy, rooted in national rivalry, search for provisional, short-run gains, and personal ambitions and suspicions. They presumably created a larger consensual base of accord that pledged member states to sacrifice temporary advantage for larger common purposes. For the federalists, Europe was already a reality and only the modalities and timing of its implementation were at issue—essentially technical questions. For de Gaulle and his followers, it was the community of interest and spirit that had still to be created through intergovernmental agreement; the federalists' community "idea" was misconceived in method and aim since it began with assumption of the nation-state's obsolescence. For Gaullists, the community spirit and method were wrong steps in the right direction. They assisted the European states in defining common interests and in coordinating

29. Quoted in Bodenheimer, *op. cit.*, p. 133.

the efforts abroad. But they were not ends in themselves. Power politics among the West European states was disciplined, not transcended, within the community for the sake of internal economic gain and external influence.

It made sense to federalist theorists to stress the problem of institution building within the Six in contrast to Gaullist emphasis on coordinating security and foreign policies toward third states. For them, the development of community institutions was tantamount to European union. It was important that union be democratically based and parallel the parliamentary arrangements already in place in Western Europe. The introduction of universal suffrage in the election of members to the European parliament was logically a high-priority item. It would bind a West European government to a mass base, obliterating national boundaries and language differences. Eventually the European group and a single community executive would pass a single budget for which it would be responsible.

Since parliamentary democracy figured so prominently in the federalist credo, only those states already committed to such a regime could become bona fide members of the community. It was closed on political grounds to fascist regimes as in Spain (the peoples of the Pyrenees) or to military juntas like Greece (the peoples of the Mediterranean). Such a supranational solution to European unity could not easily be made compatible with the East European regimes of the Soviet imperial system. De Gaulle's conception of European unity, less concerned with regime differences and opposed to traditional parliamentary democracy, was consistent with a continental grouping open to all European peoples regardless of their internal political color. External accord was the dominating criterion; French interests and objectives furnished a yardstick for agreement. The harmony between de Gaulle's vision of European unity and his definition of France's foreign policy goals was not accidental. One logically derived from the other.

The Functions of Gaullist European Ideology

The elaborate conceptual edifice erected by de Gaulle to express his view of Europe included functional parts of his foreign and domestic policy, not just the vague intellectual disposition of the French president. Adopting the goal of European union, at least in word,

disarmed or distracted many Europeanists who were initially skeptical about the implications for economic and political integration after
the May 1958 *coup d'état* in France. De Gaulle's seizure of the European banner preserved France's gains under the community treaties,
secured much-needed foreign diplomatic support for the beleaguered
French Government preoccupied with the Algerian War, temporarily
quieted the anxieties of former domestic opponents who were otherwise doubtful of Gaullist motives, and avoided conflicts at a time
when France's power was already taxed to the utmost.

De Gaulle's rhetorical embrace of European union placed him at
the front of powerful political forces already operating on the Continent. His commitment to cooperation responded in the 1950's and
early 1960's to growing concern within all of the European states
over American military and economic policies that threatened alternatively to involve them beyond their means and wishes in Third
World struggles, to dilute the American nuclear guarantee, and to
reduce Europe to economic, technological, and even cultural satel-
lization.

Gaullist ideas of European independence appealed to the psychic
needs and political aspirations of many Europeanists, including many
among the most committed in Jean Monnet's Action Committee for
a United Europe. It offered hope, if little tangible evidence, that unity
could organize over time the will and resources of the separate European states as a substitute for United States military and material
assistance. At least in its earlier formulations under the Fifth Republic, Gaullist proposals for a united Europe were able to command
the attention of nationalists among the Six without alienating supra-
nationalist forces.

The national and universal interests served by Gaullist manipulation of the symbol of European unity can be more analytically than
organically separated. Building Europe first was a worthy objective
for France and the fulfillment of national glory. Just as colonial empire offered an alternative for French energies and imagination after
the defeat of 1870, now Europe would serve a similar role. If French
imperial power balanced German Continental pre-eminence before
and immediately after World War I, so a united Western Europe,
tied closely to an emerging Third World, would offset the superpowers. The resulting equilibrium of the American, European, and

Third World *ensembles* would spell a more lasting and legitimated peace than presently prevailed under Soviet-American auspices. "For, in our time," said de Gaulle, "the only quarrel worthwhile is that of mankind. It is mankind that must be saved, made to live and enabled to advance. . . . We, who live between the Atlantic and the Urals; we, who are Europe, possessing with . . . America the principal sources and resources of civilization; . . . why do we not erect, all together, the fraternal organization which will lend its hand to the others?" [30] Europe was to be compensation for Algeria's loss. "In the twentieth century," as one perceptive interpreter of Gaullist European policy has explained, "the highest expression of power and international prestige is manifested through an independent and prominent position in the equilibrium between East and West, and through the extension of aid to and influence in developing countries, rather than through the possession of colonial empire." [31]

On the other hand, given so grandiose a dream and so inclusive and meritorious a vision, any bilateral accord or alignment that was beneficial for France was *ipso facto* enlisted, if Gaullist assumptions are conceded, in the service of these universally valid aims. The French could claim maximum tactical freedom without renouncing commitment to unchanging goals. Behavior that other states might label as opportunistic could be judged, not entirely hypocritically in de Gaulle's eyes, as France's prescience in turning propitious circumstance to its advantage; what others might condemn as a compromise of principle—for example, France's unilateral rejection in 1965 of selected majority voting prescribed by the Rome Treaty— could be viewed as a fulfillment of treaty obligations among sovereign states. The vagueness of the Gaullist European design was its strength and weakness. It was sufficiently flexible to justify successive *rapprochements* with West Germany, with Russia and the East European states, and, after 1968, again with the Anglo-American powers. France could be at once revisionist (re-established as a great power) and revolutionary (leading Europe and the Third World to unity, the end of the Cold War, and a new international system), without sacrificing gains already won (maintenance of the American

30. *Major Addresses*, pp. 43–44.
31. Bodenheimer, *op. cit.*, p. 44.

nuclear guarantee, Germany's control, EEC concessions, and a veto over Anglo-American penetration into the Common Market). Past, present, and future would thus be fused in French foreign policy. In its European (and later Third World) policies, France could at once be a revisionist, revolutionary, and a *status quo* power as suited its interests. What time frame, what conjuncture of state alignments, or what substantive issues would be placed on the international agenda by France would depend on the circumstances of the moment. Only France remained timeless and unchanging, not its behavior or its alignments, much less the pledges of its transient governments, all the more so if they issued from the discredited Fourth Republic.

The domestic import of Gaullist European ideology is worth a word, too. The Fifth Republic proposed to bring economic and political stability to France and regain its lost stature and influence abroad. De Gaulle's expansive conception of European union had great attraction for almost all sectors of French society. Nationalists could be heartened to see de Gaulle again at the head of the French state; the defeat of European supranational integration seemed assured. The Left, animated either by neutralist or Communist sentiment, could applaud de Gaulle's opening to the East in the middle 1960's, his relentless criticism of American security and economic policies, and his quest for French and West European independence; international reform contributed to domestic renovation. The Center, moderately conservative to mildly progressive, could take comfort in the Gaullist pledge to European unity although its realization would take time. Finally, conservative industrialists and agricultural groups, especially among the most efficient producers, could be assured that the Gaullist Republic would retain the economic protection and benefits of the EEC treaty.[32] Even the Atlanticists, including some in the Gaullist camp, could hope that one day Britain would accept France's conditions for entry into the Common Market.[33]

There was something for almost everyone in Gaullism. This did not mean that opposition to Gaullist European schemes and foreign policy was silenced. It was more a matter of disarming the French Europeanists, especially those in the Monnet school, or in distracting

32. Interviews, Paris, February 1970 through May 1971.
33. *Ibid.*

them. De Gaulle's view of Europe served as a club over them. His way to unity promised emancipation from the United States and reconciliation with Germany and Russia. Their way was dismissed as a reinforcement of the American presence in Europe, actively desired by many "Monnists," and an impediment to a European settlement. Not surprisingly, their opposition to the referendum of November 1962, establishing the direct election of the French president and further weakening parliamentary democracy in France, was a logical analogue of their opposition to his intergovernmental schemes for the European communities. De Gaulle's ideas of European union were then instruments in the internal struggle for power within France just as much as his success in that milieu was a springboard for his ambitious policies abroad.[34]

Phases of Fifth Republic European Policy

French European policy under the Fifth Republic may be divided into three phases. The initial phase largely covers the first presidential term of Charles de Gaulle from 1958 through 1965. It marks the Gaullist attempt to promote France as the champion of West European interests against the superpowers, as the foremost exponent of European union, and as the leader of the West European *ensemble*. Despite the Algerian War, the de Gaulle government strove to complete the first two parts of its systemic triptych for Europe—the weakening of Anglo-American economic, military, and diplomatic influence on the Continent and the assumption of France's leadership of Western Europe within a confederal union more suited to Gaullist notions of national authority than the federally oriented organization of the European communities.

Striking at NATO and the Common Market did not necessarily imply renunciation of the Atlantic or the Rome treaties. They still were useful as vehicles of national purposes. The task was not to abandon these alignments and forego their benefits. Rather, it was either to discipline France's allies to its will (hence the directorate scheme of 1958 and the Fouchet plan of 1961–1962) or to leave France's partners little choice but to tolerate greater French inde-

---

34 For an interesting account, read Robert Kleiman, *Atlantic Crisis* (New York: W. W. Norton, 1964)

pendence in foreign policy (hence the practice of the empty chair in NATO and the EEC). While preserving a place for France within both organizations, the longer range and more ambitious goal was to go beyond them to realize the Gaullist dream of ending Europe's division and of reconciling the Western and Eastern European states from the Atlantic to the Urals. The network of security, economic, and diplomatic relations that would gradually develop on bilateral lines—if not unduly inhibited by the multilateral structures of NATO and the Common Market—was expected eventually to absorb Cold War tensions, deflect the superpower struggle from Europe to the Third World, and win greater influence and esteem for France both globally and regionally where it wished to retain its traditional spheres of interest.

West Germany's support was key to the enterprise. Gaullist France concentrated initially not only on furthering France's reconciliation with Germany but also on developing a priviledged relation with its former foe. The French-German entente was the prerequisite for France's claim to speak for Europe, not just for itself. The many political and economic differences dividing the two states that were overcome in this period suggest somewhat the intense desire of the French president and German Chancellor Konrad Adenauer that the two historical enemies bury their hatreds and join in constructing a united Western Europe. The *rapprochement* succeeded, partly because the two states needed each other's help to achieve even a modicum of their dissimilar and, to an appreciable degree, competing policy aims; and partly because the national and personal emotions at play, symbolized and apparently felt by President de Gaulle and Chancellor Adenauer, urged reconciliation. Reasons of state, national emotions, and personal sympathy and respect entwined to draw the two states closer and to kindle the hope in Gaullist circles that the growing foreign policy alignment between the two states would foster European unity under France's direction.

Between 1958 and 1962, the de Gaulle government scored a number of notable advances in the pursuit of its European design. In the Berlin crisis of these years, de Gaulle skillfully forged the Franco-German entente, which subsequently weathered major differences over Britain's proposal for a free trade association and bid to join the Common Market. Gaullist France also successfully pressed Germany to accelerate the implementation of the Rome Treaty and, over serious German reservations, to include agriculture. Finally, Adenauer's Germany deferred to Gaullist ideas about European political union despite the threat that they posed to NATO and the EEC, cornerstones of postwar German foreign policy. These successes culminated in the Franco-German Friendship Treaty, signed less than a fortnight after de Gaulle's veto of Britain's application to enter the European community.

From 1962 to 1965, however, the de Gaulle government found itself engaged against the United States in the battle for German fealty. The struggle of allies for another ally's loyal support left no major area of state policy untouched. In Europe, differences between France and Germany centered primarily on Europe's relation to the United States and on the political and economic development of the Common Market. The mutual need of France and Germany for each other was too great to contemplate rupture, yet their disagreements were too sharp and profound to escape embarrassing exposure. Relations between France and the Anglo-American powers reached new lows. This downward thrust is paralleled in France's relations with West Germany. The government of Ludwig Erhard hewed closely to American security policies while preaching the not fully compatible virtues of political integration and economic liberalism in Western Europe. This period ended in de Gaulle's attempt to impose France's notions of political and economic union on its partners in the agricultural crisis of 1965–1966. Not without irony, the Gaullist bid to seize the leadership of Western Europe ended not only in isolating France within the Common Market, but also in unwittingly thrusting Germany into the role France sought.

The following discussion, including Chapter 6, traces French European policy through this first phase.

The incipient beginnings of the second phase of Gaullist European policy can be detected even before the first phase had run its course. French overtures to Eastern Europe and to the Soviet Union had begun in earnest. As early as January 1964, with the visit to the Soviet Union of Giscard d'Estaing, French minister of finance and economic affairs, France and Russia were already drawing closer together in their attitudes toward the steps that had to be taken to resolve Europe's division and toward containing, for different reasons, the expansion of the United States into the underdeveloped regions. France's intransigence within the Atlantic Alliance and its decision to set limits to West European political union through the European communities created attractive incentives for the Soviet Union to look more sympathetically on the proposition that France be accepted as the valid spokesman of the West European states. During this phase, the de Gaulle government acted as if it had already achieved its initial systemic aims in Europe and could, without United States, German, or EEC support, launch its drive for a new European security, economic, and diplomatic system beyond the Cold War.

This second phase focused on the French attempt to establish a special economic and political relation with the Soviet Union without breaking its ties with West Germany or relinquishing its security and economic guarantees under the Atlantic and Rome treaties. It was formally initiated in President de Gaulle's news conference of February 4, 1965, announcing an all-European solution for the division of Europe. It reached its high point in President de Gaulle's visit to the Soviet Union in June–July 1966 and ended abruptly and unexpectedly in the Soviet invasion of Czechoslovakia of August 1968.

The final phase, discussed below, commenced in the fall of 1968. The Czech crisis and Germany's refusal to revalue the mark in November 1968 exposed narrower limits to France's "privileged" relations with these two states than had been expected. Threats to French security and solvency, combined with the events of 1968, impelled the de Gaulle and the Pompidou regimes to place a higher value on France's ties with the Anglo-American states. Specifically courted was Great Britain, culminating in the lifting of the French veto and its successful application for membership into the European Economic Community. Progress toward full economic and political union was marked, if modest, during this period. French-German accord was still the key to the further development of European union. Paradoxically enough, even as the two middle-range powers drew closer together in their attitudes and policies toward the superpowers, they found themselves competing more for favor in Washington and Moscow than ever before. As France moved West, Germany under the Brandt government, while stressing the importance of its economic, political, and security ties with the West, moved boldly (rashly some French felt) to the East in signing the Moscow and Warsaw treaties accepting Germany's postwar boundaries. The two states also differed over the institutional development of the European communities; agriculture and monetary policy continued to plague the EEC and divide Germany and France. European political union had not advanced much beyond the aborted Fouchet plan talks of 1961–1962 except that after a decade of pulling and hauling England was to be permitted to join in the negotiations.

Phases two and three form the basis of the discussion in Chapters 7 and 8.

Franco-German Reconciliation

Introduction

Postwar French-German reconciliation began under the Fourth Republic and was completed under the Fifth. Pressured by its allies, especially the United States, successive French governments under the Fourth Republic consented to Germany's incorporation into the European Coal and Steel Community (ECSC), which pooled the coal and steel resources of the Six and appeared to be the optimal solution to a number of conflicting objectives. The European states were in desperate need to agree on common policies to speed their recoveries. Moreover, German industrial power, the economic base for three wars against France in less than a century, could be placed under a supranational authority in which France would participate as the most important member. Efforts to keep Germany divided or to separate the Ruhr, the Rhineland, and Saar, as de Gaulle had once envisioned,[35] were overtaken by the Cold War. There was the need, too, to spur Germany's economic recovery and rearmament and to integrate it politically within Western Europe. The ECSC solution provided France a means of control over German industrial development and rearmament. The supranational solutions responded also to the dream of Europeanists, like Robert Schumann whose name relabeled the Monnet plan, and provided a convenient vehicle to reinstate Germany within the Western bloc and gradually extend the legal trappings of sovereignty and the initial elements of political

35. Jouve, op. cit., I, 111–130.

equality to the West German state. In exchange for its legal and political rehabilitation within the West, Germany consented to supranational controls on its economic and security policies, conditions that the Adenauer government was more than eager to embrace for these very reasons.

The European Defense Community carried the ECSC idea to the military level. For more reasons than can be adequately discussed here, the ECSC solution applied to EDC proved unacceptable to the National Assembly.[36] It deeply touched the nerves of French national pride, sensitive to sovereignty and independence, for which so much blood had been spilled in two world wars. It provoked an unrelenting Gaullist campaign against the passage of the EDC treaty. It also raised fears in the Socialist and Radical parties, which were initially disposed to the formula, that EDC would not contain German rearmament since the conditions attached to the initial draft of the treaty proposal were not fulfilled, including the formation of a European political authority to oversee the defense agencies anticipated by the defense community, Britain's participation as a counterweight to Germany, and settlement of the Saar question.[37] The hard line laid down against the treaty by Moscow assured Communist opposition. The eleventh-hour overtures of the Soviet Union to hold out the possibility of demilitarizing Central Europe in exchange for eventual German unification attracted neutralist sentiment that was gaining ground in France as the nuclear bipolarity of the superpowers took shape and as American adventures in the Third World, sketched already in the Korean War, appeared to be on the rise. The threat of Secretary of State John Foster Dulles that the United States would be forced to make an "agonizing reappraisal" of its foreign policy if France defeated EDC backfired, unleashing anti-American sentiment on the side of treaty opponents.

The Rome Treaty, placed into operation shortly before de Gaulle's return to power, resumed the movement toward European economic and political integration and, by implication, French-German recon-

---

36. Daniel Lerner and Raymond Aron, *France Defeats EDC* (New York: Praeger, 1957); Bodenheimer, *op. cit.*, pp. 34–40; and F. Roy Willis, *France, Germany, and the New Europe, 1945–67* (New York: Oxford University Press, 1968), pp. 131–184

37. *Ibid.*, p. 35.

ciliation. In accepting the Rome Treaty, and especially the Common Market, the de Gaulle regime continued these policies, but placed them on an entirely different legal, political, and moral basis. Having no faith in supranational controls as a check on Germany or as a reliable instrument of French interests and will, de Gaulle rejected both the NATO and the European Economic communities as frameworks within which to define French-German relations. He chose instead to re-establish gradually a direct personal tie between himself and the German chancellor and, more importantly, an understanding of mutual self-interests between the two states, particularly with respect to the superpowers, to the other European states, on both sides of the Iron Curtain, and, in more muted form, to the Third World.

The Skeletal Structure of Interests

Personal and national emotions figured prominently in the first meeting of President de Gaulle and German Chancellor Konrad Adenauer at Colombey les Deux Eglises, the French executive's private residence. The setting, far removed from the protocol of Paris or Bonn, accentuated the personal bond that was to be forged between the two old leaders. Despite their different backgrounds—one military, the other mufti—their Catholicism, their mutual personal admiration, and their regard for French culture drew them together. They also "shared," as one close observer of French foreign policy notes, "a basic mistrust of the German people, as well as an acute sense of Germany's responsibilities for two world wars." [38] Both leaders understood that their peoples needed each other, notwith-

---

38. Newhouse, op. cit., p. 68. See also Grosser, French Foreign Policy, p. 66. Grosser argues that "as early as September 14, 1958, there was a sort of gentlemen's agreement between the General and the Chancellor—non-explicit, unsigned, undrafted, based on reciprocity: the Federal Republic would aid France in her Atlantic and European ambitions, and France would give firm support to the Eastern policies of the Federal Republic." The agreement, however, seems to have been more explicit on Adenauer's side since de Gaulle in his March 25, 1959, news conference effectively recognized the Oder-Neisse line as the boundary between Germany and Poland. The boundary dispute was an intrinsic part of West Germany's Eastern policy, however conceived, but it apparently escaped the gentlemen's accord observed by Grosser. Also of interest is the brief, but perceptive, analysis of the Colombey meeting offered by Schoenbrun, Three Lives of de Gaulle, pp. 297–298.

standing their different and sometimes conflicting goals. The latter problem raised the question of whose will—France's or Germany's— would prevail. European unity, as conceived by de Gaulle, would be built through an understanding between the two states later to be ratified and executed, presumably by whatever national or international instrumentalities, *including* the European communities, that they might jointly decide to use. They would avoid the error made by community founders that assumed the eventual harmony of the external policies of the Six to exist, at least in nascent form, in what they believed to be the creation of a common, supranational authority.

The Colombey meeting was a de Gaulle triumph over a skeptical Adenauer, who, despite his doubts about de Gaulle's motives, was susceptible to the French president's entreaties, placing the German and French states and peoples on an ostensibly equal political plane. "In the matter of Germany," de Gaulle was to remind Russia, "[France] has been able to master her grievances and, taking into account the changes which have occurred there, to consider this country not as an enemy, but as a partner." [39] Adenauer was even more expansive in meeting with journalists the day after the Colombey meeting. "The general . . . is not a nationalist," said Adenauer. "We are profoundly aware of the importance that our meeting assumes. We believe that it ought to be the end forever of . . . former hostility. . . . We are convinced that the close cooperation between the German Federal Republic and the French Republic is the foundation of any constructive work in Europe. It contributes to the reinforcement of the Atlantic Alliance and it is indispensable for the world. We think that this cooperation should . . . include the other nations of Western Europe. . . . We wish that it be extended to the largest possible number of European states." [40] President de Gaulle reportedly wrote the first three paragraphs of the joint communiqué from which Adenauer drew his remarks,[41] and within which are to be found all the seeds of future misunderstanding. Where Adenauer's Germany read Atlantic Alliance to mean a tight NATO organization within which Germany's armed forces were integrated, Gaullist

39. *Major Addresses*, p. 44.
40. *L'Année politique, 1958*, p. 433.
41. Roger Massip, *De Gaulle et l'Europe* (Paris: Flammarion, 1963), p. 57; Newhouse, *op. cit.*, p. 69.

France meant a traditional security pact between states. Where Germany interpreted "cooperation" to be expressed within the European communities, Gaullist France envisioned the political and economic organization for Europe on confederal, not federalist or supranational, lines. Where Germany desired an open Europe pointed to the West, and to include Britain, Gaullist France preferred to tilt Western Europe to the East and to exclude Britain until it met its tests for European unity and French continental ascendancy.[42]

In the course of the following encounters between the French president and the German chancellor, a structure of overlapping interests was outlined that gave form and substance to the reconciliation of the two states. How far the *rapprochement* could develop was largely defined by the degree to which these conflicting interests could be conciliated. On the part of Adenauer's Germany, the degree of possible accord was initially quite large, for reconciliation with France was more an end in itself than, as in de Gaulle's case, a means to other, more encompassing objectives. De Gaulle, as leader of the Free French movement and as Germany's principal French adversary during World War II, was uniquely placed to confer international respectability on Germany and to accept it as an equal European partner. He could lend his prestige, earned in combat and confirmed in victory, to Germany's political rehabilitation, one of the principal objectives of postwar German foreign policy. Moreover, a cooperative France within the European economic communities was deemed essential for the realization of Bonn's other principal postwar objectives: economic recovery, security, and unification.[43] The Common Market promised German industrialists access to French markets. Germany was still relying on the supranational features of the EEC to gain international respectability—de Gaulle's blessing was a valued supplement, not an ultimate substitute—to strengthen Germany's influence both within the Western camp and in its negotiations with the East. Given American pressures for a united Europe,[44] a strong European community appeared more firmly to tie the American nu-

42. Interview, Paris, May 1971.

43. Wolfram Hanreider, *The Stable Crisis* (New York: Harper and Row, 1970).

44. These are concisely described in Max Beloff, *The United States and the Unity of Europe* (Washington: Brookings Institute, 1963).

clear guarantee to Europe and, specifically, to Germany. From a reinforced Western position, Adenauer's Germany proposed to bargain with the Soviet Union. Adenauer hoped a strong French-German entente would buttress Germany's posture within the EEC and the Atlantic Alliance or at least not hurt its standing; certainly there was no thought that Germany would have to choose between France and these multilateral pillars of German postwar foreign policy. In addition, increased Soviet pressures on Berlin and growing doubts about Anglo-American support of Germany's foreign policy goals, especially security and unification, cautioned a prudent search for more French support on a bilateral basis, but no less directed toward larger German foreign policy objectives.

De Gaulle defined France's interest in the French-German alignment quite differently. First, France intended to maintain its war-won rights to define Germany's political future and represent German interests in East-West negotiations. Second, France expected Germany's support for the incorporation of agriculture within the Common Market in return for Gaullist France's approval of the EEC. Third, Germany was never to have nuclear weapons. This went beyond the stipulation, evidenced in the French campaign against the MLF, that Germany would never produce such devices, a right that Germany had unilaterally renounced in signing the Paris accords of 1954 that established the legal basis for its entry into the Atlantic Alliance. Otherwise France's security would be directly menaced, the *force de frappe* would be neutralized, and, worse, any possibility of settling Europe's fate, with Soviet help, would be foreclosed.[45] Fourth, and more generally, Germany was expected to support Gaullist policies within Europe and France's efforts to revise Atlantic relations. Germany could meet the first three conditions; the latter expectation, vaguer and therefore more susceptible to misunderstanding over the price that was demanded, was to be the source of most of Germany's problems with Gaullist France, especially in the post-Adenauer period.

Between 1958 and 1962, the French-German *rapprochement* was tested on six issues: (1) the Berlin crisis that roughly corresponded in length to the first phase of Gaullist European policy; (2) the Brit-

45. De Gaulle, *Mémoires d'espoir*, pp. 186–187.

ish offensive in favor of a free trade area as an alternative to the European Economic Community; (3) the acceleration of the economic customs union; (4) the incorporation of agriculture into the Common Market; (5) France's campaign for political union; and (6) France's veto of British entry into the EEC. In one way or another, these issues raised into question the assumptions and aims of Atlantic and European relations, and their resolution marked many of the important limits and possibilities of the French-German alignment in foreign affairs and, by that token, progress toward European union.

Berlin: External Alignment; Internal Conflict

On November 27, 1958, the Soviet government, in a note to the Western Big Three, denounced four-power control over Berlin as an anachronism, proposed the creation of a free, demilitarized West Berlin, and announced its intention to hand over its responsibilities, including surveillance of access routes to Berlin, to the German Democratic Republic (GDR), if an accord could not be reached between the two Germanies and the wartime allies.[46] A treaty between the Soviet Union and the East German government of Walter Ulbricht would have unilaterally terminated the Big-Four occupation regime created after World War II. The Soviet move, in the form of an ultimatum, was particularly troubling since it limited maneuverability and compromise for both sides, and immediately focused the Cold War struggle on Berlin as a major test of will. The Soviet action also menaced West Germany's claim alone to speak for Germany and outflanked its drive to isolate the East German regime diplomatically. A separate peace treaty, if acknowledged by the West, would have legitimized the *status quo* in Europe sought by the Soviets. Its own control over its Eastern empire would have been solidified, a hold shown tenuous by internal unrest among the satellites and by the steady drain of refugees leaving the East German zone for the West. A treaty would have furthermore recognized East Germany as a separate state. It would have effectively severed the constitutional link between West Berlin and West Germany and destroyed what hopes remained that Germany might still be reunited

46. E. Barker, "Berlin Crisis: 1958–62," *International Affairs,* XXXIX (January 1963), 61.

under Bonn's direction. De Gaulle made common cause with the Adenauer government, resisting Soviet threats and stiffening the West's bargaining position. Under the cover of close French-German cooperation, Berlin also served as a useful vehicle to expose the initial outlines of a Gaullist solution for Europe's division and in the process to enhance French status as a major power in Moscow and in the principal Western capitals.

The first step was accord with Germany. The second meeting of de Gaulle and Adenauer on November 26, 1958, at Bad Kreuznach, called at the French president's request, was the occasion for the understanding. In exchange for German consent to end negotiations with Britain on a free trade area, de Gaulle agreed to support Germany's campaign to resist Soviet pressures on Berlin, to bolster the eroding Anglo-American, particularly British, commitment to the city, and what appeared to be the central point of the accord, to refuse changes in Berlin's status or in access arrangements concerning the city that might have had the effect of conferring legitimacy on the East German regime.[47] The similarity between the French and German positions on Berlin thereafter obscured the divergent motives underlying their common stance and their conflicting objectives in resolving the Berlin question.

During the first phase of the Berlin controversy, from November 1958 to March 1959, the de Gaulle regime assumed a hard line in its policy regarding negotiations with the Soviet Union under threat in sharp contrast with British determination to mediate the East-West conflict. The December announcement of British Prime Minister Harold Macmillan's impending visit to the Soviet Union in early February 1959 strengthened German fears that the British might sacrifice Berlin and unification—perhaps German security, too—in a deal with the Russians. Secretary of State John Foster Dulles, with whom Adenauer had struck a particularly close personal relation, went to Europe to shore up German confidence in the American promise to defend Western rights in Berlin. Dulles' remarks to journalists that there might be other routes to German unification than elections served only to raise apprehensions.[48] France appeared uninterested in talking to the Russians or in finding new formulae to

47. De Gaulle, *Mémoires d'espoir*, pp. 191–192.
48. Newhouse, *op. cit.*, pp. 92–93.

satisfy Russian and East German political objectives. This stance dovetailed with German reluctance to engage in any talks.

The Western Big Three held firm to their occupation rights in their joint note to the Soviet Union of December 14.[49] In a separate note, the French elaborated on their position and emphasized four-power responsibility "for the settlement of the German question" and the Berlin problem. France's special status vis-à-vis West Germany was underlined at Germany's behest. The note pointedly rejected the Soviet Union's asserted right that it could unilaterally transfer its responsibilities to Pankow or create a free city of Berlin. It also broadened the agenda of discussion to include unification, European security, and a European peace treaty. France was not disposed either to discuss the Berlin question apart from these larger issues or to cede to Soviet pressures to open talks that, based on a Soviet agenda that implicitly recognized the East German state, would have prejudiced Western rights in the very act of engaging in negotiations.[50]

President de Gaulle's news conference of March 25, 1959, exposed still other facets of the French position. For the Germans, there was the reaffirmation of Western rights. Equally consoling was French rejection of proposals to neutralize Central Europe militarily, support for the Atlantic Alliance "until the day when peace is assured," and a pledge to risk even war over Berlin. The legitimacy of the West German government, "where citizens say, read and hear what they like, come and go as they please and, in complete freedom, elect their representatives and their government," was contrasted with the Pankow regime which "could not exist except by virtue of the Soviet occupation and . . . an implacable dictatorship."[51] The difference between Dulles' and de Gaulle's remarks about the appropriate route to unification was marked. De Gaulle valued the tie with Bonn enough to compromise a repeatedly asserted principle that foreign relations were between states, not regimes, however questionable or however uncertain their legal claim to legitimacy might be. On the other hand, the Soviet Union was assured that Gaullist France understood that German unification was possible only if the German people did "not reopen the question of their present frontiers to the

49. L'Année politique, 1958, p. 494.
50. Ibid., pp. 494–497.
51. Major Addresses, p. 43.

west, the east, the north and the south, and that they move[d] toward
integrating themselves one day in a contractual organization of all
Europe." [52] De Gaulle's unexpected concession, which the Federal
Republic was not to accept until twelve years later, technically kept
faith with the word given by de Gaulle to Adenauer to support West
Germany's Berlin policy. France was bound to reject Soviet attempts
to legitimate the European *status quo* without dealing with the problems of a European settlement and German unification which were
closely related to the boundary problem. Firmness on Berlin to please
Bonn did not signify a consistent view on the larger problem of Europe's division.[53] De Gaulle went beyond his pact with Adenauer and
appealed directly to Moscow. In linking unification and boundary
settlements to Berlin, de Gaulle was calling the Soviet bluff. The
French president was challenging Moscow to face the problem of a
European peace treaty that inevitably raised serious difficulties over
the definition of Soviet relations within its imperial system. Furthermore, it appeared to be no accident that in the same news conference de Gaulle linked a European settlement to the Third World.
Berlin was too small a problem for Gaullist aspirations. Its appearance on the international agenda, however, offered a convenient occasion to define the larger implication of over-all settlement of political and strategic differences between the great powers and the
right of France to play a protagonist role in the creation of a new
international order.

The second phase of the Berlin crisis revolved around the meeting
of foreign ministers at Geneva from May 11 to August 5, 1959.
Adenauer leaned all the more heavily on his personal relation with
de Gaulle as his access to Washington slipped with Dulles' fading
health and death. The French again ably steered between the Anglo-
American powers who searched for an accommodation with the Soviets over Berlin and an uncompromising West Germany. Seen from
Washington and London, France, while meticulous in negotiation,
appeared cooperative in contrast to the adamance of the German
government, prepared neither to make concessions nor to entertain
use of German troops in a clash over access routes to the city. To
the Germans, France emerged from the talks as a dependable ally

52. *Ibid.*, p. 45
53. See n. 38 above.

in contrast to British vacillation and American uncertainty and se-
crecy, especially on matters of Western nuclear policy. With its Western partners, France proposed to limit allied military forces in Berlin
to eleven thousand men, to accept the participation of East Germany
both in the four-power control over Berlin as experts and in the
administration of access routes to the city as "agents" of the Soviet
Union. The accords were designated as provisional, conceivably leading later to other modifications as political conditions changed.[54]
Nothing came of these concessions, as the surprise announcement of
early August 1959 that Soviet Premier Khrushchev would visit the
United States in September overtook the foreign ministers' meeting.
The news, according to President Eisenhower, upset Paris and
Bonn.[55] The right-of-center *Le Figaro* gave voice to Quai d'Orsay
sentiment: "This direct conversation of two colossi, over the heads
of all other nations of the world, over the head of Western Europe,"
it warned, "was precisely the objective towards which Soviet political
strategy has been tending for years." [56] Meanwhile, France reportedly
assured the Bonn government privately that it would not hold the
line in Berlin, particularly on the "agent's" doctrine and in turn Bonn
sided with the initial outlines of the French case for NATO reform.[57]

The Eisenhower-Khrushchev meeting and Soviet proposals for a
summit meeting provided a rare opportunity for France to play its
subtle balancing game aimed at producing an improved conjuncture
of bilateral relations between itself and the Western and Communist
powers in Europe that would advance its global pursuits. President
de Gaulle's November 10, 1959, news conference set the stage for
France's role in summit diplomacy that absorbed most of the third
period of the Berlin tragicomedy. Three conditions were set down
for France's participation: "an atmosphere of détente" in which
states refrained "from attacking anyone" (a convenient ploy to neutralize criticism of France's Algerian policy); careful preparation of
an agenda for discussion; and Premier Khrushchev's personal visit to
Paris. President Eisenhower had already come to Paris on September

54. Barker, *op. cit.*, pp. 59–73.
55. Newhouse, *op. cit.*, pp. 97–98.
56. *L'Année politique, 1959*, p. 466.
57. *Ibid.*, p. 470.

2–3 to confer with the French president. De Gaulle, with German help, had the Western Big Three presummit gathering held in Paris. He subsequently exchanged visits with Macmillan and toured the United States in the last week of April 1960, before the scheduled summit meeting in the middle of May. The second French atomic explosion, apparently calculated to impress the Soviet leader, took place during Khrushchev's visit to France at the end of March. Hints were dropped in the aftermath of the meeting that the Russian diplomatic position was becoming increasingly flexible and that perhaps a true détente was in the offing.

In his November 10 statement, de Gaulle publicly cited the Soviet's eroding hold on its East European satellites, including "Prussia and Saxony," internal pressures for liberalization of the regime, and the Sino-Soviet split as factors pushing the Russians to seek an agreement with the West. These sticks were matched with carrots. The anticipated personal meeting of the two world leaders in Paris was underscored and Khrushchev was complimented for having recognized the weakness of his bargaining position and for having opened the possibility of peaceful contacts with the West.[58] Suggestions were also made that France might not be fully committed to German ends; the March 25 stand on boundaries was reaffirmed, a point reiterated earlier in a Khrushchev speech before the Supreme Soviet.[59] In his talks with Khrushchev, one well-informed French journalist cited de Gaulle as saying that "if one allows time to pass, one could have two Germanies, if not three, with Berlin." [60] He was more explicit during the French presidential elections of 1965. In a television interview, de Gaulle asked rhetorically: "The Germans . . . see themselves . . . cut in two and even in three if the status of Berlin is taken into account. . . . They necessarily have ambitions. Is it necessary that Germany's ambitions be automatically ours?" [61] These passes before the Russians were incorporated in an even more expansive gesture toward the Third World where China loomed large in Gaullist for-

58. *Major Addresses*, pp. 57–58.
59. *Ibid.*, p. 68.
60. J. R. Tournoux, *La Tragédie du général*, p. 498; Newhouse, *op. cit.*, p. 103.
61. De Gaulle, *Discours*, IV, 26.

ward planning. At French insistence, the questions of disarmament (not arms control) and aid to underdeveloped states were inscribed on the summit agenda.

Still the French president drew praise from German quarters for his seemingly unyielding stand in Western presummit negotiations and in his rebuke later to Premier Khrushchev for having broken up the Paris conference over the shooting down of an American reconnaissance plane on May 1 over Russia.[62] Both in his television address of May 31, summarizing the reasons for the failure of the summit, and in his personal remarks to Premier Khrushchev, the French president took notice of the spy satellites over the United States.[63] At the conference he had vetoed Western attempts to conciliate Khrushchev with an apology from President Eisenhower demanded as a consequence of the U-2 incident.

In the lull between the end of the Paris summit and the start of the final phase of the Berlin struggle, initiated by the Soviets again in Premier Khrushchev's note to President Kennedy in their meeting at Vienna in June 1961, de Gaulle continued to play on the weaknesses of internal Western policy while advancing his larger revisionist designs for fundamental changes in Atlantic and European relations. In September 1960, he unveiled his plan for European political union that was to occupy European attention for the following two years. European union was linked to NATO reform and Europe's (and France's) larger role and responsibilities in the Third World.[64] There was also self-praise for France's generous decolonization policy and its leadership of Algeria to self-determination, themes that were to become more pronounced after 1962.

De Gaulle's attack on NATO, more than his emerging European policy, posed a particularly acute problem for the Adenauer government that had invested so much of Germany's future in the American security pledge. It was held in trust in the NATO organization as well as the Atlantic Alliance. Even the enthusiastic supporters of the French-German entente realized that it would be increasingly difficult to reconcile Germany's desire for close ties with France and its devotion to Atlantic cooperation if de Gaulle went much further

62. Newhouse, *op. cit.*, p. 99.
63. *Major Addresses*, pp. 75–77.
64. *Ibid.*, pp. 84–98.

in his disengagement from the American-dominated security grouping. Prime Minister Michel Debré and Foreign Minister Couve de Murville were dispatched on October 7–8 to Bonn to reassure the Adenauer government.[65] Bilateral accords on military bases were reached between the two states at the end of October and talks continued actively on possible French-German cooperation in fabricating arms.[66]

The de Gaulle government scored high marks in Bonn, moreover, in refusing to join or sanction bilateral talks between the United States and the Soviet Union over Berlin in the early days of the Kennedy administration. The French showed no interest in the American plan for an international access authority composed of thirteen governments, including East and West Germany.[67] They remained equally resistant to suggestions current then in American policy centers that Berlin be placed under United Nations control and that a measure of disengagement in Central Europe be contemplated. A month after the meeting in Vienna, de Gaulle issued a warning to Russia that France would not be intimidated by the Soviet Union. On September 5, 1961, he called on the West to remain firm,[68] and in his end-of-the-year message, he openly criticized direct Anglo-American contacts with the Soviet Union.[69] Two months later de Gaulle credited himself with having saved the West from a debacle: "By . . . refusing to negotiate on Berlin or Germany so long as the Soviet Union does not . . . . stop . . . threats and its injunctions . . . , we believe that we have spared our allies and ourselves the catastrophic retreat, dramatic rupture or tragi-comical engulfment, in which the conference would obviously have ended." [70] Yet in American bureaucratic circles, France gained credit for its cooperation on Western contingency planning for Berlin although, like the British, the French government was reluctant to predelegate authority for immediate Western responses to anticipated Russian moves.[71]

65. *L'Année politique, 1960,* p. 565.
66. *Ibid., 1961,* pp. 379, 441, 577.
67. Barker, *op. cit.,* p. 70.
68. *Major Addresses,* p. 156.
69. *Ibid.,* p. 160.
70. *Ibid.*
71. Newhouse, *op. cit.,* pp. 85–119.

The de Gaulle government was equally resistant to arms control proposals, either in the form of disengagement schemes for Central Europe or of bans on nuclear testing. Paris and Bonn were again made political bedfellows on this issue, but for different reasons. While both feared such accords as superpower deals over the heads of the smaller powers, the French saw the nuclear proposals as a means to deny France nuclear weapons; the Germans viewed them as East-West arms stabilization agreements that would be paid in the coinage of German political interests. Contrariwise, France no less than the other nuclear powers had incentive to block German access to nuclear weapons. De Gaulle said as much in observing, during the 1965 presidential campaign, that France had neither the same passion for unification as the Germans nor any interest in facilitating their possession or use of nuclear weapons.[72] As early as 1962, Walter Lippmann advanced the intriguing thesis, whose plausibility grew with time, that France's hard line with the Soviet Union was "founded . . . on a basic French national determination not to have to live with a large united Germany. At bottom the hard policy is directed not against the Russians," said Lippmann, "but against those Germans who want to make an opening to the East." [73] Further maneuver over Berlin and its utility for Gaullist purposes effectively ended after the November 1962 Cuban missile crisis. The remaining points on the Gaullist agenda were building the EEC to service French economic needs and to create a political grouping within the Six that might be a ready instrument for Gaullist global designs.

Casting the European Economic Community in a Gaullist Image

The Structure of Economic Interests: France and Germany

De Gaulle recognized that the Rome Treaty, especially in its creation of a common market, was generous to France—a charter for economic regeneration. If its political implications were abhorrent to Gaullist France, the commitments that it potentially elicited from France's partners, particularly Germany, to support the French economy, most notably in agriculture, were too important to reject out

72. De Gaulle, *Discours,* IV, 430.
73. Hanreider, *op. cit.,* p. 102.

of hand.[74] At French insistence the treaty defined a long period of transition to implement a common external tariff and to complete tariff disarmament among the Six. French social policy, more advanced than that of its partners on equalization of pay for men and women, workers' holidays, and overtime pay, was adopted as a model. To protect and harmonize their social progress with the competitive rules governing community industrial activity, the French were granted special permission to invoke escape clauses if their manufacturers were placed at a disadvantage. France retained special import and export charges subject to later revision by the Commission and the Council of Ministers. Guidelines for the common external tariff favored France as a high-tariff country. Assurances were made that agriculture would be included in the Common Market.[75]

Aid to France's colonial dependencies was extended through the creation of a European development fund. The contributions of France and Germany, $200 million each, accounted for the bulk of the $581 million subscribed. Of this total, French dependencies received over $511 million. The overseas departments—Algeria, Guadeloupe, French Guiana, Martinique, and Réunion—were granted access to the European Investment Fund. Meanwhile, the French retained a privileged position in the markets of association members as a consequence of traditional economic and cultural ties. The extension of the Common Market to the French dependencies supported critically important French political goals in the late 1950's: meeting African economic and political demands short of independence and settling the Algerian War on terms satisfactory to competing groups in Algeria and France as well as to former protectorates of Tunisia and Morocco.[76]

74. Useful discussions of the formation of the Rome Treaty and French success in negotiations are found in the following sources: Miriam Camps, *Britain and the European Community: 1955–1963* (Princeton: Princeton University Press, 1964), pp. 20–92; Lindberg, *op. cit.*, pp. 14–48; Baron Snoy et d'Oppuers, "La Zone de libre échange," *Chronique de politique étrangère,* XII (Sept.–Nov. 1959), 569–599.

75. Lindberg, *op. cit.*, pp. 218–282.

76. Serge Hurtig, "The European Common Market," *International Conciliation,* No. 517 (March 1958), p. 371; Ambassade de France, Service de Presse et d'Information, *A New Step in Building Europe, a Common Market for 175 Million Consumers,* European Affairs, No. 10 (New York: June 1957), pp. 9–11; Snoy, *op. cit.*, p. 598.

The Gaullist responses to Euratom and the Common Market were contrasting. On the one hand, the French government vigorously supported the Common Market. For the first half decade of the EEC's life, France was the most "European" of the Six. An alignment of convenience developed between the Commission, largely committed to federalist goals, and the de Gaulle government whose long-run objectives pointed in the opposite direction. When "community" proposals promoted French economic interests, Paris accommodated itself quite easily to Commission proposals and advanced them as its own. France successfully pressed a hesitant Germany to cast its lot with the Six in developing a common commercial and agricultural policy despite the cost to its economy. De Gaulle traded skillfully on Adenauer's desire for French-German reconciliation and his expectations for European economic and political union as the route to Germany's political rehabilitation and reunification. The Berlin problem provided a convenient lever to manipulate fears that, while commonly felt in both capitals, were weighted differentially enough to permit France to use the issue to attain more encompassing goals beyond immediate security questions.

The French position throughout the 1960's and into the Pompidou administration may be summarized as follows: a strict interpretation of treaty obligations bearing on a common commercial and agricultural policy for the Six, combined with a narrow conception of the Commission's political authority and the corresponding duty of the Six to work toward European political union through the community framework. In other words, France spurred the development of the community's economic institutions while resisting its political expansion. Toward third states, community preference became a hallowed French principle. It was the litmus test for "Europeanism" and the initial filter through which all aspirants for community membership had to pass. De Gaulle set great store on opening French industry to the competition of the Six, but not to the more rigorous demands of the open world market where the United States reigned and where an economically resurgent Germany and Japan grew apace.[77] For the French government, tariff disarmament within the Six and the erection of a common tariff wall, with escape clauses for security,

77. Interview, Paris, April 1970.

were valued instruments to reach a double purpose whose cost would be shifted partially to France's partners. The de Gaulle government never ceased to emphasize that France assured the functioning of the EEC (and hence was the "true" European). Its contribution stemmed from the economic reforms instituted by the de Gaulle government in December 1958, including the 17.5 percent devaluation of the franc, indispensable for the execution of the first stages of a community commercial policy. The fragile French economy could not have weathered the trade losses with an overvalued franc. Unlike its partners, France consistently championed the principle of community preference, particularly in agriculture, and the elaboration of community rules (consistent with the French preference for planning) regulating the national economic policy of the several states (without hampering France's diplomatic maneuverability).[78]

The French did not display the same enthusiasm for Euratom, the other creation of the Rome Treaty. The principal reasons for its disinterest and even hostility are easily perceived.[79] France's nuclear program was the most advanced within the community, and its annual expenditures exceeded those of its partners. The de Gaulle government was sensitive to the argument pressed by the Commissariat de l'Enérgie Atomique (CEA) that there was little point in giving France's research findings to its European partners.[80] Gaullists saw even less force in the federalist argument that because nuclear energy was a new area, a concerted West European program could easily be built. Because of its novelty and the bright future sketched for its application to civilian and military ends, nuclear energy was difficult to integrate within an all-European framework. Gaullist France had no wish to create European competitors for France in the peaceful and, what was expected to be, profitable development of atomic power. The CEA also argued effectively that, with limited funds available to France, it made more sense to support a national, not supranational, program.[81] De Gaulle's distaste for supranational con-

---

78. De Gaulle, *Mémoires d'espoir, passim;* Malcolm C. MacLennan, "The Common Market and French Planning," *Journal of Common Market Studies,* III (October 1964), 23–46.

79. Jouve, *op. cit.,* I, 416–419, and Scheinman, *International Conciliation,* 1967.

80. Interviews, Paris, May 1971.

81. *Ibid.*

trols, especially over France's military nuclear research, combined with the CEA's institutional resistance, shaped by scientists and functionaries, to the harnessing of the French atom to Euratom.

Objections in principle were confirmed in fact in the Hirsch affair of 1961. Etienne Hirsch, president of Euratom since February 1959, pressed the French government to adhere to the Euratom accord in two important areas. First, Hirsch's leadership was instrumental in forming a majority coalition of France's partners that overrode French objections to Euratom's decision to enter ·into contract with the United States Atomic Energy Commission for access to American technological development in enriched uranium reactors. The proposed arrangement not only conflicted with French work on natural uranium reactors but carried controls on European use of American-supplied fissionable materials that threatened to hamper the French military nuclear program. Hirsch argued that France's veto applied neither to the AEC's decision nor to other sets of decisions within the global framework of the Euratom budget. Second, he called on the French government to report to Euratom, in accordance with treaty obligations, regarding the amount of fissionable material available to it and the state of its atomic energy program. His zeal was rewarded in December 1961, when the French government refused to renominate him and instead appointed Pierre Chatenet, who was more attuned to Gaullist direction in atomic affairs.[82]

The apathy or conflicting interests of France's partners further sealed Euratom's demise. None wished to make an issue of the Hirsch incident despite its violation of the spirit, if not perhaps the formal letter, of Euratom's charter. Others, like the Italians, felt that they were not receiving enough benefits in proportion to their financial and scientific contribution. Still others eyed the Euratom bureaucracy as a threat to emerging national programs. The French fished these troubled waters. They criticized the eclectic character of the Euratom program and its modest success in industrial applications. Euratom as an organization continued, but it was forced to live within a limited budget and a snarled political and administrative framework. It has never recovered from the blows dealt to its internal administrative authority, financing, and research independence in the early days of its life.

82. Jouve, op. cit., I, 416–418.

The German government was not convinced about the economic benefits of the Rome Treaty, and especially its Common Market features. German industry was more capable of competing on the world market than its French counterpart. Germany feared that the establishment of a common external tariff based on averaging proposals among the Six, favored by the EEC Commission and France, would be too high, making German products less competitive abroad. The Erhard wing of the Christian Democratic party was committed to an open trade policy on economic and ideological grounds. The protectionism sought by the Gaullist government, however limited, under the aegis of community preference, conflicted sharply with prevailing German notions of economic liberalism. Moreover, while enthusiastic about internal tariff disarmament for industrial products within the Six, the Bonn government was wary of a common agricultural policy. Germany preferred, like Britain, to buy its foodstuffs on the open market not only to benefit from cheaper prices but also to open channels for its industrial goods. It was less expensive to subsidize inefficient German farmers, tied to the Christian Democratic party, than to support a common agricultural policy that would drain off German resources for the farms of France, Holland, and Italy. These economic and internal political costs added to those incurred under the Common Market's selective development scheme for Third World states that favored colonial states, like France. Many of Germany's trading partners among the developing states, like Ghana and Brazil, were eligible neither for Common Market assistance nor for the benefits of association. Germany was faced with the economic costs of shouldering a part of France's colonial burden and of simultaneously running the risk of political involvement in areas from which it drew negligible economic and political benefits.[83]

The first major test of will between the Erhard and Adenauer wings within the Christian Democratic party over EEC policy was on the British proposal for a free trade area within the Organization for European Economic Cooperation (OEEC) (later reorganized as the Organization for Economic Cooperation and Development). British opposition to the Common Market in the late 1950's was

83. Willis, *op. cit.,* pp. 272–292.

partially based on traditional foreign policy doctrines, rooted in four centuries of diplomatic experience and reinforced by the memory of two costly world wars. The British were slow to appreciate their weakened condition and loss of world power in 1945. Unoccupied during World War II and having emerged as a victorious power, Britain did not suffer the devastation, the humiliation of defeat, or the trauma of political rehabilitation of the continental nations. It continued to behave like a global power. With no fixed center of primary interest, it operated, as Winston Churchill observed, within three overlapping circles—the Commonwealth, the United States, and Europe.[84] Unlike France, geographically anchored to the European continent and exposed directly to its tempestuous and unpredictable political climate, Britain, protected by the Channel, looked out toward the open seas. Europe was but a part of a larger strategic, political, and economic terrain. Given Britain's special ties with the United States and the Commonwealth, Europe was often the least important of the concentric circles within which British power and priorities manifested themselves. Third-force notions that circulated in France immediately after World War II had no appeal in England.[85] Britain's brief flirtation with European unity in the Brussels Treaty of 1948 gave way rapidly to the marriage of British security interests to NATO and the Atlantic area in 1949.[86] Britain dismissed continental invitations to join the ECSC and watched from the sidelines as the West European powers wrestled with EDC, contributing through inaction to its defeat. Only after the rejection of the European army did the British fill part of the vacuum in committing troops to the Western European Union.

In the late 1950's, Britain drew even further away from Europe on economic issues. Pragmatic by experience and impulse, the British strongly preferred to resolve economic issues at hand rather than to

84. British reaction to Europe after World War II is summarized in Camps, *op. cit.,* pp. 1–53, in Nora Beloff, *The General Says No* (Baltimore: Penguin, 1963), pp. 50–60, and in Dorothy Pickles, *The Uneasy Entente* (London: Oxford University Press, 1966).

85. Edgar Furniss, Jr., *France: Troubled Ally* (New York: Harpers, 1960), pp. 3–59.

86. Paul Stehlin, "Some French Reflections on the Alliance," in *The Western Alliance: Its Status and Prospects,* ed. Edgar S. Furniss, Jr. (Columbus: Ohio State University Press, 1965), pp. 71–88.

build new institutions or to engage in what appeared to be esoteric debates over the structure of European union. Like de Gaulle, they suspected supranational organizations, and were unwilling to yield tariff authority to any international body not subject to national control. They were also convinced that their political bargaining power and economic opportunities were enhanced within the larger and more varied economic grouping of the OEEC instead of the smaller, more rigid regional arrangement, like the EEC. The OEEC balanced the British wish for economic freedom in dealing with other nations, particularly the Commonwealth and the United States, while offering an arena for the resolution of mutual trading problems.

The decision to negotiate the free trade proposal within the OEEC rather than directly with the Six created the feeling in some European quarters of British insensitivity, if not hostility, to European unity. Britain declined invitations to participate in the proceedings leading to the Rome Treaty. As these talks moved toward economic union, beginning with the Messina conference of June 1955, the British gradually re-evaluated their trade position. A British-backed resolution of July 1956 within the OEEC established a special seventeen-nation group to study the question of association between the OEEC and the EEC and, specifically, a free trade area which would include the Six as an integral, but presumably a subordinate, part. Membership in the Common Market could not be easily squared with British agricultural policy or with its Commonwealth preferential system. It would have also pointed Britain toward closer political ties with Western Europe, a notion that had little sympathy within the ruling circles of Britain's principal political parties.[87] On the other hand, a free trade area kept British agriculture and the Commonwealth system apart from continental tampering. It preserved British tariff autonomy and flexibility, permitting Great Britain, as Prime Minister Harold Macmillan reasoned in November 1956, to advance its interests within a larger arena than the Six.[88] A free trade area promised a preferential customs union, while permitting participants to control their own external tariff.

87. Britain's support of the free trade proposal is discussed in Camps, *op. cit.*, pp. 93–172. This discussion as well as the succeeding analysis of the EEC draws extensively on Mrs. Camps's excellent and exhaustive work.
88. Nora Beloff, *op. cit.*, pp. 78–79.

This seemingly technical difference between the free trade idea and the EEC formula of a common external tariff obscured the fundamental incompatibility between the two trade proposals. France stood to lose the most if the Rome Treaty were dissolved into a free trade group. Its opposition to the British plan crystallized early, well before the demise of the Fourth Republic, and hardened with de Gaulle in power. France accepted increased competition within the Six because its partners had made significant concessions to offset the economic hazards of free trade. The French objected to opening the EEC markets to other countries without requiring their corresponding pledges to assume comparable obligations.[89] French officials were convinced, too, that their electorate would be unwilling to expose French industry and agriculture to free trade and to assume the financial burdens of the EEC if their government reversed itself and accepted a free trade association. They preferred to build the EEC first and then enter into negotiations with third countries on trade liberalization from a position of economic strength, relying not only on French, but on community power. The very discriminatory features of the EEC that appealed to France repelled Britain, which viewed the European customs union as a new Continental System, menacing its access to Europe's expanding markets.[90]

London underestimated the extent to which the Six were individually committed to social and economic development through the EEC and, as in the case of Germany, to the community's political future. Liberalization of trade among the Six and the construction of a common external tariff were to be harmonized with the social policies, competitive rules, and agricultural goals of the Six. The Rome Treaty embraced the view that the community was responsible for the economic and social welfare of its citizenry. "This meant," as Nora Beloff wrote, "that power over private enterprise and planning of development, previously the responsibility of individual states, could not simply lapse: it must instead be exercised by the wider European community. This in the long run implied, and was meant to imply, fiscal, social, monetary, and ultimately political union." [91]

The French (and not a small number of other Europeans) sus-

89. Camps, *op. cit.*, pp. 133ff.
90. Nora Beloff, *op. cit.*, p. 71.
91. *Ibid.*

pected British motives. President de Gaulle's distrust of the British, formed by his Free French experience during World War II, fueled these doubts. The free trade proposal could well be interpreted as a means to divide the Six and, in particular, to pit France against Germany.[92] The Dutch and Germans were susceptible to the temptations of a free trade area. Low-tariff countries, with extensive world-wide markets that might be adversely affected by the implementation of a preferential European customs union, gained less economically from the Common Market than they had supposed. "French negotiators," as Edgar Furniss observed, "suspected that the British were up to their old game of destroying 'Europe,' seeking through the device of the Free Trade Area to deprive cooperation among the Six of any real meaning. . . . Most disastrous would be the defection of West Germany, on whose diplomatic, economic, and military support France had leaned heavily since 1955." [93] The appointment of Reginald Maudling to direct the British drive for a free trade association reinforced these suspicions. Maudling headed the OEEC committee charged with the task of developing a workable accord between the OEEC free trade proposal and the EEC's preferential system. Inexperienced and unduly encouraged by Erhard's enthusiasm for free trade and his ability to carry the Adenauer government with him, Maudling played the Germans off against the French, earning little for his efforts except their mutual ire and the scorn of Europeanists within the EEC. The British ploy seemed bent on breaking the French-German axis on which community supporters were banking.[94]

By the spring of 1958, even before de Gaulle's return, the French and British positions had hardened. Most troublesome was the problem of product origin. In the absence of a common external tariff, low-tariff states could count on a profit simply by transshipping goods to high-tariff states within the free trade area. The controls required to discourage trade diversion, while difficult enough to enforce, entailed increased restrictions on trade which a free exchange zone was supposed to reduce, not enlarge.[95] The French counterproposals, unveiled in March 1958, struck four major blows against the British

92. Camps, *op. cit.*, p. 127.
93. Furniss, *op. cit.*, pp. 456–457.
94. Beloff, *op. cit.*, p. 79.
95. Snoy, *op. cit.*, p. 613; Camps, *op. cit.*, pp. 137, 140–144.

position. They called for a common commercial policy with safe-guard clauses, sector negotiations over the global approach advocated by the English government, the subordination of trade liberalization to social harmonization, and the inclusion of agriculture.[96] The French presented their views first to their EEC partners, a move that stalled OEEC negotiations and embarrassed the British. Before action could be taken on the French suggestions, the May 1958 crisis overtook France and swept away the Fourth Republic.

In a conciliatory move, prompted by German concern, the Council of Ministers of the Six, meeting in October 1958, agreed to a community report that accepted a sector approach to resolve the problem of trade deflection. At the same time the validity of differential treatment between EEC members and nonmembers was upheld and the Rome Treaty was assigned a higher priority over other forms of economic association.

Even these terms, many paralleling French demands, were unacceptable to Paris. The French delegation to the Maudling committee insisted on a uniform commercial policy and limitations on member states' rights to change their external tariffs.[97] On November 14, 1958, Jacques Soustelle, de Gaulle's minister of information, announced a French halt to further negotiations: "It was not possible to form a free trade area as had been wished by the British, that is to say by having free trade between the six countries of the Common Market and the eleven other countries of the OEEC, without a common external tariff and without harmonization of the economic and social spheres." [98]

President de Gaulle acted quickly to enlist German support for his objections to a free trade zone and his first of three vetoes of trade talks between Britain and the Six. At his request, he met with Chancellor Konrad Adenauer at Bad Kreuznach on November 26. De Gaulle affirmed France's willingness to honor its obligations under

96. Snoy, *op. cit.*, pp. 613–615; Lindberg, *op. cit.*, pp. 119–120. The British were unlikely to have been favorably disposed to French views. They quickly rejected a more conciliatory proposal offered by the Italians, the Carli plan, that would have grouped similar products with roughly similar tariffs. Products falling outside the agreed band could then be given special remedy to meet the problem of trade diversion.

97. Lindberg, *op. cit.*, p. 142.

98. Camps, *op. cit.*, p. 165.

the Rome accord and to stand firm with Germany over Berlin. For his part, Adenauer agreed that Germany could not press the free trade proposal. De Gaulle's concession to sponsor an EEC study of a possible multilateral association between the Six and OEEC,[99] while designed to strengthen Adenauer against his opponents within his party, served eventually, with the publication of the Commission's views, to buttress the French stand. The outcome of the meeting was clear: whatever the costs to Germany's economic interests, the British free trade proposal would not be permitted to interfere with the French-German *rapprochement*.

Within a month, the British objections to the trade accord of the Six reached on December 3–4 tested the Bad Kreuznach understanding. The Council of Ministers approved 10 percent reductions in the Common Market's external tariff on a most-favored-nation basis. The Six also decided to increase quotas among themselves by 20 percent. In cases where the resulting total would be less than 3 percent of national production, increased imports to this level would be permitted. Anticipating its British and OEEC critics, the Six announced the extension of the 20 percent quotas to nonmember states, but reserved the 3 percent formula to themselves.[100]

The issue between France and Britain was joined on the restricted application of the 3 percent quota. The English government branded the action as discriminatory, singling out France for special criticism. Sir David Eccles, British negotiator within the Maudling committee, asked the extension of the community quota preference to all OEEC members. The Dutch and German delegations, hoping for increased trade liberalization, sympathized with the recommendation. The French, however, recognized that, whatever the slight cost to France of the Eccles amendment, there was the serious risk that its acceptance would establish a precedent for nondiscrimination and dilute the principle of community preference.[101] The British move threatened to expand the sphere of trade negotiations within the Six and open discussions again with OEEC. This was precisely what the Soustelle statement and the Bad Kreuznach meeting were supposed to have blocked.

99. *Ibid.*, pp. 175–176.
100. Lindberg, *op. cit.*, p. 143; Camps, *op. cit.*, p. 177.
101. *Ibid.*, p. 180.

The French called for postponement of the Eccles proposal until after January 1, 1959, when little could be done to halt the implementation of discriminatory practices feared by the British. French delegate Couve de Murville, reacting to a British hint that defensive measures might be taken if enlarged quotas were not adopted, refused to negotiate in what he characterized as an atmosphere of recrimination and threat. The French appealed directly to their EEC partners for support, emphasizing the utility of preferential treatment despite accords under OEEC and GATT. Reinforcement for the French argument came not unexpectedly from the EEC Commission and Europeanists interested in moving ahead with integration within the Six. Chancellor Adenauer also kept his part of the bargain with the French president. The Commission report fell on receptive ears. It was close to the French view on most important issues surrounding the free trade proposal. In its first memorandum to the Council of Ministers on February 26, 1959, the Commission doubted the feasibility of a trade accord among the seventeen heterogeneous states of the OEEC. Affirmed the Commission: "The Member States consider that . . . by agreeing to certain efforts and certain sacrifices in order to bring this Community into being, by accepting new disciplines and specific burdens, they have constituted an association which gives them the right to treat each other in a manner which is different from that adopted towards non-member states." [102] The following autumn, a second study group under Jean Rey confirmed the previous Commission view: that the community be built first before negotiations with third states be undertaken. Gaullist France and federalist-minded Commission members were equally opposed to OEEC trade arrangements, although again for different reasons.[103]

France Champions the Common Market:
Acceleration and Agriculture

French strategy shifted by late autumn 1959 from fending off attempts to create a free trade zone to a positive inclination to consolidate EEC progress and accelerate Rome Treaty provisions. Three changes in the European environment spurred the French effort: improved European economic and political conditions, the United

102. Lindberg, *op. cit.*, p. 147
103. Camps, *op. cit.*, p. 200.

States balance-of-payments problem, and, negatively, the British decision to organize a European Free Trade Association (EFTA).

Negotiations over EFTA played to the strong side of the French game. They distracted Britain and its trading allies (Sweden, Norway, Denmark, Switzerland, Austria, and Portugal) until November 1959 when the trade group was formally established in Stockholm. With the free trade threat held in abeyance, time was gained for the EEC to move ahead on its own. EFTA gave point to the French argument that the British were interested only in commercial advantages from the EEC and had no intention of assuming the economic obligations of the Rome Treaty, nor of subscribing to its larger political goals. The new trading bloc was portrayed, with some accuracy, as a British bargaining lever over the Six. France's charges, as plausible as they were self-serving, drove a wedge between Europeanist sentiment and those forces, especially the Dutch, that were friendly to Britain and working for an outward-looking Six and wider trading relations with OEEC states. For the immediate future, the baggage of six states trailing after Britain presented insuperable obstacles for a trade accord between Britain and the European community. EFTA weakened the British case within the EEC and reduced the incentive of the Six to reach a settlement.[104]

The perilous United States balance-of-payments problem provided an unintended boost to the French campaign against EFTA and the free trade zone. A temporary parallelism of interests, though hardly motives, crystallized between France and the United States. In Washington's view, EFTA and the free trade area in Europe erected trading barriers for American goods. If the Six also hindered the liberalization of global trade, it had the virtue of promoting political union that for larger strategic and diplomatic ends, related to the Cold War, had guided United States policy toward Europe since World War II.[105] EFTA divided Europe into sixes and sevens while seeming to provide few, if any, compensating economic benefits.[106] The United States was counting on a politically strong and econom-

104. *Ibid.*, pp. 195–197, 210–273.

105. See Max Beloff, *op. cit.*, and Henry Kissinger, *Troubled Partnership*, pp. 3–88.

106. Emile Benoit, *Europe at Sixes and Sevens* (New York: Columbia University Press, 1961).

ically integrated European community to favor global trade liberalization, encouraged by Europeanists of the Monnet school who talked in Atlantic terms.[107] Gaullists also voiced open trade sentiments toward third states that assured American listeners even as steps were taken to block British free trade initiatives. The commitment to freer trade evidenced in the EEC Commission's First Memorandum appealed equally to French and American interests. For France, the European community held out the promise of negotiations on expanded trade once it was established. For the United States, a larger economic grouping would serve a number of complementary purposes: it would bring the states of the OEEC under closer American guidance, define new rules for liberalized trade that would relieve U.S. payments difficulties, and shift some of the burden of economic assistance to the European states.

Appealing also to German and Dutch ears was the French argument that strengthening the European community would reinforce ties with the United States. In throwing provisional support behind a new international economic organization to transform the OEEC and enlarge its trade responsibilities, the French tactic also served a number of otherwise distinctly national purposes: British power was absorbed in OEEC negotiations; criticisms of EEC trade discrimination were temporarily stilled; and the prospect of French support for more liberalized trade promised to engage United States assistance, bolster the Commission's French-leaning First Memorandum in EEC negotiations, and enhance France's Third World image. Creating the Organization for Economic Cooperation and Development out of the OEEC absorbed much United States attention in 1960. Meanwhile, the EEC under French impulse accelerated implementation of the Common Market and the passage of the European Economic Community from the first to the second stage.

Political and economic conditions in Europe aligned French and Europeanist sentiment to press for speedier community integration. Both forces looked for support to Adenauer, who again put aside plans to resign from the chancellorship. Moreover, President de Gaulle remained publicly committed to the economic advancement of the EEC. The French economy was experiencing an upturn, and

107. Willis, *op. cit.,* p. 283.

French industrialists were displaying a rare confidence in their ability to compete within an open Six. Community industries were adjusting to the larger markets anticipated by an expanded Common Market. Trade boomed between Common Market partners; in the first year of operation, French exports increased 35.9 percent and imports by 11 percent.[108] Most important of all, European economic growth surged upward. Industrial production in 1958 grew 7 percent, almost twice the rate of the previous year. The stage was set to move the community forward.[109]

EFTA also challenged the EEC. The British-led trade group, even before its official creation, had reached accord in July 1959 reducing tariffs on industrial goods by 20 percent. To match the EFTA move, the EEC Europeanists proposed the acceleration of the Common Market. At a session of the Rey committee on November 17, 1959, the French turned the acceleration proposal, presented initially in a detailed plan of Belgian Foreign Minister Pierre Wigny, to their advantage. They favored the advancement of the timetable for a 20 percent tariff reduction from January 1, 1962, to July 1, 1960, and the coordination of accelerated tariff disarmament with the creation of the common external tariff. The French initiative crystallized the acceleration issue within the EEC. Outmaneuvered were the Dutch and Germans, whose interest in acceleration was linked to free trade negotiations with Britain. France tied progress on internal tariff reductions (what Germany and the Benelux wanted) to the creation of the common external tariff (about which they were far less enthusiastic). The reluctance of France's partners to move along these parallel routes exposed them to the criticism that they, not Gaullist France, were blocking European unity. As low-tariff countries, Germany and Holland were torn between their economic interests and their announced commitment to European political integration.

The acceleration issue crystallized around three problems: (1) the date of application; (2) the percentage reduction in the common external and internal tariffs; and (3) progress in other areas of community interest, including social policy, rules of competition, and, most important, agriculture. Solutions to these difficulties had implications for two larger questions: the relation of the Six to each

108. Camps, *op. cit.*, pp. 192–194; Lindberg, *op. cit.*, pp. 168–174.
109. Willis, *op. cit.*, p. 284.

other and, as a community, to third states. The French answer in principle was for community preference toward the outside world and confederal growth under French auspices within the European community. The French were to make progress on both general lines over the acceleration issue. At their insistence, community decisions were placed in the form of an accord among the represented governments, and not made the authoritative pronouncements of the Commission. Acceleration itself moved the EEC ahead at the expense of alternative arrangements with EFTA or other interested third states.

In response to the November 1959 request of the Council of Ministers, the Commission presented detailed proposals for acceleration on February 26, 1960: abolition of industrial quotas by December 31, 1961; faster internal tariff disarmament, requiring cuts of 20 percent on July 1, 1960, and December 31, 1961; speedier erection of the external tariff through a 20 percent reduction of member schedules on July 1, 1960, not a year and a half later as previously agreed upon; and more intense work on community social and agricultural policies.[110]

The German government again acquiesced more on political than on economic grounds. Adenauer overrode the opposition of the Erhard wing of the Christian Democratic party and accepted the community- (and French-) sponsored proposals despite the risks of greater division between EFTA and the EEC and a higher external tariff. French agreement to a permanent 20 percent reduction in the common external tariff and compromise on the number of exceptions that would be allowed eased the domestic political problem for the ruling Christian Democratic party and Adenauer's standing as its leader.[111] The British also unwittingly assisted the French and Commission Europeanists determined to assure the irreversibility of EEC economic integration. Prime Minister Harold Macmillan's unfortunate remarks in Washington in March 1960, reportedly expressing concern over Europe's economic division and justifying Britain's leadership of a peripheral coalition against the Continental System,

110. *Ibid.*, p. 286.
111. Paul G. Minneman, "Agriculture in France and the European Community," in *France and the European Community*, ed. Sydney N. Fisher (Columbus: Ohio State University Press, 1965), p. 6.

pushed Germany deeper into the EEC and French camps. Macmillan's untoward statements, combined with British vacillation over Berlin, German reunification, and European defense, did little to project an image of dependability in West German eyes. De Gaulle's France seemed the better bet for long-term German political objectives, the high economic costs of closer association notwithstanding.

These acceleration accords hinged, however, on a start toward incorporating agriculture into the Common Market. French, Dutch, and Italian interests largely coincided on agricultural policy in the early 1960's; Germany stood again as the outsider. It discriminated through quota restrictions against its partners' agricultural products, including French cereals and Dutch dairy products. The Fourth and Fifth Republics consistently opposed German restrictions on farm produce and insisted that agriculture's inclusion in the Common Market was the logical *quid pro quo* for the elimination of industrial tariffs. The Fourth Republic would probably have been unable to approve the Rome Treaty except for the support of farm groups who were led by government officials to expect that French agriculture would be the largest gainer from the Common Market.[112] France was the largest agricultural producer in the community. Over one-fifth of the population in the late 1950's was engaged in agricultural production. France also stood at the top rank in the ratio of actively employed labor to area of land under production. The French ratio of 6.7 contrasted with 3.2 for Germany and Italy and 4.5 and 5.0 for Holland and Belgium, respectively. France also had the largest amount of unused agricultural resources and looked expectantly on the possibility of access to a protected market of over 200 million consumers. Cereal production, France's principal agricultural commodity, was estimated to rise between 7 and 11 million tons, of which approximately half would be available for export. Beef for export was also projected to increase by 17,000 tons.[113] France's national support for agriculture exceeded $1 billion with no end in sight. The diminution of France's farm population through resettlement schemes was also expected to be costly. That 23 percent of France's population still lived on the farm, but received only 9 percent of its GNP, indicated that a major transformation of farming toward fewer farm-

112. Willis, *op. cit.*, p. 289
113. *Ibid.*, p. 388.

ers and increased production of those remaining were imperatives of modernization and industrialization if France were to maintain its economic position not only within the Six but on world markets.

Again, a change in community agricultural policy most adversely affected Germany. The German government assisted the economically inefficient, but politically potent, German farmer through a complicated system of price supports, quotas, subsidies, and tariff protection. In return most farmers voted for the Christian Democrats. No German government, much less Adenauer's ruling party, could be indifferent to agricultural interests, represented by the Deutscher Bauernverband, one of the most powerful interest groups operating in Europe.[114]

Germany's partners, with France in the forefront, pressed for approval of the acceleration accords and the beginnings of a common agricultural policy for the Six. After hard bargaining, agreement was provisionally reached at the December 1960 meeting on the Commission's recommendations to transform agriculture into a community concern, including marketing and production arrangements to be uniformly applied to the Six. Countries importing agricultural products outside the European community were obliged to pay levies, which were to be equal to the difference between the lowest world price and the community support price, less the cost of transportation to the consuming area. Farm exporters (like France and Holland) would receive, alternatively, a subsidy between the low world market price and the community figure.[115] After intense negotiations throughout 1961, Adenauer again bent his government's will over the objections of the Erhard faction and of business and subordinated German economic interests to community political development in the form of the acceleration and agriculture decisions. On January 12–13, 1962, Germany joined its partners in an agricultural accord, accepting a financial regulation based on the levy system and applicable to a number of key agricultural products, including cereals, pork, dairy products, poultry, fruit, and vegetables.[116]

Accord on financial regulation for agriculture and acceptance of community preference for agriculture within the Common Market

114. Minneman, *op. cit.,* p. 87.
115. Willis, *op. cit.,* p. 290.
116. Minneman, *op. cit.,* pp. 88–89.

capped the economic concessions made by Germany for political objectives. In agriculture, however, the Germans were partly to blame for their poor showing. German insistence on high community price supports to protect German farmers, the community substitute for the complex national system erected after World War II, meant that Germany would have to pay a higher levy on agricultural imports. The French finally concurred although they would have preferred a lower price level to check inflation, discourage overproduction, hold livestock feed costs down, and increase French competitiveness in world markets. Moreover, to lighten some of the German financial burden, a community fund was established that was financed not only by levies but also by national contributions weighted according to the amount of agricultural imports from third countries. The transition period for the implementation of a common agricultural policy was extended from six to seven and a half years.

Movement forward on agriculture assured passage of the remaining acceleration package. The Common Market, motored by German capital, passed to the second stage. The French-German axis held again. But German acquiescence more whetted than sated the Gaullist appetite. The Paris-Bonn *rapprochement* would be tested anew on de Gaulle's plan for a confederated Western Europe and on his veto of Britain's application to join the European Economic Community. We now turn in Chapter 6, which completes the analysis of the first phase of de Gaulle's European policy, to a discussion of French efforts to win Germany and Western Europe and wrest them, as de Gaulle charged, from American domination.

6

Gaullist France on the Attack

The Evolution of Negotiations: The Fouchet Plan[1]

President de Gaulle's visit to Italy on June 26, 1959, a little more than a year after his return to power, inaugurated his campaign for European political union. It resulted in a French-Italian proposal to hold regular meetings of the foreign ministers of the Six. French Foreign Minister Couve de Murville raised the idea again on November 23–24 at a meeting of his European community colleagues in Strasbourg where it was agreed that, "without prejudice to consultations in NATO and the Western European Union (WEU)," meetings could be arranged. Three encounters were organized before de Gaulle's meeting with Chancellor Konrad Adenauer at Rambouillet on July 29–30, 1960, when he first unveiled his thinking about institutionalizing European unity. Despite initial German fears about the possible diverse implications of de Gaulle's notions for the integrity of the European communities and European-American solidarity in NATO,[2] the French president went ahead with bilateral talks with the leaders and foreign ministers of the other community states between August 30 and September 18. First public exposure of de Gaulle's thinking occurred in his news conference of Septem-

1. The negotiations over European political union in the early 1960's have been studied extensively. The most comprehensive work is Robert Bloes, *Le "Plan Fouchet" et le problème de l'Europe politique* (Bruges: College d'Europe, 1970). However, the most useful for purposes of this study is Susanne J. Bodenheimer, *Political Union*. Other studies that should be examined are Alessandro Silj, *Europe's Political Puzzle: A Study of the Fouchet Negotiations and the 1963 Veto,* Occasional Paper No. 17 (Cambridge: Harvard University Center for International Affairs, 1967); Irving M. Destler, *Political Union in Europe: 1960–62* (Princeton: Woodrow Wilson School of Public and International Affairs, 1964); Jouve, *Le Général de Gaulle,* I, 316–368; and Willis, *France, Germany,* pp. 292–299.

2. Paul-Marie de la Gorce, *De Gaulle entre deux mondes* (Paris: Fayard, 1964), pp. 719–720.

ber 5 which grouped the problem of European unity with a revision of the Atlantic Alliance.

De Gaulle found the need for union not only in the commonality of West European interests to which he had earlier referred repeatedly but also in the limitations of the economic communities to be the vehicle for unification. "These organs," said de Gaulle, ruffling the sensibilities of his European federalist critics, "have their technical value, but do not have, they cannot have authority and, consequently, political effectiveness. As long as nothing serious happens, they function without much difficulty, but as soon as a tragic situation appears, a major problem to be solved, it can then be seen that one 'High Authority' or another has no authority over the various national categories and that only the States have it." [3] A European union would cooperate in "political, economic, and cultural domains and in that of defense." [4] Cooperation would be realized through regular governmental consultations prepared by specialists in these areas and through periodic deliberations of a European assembly composed of national delegates. A referendum would lend popular support and initiative to the enterprise; final authority, however, would remain with the states. [5]

Bilateral talks continued through the fall and winter of 1960, culminating in a Paris summit of the heads of state or government of the Six. Gaullist ministers Debré and Murville, in a special trip to Bonn in October, laid the foundation for the meeting, mollifying the concerns of skeptics, like Erhard and the foreign office, and reinforcing the resolve of Adenauer, grateful for France's hard-line stance on Berlin, to remain firm in his desire for French-German cooperation. Even the European federalists found favor in the summit idea although they conditioned their support on safeguards for the existing communities and progress toward a federally organized Europe. [6] Only the Dutch, who delayed progress on the Gaullist initiative, were reluctant to be courted. The principal result of the February summit was the creation of a committee, chaired by the French ambassa-

3. *Major Addresses*, p. 93.
4. *Ibid.*
5. *Ibid.*
6. Bloes, *op. cit.*, pp. 127–128.

dor to Denmark, Christian Fouchet, and charged to present concrete proposals for the May summit.

The Dutch prevented the convening of the second summit until July. Most of the elements of their position, to be reiterated and elaborated during the discussion on political confederation, crystallized early in the Fouchet talks. As a small state, jealous of its tradition of political independence and global commerce, the Netherlands built its postwar foreign policy on three principles that appeared to be challenged by the French proposal for political union. These included (1) close defense ties to the United States within the Atlantic Alliance; (2) the openness of Western European communities to other members and most particularly the participation of Great Britain in European economic and political integration; and (3) the maintenance of the limited, but real, supranational authority of the European economic communities and the gradual extension of these institutions to encompass political union. During the early Fouchet negotiations, and later in succeeding forums, these principles conditioned the Dutch to press, usually without success, for parallel discussions with Britain on political union and for assurances that the proposed union would preserve the authority of the European economic communities and the competence of NATO and that the discussion of economic and defense questions would be carried on principally within these two respective organizations. The Netherlands government resisted holding regular meetings at any level on any of the topics outlined in de Gaulle's news conference. However, if these views put the Dutch at loggerheads with the French, they were much closer to the supranational perspectives of their other EEC partners on the institutional development of the communities, including the fusion of the community executives, the election of the European Parliament by universal suffrage, the expansion of the responsibilities and authority of both agencies relative to the Council of Ministers, which represented the member states, and the extension of majority voting to larger areas of community concern.

The July summit at Bonn made more progress than the February meeting. The final communiqué, while calling for a strengthening of the Atlantic Alliance through European union and an extension of the "work already undertaken in the European Community," proposed (1) to give form to political union through closer cooperation between the Six preparatory to its institutional embodiment; (2) to develop and concert common views at the foreign ministers level; (3) to open talks beyond purely political matters on cultural, educational, and scientific relations; and (4) to charge the Fouchet committee to present a plan that would give a "statutory character" to a union of European peoples.[7]

The willingness of the French and Dutch delegations to reach some compromise was as significant as the Bad Godesberg Declaration itself. Since the meeting with Adenauer a year before, de Gaulle had dropped his suggestions concerning a revision of the community referendum. He also conceded language that tied European union to the Atlantic Alliance and accepted the June 28 resolution of the European Parliament, calling for the participation of the commissions in unity talks, the maintenance of community authority, and the direct election of the assembly as an agenda item for the Fouchet committee. The Dutch bent, too, to the pressure of their partners and agreed to regular meetings and continued participation in the Fouchet committee whose mandate was more clearly defined and authoritatively underwritten by the Bonn summit.[8]

The French plan for union, presented October 19, 1961, became the working document for the Fouchet group. It called for a council of ministers of heads of state, government, and foreign ministers, conducting its business by unanimous consent and incapable of binding a state against its will; a European parliament restricted to the deliberation of problems facing the union and to posing questions to the council, but incompetent to make decisions; and a European political commission composed of senior officials of the foreign ministries and seated in Paris, functioning as a center for coordinating and executing member decisions. The union would cooperate in foreign, defense, cultural, and science policy. Unanimity was needed for amendment of the charter. Article 16 of the treaty, which provoked considerable argument later, proposed a general revision after three years to incorporate progress made toward union. A common foreign policy and the establishment of "an organization centralizing . . . the European Communities" were also anticipated.[9]

7. *Ibid.*, pp. 150–151.
8. *Ibid.*, p. 151.
9. *Ibid.*, p. 491.

Reaction to the Fouchet plan was mixed. The delegations from Germany, Italy, and Luxembourg generally supported the French draft, differing more in detail than in principle among themselves and with the French. The Belgians and Dutch were considerably more critical. Paul-Henri Spaak, speaking for the Belgian government, wished more inclusive steps toward political union. The Dutch, seizing on the July 1961 British request for membership in the EEC, were more eager than ever to include Great Britain in the talks on political as well as economic union as a check on Gaullist ambitions.[10] These larger goals prompted a detailed criticism of the Fouchet proposal: the absence of language guaranteeing community authority and institutions, and the failure of the revision clause to specify the commitments undertaken by member states to strengthen European assembly powers, to introduce majority voting and universal suffrage, and to define the anomolous position of the political commission, which would neither function as a permanent secretariat nor as a continuing body of state representatives.

Amending their proposal to meet these objections, the French included references reinforcing United States-European defense ties within the Atlantic Alliance and respecting the institutional structure and authority of the communities. The revision clause associated the European assembly in the elaboration and execution of community policies, implicitly acknowledged the need for a fusion of the three executive agencies of the Six, and anticipated greater foreign policy coordination.

These concessions, submitted later through diplomatic channels rather than at a formal committee session, failed to blunt Dutch and Belgian demands for Britain's participation in union talks, the so-called *préalable anglais*. The foreign ministers of the Six met on December 15 and, overriding these reservations, adopted the French-German position to make membership automatic for those states which adhered to the economic community.[11] The Dutch proposal appeared premature. Economic negotiations with Britain for entry into the EEC had not proceeded very far, and the British themselves had not requested an invitation to take part in the Fouchet discussions. By the end of 1961, progress toward political union

10. *Ibid.*, p. 127
11. *Ibid.*, p. 259.

seemed sufficiently advanced for the normally skeptical, if not always cautious, *Combat* to remark that at the next scheduled summit meeting in Rome in February 1962, there would be born a "Union of Peoples." Concluded the analysis: "The Six are condemned to succeed." [12]

On July 18, 1962, less than a week after the decision of the Six to include agriculture in the Common Market, France submitted yet another formal proposal for revision.[13] It effectively withdrew, wholly or partially, previous concessions and pointed European union more directly toward the Gaullist-preferred goal of a more closed, intergovernmentally organized Six that would be more sensitive to French leadership. References to European-Atlantic defense ties were dropped. More important, the addition and deletion of language threatened the authority, structure, and functions of the communities. First, and much to the distress of European federalists, economics was added to foreign policy, culture, and defense as the areas of competence for the proposed union. Second, community guarantees were not mentioned. Third, provision for an independent secretary general was eliminated in favor of an institutionalized political commission and intergovernmental committee in foreign affairs, education, and such other fields that the council might create. Fourth, the revision clause was again silent on the role of the European parliament. Its advisory functions remained intact, but new language suggested that, while the subjects which it could debate were specifically expanded (foreign policy, defense, and education), it would be subject to tighter council direction.[14] Fifth, governments were no longer pledged to consult one another, nor were they obliged to furnish information required by the council or the political commission. Finally, the union was no longer dissoluble.

The French thunderbolt, euphemistically presented as a change in form not substance, galvanized France's divided partners in a temporary show of unity. The new French text was rejected as a basis for

12. *Ibid.*, p. 261.
13. There is some confusion on numbering the successive Fouchet plans that were developed. The first plan was submitted November 2, 1961; the second was never officially published and circulated only within the foreign ministries of the Six; the third, sometimes referred to as Fouchet 2, was presented by France on January 18, 1962, to the committee.
14. Bloes, *op. cit.*, p. 495.

discussion, and the Five developed their own counterproposals to which later bargaining revealed each delegation attached varying significance and political support. First, the Five favored language that tied European defense policies to the Atlantic Alliance although they split on how binding and comprehensive it should be. Second, economics remained partially beyond the scope of political union. The communities were assured that union would not "derogate from their competence." [15] Third, an independent secretary general was reinserted. Fourth, the revision clause spelled out the obligations of member states (1) to consider political revision at the time that the EEC passed from the second to the third stage; (2) to associate the assembly more in the process of revision and political implementation and to elect it through universal suffrage; (3) to introduce majority voting gradually into the council; (4) to integrate political and economic union without prejudice to the Rome and Paris treaties; and (5) to extend the purview of the court of justice and raise it to an official institution of European union. Fifth, the unanimity rule was slightly weakened. The Five advocated departures from majority voting in those areas where the Six had unanimously consented to its application. The Five were silent on the question whether a council decision bound states abstaining. The French would have exempted them. In cases of dispute, the Five made provision for an appeal to the European parliament for its opinion.

In meetings held between January 18 and April 17, 1962, of the Fouchet committee, of the foreign ministers of the Six, and of the leaders of France, Germany, and Italy, many of the points of disagreement were narrowed.[16] President de Gaulle's meeting with Chancellor Adenauer on February 15 at Baden-Baden and with Italian Prime Minister Fanfani on April 4 at Turin produced some noteworthy compromises. An "Atlantic clause" would be inserted

15. *Ibid.*, p. 501.
16. Observers are sharply divided on the question of the degree to which European consensus could have been reached. See n. 1 above for citations. Silj doubts seriously whether the Fouchet plan could have been ultimately acceptable, but emphasizes the tactical necessity of the Five to contain the Gaullist political offensive. Bodenheimer makes a persuasive case that, on the merits of the specific issues raised by the French proposal, the Six were closer together than might have appeared from the eventual break (*op. cit.*, pp. 76–102). Bloes remains less committal about the chances of success.

in the preamble for union, but with no mention of NATO; economics would be a subject for occasional, not regular, discussion; and the community institutions would retain their supranational character.[17] As the ministers assembled for their meeting on April 17, progress had been made on all critical questions of union except two: Britain's role in the unity talks and the revision clause.

The April 10 speech of Edward Heath, British representative to the WEU Council, complicated the settlement of the *préalable anglais*.[18] For the first time, the British discreetly requested an invitation to take part in the discussion on political union. For reasons that still remain obscure,[19] the British government also felt it expedient to take a public stand on some of the principal issues raised by the proposed union although under no obligation to do so and contrary to the advice of many of Britain's continental friends. On the one hand, the British sided with the French in favor of an intergovernmentally organized political union that went beyond the authority of the communities. They were also reluctant to assume specific commitments for a revision of the union's institutional structure at a fixed date. In words that were to be essentially echoed by de Gaulle in his May 15 news conference, Heath observed "that the substance of political integration will grow most effectively out of the habit of working more and more closely together," than from written texts.[20] On the other hand, Heath specifically underlined his government's allegiance to the Atlantic Alliance and voiced the hope that an enlarged Europe would be sympathetic to closer association with the EFTA states, including the neutral powers of Sweden, Switzerland, and Austria, and with the British Commonwealth.

The British action prompted the Dutch and Belgians to reaffirm their insistence on British participation in the European discussions on political union. Finding no way to overcome these objections, the foreign ministers adjourned shortly after French Foreign Minister Couve de Murville received a divided answer to his question: "Are

17. Gorce, *op. cit.*, p. 721; Bodenheimer, *op. cit.*, p. 63; Bloes, *op. cit.*, pp. 258–261.

18. Western European Union, General Affairs Committee, *A Retrospective View of the Political Year in Europe, 1962* (Paris, March 1963), pp. 26–30. Hereafter cited WEU, *Political Year, 1962*.

19. See Silj, *op. cit.*, pp. 3–24, 65–79, 80–105.

20. WEU, *Political Year, 1962*, p. 29.

we in agreement to continue our work, to agree on a text, to communicate it to the British, and, if they have no major objection, to sign it and put it into effect?" [21] Neither the Dutch nor the Belgian delegations would sign a treaty without Great Britain. Attempts by the Italian government in succeeding months to revive the discussions on union, with quiet French and German backing, came to nothing. By the summer of 1962, the European states were turning to other problems that seemed more susceptible to resolution. The French government, having secured agriculture's inclusion in the Common Market and the end of the Algerian War, similarly revised its tactical position in Europe, away from multilateral negotiations to preferred bilateral dealings with key states. Gaullist Europe prepared to move toward its conception of Europe outside, and even in spite of, a common West European political framework.

The Collapse of the Fouchet Plans: Implications for European Union and Gaullist Foreign Policy

The breakdown of the Fouchet talks affected European union and Gaullist global objectives more profoundly than the participants were able, or willing—as in France's case—to discern at the time. The broad internal and external dimensions of the problem of European union, beyond those raised in signing the Rome Treaty, were never more clearly articulated. So long as no state proposed a formal union, there was no need to face the embarrassing question of what kind of union to establish. Avoided, thus, were the subsidiary questions of what would be the aims of union, the competence and authority of its communal (or intergovernmental) institutions, and its relation to the existing economic communities. These questions of internal organization, as the French and Dutch delegations were so acutely aware, also raised more fundamental problems of the external relations of such a union. Specifically, how would European union relate to the security and economic ties with the United States within the Atlantic Alliance and what would be its impact on East-West relations and the eventual settlement of World War II, includ-

21. Bodenheimer, *op. cit.*, p. 137. Spaak offers his own rationale for his actions that rather closely parallel Bodenheimer's analysis. Paul-Henri Spaak, *Combats inachevés* (Paris: Fayard, 1969), pp. 357–380.

ing the end of Europe's and Germany's division. Once Gaullist France pressed the issue of union for its own ends, these troubled problems could no longer be ignored. Once raised, none of the Six could henceforward claim to support European union without simultaneously offering answers to the more inclusive agenda items.

The French initiative forced France's partners, less eager than President de Gaulle, to relate their allegedly uniform commitment to European union to their particular national objectives and interests. The discussion revealed, as most sensed or were soon to discover, that each state's conception of union was shaped more by the instrumental value that it placed on union in reaching other goals than by its abstract commitment to union as an end in itself. After the Fouchet collapse, appeals to community spirit that had previously helped to overcome national differences, which might well have remained unresolved if left solely to calculations of advantage, had lost some of their intellectual, not to mention emotional, force. Nor could the Six so easily hide from public notice the formidable difficulties of achieving a more perfect European union. The brave front of the Five in the face of the revised French plan of January 18 was not entirely convincing, as the bilateral compromises reached between France, Germany, and Italy before and after the April 17 meeting attested. Even enthusiastic unionists like Spaak, who refused to believe that the April 17 adjournment was sine die, were sobered by the adamance of the French and Dutch delegations in holding to their respective positions.[22] For better or worse, the Fouchet negotiations left a legacy of heightened consciousness about what separated, not united, the European states. Blurring these divisions was of course no prescription for their reconciliation, but recognizing them more clearly was only an invitation, not a formula, for overcoming them. The agenda for union was longer than states had been willing to admit; the principal issues to be settled more intractable than hitherto foreseen.

However difficult were the logical and substantive problems raised by political union, they paled before the problem of generating sufficient political will among the Six to cooperate in areas where tenta-

22. Silj, op. cit., pp. 25ff; Bloes, op. cit., passim.

tive accord could be struck.[23] The issue of European unity revealed not only the divergencies between the Six but also the contradictions on which their respective foreign policies were founded. The Dutch case is particularly instructive as counterpoint to the French position.

The Dutch concluded after World War II that neutrality no longer served their defense, economic, or diplomatic interests. Recognizing the need to cooperate with their North American and European partners to achieve national objectives posed a novel problem for Dutch foreign policy that in many ways was structurally similar to that facing the other states of Western Europe: how to contribute in the construction of a set of international relations that responded to Dutch interests and simultaneously maximized national independence, externally and internally. As a small power, having more to adapt to alternatives made available by stronger states than to originate plans of its own design, the solutions seized upon by the Dutch were bound to be evaluated more on the strength of their political feasibility than their logical consistency. The Atlantic Alliance provided an acceptable security framework; the European communities, once postwar rehabilitation had been achieved, formed an important part of the Dutch answer to their welfare and economic goals. The limited scope and supranational authority of the communities had two advantages. They minimized the amount of national sovereignty and flexibility that had to be relinquished and maximized the institutional and juridical guarantees for the Netherlands, as a small state, against the feared encroachments of its larger neighbors. The universal character of community law appealed to the Dutch sense of fair play and moral rectitude.

The communities, moreover, afforded a testing ground for political union at low risk. If the Rome and Paris treaties conceded a great deal in principle, committing member states to eventual economic and political integration, the operating procedures and accepted customs of the communities were more modest; these were sensitively attuned to the subtle variations of interest of the participating states, their particular domestic constraints, and their reluctance to accept

23. Bodenheimer makes this case in her excellent analysis of European political union; the whole book is eminently worth reading, particularly her analysis of Dutch foreign policy on which the evaluation above heavily draws. Bodenheimer, *op. cit.*, pp. 152–196.

limits on their freedom of action. Each of the governments could talk a good game of union before their respective constituencies— and could seriously play at it on occasion as the negotiations over agriculture demonstrate—but each could still count on large measures of independence in foreign affairs. Time would supposedly resolve the contradictions prompted by this not entirely candid mode of behavior; reconciliation would await the future, measured more by a Greek than a Gregorian calendar.

The French plan for union forced unwanted choices on the Netherlands. Gaullist dislike for NATO threatened the foundation of Dutch security policy, and the proposed French confederation appeared to be a vehicle for loosening transatlantic ties. Moreover, French confederal notions, combining broad aims for union with new institutional machinery favoring the larger European states, challenged the fragile bond of juridical, institutional, and implicit intergovernmental understandings within the communities that protected Dutch interests. No less than the French, the Dutch were aware of the contradiction, first, between their announced commitment to European unity and their acceptance of the United States security guarantee and, second, between their support for the supranational development of the communities and their unswerving determination to bring Britain, as much opposed as Gaullist France to any weakening of its national authority, into the West European economic and political integrationist movement.

These logical embarrassments were of lesser consequence, however, than the Gaullist danger that threatened to unravel the crazyquilt design of security, economic, and diplomatic ties that the Dutch had tirelessly woven since World War II. That this pattern of political alignments was not compatible with a Gaullist Europe was often obscured by the Dutch in quibbles with partners over narrow questions of procedure and definition during the Fouchet talks. The British appeared to be the ideal partners. There were traditional ties and sentiments to count on. The pragmatic disposition of the British who were skilled in managing conflicting foreign policy relations, like those on which Dutch policy rested, worked to the mutual advantage of the parties concerned. Even before the British, the Dutch saw the value of limited economic and political cooperation with their continental neighbors, but not to so inclusive a degree as to jeopardize security interests or turn the low countries inward, away from their open commercial tradition. Wanting more supranational development of the communities was consistent with Dutch democratic leanings. Given the circumscribed foreign policy concerns of the Brussels agencies, these were of minimal immediate danger to Dutch national authority. Besides, the Dutch saw advantage in maintaining "a certain 'institutional balance' among the Council, the Commission, and the European Parliament (the latter two being encouraged in the directions favored by the Dutch government) so as to counter growing French influence in daily activities and in the planning of the Brussels institutions." [24] They were, however, willing to concede ground on supranationality if Britain was to become a member of the European union and the economic communities. Its presence offered more assurance than treaty pledges, taken lightly by a revisionist and revolutionary France, that Dutch interests would be honored. For the Netherlands and for its partners, the goal of European union and the competing plans for integration or confederation could be evaluated, not on their abstract merits, but, finally, only in terms of their implications for the existing network of satisfactory bilateral and multilateral relations already painfully and precariously knitted together.

It was not surprising then that each of the Six, as Dutch behavior suggests, would have a different evaluation of the aims, powers, and institutional make-up of the proposed union. Confederal union was, as de Gaulle indicated to one of his better biographers, but a means. Even the collapse of the Fouchet talks served French purposes,[25] notwithstanding its rejection. First, it forced France's partners to confront the logical contradictions of their political commitments. Second, it focused attention on the imperfections of existing community institutions to realize these conflicting objectives. Third, it afforded the opportunity for France to propose, however vague and ill-defined the outline, its own formulae that purportedly would resolve or attenuate these contradictions through intergovernmental arrangements that would promote France's leadership role. And, fourth, it served notice that failure to rationalize foreign policy differences along French lines freed France to pursue its objectives out-

24. Silj, *op. cit.,* p. 52.
25. Interview with Paul-Marie de la Gorce, Paris, March 1971.

side the framework of the Six (as the rejection of the directorate justified in de Gaulle's mind France's gradual disengagement from NATO). On the other hand, acceptance of French European proposals promised to advance Gaullist aspirations in the very directions most feared by the Dutch. Like the nimble acrobat who must mount to the top post of a circus pyramid, France would reach new and dizzier heights of international performance and prestige on the strength of its partners' support.[26]

That the Dutch were reluctant to back the French effort was clear from the start. How steady France's partners would be depended less on their enthusiasm for France's ascension or for the construction of a French-modeled pyramid than on how well union served their particular drives. The Belgians felt that the Fouchet plans did not go far enough toward federal union while the Dutch were concerned that they went too far; alignment on Britain's participation was a temporary liaison of convenience designed, paradoxically enough, to achieve different results. The Belgians, through Spaak, looked for leverage to elicit concessions from the French; the Dutch, through Joseph Luns, were pleased, at a minimum, with no progress toward political unity unless the British were present as a counterweight to the French-German entente.[27] The Germans, eager for reconciliation with France, still less apprehensive than their partners about ultimate Gaullist aims, and more sensitive to the larger questions of East-West relations and their own division, saw even Gaullist-styled European union as a positive step toward a stronger defense posture and closer political ties between the West European states. The Italians saw themselves in the middle. Sympathetic to political union and community development, they were also concerned about maintaining good relations among the Six and between Europe and the United States. With less immediate interests at stake, the role of mediator came more easily to Italy than to its partners. However, when pressed to align on the French-German axis after the April 17 debacle, Italy realized soon that joining a Paris-Bonn grouping to overrun the small

26. Hoffmann, *Daedalus,* 1966, pp. 862–915, discusses the "escalator" effect that Europe was to play in Gaullist designs for France.

27. Delineation of these competing national concerns is more fully treated in the works of Bloes, Bodenheimer, and Silj. See n. 1 above. Only the major divisions can be suggested here.

powers would merely mortgage the day when Italian interests might similarly be adversely affected. The defeat of the small states would, in effect, undermine the very rationale that encouraged Italy's assumption of a mediating role: to keep a certain balance of forces in equilibrium within Europe. For its part, Luxembourg, unable to agree with its Belgian and Dutch neighbors and with the French-German position, seriously weakened what modifying role it might have played.[28]

Seen from the perspectives of the six states searching for union—and failing in the Fouchet affair—no one state can be fully blamed for the breakdown of talks. Each quite naturally evaluated union from its own perspective; each differed often as much from the French plan as between themselves. There is still force in the carefully argued conclusion reached by one analyst that the Fouchet episode, as far as the behavior of the Six can suggest, supports the view "that there is an autonomous sphere of foreign policy and defense, that disputes about foreign policy cannot necessarily be resolved through the community method, and that the gap between economics and foreign policy will not be bridged through institutionalized 'spill-over.'" [29] Questions of economic and welfare policy could not be kept out of the meetings of the heads of state and government, according to de Gaulle, for such questions were subject to the determination of the participating states and could not be arbitrarily excluded from their concern, however previous treaty commitments might be interpreted.[30] As later experience was to demonstrate, economic integration might develop quite far—witness agricultural policy, the fusion of the community executives, even the survival of the communities after the crisis of 1965–1966—without leading to a political integration that confirmed the hopes and calculations of community federalists. In one sense at least, de Gaulle's assumptions about state behavior were confirmed. They acted on their own interests as they separately perceived them, and movement toward union was evaluated as but a part, however important, of a larger set of relations that each was working to keep or strike.

28. Silj, *op. cit.*, pp. 29–33, is helpful on Italy. Bloes presents the most detail on Luxembourg's role, *op. cit.*, *passim.*
29. Bodenheimer, *op. cit.*, p. 24.
30. *Major Addresses*, p. 175.

It was the over-all conjuncture of satisfactory, if refracted, relations, not the realization of just one political outcome—presented under the rubric of European union—that was sought. Even the calculating French were willing to admit their mutuality of interest with their partners, not only in the original proposal for union, but in their disposition, manifested throughout the discussion and especially in their bilateral contacts with their partners, to compromise on some essential points of their own proposals. On the other hand, the self-serving character of the French initiative, seen perhaps most sharply in the January 18 revision, tended to encourage each of the Six also to adopt a narrow national strategy which was only briefly and imperfectly papered over by the makeshift hastily fabricated by the Five to meet the French challenge. If Gaullist assumptions were borne out, it appears plausible to argue that French behavior was as much the source of an "induced response" on the part of its partners as an anticipated reaction on France's part to their nationally biased behavior.

France, the Five, and France's partners separately gained little from the Fouchet collapse. The failure of unity talks suggested narrower limits to French maneuverability and influence than the Gaullists were willing to concede for some years to come. A small state, like the Netherlands, handily withstood French pressures; Luns held de Gaulle to a draw in a test of wills. France's inability to outmove or compel its weaker partner to toe a French mark raised the reasonable prospect that it would equally fail once Germany refused to submit itself to French direction. Then it would be more moved than mover. Dutch intransigence taught de Gaulle no lesson about the limits of French diplomacy, which remained wedded until the late 1960's to a high evaluation of its potential influence. Furthermore, bilateral diplomacy, as the preferred French technique, hardly proved itself an all-purpose tool. If it overcame many of the reservations voiced especially in Germany and Italy, it backfired noticeably with Belgium and Holland. It created the impression, not far from the truth, that France expected the small powers to acquiesce in what was decided between Paris and Bonn, with the approval, more or less, of a timid Rome. Curiously enough, rather than caution Gaullist France about its dependence on allies, the breakup of the Fouchet meetings emboldened it to embark further on its ambitious program for Europe, first with Germany and later with the Soviet Union, parading its dubious claims to original power as a sufficient weight to transform inner-European and transatlantic relations without the assistance either of the Six, as a bloc, or of Germany, its strongest partner.

The Five were not victors, either. If they were able to agree that the maintenance of community integrity and American defense ties were irreducible common interests, they failed to blunt the Gaullist challenge. They were slow to seize on French concessions to keep the talks from folding. Buoyed by the success of the communities to which Gaullist France itself had contributed and because of which Britain wished to join the Continent at long last, the federalists believed that they could press ahead toward their most precious objectives. "In order to achieve a distant objective," as one observer concluded, "they failed to see that the most urgent task was that of 'containing' de Gaulle." [31] To be sure, Gaullist France carefully cast its concessions toward the Atlantic Alliance in terms of a traditional guarantee pact, not NATO, and stressed the principle of economic integration while depreciating the community's authority to define economic policy independent of the member states. The task facing the Five, if later experience offers any guide, was to make more difficult a strategy of the lone ranger and to hem France as much as possible within a multilateral setting. "A political union, by expanding the area of common interests and consultation, would have allowed France's partners to bargain from a more solid position. The *de-ut-des* would have applied not only to Communities but also to other problems closer to de Gaulle's heart." [32] The federalists could fear with reason that the council of the proposed union might become a court of final appeal for the community, but the breakdown of the Fouchet talks led to yet an even more unfortunate result. Instead of a multilateral court of appeals for the Six on which would sit their respective representatives, France alone decided to monopolize the appellate bench.

If the Dutch can be faulted less on this score, their forcing of France's hand with Britain suited de Gaulle's manner of play. Gaullist France had no intention of sharing European leadership with

31. Silj, *op. cit.*, p. 127.
32. *Ibid.*, p. 131.

Britain. If Heath struck a responsive chord in Paris in approving de Gaulle's intergovernmental notions, his equally vociferous support for Atlantic ties and Britain's world leadership role nullified his positive gesture. Heath hinted strongly that Britain was finally ready to make Western Europe the center ring of its global diplomacy. But once Britain's membership in the Common Market was approved, this would involve both the EEC and the EFTA states, including the neutral group of Sweden, Switzerland, and Austria, and perhaps some Commonwealth states in associate status. Britain's European policy was to complement, not supplant, its relations with EFTA and the Commonwealth states, with the EEC states cast in supporting roles for the British global show. Heath's future could hardly be attractive to an aspiring and ambitious France eager to secure its own world role in a new political grouping. Having displayed no interest in playing the attendant lord to the United States, Gaullist France showed, by its veto of Britain's membership bid in the EEC, even less willingness to share with Britain what little influence any state might be able to exercise over the development of a common West European foreign policy.

De Gaulle's Veto of Britain's Entry into the Common Market

The case advanced by the Conservative government for Britain's membership in the Common Market paradoxically made much of the Gaullist argument, explicitly stated or implicitly understood, why it should be denied entry. Political and strategic considerations predominated. Britain's security and world role appeared to be better protected if Britain directly exercised its influence on the Continent. No longer able to afford a posture of isolation, it was better, said Prime Minister Macmillan, " 'to play our role to the full and use the influence we have for the free development of the life and thought of Europe.' " [33] Britain's world mission had not so much changed as had the stage on which it played its role. " 'Our right place,' " Macmillan went on, " 'is in the vanguard of the movement towards the greater unity of the free world, and . . . we can lead better from within [Europe] than outside.' " [34] A Britain within Europe would stabilize what was still viewed as a shaky West European formation.

33. Camps, *Britain and the European Community,* p. 359.
34. *Ibid.*

France remained in turmoil, and Algeria might at any moment topple de Gaulle. Adenauer's rule might also collapse due to the chancellor's advanced age, and the inherent fragility of German politics built on an uncertain democratic tradition and a divided country with unsatisfied foreign policy claims. Britain's membership in the Common Market would also assure its special relation with the United States. On the one hand, Britain would be doing what America wanted most: building a united Europe, economically and politically, within an Atlantic community responsive to American defense influence. On the other hand, if Britain crossed the Channel any choice in Washington's mind between Britain and the EEC states would be precluded, and it would block Gaullist "third force" notions.[35]

Economic concerns were of great moment, too. The EEC threatened to discriminate against British products, already facing brisk competition in world markets. Britain, as the Dutch hoped, would keep the Six open commercially but would not be a member of an inward-looking Europe. " 'Certainly,' said Macmillan, 'this island could never join an association which believed in such medieval dreams.' "[36] As part of a larger economic grouping, Britain would gain through increased specialization, cheaper production costs, a greater variety of consumer goods, and economic growth through increased exports. Following logic applied already by the Gaullists in France, the British government hoped that industry would be stimulated and modernized by more competition.[37]

Negotiations between Britain and the Six dragged on between October 1961 and de Gaulle's veto of Britain on January 14, 1963.[38] The first phase of the discussions, lasting until the summer of 1962, turned largely around British Commonwealth ties. Political obligations, emotional and historical bonds, and shared economic benefits

35. That the Kennedy administration was enthusiastic about British entry into the Common Market is documented in the following: Schlesinger, Jr., *op. cit.*, pp. 842–923; Kraft, *op. cit.*

36. Camps, *Britain and the European Community*, p. 359.

37. *Ibid.*, p. 107.

38. For a lengthy summary of these negotiations and the immediate background leading to them, see *ibid.*, pp. 274–413, 434–519. Shorter, less thorough, journalistic accounts may be found in Nora Beloff, *General Says No*, pp. 95–178; and Kleiman, *Atlantic Crisis*.

still tied Britain to the Commonwealth. Ending Commonwealth preferences would have been a blow to agricultural products from Canada, Australia, and New Zealand. Ninety percent of New Zealand's meat and dairy production was destined for the British market. Large amounts of Canadian cereals and Australian wheat, meat, butter, and sugar products were marketed in England. Tropical fruit imports from Britain's former African colonies were also menaced; under EEC rules, Ivory Coast cocoa, for example, would be favored over the same product from Ghana. Light manufactured products, principally textiles, from India and Hong Kong posed equally troublesome problems. Asserting a moral obligation to protect its Commonwealth associates and a less articulated but no less real interest in preserving access to traditional markets, the British government pressed for comparable outlets and a long transition time to adjust trade patterns. After ten months of tedious negotiations the only progress was a trade agreement between the Six and India, Pakistan, and Ceylon and an EEC pledge to place Britain's former African and Caribbean dependencies on the same footing as the former colonies of the Six. Both accords were contingent on Britain's entry into the Common Market.

British agriculture was the major rub once negotiations resumed in October 1962. The British agricultural program contrasted sharply with the EEC levy system. British farmers, representing only a small part of the economy, enjoyed high subsidies to compensate for the low level of food prices resulting from British buying on the world market. Adoption of EEC practices promised to cost the United Kingdom more than 1.3 billion pounds, not to mention dislocation of traditional trading relations that provided a significant share of its export markets for processed goods.[39] Great Britain would have to discriminate against many of its trading partners in favor of the Six. A common external tariff accentuated Britain's balance-of-payments problem. The anticipated increase in European trade, already on the rise in the early 1960's, and the modernization of Britain's economic plant would be long-run gains. To complicate the problem, the French opposed any compromise on agriculture,

39. Department of Economic Affairs, Central Office of Information, *Britain and the EEC: The Economic Background,* London, Her Majesty's Stationery Office, pp. 36ff.

insisting that the British adopt the financial regulations supporting Common Market agriculture. The French also sponsored the Baumgartner plan that advised higher world prices for foodstuffs, a measure favoring agricultural exporters, and the creation of a special international fund to buy and distribute food surpluses to underdeveloped states. French interest and humanitarian purpose again marched in lock step. Progress on these varied issues was slight. As 1963 began, the Six made only minor concessions on the timing of tariff applications against EFTA and the gradual elimination of Britain's deficiency payments system.[40]

Further negotiations were abruptly halted when President de Gaulle vetoed Britain's entry into the Common Market at his news conference on January 14, 1963. The French president's public case hinged on two propositions: that Britain could not accept Common Market rules and that to make the Common Market acceptable to Britain would endanger the EEC and the possibility of European economic and political unity. Evidence for the first proposition took several forms. Unlike Britain, the Six were allegedly approaching cohesion "from the standpoint of their economic development, their social progress and their technological capability." [41] They shared a common civilization and confronted a common threat. The Six were committed from the outset to political and economic union. Britain had refused to participate, hindered community progress in proposing the free trade zone, and created a rival trading bloc that it now proposed to lead into the EEC.[42] De Gaulle found it implausible to believe that Great Britain could "place itself, with the Continent and like it, within a tariff that is truly common, give up all preference with regard to the Commonwealth, cease to claim that its agriculture be privileged and, even more, consider null and void the commitments it has made with the countries that are part of its free trade area." [43]

Adjustment of EEC policy to suit British interests would have endangered EEC cohesion, according to de Gaulle. Britain's entry, along with its EFTA partners, would "completely change the series

40. Nora Beloff, *op. cit.,* pp. 148ff.
41. *Major Addresses,* p. 212.
42. *Ibid.*
43. *Ibid.,* p. 214.

of adjustments, agreements, compensations and regulations already established between the Six." [44] The internal weakness of an "11-member, then 13-member and then perhaps 18-member Common Market" would make the EEC prey to American economic influence and dominance. The British had already made it clear that a compelling reason for their "decision to join the Community had been the conviction that the shortest route to a genuine Atlantic partnership led through British membership in the European Community." [45] European security dependency on the United States would be extended to economic and technological spheres. De Gaulle had earlier referred obliquely in his remarks to the Nassau accord. Unlike Britain, the Six supposedly had a "feeling of solidarity because not one of them is linked on the outside by any special political or military agreement." [46] De Gaulle drove home the point to Europeanists that granting EEC membership to an unreformed Britain that proposed to shape Europe to its own interests, treating the Six more as suppliant, was tantamount to a nullification of European independence. Great Britain's ambiguous posture, voiced in Macmillan's July 1961 address to Parliament and reiterated in Heath's April 10 speech a year later, about what commitments it was prepared to make toward Europe provided another opportunity for Gaullist France to pose as the defender of Europe's independence and the champion of European unity. That either image had any relation to the truth derived less from the evident inconsistencies of the French position than from the visibly greater uncertainty and vacillation projected by Great Britain.

The larger dangers posed by Britain's membership in the Common Market to French foreign policy goals remained unarticulated, but even more keenly felt in Gaullist quarters. Britain was an immediate threat to French continental domination. Britain and Germany had parallel interests in agriculture, and the January 1962 EEC agreement was only a partial victory for French agriculture. Important areas remained outside the EEC plan, and what had been agreed upon was scheduled for re-examination in three years. A German-British axis could not be ruled out. Moreover, Britain's weight would

44. *Ibid.*
45. Camps, *Britain and the European Community*, p. 504.
46. *Major Addresses*, p. 212.

probably upset the delicate balance between protectionism and free trade struck by French negotiators with their Common Market partners. A more open Six might prove too competitive for France's fragile industries. As one close observer of EEC has noted, the French feared that "the British would ally themselves with the Dutch and the Germans in pushing the Community toward making important concessions in the forthcoming Kennedy Round [with the United States]; they would carry their EFTA allies along with them into the Community; they would in fact isolate France and jeopardize de Gaulle's efforts over the years." [47] In addition, Britain, like France, had long experience and continued interest in global affairs. De Gaulle recognized that powerful elements in the community would look to Britain, not France, for leadership if Britain joined the EEC. More unsettling were Britain's external community allies—the United States, EFTA, and even the Commonwealth. As the Fouchet talks amply demonstrated, France could not have its way with the Five. How was it to impress its will on ten or more states, including the American colossus, and advance its plans for Europe?

De Gaulle's cavalier veto of Britain's membership served subsidiary purposes. The dramatic announcement, coupled with the simultaneous rejection of the Nassau offer, made shambles of the Kennedy administration's "Grand Design." Saying "no" to stronger states was a form of psychic income on which the Gaullist regime throve, valued all the more if France's principal ally-adversaries were frustrated. The veto settled some old scores with Britain, dating from World War II when France was often treated as a second-rate power. It also reaffirmed the Gaullist insistence on retaining maximal flexibility in foreign policy maneuvering. In failing to consult with his partners, precedent having been established as early as the Hirsch affair in Euratom, de Gaulle served notice that France did not feel bound by the community spirit or method.

Logic and circumstance conspired to elicit the de Gaulle veto and to make it stick. De Gaulle played skillfully on European suspicions, bred over many years, about England's motives. Evidence was offered that neither the British public nor important interest groups, such as the National Farmers Union, nor the Labor party would support

47. Silj, *op. cit.*, p. 94.

Britain's membership in the EEC. Britain's policy toward the Fouchet plan, marked especially by Heath's speech of April 10, suggested that Britain would not ally with the federalist wing of the European integrationist movement, nor strengthen European economic and security ties free from American prompting. De Gaulle would reason that France would not be more isolated within the Six in vetoing Britain than in permitting its entry that boded ill for Gaullist aspirations. The French president could also bank on the Five to accept, however reluctantly, his decision rather than risk what progress had been made. "British membership was worth a battle," as one close observer of the behavior of France's EEC partners notes, "but not a deadly war." [48]

The British also badly handled the EEC negotiations. The first several months of talks focused on peripheral issues; next Britain refused to cut bait on Commonwealth ties; then, to the exasperation of its supporters, it delayed reaching accord on issues within range of agreement, such as proposals on zero tariffs on aluminum and other raw materials;[49] and, finally, it displayed a mean spirit of compromise on agriculture, insisting on exceptions foresworn already by the Six among themselves while demanding an eight-year transition period. There was some suspicion in Gaullist quarters, too, that the British were waiting for de Gaulle's defeat in November 1962 on the crucial issue of a popularly elected president. In winning handily, de Gaulle frustrated this muted hope and effectively isolated domestic opposition to his European policies. As early as May 1962, he had forced, through his intemperate if calculated criticism of the European communities and their federalist advocates, the resignation of Centrist members of his government who favored greater European supranational integration. Having won the May and October encounters at home, and with his enemies divided at home and abroad, as much against themselves as against his regime and its policies, de Gaulle met little effective opposition to his veto. When West Germany signed a treaty of friendship on January 23, 1963, less than a fortnight after the British rejection, his diplomatic success was assured, if only temporarily.

48. *Ibid.,* p. 103.
49. Kleiman, *op. cit.,* pp. 80–98.

Testing the Limits of French Leadership in Western Europe[50]

The Battle for Germany

If blocking England as a rival for the leadership of Western Europe was crucial, harnessing Germany, as the major prize of the East-West conflict, was indispensable for the success of Gaullist ambitions in Europe. What then could have been more fortuitous than the Adenauer government's request that the two former antagonists sign a friendship treaty? The Fouchet plan would then be realized bilaterally, where it really counted, between France and Germany. Agreement was rapidly reached on the details of the treaty: periodic meetings of heads of government and state and ministers of foreign affairs, defense, education, and culture; an interministerial commission to coordinate policies; a joint pledge to "consult each other, prior to any decision, on all questions of foreign policy . . . with a view to reaching . . . an analogous position."[51] For Adenauer, the treaty culminated a life's work to reconcile two antagonists. For de Gaulle, it validated his decision to exclude Britain and opened the way for the implementation of his European vision.

The entente, however, foundered quickly. There was a fundamental conflict between the goals of the two states that the mere creation of consulttaive mechanisms could not bridge. France's modest military and economic resources compelled German leaders, however much they valued the French connection, to look beyond it for the realization of their larger security, welfare, and diplomatic objectives. The United States remained the guarantor of German security; the EEC, with Britain's entry, was the means for freer and enlarging global trade; a West European political union, tied closely to the United States, completed the process of Germany's rehabilitation as an equal member of the European and Atlantic communities. From this "situation of strength" Europe's division and Bonn's

50. For more detailed exploration of French policy during this period, consult especially John Newhouse, *Collision in Brussels: The Common Market Crisis of 30 June 1965* (New York: W. W. Norton, 1967); Miriam Camps, *European Unification in the Sixties* (New York: McGraw-Hill, 1966); Willis, *op. cit.*, pp. 312–365; and Jouve, *op. cit.*, I, 585–725.

51. WEU, *Political Year, 1963*, pp. 23–30.

legitimacy as the sole representative of the German nation could be negotiated with the East.[52]

Even as Adenauer hailed the new era of Franco-German collaboration, he was unsuccessfully urging de Gaulle to reopen negotiations with Great Britain or, at a minimum, to authorize the EEC to evaluate the negotiations. These overtures were formally rebuffed on January 29, 1963, at a meeting of the foreign ministers of the Six, despite the strongly expressed wish of France's partners to continue the talks.[53] This clash foreshadowed a change in the German government's attitude toward its partners, particularly France. The signal was given in Foreign Minister Gerhard Schroeder's speech to the EEC Council on April 23. The Schroeder proposals gave some point to the remarks of Walter Hallstein, EEC head, two weeks earlier: "We must refuse to return to power politics. . . . The worst course we could follow would be ourselves to forsake the Community method and revert to those older methods of hegemony, coalition, reprisal, and blackmail." [54] France's violation of the community method occasioned Germany's own proposals for changes in the making of community policy. Under French tutelage, Germany was learning to use French negotiating techniques and bargaining ploys without necessarily following French policies—being Gaullist without succumbing to Gaullism.

Schroeder asserted a previously muted claim: German equality with its partners within the EEC: "I believe that this crisis of confidence [France's veto] can only be overcome provided the Community spirit is put first, that the principle of equal rights among the member nations is respected, and lastly, that each country is prepared, now and in the future, to make concessions." [55] The test of equality and *ipso facto* the new community spirit was to be the "synchronization" of benefits and concessions or, more antiseptically stated, "parallel" progress of the community in its several sectors. The *quid pro quo* rule had been ignored to Germany's disadvantage.

52. For further analysis of German policy in a global framework, see Karl Kaiser, *German Foreign Policy in Transition* (New York: Oxford University Press, 1968).
53. WEU, *Political Year, 1963*, pp. 32–41; Willis, *op. cit.*, p. 313.
54. *Ibid.*, p. 46.
55. *Ibid.*, p. 49.

Opening German agriculture to the Common Market was premised
upon enlargement (Britain's entry); aiding underdeveloped states
(mostly former French colonies) was contingent upon sympathetic
treatment for Germany's economic clients (such as Turkey). Germany's claims were pointedly directed at France: "Germany does
not demand any *préalable* to use the French word," said Schroeder.[56]
Progress toward France's demand for a common agricultural policy
was hostage to some satisfaction of larger German economic and
political interests. These included, as Schroeder explained, Britain's
eventual membership in the EEC, broadened international trade and
alliance ties through concessions to the United States within GATT,
opening of Black African markets still dominated largely by French
firms, strengthening of the European Parliament, merger of the community executives, and movement toward political union. Schroeder's
listing conflicted at every point with France's EEC agenda. The clash
was symptomatic of a duel between two sharply opposed visions of
Europe—Gaullist and German.

The preamble to the Franco-German treaty passed by the Bundestag on May 8 formally crystallized the differences in world view
between the two states. Over the objections of Chancellor Adenauer,
the Bundestag solemnly subordinated the French-German entente to
Germany's multilateral obligations to the Atlantic Alliance, the EEC,
and even GATT. Nor was the proposed treaty to dilute ties with the
United States and Britain. All of the graven images condemned by
de Gaulle as obstacles to his European Europe were affirmed: "collective defense within the framework of the North Atlantic Alliance,
and the integration of the armed forces," "the unification of Europe
. . . by the establishment of the European Communities, with . . .
Great Britain," "the further strengthening of those Communities,"
and "the elimination of trade barriers" between the United States,
Great Britain, and the EEC.[57]

The immediate cause of the Franco-German rift, the multilateral
nuclear force, has already been discussed.[58] The American proposal
seriously hampered closer French-German cooperation—admittedly
a partial aim—and greatly aggravated the problem of alliance cohe-

56. *Ibid.*
57. *Ibid.*, p. 64.
58. See Chapter 2, pp. 114–120.

sion.[59] The Erhard government's enthusiasm for German access to nuclear weapons, echoed in his maiden speech as chancellor on October 18, 1963, menaced the Gaullist scheme for Europe. A nuclear Germany, even under American reign, isolated France within the Western camp, armed a former enemy, elevated Germany's Western standing, prompted Franco-German competition, effectively precluded progress toward détente with the Soviet Union, and nullified France's desired role as interlocutor between East and West.

Despite repeated warnings from the French,[60] the Erhard government pressed ahead on the MLF.[61] The controversy culminated in late fall of 1964 and was linked closely to other Franco-German differences, particularly those leading to the Brussels crisis within the EEC. In his news conference of July 29, 1963, President de Gaulle again set out the choices for Germany: Europe under French leadership, or an Atlantic community under American hegemony. The MLF was the French test of Germany's commitment to Europe. Threats issued from Paris that even the French-German treaty might be renounced.[62] On November 5, Prime Minister Pompidou painted a bleak picture if Germany joined the MLF: "If the multilateral force were to lead to the creation of a German-American military alliance, we would not consider this as being fully consistent with the relations we have with the Federal Republic . . . based on the Franco-German Treaty. . . . We may ask if such . . . a force would not destroy Europe and provoke certain other countries. We may even wonder whether, in the last analysis, it is not more or less directed against France." [63] Less than three weeks later, de Gaulle drew a more optimistic future for Europe if Germany joined France in political union through closer defense cooperation.[64] The choice posed by these carrot and stick techniques became moot when, to forestall further allied friction, President Johnson shelved the MLF in December 1964.

59. Kissinger, *Troubled Partnership*, particularly Parts II and III, pp. 31–159.
60. Newhouse, *Collision in Brussels, passim.*
61. WEU, *Political Year, 1963,* p. 111; *ibid., 1964,* pp. 21, 71; Willis, *op. cit.,* pp. 312ff.
62. Camps, *European Unification,* p. 28.
63. Newhouse, *Collision in Brussels,* p. 40.
64. De Gaulle, *Discours,* IV, 315.

By this time France, not surprisingly, was looking beyond its partner to realize its European objectives, for Germany was both the object and tool of the Gaullist policy. In his news conference of February 4, 1965, President de Gaulle outlined his plan to resolve the German problem. Rejecting both Soviet and American expectations that each could impose a solution, de Gaulle focused on the responsibilities of the European states to assume a larger share of the burden. For de Gaulle, the conditions of European peace were as many as they were complex: liberalization of the Russian regime and the East European empire, Germany's settlement of its frontiers and its agreement on armaments, West European economic integration and political union, including a common defense policy, and the establishment of a European system of states from the "Atlantic to the Urals in harmony and cooperation with a view to the development of her vast resources . . . so as to play, in conjunction with America, her daughter, the role which falls to her in the progress of two billion men who desperately need it." [65] The German problem would eventually be solved by ending the Cold War and housing Germany within a larger European political and security framework and a still more grandiose North-South scheme. It was no accident that the February news conference both attacked American Atlantic hegemony and argued for a return to a United Nations led by the permanent members of the Security Council, a position urged by the Soviet Union and France in the wake of the Congo crisis.

De Gaulle's vision, whatever its utopian features, had important practical implications for the French-German entente. German unification, if not abandoned outright, was downgraded as a goal. Under French guidance, Germany was assigned major responsibility for ending the East-West conflict and its own division. This meant, first, the settlement of its border disputes with Czechoslovakia and Poland; in other words, denunciation of the Munich agreement and recognition of the Oder-Neisse line. Germany should also renounce nuclear weapons and the MLF and reverse its insistence on the formula of détente through unification.[66] Only the Soviet Union could grant Germany unification; compelling Russian consent based on a strong Atlantic Alliance had already proven bankrupt. A West Euro-

65. *Ibid.,* IV, 341–342.
66. *Ibid.,* IV, 430; Kaiser, *op. cit.*

pean foundation would be less threatening to the East, yet an adequate bargaining base to confront a progressively less cohesive Eastern bloc. The tests of West European unity were also Gaullist: a common agricultural policy tied to a loose confederation of states capable of defending themselves, presumably around the French *force de frappe*. The need for the American nuclear guarantee would diminish in proportion to the improvement in East-West relations in Europe; moreover, a growing convergence of foreign policies of the European states would necessarily reduce the strategic military dependence of the West European states on the United States.

Even before the February 4 statement, French European policy was aligning on Soviet détente moves aimed more at Germany than France.[67] France's credibility as the valid European interlocutor was still in question. In early 1964, Giscard d'Estaing visited Moscow, followed shortly thereafter by the sojourn in Paris of a Soviet vice-president. In early 1965, Soviet Premier Kosygin suggested to the French ambassador in Moscow that the two governments hold more regular talks since their views on a number of subjects (Vietnam, UN financing) were in accord. In March 1964, a Soviet parliamentary group arrived for a week's stay in Paris.[68] In September, the French government, to Bonn's irritation, noted its intention to consider the extension of long-range credits to Eastern Europe. In January 1965, French Minister Alain Peyrefitte announced the Soviet Union's decision to adopt French color television for its system (the Germans demurred); six months later a modest agreement on the peaceful uses of atomic energy was reached. Gains were scored on the diplomatic front, too. In January 1965, the Hungarian foreign minister expressed interest in France's idea of a European Europe; Rumania went further and signed a five-year cultural pact with the de Gaulle government. These preliminary movements culminated in the visit of Soviet Foreign Minister Andre Gromyko in April. The joint communiqué expressed opposition to United States policy in Vietnam (Erhard supported it), determination to settle the German question

---

67. Thomas W. Wolfe, *Soviet Power and Europe, 1945–1970* (Baltimore: Johns Hopkins Press, 1970), pp. 100–127. See also Michel Tatu, *Le Triangle Washington-Moscou-Pékin et les deux Europe(s)* Paris: Casterman, 1972), pp. 102ff.

68. WEU, *Political Year, 1964,* p. 12.

peacefully, Soviet agreement to re-examine France's proposal for five-power nuclear talks on disarmament, strengthening of the UN Security Council, and interest in closer bilateral economic, scientific, technological, and cultural ties. French Foreign Minister Couve de Murville was also scheduled to go to Moscow in the fall. Perhaps most alarming to the Germans, however, was the gratuitous interpretation of the Paris meeting offered by Gromyko to reporters as he left. He allowed that the two governments had agreed on the permanence of Germany's eastern boundaries, the existence of two German states, and the unacceptability of Germany's acquisition of nuclear weapons.[69] The Quai d'Orsay discreetly demurred.

Gestures to the East were balanced by assurances to Germany that on the key questions of Western rights in Germany and Berlin and on Bonn's claim to be the only legitimate representative of the German people France was steadfast.[70] The de Gaulle record on the French-German *rapprochement* had weight, too. Soviet attacks, culminating in a propaganda campaign against the friendship treaty, were turned aside with little ado. Cooperative ventures, such as the Moselle project, went forward, and whatever the depth of difference between the two states, they continued to meet within the terms of their treaty arrangements.

Fear of a reversal of alliances was exaggerated.[71] Gaullist objectives in Europe required an enlargement of global politics coupled with an intensification of bilateral relations between the European states. Needed was a more subtle and complex global balance among a larger number of states covering an expanded geographic reach and encompassing a wider spectrum of policy issues. Formed would be a bewildering pattern of bilateral ties across East-West and North-South axes. Moscow and Eastern Europe had first to be engaged in détente diplomacy to end the Cold War in Europe. The proper mix of incentives to elicit Soviet cooperation was to be found both within and outside Europe. The man of June 18 was again counting on changes in the problems and structure of global politics to ease France's and Europe's difficulties.

There was something for everyone in the Gaullist scheme, but not

69. Newhouse, *Collision in Brussels,* p. 91.
70. WEU, *Political Year, 1964,* pp. 74–75.
71. Carmoy, *Foreign Policies of France,* pp. 402–415.

enough to satisfy anyone. Total satisfaction could only be at the expense of one or more of the participants in the global contest. Besides, a modest-sized France stood, in the Gaullist calculus, to profit from the differences among its rivals rather than facing them directly in a test of wills. The Gaullist preference for bilateral relations between states was not conceived to operate in a vacuum, but their proper expression required a global stage. The sweep of the Gaullist global game is suggested by the maneuvering already manifest in early 1965. France's recognition of Red China, without previous consultation with Bonn, demonstrated not only its own independence to the Soviet Union but also, in a cross-cutting twist, upgraded Moscow's principal Asian rival. On the other hand, France responded favorably to Moscow's diplomatic signals calling for détente in Europe and aligned its Vietnam policy with that of the Soviet Union. Neither position, of course, damaged France's stature in Peking. Meanwhile, a Gaullist-styed political union in Europe promised to reduce American influence there and be less menacing to the Soviet Union. Diminishing American power in Europe would entice (while growing Chinese pressure would induce)[72] the Soviet Union to make peace eventually with its European neighbors. There would slowly emerge a Europe from the Atlantic to the Urals drawn together by history, culture, and national interests, but still sufficiently differentiated within to permit a measure of national independence and initiative.

Under French aegis Germany would be drawn within a larger European framework in which to realize its foreign policy goals, including reunification, without being compelled to forego either the EEC (how else would France's economic interests be protected) or the Atlantic Alliance (a useful residual guarantor of French and West European security interests in the Cold War setting). De Gaulle believed, as one perceptive commentator observed, that European and German unification could succeed only if the Soviet Union and West Germany composed their differences, "not as in 1922 and 1939 against the Western countries, but in accord with them." De Gaulle also felt "that France tied to Bonn and progressively improving its relations with Moscow [was] best placed to move this conception

72. See, for example, de Gaulle, *Discours,* IV, 22, 178–182.

gradually forward." [73] The best assurance for France would be a Germany still somewhat linked to the West in the Atlantic Alliance and the EEC and coaxed simultaneously into a larger European and even global network. That would imply running an immediate risk of loosening Germany's multilateral ties for a long-run gain: settling Soviet-German differences through French mediation and, to a degree, arbitration. Tying both competitors (one actual, the other potential) to a European structure of cooperation in as many areas as possible appeared to be the best guarantee of French long-run security objectives and global aspirations.

On this larger diplomatic stage, French expertise and experience in political leadership could be given full scope to enhance France's European and world-wide standing; self-interest and universal mission were again joined. The task facing French diplomacy in Europe was considerably more challenging than that of reversing alliances— trading the Soviet Union for the United States; it was to encourage a global realignment of forces favorable to France's (Gaullist-defined) interests. Such a system of politics was inherently more uncertain and fluid than bloc politics, particularly with respect to the relations between the major powers of the Soviet Union, the United States, and China, but, paradoxically, the French president seemed to believe that it bid fair to lower tensions in Europe and deflect the Cold War to other parts of the globe. A "European Europe" required an international politics in which formal alliances and tacit alignments were increasingly more conditional and tenuous. There would be greater room for diplomatic maneuver for all states. In such a world scene the smaller European states from the Atlantic to the Vistula would pass from the status of stakes to participants in global diplomacy. How a loosely organized Europe could both extricate itself from the great power struggle and actively participate to influence effectively global politics were questions that went begging. However fanciful these implications of Gaullist worldly maneuvering may appear, they were rooted solidly in the understanding that the old formulas to solve the German question and end the Cold War in Europe were being overtaken by forces in Europe and around the globe and that even the most vigorous supporters of the postwar political axioms were, as the frustration of the Grand Coalition's Eastern policy suggested,[74] increasingly disenchanted with their own expectations.

The Battle for Western Europe

These visionary possibilities, alluded to repeatedly by de Gaulle, hinged on winning the battle for Germany. The campaign had been going badly since the signing of the friendship treaty. As early as July 1963, de Gaulle was comparing it to a fading rose.[75] A year later he was more precise, succinctly listing the points of friction:

Whether it is a matter of the effective solidarity of France and Germany concerning their defence, or even of the stand to take and the action to pursue toward the East, above all the Moscow satellites, or correlatively of the question of boundaries and nationalities in Central and Eastern Europe, or of the recognition of China and of the diplomatic and economic mission which can be opened to Europe in relation to that great people, or of peace in Asia and particularly Indochina and Indonesia, or of the aid to give to the developing countries in Africa, Asia, and Latin America, or of the organization of the agricultural common market and consequently the future of the Community of the Six—one could not say that Germany and France have yet agreed to make together a policy and one could not dispute that this results from the fact that Bonn has not believed, up to now, that this policy should be European and independent.[76]

De Gaulle was driving a hard bargain with Germany. French policy was the standard for Europe. Deviation was tantamount to the rejection of an independent Europe and, concomitantly, French leadership. Germany had failed on the MLF question to live up to French expectation. It had scored poorly on Third World problems. Its Eastern policy was retarded, prompting France to initiate Germany's policy on its behalf. One final major test remained: the regulation to finance the Common Market's argricultural program.

The agricultural problem was the thorniest issue between France and its partners. It was Paris' index for measuring the commitment of the Six to political and economic union. The accord reached on January 14, 1962, provided in principle for the gradual incorporation

74. Kaiser, op. cit., pp. 100ff.
75. L'Année politique, 1963, p. 280.
76. WEU, Political Year, 1964, p. 85.

of agriculture into the Common Market and the community's financing of the agricultural program until June 30, 1965. By the end of 1963 approximately three hundred regulations were published on a product-by-product basis. Wheat and feed grains, however, were uncovered. Their combined importance for the raising of pork, poultry, and eggs comprised one-third of the value of the community's agricultural production[77] and the major share of France's output. The French fixed December 15, 1964, as the deadline for a grain accord. This thinly veiled threat to withdraw from the community, combined with a more flexible French stand on Kennedy Round negotiations desired by Germany, opened the way for an agreement on a common price for grains on December 14.[78]

Anticipating the June 30 deadline, the EEC Commission proposed in April a complex three-part procedure to finance the community's agricultural program. It linked the financial regulation for agriculture to two other problems: raising revenues for over-all community expenditures and strengthening the role of the European Parliament. First, the Commission provided for the gradual community absorption of agricultural expenditures, including market intervention, export rebates, and structural reform. A single market system for agriculture was scheduled for July 1, 1967, the date when a common external tariff would be applied and the industrial customs union favored by Germany would be established. Second, the Commission proposed that levies from agricultural imports and tariffs from industrial products be assigned to the community. France had strongly supported the principle that levies be paid directly to the community to finance the agricultural program. The Commission estimated that agricultural expenditures would reach $1.344 billion by July 1, 1967; revenues from levies and tariffs were estimated at $600 million and $1.7 billion, respectively, for a total of $2.3 billion. Third, the Commission recommended enlarging the budgetary powers of the European Parliament to oversee the community's expanded resources and provide, as

77. The most extensive treatment of the agricultural problem is found in Hans Peter Muth, *French Agriculture and the Political Integration of Western Europe* (Leyden: A. W. Sijthoff, 1970); a summary treatment is presented in Leon N. Lindberg and Stuart A. Scheingold, *Europe's Would-Be Polity* (Englewood Cliffs: Prentice-Hall, 1970), pp. 141–163.

78. Muth, *op. cit.*, pp. 157–158; *Gazette de Lausanne,* June 10, 1965, p. 1.

some delegations desired, greater democratic control of the Commission and Council. The community's budget sent to the Parliament after Commission and Council approval would be subject to amendment. Revisions accepted by the Commission would stand unless the Council overturned them by a five-sixths majority on a straight vote of the member states. If the Parliament and the Commission disagreed, the Commission's position could be sustained by a four-sixths vote of the Council.[79]

The Commission plan occasioned a French decision to draw a battle line on the agricultural issue and, for good measure, to press its partners on the political issues that still remained on the EEC agenda since the breakdown of the Fouchet talks. Before turning to President de Gaulle's news conference of September 9, 1965, which summarized the French case, some of the events surrounding the June 30 rejection of the Commission's suggestions should be kept in mind to place the agricultural problem within the context of European politics. EEC President Walter Hallstein ill disposed the de Gaulle government to his Commission's proposals. He blundered tactically in first presenting its views in March to the European Parliament instead of to the Council. He had, moreover, reportedly violated French notions of protocol in the same month during his trip to the United States where he was allegedly received as the head of an independent government.[80] Between these two incidents, and perhaps related to Hallstein's behavior and picture of himself as acting from an independent base of political authority, French Foreign Minister Couve de Murville announced that the French president had canceled France's participation in a foreign ministers meeting to be held at Venice in May. The meeting depended upon at least two conditions: greater lower-level progress on agriculture and on the development of a common foreign and defense policy among the Six. The target of this surprise announcement was Germany. It had actively sought the Venice convocation. Shelving MLF was not enough. More positive pledges of support for Gaullist foreign policy aims were required. The MLF had to be buried; France's agriculture demands had to be honored.

79. John Lambert, "The Constitutional Crisis: 1965–1966," *Journal of Common Market Studies*, IV (May 1966), 195–228.

80. Newhouse, *Collision in Brussels*, pp. 86–88.

France's cancellation of the Venice meeting was a harsh personal blow to Chancellor Erhard. He had pinned his hopes and the prestige of his government on eliciting France's cooperation for a German initiative on political union. The French rebuff was particularly sharp after the German concessions on agriculture at the December 1964 session of the EEC Council. Erhard had long played the role of expectant suitor. As early as January 1964, the German chancellor publicly placed progress toward West European union—closely linked in German thinking to strong Atlantic ties and a position of strength toward the East—at the top of his list of priorities.[81] The German proposal for political union of November 4, 1964, submitted to the member states of the EEC, steered a course between the extremes of Gaullist confederal and European federalist thinking. It conceded the Gaullist argument that community institutions were limited instruments for closer European cooperation on foreign defense and cultural policy. Multilateral consultations in these areas after the Fouchet model would supplant the special French-German bilateral relation. On the other hand, the European communities would "remain the vehicles of unification in the economic and social policy fields." Specifically recommended was the amalgamation of the community organs and their executives, points later ratified in a separate treaty by the Six states, and the enlargement of the European Parliament's powers in community lawmaking, budgetary oversight, and relations with third states.[82] If Gaullist go-slow consultative arrangements were accepted as a starting point toward political union, "the ultimate aim of the German Federal Republic," noted the draft treaty, was "still a democratic Europe which is *federal,* and politically and economically united." [83]

The German proposal carried the clear message that concessions on political union were the German government's immediate conditions for progress in other areas of Six concern. Foreign Minister Gerhard Schroeder's "synchronization" principle was carried to the level of political unification. The uneven development of unification "may be temporarily acceptable," said the proposal. "[B]ut European unification will only attain its goal when equivalent success has been

81. WEU, *Political Year, 1964,* p. 31.
82. *Ibid.,* p. 11.
83. *Ibid.,* p. 109.

achieved in all the main areas." [84] In his meeting with de Gaulle at Rambouillet in January 1965, Erhard believed that he had secured de Gaulle's consent to a summit conference. Armed with what he believed was de Gaulle's acceptance of the procedure, if not the substance of a plan for political union, Erhard successfully secured the consent of the other EEC partners, with Italy's active cooperation, to the May meeting of the foreign ministers of the Six. France's withdrawal undid these efforts and weakened further the basis for a compromise.

The regular semiannual meeting between the French president and the German chancellor, held June 11–12, registered the long list of differences still separating the two states. French Eastern policy still partly hung over the conference. The appointment of Valerian Zorin, who headed the Soviet embassy at Prague during the 1948 *coup d'état,* as ambassador to France did little to clear the air.[85] The two governments were able to make progress on peripheral questions of industrial cooperation and even on narrowing their disagreement on the principle of parallel progress in different EEC sectors. But on the essential question of an agricultural regulation the German government continued to cling to the notion of a ceiling on national contributions; omitted, too, from mention was the amount of money West Germany was ready to commit to the agricultural fund and the length of time that the new regulation would run. The de Gaulle government was equally ambiguous on Erhard's call for a summit conference. As the two leaders parted, rival interpretations of the range of agreement quickly appeared in newspaper accounts. The Bonn government preferred the view that de Gaulle had accepted the idea of a European summit by the end of the year; the French countered that, although there was an accord on principle to convoke a summit, movement was conditioned by the resolution of a number of outstanding problems. And agriculture was first among them.[86]

The preconference maneuvering before the Brussels meeting of

84. *Ibid.,* p. 108.

85. *Combat,* May 27, 1965, p. 9.

86. Consult *Journal de Genève,* June 14, 1965, p. 14; *Le Monde,* June 15, 1965, p. 1; *ibid.,* June 16, 1965, p. 1; Newhouse, *Collision in Brussels,* pp. 95ff; and Willis, *op. cit.,* pp. 335–336.

June 28–30 to decide the agricultural regulation was similarly inconclusive. Two weeks before the conference, France dropped its insistence that levies directly support the community's agricultural program once common price accords were put into effect. If the French proposal were adopted, the community would not have had its own resources until 1970 and, therefore, the question of the European Parliament's authority over the community budget would be moot. So strong was France's opposition that the de Gaulle government was even prepared to maintain a higher level of national contribution to finance the regulation. A meeting of French and German officials a week before the Brussels confrontation did little more than state previous positions. The appearance of French flexibility on the question of the June 30 deadline, independent community resources, and the European Parliament proved illusive.[87]

French Foreign Minister Couve de Murville chaired the Brussels assembly. Following the logic of his proposal of a fortnight before, he defined the issue of the meeting narrowly to financial regulation for agriculture. Germany, Italy, and the Netherlands refused to dismember the Commission's recommendations. Italy added an additional grievance to the agenda. Since the agricultural regulation had been first written in 1962, Italy had become a net importer of foodstuffs. It found itself paying more into the community fund than it was receiving. It was reluctant under these circumstances to consent to any regulation without knowing in detail what its financial obligations would be. Inconclusive exchanges over the power of the European Parliament, the timetable for resolving farm problems, the transfer of most costs to the community budget, and the distribution of the financial burden set the stage for the closing session on June 30. Last-minute threats issuing from the French delegation that the community was on the brink of collapse and an eleventh-hour French offer to carry part of Italy's burden had no appreciable effect. Germany, Italy, and the Netherlands still insisted on examining the Commission's package as a whole. German Foreign Minister Gerhard Schroeder underlined his government's commitment to the enlargement of the European Parliament's powers. Only hours before, the

87. Newhouse, *Collision in Brussels,* pp. 100–106; Lambert, *Journal of Common Market Studies,* 1966, p. 206.

Bundestag, in approving the treaty to merge the community's executives, had unanimously passed a protocol to this effect. The Germans had not budged on the issue of the European Parliament since Schroeder's synchronization speech. Dutch resolution was of even longer standing. Some additional narrowing of differences on the duration of the financial regulation (Italy and the Netherlands held out for two years while the others accepted five) was insufficient to prevent the French chairman from closing the session sine die.

France moved quickly to bring the EEC to a halt. It struck at the authority of the communities and, specifically, the Commission and the Council to act legitimately in its absence and without its consent. On July 6, the French permanent representative was withdrawn. Moreover, France refused to participate in the work of the EEC and ESCS councils or to assist in preparations for their meetings. Boycotted, too, were negotiations authorized by the EEC Council and conducted under Commission direction, including work on day-to-day problems leading to economic union. That the French were not burning all of their bridges behind them is suggested by their continued participation in lesser areas of community concern, such as meetings on the association of Greece and Turkey, and, significantly, in common agricultural policy discussions.[88] These remaining lines of communication signaled that some basis for compromise might be found.

President de Gaulle's September 9 news conference exposed the French demands that went well beyond agriculture to include West European political cooperation and an improvement in East-West relations. First, agriculture was a *sine qua non* for French participation in the community; its inclusion had already been authorized, according to the French president, but France's partners had reneged on their commitments of January 1, 1962, and December 14, 1964. Second, the financial regulation had to be tied to a confederal, not federal, Europe. This part of the Gaullist critique took two forms. On the one hand, even if the June Brussels meeting had written an acceptable financial regulation, French agriculture would still not have been sufficiently protected since the Rome Treaty stipulated that, as of January 1966, majority voting would be introduced into

88. *Ibid.,* pp. 210–211.

Council proceedings. What was once adopted unanimously could thereafter be undone by a majority. On the other hand, the Rome and Paris treaties were extracted from a weakened France incapable of asserting its own interests. The independent executives and bureaucracies that were created were "destined to infringe upon France's democracy in settling problems that dictate the very existence of our country. . . . Obviously," de Gaulle went on, such a situation "could not suit our purposes once we were determined to take our destiny into our hands." [89] These "basic errors or ambiguities," to use de Gaulle's words, made the crisis "inevitable." [90]

Third, the Commission had worsened an already intolerable arrangement: more revenue would be collected than the agricultural regulation required; the states would further lose control of the community budget; increasing the European Parliament's powers would deepen the "errors" already embodied in the Rome Treaty and would only exacerbate the usurpation of power demanded by the Commission; and, finally, the complex voting procedures on the budget were calculated more to enhance the power of the Commission over the Council than that of the European Parliament.

The implications of the Commission's position bore directly on East-West relations. Only a confederal Europe could be open to West and East European states and be the basis for ending Europe's division. The Commission's Europe dissolved France into a federation called "European" which would actually be "Atlantic." [91] That would create an insuperable barrier for cooperation with the East European states. Confederation "alone," concluded de Gaulle, "seems to France to be consistent with what the nations of our continent actually are. It alone could one day make possible the adherence of countries such as Britain or Spain which, like ours, could in no way accept the loss of their sovereignty. It alone would make the future entente of all Europe conceivable." [92]

The Olympian stance of the French president, much like Fouchet 2, again unified the Five around the essential community principles. They decided that Council meetings were bona fide sessions under

89. De Gaulle, *Discours*, IV, 378.
90. *Ibid.*, IV, 377.
91. *Ibid.*, IV, 377–381.
92. *Ibid.*, IV, 379.

community rules. A written procedure was adopted to elicit France's consent on important decisions taken during its absence within the Council. This position underwrote the authority of the Council to make decisions and countered the French view that a member state might veto majority decisions duly reached by the Council under rules set down by the Rome and Paris treaties; continued meetings of the Council during the crisis reaffirmed its authority and the independent communities. In searching for a compromise with France, the Five insisted, as their communiqué of October 25–26 indicated, that it be found "within the framework of the Treaties and of their institutions." [93] Bilateral contacts with the French government were not ruled out, but a compromise on the community crisis would have to be agreed upon in a multilateral setting appropriate to the letter and spirit of the community charters.

The French government rejected the Council's proposal to meet in Brussels in special session without the Commission (as provided for in community practice). The mode of rejection characterized the French position. The chairman of the Council, the Italian delegate Mr. Colombo, communicated the views of the Five to France directly. France replied through normal, bilateral diplomatic channels. The Italian ambassador in Paris was contacted, and on one occasion Couve de Murville conveyed the views of the French government to Mr. Colombo during the closing session of the Vatican Council on December 8. The initial results of the French presidential election in December gave impetus to these efforts for a meeting. President de Gaulle was forced into a runoff partly because of the large number of votes (approximately one-fifth of the total) garnered unexpectedly by Jean Lecanuet who ran as a strong Europeanist.[94] After some additional haggling and maneuver, the Five and France agreed to meet in special session at Luxembourg, another community seat, without the Commission. The breakdown in the use of a written procedure over the approval of the community budget further urged some timely solution to the impasse.

A compromise was worked out at two sessions on January 18 and

93. "Declaration by the EEE Council of Ministers, October 25–26, 1965."

94. Muth, *op. cit.*, pp. 214–248, contends that the agricultural crisis had little effect on peasant voting behavior. Lecanuet's support, however, was broader, including European federalists and conservative opponents to de Gaulle.

28–29. Two principal political issues were tackled: the relation of the Council to the Commission and majority voting within the Council. French Minister Couve de Murville first presented a set of ten demands. The general aim was to narrow the Commission's discretion and to submit it to tighter Council control. The Commission's independence was not directly attacked so much as its powers were submitted to a more restrictive interpretation.

The Council was asserted as the source of new authority for the Commission. The latter was advised to be specific about how it planned to use its delegated powers and to be apprised of the Council's continuing oversight functions. Moreover, the Council, according to the French commandments, was to reclaim its allegedly usurped prerogatives in receiving the credentials of ambassadors and in conducting relations with third states. These foreign affairs responsibilities were to be placed under closer Council management.

Conspicuous by its absence was mention of the European Parliament. In addition, only vague references to the "commitment, ordering, and carrying out of the community expenditures" [95] remained of the French attack on the Commission's plan for community resources. These two issues, which prompted the crisis, lost urgency in direct proportion to the political escalation of the conflict between France and its partners. As early as July 22, 1965, the Commission had backed away from these parts of its own recommendations. It concentrated on finding a compromise for the financial regulation and softpedaled its previous insistence on revenues from industrial tariffs and agricultural levies. The response of the Five to the French decalogue was a conciliatory heptalogue, which took issue with specific points of Murville's memorandum, but implicitly accepted the French agenda for the Council. Without yielding on principle—that the authority of the communities and the initiative and independence of the Commission remain intact—the Five underscored the obvious in calling for closer Commission-Council cooperation. The presidents of both bodies would receive ambassadors; greater information flow on actions affecting both organs would be encouraged; and the execution of budgetary and information policy were to be placed under closer Council scrutiny.

95. Lambert, *Journal of Common Market Studies*, 1966, p. 223.

The question of majority voting proved more intractable. President de Gaulle had overstated the French case in arguing that all Council decisions would be subject to majority vote. The Rome Treaty provided for carefully weighted majority voting in selected areas. Furthermore, the Hirsch affair sharply defined the limits beyond which a major state could be compelled to accept a decision when overridden by a majority of its partners. Euratom was further crippled, and Hirsch was sacked. That there may have been some truth in de Gaulle's insinuation of collusion between the Commission and some of France's partners is of less significance than the larger point that the community depended on the mutual recognition of the member states of each other's special needs and particular national interests. De Gaulle was characteristically unwilling to accept even the possibility of being overruled by his partners. The controversy turned then on whether a member state could be permitted to veto community decisions reached in the Council. The Five were adamant that the treaty rules should stand; France was unmovable that decisions of importance be reached unanimously. In their final communiqué, the Five and France agreed to disagree: "The French delegation considers that, when very important issues are at stake, discussion must be continued until unanimous agreement is reached. The six delegations note that there is a divergence of views on what should be done in the event of a failure to reach complete agreement." [96]

With the adoption of these political ground rules, the Six proceeded to negotiations on the substantive issues still on their agenda. The most pressing were agriculture, tariffs, and trade. The former remained uppermost for the French; the latter for Germany. The other EEC states had a crucial interest in the outcome of both issues. On May 11, after another marathon session, the Six agreed on an agricultural financial regulation to run until the end of 1969. Agriculture would enter the Common Market on July 1, 1967; the industrial sector would be completed a year later. Ninety percent of all levies would go to the community to support the agricultural program. National contributions would supply the rest. Council members agreed to set in motion procedures for the European Parliament's ratification of community revenues by the end of the transition pe-

96. *Ibid.*, p. 225.

riod. Germany received assurances about the manner in which the financial regulation would apply to Common Market pricing and market arrangements, a liberal approach to Kennedy Round negotiations, and the exclusion of East Germany from the agricultural benefits accruing under the community plan.[97] The community had survived its worst crisis. France had its agricultural regulation on terms that were about the same as it would have likely received a year earlier. But agriculture, despite its crucial importance for France's hopes of economic independence and industrialization, was a tool for larger ends. The stake was Europe itself.

French European Policy and the Community Crisis

The crisis provoked by France had a noticeable impact on the spirit, mode of procedure, and distribution of power within the community. The community and the Western Europe states moved closer to Gaullist confederal notions, while the European federalists lost ground. The crisis also had important implications for France's leadership hopes in Western Europe and for the evolution of East-West relations.

The Hirsch affair, the Fouchet negotiations, and the British veto had already evidenced a decline in community spirit. The member states had, of course, always acted on their own interests; to a significant degree the Rome and Paris treaties are a register of compromise among member states over divergent perspectives and interests. But periodic appeals to common interests still yielded impressive results; the fiction of unity did have some positive effects. De Gaulle's style of negotiation made it increasingly difficult to sustain the fiction either intellectually or politically. Issuing ultimata and explicitly pursuing particularistic goals set an example for other EEC states to follow. Appeals to unity necessarily had less force in such a negotiating framework. France had provided ample precedent for Italy's demands that the agricultural regulation lighten its financial burden. The Germans similarly sought certain gains: concessions on European union, bargaining support with the East, status equal to its partners, particularly France, within the Six, and trade allowances. The synchronization formula and pleas for parallel progress were less abstract and politically neutral than they appeared on the surface.

97. Newhouse, *Collision in Brussels,* pp. 157–159.

Drained increasingly of spirit, the community method was bound to suffer. The Luxembourg accord seemed to end in a draw between France and the Five. The Rome Treaty was affirmed; French hints to revise the document were resisted; negotiations leading to France's return to the community fold were technically conducted within a multilateral framework; and the Commission's right of initiative remained intact. Nevertheless, France's refusal to accept the discipline of the treaty was tantamount to a weakening of the treaty itself. If the Five did not formally accept France's confederal notions, they could do little to offset its view that any state could assert a veto over community decisions when its vital interests were at stake. The practical import of the French assertion was to encourage other states to press their claims. The crisis loosened the bonds of the states within the Six without yielding consultative mechanisms, like those proposed under the Fouchet and German plans, that might have compensated somewhat for the community's enfeeblement. The French freed themselves from an obligation to concert their policies with those of their partners. That such a restraint would hardly have been compelling is suggested by the history of the Franco-German treaty. That it would have at least placed the onus on France for noncompliance is no less true. Germany, too, began to display reservations about its commitment to majority rule as its principal partner claimed exemption. Germany stood with the Five on principle, yet temporized on what it might be able to accept of community decisions when the concrete problems of agriculture and trade were before the Six.

As the authority of the community diminished, so also did the Commission's relative power within it. The balance tilted noticeably toward the Council which was organizationally less equipped to exercise community authority and implement the complex programs of the Six. The Commission's agricultural proposals of April and July were largely rejected. French enthusiasm for establishing community resources flagged. The Five were skeptical in different degrees about granting increased budgetary discretion to the Commission; the controversy with France over the very existence of the community merely muted their reservations temporarily. The problem was not that the Five preferred the Gaullist alternative. They clearly did not. Faced by French obstinacy, they lacked sufficient political will to insist on an alternative move in harmony with the development of the community as the path toward union. Movement toward a stronger European Parliament was effectively blocked. However much the Luxembourg accord and the ensuing heptalogue protected the Commission's treaty position, its exclusion from the negotiations was conspicuous. It was also advised to restrain the public statements of its members and, in effect, to be more prudent in asserting its rights to deal directly with third states. The crisis did nothing to increase the Commission's prestige. The subsequent French veto of Walter Hallstein as head of a unified community executive further weakened the claim that the Commission (or its president) was the authentic voice of the community. French logic and maneuvering created the unfortunate impression that commissioners were either tainted by national prejudice or mere technicians. Both views narrowed the independent political role of the Commission under the community charters. The enlargement of the Commission to fourteen members at the time of its fusion complicated the task of asserting community position above the competing demands of the member states. The requirements for consensus increased with members as the support among member states for the community method lessened.

This pessimistic evaluation can be exaggerated. The community and the Six *did* surmount the crisis. The Five fashioned a mutually acceptable approach to keep the community running in France's absence, to maintain a united front before French intransigence, and to resist compromise of fundamental community principles. For all its scorn and censure of its partners' behavior, the French government carefully refrained from cutting all of its ties with the community. All of the participants understood that their economic and social welfare goals were intertwined. Realization of these material objectives was prerequisite for de Gaulle's larger political schemes. He had recognized the connection during his presidency of the provisional government and used it in his tough dealings with his partners. The Six also made tangible progress on the agricultural issue in May and drew toward a common position in Kennedy Round trade talks once some of the important political problems raised by

France were provisionally decided. The argument that the crisis demonstrated the inner strength of the community can be overstated, but it cannot be entirely dismissed.

France's hold on the foreign policies of the Six was similarly tested and found wanting. Holland checked France in the Fouchet negotiations. Germany played the major role during the agricultural crisis in blunting Gaullist demands. No amount of diplomatic bombast could deflect attention from the fact that France was the *demandeur* on the agricultural regulation. Its dependence on its partners and, specifically, on Germany was abundantly clear. By default, moreover, France placed Germany in a leadership role which it was reluctant to assume until the outbreak of the crisis. Gaullist policy did not intend to promote German leadership in Western Europe, but its inflexibility produced the same result. In attempting to loosen Germany's ties to the Atlantic Alliance and to redefine the European Economic Community, it sought to fill the resulting void through its privileged relation with Bonn. Gaullist France was willing to risk a Germany more independent of these multilateral ties if its own hold could be proportionately increased and if it could successfully play the interlocutory role between Germany and its East European neighbors. The de Gaulle government failed to dislodge Germany from the American field of attraction or to reduce its commitment to the European communities. Indeed, its stature rose in both organizations as France postured outwardly. Moreover, Gaullist policies hastened the day when Germany would begin moving eastward on its own, without France as broker or mediator, and much less as arbiter. As Germany learned to be more assertive in the West and in the East, France again found itself facing not only a more independent-minded partner, but an increasingly formidable competitor.

De Gaulle, however, did make the crucial point that the development of West European economic and political union depended on a closer alignment of the foreign policies of the West European states. Community authority and institutions were insufficient for the task. The community's future itself ultimately hinged on the outcome of the separate decisions of the several states on European defense, German unification, the enlargement of the community, and Britain's entry into the EEC. It also depended on factors beyond the capacity of the Europeans to decide. These included America's commitment to European security, economic well-being, progress toward union, developments in the Soviet bloc, the improvement of East-West relations, and, finally, trends in international politics shaped by regional conflicts, like the Arab-Israeli War, and the evolution of global politics increasingly influenced by the weight of China and Japan. De Gaulle specifically tied West European independence to progress in East-West relations. An integrated Europe along federalist lines, dependent on the United States, remained an insuperable barrier to détente in Europe. It seriously hampered the initiation of negotiations aimed at settling Europe's differences and at solving the German problem.

Attacking the Europeanists who sought closer relations between the community and the United States was also good politics. It ingratiated France in Moscow. It was the logical complement to France's withdrawal from NATO shortly after the Luxembourg accord. Both organizations were central objects of Soviet attack.[98] On the one hand, drawing closer to Moscow did not preclude benefits from continued, if more specifically conditional, participation in both organizations that was more coherently related to Gaullist presumptions and ambitions. Contrariwise, failing to discipline Germany reduced France's standing as an effective Western broker and its credibility in a balancing role within Western Europe and the Atlantic community. But France's policy toward the communities and Germany opened the way for a French initiative to the East from which Germany could later draw guidance. The limitations of French influence on Germany and the other EEC partners, evident in the Fouchet collapse and the EEC crisis, did not inhibit the French government from attempting to exploit its enhanced standing in Moscow. That there were limits, too, to France's influence on Russian policy and behavior, few Gaullists would later contest. That these constraints were so narrow as to be nonexistent at times is suggested in the Czechoslovakian invasion of August 1968.

98. Charles Zorgbibe, *L'Europe de l'est face au marché commun* (Paris: Colin, 1971); Robert Legvold, "European Security Conference," *Survey,* No. 76 (Summer 1970), 41–52.

7

De Gaulle's Europe:
Atlantic to the Urals

The Politics of Independence Wanes

The Common Market crisis marked the close of the first phase of de Gaulle's European policy. It terminated, not accidentally, just as the final scene of de Gaulle's attack on NATO was about to begin with France's formal withdrawal from most activities of the military organization. In de Gaulle's mind, the NATO and the EEC organizations, notwithstanding the critical importance of the treaties on which they were based for France's security and solvency, constricted France's independence and inhibited realization of a fuller measure of national influence and status in world affairs. They also blocked completion of de Gaulle's larger European design. Assaults on these multilateral organizations formed the Western theater of his European strategy to upstage the United States military, economic, and diplomatic role in Europe and to assume progressively the political leadership of the European Six. Both these objectives, as Chapter 5 sketched,[1] were preparatory to the opening of his Eastern campaign. France's *grandeur* was identified finally with the reconciliation of the East and West European states under French auspices and the end of Europe's geographic and political division into two military blocs.[2] France's lead toward détente in Europe would presumably set in motion an international politics in Europe beyond the Cold War in which France would enjoy a protagonist role. National interest and universal mission would find new expression in French foreign policy.

This chapter explores the systemic and national objectives underlying France's initiatives in East Europe and the factors that led to the setback of the second phase of de Gaulle's European policy. It

1. See above, Chapter 5, pp. 235–247.
2. *FFP*, July–Dec. 1968, pp. 22–24.

concludes with a sketch of its policy toward Western Europe up to
the crises of 1968 that, as the next chapter indicates, opened the
third phase of France's European policy under the Fifth Republic.

Phase Two of France's European Policy

Background Considerations

Gaullist France's Eastern initiatives were launched quietly. France
moved East before its Western flank was secure. The Western
European states resisted de Gaulle's overtures to weaken their defense and economic ties with the United States, to second his criticism
of American Third World policies, or to follow France's foreign
policy lead in Eastern Europe. Neither Gaullist persuasiveness in the
Fouchet talks nor pressures during the agricultural dispute could
reshape the EEC to fit a French form. The possibilities of the French-
German entente were temporarily exhausted. Under the Erhard
regime, Germany remained wedded to NATO defense policies and
conditioned to American economic and monetary signaling. German
support for European community institutions remained strong, but
its willingness to underwrite the community's common agricultural
policy was still uncertain. There were increasing signs, too, of another English campaign to storm the gates of the Common Market.
The French questioned whether their partners within the community
would be any more resistant to the British assault than before.[3] The
Dutch never wavered in their support for British membership. Bonn's
ties with Washington were so close in the middle 1960's that the
French sometimes wondered whether the American Trojan horse was
already within the gates of the European grouping.[4]

There were, however, sufficient positive signs of a stabilized Western flank to risk an Eastern offensive. France had successfully blocked
federalist attempts to strengthen community institutions and authority
without destroying those aspects on which France depended economically. Britain was held at bay, but had helped France snuff the
MLF, although elements within the Erhard government still raked

3. This theme runs throughout French statements on British entry. See, for
example, *ibid.*, July–Dec. 1967, pp. 102–105, 139–142.
4. The joint communiqué of German Chancellor Erhard and President Johnson, September 28, 1966, is found in WEU, *Political Year, 1966*, pp. 182–184.

the coals of the dying proposal to keep the nuclear fires burning.[5] Most important, de Gaulle had exposed the nationalistic roots of the American design for Atlantic union. Adherents on both sides of the Atlantic, as de Gaulle charged—abusively on occasion—were not fully candid about the self-serving interests that partially underlay the scheme most eloquently articulated by the Kennedy administration[6] and only reluctantly abandoned by its successor.[7] French tactlessness in pressing national concerns in alliance bargaining could and did increase frictions. Alliance ideology, whether Atlanticist or federalist, was useful to smooth national differences and postulate a more optimistic future in which competing objectives might be compatibly managed. Nevertheless, neither rationale could obscure, once tested by a willful France, the conflicts of aims and strategies of the member states within the two principal Western groupings. At play, too, as de Gaulle's behavior dramatized, were disparate national styles and clashing personalities. These were not easily housed within the simpler designs of federalist or Atlanticist ideologies. Gaullist aspirations for France were functionally related to the subtle manipulation of these disparities and divergencies. France's bargaining position within the West played on the conflicts and tensions of other states. Increased tensions within the West, moreover, cast a more favorable light on the prospect of political accommodations with the East.

If these negative successes fell short of Gaullist hopes in Western Europe, they were not negligible when measured against the strength, determination, and resourcefulness of France's opponents. After 1966, there were few, if any, tangible gains to be made in the West as long as de Gaulle doggedly persisted in his policies toward his Western allies. The most attractive alternative to realize Gaullist

5. *Ibid.*, p. 316.

6. President Kennedy's speech appears in *Department of State Bulletin*, XLVII (July 25, 1962), 131–133.

7. Useful discussion of the MLF within the Johnson administration is found in Philip Geyelin, *Lyndon Johnson and the World* (New York: Praeger, 1966), Chapter 7, pp. 159–180. Two spokesmen of the Atlantic Community thesis are Cleveland, *The Atlantic Idea,* and George Ball, *The Discipline of Power* (Boston: Little, Brown, 1968). See also Chapter 5 of Henry Kissinger's *Troubled Partnership,* pp. 129–161.

aims of maximizing national independence and big-power status for France was to test Soviet reactions to a détente policy.

There were some grounds to expect a favorable Soviet response. A new offensive to limit American influence in Europe and to isolate West Germany was taking shape in Soviet diplomacy after the hesitance and caution displayed in the immediate aftermath of Khrushchev's toppling in October 1964.[8] Gaullist France earned Soviet attention in its challenge to EEC and NATO. The movement toward détente, begun even before President de Gaulle's February 4 speech,[9] had not faltered during the exchange of visits of foreign ministers—Gromyko in April 1965 and Murville in the following October.[10] France might be useful in fostering Soviet designs which, despite their differences from French objectives, temporarily overlapped in part.

Settling the Cold War in Europe, according to French reasoning, held possible attractions for the Soviet Union. Loosening EEC and NATO ties opened the way to détente with the East. Checking the United States in Europe and the Third World was a sufficiently ready, if eventually insufficient, basis on which to proceed. The strategic superiority of the United States was a constant source of concern to Russian leaders. France's détente policy held promise of diplomatic gains for the Soviet Union's campaign for respectability and recognition of its special interests in Eastern Europe. Security ties between the Soviet Union and the East European states might be

8. Lawrence L. Whetten, *Germany's Ostpolitik* (London: Oxford University Press, 1971), p. 16; Thomas W. Wolfe, *Soviet Power and Europe: 1945–1970* (Baltimore: Johns Hopkins Press, 1970), pp. 280–281. Wolfe divides Soviet policy toward Europe into four phases after the downfall of Khrushchev. The first was subdued in foreign policy and focused on domestic problems. The second, beginning about the time of the 23rd Communist Party Congress in April 1966, sought to better relations with Western Europe, to isolate West Germany, to weaken the United States in Europe, particularly in attacking U.S. Vietnam policy, and to convene an all-European conference to solidify its hold on East Europe. In outward form, if not motivation, these objectives corresponded to French policy with the crucial exception of Germany.

9. See above, Chapter 6, pp. 321–325.

10. For appropriate newspaper commentary, examine the remarks of Georges Broussine in *La Nation*, Feb. 2, 1965; *Gazette de Lausanne*, March 1, 1965, p. 1; *La Documentation française, articles et documents*, No. 0-1679-80, May 8–11, 1965; *Combat*, Oct. 31, 1965; *Le Monde*, Nov. 3, 1965, pp. 1, 3; *Le Monde*, April 4, 1965, p. 1.

accepted by the West, its social and economic penetration of the region recognized, and boundary disputes conclusively defined in its favor. France and the Soviet Union were agreed, moreover, that Germany should not have access to nuclear weapons. Relieved of Western pressures and the threat of a resurgent Germany, the Soviet Union could concentrate on meeting the Chinese challenge, to which de Gaulle publicly alluded as early as 1959.[11] The growing parallel between Soviet and French Third World policy—in the United Nations, the Middle East, and Asia—added to the attractions of working together. Soviet policy was open to ways to lessen the chances of war in Europe provided its policy objectives, especially in Eastern Europe, were not jeopardized. There was the possibility, moreover, of greater access to Western products, technology, and scientific development, an appeal for the consumer-oriented faction within the Kremlin.

Meanwhile, prospects of progress with the United States or with West Germany appeared slim. The United States was holding firmly to Western Europe while expanding its commitments to the Third World. The Vietnam escalation was hardly reassuring. Movement in German foreign policy, in the Erhard government's spring peace offensive in 1966 and the more fundamental shift under the Grand Coalition in 1967, seemed keyed in Soviet estimates to building bridgeheads to Eastern Europe rather than bridges as President Johnson intimated.[12] Soviet rule in Eastern Europe was challenged and East Germany risked being isolated diplomatically within and outside the Warsaw Pact.

Risks Run in Moving Eastward

France ran three sets of risks in moving East. First, there was the possibility that, as critics charged, the Soviet Union's hold on Eastern Europe would be tightened through détente while its influence in the West would expand if other states followed France's defection or sought to strike a bargain with the Soviet Union. The

11. *Major Addresses,* p. 58. See also observations of C. L. Sulzberger with respect to the trip of André Malraux to China in summer 1965, *New York Times,* International edition, Aug. 23, 1965, p. 6.

12. President Lyndon Johnson, "Making Europe Whole: An Unfinished Task," *Department of State Bulletin,* LV (Oct. 24, 1966), 622–625.

French rebuttal was as complicated as the criticism. As the discussion below further elaborates, détente between the blocs and between the individual states was viewed as eventually leading to a greater liberalization of relations within the blocs "between the state and the citizens." [13] France's initiative in the East would presumably neither damage the West's negotiating position as critics alleged nor, insofar as Germany was concerned, concede as much to the Soviet Union as its declaratory statements might otherwise have implied. The German government reportedly concluded that de Gaulle would remain within a narrow bargaining framework so as neither to alienate ties with Germany nor prejudice talks with the Soviet Union.[14]

The risks of *ouverture* were acceptable to de Gaulle because France could be relatively assured that NATO and the EEC would not immediately disintegrate under French fire. Nor would it be correct to say that that was de Gaulle's intent. The Washington, Rome, and Paris treaties served French economic, military, and diplomatic objectives as long as the institutional structures deriving from them did not hinder the achievement of its narrower national and wider European purposes.[15] As for the American guarantee, the de Gaulle government tacitly conceded the premise of President Johnson's "bridge building" speech of October 1966 that the Atlantic Alliance was a prerequisite for détente. Paris disputed suggestions, however, that conformity was the price to be paid for American military support. The French reasoned that the United States would remain in Europe whatever they did. Loose talk by the American NATO ambassador that, in the event of war, France would be an occupied country as a consequence of its withdrawal from NATO unwittingly lent weight to French calculations.[16] Indeed, containing the United States, as noted in Chapter 2, was portrayed by France as the more pressing problem in the 1960's.

Furthermore, Gaullist France could count on the European community remaining intact. Its membership in the Western grouping bolstered its negotiating position with the East European states.

13. *FFP*, 1966, p. 25.
14. The report of Roland Delcour, *Le Monde,* Oct. 30, 1965, p. 1, and the analysis of André Fontaine, *ibid.,* Nov. 3, 1965, pp. 1, 3.
15. De Gaulle makes his point clear in *FFP*, 1966, p. 157.
16. Interview, Paris, Dec. 1965.

France wished to protect the tangible economic benefits of financial regulation for agriculture, the stimulus of increased trade, assistance for modernization, and the promise of future community coordination in areas of special French interest, such as transportation, taxation, welfare, and monetary policy. If the French were bearish about the EEC's institutional development, they were in the forefront of efforts to enlarge the scope of the community's cooperation through the pragmatic alignment of national economic policies rather than through centralized Commission directives.

De Gaulle had no difficulty in arguing that the strides made toward economic and political union in West Europe would be imperiled unless political détente succeeded with the East: "From the moment we speak of Europe, how can we deny France has done everything for it to take shape and materialize in the Western world in some form other than futile speeches? Moreover, even if one day the economic group of the Six is supplemented by their political concert, nothing either valid or sound would have been done regarding Europe, so long as its peoples of the West and its peoples of the East have not reached agreement. The solution to a problem as serious as that of the future of Germany is not conceivable otherwise." [17] To the Soviet government, on the other hand, the French government insisted that their support for the Common Market and European unity, conceived along de Gaulle's confederal lines, posed no threat to Eastern Europe.[18]

Risks run with Germany were potentially higher. These were of three kinds. There was, first of all, the danger that West Germany would be drawn closer to the United States. The MLF, which threatened to reduce NATO to a Bonn-Washington axis, failed partially as a result of French opposition. France's departure potentially simplified alignment between the two governments on major policy issues.[19] On the other hand, French influence in Bonn was still present. More importantly, the possibility of French concessions on East Ger-

17. *FFP*, 1966, pp. 159–160. See also remarks of Couve de Murville, *ibid.*, pp. 165–175.

18. Couve de Murville, *La Politique étrangère, 1958–1969* (Plon: Paris, 1970), pp. 191–234, sketches France's policy toward the Soviet Union and Eastern Europe during his tenure as foreign minister.

19. *Le Monde*, April 30, 1965, p. 1.

many and East Berlin remained hostages to French diplomacy. In any event, de Gaulle was confident that Germany would gradually recognize that the Soviet Union, not the United States, held the key to German unification and to better relations with the East European states. Logic and interest would eventually turn Germany eastward, too, and hopefully under French patronage.[20]

More problematic was the possibility that Germany would become more nationalistic. One or two paths, both adverse to France, might then be followed. Some worried that Germany might again seek to accommodate the East in a new Rapallo. This fear seemed overdrawn for the French. After World War I, Germany and the Soviet Union were two outcast powers who needed each other for international respectability and recognition. Their situations and circumstances had changed radically in less than half a century. The Soviet Union was a superpower with an empire to protect. Germany was a powerful economic giant and a rising political power in European politics. Its defense and economic policies and its governmental regime were firmly tied to the West. These ties gained for West Germany moral and political respectability, enormous economic benefits, and, as de Gaulle perceived in his first talk with Adenauer, diplomatic support for its Eastern policy of strength.[21] It was not reasonable to expect Germany to reverse its policies overnight, abandon the West, and place its trust in a policy of political accommodation or even appeasement of the Soviet Union because of France's flirtation with East Europe. The United States and France's European allies could keep Germany from going too far eastward if it should, under Gaullist prodding, go beyond France's lead. In drawing Germany into the détente sweepstakes, de Gaulle had no intention of losing the prize of a special and privileged relation with the Soviet Union.

Finally, there was the possibility that German nationalism, as the Soviets repeatedly claimed, would grow increasingly intransigent and revisionist. The de Gaulle regime also marshaled retorts to these objections. The Franco-German reconciliation mocked Soviet charges of an emergent German security threat to Europe. No less than the

20. *FFP,* 1966, p. 47.
21. See also the supporting remarks of Foreign Minister Maurice Schumann, *PEF,* July–Dec. 1970, pp. 75, 171–172.

other victorious states of World War II, France held firmly to its four-power rights while the Soviet Union's attacks on Berlin would have diluted them. Moscow could be expected to oppose any Nazi resurgence and in that case it would enjoy France's (and West Europe's) support. In addition, a Paris-Moscow accord to prevent any expansionist policy from taking root in Germany was implicit in de Gaulle's courting of the Kremlin.

On the other hand, France saw deterioration in German relations as highly improbable. France held insurance on a number of points. The German nation, as de Gaulle and his close collaborators were careful to underline, was divided and its boundaries unsettled. It lacked the marks of full sovereignty.[22] France's credentials in the effort to keep Germany from nuclear weapons were as impeccable as those of the Soviet Union, and after the MLF it could point to more tangible results. French troops remained in Germany after France's NATO withdrawal at the invitation of the German government.[23] There was always the *force de frappe* in reserve. De Gaulle could hope, too, with less justification as time unfolded, that the moral liability of the German nation for the outrages of World War II still acted as a restraint on the Bonn government. Brandt's *Ostpolitik* would demonstrate that a German regime could be nationalistic and peaceful and still assert its interests, even at the risk of opposing France.

As these various restraints eroded in the late 1960's, Gaullist apologists were equal to the change in fortune. The rationalization gradually emerged that Germany would have become increasingly nationalistic in the future anyway.[24] (What other expectation was plausible given the Gaullist conception of state behavior?) So it was better sooner than later to strike a bargain with the East that might eventually be made acceptable to Germany. In any event, time was not on the side of the de Gaulle regime or de Gaulle personally. Multilateral checks, as France was keen to show, were ultimately incapable of confining the expression of determined national drives. The best way to tame the Germans was to have them tame themselves. De Gaulle's multipolar scheme for Europe was ostensibly

22. *FFP*, 1966, pp. 46–47.
23. *Ibid.*, pp. 218–221.
24. Interviews, Paris, Feb. 1970, to May 1971.

responsive to Germany's most emotionally felt demands for unification—over the long run—and promised a new international politics in which these unrequited hopes would find a fuller measure of realization without contesting France's political ascendancy in Western Europe.

The third possible risk to de Gaulle's Eastern policy was domestic. Internal support for his initiatives abroad could not be taken for granted after the 1965 election. De Gaulle was forced into a *ballotage* partly because of the impressive first-run showing of confirmed Europeanist Jean Lecanuet.[25] De Gaulle's victory settled temporarily the question of domestic support for his Western policies. His electoral success opened the way for his withdrawal from NATO in much the same way that the defeat of his opponents on the question of the direct election of the president paved the way for his veto of Britain's application in the Common Market.[26] De Gaulle's Eastern policy could also be calculated to divide the Left in France, fractionalized already by its own inner personal and political quarrels. The prospects of profitable trade and of more numerous and extensive technical and scientific exchanges with the East would tempt wary conservatives and moneyed interests. The French economy would be further stimulated, and France would steal a march on its economic rivals in the West for Eastern markets.

The high stakes to be won from an opening to the East appeared to warrant the potentially high risks. What other options were available to France to diminish the threat of war in Europe, blunt further American penetration, moderate Soviet external behavior, and win for France a privileged position in European politics?

Systemic and National Stakes of Détente

The anticipated systemic benefits of détente, suggested in the preceding chapters, were not to be denied de Gaulle. Transforming the reciprocal perceptions of the German and Soviet threat would begin the process of dissolving the military blocs. Criticizing United States behavior was a convenient distraction from Europe's problems and

25. The results of the first ballot were 44.64% for de Gaulle, 31.72% for François Mitterand, and 15.57% for Lecanuet. Three candidates split the remainder of less than 10% of the vote.
26. Kleiman, *Atlantic Crisis, passim.*

a means for resolving them. Fear of American expansion into the Third World could be played upon to encourage Soviet *rapprochement* with Western Europe. If the German and Soviet threats were illusions relative to each other and the United States challenge was the reality—economic and political for Western Europe, military for the Soviet Union and its Eastern clients—then what justification was there for the retention of the NATO and Warsaw organizations as rival European groupings? Soviet accommodation on a German settlement would decrease the West European need for the American security guarantee. It would also permit the West Europeans to meet United States economic, technological, and scientific competition more effectively, with indirect support from the Soviet Union and Eastern Europe in the form of trade outlets and opportunities for scientific, technological, and industrial exchange. Western Europe's client status would be reduced. Greater East-West European exchanges of all kinds would, accordingly, contribute to Europe's emancipation from the control of both superpowers.

European politics would move under the spur provided by France's détente policy from a bloc system to an interpenetrated security and economic system. The French expected the Soviet hold on Eastern Europe to relax gradually. As security fears declined, the Soviet need for its Eastern empire would lose some of its attraction and much of its rationale. East European pressures for liberalization could be counted upon to accelerate tendencies toward polycentrism within the Eastern bloc. As this trend gained momentum, the Soviet Union's capacity to direct the foreign policies of the East European states and to establish their internal economic and social priorities would be weakened as bilateral ties in an expanding number of policy fields developed across bloc lines. French détente policy allegedly responded to the national sentiment of West and East European states. They were given incentive in France's example to assert their national claims and not subordinate them to bloc priorities in deference to superpower directives or squander resources in intrabloc bargaining. In his news conference of September 9, 1968, President de Gaulle summarized these great expectations while lamenting the damage inflicted by the Soviet invasion of Czechoslovakia:

Since 1958 we French have not stopped working to end the system of the two blocs. Thus, while maintaining close relations with the countries of Western Europe and, with respect to Germany, going so far as to change our former enmity into cordial cooperation, we have gradually detached ourselves from the military organization of NATO which subordinates the Europeans to the Americans. Thus, while participating in the Common Market, we have never agreed to the so-called "supranational" system for the Six which would engulf France in a stateless entity and whose policy would be none other than that of the protector from across the ocean. Thus, our will not to risk this Atlantic absorption is one of the reasons for which, to our great regret, we have up to now deferred Britain's entry into the existing Community.

At the same time, while we were making the advent of a Communist regime at home impossible, we have renewed with the countries of the East, and first with Russia, growing practical relations. In this way we were, it is true, encouraging common economic, scientific, technical and cultural progress, but we were also promoting political détente, we were again beginning to knit, with the countries around the Vistula, Danube, and the Balkans, the special ties which for many centuries have bound us to them in so many respects. We were intimating to the great Russian people—whom the French people has throughout history, for purely emotional reasons, considered to be its appointed friend—that all of Europe expects from it something quite different and much better than seeing it shut itself in and chain its satellites behind the walls of a crushing totalitarianism.[27]

This was a rare admission that the transformation of Communist regimes, in Eastern Europe and in the Soviet Union, was an important Gaullist consideration linked to its quest for national independence. National and personal liberty were seen converging in the future; both were in the service of Europe freed from the Cold War.

Gaullist France believed it was setting in motion a chain reaction, beginning with economic, technological, scientific, and cultural exchanges between the West and East European states—and first of all with the Soviet Union—that would erode over time the American and Soviet imperial systems in Europe. International politics in Europe would move along a wider track than tests of military strength and spiraling arms races. Gradually replacing the ministry of defense would be the ministries of foreign affairs, finance and economics, science and technology, and education in the management

27. *FFP,* July–Dec. 1968, p. 23.

of interstate relations. Europe would not be militarily neutralized. De Gaulle had consistently rejected that enduring theme of the French Communist Left. Europe would, however, be rendered politically neutral in the Cold War struggle between the superpowers. The European political agenda, focused for over a generation on military security questions, would be redefined, and political problems, the roots of security fears, would again head the list of European concerns.[28]

According to the French proponents of détente, changes in the threat perception of the European states toward each other would encourage greater confidence in the development of intra-European relations. General Ailleret, de Gaulle's chief of staff, published an authoritative reinterpretation of the military threats facing France.[29] He dropped the traditional accent on the threat coming from the East. His trip to the Soviet Union in spring 1968 confirmed the new French understanding. Agreement between the West and East European states in less volatile areas than politics, such as trade and cultural exchanges, would presumably lead to talks about political differences and eventually to a resolution of the German problem and the erection of a new European security system whose outline, admittedly, could only be dimly seen in the middle 1960's.[30] Couve de Murville, as foreign minister, spoke of "prompting better relations between the European countries" and also of organizing "détente in Europe, which should make possible the solution of the German problem." [31]

France's détente policy would, in Murville's term, "trigger" a movement toward East-West cooperation that would advance its systemic designs.[32] National sentiment and interests, expressing themselves more through normal diplomatic channels than through multilateral economic and security organizations, would motor the détente process. The importance of these multilateral groupings would vary according to the interest of the states composing them, and not respond primarily to the convenience of the superpowers. These *en-*

28. Prime Minister Georges Pompidou makes this point, *ibid.,* Jan.–June 1967, p. 6.
29. Ailleret, *Revue de défense nationale,* Dec. 1967, pp. 1923–1932.
30. *FFP,* July–Dec. 1968, p. 24.
31. *Ibid.,* 1966, p. xii.
32. *Ibid.,* p. 169.

sembles would be subordinated in diplomatic practice to intrastate ties based on bilateral accords.

Checked, too, would be the proclivity of international bureaucratic agencies, such as the Brussels complex of the European communities, to introduce themselves between states or between the governments of the states and their constituencies. Similarly, no one state would be permitted to dominate an international grouping or use clients to exert their influence indirectly. De Gaulle projected the image of a new international process and structure for European politics. The NATO, Warsaw, EEC, and Comecon groupings would be gradually drawn into a larger and stronger mesh of essentially bilateral alignments. States would conduct their relations with each other on the basis of what bilateral and multilateral mix suited their national needs and dispositions. As these alignments developed and became institutionalized in international practice, coordinating mechanisms, resembling the committee arrangements of the Fouchet plan, would be established. The Fouchet plan, blocked by France's smallest West European allies, would then be realized in modified form through Soviet and East European adoption of French notions of diplomatic practice.

The de Gaulle government's announced systemic hopes went further. Détente would eventually lead to entente and cooperation with the Soviet Union and result in common policies toward the Third World. Europe from the Atlantic to the Urals would be achieved through the slow, glacial alignment of the foreign policies of the European states. De Gaulle specifically identified possibilities of East-West European agreement in a number of important areas relative to Third World issues, including fixed prices for raw materials, currency reform, transfer of technological information, and training of indigenous cadres.[33] Such a Europe would act as a unit in world affairs.

It stretches credibility to believe that de Gaulle placed much confidence on so bright a future. Gaullist France's play on the vulnerabilities of other states and on their conflicts with each other for national advantage and de Gaulle's conception of international relations as built more on the tendency of states to clash rather than to

33. *Ibid.,* p. 198.

cooperate with each other could not be easily squared with such sanguine hopes. But the triptych of détente, entente, and cooperation, for all its rhetorical inflation, did have at least two uses. It was a slogan to rally domestic and West European support for the Gaullist Eastern schemes. Moreover, by posing an optimistic future the de Gaulle government obscured the profound differences between France and its Western allies, on the one hand, and the Soviet Union and most of its satellites, on the other. Deliberate obfuscation was a way to open negotiations on old problems and to define possible areas of accord that had hitherto been slighted or escaped clarification.

Through détente new participants, with their own special interests, talents, and strengths, would be drawn into international politics. New centers of power and achievement would arise to balance the superpowers, if not on strategic grounds, then in areas where, through specialization on the part of small states, larger states were vulnerable to competition. As the capacity of the superpowers to manipulate the perception of exterior threats of their clients diminished, they would have increasing difficulty ruling them or reducing them as pawns in their own power game. European politics would become more stable as new interests were created across bloc lines. Smaller and middle-power states would have a greater sense that their claims were being articulated and adjudicated within an international political process, partially of their construction and responsive to their national demands. The European states would presumably develop a heightened sense of legitimacy in the new order as more states participated directly in shaping their security, economic, and diplomatic arrangements. Stability would correspondingly be promoted as all states, large and small, perceived themselves as having a stake in the international system.[34]

These benefits of a multipolar system would allegedly redound to France's national advantage. There was self-proclaimed prestige

34. President Richard Nixon's *Foreign Policy Report* gives expression to this Gaullist point, "U.S. Foreign Policy for the 1970's: The Emerging Structure of Peace," *Department of State Bulletin*, LXVI (March 13, 1972), 314–315. It contrasts with President Nixon's address to the UN General Assembly in the fall of 1970, which stressed Soviet-American responsibility for peace, *ibid.*, LXIII (Nov. 16, 1970), 601–606.

in being the vanguard of the multipolar international order. Every state might still be Gaullist. The Soviet Union would accord France the big-power status that the United States and France's European allies withheld in the Atlantic directorate scheme and in the Fouchet plan. As one French observer noted, "This gratification . . . had definite political value. While one of the superpowers forever insisted on its economic, military and technological superiority, the other [was] ready to speak to France as an equal, even if the cold facts prove the inequality of resources and potential." [35] The appearance projected was of a France capable and assured of acting alone on its own behalf (and that of Western Europe) rather than a client deferentially conceding its freedom of maneuver to stronger allies.

France's international roles would be more clearly defined and its ability to play them would be strengthened as the international system moved from the politics of blocs to the atomistic politics of states, forming and dissolving in fluid coalitions. De Gaulle and his collaborators openly asserted France's utility as an "interlocutor" between the West and East European states and, more particularly, between Germany and its Eastern neighbors. [36] The roles of balancer and arbiter in intra-European disputes could then be plausibly entertained as European interstate politics moved from coercive to noncoercive forms of competition. France's proven diplomatic skill and experience would carry more weight finally than the *force de frappe* in influencing the daily behavior of other states. Its progressive political attitudes in the Third World and in Europe would prepare the ground not only for the expansion of its diplomatic influence but also for the penetration of foreign markets. Through domestic social and industrial modernization, including the reform of agriculture, it would equip itself for new forms of international competition. [37] France's cultural attraction, still valued highly by the French, would give additional prestige and influence in a multipolar system than under

35. Alfred Grosser, *Franco-Soviet Relations Today*, Rand Corporation, Memorandum RM-5382-PR (Santa Monica, Calif., Aug. 1967), p. 46.

36. Read the remarks of Couve de Murville after his visit to Hungary, *FFP*, 1966, p. 104.

37. This is the thrust of Robert Gilpin's analysis of French scientific policy in his excellent *France in the Age of the Scientific State*.

the bloc direction of two superpowers. French culture and its progressive foreign policy positions were the advance elements of its expansionist economic and diplomatic policy. What power, prestige, and privileges would flow from France's enhanced ability to assume a large and more significant diplomatic role in world politics would bolster France's North-South posture as its efforts in the Third World, as Chapters 9 and 10 suggest, would buttress its East-West position. Progress in foreign and economic areas would spell increased domestic stability and regime support.

Phase Two of French European Policy in Action

The détente process, set in motion almost two years before by the French,[38] reached its peak with the announcement of January 12, 1966, issued by Valerian Zorin, the Soviet ambassador to France, that President de Gaulle would visit Moscow in June. Soundings from the Soviet Union were favorable. Communist party chief Leonid Brezhnev singled out Russia's improving relations with France as a possible "important element of European security." [39] This promising tone contrasted with the Soviet response to the Erhard government's peace note sent to most countries of the world. The Bonn initiative was remarkable because it was one of the first signs of a shift in German foreign policy from deference to allied interests to a more direct assertion of its claims or, in other words, from multilateral to bilateral diplomacy along the Gaullist mode. Europe remained the center of focus, but there were suggestions of a new international role for Germany, beyond big-power dependency, once a European settlement was achieved. As for this immediate issue, the note called for better bilateral relations with Eastern Europe, accord on Germany's frontiers within the framework of a peace treaty, and the voiding of the Munich Treaty as a consequence of the unlawful acts of the Hitler regime. Germany also affirmed its previous renunciation of atomic weapons production and willingness to sign a mutual pledge with other states renouncing the use of force in resolving differences.[40] These departures from past practice, initially more

38. Wolfe, op. cit., describes the initial Soviet flirtation with France in 1963–1964, pp. 116–119.
39. FFP, 1966, p. iv.
40. WEU, Political Year, 1966, pp. 97–100.

stylistic than substantive, were overshadowed by the reassertion of traditional claims—commitment to NATO and the EEC, the exclusive right to speak for all of Germany, and continued economic and legal ties with West Berlin. Foreign Minister Gerhard Schroeder set the record straight in remarks made in August 1966: "Our relations with the Eastern European countries—necessary though these may be—cannot make progress by our sacrificing basic positions with regard to the German question." [41]

The official Soviet reply of May 17 chilled the détente atmosphere. Demanded were Germany's renunciation of all access to nuclear weapons, its signing of a nonproliferation treaty, the establishment of nuclear free zones in Central Europe, the stoppage of flights over European states by planes bearing nuclear weapons, the evacuation of all foreign bases and troops from the European states, acceptance of the frontiers growing out of World War II, recognition of East Germany, special political status for West Berlin, a decrease in size of the *Bundeswehr,* and the convening of an all-European conference "to discuss the questions of ensuring security in Europe and organizing general European cooperation." [42] These Soviet conditions were tantamount to German capitulation. German acquiescence would have rendered the pursuit of détente, as a prelude to a European settlement, meaningless.

The success of the French détente venture and the prospects of France's ability to play an interlocutory role in Europe depended on how well de Gaulle could square these conflicting positions of France's two most powerful continental neighbors. Fears that his government would tilt too far to the East proved unfounded. Even before de Gaulle left Moscow, in counterpoint to the dramatic withdrawal from NATO, the French were discreetly assuring their Western allies of France's fidelity. In his regular semiannual meeting with Chancellor Erhard on February 8–9, within a fortnight of the Luxembourg settlement, President de Gaulle and his German colleague toasted the proposition of a search for European political cooperation. Both statesmen carefully sidestepped translating their

41. *Ibid.,* p. 47. See also Erhard's statement of September 1966: "We shall not abandon any of the positions we have so far taken on German participation in Western nuclear defence" (*ibid.,* p. 52).

42. *Ibid.,* pp. 143–150.

varying interpretations of such cooperation into a French and German political idiom.[43]

These differences in approach to East-West problems were assuaged somewhat, a month later, when France stood with its Anglo-American adversaries in opposing East Germany's recognition.[44] In April, Prime Minister Georges Pompidou publicly affirmed France's continued close ties with Germany.[45] Foreign Minister Couve de Murville appeared on German television to assure his listeners that France did not intend to enter into any military accords with the Soviet Union. He denied, not without mental reservation (given his own and Gaullist pronouncements to the contrary), that France had taken an official position on the questions of German access to nuclear weapons and frontiers.[46] These problems were to be resolved, respectively, within an all-European security framework and by the four occupying powers.

Broad hints were dropped, too, that France might entertain another British application for entry in the European community. Before journalists in Paris, Prime Minister Pompidou on January 12 remarked that his government was "still in favor of seeing economic Europe become broader, and would favor the entry of a Britain who would accept the rules of the Common Market and a *rapprochement* with Europe." [47] During his July visit to Britain, Pompidou expressed pleasure that "on the British side, the possibility of participating in . . . the Common Market, seems closer than several years ago." [48]

Close examination both of France's announced *and* operational policy toward Europe casts doubt on the bald charge of Gaullist critics that de Gaulle was preparing to abandon the West and, like Francis I, deal with an Eastern empire, temporarily strengthening

43. *FFP*, 1966, p. 15.
44. *Ibid.*, p. 24.
45. *Ibid.*, p. 12.
46. *Ibid.*, p. 65. On Czech television in July 1966, Murville is quoted as saying, "We do not recognize the Government of East Germany, which is not particularly representative. Conversely, we agree on the problem of frontiers and on the fact that Germany must not have nuclear weapons. At the present juncture, nothing can be done without new links between Eastern and Western Europe" (*ibid.*, p. 44).
47. *FFP*, 1966, p. i.
48. *Ibid.*, p. 98.

France, but irreparably weakening Western Europe and the Atlantic Alliance.

De Gaulle's tour of the Soviet Union was masterfully conducted. If his travel log and ceremonial doings were the only aspects of the trip that mattered, the misleading impression would have been given of growing French-Russian solidarity. De Gaulle became the first Western statesman to visit a Russian missile site. His travels took him throughout Russia, even beyond the Urals, a subtle reminder of the Soviet Union's European and Asian dimensions. Extensive, too, were de Gaulle's contacts with the Russian people at all levels, including a speech at the University of Moscow and an address on Russian television.

The political results of the voyage, however, were considerably less dramatic. The Russian leaders, according to one prominent journalist accompanying the French delegation, listened with growing impatience to de Gaulle's lengthy lectures on his vision for Europe.[49] They waited vainly for some break in France's refusal to recognize East Germany, resistance to a special status for West Berlin, and reluctance to be drawn quickly into supporting the Soviet proposal for the convening of a European security conference. Instead de Gaulle pleaded the German case in Moscow[50] and affirmed France's commitment to liberal democracy (another Gaullist lapse into regime politics). While condemning bloc politics and the American military intervention in Vietnam, de Gaulle acknowledged in his presentations an important role for the United States "in the pacification and transformation of the world." [51]

Little, too, was said about Soviet interest in disarmament and especially arms control problems. The final communiqué was restricted to mutual confessions of regret over the slow progress in

49. Interview, André Fontaine, *Le Monde,* April 1971. In an article appearing during de Gaulle's trip, Fontaine characterized the Russian-de Gaulle exchange as: "They played their record and I played mine" (*Le Monde,* June 28, 1966, p. 2).

50. Bonn's reaction to the de Gaulle visit was outwardly favorable (*Combat,* June 27, 1966, p. 1). Said Erhard during an electoral address: "We ought to be grateful to General De Gaulle for having pleaded in Moscow the German case with so much frankness."

51. Read de Gaulle's toast at the Kremlin, *FFP,* 1966, pp. 82–83. Grosser, *Franco-Soviet Relations,* presents a useful summation of the results of the trip, pp. 41–46.

these areas. Passing mention was made of the utility of discussing disarmament among the nuclear powers, a point conceded by the Soviet Union a year before, but whose enthusiasm for the more cumbersome arrangements of the Geneva disarmament discussions had not entirely flagged. (France abstained from these talks.) No concession was made, moreover, to the Soviet agenda that featured accords on nonproliferation, test ban, nonnuclear zones, and the barring of ABC weapons. Similarly, there was no reference to decreasing bloc forces or ending foreign bases or the stationing of foreign troops in European states. In banishing all foreign contingents from France, the de Gaulle government was quite prepared to reach an agreement with the Germans on the conditions under which French armed forces would remain.

As if to compensate for the lack of progress on these critical political and strategic issues facing Europe, the accent of the joint communiqué was placed on secondary matters where agreement could be reached.[52] Two accords were signed on technical, scientific, and economic cooperation and on joint space exploration. A French-Soviet committee was established to examine additional areas of cooperation. French contacts with Eastern Europe were officially recognized and blessed by the Kremlin. The commercial agreement of October 30, 1964, was updated and more optimistic target levels for trade exchange were defined. A consular convention was also to be negotiated. The political process of negotiation between France and the Soviet Union was also more formally institutionalized. Regular meetings between the two governments and a direct communications link, a copy of the Moscow-Washington hot line, were decided upon. Plans were laid for the exchange visits of government, technical, and professional personnel.

Much of the anticipated success of the French détente strategy depended on how well bilateral ties between France and the East European states developed in scientific, technological, economic, and cultural areas. Progress, while notable when compared to the absence of movement on security and German questions, still fell be-

52. The communiqué is found in *FFP*, 1966, pp. 87–89. Also of note is the Franco-Soviet communiqué of April 29, 1965, in the wake of Soviet Foreign Minister André Gromyko's visit to France, found in *La Documentation française*, No. 0-1679-30, May 8–11, 1965.

low French expectations. Russian assessments of future Franco-Soviet cooperation were more precisely drawn two years later in the Czech invasion. A sketch of their development before the Czech crisis indicates their modest proportions.

An elaborate committee network grew out of the June 30 communiqué. By the end of 1966, so-called "Large" and "Small" committees were created which began operating in January 1967. The French minister of economics and finance and a deputy-chairman of the Council of Ministers of the Soviet Union (who was also chairman of the State Committee for Science and Technology) jointly chaired the Large Committee. Michel Debré's presence as the French chairman underlined the importance attached by Paris to the group. Its task was to examine over-all trade, technical, and scientific relations between the two states and define new avenues for cooperation. The Small Committee, composed of lesser officials, was charged with following the execution of those accords reached between France and Soviet Russia. By 1970 these two committees spawned other committees to oversee commercial progress, the development of French color television for the Soviet Union, and the peaceful uses of atomic energy. Also organized were eighteen working groups for space, specialized industrial development, and the exchange of economic information.[53] The establishment of the first Soviet Chamber of Commerce in a Western state added to the esteem accorded by the Kremlin specifically to France.[54]

Soviet Premier Kosygin made much of the future possibilities of cooperation between the Soviet Union and France during his visit to Paris in December 1966. In his speech at the Sorbonne, Kosygin stressed the theme that isolation in technological, scientific, and industrial development retarded growth and diminished national strength.[55] Vladimir Kirilin, the Soviet co-chairman of the Large Committee, similarly expressed enthusiasm for French technical prowess and expressed eagerness to exploit as many parts of French technology

53. The results of Soviet-French relations from this period through 1970 are summarized in Premier Ministre, Comité Interministériel pour l'Information, "La Coopération franco-soviétique," *Actualités-documents,* May 1970. Hereafter cited "La Cooperation franco-soviétique."

54. *Le Monde,* Dec. 3, 1966, p. 2.

55. *Ibid.,* Dec. 4–5, 1966, p. 2.

as possible to improve the Soviet economy.[56] One French report summarized the feeling in some governmental quarters about the genuineness of Soviet interest in importing Western technology into Russia: "The Soviet Union realizes that, if she pursues the road to isolation, there will soon be only one great power in the world, the United States." [57] *L'Humanité,* the French Communist party newspaper, seconded this theme: "The Soviet Union wants to buy industrial equipment and commercial goods it needs to raise the living standards of the population, and it wants to sell the raw materials of which it has practically inexhaustible reserves." [58]

The sentiments expressed by Kosygin and Kirilin flattered French sensitivities. In contrast to the United States, which had discriminated against French science, evidenced by the differential application of the atomic energy legislation to Britain and France, the Soviet Union seemingly accepted France as an equal. Whereas the substantive acquisition of Western know-how was a serious Soviet concern, the French were as pleased with the esteem accorded them by the Soviet Union as with the content of the agreements that were reached.

The number of technical, scientific, and trade accords were more impressive than their practical import. Between October 30, 1964, and February 3, 1967, eleven "nonpolitical" accords were signed, stressing cooperation in nuclear energy, color television, space, health, and medicine.[59] The French, for example, installed a bubble chamber at the Soviet nuclear installation at Serpukhov. Teams of physicists worked on experiments in rapid neutrons. In space, after some false starts, work groups were organized in pure research, meteorology, and telecommunications. The medical and health fields came into prominence as a common subject of concern in the accord of January 9, 1969. Within the framework of these several agreements, specialized studies in such fields as water resources (February 8, 1967), aeronautics (March 1, 1967), and maritime problems (April 20, 1967) were pursued.[60] The development of

56. Grosser, *Franco-Soviet Relations,* pp. 56–57.

57. *Ibid.,* pp. 48–49.

58. Quoted in *New York Herald Tribune,* International edition, Dec. 10–11, 1966, p. 1.

59. These accords and cooperative ties are too numerous to explore here. They are outlined in "La Coopération franco-soviétique."

60. *FFP,* Jan.–June 1967, *passim.*

bilateral ties was retarded considerably after February 1967, for reasons speculated about below. Cultural relations progressed more slowly throughout this period. Almost two years passed before the cultural accord of December 20, 1968, was signed. The French admitted that the cultural relations "remained stationary, if compared to scientific and technological exchanges." [61] For the Russians, technology preceded culture, not the reverse, as the French tended to approach the problem of penetrating another state.

Considering the number of operating committees and the accords that were formally reached, the French did not achieve any significant lead over their Western competitors in reaching the Russian market. Table 1 compares exports and imports of France, West Germany, and the United Kingdom between 1966 and 1971. France enjoyed a significant jump in its exports to the Soviet Union after 1966 when French complaints and pressures about balancing their trade with the Soviet Union eventually had some effect. Thereafter, progress was not as rapid. Monthly averages in sales tripled in the first two years after the de Gaulle visit, but they later stagnated. The French largely balanced their unfavorable position vis-à-vis the Soviet Union. They succeeded perceptibly better than Great Britain although exports were at about the same level. The rapid improvement in German-Soviet trade clearly outdistanced French efforts despite heightened tensions between the two states in the midst of France's best efforts on behalf of détente.

France and Eastern Europe

The de Gaulle government busily engaged itself in re-establishing France's diplomatic presence and importance in East European capitals. A generation had almost elapsed since the debacle of Munich destroyed the fragile entente formed between France and the East European states after World War I. The fundamental choice facing France was whether to proceed without the Soviet Union's approval or acquiescence. The French answered the question well before de Gaulle's visit to Moscow. Bypassing the Soviet Union and dealing directly with its satellites would have been consistent with the strategy used within the Atlantic Alliance. But it was judged too

61. "La Coopération franco-soviétique."

Table 1. Trade of France, West Germany, and United Kingdom with the Soviet Union, 1966–1971* (monthly averages in millions of dollars)

	1966		1967		1968		1969		1970		1971	
	Import	Export	Import	Export	Import	Export	Import	Export	Import	Export	Import	Export
France	14.30	6.30	15.59	12.94	15.23	21.37	17.06	22.01	16.96	22.76	21.64	21.29
West Germany	20.44	11.28	22.07	16.50	24.36	22.78	27.85	33.81	28.47	35.20	30.53	38.39
United Kingdom	29.27	11.75	28.19	14.86	31.62	20.79	39.43	19.43	44.01	20.43	41.76	18.06

* Organization for Economic Cooperation and Development, Series A, *Over-All Trade by Countries*, October 1970, pp. 58, 60, 62, 64, 110, 112; January 1972, pp. 58, 60, 62, 64, 110, 112; and October 1972, pp. 58, 60, 62, 64, 110, 112.

risky. Attacking an ally on whom one still depended carried less potential costs than assaulting an adversary who was still to be tamed and transformed through détente. During the visit of Ian Maurer, Rumanian president of the Council of Ministers, to Paris in July 1964, news reports allegedly placed by official sources observed: "French government circles are anxious to avoid anything which might give the impression that President Maurer's visit is directed against the USSR. Rumania has adopted an attitude of detachment toward Moscow. She refuses to align herself with Moscow or Peking in the conflict which divides them. She does, however, belong to the socialist camp, and *no one in Paris has any notion of making her leave it.*" [62]

The Rumanians were reported to have urged a more ambitious strategy on the French during Foreign Minister Couve de Murville's visit there two years later, but to little avail. The de Gaulle government traded the confidence of the East European states in its reliability for what it apparently calculated would be the retention of its interlocutor role between Germany and the Soviet Union. As suggested below, however, it was overtaken by events in 1968 and was not able to play this role. Its reserve before the Soviet Union also meant that the de Gaulle government denied to itself what it did best: public exposure and criticism of superpower pretensions. French diplomatic tact in confronting Soviet imperial control, temperate when compared to its thrusts against American hegemony, and cautious relative to the risks run by Rumania, Yugoslavia, and Czechoslovakia, lacked much of the heroic posturing normally attributable to Gaullist foreign policy behavior.[63]

Rapprochement between East and West was conceived as a prerequisite to the more hazardous course of creating a new European politics. For the while, it appeared important to avoid a choice between Germany and the Soviet Union or to make any untoward move that might tarnish French credibility with one or the other of these two key states. Prudence proved the better part of Gaullist valor. Top priority was assigned to both states with the hope of alienating neither. Lesser attention was necessarily directed toward supporting

62. Quoted in Grosser, *Franco-Soviet Relations,* p. 59. Emphasis added.
63. This theme is driven forcefully home in Michel Tatu, *Le Triangle Washington-Moscou-Pékin,* pp. 94–133.

the independence struggles of the East European states. (De Gaulle did not visit any satellite capital immediately after his visit to Russia.) French efforts aimed at muting, manipulating, and managing the antagonisms between Germany and the Soviet Union, not inflaming them. The French rationalized their circumspection on the grounds that short-run Soviet control of East Europe would eventually give way to long-term polycentrism once the tensions of the Cold War were dissipated. And France would be the honest (if interested) broker striking the bargain. Its commission would be peace in Europe and the prestige and influence deriving from the performance of so critical and historic a role. The significance attached by the Gaullist government to its leader's pilgrimage to the Soviet Union was less in terms of its tangible results—which were meager—than in the attitudinal change it sought: to transform Soviet and German attitudes about each other as threats to their respective security; to demonstrate through French friendship to both states that Germany was not embarking on a revanchist policy and that the Soviet Union was not preparing to use force to achieve its aims. For de Gaulle, the first matter of business was of epic proportions, of war and peace. The troubling details of political settlement would come later.

Even with Soviet acquiescence, French penetration into Eastern Europe was undramatic. The patterns of relations that were developed varied with each state.[64] Formal exchanges of prime ministers, presidents, foreign ministers, and lesser officials and technical professional and scientific groups grew apace after 1964. In 1964 and early 1965, the foreign ministers of all the Eastern satellites and Yugoslavia visited Paris; only Poland sent a nonparty official, President Czyrankiewicz in September 1965. French Minister Couve de Murville returned the visits in 1966. How far the road was to be traveled in bettering relations may be suggested by the mission of Christian Fouchet, French minister of education, to Czechoslovakia in May 1966. He was only the second French minister since 1939 to visit Prague. A year before, Louis Joxe, in the Pompidou cabinet, signed a long-term

64. These exchanges between French and East European officials are too numerous to mention here, but their cumulative effect merits notice. See *FFP*, 1966, 1967, 1968, *passim*, for a chronicle of these exchanges. French Foreign Minister Couve de Murville makes much of the opening to the East under the de Gaulle administration in Couve de Murville, *op. cit.*, pp. 191–234.

trade accord and another dealing with scientific and technical collaboration.[65] That these visits were being made at all was considered more important and critical to the French than their dubious practical results.

France also enlarged the network of its bilateral committee arrangements with all of the East European states, including apostate Yugoslavia and neutral Austria. Like their Soviet analogues, they dealt with "nonpolitical" areas already mentioned. The functions and competence of these committees varied with the interest of the parties. Their very formation was considered as important as the specific purposes they served. They were vehicles by which to normalize and institutionalize relations between France and the East European states. Their existence, unique in East-West relations, implied a special relation that advanced, in Gaullist eyes, France's logical role as an interlocutor between East and West. They were to be motor forces, too, encouraging the expansion of specific ties with the East European regimes along the lines with those accords reached respectively with Rumania and Czechoslovakia in such politically innocuous areas as veterinary services (February 1967) and the organization of a French library in Prague (April 1966). The increasing tempo of visits and exchanges between French and East European officials and peoples, the accumulation of bilateral agreements in defined policy areas, the creation of a new process of foreign relations between East and West through the multiplication of committees were so many means to nurse notions of East European independence in Moscow and to increase French influence and status east of the Oder-Neisse. All were parts of the Gaullist effort to have France participate on a global scale in world politics.

Technical, scientific, and economic concerns dominated the East European agenda. France signed trade accords with all of the states except East Germany with which relations could not be officially recognized. Five-year spans were the vogue. All of the states, too, adopted French color television. Cooperation in nuclear energy particularly attracted Bulgaria and Czechoslovakia. Rumania and Hungary focused on industrial exchanges; both contracted for assistance from Renault as the Soviet Union had already done. Poland signed

65. Grosser, *Franco-Soviet Relations,* p. 58.

similar agreements in these areas. Contracts between Paris and the Chambers of Commerce of these states were multiplied.

As with the Soviet Union, trade figures between France and East Europe did not reflect the pace and range of the diplomatic activity. Over-all trade with China and the Soviet bloc states represented less than 10 percent of France's commercial trade. French Foreign Minister Couve de Murville admitted before a Council of Ministers meeting after his trips to Hungary and Czechoslovakia: "The situation was not satisfactory." [66] These sentiments were no less applicable to the other East European states. Between 1966 and 1971, West Germany's trade with Eastern Europe was twice that of France's and was approximately equal to the combined total of France and Great Britain. France had political concessions to sell, but these were not highly negotiable in the marketplace.[67]

If trade relations lagged behind diplomatic contacts, so cultural exchanges lagged behind both. Like the Soviet Union, the East European states showed less interest in this area. Published statements of the French Council of Ministers noted the dim prospects for cultural penetration. Rumania and Poland offered the best opportunities for exchanges. The ties with Poland were of long standing, dating from before the Napoleonic period. Rumania, whose language was the most closely related to French, was similarly disposed. The political deviationism of France and Rumania within their respective blocs also encouraged more interest in the other's cultural settings. In 1963, only $6 million in French books were sold to Rumania; two years later the figure was $88 million. When the Russian language was dropped as obligatory in Rumania, 65 percent of the students chose French as their first language. Prospects for the expansion of French culture were slimmer in the other East European states. In some, like Yugoslavia, the teaching of French had actually declined.[68]

No one factor explains the slow political progress registered by France in its détente policy, nor its equally dubious success in less

66. *FFP*, 1966, p. 251.
67. Organization for Economic Cooperation and Development, Series A, *Over-All Trade by Countries*, Oct. 1970, pp. 58, 60, 62, 64, 110, 112; Jan. 1972, pp. 58, 60, 62, 64, 110, 112; and Oct. 1972, pp. 58, 60, 62, 64, 110, 112.
68. *FFP*, 1966, p. 253.

sensitive areas. By early 1967, France appeared to have less to offer these states than did other Western powers, especially Germany. Premier Kosygin's visit to Paris in December 1966 marked the high point of Franco-Soviet collaboration relative to that enjoyed by France's Western allies. The Kosygin visit offered an opportunity for the Soviet Union to project an image, as newspaper accounts suggested, of reason and maturity in seeking a peaceful solution to common European problems. This was part of the Russian offensive aimed at Western Europe. Affirming the Franco-Soviet accord communiqué of the previous June 30, Kosygin commended France's role in opposing bloc politics and lauded its efforts to bring a new basis of understanding among the European states.[69] His public remarks, while noting differences between the two states, acknowledged a similar disposition regarding the unsettled political questions facing Europe and the Third World.

Kosygin's optimistic observations contrasted with his failure to budge France on the German problem, the Soviet proposal of a European security conference, and the nonproliferation treaty. French policy toward the Third World was in step with Soviet views, particularly in the Middle East and Vietnam, but its utility in the underdeveloped states did not outweigh the great value attached by the Soviet Union to the retention of its possessions and influence in Eastern Europe. Nevertheless, French-Soviet relations remained outwardly cordial throughout 1967. They appeared especially close during the Six-Day War of 1967. Visits of Prime Minister Georges Pompidou and Foreign Minister Couve de Murville in July 1967 [70] and Minister of Information Georges Gorse the following November[71] affirmed the détente process begun three years before. General Ailleret appeared at the Moscow May Day ceremonies, and his Soviet counterpart, Marshall Zakharov, visited Paris in October. Ailleret's reinterpretation of the strategic threats facing France, as no longer coming from the East, appeared in December 1967 [72] and prepared the way for the visit of Defense Minister Pierre Messmer to the Soviet Union in spring 1968.

69. *Le Monde,* Dec. 3, 1966, p. 2.
70. See dispatches of *Le Monde,* July 4–11, 1967.
71. See *ibid.,* Nov. 16–22, 1967.
72. See above, Chapter 3, for a discussion of the Ailleret doctrine.

Meanwhile, Soviet officials drew on the criticisms articulated by de Gaulle in their offensive against the United States role in Europe—dollar and technological dominance, American military presence, and the continuation of NATO.[73]

If the de Gaulle government was bent on extending relations and on playing fully its self-assigned détente role, the Soviet Union was showing signs of disinterest by mid-1967 and, by mid-1968, the Franco-Soviet *rapprochement* had passed its peak. De Gaulle's utility for Soviet diplomacy and economic goals had largely been exploited. France could not give what was at the disposal of the United States and Germany: their consent or acquiescence in Soviet aims for the *status quo* in Europe. The greater resources and economic development of Germany and the United States meant both had more to offer than France in technological, scientific, and commercial exchanges and assistance. Some accord with the United States was essential, too, to Soviet aims in Europe and the Third World on arms control. The French might weaken the United States negotiating position by attacking alliance solidarity, but could not control the timing or substance of United States negotiations with the Soviet Union. Despite its differences with the United States over Vietnam, the Soviet Union was eager to sign the nonproliferation treaty, to induce other nonnuclear states, particularly Germany, to adhere to the document, and to enlarge gradually the scope of strategic arms limitation talks. Here the French had little to offer; and that which they might have provided was stiffly refused.[74]

The nonproliferation treaty (NPT) indicated that the United States was willing to trade on some of its political capital in Bonn.[75] The June war illustrated, too, that the superpowers regarded themselves as the principal arbiters of the Middle East conflict. Premier Kosygin's two meetings with President de Gaulle before and after his trip to the United Nations after the Six-Day War did not compensate for the hastily prepared meeting at Glassboro between Kosygin and President Johnson where the two leaders addressed each other as equals on the

73. Wolfe, *op. cit.*, pp. 325–330.
74. See the French note on disarmament of August 1968 to the Soviet Union, *FFP*, July–Dec. 1968, p. 17.
75. Wolfe, *op. cit.*, pp. 323–324.

Middle East crisis.[76] By June 1967, the United States began to upstage France in its own play for a leading détente role. If military-strategic matters still dominated the formal NATO agenda, the NATO ministers conference manifested a novel sensitivity to the political currents running deeply in European capitals. It officially approved the new accent on political détente over defense and encouraged all members, with Germany in the forefront, to probe bilaterally for progress in East-West relations.[77]

After December 1966, Germany increasingly assumed the center of the stage of détente maneuvering in the West. The Grand Coalition formed by the Christian and Social Democrats shortly after Premier Kosygin's visit to Paris departed perceptibly from the Adenauer-Erhard Cold War line. Early during his tenure as German chancellor, Kurt Kiesinger subtly shifted the declared priorities of German foreign policy: "We are not saying détente first and then reunification. We are saying détente. And while pursuing this policy we—and the others— must never lose sight of the problem of German reunification." [78] Kiesinger acknowledged that Germany was partly to blame for the falling out with France. It would follow France's example toward détente: "I wish to draw your attention to the aspect of my talks with President de Gaulle which is of the greatest importance for our future, i.e., cooperation between our two governments in the vast field of European policy towards the East. The Federal Government's aim is to relax and ease Germany's relations with the Eastern European countries and the Soviet Union. This new intention accords with the intention of the French President, in particular, because this policy, *our* policy, is directed against no one, not even Russia." [79]

In following France's lead, the Bonn government did not suggest that it would defer to France's leadership in improving relations with Eastern Europe. De Gaulle, as one acute observer noted, could be credited with having instructed Germany in its responsibility for

76. This is the general impression drawn by Prime Minister Harold Wilson from his talk with de Gaulle and confirmed by the author in interviews with French officials. See Harold Wilson, *The Labour Government, 1964–1970* (London: Weidenfeld and Nicolson, 1971), pp. 404–406. There was some doubt in de Gaulle's mind whether any state had control of the Middle East.

77. WEU, *Political Year, 1967*, pp. 97–98.

78. *Ibid.*, p. 75.

79. *Ibid.*, p. 58. Emphasis added.

détente.[80] He took Bonn to school on how to press its interests through its own efforts. The outward trappings of German policy may have been French in inspiration, but they were motored by German concerns and managed by the Bonn government. The French had already unwittingly contributed to the new sense of German confidence in foreign policy in thrusting the Federal Republic into the leadership of the Five during the agricultural crisis of 1965–1966. The slowdown in Western integration and the decline of Atlantic cohesion also weakened Bonn's hopes of increased stature in the West. This dismantling process advised Bonn against relying almost exclusively on its Western base to exert pressure in the East. The Johnson administration's interest in the NPT and its bridge-building efforts in Eastern Europe, not to mention France's active Eastern diplomacy, also raised the specter of an East-West accord at Germany's expense. Doubts were raised in Bonn, mixed with complaints, about the failure of the American government to keep the Federal Republic adequately informed about its plans, particularly with respect to arms control talks with the Soviet Union. It became increasingly more plausible to accept the de Gaulle argument of placing détente ahead of unification as an immediate goal of German foreign policy. The Berlin Wall would not collapse through a policy of "maintained tensions," and the East European states would similarly not bend to Western pressures. They would be more bound than ever to the Soviet Union.

The Grand Coalition departed in a number of operationally important respects from the policies of its predecessors. The Bonn government sought to relieve tensions with the Pankow regime without recognizing its authority in the hope of improving the daily lot of the East German citizenry and in opening communication and contacts between the two Germanies and the German people across their divided borders. In his maiden speech to the Bundestag, Chancellor Kiesinger called for better relations with Eastern Europe and, as a gesture of conciliation, referred to the GDR by name rather than to "Middle Germany" or to the "Soviet Occupied Zone." [81] Furthermore, the coalition regime, like the Erhard government, was prepared to declare the Munich Treaty null and void and to affirm its interest in

80. Karl Kaiser, *German Foreign Policy in Transition* (London: Oxford University Press, 1968), pp. 97–100.

81. Whetten, *op. cit.*, p. 19

border settlements with Eastern Europe within the framework of a general peace treaty. More significant was the abandonment of the Hallstein doctrine in establishing diplomatic relations with Rumania (January 1967) and Yugoslavia a year later. Overtures, too, were extended to Hungary, Bulgaria, and Czechoslovakia after the Moscow government had rebuffed early West German efforts to improve relations with them. In relinquishing the Hallstein doctrine, Bonn weakened its case to speak for all of Germany, but its more effective diplomatic moves tended to isolate East Germany within its own bloc.

The Soviet Union and its closest northern satellites yielded little to the new winds out of Bonn. Largely adopted, with some discreet reservations, was the East German thesis of resistance to West German conciliatory moves. With Rumania demurring, the other East European states signed a series of bilateral accords supporting each other's existing boundaries and sovereignty. Poland was particularly pointed about the conditions for détente: the recognition of East Germany, West German renunciation of nuclear weapons, and acceptance of its western boundaries.[82] The Soviet Union also reaffirmed its security ties with its satellites.[83]

It was in this depressing diplomatic setting that de Gaulle made his first trip to an East European capital in September 1967, shortly after his controversial visit to Canada where he aroused already inflamed French opinion in his call for a free Quebec.[84] In Poland, the reception was officially colder and the rebuke to French policy more blunt than the restrained request of the Ottawa government that de Gaulle's welcome had been exhausted after his appeals to French nationalism had so disturbed Canadian domestic tranquillity.[85] The voyage to Poland, in some ways a sentimental return of an old soldier to the scene of past glories as a young officer,[86] marked the low estate to which

82. *FFP,* July–Dec. 1967, p. 39.

83. Soviet relations with its East European clients are expertly discussed in Whetten, *op. cit.,* pp. 35–65, and Wolfe, *op. cit.,* pp. 348–426. Also helpful is Karl E. Birnbaum, *Peace in Europe* (London: Oxford University Press, 1970), especially Chapters 1–2, pp. 1–77.

84. *FFP,* July–Dec. 1967, pp. 16–27. At Montreal, de Gaulle roused the crowds by referring to a "free Quebec," the motto of French-Canadian separatists.

85. *Ibid.,* p. 22.

86. Jean Lacouture, *De Gaulle,* trans. Francis K. Price (New York: New American Library, 1965), pp. 21–23.

French esteem had fallen in Eastern Europe. De Gaulle's open acknowledgment of Poland's borders, a recognition he alleged had been extended as far back as 1944, earned the public declination of the Bonn government.[87] His suggestion that Poland manifest more national independence was met with an unanticipated retort from Polish Premier Wladyslaw Gomulka. It did not spare French feelings about their reliability as a potential ally or usefulness as an interlocutor between East and West. "During the period between World War I and II," said the Polish leader, "Poland and France were bound by a political and military alliance. . . . This alliance did not work well. . . . It was not able to protect either Poland or France from the catastrophe of defeat and occupation by Hitler. Alliance with the Soviet Union, together with the treaties of friendship, cooperation and mutual assistance concluded with the Socialist States of Central, Eastern, and Southern Europe, including [sic] with our Western neighbor the German Democratic Republic . . . is the cornerstone of the policy of the Polish People's Republic and the principal guarantee of her security."[88] De Gaulle's deferential regard for Soviet power and influence in Eastern Europe did little to add credibility to his counsel for more national independence. The risks would be run in Warsaw, not Paris.

Gomulka's candor, if it did not reject the possibility of East-West détente, did much to shatter French expectations of Soviet and East European interest in French leadership. By fall 1967, the Middle East crisis had overshadowed the German question and France was again crowded out by the superpowers. The Czechoslovakian upheaval, beginning in early 1968 and ending with the Soviet and satellite invasion of August 1968, dispelled most of the remaining fancies about French influence on Soviet behavior.

West European Policy, 1966–1968

Before examining the impact of the events of 1968 on France's European posture, it would be helpful to relate France's *Westpolitik* to its *Ostpolitik*. One reinforced the other. The Luxembourg accords of early 1966 essentially defined Gaullist France's policy toward its

87. *FFP*, July–Dec. 1967, p. vi.
88. *Ibid.*, p. 39.

West European partners. Preserving these gains, particularly in agriculture, and preventing further erosion of France's position within the European community were the dominant aims of the de Gaulle government in the West as it turned its primary attention toward the East. The decision of the British Labor government to apply again for entry into the Common Market threatened the delicate political and economic balance within the West European grouping that still favored France's leadership role. Stopping British entry absorbed most of the thrust of France's policy toward Western Europe until de Gaulle's resignation in April 1969.

As early as February 10, 1966, in a speech before the House of Commons, British Prime Minister Harold Wilson raised the possibility of reapplying for membership in the EEC. Domestic opposition to entry was strongest within Wilson's own party; the most formidable foreign obstacle remained President de Gaulle. There followed over a year of delicate negotiations with the member states and the careful cultivation of domestic opinion to lay the ground for a new application. These are too complicated to recount here.[89] Only those aspects bearing on French policy and responses need concern us.

A number of important factors advised another attempt to enter the Common Market. Economic considerations included sluggish growth, retarded industrial modernization, insufficient investment, chronic balance-of-payments problems, and continuing trouble with sterling's stability. These problems impelled London to seek a solution to national economic ills by turning once again to the Continent and the market and stimulus offered by almost three hundred million potential consumers.

Also pointing Britain toward the Continent was the gradual wither-

89. For a general discussion of British negotiations over entry, see the annual numbers of the WEU publication *A Retrospective View of the Political Year in Europe* (Paris). Of particular interest is its publication, *The British Application for Membership in the European Communities: 1963–68* (Paris, May 1968). For a French account that is balanced and informed consult Françoise de la Serre, "L'Adhésion de la grande-bretagne aux communautés européenes: la seconde candidature, 1967–69," *Notes et études documentaires*, No. 3882–3883, April 19, 1972. For a journalistic account see Merry and Serge Bromberger, *Jean Monnet and the United States of Europe*, trans. Elaine P. Halperin (New York: Coward-McCann, 1968), chap. 19, pp. 317–340.

ing of the special relation with the United States. Security aspects remained strong, and British strategy was still entangled in American nuclear policy. But United States foreign policy, especially in the Third World—Vietnam and Santo Domingo were cases in point— caused embarrassment. American economic competition and investment penetration into British industry were also increasingly troublesome aspects of Britain's difficulties with its North American ally. Help might be found in Europe. The Luxembourg accords that weakened the development of centralized supranational authority and institutions within the community facilitated British re-evaluation of the European option to improve its economic position to meet foreign competition.

These re-evaluations of Britain's position pointed to the larger political reasoning that underlay the previous attempt to join the Brussels organization. British leaders of both parties understood that England could no longer play a global role alone. It needed a larger policy framework within which to exert its influence abroad. The political neutrality of most EFTA members precluded reliance on this vehicle. The Commonwealth, divided and incoherent, no longer provided an adequate basis for a global role. The Soviet Union's settlement of the border clash between India and Pakistan in 1965 and British impotence in the face of Rhodesian independence were symptomatic of the Commonwealth's reduced political significance. Nor did the United States respond, as in the immediate postwar period, to British prompting.[90]

London articulated an elaborate case for entry before its European auditors.[91] First, Britain would presumably add weight to Europe's capacity to play an independent role in global politics. Together (and implicitly under British leadership), the West European states would make their political influence felt in the Third World and in the calculations of the superpowers.

90. For a highly readable analysis of American-British relations, sprinkled with insights, see Richard E. Neustadt, *Alliance Politics.*

91. Four speeches that, together, summarize most of the British case are those of Prime Minister Harold Wilson before the Council of Europe in Strasbourg (Jan. 23, 1967), Foreign Minister George Brown (Feb. 22 and July 4), and Lord Chalfont, Minister of State for Foreign Affairs (Sept. 15). These are found in WEU, *British Application for Membership,* pp. 45–47, 51–53, 59–68.

Second, only through European cooperation could the United States economic challenge be met in trade, investment, and technological development. Wilson advanced a proposal to pool the scientific and technological resources of Europe to meet the United States competitive advantage. Speaking to the French point of alleged irreconcilability of Britain's commitment to the Atlantic Alliance and the preservation of national independence, Wilson said, "Loyalty to NATO and the Atlantic Alliance never means subservience. Still less must it mean an industrial helotry under which we in Europe produce only the conventional apparatus of modern economy, while becoming increasingly dependent on American business for the sophisticated apparatus which will call the industrial tune in the '70's and '80's." [92] Avoiding the stigma of *demandeur,* George Brown, the British foreign secretary, echoed Wilson's optimism regarding the technological skills and resources that Britain would bring Europe: "Britain alone spends on technological research and development 70 percent of the combined expenditures of the Common Market countries. We can bring to the Community a large and a highly developed industry. We can bring an outstandingly efficient agriculture and we can bring our political standing as a major nation of the world occupying a central position in the Commonwealth." [93]

Third, the Labor government rationalized Britain's defense role.[94] In withdrawing from east of Suez, it oriented its defense policies more toward Europe and anticipated increased cooperation within this area.[95] The Wilson government turned the Gaullist criticism of Britain's foreign policy to its advantage: British entry into the EEC was the precondition for European independence from the United States and the end of superpower dominance of international politics. Meanwhile, the British displayed their credentials as a progenitor of détente, even before de Gaulle had raised this standard.

British tactics in persuading the Six were as painstaking as the brief for entry.[96] The Labor government accepted the common agri-

92. *Ibid.,* p. 45.
93. *Ibid.,* p. 52.
94. See Pierre, *Nuclear Politics,* pp. 295ff.
95. WEU, *British Application for Membership,* pp. 59–68.
96. Useful for an understanding of British policy and the problems of Common Market entry are the memoirs of Harold Wilson, *op. cit.,* and George Brown, *In My Way* (London: Gollancz, 1971), especially pp. 209–223.

cultural policy and called more for adjustments in EEC policies than for a fundamental change in the Brussels organization or in the arrangements reached among the Six after ten years of working together. The burden of the common agricultural policy would be partly compensated through assistance to Britain's regional development that would bring in new investment and support funds from the European community. The efficiency and high productivity of British farmers placed them closer to the French than many realized. Britain produced thirteen million tons of cereals to France's twenty million.[97] Both states had an interest in keeping production down and in cutting farm prices lower than Germany insisted upon to subsidize its inefficient agriculture. Solutions to sterling's problems were also at hand, argued the British, without undue risk or cost to the community. Britain's trade was in surplus, albeit temporarily; sterling as a reserve currency was really an international monetary problem to which the EEC states were already heir; and in any event Britain was prepared to consider alternatives to present policies to minimize any transfer of financial obligations to the Six on Britain's entry. Finally, special arrangements would have to be found for New Zealand dairy and meat products and Commonwealth sugar. To a lesser degree of significance, Australia and Canada still posed some difficulty, but they did not raise insurmountable barriers for Britain's application.

Discreetly dropped from Wilson's program for entry were the more rigorous conditions for application set out by Hugh Gaitskell, Wilson's predecessor as head of the Labor party.[98] Moreover, in accepting the Rome and Paris treaties, the British government foreclosed long negotiations over principle which had so retarded the talks in 1962–1963. Prime Minister Wilson's tour of European capitals in early 1967 lent personal assurances to British governmental pledges issuing from Whitehall, the podiums of the WEU,

97. Wilson, *op. cit.*, pp. 339–340.
98. George Brown quotes Gaitskell's condition in his speech before the Socialist International in Stockholm of May 6, 1966: "First, safeguards for trade and other interests of our friends and partners in the Commonwealth; second, safeguards for our EFTA partners; third, safeguards for the position of British agriculture; fourth, freedom to pursue our own foreign policy; and fifth, the right to plan our own economy" (WEU, *Political Year, 1966*, pp. 138–139).

the European Parliament, and other European forums.[99] On May 11, 1967, Britain formally submitted its application to the EEC for entry.

The French response was initially cautious and reserved. Hints were broad enough during Prime Minister Wilson's trip to France in early February and even before to warrant serious doubts that French objections to British entry had been overcome.[100] President de Gaulle was clear on this point in his impromptu meeting with British Foreign Minister George Brown in the midst of a NATO meeting in December 1966. According to Brown's account, "De Gaulle was adamantly against us [Britain]. He regarded the continent as France's place and the Atlantic Ocean and the United States as Britain's place. . . . He said that he had had a lot of trouble getting the five hens to do what France wanted, and he wasn't going to have Britain's coming in and creating trouble all over again, this time with ten. All this, however, was exceedingly friendly." [101]

The French president was less colorful, but more explicit, in his news conference of May 16, less than a week after Britain's application. Most of the objections to British entry already stated in the January 1963 veto were reiterated:[102] Britain's distance in history, its geographic and strategic position relative to the Continent, its different economic system, including its agricultural program, its close economic, political, and cultural ties to the Commonwealth, EFTA, and the United States—all these factors remained as insurmountable obstacles in the immediate future to British acceptance of a French-conceived independent Europe.[103] These conditions of British life, if incorporated into the EEC, challenged French leadership of the Six in regional and global affairs and its capacity to shape community policies to serve its economic interests, particularly in agriculture.

For most practical purposes, completion of the European community along lines set out in Paris was a prerequisite of enlarge-

99. Wilson toured the capitals of the Six in early 1967: Rome (Jan. 15–17), Paris (Jan. 25–27), Brussels (Jan. 31–Feb. 1), Bonn (Feb. 14–16), Hague (Feb. 20–27), and Luxembourg (March 7–8).

100. Wilson, *op. cit.*, pp. 334–345.

101. Brown, *op. cit.*, p. 220.

102. See Chapter 6, above, pp. 309–315.

103. De Gaulle's news conference is found in *FFP*, July–Dec. 1967, pp. 135–146.

ment.[104] De Gaulle dismissed British acceptance of EEC principles as a negotiating tactic, foreshadowing an inevitable transformation of the EEC into a free trade area and exposing Europe to overweening United States influence. At the same time, French officials, anticipating their critics, reaffirmed France's commitment to an enlarged trading and competitive area pictured as the key to France's own modernization. It was asserted as self-evident that the British would never be able to accept the financial burdens of the community's agricultural policy, whatever the London government promised or otherwise believed. The increased charges for agriculture would undo further Britain's balance-of-trade deficits and weaken sterling. This was a new element of the French rebuttal. It countered much of Britain's brief for entry which, as Prime Minister Wilson himself admitted, hinged on balancing Britain's trade deficits and strengthening the pound.[105] The French thrust might well be considered as a link in the "gold war" against the dollar and, according to the French, its minion, the pound sterling.[106] Finally, Britain's presence in Western European councils might undermine France's Eastern policy and its play to become the privileged partner of the Soviet Union within Europe.[107]

De Gaulle preferred to see nothing new in the British stance if it conflicted with his already hard and fast notions of British policy and equally settled views about France's political destiny. The change in Labor's attitude, the large vote of the House of Commons in support of the government's decision to apply for membership,[108] the acceptance of the community treaties and the common agricultural policy, and the reorientation of Britain's technological, scientific, and defense policies toward Europe were conveniently overlooked in the French rebuttal. It was as if nothing had changed in British policy,

104. See the speeches of Couve de Murville and André Bettencourt, *ibid.*, July–Dec. 1967, pp. 103–104, 122–123.

105. Wilson, *op. cit.*, p. xvii. Said Wilson in the opening sentence of his *Memoirs*: "This book is the record of a Government all but a year of whose life was dominated by an inherited balance of payments problems."

106. See Chapter 4, above.

107. De Gaulle critically refers to this threat in Britain's challenge to a European Europe, *FFP*, Jan.–June 1967, p. 68.

108. The vote was 488 to 62, with 80 abstentions, in favor of the British application.

nor would soon change in France's internal position or in Soviet-American policy toward each other or in their views of Europe's (and France's) role in world affairs. The French moved forward, as in a dream, to use a favorite de Gaulle simile, applying their policy of resistance to British entry, yet all the while that policy and its assumptions about France's power in Europe—specifically, toward Germany and the Soviet Union on which they were based—were rapidly eroding.

The cold water abruptly splashed on the British application by de Gaulle continued to gush from the Quai d'Orsay. The French stalled for time rather than refuse outright to review the British application. After some uncertainty over whether France would attend a summit of heads of state commemorating the tenth anniversary of the EEC treaties, President de Gaulle acknowledged the wish of his peers at the summit on May 29–30 that the British proposal for entry be studied. Meanwhile, André Bettencourt, French secretary of state for foreign affairs, said before the WEU Council in early July that it would be impossible to decide on Britain's Common Market application. There followed additional statements of November 11 and 16 to discourage hopes that the thorny legal and economic problems posed by the British candidacy might be resolved.[109] Foreign Minister Couve de Murville's addresses before the National Assembly in June and November 1967 re-echoed the themes struck in de Gaulle's May news conference.[110] These pronouncements prepared the way for the French president's refusal of November 27 to discuss the British request short of a complete transformation of British foreign and economic policy suitable to French conditions, many that remained vague and ill-defined since they turned more on implicit political considerations than on explicit economic factors.[111] Fortuitously strengthening de Gaulle's case was the unexpected devaluation of the pound on November 18. It seemed to confirm dire French prognostications of the adverse effects of permitting Britain's membership in the Six. Nor was the French president below selecting only those parts of an EEC commission report that underlined the difficulties which a weak trade and currency position

109. *FFP*, July–Dec. 1967, pp. 109–113, 121–127.
110. *Ibid.*, Jan.–June, 1967, pp. 96–100; *ibid.*, July–Dec. 1967, pp. 102–106.
111. *Ibid.*, pp. 138–141

posed for British adhesion, although the EEC Commission actually favored opening negotiations with Britain.

There was a positive side to the French case, too. England was allegedly not needed to bolster Europe against the United States. The success of the EEC during the Kennedy Round of tariff negotiations among the major Western trading nations was cited as proof of increased European bargaining power vis-à-vis the North Atlantic giant, all the more so, since, as Murville charged, "Great Britain was at the . . . side [of the United States]." [112] The French could also point, and not without some justification, to other elements of progress made within the Six toward greater economic cooperation. These included the increasing charge of agriculture as a community obligation, the application of the value added tax (TVA) in all states to increase community revenue and harmonize tax policies, the installation of a single executive (despite the quarrel over retaining Walter Hallstein as the first president), and the gradual implementation of the May 1966 accords.[113]

These maneuvers culminated at the Council of Ministers meeting of the Six in December 1967, convened to hear the British request. The conference ended in an impasse. France refused to discuss the possibility of Britain's entry as premature. De Gaulle had already bound his foreign minister in his November 27 news conference: "For the British Isles really to be able to moor fast to the continent, a very vast and very far-reaching mutation is still involved. Everything depends, therefore, *not* at all on negotiations . . . but rather on the determination and action of the great British people, which would make it one of the pillars of a European Europe." [114] The problem was still Britain's hesitancy (shared by some of France's EEC partners) to join a Europe of dominantly French design. But the French president held firm to his understanding of West Europe's political future and France's privileged position within it. "What France cannot do is to enter now, with the British and their associates, into negotiations that would lead to destroying the European construction to which she belongs. . . . For Europe to be able to

112. *Ibid.,* p. 104.
113. Hallstein resigned as president when a French-Five compromise would have permitted him to remain only one year as president.
114. *FFP,* July–Dec. 1967, p. 141. Emphasis added.

counterbalance the immense power of the United States, it is necessary not at all to weaken, but to the contrary to strengthen the Community's ties and rules." [115]

The foreign ministers communiqué of December 22 noted the disagreements between France and its partners. The Five wished negotiations to proceed parallel with London's efforts to stabilize the British economy; the French wished a fundamental overhaul of its internal economy and a restructuring of its external relations. The question of opening talks with Britain remained on the EEC agenda with no decision taken until December 1969, when France, under great domestic and foreign pressure and with de Gaulle gone from the scene, finally acceded to examine the British petition.

What is perhaps most striking about French behavior during this period, when contrasted with the 1963 veto, was the greater reserve exhibited in diplomatic maneuvering. Britain was not rejected; the decision to entertain Britain's application was instead shelved indefinitely. French tergiversations to justify deferral of the decision on British entry were symptomatic of its declining ability to control its partners. Gaullist France's lessening influence on the Five was of a piece with the frustration of the Fouchet plan and the blockage of the French power play in 1965–1966. French economic strength and the domestic political health of the de Gaulle government were increasingly dependent, notwithstanding France's protestations of legal and moral independence, on the cooperation of its partners.

As the decade reached an end, France's dependency would become more evident, even to Gaullist advocates like Michel Debré. The financial regulation for agriculture came due in December 1969. Progress in other areas of French interest was impossible unless favorable actions were taken on Britain. France's *Ostpolitik* was largely immobile by early 1968. Germany's initiatives and Soviet and East European defensive reactions (including Rumania's intransigence) overtook in importance France's Eastern posturing. Furthermore, France's products, as inflation rose, were being priced out of world markets by the close of 1965. Its large gold reserves were of little use in improving its competitive position or in increasing the

115. *Ibid.*

production and distribution of real goods in France to meet rising social demands for a higher standard of living.

The remainder of 1968 and much of 1969, until de Gaulle's resignation in April 1969, saw the Five put varying amounts of pressure, with little immediate success, to bring France to heel on the British question. Germany's weight, which was potentially greatest, could not be brought to bear fully on Paris. The Kiesinger government was too internally unstable and had committed itself from the start to healing the rifts between the two states. It looked, too, for support from France for its Eastern policy.[116] Chancellor Kiesinger reportedly had "neither the means nor the intention to exercise pressure on Paris to promote the accession of the United Kingdom to the EEC." [117] The Kiesinger-de Gaulle meeting of February 1968 hit on a compromise acceptable to both parties. Germany would defer to French objections to negotiations in practice while both would agree on enlargement in principle. France went along with the German proposal to take steps toward greater commercial and technological cooperation between Britain and the Six, leading to a reduction of trade obstacles for industrial products. Each state could attach its preferred interpretations—Germany could believe these steps would lead to British membership; France, to associate status. The *Economist* cut to the heart of the matter when it observed that for the while, given German policy aims in the East, a movement toward lowering trade barriers with Britain and its EFTA neighbors fostered German economic interests adequately enough. To force British entry into the EEC might cost France's political support, still valued as important, and upset the delicate balance of forces within the German coalition government of the SPD and CDU.[118]

The Benelux countries and Italy were as disposed to British entry as ever. These states floated a number of plans and proposals in the course of the succeeding eighteen months in an attempt to bypass the French roadblocks to negotiations. On January 18, the Benelux states issued a joint statement assessing the state of the community and outlining the steps toward "avoiding increased discrepancies

116. Wilson, *op. cit.*, pp. 367–368.
117. WEU, *Political Year, 1967*, p. 13.
118. *Economist*, March 16, 1968, p. 25.

between the Common Market and the applicant countries." [119] The Commission was encouraged to continue its study of enlargement. The route to cooperation was through a wider and well-defined framework of economic consultations "between the Commission, the member States, and the applicant States." [120]

Going beyond the community, the three small states supported greater consultations between the Six and Britain in areas not covered by the Rome and Paris treaties.[121] Foreign policy was cited as a field where fruitful bilateral harmonization might be pursued. Although designed as a means to circumvent the implicit French veto on negotiations, it played into French hands since the de Gaulle government had been insisting for almost a decade on state-to-state negotiations outside the community framework as the principal outlet for state action. The Dutch refusal in March 1968 to participate in talks within the community on technological and scientific cooperation, if aimed at paying in kind France's policy of *la chaise vide,* also gave the Paris government the argument that their partners, not they, were the obstacles to closer European cooperation.[122]

With the small states taking the lead, the Five, tacitly supported by the British foreign office, continued to apply pressure on unyielding France. British Foreign Secretary Michael Stewart, who had since replaced George Brown, announced Britain's refusal to entertain any steps toward greater cooperation between the Six and England that would not result eventually in Britain's joining the EEC.[123] There was no compromising on this point. Belgian Foreign Minister Pierre Harmel, who had already expressed his anxiety to Prime Minister Wilson about the dominance of the Six through a Paris-Bonn axis,[124] again seized the initiative. He proposed an elaborate plan that would have used the WEU "to strengthen European cooperation in the political, military, technological, and monetary fields." [125] While Germany officially temporized (with Foreign Minister Willy Brandt's

119. WEU, *Political Year, 1966,* p. 86.
120. *Ibid.*
121. WEU, *British Application for Membership,* pp. 93–95. The Italian plan of February 23, 1968, parallels the thinking of the Benelux countries.
122. *L'Année politique, 1968,* p. 230.
123. WEU, *Political Year, 1968,* p. 35.
124. Wilson, *op. cit.,* pp. 341–343.
125. WEU, *Political Year, 1968,* pp. 140–143.

statements at an SPD political rally unofficially manifesting a more open policy toward Britain),[126] Italy joined the Benelux in pressing the British case. In what was to become a basic bargaining point in the position of the Five, Harmel linked the completion of the community to enlargement. There might be no common agricultural policy unless the British application were seriously examined. Harmel spoke, too, of compulsory consultations among the Seven in foreign affairs. In turnabout as fair play, he paraphrased de Gaulle in his closing remarks: "Let us build the Europe of European desires, everywhere possible, as we have so often said." [127]

From fall 1968 through the spring of 1969, the struggle within the EEC shifted to the WEU battleground. On October 7, the Political Committee of the WEU approved the Harmel proposal by a vote of 12 to 3. A week later, the WEU Assembly concurred, but with Gaullist deputies abstaining. The Assembly majority also supported the creation of a "political conference" as well as an independent political committee to execute the Harmel plan.[128] At the Rome meeting of the Permanent Council of the WEU on October 21–22, the French, following the tactic used in Brussels the previous December, reluctantly agreed to place the question of "working groups" to implement the Belgian initiative on the WEU agenda, but not to accede to their creation. They were prepared, however, to permit the establishment of committees to explore ways to improve technological and commercial relations between the Six and third states consistent with the French nine-point proposal of November 1968 to the European Economic Community to advance technical and economic cooperation within the Common Market.[129]

Matters came to a head at the regular WEU session of the Permanent Council in Luxembourg on February 5–6. The French objected to the Italian proposal of compulsory consultations "on all matters which are not the object of any formal provision of the Rome Treaty and notably on the political organization of Western

126. See, for example, Brandt's remarks in favor of British entry in *ibid.*, 1968, p. 81; *ibid.*, 1969, p. 108. There is also the Ravensburg affair in which Brandt is quoted as sharply criticizing President de Gaulle as "obsessed with power" (*L'Année politique, 1968*, p. 217–218)

127. WEU, *Political Year, 1968*, p. 143.

128. *L'Année politique, 1969*, p. 295.

129. *FFP*, July–Dec. 1968, p. xiv.

Europe." [130] British Foreign Minister Michael Stewart's invitation to hold a special meeting in London of foreign ministers on the Middle East forced the issue. On February 11, 12, and 13, the Gaullist government successively issued warnings that it would not participate in the London talks. When the group met on February 14, France extended its policy of the empty chair to the WEU.

The French case turned on a strict interpretation of the WEU charter. They insisted on unanimity both on the timing of meetings and on the agenda items for discussion, and argued further that the list of subjects to be discussed by the WEU overlapped with the EEC. The former overstepped its competence while intruding on that of the European community. The French made little effort to hide the political significance of the maneuvering of its WEU partners. They deplored use of the WEU as a means of forcing a reconsideration of the Brussels stalemate to bar review of the British request for entry into the EEC. Placing the issue of the Middle East on the WEU agenda and calling a special meeting of the Permanent Council were precedent-setting moves to this long-range aim: "It is quite obvious that his maneuver [of the London meeting] by creating a precedent on the Middle East," said officials of the French government, "is in fact designed to introduce the practice of permanent discussion on every problem and that in the final analysis, its purpose is to debate the various aspects of Britain's candidacy to the Common Market, that is, to make the Council of Ministers of the WEU a court of appeal for the Council of Ministers of the European Community." [131]

The implications of the WEU controversy were significant from two points of view. First, the strict constructionist position adopted by the French, matched with its legal-minded, defensive posture in the EEC, signaled a further shift in the relative power position of France vis-à-vis its European allies. Weakened internally and beset externally after 1968, as sketched below, French diplomacy had to rely increasingly on legal claims to bolster its economic and political objectives. This was to become a distinguishing feature of French diplomacy under the Pompidou regime, going beyond Europe in its application to the European community, the Middle East, and mone-

130. *Ibid.,* Jan.–June 1969, p. vi.
131. *Ibid.,* pp. 54–55.

tary policy. The Brussels impasse of December 1967 was one of the first steps of French enfeeblement in the struggle with its partners; the WEU controversy provided additional symptoms of waning French influence in Europe.

Second, and not without irony, Gaullist France was placed in the uncomfortable position of defending EEC prerogatives and competence against the alleged encroachments of those who would have used the WEU to weaken EEC autonomy. This placed the de Gaulle government in a curiously reversed role compared to its proposals for political union in the early 1960's. Almost a decade earlier it appeared bent on weakening the EEC organization as a means of enhancing French power in Western Europe. Acceding to a broader mandate for WEU and to the creation of working groups in "political, military, technological, and monetary" fields would have placed France somewhat in the position of implementing a political grouping similar to its Fouchet plan, but aimed at circumventing France's veto of Britain and at reducing its role and influence in European councils. If a majority on the Permanent Council of the WEU could control its agenda and impose compulsory consultations on its members, France would experience increased difficulty in resisting discussion and action on those initiatives of its partners with which it disagreed. The working groups, moreover, threatened to evolve into coordinating committees in the principal areas of concern to the West European states, much like those suggested by de Gaulle a half decade before. Against its will, but now outmaneuvered and outvoted within the WEU, Gaullist France would have found its foreign policy constrained in timing, form, and substance by its WEU allies. There was the possibility, too, of British candidacy being forced upon France without an adequate *quid pro quo* being extracted from its partners, viz., the agricultural regulation. There would be little hope then of the French cock ever being able to rule the European roost, a dim prospect at any time, but largely precluded if it did not hold firm in the WEU tilt of European wills.

The French White Paper on the WEU controversy testified to the frustration of France's diplomacy within the EEC and its isolation within the community: "Great Britain is a candidate to the Common Market. This candidacy provoked on December 19, 1967, a state of discord between France and its five partners. Since then, and despite French proposals to unblock the Common Market (commercial arrangements, Plan Debré), Great Britain has mainly sought to isolate France within the EEC." [132] Paris did not protest all too much, for such was the case. However, the protest was more plaintive than constructive. To escape "a diplomatic Waterloo," as Michel Debré was later to write,[133] Pompidou's France would be compelled, after the events of 1968 further weakened its position, to accept enlargement—and to do so not altogether reluctantly.

132. Secrétariat d'Etat auprès du Premier Ministre chargé de l'Information, *La France et la crise de l'U.E.O., Actualités-documents,* No. 26, March 1969, p. 13.
133. Reported by André Fontaine, *Le Monde,* April 16–17, 1972, p. 7.

8

Pompidou's Europe: Britain within the Continental System

The Politics of Interdependence Rises

As in other policy areas, 1968 marks a turning point in France's policy toward Europe. Domestic upheaval and structural changes in regional and global power relations compelled a profound re-examination and refashioning of France's European posture. This chapter first sketches the weaknesses of de Gaulle's European policy and approach, exposed by the events of 1968, and outlines the domestic and international conditions that prompted a French redefinition of the foreign policy priorities and alignment strategies to be followed in Europe.

These general considerations are then related to the major innovations in French European policy since 1968. The principal topics on the European agenda were in the West. They included completion of the transitional phase of the Rome Treaty, the enlargement of the European grouping with the proposed entry of Britain and some of its EFTA partners—Ireland, Denmark, and Norway—and the strengthening of the West European community, leading to greater economic integration and political union. In the East, the problem remained the terms and direction of détente. But, whereas France led the forces of détente before, it was now constrained to temper or adapt to initiatives taken by others, principally West Germany and the superpowers.

The End of the Gaullist Line in Europe

By 1968, Gaullist France could no longer pretend to have an independent foreign policy or claim a big-power role in Europe and in world politics. First, the student and worker strikes threatened the government's overthrow, weakened France's international standing and influence, and struck at President de Gaulle's own personal prestige and stature. The domestic economy was brought to a stand-still. Internal social needs could no longer be enlisted so freely or subordinated to Gaullist foreign policy schemes. Most Frenchmen were unwilling to incur indefinite privation for enhanced international prestige of dubious material benefit. If fear of turmoil and incipient revolution induced most to vote for order over disruption in electing a Gaullist majority to the National Assembly in June 1968, the depu-ties needed little instruction, least of all those in the government, that they could ignore domestic concerns only at their own peril. They would have to address themselves to basic reforms in social legisla-tion and economic policies. The structure of higher education would have to be renovated. Responding to labor demands would hence-forward have to be high among the government's priorities. Foreign policy would be more servant than master of the nation's internal economic and social betterment. President de Gaulle's resignation on a question of domestic policy—regionalization and Senate reform—and the elevation of Georges Pompidou to the presidency consecrated the reversal in priorities between foreign and domestic imperatives.

The weakening of France's economic and political fiber, the warp and woof of the de Gaulle government's claim to international re-spect, accented its dependency on its European partners and on the United States. While the de Gaulle regime accepted the completion of the Common Market industrial union on July 1, the May events forced Paris to request temporary delays and exceptions in its appli-cation. The United States, Britain, and the Five moved quickly, if not enthusiastically, to ease France's strained economic situation in the form of financial assistance, trade concessions, or acquiescence to the protective moves by the de Gaulle government. These con-tinued throughout the franc crisis of fall 1968. The unwillingness of the German government to revalue the mark upward at French (and Anglo-American) insistence dramatized the role of *demandeur* that the de Gaulle government, reluctantly, was compelled to assume. French economic and political well-being was a function of the as-sistance and cooperation of its Western partners.

The rise of Germany also gave Gaullist France pause. In his talks with British Prime Minister Harold Wilson in June 1967, President de Gaulle had expressed serious doubts about the likelihood of France's retention of its then currently ascendant, if not commanding, position in Western Europe. "Did he [de Gaulle] not fear," recounts Wilson, "that post-de Gaulle France, particularly if his forecast of a period of anarchy and division were realized, would be relegated to a second-class status against the power of a strong Germany? He warmed to this theme. *'Les Allemands,'* he said, *'seront toujours les Allemands.'* He had no doubt what would happen—but he would not be there to prevent it. . . . Would he want to see a Europe with, on his estimate, a weakened France, but without the balancing factor of Britain? He said he was very well aware of these questions. But he would not then have the responsibility." [1] The German refusal of monetary help a year and a half later confirmed this pessimistic appraisal of France's prospects and prompted similarly lugubrious conjecturing by de Gaulle of France's political future in an interview with Cyris Sulzberger after his resignation.[2]

Not two cocks (Britain and France), but three were in competition for the hens of Western Europe. Germany was no military threat to France, but its political and economic weight in Western Europe was another matter. Its Eastern policy, if patterned after the French lead, was still German, vigorously pressed by a chancellor committed to reconciling his nation with its Eastern neighbors and to increasing its freedom of maneuver in foreign policy. After 1968, France faced a Germany emerging from its penitential and subservient condition, possessed of a political will of its own and a government determined to assert its interests and objectives even at the risk of direct conflict with France.

The invasion of Czechoslovakia by the Soviet Union and five of its satellites, including East Germany, in August 1968, also thrust at French hopes in Eastern Europe. The French president had tended to define détente as a change in the threat perceptions of the West and East European camps and, specifically, of Germany and the Soviet Union of each other. Of less moment to Gaullist détente aims was any challenge to Soviet rule in Eastern Europe or the maintenance of Communist regimes in these countries. French hopes were linked to the tenuous expectation that liberalization within the Soviet empire and other Communist regimes between the state and its

1. Wilson, *Labour Government,* p. 412.
2. C. L. Sulzberger, *Herald Tribune,* International edition, Nov. 11, 1971, pp. 1, 4.

citizens would be the inevitable by-product of enlarging ties with the Western states, a decreased feeling of anxiety over Germany, and the gradual disintegration of the NATO and Warsaw military blocs.

The Soviet Union looked at détente differently in the late 1960's. Crucial—many would argue of controlling importance—[3] was the Soviet fear that a trend toward social democracy would undermine one-party rule in Eastern Europe and erode the legitimacy of the Communist regimes in the satellite states, perhaps even with repercussions in the Soviet Union. More immediate was the concern that political reforms in Czechoslovakia would weaken Soviet control of its clients and simultaneously open them to Western penetration, enlarging the success already made by Germany in Rumania and Yugoslavia. These anxieties were sufficient to override the damage done to the image carefully nurtured by the Kremlin of the Soviet Union as a moderate power with limited goals in Europe. Military security in Central Europe and political stability among the Eastern satellites were still closely identified in Soviet calculations.

The Czech affair left little doubt about the significant differences between French and Soviet views about détente in Europe. French officials had identified four levels of détente: between blocs, between individual states in East and West Europe, between the superpowers and their respective European clients, and between the Communist regimes and their citizens. Only the first element appeared to be developing while the others lagged behind roughly in the same order.[4] For the Soviet Union, cooperating with France was useful to extract concessions on Germany and to undermine the EEC and NATO.[5] Détente was not meant to facilitate Western and French access to the East European states. The Czech invasion mocked the Franco-Soviet communiqué of June 1968: "for France as for the Soviet Union, the primary objective [of détente] is . . . the progressive development of relations between all European countries through the respect of the independence of each and . . . non-intervention in its domestic affairs." [6] The Brezhnev doctrine, in claiming a right to intervene on

3. Wolfe, *Soviet Power and Europe,* pp. 386–426.
4. *FFP,* July–Dec. 1968, pp. 25, 59–60.
5. On Soviet policy toward the EEC before 1969, see Zorgbibe, *op. cit.,* pp. 5–34.
6. "La Coopération franco-soviétique," p. 17.

behalf of threatened Communist regimes, insulted French sensitivities. Why not on behalf of a local Communist party in Western Europe? The swift military success in Czechoslovakia also raised serious questions about the limits of Soviet strategic and diplomatic intentions in Western Europe.[7] There was the additionally unsettling point that the Soviet Union asserted, under the United Nations Charter, a right to intervene in West Germany if, by its own definition, another fascist regime were to be installed.

As German economic and political influence rose in the European community and in East-West relations and as the Soviet Union retightened its grip on Eastern Europe and again cast a troubling shadow over Western Europe, American power appeared paralyzed in Southeast Asia and moribund in Europe. Domestic strife, centered, like France's, in its universities, contributed to the growing image of the United States as a declining force in international relations. Almost overnight, it lost its formidable specter as *the* superpower. Conventional wisdom in Europe seized on the picture of an America overextended abroad, fatigued by its global responsibilities, distracted by domestic problems, and confused about its national objectives and global role. Only a few years before the popular mood, inspired by Gaullists and their critics alike, worried about the American challenge.[8] Now they feared the superpower balance that had favored the United States since World War II might tilt toward the Soviet Union in the 1970's and 1980's.[9]

Two potentially reinforcing tendencies in American policy toward Europe and the Soviet Union deepened European fears about the implications of apparently developing American impotence and decreasing interest in Europe. One direction pointed toward efforts by Washington to lower the cost of the American posture in Europe,

7. *FFP,* July–Dec. 1968, p. 112, paragraph 3 of the NATO minister's communiqué of November 16. The application of the Brezhnev doctrine to French domestic politics has been openly debated. *Le Monde,* Oct. 7, 1972, p. 11.

8. See Chapter 2.

9. Pierre Gallois, *L'Europe change de maître* (Paris: L'Herne, 1972). The observation of Sicco Mansholt, vice-president of the European Economic Community, in his widely reported memorandum on Europe's historic mission, is relevant: "The United States is on the way to decline and it will be extremely difficult for us to keep it from total dissolution" (Commission des Communautés Européennes, Secrétariat Générale, Feb. 14, 1972, p. 3).

shifting the defense burden, economic and military, to the European states and reducing the American strategic and political commitment to the region. Gone was any mention of a Grand Design. If American policy toward Europe had earlier suffered from excessive ambition, it risked self-abasement in the closing years of the Johnson administration. The burial of the MLF extinguished the last hopes of a Grand Design for the Atlantic community. Europe's role in American global policy was accordingly reduced. By President Johnson's own estimate, Europe was to assume more the aspect of a countinghouse than a military bastion to which the United States could appeal for relief in the form of trade and monetary accommodations, increased purchases of American military equipment, and larger European defense spending. These remedies would relieve growing American balance-of-payments deficits. These were to be Europe's contribution to Western defense as the United States struggled with the Vietnam War presumably to protect alliance interests in Asia.[10]

Quiet troop transfers from Europe to other theaters and talk of military disengagement, centered around the Mansfield amendment, deepened French and European anxieties about the American strategic and political guarantee. The Nixon Doctrine, emphasizing more self-help by American allies for their own defense, meant that the Republican administration no less than its Democratic predecessor, desired some measure of global and European military disengagement and a more precise and restrictive definition of American commitments abroad.[11] The prospect of at least partial American military withdrawal became, in the minds of Europeans, more a question of when and how much, not whether.

United States presence in Europe had served the conflicting purposes of countering Soviet pressures and checking German national aspirations and of furnishing a highly visible target useful to France in coalescing European opposition to the United States. Playing on the fear of alleged American undependability in European circles was a reasonable tactic as long as Gaullist France could rely on the

10. Lyndon B. Johnson, *The Vantage Point* (New York: Holt, Rinehart, and Winston, 1971), chap. 14, pp. 305–321.

11. For a representative statement of the Nixon Doctrine as applied in official pronouncements to global politics, see "United States Foreign Policy for the 1970's," *Department of State Bulletin*, LXIV (March 22, 1971).

American security pledge. As the United States evidenced diminishing resolve in supporting its previous level of global and regional commitments and as the Soviet Union multiplied its efforts to expand its influence in Western Europe, Gaullist criticism risked becoming a self-fulfilling prophecy, encouraging results it least wished, before adequate European institutions and cooperative efforts could assume former United States obligations. At the same time, the nationalistic drive on which Gaullist policy was predicated inhibited timely and effective development of adequate substitutes.

There was also the possibility, which did not necessarily conflict with the American sentiments for disengagement, that the superpowers might reach a military and political accommodation at the expense of the West European states. Collusion, not collision, between the superpowers became the more immediate threat to French and European ambitions.[12] France had nudged European and global politics toward its oligarchical ideal of international relations only to discover that the superpowers could display diplomatic skill equal to France's in adjusting their policies to each other's claims and dispose greater resources than the Paris government in meeting only those demands of their clients that suited their foreign policy interests and domestic political imperatives. To preserve their strategic superiority and to minimize the costs and risks of an arms race, the superpowers calibrated their diplomacies finely enough to retain their predominant positions globally while permitting expression of greater divergencies, from states within their camps. In the forefront of these efforts were the nonproliferation treaty under the Johnson administration and the strategic arms limitation accord signed by President Nixon in May 1972. NATO's slow and groping movement toward mutual balanced force reductions (MBFR) marked another area of gradual superpower alignment progressively beyond French and European influence to shape decisively.[13]

Within a framework of growing strategic stability, mutually accepted and ratified by successive executive understandings and solemn

12. The felicitous phrase is Stanley Hoffmann's in "Franco-American Differences over the Arab-Israeli Conflict, 1967–71," *Public Policy*, XIX (Fall 1971), 539–565.

13. See the two articles on French foreign policy appearing in the *Manchester Guardian*, Oct. 13 and Nov. 4, 1972, pp. 14 and 15, respectively.

treaties between the two superpowers, the international system gave evidence of becoming increasingly multipolar, after the Gaullist model, in most significant areas of nonmilitary state activity. Not France, but China, Germany, and Japan were the principal propelling forces. France found its security, as before, in the hands of the giant states while pressed increasingly elsewhere by others. As Chapters 9 and 10 suggest, France's bid to speak for the Third World similarly met with dubious success. In the Mediterranean and North Africa, where France struggled to preserve and deepen its special ties, the states demonstrated surprising skill and remarkable resourcefulness, with Algeria in the forefront, in pressing their interests to France's disadvantage.

After 1968, there was a heightened recognition in French official circles, including de Gaulle himself, that France had not fully benefited from the alignment mix molded and managed under the Fifth Republic. The events of 1968 indicated that France could not fully achieve its security, economic, and diplomatic goals, nor could its liberal institutions be adequately insulated from internal buffeting, without appeal for help to the other Western democracies, including the Anglo-American states. The Atlantic security framework was needed to offset rising Soviet strategic power and political influence in Western Europe. It also acted as a subtle restraint on German foreign policy. Association with the English-speaking democracies tended, too, to support free institutions so sorely tested in the early and late 1960's from the Right and the Left.

There was greater appreciation of the argument, too, that France and French industry had not exploited with sufficient imagination and enterprise the possibilities of the British and American markets, opportunities for reciprocal investment, and benefits from the transfer of technology. How then to keep the United States military presence in Europe and encourage freer exchange between both sides of the Atlantic while limiting as much as possible American influence on France's economic life, defense arrangements, and diplomatic maneuvering?

Nor could France do without Germany although it could no longer exercise the same degree of influence over Bonn's foreign and economic policy as during the Adenauer period. Obvious enough was Germany's importance to the operation of the Common Market and to the support of French agriculture on which Paris pinned so much of its economic hopes for modernization and industrialization. There was no turning back the clock on the reconciliation process almost a generation in train. Germany was still key to a peaceful Europe, and its participation in Western Europe was indispensable for regional stability whether United States military and political disengagement grew apace or not. But how to draw on German resources and support while containing Germany as an economic and political force in Western Europe? And how to prevent it from gravitating, perhaps irretrievably, toward the East in pursuit of its yet unrealized, albeit long-term, goal of unification? What would France do, moreover, to prevent Central Europe, under German influence, from playing West against East for its own advantage?

Czechoslovakia also raised latent French fears about Soviet power and purpose in Europe. There was the need, alternatively, to resist Soviet encroachments and to accommodate this Eastern giant in hope of satisfying its appetites and of hedging against the possibility of a precipitate American withdrawal. Meanwhile, France's policy line toward Europe had to be flexible enough to meet the possibility of collusion between the superpowers. This posed another serious question. How could France, with or without the help of its European partners, affect superpower relations sufficiently to make its influence felt in Moscow and Washington? To these competing demands should be added the search for United States and Soviet support for France's position within Europe and the Third World. There was also the temptation of markets, technological and industrial cooperation, and joint scientific and cultural ventures that were desirable in their own right and complements to the détente process.

De Gaulle's resignation in April 1969 left the Pompidou regime with the formidable task of forging alignments more responsive to France's varied problems and needs from a position of internal and external weakness. It was confronted, ironically, with adapting France to a multipolar world, presumably of Gaullist urging, in which France found itself increasingly outpaced and outwitted. The feasibility of a confederal Europe restricted to the Six under French leadership and joined to Eastern Europe by a special Paris-Moscow understanding was gone. The alternative visions of Gaullist opponents were also fading. Like de Gaulle, supporters of an Atlantic community and a federal, supranational Europe were overtaken by events. European and global politics were too complex to be channeled into such narrow forms and processes. They neither reflected the relative power positions of the European and North American states nor their contrasting circumstances and objectives. Continuing the confining alignment strategies pursued by the de Gaulle regime to promote France's foreign influence and domestic prosperity risked further erosion of France's tenuous external position and internal stability.

Redefining France's European policy carried its own hazards in domestic politics. The Pompidou government could not repudiate all or part of its Gaullist past without undermining the support of its most loyal followers. Affirmations of the Gaullist legacy had to be harmonized with moves to circumvent its strictures. The delicacy of the Pompidou government's position can be somewhat discerned in its slogan, *continuité et ouverture*. The old would be preserved (a bow to Gaullist stalwarts and the old president who watched silently from Colombey). The government would not make changes, but would be "open" to opportunities in Europe to advance French interests (and simultaneously be attentive to possibilities to widen the base of the government's electoral support). That the task was not easy is suggested in the feeling of some Gaullist followers who considered Pompidou a usurper and charged him with betrayal of the Gaullist creed.[14] Others could not conceive of Gaullism without de Gaulle.[15] Still others saw him as a worthy heir to de Gaulle's mantle and to his mission: *"Il est un Gaullist dur,"* said one long-time observer of the Gaullist phenomenon and an active participant himself in the movement.[16] Could France under the Pompidou government cooperate more closely with other states to elicit the support it needed, and yet preserve a measure of national independence, in form if not in substance, acceptable to national and Gaullist sentiment?

The discussion below traces the evolution of France's policy toward Europe under the Pompidou regime as it responded to the external and internal constraints and pressures of the post-de Gaulle

14. Phillippe Alexandre, *The Duel: De Gaulle and Pompidou,* trans. Elaine P. Halperin (Boston: Houghton-Mifflin, 1972). Also examine Louis Vallon, *L'Anti-de Gaulle* (Paris: Le Seuil, 1969).

15. Interview with André Malraux, "Gaullism without de Gaulle Is Idiotic," *New York Times Magazine,* Aug. 6, 1972, pp. 7, 55–58.

16. Interview with Paul Marie de la Gorce, April 1971.

era. Europe was the crucible of the Pompidou government's foreign policy. Western Europe was to be the principal vehicle for the realization of France's domestic and foreign policy goals. In a superficial sense, it marked a return to the thinking of the Fouchet plan era. Western Europe was to reinforce and radiate French influence. But the differences were more interesting than the similarities. These suggested a different conception of the West European community, of France's regional and global role in world politics, and even of such traditional Gaullist shibboleths as independence and *grandeur*. These changes largely crystallized in the meaning that the Pompidou regime attached, through its pronouncements, decisions, and behavior, to its own triptych of "completion, enlargement, and strengthening" for the West European community.[17] Around these three terms was formed much of the European initiative taken under the Pompidou regime in its years in office.

The Tricolor before a Western Wind

The Soames affair suggested that President de Gaulle may have changed his mind about excluding Britain from Europe and was contemplating yet another European grouping more suitable to the post-1968 period in which Britain's role would appreciate significantly. On February 4, 1969, Christopher Soames, the British ambassador to France and kin of Winston Churchill, was received at his request by President de Gaulle. The meeting has since been subject to rival French and British interpretations.[18] According to the British ac-

17. Comité Interministériel pour l'Information, *L'Avenir du marché commun* (Paris, Nov. 1969).

18. There is no dearth of material on the affair although as a body it remains inconclusive. See the following useful accounts: Wilson, *op. cit.,* pp. 610–618; Newhouse, *De Gaulle and the Anglo-Saxons,* pp. 337–341; *L'Année politique, 1969,* pp. 226–227; and Roger Massip, "Complot contre le marché commun," *Revue politique et parlementaire,* (March 1969), 5–8. Newspaper accounts of special note include André Fontaine's *Le Monde* pieces, Feb. 1969, p. 1, and Feb. 21, 1969, p. 3; the London *Times* accounts of Parliament's debate of the affair are in the issues of Feb. 25–26. For associated comments, see *Le Figaro,* Feb. 24, p. 4; *New York Times,* International Edition Feb. 21, 27; and Leonard Beaton in the *Observer,* Feb. 23. Prescient is Guy de Carmoy's, "The Last Year of De Gaulle's Foreign Policy," *International Affairs,* XLV (July 1969), 424–435. In this vein, an early sketch of Pompidou's policies appears in Wolf Mendl, "After De Gaulle: Continuity and Change in French Foreign Policy," *World Today,* XXVII (Jan. 1971), 8–17.

count, President de Gaulle spoke of possible British entry into the EEC. For de Gaulle, such a move would necessarily transform the grouping into a free trade association which he reportedly found, in contrast to repeated public disclaimers, to be a conceivably desirable prospect. A major rub would be agriculture where speculation turned to the need for special arrangements. De Gaulle was to have proposed that this larger West European association be under the quadripartite direction of France, Britain, Germany, and Italy. Such a Europe could eventually become independent of the United States. With its own defense, economic, and diplomatic policies, it could do without NATO and the American military presence. Britain was invited to consider secret bilateral talks with France to explore these possibilities for mutual advantage.

These Gaullist ruminations might well have been buried in the ambassador's cables to London but for their exposition during Prime Minister Harold Wilson's visit to Bonn on February 11–12. While Wilson minimized the significance of de Gaulle's suggestions, he acceded to Foreign Office coaxing and revealed the French proposition and the English demurrer to the Germans (and to France's other partners). This step was taken partially to avoid what was felt to be a de Gaulle trap to test British sincerity about its European intentions.[19] There was the added motive, advanced by some observers, of "banking credit in Bonn." [20] This latter view gained some basis in the importance attached by the British diplomatic establishment to the British-German communiqué approved by Wilson and Kiesinger, calling for Britain's entry into the EEC.[21] Since the Soames affair broke at a time when Britain and France were locked in battle over the WEU and its use as a British shortcut to Brussels around Paris, it may have been a ploy to embarrass the de Gaulle regime.

Official French pronouncements flatly rejected the British understanding of what had happened: dissolving NATO had not been discussed; France did not seek to undermine the EEC although British entry would inevitably require adjustments; and no "directorate" had been suggested.[22] The French reportedly viewed the British breach

19. Wilson, op. cit., pp. 610–618.
20. Newhouse, De Gaulle and the Anglo-Saxons, p. 339.
21. Wilson, op. cit., pp. 610–611.
22. Le Figaro, Feb. 24, 1969, p. 4.

of diplomatic practice as self-serving and not a little vindictive. In leaks to the press, they pictured the British action as an attempt to drive a wedge between France and its EEC partners. Others conjectured that the British sought to color President Nixon's favourable impression of France and to hurt the newly developed *rapprochement* to be strengthened by his visit to Paris in early 1969. Still others, even more suspicious, saw Britain intervening in French domestic politics to weaken de Gaulle in the upcoming April referendum.[23] The poisoned political atmosphere, generated so rapidly by British indiscretion, suggested that there was little possibility that the Entente Cordiale would be resurrected while President de Gaulle was in office. The political, even psychic, basis for mutual trust and cooperation between the two countries and their foreign offices was conspicuously absent.

After a series of spirited exchanges (one French diplomat, for example, accusing the British of "diplomatic terrorism"), the affair cooled as rapidly as it had boiled over. The skepticism harbored by both sides at the highest political and bureaucratic levels was so profound and the historical experience so colored by previous misunderstandings and misadventures that the truth of either version may never be known. What is interesting is that the controversy should have arisen at all in light of past Gaullist attempts to keep Britain out of Europe. De Gaulle, however tentatively, appeared to be breaking new ground regarding Britain's role in Europe at the very time that his government's exterior behavior and official pronouncements were steadfastly opposed to its entry.

President Pompidou's election campaign signaled an opening to the European and Atlantic wings of the sprawling Gaullist camp and to associates in the center and right of French politics like Giscard d'Estaing's Independent Republicans and Jacques Duhamel's Center for Democracy and Progress. Outflanking Alain Poher, his principal opponent and an outspoken Europeanist, Pompidou early proposed a European summit to advance economic cooperation and union. Jacques Chaban-Delmas, President Pompidou's choice as prime minister, hinted in his initial address to the National Assembly at the priorities that had to be addressed on the European agenda. Stressed

23. Massip, *Revue politique et parlementaire,* 1969, pp. 5–6.

was French economic development. France had to be open to world trade. "This opening," said the premier, "must be first directed toward Europe, for economic . . . but also for political reasons." [24] British membership was broached. "We clearly affirm that we are ready in the matter of European construction to go as fast and as far as our partners are themselves inclined to go." [25]

On July 10, President Pompidou reinforced the foundation of his European edifice. The hitherto unspeakable subject of British entry was again raised for serious examination once the Common Market was completed—that is, when a regulation for agriculture was definitely written. A French "veto" of Britain was pointedly denied. By the end of July, the French negotiation position had sufficiently crystallized to permit Foreign Minister Maurice Schumann, an Atlantic and European-oriented Gaullist, to urge, at the EEC Council of Ministers meeting on July 22, a summit meeting of heads of government and state.[26] He specifically repudiated the Gaullist assumption that Britain could not be absorbed into the Common Market without creating a free trade zone: "It is not at all inevitable," Schumann argued, "that the entry of Britain and of new members will result in a weakening of the organization." [27] The Pompidou triptych put strengthening and completing the community ahead of enlargement. The order was not accidental. Completion was a precondition for the others. Strengthening the community, presumably along French lines, such as monetary union, without elaborate institutional controls, would promote French interests. It would also disarm orthodox Gaullists at home who held the General's publicly sanctioned view that Britain's entry meant the dissolution of a French-inspired independent Europe into a free trade zone susceptible to American influence and under British direction.

After some confusion over timing and dates, including a seasonal crisis within the Italian government, the summit meeting was held on December 1 and 2 at the Hague.

24. *FFP*, Jan.–June 1969, p. 137.
25. *Ibid.*
26. *Ibid.*, July–Dec. 1969, p. 13–14.
27. *Ibid.*, p. 14.

Completion of the Rome Treaty

France's partners and the Brussels Commission ordered the priorities of the French triptych differently and attached different meanings to each term. German Chancellor Willy Brandt was no less mindful than his predecessors of Germany's unfinished business with its eastern neighbors. A strong and enlarged West European base from which to negotiate with the East was still highly desirable, if not necessarily indispensable as before. There was also the problem of dispelling doubts about the new German Socialist government's commitment to closer West European cooperation. Brandt's passionate plea for Western unity captured the headlines that were supposed to have been reserved for the French president,[28] whose call for the meeting had been the principal impulse for the Hague meeting.[29] Brandt stressed enlargement and the community's internal development, including its multilateral institutions. Progress in these areas would enlist Western Europe into Germany's service. Completion, which was identified by the Pomidou regime with a definite regulation for agriculture, was Germany's burden to shoulder for the community, and was of lesser interest to Bonn.

The smaller states, in their public statements, attached greater weight to Britain's entry than did France, but the differences can be exaggerated. Italy's expectations of gain from the agricultural program had never been realized. The Netherlands, France's principal antagonist on the British issue, was no less interested in the success of the agricultural negotiations than Paris since they stood to profit most from a community-based program measured in per capita benefits. On the other hand, the Commission, under the outspoken Belgian Jean Rey, tended toward the French position, but stressed

28. West German leaders have been clear about the close relation between *Ostpolitik* and Germany's Western ties. See Willy Brandt, "Germany's Prospects," *Atlantic Community Quarterly*, VIII (Spring 1970), 36–42; Helmut Schmidt, "Germany in the Era of Negotiations," *Foreign Affairs*, XLIX (Oct. 1970), 40–50.

29. Most of the text of Chancellor Brandt's remarks before the summit may be found in the London *Times*, Dec. 2, 1969, pp. 6–7. Useful summaries of the conference are found in *Le Monde* and *Le Figaro* of this period. In this vein, see *L'Express*, Dec. 8, 1969, pp. 62–63, and *Le Nouvel observateur*, Dec. 8, 1969.

greater progress in institution building and in creating an economic and monetary union after the Barre plan within the framework of the Rome Treaty.

The French terms of compromise generally prevailed. Opening discussions on enlargement were to depend on four conditions: (1) the incorporation of all major farm products within the EEC's agricultural program; (2) agreement on substituting the community's own financial resources (so-called *"resources propres"*) for national contributions to underwrite the agricultural program; (3) treaty passage of these arrangements by the member parliaments; and (4) unreserved acceptance of these financial stipulations by the candidate states. In contributing funds to the community, according to the French, the member states were establishing a permanent basis for the community's own resources. Foreign Minister Maurice Schumann elaborated French legal reasoning before the National Assembly: "The thought of the authors of the Rome and Paris treaties reflects constructive wisdom. Both had foreseen the replacement of national contributions by [the community's] own resources; both had subordinated it to the unanimous approval of the council, then to the adoption of the necessary dispositions by the member states. In sum, *they wished that the fact might precede the right and that the right might sanction the evolution by making it irreversible.*" [30] France did not come to the Hague as a petitioner, but as a plaintiff seeking redress for the community's failure to implement preceding agreements.

The Commission and the Six moved speedily to define the details of the agricultural accord once the Hague meeting gave the green light to go ahead. By the end of December a financial regulation was outlined. The Council of Ministers gave final approval on April 20–22. Italy received compensation for the heavy charges incurred on levies and in organizing wine and tobacco markets more suited to its interests. Over a period of five years, to be completed in 1975, the community's own resources would replace national contributions. These would be drawn from agricultural levies, customs duties, and the newly installed value added tax (TVA) urged on member states by France.[31] A ceiling of 1 percent was set for the latter tax.

30. *PEF,* Jan.–June 1970, p. 187. Consult Schumann's statement for an outline of the French position in the problem of the community's own resources, pp. 187–190.

31. *L'Année politique, 1969,* pp. 323–326, details the accord.

Enlargement

Negotiations on enlargement opened on June 30, a week after the French Assembly overwhelmingly passed the treaty governing community resources. They concluded a year later with the acceptance of Britain, Ireland, Denmark, and Norway into the Common Market. These negotiations are too complex and cover too great a span of time to be usefully detailed here. For our purposes, it will be sufficient to focus on the principal problems raised by enlargement, particularly the British application, the way in which they were settled, and the French position. The Pompidou administration's management of the enlargement negotiations and the decisions and compromises reached in finally lifting the veto on Britain portended a major shift in French European policy. They projected, too, a substantial difference in the Pompidou and de Gaulle images of Europe and France's place within it.

Accepting Britain's entry into the Common Market was no easy matter for the Pompidou government. The Gaullist legacy weighed heavily on French policy. It allowed little room for compromise between another veto, ostensibly to protect Europe's independence, and what was repeatedly pictured as the inevitable dissolution of the Brussels pact into an Anglo-American free trade association if Britain entered. But, the gains France had already made on completion might be lost unless Britain became a member. Additional community help on French economic and political problems was not likely to be forthcoming.[32] The Pompidou government's bargaining stance reflected these conflicting demands. It had to be simultaneously responsive to the Five, the British, and French domestic opinion, particularly that of unreconstructed Gaullists. It had to be sensitive, too, to its own need for survival and to France's best interests abroad.

First, President Pompidou and his ministers, through quiet diplomacy and public statements, worked to create a favorable climate for negotiations, reassuring to skeptics at home, yet encouraging to Britain and its EEC supporters. During a visit to London in January 1970, Foreign Minister Maurice Schumann underlined France's favorable view of the British application. Unlike his two predecessors, Michel Debré and Couve de Murville, Schumann—fluent in English,

32. This is the general theme struck by officials interviewed in Paris and Brussels in 1971 and 1972.

perfected as a Free French official and liaison officer with English troops during World War II—was disposed to British membership. He did not share the many Gaullist suspicions of British motivation. As before, political factors were controlling, but they led to different conclusions and implications than those voiced by de Gaulle. Repeating a theme already struck at Brussels, Schumann remarked, "In the long-run, there cannot be any Europe without Great Britain for numerous reasons, and in particular because without Great Britain's action thirty years ago, there would not have been any Europe worthy of the name." [33] Murville, two years earlier, had waxed enthusiastic on the theme that the Europe of the Six could well do without Britain's help. Schumann resurrected the long dormant Entente Cordiale. "It existed before the European Community," he said.[34] It had not lapsed. It was to be the foundation stone of Europe's enlargement. Where de Gaulle had seen only profound differences between England and France, Schumann catalogued the cultural, technical, and commercial ties between them. "The profound solidarity that [the Entente Cordiale] expresses is not translated only by the problems that the United Kingdom's adhesion to the Common Market poses. It is at once necessary and comforting to note that never . . . have the ties of all sorts which unite our two peoples been so many and so deep." [35]

President Pompidou lent a helping hand. When the British continued to drag their feet after six months of bargaining on the question of increasing their contribution to the community above 3 percent in the first year of transition, President Pompidou used levity as a prod where de Gaulle had terminated further discussion with two vetoes. "One readily recognizes three qualities in the British, differentiating them from others: humor, tenacity, and realism. It comes to mind that we are still at the stage of humor." [36] As negotiations neared completion but were still blocked on the critical questions of the British pound as a reserve currency, New Zealand dairy products, and, again, Britain's budgetary contribution to the community, President Pompidou met with Prime Minister Heath to resolve these is-

33. *PEF,* Jan.–June 1970, p. 36.
34. *Ibid.,* and *Le Monde,* Sélection hebdomadaire, Nov. 15–21, 1973, p. 1.
35. *PEF,* Jan.–June 1970, p. 36.
36. *Ibid.,* Jan.–June 1971, p. 54.

sues. Even before entering office, he reportedly assured a British visitor that "if he were ever elected [president], he would have Britain enter the Common Market." [37]

If the Pompidou government was careful to create the impression of bargaining in good faith and to accept as genuine British declarations of commitment to Europe, it was still intent upon applying rigorous tests to British "Europeanness." The French drove a hard bargain initially on the principal issues between Britain and the Six, even as their desire for British entry quickened. Differences included, most especially, Britain's application of community preference to agriculture and Commonwealth relations. The French White Paper on Britain's entry made this point clear: "Community achievements could not be placed in question: Thus, for example, with respect to the common agricultural policy, by the very fact of the deposit of their candidature, the candidate countries engage themselves to accept the principle . . . of Community preference and the measures taken by the Six Member States for its application." [38] Associated issues, also of great significance, were Britain's share of the community budget, transitional arrangements to adapt its economy to community rules and policies, and the role of the pound as a reserve currency. Of lesser significance, and most easily resolved, were Britain's accession to the Second Yaoundé Convention between the Black African states and the community, special arrangements for British dependencies, Britain's incorporation into Euratom and the European Coal and Steel Community, and its absorption into community institutions, including the place of the English language in conducting community business.[39]

By December 1970, Great Britain accepted the community financial system and the association accords with the Black African states in which its own former colonies would participate. By February, the modalities and the period of adjustment of British industry to the

37. *Le Monde,* April 16–17, 1972, p. 7. Quoted in an article by André Fontaine.

38. Comité Interministériel pour l'Information, "La France et l'adhésion de la grande-bretagne à la C.E.E.," *Actualités-documents,* Oct. 1971, No. 82, p. 4. Hereafter cited as "La France et l'adhésion."

39. For a review of these problems, see European Commission, *Fifth General Report on the Activities of the Communities: 1971* (Brussels, 1972), pp. 7–68. Hereafter cited *Fifth Report of the Communities.*

community system were also in place. By mid-May 1971, Britain agreed, as in the case of industry, to a five-year transition for agriculture. It is difficult to underestimate the importance and the difficulty of this concession. The Labor government's White Paper on British entry acknowledged that the community's agricultural program would require a profound reorganization of Britain's domestic subsidy system, alignment on the higher agricultural price levels of the Six, and the payment of large levies that would additionally unsettle Britain's already precarious balance-of-payments position.[40]

Four major problems required political resolution by the end of May 1971. First, there was the Commonwealth Sugar Act due to expire at the end of 1974. Second was finding an outlet for New Zealand butter and cheese. Exceptions conflicted directly with the principle of community preference. A favorable solution to these problems would help sway British opinion toward joining the Common Market since strong emotional and commercial ties to the Commonwealth and New Zealand in particular still lingered. Third, the level of Britain's contribution to the community budget was still in question. The British refused to contribute more than 3 percent to the community budget in the first year of transition and looked to a leveling off at under 15 percent. The Commission proposal was closer to 10 percent for the first year, leading to a plateau in excess of 20 percent at the end of the transition period. French negotiators were particularly concerned that the British would not be able to afford entry into the community after a five-year transition period unless contributions began at a higher level and increased successively to an annual level greater than that proposed by the British. There was the latent fear, expressed outside meeting rooms, that Germany and Britain might join at the end of the transition period to amend the agricultural program, relaxing Britain's obligations to support it and, subsequently, undermining one of the principal reasons for French participation in the EEC.[41]

40. The White Papers issued by the Wilson and Heath governments, respectively, in 1970 and 1971 differ sharply on their estimates of the cost of British entry. The Heath figures are lower and more optimistic. Great Britain, Command Paper 4289, *Britain and the European Communities*, Feb. 1970, p. 21. The Heath paper is Command Paper 4517, 1971, especially pp. 11–17, 21–25.

41. Interviews, Brussels, April and May 1971.

To these problems the French added, in March 1971, a memorandum on sterling. The goal of European economic and monetary
union was incompatible with sterling's reserve role. France was intent on linking enlargement to community strengthening, translated
into French as support for the variable fortunes of the franc and the
French economy and, more broadly, as the development of a solid
West European front vis-à-vis the United States. The pound's chronic
instability, deriving from Britain's balance-of-payments deficits and
its exterior financial obligations, posed the possibility of increased
charges for the community as a whole. The agricultural program,
resting more on a financial arrangement than on an agricultural system to cope with surpluses, and an excess of productive farm resources, would also be threatened.[42]

Progress on these various matters was left to the Pompidou-Heath
talks in May 1971. Both leaders were careful to preserve the niceties
of protocol: that the outstanding questions on the Brussels agenda
would be left to the Six and the candidate states to decide. Meanwhile, the joint communiqué, press releases, and news conferences
made clear that these items were very much on the minds of the two
leaders. Following the example of his predecessor, Pompidou preferred to strike a pose of high politics: "One should not believe that
the problem of Great Britain's entry into the Common Market consists in resolving, for example, the problem of sugar of Commonwealth countries. One can always resolve the sugar problem. . . .
The test, moreover, is that a solution has been found. The truth is
that there is a conception of Europe and it is a question of knowing
if Great Britain's conception is truly European." [43] Pompidou, like
de Gaulle, was to be the guardian of the weights and measures for
Europe. The joint French-British communiqué of May 21 presumably met the French president's test: "The President of the Republic
and the British Prime Minister," concluded the message, "consider
that it is desirable and possible to reach a rapid accord on the principal parts of the negotiations which are being examined by the conference on adhesion and notably the interesting problems of New

---

42. Atlantic Institute, *A Future for European Agriculture* (Paris: Atlantic
Institute, n.d.), argues this case persuasively.
43. *PEF*, Jan.–June 1971, p. 168.

Zealand and British contribution to the financing of Community expenses." [44]

The fruit of the Pompidou-Heath summit was harvested at successive ministerial meetings of the Six in June. The Commonwealth Sugar Act was permitted to run its course through 1974, two years into the transitional period. Thereafter its renegotiation would be a community charge. Britain was allowed to import butter from New Zealand up to 80 percent of its 1973 level at the end of the transitional period in 1977. In the same period cheese would diminish to 20 percent of its 1973 total. The community would re-examine the New Zealand butter problem and make changes as appropriate to conform to community policies, but not at an expense too burdensome for New Zealand to bear. Community fisheries policy was also to be redefined in the future to ease Britain's adhesion and that of its EFTA partners.

A similar disposition to be constructive developed on the two remaining issues of importance—British monetary policy and its financial contribution to the community. France accepted the British government's declaration to seek the progressive and ordered disappearance of official sterling balances, to align the pound with other European currencies, leading in the long run to an economic and monetary union. The French proposal to base British contributions on the anticipated growth in British GNP was also helpful in bringing about basic accord on that subject. Britain would begin payments in 1973 at 8.64 percent of the community budget while participating as a full member in the community's deliberations; it would increase these proportionally each year until the end of the transition period in 1977 to a level of just under 19 percent.[45]

At least two plausible, and not necessarily incompatible, lines of explanation may be advanced to explain the lifting of the French veto. The first is the simplest: future cooperation within the EEC on matters of interest to France depended on a bona fide effort to examine Britain's credentials for entry. With necessity dictating invention, the French government could be said to have immediately set about turning Britain's joining to its advantage. The financial

44. *Ibid.,* p. 180.
45. See n. 39 above for the details of settlement made to Britain.

regulation for agriculture was set in place before France would consent to talks on the British dossier. The candidate states were obliged to accept the principles of the Rome Treaty and the basic accords and procedures worked out by the Six over a decade. De Gaulle had argued, with some persuasiveness, in his first veto of Britain's application that its presence and participation at Brussels would foreclose progress toward an independent (and French-led) Europe. But the lesson drawn by the Pompidou regime from the breakdown in inner Six bargaining after the second veto in 1967 was that Britain's absence similarly prevented movement toward economic integration, political union, and the creation of an independent Europe. The Five could not compel de Gaulle to accept a Europe with Britain. But they could reject a Gaullist-led Europe.

This line of analysis, while not necessarily incorrect, is not fully satisfying. The concessions made by France in the negotiations, the short- and long-term domestic and foreign policy risks run by the Pompidou government in making them, and the solicitude of the Paris regime, particularly in the final six months of negotiations with Britain, strongly suggested that more was at stake than agriculture; that larger political and economic considerations disposed the Pompidou government to Britain's membership; that Britain was the centerpiece of an entirely different vision of European and global politics than that projected for over a generation by Charles de Gaulle; and that, indeed, Britain's entry was welcomed by the Paris regime once the conditions raised in the Brussels negotiations were met. That these matters were masked in the cryptic phrase of *"continuité et ouverture"* rather than openly announced was hardly surprising. The Pompidou regime, not yet fully in control of itself or its supporters, much less its opponents, could not openly repudiate a past on which an important part of its credentials to rule was based. It was not ready, either, to permit Britain's entry without attempting to discipline London to Paris' needs and, where failing, to preserve the fiction for the sake of domestic political consumption. Besides, as those experienced in dealing with them readily attested French negotiators thrived on diplomatic bargaining.

The significant concessions made by the French measured the political and economic importance attached to Britain's entry. Pompidou's France went well beyond what the Five might have reasonably expected of France (or of themselves) in accommodating community policies and rules to Britain's situation on entry.[46] France blinked at the significant exceptions to community preference embodied in the arrangements for Commonwealth sugar and New Zealand butter and cheese. In the latter case, exemptions from rigid application of community preference were to be allowed even after Britain's transition period. The actual material cost of the French concessions was perhaps not great. They were important as a matter of principle and because the French negotiating position within the Six leaned on assertions of legal right and moral obligation to protect France's economic interests and gains. Derogations from community preference potentially established dangerous precedents that could be used by other states later to weaken further community cohesion and point the Brussels group to a free trade zone. These possibilities were real enough. The agricultural burden fell heavily on Germany and, in the absence of periodic adjustments and compensations, on Italy. The sugar and New Zealand compromises were not without some serious risk to the over-all French position in the EEC. France had to rely increasingly on formal bargaining chips, lacking economic and political weight as Germany had to carry its interests forward.

France also accepted British pledges of monetary support where de Gaulle had demanded concrete changes in Britain's financial position, including an end to controls on capital transfers, rectification of its balance of payments, and the end of sterling's reserve role. That solving these problems might depend partially on access to the European community's markets did not bend the French president's resolve to exclude Britain from the Continent for political reasons. The Pompidou government had incentive to be more understanding. Indeed, it was willing to risk that the British would, without formal commitments, ultimately support a French-defined European monetary and trade position toward third states, and most particularly toward the United States. It did not insist on reducing sterling's role as a precondition for entry as de Gaulle had implicitly demanded in his second veto. It accepted the Heath government's word that ster-

46. Prime Minister Heath makes much of these concessions in his government's White Paper on British membership, Command Paper 4517, *passim*.

ling balances would be decreased and that Britain would gradually align the pound on the other community currencies. Referring to his talk with President Pompidou, Prime Minister Heath emphasized his freedom of maneuver in defending the terms of Britain's adhesion to the Common Market: "We have given no undertakings as to how fast or by what means these developments [reduction of sterling balances and alignment] could or should be brought about. These would be matters for discussion after our entry, when we should be a full member of the Community with all the rights of a member. . . . We have made clear the . . . conditions which any proposal for reducing the official sterling balances would have to satisfy: notably, of course, the protection of the interests of balance holders and the avoidance of unacceptable burdens on our balance of payments." [47]

Paris was also conciliatory on the question of Britain's level of contribution to the community and on the transitional arrangements for entry. Provision was made for additional time and exemption from the 19 percent standard after 1977 should circumstances prevent Britain from assuming its full share of the community's financial burden. These adjustments, as Heath intimated, were made at no expense to Britain's voting rights in the EEC during the transition period. Additional concessions were made, too, for the gradual relaxation of Britain's control on capital flows, for labor movements into Northern Ireland, for fishery rights to protect Britain's industry, and for special products of unique interest to Britain. The London government also expected that Britain's contribution to the European Investment Bank and to the reserve fund of the ECSC of approximately $90 and $55 million, respectively, would either remain or be spent in Britain. [48]

There was also a keen awareness demonstrated in French and community circles of the delicacy of the Heath government's position in Britain as most of the rank and file of the Labor party under former Prime Minister Harold Wilson abandoned its support of the Common Market proposal and geared for a battle over approval. The Pompidou government avoided any moves or statements before parliamentary passage of the final treaty in principle that might have un-

47. *Ibid.*, p. 33.
48. *Ibid.*, pp. 33ff.

dermined the Conservative government's position before British public opinion and Parliament. The occasions were at hand to feign interest in British entry while permitting the regime to founder on the issue at home. Pompidou, as some informed opinion in England believed, had no taste for this double game.[49] Whether deliberate or not, similar reserve was not exercised at the time of the Norwegian referendum on entry in September 1972. A few days before the vote, President Pompidou had affirmed his support for Spain's eventual entry into the European community, a prospect bitterly opposed in the Scandinavian states.[50]

A fuller and more satisfactory explanation of the French change in attitude, reflected in the compromises and concessions facilitating Britain's joining the Brussels group, must be found in the radically different circumstances of France's domestic and international position and in the Pompidou government's response to them. After 1968, it was pointless, perhaps even mischievous, to keep Britain out. Much of the justification for its exclusion had rested on political and economic assumptions that were undermined by the events of that year. First of all, France's European options were exhausted by 1968. When de Gaulle played France's European card, potentially its strongest lead, he tended to weaken, not strengthen, France's position. His uncompromising stances often repelled his natural partners, propelling them either into direct opposition to France or, tantamount to the same thing, into the camp of France's adversaries. Or, like Achilles, Gaullist France would sulk in its tent and risk having its European partners look elsewhere for mutual assistance. President Pompidou had little taste for multiplying opponents when beset already with enough problems not of his government's doing.

Britain held the key to better relations with the Five. The British option also held promise of strengthening France's European posture and West Europe's as well in regional and global politics. France's

49. See the commentary on the Pompidou-Heath meeting in the London *Times* of May 18–22, *passim,* especially the editorial comment.

50. Comité Interministériel pour l'Information, *Actualités-documents,* "Conférence de presse de M. Georges Pompidou," Sept. 21, 1972, p. 13 (hereafter cited "Conférence de Pompidou"): "As for Spain, . . . I am a partisan of its entry into the Common Market and I wish it can do so as quickly as possible while knowing that there are still economic difficulties and political objections according to some." The Norwegians were among those "some."

material power was modest by any measure. Its economic and political independence, without outside assistance, was accordingly circumscribed.[51] Its global role depended on how well it could magnify its voice in European affairs. These calculations were apparently not far from de Gaulle's mind in his talk with Soames. It took his successor, freed from antiquated habits born of an educational formation stretching back to the nineteenth century and hardened by over a generation of struggles with British leaders, to explore the positive aspects of a revived Entente Cordiale and its value to the European community. Germany would be a partner, not an opponent, of the grouping. A Britain tied to Europe in a new Continental System held out the possibility of more tangible realization of a distinct French and European policy despite the added difficulties of concerting policy and action with nine states within the Common Market. It held some possibility of success where Gaullist gestures, deprived of sufficient backing, were often only of glancing impact on the behavior of other states, notwithstanding the rhetorical eloquence and fascinating dramatic posturing that surrounded them.

Britain's closer and more formal institutional participation in West European economic and political life promoted the multipolar politics de Gaulle heralded as the systemic guarantee of France's independence and the expansion of its influence. Britain's participation in Europe was indispensable if, as Schumann observed, there was to be a Europe worthy of the name. As thirty years earlier, France's future (and that of democratic Europe) still hinged on the question of whither went Britain. Pompidou made the point in his call for a massive vote in favor of the referendum on Britain's entry into the Common Market:

We have seen . . . created enormous *ensembles* founded on territory, mass population, economic power or on one or the other of these elements. . . . In face of that, what is the situation of the European nations? A very small territory, with a medium-sized population, an economic capacity which is great, but which, in absolute value, remains limited. If,

51. See Edward L. Morse, *Foreign Policy and Interdependence in Gaullist France* (Princeton: Princeton University Press, 1973). Morse focuses on the limits of Gaullist foreign policy as a function of interstate and transnational interdependence. The book, however, arrived too late to be incorporated into my analysis.

on the contrary, thty are put together, then one obtains a power equal in many areas to any other * * * * But if Europe is not formed, the European nations will be completely eclipsed by all these great *ensembles*. . . . From that point of view, moreover, history can come to our aid insofar as these [West] European nations have the habit and, therefore, have acquired the need to play a global role.[52]

The similarity of British and French positions was accented. Both peoples shared a strong commitment to their national institutions and culture. Both had broad experience in world affairs and yearned still to play a larger role than their means permitted. Both had fallen as global powers and no longer, separately, could be classed in the same category as the United States and the Soviet Union. Their rights in Europe, centering around the four-power accords after World War II, were eroding through Germany's reconciliation with the East and West and, more importantly, through the evolving alignment of the superpowers on strategic and political matters affecting Europe. As Chapter 10 indicates, both were given subordinate status in the Rogers plan of fall 1970 for an Arab-Israeli settlement and, more critically, in the hasty cease-fire organized by the superpowers to bring a halt in the Yom Kippur War of fall 1973.

A European Britain offset rising German economic and political power while mooring Germany, with its active cooperation,[53] to a West European framework. Britain had refused to accept these responsibilities in the European Defense Community proposal of the middle 1950's. Brandt's Germany could count on Britain's support for its *Ostpolitik*. Britain and France were agreed that Germany's reconciliation with the East, whatever the long-run risks, was preferable to the tensions of the Cold War. These benefits were in addition to the obvious economic and commercial advantages to be had from Britain's joining the Common Market as pressed so assiduously a decade earlier by Chancellor Erhard. The British were not unsympathetic to Brandt's efforts to anchor Germany to the West while keeping his options open in the East. There was a growing convergence, too, between London and Paris of their modest assessment of what could be prudently derived from détente with the East.

52. "Conférence de Pompidou," March 16, 1972, pp. 17–18.
53. Chancellor Brandt remarked at the Hague summit: "Those who fear the weight of the Federal Republic, for this very reason, should be favorable to the enlargement of the Community" (*L'Express,* Dec. 8, 1968, p. 62).

Neither Pompidou nor Brandt was unmindful of the moderating influence Britain would presumably have on inner West European politics. There was Britain's long commitment to democratic institutions where Germany's experience was wanting. President Pompidou referred to this latter point in his news conference of March 16, 1972: "To be associated closely with the oldest democracy of the world is to underline that France remains faithful to a representative regime, that is to say, to the choice of leaders by the people through free elections and plural parties." [54] The Fifth Republic's institutions, it might be added, were no more firmly installed than those of its German counterpart.

Britain also appeared prepared to play a larger world role through Europe and to provide a better balance within the Western alliance between the superpowers and between the states of Western Europe itself. Prime Minister Harold Wilson had already alluded to Britain's utility as a makeweight to balance the United States in the Atlantic grouping and Germany in the Western European community and as a useful partner in the successful management of détente politics in the East. The Heath government quoted Wilson's own remarks in retort to his defense of anti-Market forces in the parliamentary debates on adhesion: "Together we can ensure that Europe plays in world affairs the part which the Europe of today is not at present playing. For a Europe that fails to put forward its full economic strength will never have the political influence which I believe it could and should exert within the United Nations, within the Western Alliance, and as the means for effecting a lasting détente between East and West; and equally in contributing in ever fuller measure to the solution of the world North-South problem, to the needs of the developing world." [55] These sentiments might have been expressed by de Gaulle on behalf of France. There was nothing in Heath's record to suggest that he did not subscribe to these views of Europe's and Britain's role in realizing its potential strength in world councils.[56]

Changed global conditions made Castlereagh's proposal for a greater British commitment to the European continent more attrac-

54. "Conférence de Pompidou," March 16, 1972, p. 10.
55. Command Paper 4517, pp. 9–10.
56. Pompidou affirms as much in his news conference of March 16, p. 19, n. 54 above.

tive than when it was first advanced a century and a half ago. There was no power then capable of ruling the Continent after Napoleon's defeat. Outward pressures, generated largely by the superpowers and the Third World, pushed the European states inward, on themselves, for mutual help as a precondition to their ability to influence events exterior to them, as before, when power vacuums abroad were an invitation to European imperialism and the projection of the European balance of power into the industrially backward parts of the globe.

The risks and costs of Britain's entry to the line of policy laid down previously by de Gaulle should not be minimized. First, there was the double risk, recognized by President de Gaulle from his early days in office, of the European community's dissolution into a free trade zone and its susceptibility with Britain in Europe, to United States pressures and influence. President Pompidou met the first problem directly in calling for French approval of Britain's candidacy: "If one admits that Great Britain could not remain forever outside [the Common Market], the question is then posed of the conditions of its entry. Was it a question . . . of dissolving the Community in a kind of vast Atlantic free exchange zone dominated in fact, whether one might wish it or not, by the United States? Was it, on the contrary [a question] of anchoring Great Britain solidly to Europe, to give it its true dimensions and possibilities and to mark the identity of this Europe vis-à-vis the world, including the United States, friend certainly, but situated finally on another continent." [57]

In dealing with Britain, the Pompidou government followed two courses. On the one hand, as already described, Britain was obliged in principle to accept the Rome Treaty and all of its works. Despite the concessions made by the French, success in securing British consent was not negligible. London, too, had to abandon traditional practices and policies. In a sense, President Pompidou drew profit from the work of his predecessor. De Gaulle, as much as anyone, was instrumental in preparing Britain for Europe. His intransigence helped prod a reluctant Great Britain to reconsider its fading global position and to strengthen its continental commitments. For almost ten years it carefully marshaled its forces and transformed its internal structure and external alignments to meet some of the exacting tests established by Paris. There was less ambiguity and vacillation about accepting community rules and principles when the British made a second attempt to join in 1967. Requests for exceptions were fewer in number than before and of lesser magnitude. Canada and Austria, for example, were able to fend for themselves. Where the Six were firm—a five-year transition period with supplementary adjustments —the British proved conciliatory. Negotiations were not permitted to drag on interminably, nor to bog down on minor points as in 1961–1962. Its trade with the EEC countries continued to advance at a faster rate than with the Commonwealth and other trading areas and held about even with the EFTA group.[58] Neither the Wilson nor the Heath governments could be accused, as Macmillan had been— and not altogether unjustifiably—of seeking to dissolve the Common Market from without or, failing that, to lead it from within. Heath's credentials as a European were in good order. There was enough of a change in the British position to have warranted serious examination of its dossier, based on de Gaulle's own criteria.

On the other hand, the French pressed the case for strengthening of the community. The difficulties surrounding enlargement, with the absorption of Britain, Ireland, and Denmark into the Common Market, are still too great at this writing to speak with any certainty about the outcome of this campaign. It is here where the Pompidou government was accepting risks, refused by the de Gaulle administration, that the EEC would not backslide and that its momentum toward economic integration and political union would not be blocked. De Gaulle had been unwilling to run these risks and to profit from the possible opportunities they offered. It was an implicit admission of weakness on the part of Gaullist diplomacy to deny Britain's entry into Europe rather than to be confident to draw on Britain's presence and turn its weight to France's (and Europe's) advantage as circumstances required.

The costs to Gaullist aims in lifting the veto on Britain should not be minimized. First, dependence for the immediate future on the United States military guarantee was openly acknowledged. Britain would not relax its security ties with the United States as de Gaulle

58. *Le Monde,* July 24, 1971, p. 2.

had required as a condition to entry. The Pompidou government needed little inducement to relent on this crucial point. Under the impetus of increasing American withdrawal symptoms, of growing superpower accord, and of heightened Soviet diplomatic activity in Europe, the Pompidou government wished to maximize the American security commitment while minimizing the cost to France—in economic support or diplomatic maneuverability—of relying on American military presence to service French and European security needs. On several occasions Pompidou tried to justify a logically self-contradictory but politically attractive policy that accepted—indeed insisted upon—the necessity of American troops in Europe while resisting responsibility to pay in economic and political coinage for the protection. His statement before the second European summit conference on October 19, 1972, is representative:

Western Europe, liberated from Armies thanks to the essential contribution of American soldiers, reconstructed with American aid, having looked for its security in alliance with America, having hitherto accepted American currency as the main element of its monetary reserves, must not and cannot sever its links with the United States. But neither must it refrain from affirming its existence as a new reality. Whether the matter concerns trade discussions, towards which we are disposed since our record is clean, or whether it concerns the reform of the monetary system, which must necessarily include a return to the convertibility of the dollar, a new definition of reserve instruments, the development of trade and the control of speculative capital, solutions can be devised.[59]

A Britain in Europe would be added collateral against the possibility of too rapid a United States withdrawal from Europe. Its traditional ties and language links drew the United States to Britain more than verbal pledges or treaty obligations, yet, expectedly, at sufficient distance to permit Europe freedom for maneuver in world politics. Britain's membership in the EEC was also a hedge against American disengagement if Western Europe were forced to deal with the Soviet Union alone and, not inconceivably after Suez, in opposition to a joint accord between the two superpowers.

There was a less obvious purpose at issue in a closer French-United

59. Ambassade de France, Service de Presse et d'Information, No. 72/162, *European Summit Conference*, Oct. 19, 1972, p. 3; hereafter cited as *European Summit Conference*.

States alignment, encouraged, if not assured, by Britain's presence in Western Europe. France seemed to have gained little from its direct opposition to the United States. De Gaulle had cast France, sometimes apparently only for ephemeral psychic purpose, into the role of America's principal opponent in Europe. In drawing fire, France exhausted its limited resources in a struggle with its major security ally. President Pompidou, abhorring open conflict to a fault and sensitive to French weakness, preferred accommodating United States power where possible and adjusting to it when necessary. Better to work with United States influence than against it, even at the cost of a questionable international prestige in earning its ire. This was a commodity of doubtful economic and political marketability at home when the dominant objectives of the government after 1968 were addressed to the prosperity and welfare of Frenchmen, not the *grandeur* and independence of the French nation. In his television address to the nation on the British referendum, President Pompidou subtly signaled the shift in priorities. " 'What good is Europe?' say people with a short-run view. 'Take care of France,' and, of course, *the government's task is to think first about France and about Frenchmen, about their prosperity, about their welfare, about the grandeur and independence of our country.*" [60] The French, here and now, counted more than the more abstract ideals of national *grandeur* and independence. Their well-being of the moment mortgaged for the while the realization of national ambitions.

At a more theoretical level of analysis, de Gaulle's conception of international politics, based on different hierarchies of states,[61] might have prompted him to be more flexible with respect to the conditions of enlisting American influence in France's service. Years of opposition to real and imagined American encroachments on French (and European) prerogatives—in its inception a foil to decrease American influence and expand France's—risked becoming an end in itself, like some conditioned response that persists though the outside stimuli initially inducing behavior no longer exist and, indeed, are prompting a contrary response.

The Pompidou government, while not fully abandoning the de Gaulle image of a United States as competitor and challenge to

60. *Le Monde*, April 13, 1972, p. 6.
61.See abo ve, Chapter 1, pp. 54–61.

French and European independence, widened France's conception of America's role in Europe. It reinforced the stance, only dimly visible in the closing months of the de Gaulle years, of reducing French criticism of United States policies in Europe and the Third World, a posture abetted by the Paris peace talks and the United States monetary assistance during the franc crisis of 1968. The Pompidou government additionally accented France's close relations with the United States within the Atlantic Alliance while minimizing its participation in NATO activities.[62] If American and French monetary policies and economic interests still sharply conflicted, the gold war was quietly ended.[63] Adopted was a set of competing strategies, at least partially explicable and rationalized by France's diverse objectives, aimed at improving its continental position in the immediate future while ostensibly strengthening the West European grouping vis-à-vis the United States and the Soviet Union even at the risk of French autonomy in the long run.

The second major cost of Britain's entry was Britain's presence itself. De Gaulle considered Britain a competitor for power, to be excluded whatever the pretext. The Pompidou government accepted Britain as a partner with which the increased power and authority of the European community, if not necessarily the Brussels organizations, would have to be divided. There was no way to draw Britain into Europe except to share power, and an enlarged Europe would project French influence on a global screen. There is perhaps merit in the argument, as some have insisted,[64] that a Europe with Britain was a Europe repugnant to de Gaulle under almost any circumstances; that he preferred a France isolated and weak, even at the risk of losing the economic benefits of the Common Market and the common agricultural policy, if he could not have his larger Europe from the Atlantic to the Urals, resting on French-Soviet cooperation with German acquiescence. Only a Europe bearing his and France's stamp was acceptable.[65] The Pompidou government was prepared to share power with Britain in the European community. There was

62. See Chapter 3 above, pp. 140–145.
63. See Chapter 4 above.
64. Newhouse, *De Gaulle and the Anglo-Saxons, passim.*
65. This point is drawn, with some reinterpretation, from Stanley Hoffmann, *New Republic,* April 12, 1969, pp. 20–23.

always the safety valve of unanimity to preclude undesirable actions pressed by Britain or France's other partners. Besides, on the question of unanimity, Britain shared France's antipathy to supranational controls.[66] A policy of interdependence meant cooperating, as an equal, with others. De Gaulle had implicitly conceded as much in pressing the CAP. He recoiled from the logical consequences of the new politics—that France's independence would be harnessed to a larger European community. His successor was left the difficult task of reconciling national independence with France's need for allied interdependence.

Strengthening the Community

Community Dimensions of Strengthening. Within the Pompidou regime's frame of reference, the European community, as a political entity, was distinguishable from the states that presently, or could conceivably, compose it and from the institutional framework, practices, and policies of the Rome Treaty. The West European community could be defined by its common elements and, more importantly, by the political acts of will of its diverse peoples, affirming a community reality. History, recognized Pompidou, produced European division rooted in differences of language, national pride, and the memory of past slights and quarrels.[67] But these barriers, he intimated, need not be as formidable or as impassible as de Gaulle had believed. The states of Western Europe were being pushed closer together by "geography, life-style, a certain conception of democracy, and an evident political and economic interest." [68]

At issue was the political will of the individual states and their people to affirm the community over their diverse national conditions. De Gaulle had been reluctant to pose this question to the French people. Pompidou raised the issue before the French voted in the referendum on Britain's entry of April 1972: "It is a question of making Europe. . . . The objective is certainly not easy to attain and there are and will continue to be many obstacles at home and abroad, but what is essential is the undertaking and, what is most important, is political determination. Now, I affirm here that France has this

66. Command Paper 4517, *passim.*
67. "Conférence de Pompidou," March 16, 1972, p. 18.
68. *Ibid.*

political determination." [69] The French people living now were to
have a free and unencumbered right to make such an affirmation.
The affirmation, indeed, was implicitly rendered already: "How could
we . . . [turn back on ourselves]," asked Pompidou in his television
address of April 12, "when for twelve years we have ceased to live
in a closed circuit?" [70]

In Pompidou's view, political authority sprang from the French
people of the moment. They had a right to authorize their government to consign part of national authority to a European community of which they and the French nation were a part. This point
was struck in the letter sent to each French voter explaining the referendum and soliciting his support: "France is ready to play the
role in . . . Europe to which its geographic situation, its past, the
work of its people, [and] the prestige of its culture destines it. . . .
I believe in France, and I believe in Europe. You [French] do, also,
I am sure of it! You will prove it by responding to the question which
is posed to you and on which each of you will pronounce freely." [71]

The European community, no less than the French people with
their unique language and nationhood, was a product of history. Its
vitality and future, moreover, depended on French will and witness.
That France's commitment to Europe was at issue in the referendum
on enlargement was suggested in Pompidou's announcement of the
proposal to be put before the French voters: "This adhesion [of
Britain] goes very far beyond the simple notion of Community enlargement. It is not simply the exterior role of Europe which will be
modified by it, it is the internal future of Europe and of the European nations and, consequently, the future of the French in every
area." [72]

The European community was also defined by its difference from
other states and groupings. This was the message repeatedly asserted
by President Pompidou at Brussels in his official visit to Belgium on

69. *Ibid.*

70. *Le Monde,* April 13, 1972, p. 6. It is interesting that Pompidou says
twelve, not fourteen years. That would place the decision for entry into a multilateral Western Europe around the time of the acceptance of the common
agricultural policy, not coterminous with the establishment of the Fifth Republic.

71. The full text appears in *L'Humanité,* April 1, 1972, p. 4.

72. "Conférence de Pompidou," March 16, 1972, p. 19.

May 24–25, 1971, shortly after his historic meeting with Prime Minister Heath in Paris. With Britain joining the Continent, the Western European community could look to the day when it could declare its independence from the United States. The French president's remarks bear reading. They stress the peculiar features of West European life—its traditions, policies, institutions, interests, and languages. These elements marked Britain as more European than Atlantic. Prying Britain from the American grasp to labor within a European framework, compatible in form with Gaullist strictures, appeared to be an animating political motive of the Pompidou regime. It elaborated on the theme of "get away closer" from the United States already seen in security and monetary affairs.

To be European, that means to be distinguished from the rest [of the world], from Asia, from the Soviet world, but also from America. . . . It is not difficult to distinguish ourselves from Asia; . . . it is not difficult, either, to distinguish ourselves from the Soviet world . . . because we have different regimes. . . . As for the United States, we ought to distinguish ourselves from it because if we do not distinguish ourselves from it, we will be Americans; . . . we do not wish to be American; we wish to be European. But we have very close ties: born of a political and social regime (we are in the same democratic universe), extremely close commercial and economic and monetary ties (our entire monetary system is linked to the dollar), [and] political and alliance ties with the United States (all of the countries who are in the Community, almost all of those who are candidates for adhesion, are allies of the United States within the Atlantic Alliance).[73]

Whereas Gaullist policies and style had driven Britain into closer league with the United States, Pompidou attempted through persuasion, accommodation, cajolery, and specific binding commitments to loosen Britain's Atlantic ties in favor of European (and French) interests and to confine its principal decision-making priorities within a European framework of French confederal design, resting on the assumption of continued and close bilateral contacts between the two governments. One need not take Pompidou's identification of France with the cause of European community too seriously to recognize that, for all its purely rhetorical character, it served as a handy

73. *PEF,* Jan.–June 1971, p. 194.

ideological whip to bring France's partners (and domestic critics) into line. As the discussion below suggests, the particular and parochial needs of France and the Pompidou government paraded behind the newly unfurled West European community standard.

Strengthening National and Presidential Authority. Communal considerations surrounding enlargement and strengthening formed the surface tensions of the referendum. They obscured, however, a complex web of other domestic and foreign policy issues that were central to President Pompidou's unexpected use of the referendum device to strengthen France's hand in Europe and his position at home and abroad. The European community was viewed, first of all, as a medium through which French influence might more effectively be radiated abroad. President Pompidou articulated this objective in his television presentation on behalf of a massive "Yes" vote: "France cannot maintain and increase its role in the world except by uniting with other European nations, including England," he said. "The added means will permit [us] to speak as an equal to anyone." [74] Like de Gaulle, Pompidou saw the European community as an extension of France, but he displayed more flexibility than de Gaulle in exploiting its possibilities.

Second, Pompidou linked the referendum to the upcoming European summit conference that he had proposed in August 1971 to deal with the monetary and trade crises engendered by President Nixon's decisions to cut the formal tie between the dollar and gold and to place a 10 percent surtax on imports. In voting to enlarge the Common Market and to increase France's participation in the politics of European unity, the French electorate would, willy-nilly, be voting to enhance the position of the French president since he was France's principal voice in foreign affairs. In campaigning for massive approval of his referendum question, President Pompidou alluded to his meeting with President Nixon in the Azores the previous December to illustrate how domestic support of the president strengthened France's hand in world councils. His influence there was allegedly due to his solid domestic position and to his virtual

74. *Le Monde,* April 13, 1972, p. 6. Note the ambiguity of the last sentence. It is not clear from the context whether France or Europe is meant. It would appear to be a deliberate obfuscation to permit Pompidou to straddle the nationalist and Europeanist camps.

status as the representative of the European community and of its collective political will.[75] Support of the referendum would underwrite his new West European orientation (and the other parts of his governmental program), bolster Gaullist rule and his own personal power among Gaullists and non-Gaullists, reinforce the presidency within Fifth Republic institutions and, in the bargain, increase France's weight in Brussels and, through the European grouping, in world politics.

De Gaulle and Pompidou did not differ theoretically in their views about how foreign and domestic politics could be made to work to strengthen the position of the French president. They tended, however, to approach the problem from opposite ends of a spectrum. After the end of the Algerian War, de Gaulle largely used domestic politics to enhance his stature abroad; Pompidou, for whom domestic objectives were of more urgent concern, was inclined to follow a reverse course. The end results of Gaullist and Pompidou strategies, in principle, would presumably be similar, but government priorities would be inevitably affected once one or the other approach was adopted to realize these diverse personal, institutional, and domestic and foreign policy goals. The April 1972 referendum on a foreign policy issue that had already been favorably decided—President Pompidou admitted that the champagne had already been drunk at Brussels in celebration of Britain's entry—appeared to be a safe device by which to renew and enlarge the French president's mandate at home.

Indeed, the April referendum said a great deal about Pompidou's conception of his authority as president and the political expectations he had of himself and of the French people. These were intimately related, finally, to France's relation to Europe. Lacking de Gaulle's personal prestige, authority, and historical credentials, and endowed with a more reserved personality, President Pompidou viewed himself as ruling more by persuasion and manipulation than by command. He did not claim any special privilege or right to rule other than those conferred by the French electorate. "As for legitimacy, I hold my legitimacy from the free election of the French people who have carried me where I am and before whom I alone am re-

75. *Le Monde*, April 13, 1972, p. 6.

sponsible," [76] he said. Even *grandeur,* however characterized, would have to meet an electoral test not only as a matter of practical politics but also of moral legitimacy. In his remarks to the newly elected National Assembly in April 1973, President Pompidou defined his authority in terms of a public consent that was a function of the government's capacity to respond to French welfare demands: "France's *grandeur,* which we do not renounce," he observed, "cannot be conceived without the consent of the French people, a consent which depends in large part on the response that will be given to their aspirations. These aspirations are, first of all, social." [77] Contrast this view with de Gaulle's conception of his authority, discussed in Chapter 1, that rested ultimately on his self-defined contract with France, and not the French people.

In resting his rule on a majority of the French voters, Pompidou traded a theoretical limitation, not found in de Gaulle's conception of his legitimacy, for a practical expansion of effective presidential authority. De Gaulle's more expansive understanding of his political authority and legitimacy were essentially voided by the events of 1968. De Gaulle had rested his authority on the French nation, beyond the French voters of the moment or the National Assembly. Still less did it depend on the political parties which reflected the refracted sentiment of the French electorate. But in the aftermath of the May crisis, de Gaulle had to rely on these previously scorned instruments to cling to the appearance of power. The May events amounted to an unscheduled referendum on ten years of Gaullist rule. De Gaulle's foreign policy hopes for *grandeur* were undermined by the implicit withdrawal of confidence in his rule. After the decisive Gaullist legislative victory of June 1968, de Gaulle would be able to rule France, but not govern it effectively until he addressed himself to the social and economic welfare questions raised by the spring upheaval. That he had difficulty in reorientating his priorities and in convincing the French populace of his reformist intent was suggested in his final conversation with André Malraux. "Why did you leave on a question so secondary as that of the regions," asked Malraux. "Because of the absurdity?" "Because of the absurdity," replied de Gaulle.[78]

76. *Le Figaro,* Jan. 22, 1972, p. 8.
77. *Le Monde,* April 5, 1973, p. 1ff.
78. Malraux, *Les Chênes,* pp. 30–31.

President Pompidou added welfare to de Gaulle's foreign and security concerns as governmental imperatives. The welfare of the French populace was related closely to Europe's enlargement and to a greater role for France in West European economic and political development. Whether or not these goals had been achieved was left to the decision of the French electorate. Otherwise, the streets might settle the question at the cost of liberal institutions. Moreover, on the makeup of France's government, Pompidou, like de Gaulle, opted for presidential over parliamentary primacy. The prime minister served at the pleasure of the president. De Gaulle's dismissal of Pompidou after the latter's brilliant engineering of the parliamentary election victory in June 1968, and President Pompidou's dismissal of Jacques Chaban-Delmas after (some intimate *because*) he had just been given a vote of confidence by the National Assembly in May 1972, left no doubt on this question.[79] Not surprisingly, Pompidou rested his claim of superiority on his election by universal suffrage, a legacy of the 1962 referendum launched by de Gaulle.[80]

April, however, was a cruel month for Pompidou as it was for his predecessor three years before. It began auspiciously enough. Such rivals as orthodox Gaullist Michel Debré and European federalist Jean Monnet joined in supporting the referendum. They preferred to see what they desired most in the ambiguous statement of the referendum question. Monnet saw it as a step to European unity; Debré, as a means by which France might again influence European and global politics through increased political and economic cooperation among the West European states. The ambiguous wording of the referendum permitted the voter to attach a strict or loose construction to its meaning, depending on his priorities and values.[81]

79. See the penetrating analysis on this point by Pierre Viansson-Ponté in *Le Monde,* Sept. 7, 1972, pp. 1, 4.
80. See President Pompidou's press conferences of September 1972 and January 1973, *Le Monde,* Sélection hebdomadaire, Sept. 21–27, 1972, pp. 1–2; *ibid.,* Jan. 4–10, 1973, pp. 1–2.
81. The referendum question was as follows: "With the new prospects that open for Europe, do you approve the bill submitted to the French people by the President of the Republic authorizing ratification of the treaty concerning the membership of Britain, Denmark, Ireland, and Norway in the European Communities?" (Ambassade de France, Service de Presse et d'Information, *France,* April 1972, p. 3).

Pompidou's surprise referendum proposal caught his opponents off guard. Adversaries, like Europeanists Jean Lecanuet and Jean-Jacques Servan-Schreiber, were drawn into his camp on the issue, however much they opposed his policies or his personal rule. Division was sown among the Left. The Communist party opposed the referendum; the Socialists advised abstention. Pompidou argued the case for European unity while the Communists asserted that French national interests would be sacrificed in enlarging the community. The publication of a memorandum by Sicco Mansholt, written to Commission president Franco Maria Malfatti, calling for a reordering of Europe's goals from unlimited economic growth to greater emphasis on the quality of life and controls on economic activity, offered grist for the Communist mill.[82]

The outcome of the referendum was a blow to the European movement and for the French president. Only a little over 53 percent of the registered voters cast ballots. Of these, approximately 68 percent voted in favor, representing only slightly more than one third of the registered voters. The results were too scattered and mixed to know whether the vote was directed at Pompidou's leadership or at the European idea, or at both. The two became so confounded by the time of voting as to make their separation difficult. The support of the French electorate for a strengthened West Europe remained to be tested.

President Pompidou and Community Institutions. Adherents and opponents of the Pompidou regime could agree that the European community, however defined, should be distinguished from the Rome Treaty and the institutions and processes flowing from it. The Pompidou regime was very reserved about any moves to increase the status of the community institutions, particularly the Commission or the European Parliament. This attitude manifested itself in the decisions surrounding the negotiations among the Six about the procedures to be established for the enlargement talks and about the European Parliament's authority to oversee community resources.

Like de Gaulle, President Pompidou accepted the European com-

---

82. Commission des Communautés Européennes, Secrétariat Général, Feb. 11, 1972. See also the early April 1971 issues of *L'Humanité* for critical commentary. President Pompidou was closer to *Humanité* than to Mansholt on the issue. *PEF*, Jan.–June 1972, p. 201.

munity as coterminous in its beginning with the nations comprising it. The possibility of political union and of a community government was seen to arise from the separate consent of the particular governments, acting on the authority vested in them through their separate constitutional processes.

President Pompidou also introduced a shade of difference from Gaullist doctrine, initially of more theoretical than practical import, in how a community government might arise. He foresaw the possibility of each state eventually appointing a minister of European affairs. The post would become necessary as the "questions which will be debated at the European level will be more and more numerous and meetings more and more frequent." [83] What was significant was that the possibility of a governmental authority for the community beyond that of the individual states, but approved by them, was held open. "One can even think, or imagine," said Pompidou in his news conference of January 21, 1971, "that in a final phase these ministers will no longer have any but strictly European attributes and will no longer belong to national governments." [84] Once this governmental or executive authority was established, the question of creating and widening the authority of parliamentary institutions would arise. To dispel doubts, President Pompidou specifically repudiated the notion of governmental union through the Brussels Commission or through its technical services: "That [the European confederation] might be made through technical organisms, [or] through committees is an illusion already swept away by the facts. . . . The government of Europe can arise only out of the gathering of national governments, joining together to take decisions that are valid for all." [85]

The French position on what framework to adopt for negotiation between the Six and the candidate states reflected Pompidou's views. France insisted that the negotiations be led by the "Community as an entity," operating through the Council of Ministers and its president, "with the assistance of the European Commission." [86] Rejected was the Commission proposal to act as the agent of the com-

83. *Ibid.*, 1971, p. 53.
84. *Ibid.*
85. *Ibid.*
86. "La France et l'adhésion," p. 4.

munity along the lines of the role it played in the Kennedy Round discussions.

The French conception of state-to-state bargaining prevailed. The permanent representatives in Brussels were assigned a greater role than before as instruments of Council deliberations. The Commission and its directorates were to be utilized ostensibly to detail the implications of policies reached by higher political authority and to provide the necessary technical backup for the talks. After a decade of exhausting battle to retain its independence and increase its authority, the Commission accepted its subordinate role with but a hint of chagrin: "In light of the outcome and achievements of the Conference [on enlargement] it should be said that this procedure [of working through the Council and the permanent representatives] decided upon by the Council—*which may sometimes have seemed somewhat cumbersome in its workings*—owes its success largely to the complementary nature of the two institutions, the Council and the Commission." [87]

The French conceded some slight ground, too, to the European Parliament regarding its authority to oversee the community's own resources. It was permitted to increase the nonobligatory expenses of the community budget, subject to a qualified majority vote of the Council. These items, however, represented little more than 3 to 5 percent of the budget, of which 80 percent constituted fixed costs and salaries.[88] Specifically dismissed by French officials, contrary to views expressed by the European Parliament, was power to reject the community's budget as a whole.[89] Finessed for the while, too, was any increase in the popular support of the European Parliament through the direct election of delegates. The Hague conference of 1968 consigned this problem to committee discussion, and the summit conference of October 1972 registered little progress in this area.[90]

The commission was also held in its budgetary operations to an amount carefully determined by its projected needs as approved by

87. *Fifth Report of the Communities,* p. 34.

88. French Foreign Minister Maurice Schumann cites 5 percent. *PEF,* Jan.–June 1970, p. 189; *L'Année politique, 1970,* p. 258, suggests 3 percent.

89. *L'Année politique, 1970,* p. 258.

90. Comité Interministériel pour l'Information, "La Communauté européenne après le sommet de Paris," Dec. 1972.

the Council.[91] The problem of budgetary surpluses that might be used for community-wide programs at Commission discretion, an important problem during the 1965–1966 crisis, was rendered essentially mute by tight Council control over the community's purse strings. The Council emerged as the principal agent of control over the community budget. The Commission was reduced to technical commentary and recommendations; the European Parliament was permitted "high sentence," to use a phrase of T. S. Eliot, but little power.

The major difference between the de Gaulle and Pompidou governments on community institutions was the latter's greater willingness to discuss changes in the relations between the organs of the community; but it was reluctant to go beyond talk. Even if President Pompidou had wished to go farther, the Gaullist majority in the National Assembly was resistant. There was also Michel Debré, the conscience of the orthodox Gaullists, who was on record opposing any increase in the budgetary powers of the European Parliament.[92] The Five were constrained, with France's consent to enlargement in the offing, from pressing the case for community institutions very far. The Dutch were less vocal on the issue when compared with their pronouncements during the Fouchet plan struggle.[93] The larger states of Britain and Germany were finding the French argument increasingly persuasive and congenial to the pursuit of their separate and not always compatible national aims.[94]

The Pompidou regime was wary of ideological debates over community institutional development. The existing EEC institutions were held to a strict construction of their powers. The approach to community action on matters falling outside the terms of the Rome Treaty was, according to President Pompidou, to be "rigorously pragmatic." [95] In these broader realms the states were to retain their capacity for initiative,[96] and they were "to decide exactly when they

91. Interviews, Brussels, May 1971.

92. L'Année politique, 1970, p. 239.

93. For a recent sketch of Dutch attitudes toward European union see the thoughtful article by Robert Wood, "European and the Communitarian Images in Dutch Foreign Policy," International Spectator, XXVI, 836–846.

94. This is the conclusion of Professor Roy Price's analysis of the European community in mid-1972, in "Political Aspects of an Enlarged European Community," International Journal, XXVII (Winter 1971–1972), 94–112.

95. European Summit Conference, pp. 7–8.

96. Ibid

wish to submit these matters to Community procedures, including the action of the Commission and the other organizations." [97] Paris also pressed for the creation of a political secretariat within the EEC to be located in Paris, a proposal that met with little enthusiasm in the other major capitals of the Brussels organization.

In lieu of the institutional development of the community, the Pompidou administration, much like its predecessor, accented the need for substantive agreements in specific policy areas preceding their implementation through community institutions. A basic tactic of the Pompidou regime was to reach accord with its partners on a specific item of concern to France and to wrap the mantle of a European obligation around it to solidify the gain. Deviation from the agreement was then treated, as exemplified during the negotiations over agriculture and the monetary crisis of May 1971, as a legal transgression and a blow to European integration. In this way stronger powers, like Germany, could be held to greater accountability in terms of specific French interests of the moment without tying France's hand too tightly by the creation of community institutions, invested with general authority to act in a given policy area and perhaps susceptible to control by the strongest power within the EEC, that is, Germany.

The Pompidou regime, however, concentrated most of its efforts on the political, not the legalistic, elements of expanding France's influence and economic potential through Europe. It was prepared to accept the implications of the 1965–1966 compromise from which de Gaulle recoiled. Pompidou compared decision making within the community to coalition politics within a government.[98] A European confederation and a European policy would arise from the compromises reached within the coalition. Leadership, too, was to be apportioned and was not necessarily attributable to any one state as a product of a self-assigned historical mission, legal claim, or material strength.

The contrast between Pompidou's and de Gaulle's understanding and approach to European unity is revealing. Pompidou was more disposed than his predecessor to treat France's partners as equals

97. *Ibid.*
98. *PEF*, Jan.–June 1971, p. 170.

than as subordinates, creating thereby a more favorable climate for unity talks. Like de Gaulle, Pompidou believed that the articulation of a common political will had to precede the formation of community institutions,[99] but the old general had effectively halted the search for accord in vetoing Britain's second request to enter the Brussels grouping. Pompidou widened the agenda for discussion of areas of cooperation and for a more equitable sharing of community responsibility and authority in the definition and pursuit of common objectives. Under his aegis, Britain and France were reconciled on the terms and processes by which European union would proceed, including the participation of a larger number of interested states. These moves were, paradoxically, closer to Gaullist conceptions for the stable and legitimate functioning of interstate relations than de Gaulle's practice of his own political preachments would admit. President Pompidou also introduced helpful, if modest, changes in the French position on community institution building. Through these varied ways, the Pompidou government kept alive the Western European option, as an instrument of French foreign and domestic policy, that had been neglected under the de Gaulle administration in its last years in office.

A new kind of summitry was also basic to the Pompidou strategy in Europe. Pompidou took the lead in convening the summits of December 1969 (Hague), October 1972 (Paris), and December 1973 (Copenhagen). Reacting, moreover, to the Middle East crisis of fall 1973 in which the European states had been excluded by the superpowers from effective participation in arranging peace negotiations, he proposed regular summit meetings of the Nine. They aimed at developing common positions on political questions, such as the Middle East, monetary affairs, and inflation controls.[100] This call was related to parallel French efforts to organize a unified European position, with the president of the Council of Ministers of the EEC acting as spokesman, in discussions requested by the United States in April 1973 on redefining European-American relations. These initiatives resulted in declaratory statements at the September 1973 meeting of EEC foreign ministers in Copenhagen and at the Decem-

99. *Ibid.*, Jan.–June 1972, p. 201.
100. *Le Monde*, Nov. 2, 1973, p. 4.

ber summit.[101] These served to establish an agenda for talks with President Nixon's announced tour of European capitals in 1974, to define the separate political and economic identity of the Nine, and to provide guidelines for the realization of union by the end of the decade.

Whereas de Gaulle preferred summit diplomacy on a world scale between France and the great powers, Pompidou stressed West European summitry as a means of enhancing French prestige and power and that of the European community. Regional strength preceded global power, not the reverse. The inversion of Gaullist principles was necessary because France could not influence global politics without the weight and assistance of its European partners. In addition, European unity was seen by the Pompidou regime to occur initially through economic and political cooperation rather than through security as under the Fouchet plan. The former involved sharper and more evident differences between the United States and the West European states which facilitated the identification of a European position. Security problems raised too many intractable and emotional issues to be a promising route to European unity in the immediate future. In Pompidou's mind, economic and social welfare questions were of greater moment, too, for regime stability in France. There was also a difference of temperament and experience between de Gaulle and Pompidou, inclining the former to questions of military pomp and power, the latter to wealth and well-being.

Pompidou's Europe: From the Thames to the Elbe

Pompidou's Europe—the Europe out of which unity was sought—stretched from the Thames to the Elbe and from the North Sea to the Mediterranean. On the Continent, it covered an area that, according to President Pompidou's estimate, encompassed Napoleon's empire.[102] Beyond lay the remains of the Prussian empire, the diverse Slavic states, and Russia—all with a different history, economic system, political experience, and institutions. Pompidou's Europe, by his own reckoning, was Western, Christian, capitalist, and democratic.

101. *Ibid.*, Sept. 12, 1973, pp. 1, 6, and *New York Times*, Dec. 15, 1973, pp. 1, 6.
102. "Conférence de Pompidou," March 16, 1972, p. 19.

These differences were underscored in his speech, welcoming Party Secretary Leonid Brezhnev to France, the first Western country to be visited by the Soviet leader.[103] Similar allusions can be found in Pompidou's statements during his visit to the Soviet Union in October 1970.[104] Reaffirmations appeared in his pronouncements in Brussels and at the Paris summit in October 1971 and in the announcement of a referendum on British entry into the EEC:[105] "France had adopted, in the final analysis in response to General de Gaulle's appeal, quite different institutions [from those of the Soviet Union]. . . . [I]ts economic and social organization, even if it is far from corresponding to the theoretical model of liberal capitalism, attach it to the Western world . . . . [I]ts alliances, as the active part that it takes in European construction within the framework of the Communities, are integral parts of its policy." [106] The Nine shared these characteristics. They also had, as President Pompidou noted, "a similar Christian and rationalist civilization. . . . There is not any European country, but there is European man, there is a European civilization, and it is a question of reserving and adapting it to the evolution of the world and to the aspirations of youth." [107] These differences between a Western France and an Eastern Soviet Union, each linked to different security systems and alliance networks, were advanced by France in its discreet demurrer to Soviet entreaties that the two states sign a friendship treaty during Leonid Brezhnev's visit in 1971.[108]

That these distinctions may not have been viable when applied to Eastern Europe was of more intellectual than political relevance since, for the Pompidou regime, they provided a vague rationalization of its European policies and approach. There was no longer mention of de Gaulle's Europe from the Atlantic to the Urals. The French tricolor flew on a Western, not Eastern, wind. It symbolized a new triptych: "completion, enlargement, and strengthening." Downplayed, though not entirely disregarded—certainly in the bi-

103. *PEF*, July–Dec. 1971, pp. 159–162.

104. *Ibid.*, July–Dec. 1970, pp. 77–113.

105. *Ibid.*, Jan.–June 1971, pp. 182–198; *European Summit Conference*, p. 4; Conférence de Pompidou," March 16, 1972, pp. 17–20.

106. *PEF*, July–Dec. 1971, p. 162.

107. Conférence de Pompidou," March 16, 1972, p. 21.

108. Interviews, Paris, September 1972.

lateral communications and exchanges between France and the Soviet Union—was the Gaullist slogan of "détente, entente, and cooperation." The latter was struck for different purposes and aimed
at developing a different alignment of states in Europe than that
which inspired the European policy of the Pompidou administration.

There is little to add beyond what has already been covered regarding the Eastern policy of France under the Fifth Republic.[109]
De Gaulle's détente policy was not so much abandoned as it was
subordinated to a newly manifested French interest in building and
participating within a larger West European grouping. The shift,
already anticipated in the Soames affair, was logical enough since
Germany and the United States assumed, not always in harmony with
each other, Western leadership of the détente process. Pompidou's
France, whatever its reservation about Germany's independent initiatives in Western Europe, was consistent in supporting the Brandt
government's *Ostpolitik*. The German treaties with the Soviet Union
and Poland, signed in 1970, and the accord between the two Germanies initialed two years later were welcome even if they were
reached through German enterprise, without France playing a significant interlocutory role. Along with the four-power accord on
Berlin of September 1971, these agreements were tantamount to a
formal liquidation of the Cold War in Europe. France's secondary
role in their formulation, quite aside from the notable contribution
of the de Gaulle regime to the larger détente process, was a source
of smoldering anxiety within the Pompidou government.[110] But, after
all, a major feature of de Gaulle's European policy was to promote
German reconciliation with its Eastern neighbors. It should not have
been too surprising, following Gaullist admonitions, that Germany
would do so itself rather than through an intermediary. In the foreseeable future, France could not ask for much more than a Germany
reconciled, at least temporarily, to its own division.

On the other hand, France continued to assert its four-power rights
to preserve what little legal leverage it still possessed over Germany's

109. See above Chapter 3, pp. 146–162; Chapter 6, pp. 316–325; Chapter 7,
pp. 350–375.
110. Interviews, Paris, February 1970 through August 1971; also September 1972.

future.[111] Germany's ability to play West against East Europe, should it be so inclined in the future, would be constrained. In stressing the multilateral commitments of the Rome and Paris treaties and in appealing to the community responsibilities of the Nine, Pompidou's France worked more consistently than de Gaulle's to ensnare West Germany into a network of legal, moral, and political agreements that would bind it closer to its West European partners. Completing the regulation for agriculture was the first major step. Here, Pompidou and de Gaulle were in lock step. Permitting Britain's entry was the second. Bonding Bonn to a French-defined monetary and economic union was the third. These latter two initiatives, as the discussion above indicates, were innovations of the Pompidou years. They also gave further evidence of French interest in greater multilateral decision and action that, over time, did not preclude the possibility of increased supranational controls over the member states of the community. The agenda for discussion of union was widened, even if concrete institutional mechanisms remained to be fashioned.

Greater accord on the United States security role in Europe and on Britain's participation in the EEC aligned France and Germany more closely than ever before—and within a larger European grouping. Chancellor Brandt was a willing partner, eager, like Pompidou, to seize the West European banner, as much to promote narrow national interests and enhance his own domestic political position as to demonstrate, not totally disingenuously—as much as one can surmise from the public record—an attachment to a larger community interest. It seemed altogether fitting that Chancellor Brandt should have presented President Pompidou with a Max Ernst painting on the latter's sixtieth birthday that fell during one of the two annual state meetings between the two leaders under the 1963 treaty. Like the multiplicity of bewildering lines and points marking Ernst's work, the French-German reconciliation was to be similarly built toward a culminating vision or ideal that itself could not be fully foreseen and that was quite apart and beyond the specific lines and points of accord composing the relationship. Only time would tell if enough political determination would be present on the part of both nations

111. *Le Monde*, Oct. 12, 1972, p. 1.

and whether domestic pressures and international circumstances would favor an enlarging alignment leading to European confederation. Germany's division and the maintenance of the Soviet imperial system still posed formidable political obstacles to the realization of such a grouping. The referendum of April 1972 and the legislative election of March 1973 afforded little comfort to supporters of greater West European cooperation.

Toward Eastern Europe, the Pompidou regime attempted to straddle the de Gaulle policy that searched for a special relation with the Soviet Union and a more cautious posture that hedged against the risks of such a bilateral relationship, where Paris would be the stalking horse of Moscow, by strengthening French ties with the states of the North Atlantic and Western Europe. The Soviet Union had been quite adept since the Czech invasion in pursuing a strategy of dividing diplomatic labor within the Warsaw Pact. By relying partially on its clients as bargaining agents, the Brezhnev regime was able to extract political concessions from Western states that Khrushchev's overbearing and blustering diplomacy had failed to produce. This was to turn Gaullist doctrine against France.[112]

President Pompidou's France transformed de Gaulle's Eastern policy by placing it within a global and regional framework with a more defined Western cast. The number and pace of economic, technological, industrial, and cultural exchanges between France and the East European states continued. These channels of communication and cooperation were, indeed, deepened after de Gaulle's parting.[113] Progress could even be detected with those states, like Poland, where relations had lagged before.[114] Like de Gaulle, the Pompidou government was cautious about managing the détente process in Eastern Europe to preclude too precipitate a loosening of Soviet-East European ties, like the Czech spring, that might undo the glacially developed improvement in East-West relations in Europe. This caution marked France's approach to the preliminary Helsinki negotiations

112. Whetten, *Germany's Ostpolitik, passim.*
113. These are listed in the chronologies of the semiannual publication, *Politique étrangère de la france.* See also President Pompidou's evaluation of French-Soviet relations, *Le Monde,* Sélection hebdomadaire, Jan. 11–17, 1972, p. 5.
114. *Le Monde,* Oct. 7, 1972, pp. 1–2.

surrounding the convening and development of the European Conference on Security and Cooperation. The Paris summit of October 1972 did not raise the issue to a matter of joint accord. Cooperation was largely confined to the circulation of working papers among the member states within the terms of the Davignon plan to have periodic meetings of the foreign ministers of the European community. The Nine were able, however, to agree on proposing an agenda for the Helsinki meeting.[115]

Vestigial remains of Gaullist objections to bloc politics also appeared to play a part in Pompidou thinking although how much would be difficult to say with accuracy. The French could not easily push a West European position at the Helsinki meeting. To achieve the effect of a common position without obvious embarrassment and at a cost of arousing a wary Kremlin, French diplomacy under Pompidou stressed the political, cultural, and economic, not security, aspects of West European unity, while in other forums, like the WEU Assembly and the National Assembly, greater community efforts in defense were urged.[116] The Pompidou government succeeded in tempering previous Soviet hostility to the Brussels grouping, which had been viewed as a cover for United States imperialism and German revisionism. While France retained a right to develop its own trade and economic relations with the Soviet Union, it agreed to cooperate in defining a common commercial policy toward the East.[117] The Paris summit authorized work to commence on such a plan.[118] At the same time, France and the Soviet Union worked toward completion of a ten-year economic accord. Harmonizing these conflicting imperatives would be one of the critical tests of the Pompidou regime's successor in reconciling a Gaullist past, rooted in national concerns for autonomy, with France's future need for cooperation with its European neighbors.

115. *Ibid.,* Jan. 7, 1973, p. 5.
116. See Chapter 3 above.
117. *Le Monde,* Sélection hebdomadaire, Jan. 11–17, 1972, p. 5.
118. "La Communauté européenne après le sommet de Paris."

PART III

FRENCH INTERNATIONAL POLICY
IN THE THIRD WORLD:
NORTH AFRICA AND
THE MIDDLE EAST

9

From the Algerian Revolution to a Revolution in World Politics

The Third World in the Gaullist Global Setting

Identifying French and Third World interests and aspirations was critical to the Gaullist attack on superpower rule. Over time, with the rise of a strong China of continental proportions, the Third World might be called into play to balance the United States and the Soviet Union in the Old World. Realignment efforts were flawed, however, as long as France retained any remnants of empire. Keeping Algeria and Black Africa in colonial status compromised the force of Gaullist France's criticism of superpower hegemonic pretensions; it diluted, too, its appeal to the developing states to enlist in the French-led resistance movement to American and Soviet pressures and blandishments. The origins and mandate of the Fifth Republic hardly eased its task of reorienting France's Third World posture. The Gaullist regime was charged by its principal progenitors—a mutinous professional army corps—to preserve, not dissolve, the empire.

Colonies had outgrown their usefulness. They were an increasingly intolerable burden for the French nation and an insurmountable obstacle to the realization of de Gaulle's global aims. Twelve years of bitter colonial fighting, sustained by enormous losses in French blood and treasure, testified to the determination of colonial peoples to govern themselves. Foreign wars polarized domestic opinion. Devastated by invasion, disillusioned in defeat, and distracted by reconstruction, the French were increasingly divided against themselves: neither willing to support an empire, nor prepared to rid themselves of old habits or outdated notions of a world role whose validity depended on foreign possessions. Meanwhile, the economic costs of colonies exceeded their benefits, and the gap widened with each passing year. Compelled to use force to pacify rebellious foreign populations, French self-esteem and stature abroad inevitably deteriorated.

Lacking credibility, attempts to expand France's influence among the developing states, such as the Fourth Republic's plan to share North African resources, proved abortive from the outset.

The delicate task confronting the Gaullist Fifth Republic was to marry necessity with a national opportunity: to inter the remains of French empire and create a new image and source of influence among the developing states while avoiding its predecessor's unfortunate fate. The objectives served by colonialism would still largely be honored— *grandeur*, security, economic gain, cultural radiation, a sense of universal mission, and moral vindication. However, the modalities by which these aims were to be achieved were transformed by the rise of the Third World, Western Europe's economic and political regeneration, and superpower nuclear stalemate. These structural changes in world politics created opportunities for maneuver if France's colonial past could be shaken.

The rise of a host of nation-states in the Third World played to the strong ideological suit of Gaullist foreign policy. In its campaign against imperial America, France posed as the champion of national independence. Its own seeming emancipation, whatever the real circumstances of American domination may have been, was advanced as a model for emulation. Gaullist policies were partly premised on the assumption that this image would be turned to France's advantage once its colonial burden had been lifted. Encouraging national centrifugal forces, while perhaps risky for international order, inevitably complicated superpower rule and created opportunities for French initiative and leadership.

These visionary possibilities were also enlisted in de Gaulle's promotion of France's particular interests with Third World states. While Gaullist rhetoric kept France's bond with its self-assumed global responsibilities, French diplomacy scratched for privileges and concessions from Third World states. Not surprisingly, it concentrated its attention in North Africa, the Middle East, and Black Africa where France had traditionally exercised significant influence. Gaullist France could claim to be both revolutionary (opposed to big-power rule) and revisionist (possessed of a special right, founded on nuclear weapons and traditional and legal precedents, to global leadership and an elevated status among nations). It could be selfless and self-interested without fear of logical inconsistency or political hyprocrisy. The systemic interests of Third World states and those of France were portrayed as congruent. For de Gaulle, strengthening France's role in world politics, as Chapter 1 suggests, was tantamount to bolstering efforts to resist superpower domination. The argument had ideological attraction. Some states, like Tunisia, even appeared ready at times to go beyond lip-service support of Gaullist claims. The posturing was less than convincing, as the discussion below of the Algerian case makes clear, when the record of France's bargaining with Third World states is examined.

France's relations with the states of North Africa—Algeria, Tunisia, and Morocco—and response to the Middle East wars of 1967 and 1973 illustrate this dualism most pointedly. Relations with the states of these areas will form the basis for the discussion of France's approach to the Third World in this and in the next chapter. Under the de Gaulle and Pompidou regimes, France's experience in these regions suggests the difficulties faced by a middle-range power in its attempt to develop a viable position in the Third World that simultaneously advanced its particular interests and afforded an outlet for its leadership ambitions. Out of its manifold bilateral ties with the Mediterranean states—security, economic, diplomatic, and cultural—Gaullist and Pompidou France sought not only to make advantageous gains that drew on the special circumstances of each state, such as Algeria's oil, but to forge from these relations a larger global or, at least, regional role appropriate for the postcolonial era. From this perspective France's position on the North-South axis is viewed largely as a means to an end. It potentially offered leverage in the East-West struggle, placing France accordingly in a more competitive position in the Third World among the other developed states.

Altruistic motives should neither be entirely discounted—nor exaggerated. There exists evidence of a genuine concern in French foreign policy for the depressed conditions of Third World life, and especially for the peoples of its former dependencies. There was a general feeling among many groups, in and out of the government, that France owed her colonies a better fate, for example, than that of the Belgian Congo. Below the surface of high moral purpose, moreover, was the sentiment shared by many French, whatever its validity in fact, that France's *protégés* were better prepared—*mieux élevés*—for independence than those of their competitors. There were benefits to be drawn from this claim, too, in jockeying for position among the developing states. Finally, there was agreement, as the Jeanneney report recognized,[1] that political independence did not relieve the chronic economic and even cultural dependence of the new states on their former masters. France's extensive aid program, commenced under the Fourth Republic and continued under the Fifth, responded in part to these varied concerns.

Even if the carefully weighted figures furnished by OECD are used, France's aid effort compares favorably with those of the other leading Western industrial states and Japan. It ranked second only to the United States in the total amount of public resources granted to less-developed countries. In 1968, France spent $855 million compared to $3,314 million for the United States. This sum was $300 million more than West Germany and twice as much as Great Britain. In 1968, French public development assistance expenditures represented .68 percent of GNP, the highest of the OECD countries. The American figure for the same period was .41 percent; West Germany and Great Britain reached .45 percent and .42 percent, respectively.[2]

The number of individuals occupied in technical assistance programs also provides a measure of the relative generosity and size of French contributions abroad. In 1968, France had 42,613 personnel engaged in technical and cultural assistance. If the United States, with 29,109 effectives in this field is excluded, France's total exceeded all other OECD countries combined. France stood second to the United States in the number of students and trainees. In 1968, the French total was approximately 80 percent of the American level of 20,855.[3] However, the French financial and technical assistance program was also in secular decline in relation to GNP, a trend then reflected in the statistics from other OECD states. During the 1960's, France's financial assistance program declined from a high of 1.38 percent in relation to GNP to the 1968 low. Most of French aid, like that of its other OECD members, was bilateral and closely tied to specific French foreign policy and economic interests. French planning goals

1. La Documentation Française, *La Politique de coopération avec les pays en voie de développement*, Paris, Nov. 1964.
2. Organization for Economic Cooperation and Development, *Development Assistance, 1969*, p. 308.
3. *Ibid.*, pp. 320–325.

for the 1970's (based on measures that inflate the amount of actual flows of aid abroad) envisioned expenditures approaching 1 percent of an enlarging GNP.

But it was the Third World as a means to larger global purposes that was a significant feature of Gaullist Third World policy. The de Gaulle government recognized from the outset that the result of the East-West struggle, and France's influence upon it, would depend increasingly on the relations between the industrial states and the underdeveloped world. The expansion of the Cold War in the 1950's and its increasing tendency to shift in focus to the Third World made this inevitable. French policies toward the Third World tended to fall into three periods that roughly paralleled the pattern of relations toward the Atlantic Alliance and Europe. The first, from 1958 to 1962, was focused on freeing the Black African states, a relatively easy task, and on ending the Algerian War. De Gaulle understood that France's margin of maneuver in the Atlantic Alliance and in Europe as well as the Third World hinged on the completion of decolonization. Algerian independence was the principal problem. The resistance of important sectors of French public opinion and especially the army, which had borne the burden of maintaining the empire, was the major stumbling block. The task facing the de Gaulle government was to reconcile or isolate these groups and to convince the nation that, in the absence of France's withdrawal to the hexagon, there would be little chance of preserving its influence and interests in the Third World. Moreover, de Gaulle had come to accept the view that unless the European states interred the remaining vestiges of colonialism, they ran the risk of forcing the new states into the Soviet or American camp. The unity displayed at Bandung in 1955 by the emerging states left a deep impression on de Gaulle. This added another dimension to the Algerian rebellion; the problem was to end the war and still retain close relations with an independent Algeria resistant to Soviet (and American) enticements and threats and responsive to West European and, specifically, French influence.

From 1962 to 1968 Gaullist policy toward the Third World moved to the offensive. It proceeded along two not entirely compatible lines. First, Gaullist France, no longer preoccupied after 1962 with the Algerian rebellion or with army insurrection, opened a crusade in the Third World against the hegemonic rule of the superpowers. It attempted to establish an interlocutory role between the developed Western states and the Third World, paralleling its search for a similar role between the Atlantic Alliance and the Warsaw bloc states in Europe. The newly created states were alerted to the dangers of being drawn into the Cold War conflict or becoming indentured to the United States and the Soviet Union. They were encouraged to follow France's increasingly neutralist lead in the global struggles and to develop either closer ties with France and Europe, as a substitute for superpower dependence, or to nurture contacts among themselves beyond superpower dictate or influence. Gaullist France projected a revolutionary image of itself as a Western liberal state prepared to deal with any other state, whatever its regime. Algeria became the keystone of this new posture. France's close ties with its former Black African dependencies and de Gaulle's trips to the far corners of the globe, including Latin America and French Canada, complemented the attempt to become the principal Western spokesman of the developing states.

At another level, France encouraged Third World states to resist what was pictured as growing American expansionism. On a global scale, the United States was progressively identified as the major threat to peace. France made common cause with those Third World states, particularly among the Arab nations, opposed to United States military presence and political and economic influence in Southeast Asia, Latin America, the Mediterranean, and Africa. Into the vacuum created by a United States at bay would presumably radiate the influence of an expectant Gaullist France. This posture also appeared calculated to pay added dividends in aligning France and the Soviet Union in the Third World. After the Cuban missile crisis in 1962, the Soviet Union assumed, in Gaullist eyes, the aspect of a declining force in the Cold War conflict. The setback in the Caribbean created incentives to draw diplomatic solace and sustenance from a France which was still discreetly retaining its place in the Atlantic Alliance. De Gaulle could see a reasonable prospect of advancing France's regional aims in Europe as a partial trade-off for qualified support of Soviet Third World policy. The major exception was, of course, China, which was to be an additional, delicately balanced counterweight to check possible Soviet ambitions. France's Third World and European policies would be harmoniously sewn in an embroidery—a new Bayeux masterpiece—expressive of France's global *rayonnement* and claims.

The final period of French Third World policy commenced with the 1968 crisis. For most of the de Gaulle years, France had claimed a right to exert influence in regional affairs because it was allegedly a global power. After the exposure of French weakness in 1968, Paris increasingly assumed the posture that the reverse was true. Under President Pompidou, France's regional position, especially in the Mediterranean, was accentuated. More visibly concerned with France's modest size and capacity to influence events abroad than its predecessor, the Pompidou government deflated Gaullist global hopes and softened previous rhetorical attacks on American and Soviet hegemonic rule. Post-de Gaulle France concentrated on the meticulous weaving of a web of bilateral relations with each Mediterranean power from whatever material appeared at hand in order to promote France's specific interests and to shield them as much as possible against superpower penetration.

Algeria and North Africa

Ending the Algerian War

The Third and Fourth Republics owed their lives to military defeats, respectively, in the Franco-Prussian War and World War II. The Fifth Republic arose out of the internal turmoil and incipient military insurrection surrounding the Algerian War. Begun on November 1, 1954, the Algerian War sapped the waning strength of the Fourth Republic. Successive French governments, enfeebled by interminable ministerial changes and parliamentary maneuvers, proved progressively incapable of dealing with the Algerian rebels. When the Pflimlin government came to power in May 1958, widespread fears developed that concessions would be made to the Algerian rebels; even that independence might eventually be granted. Paris' temporizing disquieted *colon* and army groups in Algeria. On May 13 open revolt occurred in Algeria, and committees of public safety were established to exercise governmental functions and responsibility. With the open collusion of army forces, pressures were applied on the government of Pierre Pflimlin to resign in favor of General Charles de Gaulle. On May 15, de Gaulle announced his availability. On June 2, the National Assembly charged him with the responsibility of formulating a new constitution and of ruling by administrative decree until a new governing regime could be instituted.

De Gaulle writes in his memoirs that he was convinced upon entering office that the only feasible solution of the Algerian War was independence. There is evidence that he had expressed this view as early as the middle 1950's.[4] However clear his policies are in retrospect, they were fundamentally ambiguous in their initial stages of application. His cryptic, "I have understood you," which he addressed to the cheering crowds of Algerians during his June trip after investiture was a master stroke of dissimulation. It gained him time to measure his opponents and to build support for his policies. His initial tasks were to assert his undisputed claim to make French policy, to establish the authority of his government, and to assure the legitimacy of the Fifth Republic. He lost no occasion to underline his personal authority. To later conspirators, like General Salan, who was the military commander in Algeria, he made clear, no less than he had to General Giraud a score of years earlier, that *"Le Ministre de l'Algérie, c'est moi."* [5] He drew sustenance from his exposure before the Algerian masses. The smashing referendum victory on the new constitution of September 28, 1958, and de Gaulle's subsequent election as president in January enhanced his personal power and strengthened the position of his government in dealing with the Algerian question. Of those votitng, 79.2 percent approved the Fifth Republic, and despite FLN pressure to boycott the election over 90 percent of those voting in Algeria consented to the new regime.[6]

De Gaulle's hesitancy was understandable enough. If independence was the eventual goal, it would have to pass through the lines of the opposition camps which had destroyed the Fourth Republic over the issue. First, there were the *colons*. They opposed any step that would lead either to more autonomy for the native population or to reforms that would equalize the positions of all inhabitants. Either road threatened their local dominance. Reforms would require sharing political power with the Muslim majority. There was the possibility, too, of European subordination to the Arab population. More auton-

4. Interviews, Paris, 1970–1971.
5. Guy de Carmoy, *Les Politiques étrangères de la France* (Paris: La Table Ronde, 1967), p. 251.
6. De Gaulle, *Discours,* III, 47.

omy weakened the veto power of the *colons* and threatened to place
their fate in the hands of the indigenous groups that they had for so
many years subjugated. As Gaullist policy slowly moved toward self-
determination as the ultimate solution for Algeria, frustrated *colons*
joined with disenchanted army personnel to form the nucleus of the
OAS, the European secret terror organization that represented the
final, desperate attempt of the *colons* and their supporters in France
to keep Algeria French.

Second, there were the non-Communist, but anti-de Gaulle, political parties. They feared for their positions and for the preservation
of republican government if the army further intruded into politics.
They vainly sought a solution to the war that would preserve Algeria's
subordination to the Metropole. Those on the Left clung to the hope
of retaining Algeria through broad political and economic reforms;
those on the Right suspected such proposals as ineffective or, to the
degree that they encouraged native demands, mischievous. Only the
Communists consistently condemned French colonialism. The governments of the Fourth Republic were more the prisoners than the
masters of these conflicting tendencies. Lacking ministerial cohesion,
the constantly changing governments of the Fourth Republic proved
incapable of pursuing a coherent Algerian policy or of defending the
regime against its domestic and foreign enemies.

Finally, there was the army. The feckless and confused handling
of the Algerian War by successive Fourth Republic governments
prompted the army command to assume an increasing role not only
in the prosecution of the war but also in the administration and politics of Algeria. As responsibilities enlarged, its political neutrality was
correspondingly compromised. To discharge its duties and to suppress
the rebellion, the army was led to make its own arrangements with
the *colons* and Muslim population. Lacking firm civilian direction and
clearly articulated political objectives for the conduct of the war, it
developed its own Algerian policy, resting on forceful rebel suppression, political reform, economic development, and the eventual integration of the European and Muslim populations. Its firm views conflicted with the indecision of Paris and the tendency of the delicate
coalitions that were struck to accede to rebel demands too readily.

Whatever the commitment of the army's leadership to reform in
Algeria, the immediate effect of its posture was alignment with the

European *colons* and cooperating Muslims in order to preserve a French Algeria. Any notion of independence was rejected as contrary to the army's self-defined mission. Independence appeared impolitic and dishonorable. It meant abandoning the Europeans and Muslims supporting the suppression of the rebellion. Thousands of Muslims had been conscripted or joined the French army in the effort to provide internal security against terrorism and to isolate the rebel forces stationed in Tunisia and Morocco. Many in army circles felt, moreover, that the war could be won if Paris were determined to press a vigorous campaign. Building on its experience in Indo-China, the army developed effective counterguerrilla tactics. The conciliatory policies of the Fourth Republic threatened to deny the army a victory which seemed close at hand, to break its pledge of protection to the Muslim and European populations, and to rob the war of its rationale, to create a security framework within which reforms could be implemented.[7]

The *colons,* the army, and the parties—each for their own conflicting reasons—placed confidence in de Gaulle to resolve the war to their satisfaction. De Gaulle's assets were his great personal prestige and his still publicly unarticulated views about Algeria. According to his defenders,[8] de Gaulle initially threw his weight behind the policy of a French Algeria more from a sense of responsibility to explore for himself the possibility of a compromise and from an awareness of the frailty of his government's position than from a deep conviction that anything less than Algerian independence could end the rebellion. In his May 19, 1958, news conference de Gaulle assumed that Algeria must remain under French control.[9] A four-point effort, consisting of economic development, political reform, forceful pacification, and the diplomatic isolation of the rebels, was early launched to

7. Excellent for their discussion of the Algerian War are the works of Ives Courrière, including *La Guerre d'Algérie: les fils de la Toussaint* (Paris: Fayard, 1969). For civil-military relations, see Jacques Fauvet and Jean Planchais, *La Fronde des généraux* (Paris: Arthaud, 1961); Merry and Serge Bromberger, *Les 13 complots du 13 mai* (Paris: Fayard, 1959); Edgar S. Furniss, Jr., *De Gaulle and the French Army* (New York: Twentieth Century Fund, 1964); John S. Ambler, *The French Army in Politics: 1945–1962* (Columbus: Ohio State University Press, 1966).

8. Louis Terrenoire, *De Gaulle et l'Algérie: Témoignage pour l'histoire* (Paris: Fayard, 1964), and Interviews, Paris, 1970–1971.

9. De Gaulle, *Discours,* III, 8.

end the insurrection. On October 3, 1958, less than a week after the referendum on the constitution, de Gaulle announced a sweeping plan for the economic development of Algeria at a cost of approximately $200 million a year. Investments in Sahara oil and gas were accelerated; oil production reached ten million tons in 1961 compared to one million three years earlier. The surface intent of the Gaullist government in these initial years was to tie Algeria and France closer together and reduce the independence drive.[10] Having a large domestic supply of oil for the first time also weighed heavily in French calculations. Private and public investment in Algeria in 1959 totaled more than $400 million.[11]

Emphasis was also placed on voting reform. The constitution provided for a single electoral college of Muslims and Europeans. Muslim women were permitted to vote for the first time. De Gaulle moved much further than the Socialist Mollet government in installing an electoral system for Algeria which could more accurately register Algerian preferences. He called attention to the Algerian support of the Fifth Republic in the September referendum and noted that for the first time Algerians and Europeans would together elect legislative deputies on November 30, municipal officers in April 1959, and senators in May. The results of the legislative election reinforced the integrationist image of the first Gaullist days in office as most of the deputies favored a French Algeria.[12]

Establishing a process to register accurately public opinion in the Metropole was no less important than in Algeria. The French public had remained more a spectator than an active participant in the Algerian drama. If it could be won to the Gaullist policy and its support authenticated in open referenda, opponents would be trapped between acquiescence or revolt. The strategy was dangerous. Using public opinion was a two-edged sword. Once won, however, it was a decisive weapon; it would not only deny a stake in the struggle to the opponents, but it was a club with which to disarm them.

Meanwhile, plans were laid to launch a vigorous attack against the rebel structure in Algeria. The drive which was begun in 1959 sought

10. Interviews, Paris, 1970–1971.
11. De Gaulle, *Discours,* III, 119.
12. Henri Grimal, *La Décolonisation: 1919–1963* (Paris: Colin, 1965), p. 372.

to identify and destroy the rebel organization in the interior, to break its ties with the liberation army in the Tunisian and Moroccan sanctuaries, to accelerate the pacification effort, and to institute a larger civic action program among the populace. By the end of 1959, de Gaulle announced a 40 percent drop in the number of rebel incidents. The Muslim population appeared more disposed to cooperate with the French army. In January, 43,400 Muslims served in the French army; at the end of 1959, the number rose to 182,000, of which 129,000 were regular troops and the remainder auxiliaries. The de Gaulle government also pledged amnesty to rebels abandoning the struggle, a move that yielded disappointing results.[13]

A concerted diplomatic campaign was also set in motion to strengthen France's international position. Reference has already been made to de Gaulle's directorate scheme that partly aimed at garnering support for his Algerian policies. Overtures were also made to Tunisia and Morocco, former French protectorates which had gained their independence in the middle 1950's. They were encouraged to believe that they could share in the development of Saharan oil and gas as part of a movement toward greater French-Maghreb unity. Aid and commercial talks were opened, and a French-Tunisian pipeline agreement was reached in late 1958. Paris indicated a disposition to redefine France's military presence in both states, including the important naval base at Bizerte. Efforts were made, too, to block United Nations discussion of the Algerian question.

Much of this diplomatic offensive failed. Neither Britain nor the United States wished to be ensnared in the North African conflict. Similarly, French efforts in the Maghreb were severely limited by the Algerian War and the presence of French troops in Tunisia and Morocco. The United Nations rejected the claim that Algeria was an internal problem. United Nations involvement in the Congo in 1960–1961 further weakened the French attempt to restrict the peacekeeping activities of the world organization and, implicitly, limit its competence to deal with the Algerian question.

This broad offensive damaged, but did not defeat, the revolution. As the war continued at great human and material sacrifice to France and at the expense of its freedom of maneuver elsewhere, especially

13. De Gaulle, *Discours,* III, 55–56.

in Europe, de Gaulle moved to implement his views on independence. As early as July 13, 1958, he acknowledged a separate Algerian personality.[14] Three months later he distinguished between the Algerian and French communities in Algeria.[15] On January 30, 1959, he conceded that the destiny of Algeria belonged to the Algerians.[16] On March 25, this destiny was still considered to be linked to France's, but the development of a "new personality" for Algeria was envisioned. How this destiny might be joined was further exposed in de Gaulle's important news conference of September 16. Three solutions were outlined: secession, *francisation* (integration or assimilation), and cooperation under which the Algerians would govern themselves, but in some kind of association with France. For the first time, the word "self-determination" was employed and a promise was made that the will of the Algerians would be expressed in a referendum as soon as the pacification effort could provide adequate security.[17] De Gaulle stated no explicit preference between *francisation* and cooperation. Only secession was scorned as an unreasonable, although conceivable, course. In de Gaulle's mind it would entail "appalling misery, frightful political chaos, generalized slaughter and, soon, the bellicose dictatorship of the communists." [18]

The FLN remained uncompromising despite furtive signs of a will to negotiate. Independence would be taken from, not granted by, France. Determined to resolve the struggle, the de Gaulle government gradually widened the scope of its definition of Algerian self-determination. In his news conference of September 5, 1960, de Gaulle came close to conceding that Algeria's future would have to be placed in the hands of the Muslim majority. "There is an Algeria, there is an Algerian entity, there is an Algerian personality. It belongs to the Algerians, through suffrage, to decide their destiny." [19] Resolution of the conflict was needed to head off internal challenges to the de Gaulle regime or outside intervention, or both.

In November, de Gaulle openly proclaimed his commitment to the

14. *Ibid.*, p. 25.
15. *Ibid.*, pp. 48–49.
16. *Ibid.*, p. 78.
17. *Ibid.*, pp. 119–122.
18. *Ibid.*, p. 121.
19. *Ibid.*, p. 239.

eventual creation of an Algerian republic. What had previously appeared to be a deliberate policy of ambiguity was presented as the realization of a preconceived plan: "Having taken the leadership of France again, I have . . . decided, in her name, to follow a new course. This course leads . . . to an . . . emancipated Algeria, . . . an Algeria which, if the Algerians so desire—and I think this is the case—will have its own Government, its institutions and its laws." [20] On November 16, a referendum was announced that posed the question of whether the government could submit a bill for Algerian self-determination. Held on January 8, 1961, the referendum overwhelmingly endorsed the measure by 75 percent of those voting in France and by 70 percent in Algeria.[21]

The referendum effectively freed de Gaulle from *colon* and party pressures. He had already weathered a *colon* attempt in January 1960 to overturn his government. Except for scattered units and individuals, most of the army remained loyal, and after a week of open opposition to the Paris government, the barricades in Algeria quietly came down. Assurances that the European population would not be abandoned mollified the army; self-determination would allegedly neither sacrifice French interests nor previous commitments. Shortly after the collapse of the barricades, those suspected of sympathy for the *colon* insurgents were, like Jacques Soustelle, eased out of office or dismissed. The army's psychological warfare units were dissolved and its political responsibilities were reduced and placed under tighter civilian supervision. De Gaulle toured army emplacements in Algeria to affirm his personal authority and spurred French units to vigorous suppression of rebel forces. Consistent with France's great power status, independence would be granted, not conceded.

Retaining army confidence was the key to de Gaulle's evolving Algerian policy. Renewed pursuit of the rebels, increased participation of the Muslim population in the political and economic life of Algeria, and repeated pledges that the Europeans and Muslims cooperating with France would be protected maintained army allegiance. All of these actions were consistent with a French Algeria. Even some form of self-determination in association with France,

20. *Major Addresses,* p. 100.
21. De Gaulle, *Discours,* III, 275.

along the line of a Black African solution, could conceivably be accepted as the basis for a new Algerian-French relation. The fear grew, however, in army circles that de Gaulle was prepared not only to bargain Algeria away but also to consign the fate of the Muslim and European populations to rebel disposition.

Dissident army officers moved against the Gaullist regime on April 22, 1961. Generals Challe, Salan, Zeller, and Jouhaud established a high command in Algeria and in cooperation with scattered army elements, particularly among the paratroops, arrested the delegate-general of the Paris government and the minister of public works. In a nationwide radio and television address on April 23, President de Gaulle publicly ordered all French troops to disobey their mutinous officers.[22] Unable to rally popular support or command French troops, composed largely of conscripts, the rebellious army officers were put in flight, driven underground into the ranks of the OAS, or placed under arrest.

The *colons* could be isolated, the army disciplined, and the parties dispersed, but the de Gaulle government could not apply decisive pressure on the rebels through military force or diplomatic maneuver. Informal and personal contacts had reportedly been made between French officials and rebels. De Gaulle had established personal contact with FLN leadership immediately upon entering office.[23] On June 25–29, 1960, representatives of the Algerian provisional government and the Gaullist government met at Melun to review the prospects of an accord. Time inevitably worked for the rebels. The referendum of January 1961 registered the desire of French public opinion to end the war. The generals' uprising reaffirmed the need for an early cessation of hostilities to control the armed forces. The possibility of outside pressure, from the United Nations or the superpowers, to intervene in the conflict still could not be excluded. Formal negotiations were opened within a fortnight of the Gaullist victory over his mutinous generals. They continued irregularly for ten months from May 1961 until March 19, 1962, when a settlement was reached at Evian. What the *colons* and army had most feared had come to pass. The French people, comforted by the hope that the guarantees writ-

22. *Ibid.*, pp. 306–307.
23. De Gaulle, *Mémoires de l'espoir,* p. 64.

ten into the Evian accord to protect the European minority would be honored, accepted this solution. The Evian referendum in April was approved by over 90 percent of those voting in France and its overseas territories.[24]

France and the New Algeria: Search for Privileged Relations

Three general considerations underlay Gaullist policy toward an independent Algeria: (1) a concern for the preservation of Fifth Republic institutions and the maintenance of the Gaullist government in power; (2) a desire to fashion from the French-Algerian relation a new image and a new leadership role for France in the Third World and, consequently, to strengthen France both on the East-West and North-South axes in global politics; and (3) a determination to establish a privileged relation with Algeria that would protect as much as possible of France's former colonial interests, particularly oil, under conditions of Algerian self-determination.

The Domestic Dimension

The Algerian War was the crucible of the Fifth Republic and the de Gaulle government. It had toppled at least four ministries under the Fourth Republic—Guy Mollet, Maurice Bourgès-Maunoury, Félix Gaillard, and Pierre Pflimlin—and destroyed the regime. De Gaulle used two mutually exclusive arguments in justifying the Evian accords: that Algerian self-determination was inevitable and that France's grant of Algerian independence was intrinsically meritorious and civilizing.[25] The April 8 referendum asked the French to affirm an action to which there was no feasible alternative. But without choice, how could there be merit? Strict logic again bowed to political necessity. De Gaulle tied the institutions of the Fifth Republic and the future of his government to public approval of his Algerian policy: "If the common-sense solution pursued here without respite for nearly four years had finally prevailed over the frenzy of some, the blindness of others, the agitation of many, it is in the first place due to the Republic, which was able to reorganize its institutions and make them function in such a way that the stability of the powers, the

24. De Gaulle, *Discours*, III, 401.
25. *L'Année politique, 1962*, p. 631.

authority of the State, the continuity of plans, are now replacing the crises, the abandonment, the helplessness, in which it previously floundered." [26]

But the need to depict the end of the Algerian War as a success played into the hands of the FLN. A tacit alignment of interest was created between the FLN and the Gaullist government—and between the FLN leadership and de Gaulle personally—that freed the Algerians to challenge French interests defined at Evian almost immediately without great fear of reprisal. Once the war was over the French government could no longer enforce its rights under the Evian accords through military force. That was tantamount to reopening the war. Left with few levers of influence over the revolutionary regime, it could protest Algerian incursions, cut off aid, freeze Algerian assets, or harass Algerians living in France. None of these instruments promised to be effective against a regime determined to complete its internal revolution.

For all its failings, there appeared to be no feasible alternative to the Ben Bella regime in 1962. The withdrawal of assistance and trained personnel, including approximately 10,662 administrators and 12,500 technical assistants and teachers, could only have worsened internal disorder.[27] There was the strong possibility, too, that the example of Castro's Cuba might be followed. Any attempt to hamper the Ben Bella regime's consolidation of power would thrust it further into the Soviet camp. Ben Bella, a medaled hero of the Soviet Union, had already evidenced a pronounced Marxist bent; Russian technicians and aid were pouring into the new nation; and the Soviet Union enjoyed a reservoir of good will for its support of the rebellion. There was also the example of Guinea, which, with considerably less resources than Algeria, had denounced its ties with France in 1958. The ease with which France granted the Black African states independence in 1960 and the close security, economic, and cultural relations between them overshadowed Guinea's departure. But if Guinea could be dismissed, Algeria could not. Its history weighed too heavily upon the French consciousness. It was too important for the global

26. *Major Addresses,* pp. 163–164.
27. Teresa Hayter, *French Aid* (London: Overseas Development Institute, 1966), p. 137.

ambitions of the French president. Its oil and economic outlets were too enticing. Its significance for French security was too compelling.

Algeria: Gateway to the Third World

Algeria appeared to be the pivot of Gaullist France's efforts to increase its access to the emerging states. It was a key communications link with North Africa, the Middle East, and Black Africa. Its Arab-Islamic culture, 130 years of contact with France, and extensive relations with Black Africa placed it in a potentially important interlocutory role among the three cultures. Its zeal and successful revolutionary struggle were an example for other dissident groups seeking to achieve rapid social change, through violence if necessary. As Jean de Broglie, Secretary of State for Algerian Affairs, said in an oftenquoted statement of November 4, 1964: "Certainly, while pursuing her policy of cooperation with Algeria, France defends certain interests and strives to counterbalance the tendency of this country to slide towards communism. But Algeria is also and especially the 'narrow door' through which we are penetrating the Third World. A falling out between France and another North African state is only a simple bilateral tension. A falling out with Algeria would go beyond the limits of Franco-Algerian relations and would peril the efforts of our diplomacy in the whole world." [28]

De Gaulle's meeting with Ben Bella just before his March 1964 trip to Mexico confirmed this view. De Gaulle made a special point of seeing Ben Bella to underline his amicable personal relations with the Algerian leader despite the mounting differences dividing their countries. It was important for the French president, on the eve of his visit to Latin America, to project the image of an excellent rapport between France and revolutionary Algeria (and between himself and Ben Bella personally) whatever the facts of the matter. Where the United States had failed in Cuba, a generous and benevolent France would succeed in Algeria.

Closely linked to Algeria, France could establish in a stroke its anticolonial credentials after decades of moral and political suffrance as a colonial power. Algeria's blessing would wash away past sins and identify France with the aspirations of the most militant revolu-

28. *L'Année politique, 1964*, p. 326.

tionary states. Franco-Algerian relations would be a model for the other industrial states to follow. Through aid and recognition of national independence—French resistance to American encroachments in Europe was relevant counterpoint—Gaullist France purported to present a long-range plan and posture for arresting the growing gap between developed and underdeveloped states. Algeria would be the key to resolving the North-South split and, covertly, to expanding French influence in the underdeveloped areas. Meanwhile, behind the façade of Franco-Algerian harmony, France would be insulated from critics who might attack its overbearing influence in the Black African states or its military intervention, as in Gabon and later in Chad, or wherever intervention might be advised.

Algeria needed no coaching in revolutionary fervor.[29] The FLN's Charter of Tripoli pledged the Algerian state to the eventual nationization of foreign property. The Cuban revolution was adopted as a model. Ben Bella made a personal visit to Cuba to establish contact with Fidel Castro and took the occasion to condemn American imperialism, little checked by his visit shortly before with President Kennedy, who, as a senator, had supported the Algerian rebellion. In international conferences the standard themes voiced by the Algerians were the denunciation of colonialism and the indispensability of revolutionary methods for social change. The Algerians assumed a visible role in the Cairo conference of nonaligned nations in 1964.[30] They successfully secured accord to have another plenary session of anticolonial states, after the pattern of Bandung, at Algiers in 1965. The meeting was, however, flawed from the start when Houri Boumedienne overthrew the Ben Bella government shortly before the opening session. The Moscow-Peking split made unity among the delegations impossible. Moderate regimes, like Bourguiba's Tunisia, were increasingly wary of supporting international assemblies that

29. An excellent summary of the first years of Algerian independence appears in I. William Zartman, "Les Relations entre la France et l'Algérie depuis les accords d'Evian," *Revue française de science politique*, XIV (Dec. 1964), 1087–1113.

30. *Annuaire de l'Afrique du nord, 1964*, pp. 160–161, published under the auspices of Le Centre de Recherches sur l'Afrique Méditerranée, Aix-en-Provence (Paris: Editions du Centre National de la Recherche Scientifique, 1965). Hereafter cited *Annuaire* with corresponding year. This is an indispensable research tool for the Maghreb.

were dominated by their enemies at home and abroad.[31] This temporary setback stifled, but did not snuff, Algerian enthusiasm for revolutionary causes. Alone among the Maghreb states it participated in the Cuban meeting of 1966 organized to concert Third World revolutionary activities around the globe.[32] Like Cuba, it afforded haven and example to revolutionary groups.

Algeria served, too, as a political bridge to Africa. Early upon gaining independence, Algeria joined the Organization for African Unity (OAU) and attempted to instill a revolutionary consciousness into the group. The good offices of the OAU were accepted to resolve the Algerian-Moroccan border dispute which had led to military clashes. The Algerians encouraged efforts within the OAU to support revolutionary groups working against Portuguese colonialism and the white supremacist states of Rhodesia and South Africa. Relations with Great Britain were broken over Rhodesian independence in 1965.[33]

The Boumedienne regime focused its attention on arranging a marriage of convenience between Arab and Black African states against Israel, a policy thrust that an ambitious France under de Gaulle could not ignore. In return for support against Portugal and South Africa, the Black African members of the OAU were urged to side with the Arabs. These matchmaking attempts met initially with meager results as the Black African states were reluctant to choose between their Israeli and Arab suitors and displayed no interest in being drawn into their quarrels. Algeria's disenchantment was expressed in its boycott of the Congo summit of 1967 despite the skillful maneuvering of Mauritania's Ould Daddah to guide OAU assembly approval of a resolution inviting Israel's retreat from Arab territory. The Algerian campaign to bring Arab and Black African states together finally bore fruit in November 1973, when a special session of the OAU, called at Algiers' behest, supported the Arab position in the Yom Kippur War by an overwhelming majority. In repayment, the Arab states were expected to assist the states south of the Sahara in their struggle with white Portugal and South Africa.[34]

31. Ibid., 1965, pp. 210–211.
32. Ibid., 1966, pp. 280–281.
33. Ibid., 1965, p. 209.
34. Ibid., 1967, pp. 338ff. Le Monde, Sélection hebdomadaire, Nov. 15–21, 1973, p. 1.

For the de Gaulle regime, moreover, the Algerians appeared to synthesize the dynamic tendencies of Arab politics: Islamism, Arabism, nationalism, and socialism. Islam was a force in Algerian daily life. Despite Algeria's revolutionary rhetoric, traditional practices, such as the restrictions on women appearing in public places, were respected.[35] For the Algerians, the Palestine problem and the creation of the state of Israel were cast in the terms of a struggle of the progressive Arab states (and national liberation movements everywhere) against Western imperialism and, specifically, perceived American expansion. As one observer has remarked about Algerian ideology: "The struggle with Zionism and imperialism over Palestine was but one battle in a larger war against capitalism and imperialism—the proven enemies of Third World independence and socialism." [36] From this point of view, the Algerian search for national self-identity became partly but importantly defined by the global tension between socialist and capitalist ideologies. The Algerian revolution was justified as a national struggle for Muslim self-expression and as an instrument of Arab unity and socialism. As long as it could retain Algeria's confidence, a progressively more difficult goal in the 1960's, France could strengthen its prestige, if not influence, in intramural Arab politics.

In improving France's standing on the North-South axis, the Franco-Algerian alignment was calculated to reinforce France's position in the East-West struggle between the superpowers. Both France and Algeria agreed on condemning United States involvement in Vietnam and resisting American penetration of the Middle East. France could be portrayed as the only progressive Western state and enjoy a privileged position among the Western powers in competing for Third World favor. Algerian neutrality, like France's, was bent toward the East. Algerian revolutionary preachments and efforts to reorder Third World relations in favor of more radical reformist regimes struck a responsive chord in Gaullist desires to revise great power relations. For different reasons and from different perspectives, both states shared a global revolutionary interest. While France did not explicitly

35. Edward Behr, "Algeria," *Newsweek,* European edition, July 20, 1970, pp. 14–17.
36. Richard A. Roughton, "Algeria and the June 1967 Arab-Israeli War," *Middle East Journal,* XXIII (Autumn 1969), 433–444.

encourage Algerian export of revolution, it did nothing publicly to temper incendiary pronouncements that were aimed at the Anglo-American states, though it is highly doubtful that it would have been successful if it had tried.

Algeria also provided a useful testing ground for Soviet-French differences on the long-range trend in interstate relations. The French emphasized the lasting force of nationalism; the Soviets insisted on the gradual transformation of international politics through wars of national liberation, leading to the eventual victory of socialism. De Gaulle rejected the notion of a coherent evolution toward a homogeneous bloc of socialist states. In its relations with Algeria, Gaullist France asserted a willingness to cooperate with any state, no matter its regime or the crimes attributed to it. The test always, as the Evian accords made abundantly clear, was the mutual self-interest of the states. The French rested the hope for détente in Europe on improving relations with individual socialist states and, more particularly, with the Soviet Union; global détente was to be placed on a similar basis. Algeria was to be the key to Gaullist strategy that sought to accelerate the centrifugal force of nationalism operating in the Third World to the detriment of the superpowers and, simultaneously, to increase its relative power through reciprocal reinforcement of its positions on the North-South and East-West axes.

French-Algerian Special Interests: Evolution to 1968

The most striking feature of the Evian accords was that they were obsolete from the moment they were reached. They ended military hostilities between France and Algeria, but they neither resolved conflicts of interest nor went very far toward defining the common interests between the two states. The document was conspicuously silent on Algeria's view of its political objectives as an independent state. These awaited the creation of the Algerian state and the outcome of the power struggle between rival factions in the FLN leadership. Those French interests that were defined were responsive more to the larger global objectives of the de Gaulle government and to the internal necessity of maintaining his regime in power than either to the views of the *colons* and their Metropole and army supporters or to Gaullist critics among the parties who could not be reconciled either to keeping or freeing Algeria. The Algerians did not view Evian as the end of the struggle. It marked more a change in the means by which the conflict would be fought than a resolution of the divergent interests. Instead of military threats and armed reprisals, the struggle moved to the level of tortuous diplomatic maneuvering, veiled threats, bombast, and hard bargaining behind the scenes. For military campaigns and reprisal raids, France substituted threats to cut or diminish its aid; for terrorist incidents, the Algerians unilaterally revised specific French rights, private and public, or broadly hinted that France's privileged position might be terminated. The Algerians rationalized their exactions from the French as little enough compensation for years of exploitation.

The Algerians learned their French lessons well. State interests justified Algerian incursion on French interests. Evian itself had raised the trading process to the level of moral virtue. "The relations between the two countries will be founded," the Evian document observed, "in mutual respect of their independence, *on the reciprocal exchange of benefits and the interests of the two parties.*" [37] The Algerian leader Ben Khedda had similarly placed French-Algerian relations on the basis of mutual self-interest: "The cooperation that the state of Algeria will establish with France will be founded on the equality and the mutual respect of the sovereignty of the two states as well as *on the reciprocal advantages and interest of the two nations.*" [38] From the Algerian point of view, the Evian pledges tended to be reduced to bargaining points. These written concessions served the function of quieting French public and press opinion and of disarming critics. The stipulations of the Evian accords that would actually be executed would largely depend on the rival pressures that each state could apply to the other end, concomitantly, on the reciprocal perception of each of how much one side valued its relation with the other.

The transition to Algerian independence proved more difficult for both states than the signing of the Evian agreement suggested. Animosities still smoldered below the surface of French political life.

37. Ambassade de France, Service de Presse et d'Information, *Texts of Declarations Drawn Up in Common Agreement at Evian, March 18, 1962, by the Delegations of the Government of the French Republic and the Algerian Liberation Front,* p. 7. Hereafter cited *Evian.* Emphasis added.

38. *L'Année politique, 1962,* p. 630. Emphasis added.

Each Algerian violation of the peace document brought renewed criticism from opponents to de Gaulle's Algerian policies and anguished claims of self-justification for the lost cause of a French Algeria. De Gaulle could hardly let Algeria go. Vindication of his personal leadership and France's global mission significantly depended upon the success of the postwar relations. There were also concrete interests to protect—oil, diplomatic access, military bases, commercial advantages, financial assets in Algerian institutions, and cultural pre-eminence—and the French citizens to harbor. Breaking cleanly with Algeria would have placated only those elements who still refused to accept an Arab Algeria; it would have been an admission that they were right. Retributive measures might have yielded temporary solace, but also taken away hope of establishing a viable bargaining relation with the former principality. Abandonment would have left Algeria to its own devices and sparse means. This fate was not without moral reproach. It would have also opened the way to foreign intervention, which was one of the driving forces leading to a settlement in the first place.

All of these concerns joined to keep Algeria at the center of French attention in the years immediately following the Algerian War. Fascination with Algeria, however, had a number of conceivably avoidable adverse effects. It narrowed France's base among the Arab states. Partly by choice, partly by circumstance, France relinquished some of its position among the moderate Maghreb states of Tunisia and Morocco despite their affinity for French culture and their attraction to the political leadership of Paris. France also concentrated a heavy proportion of its aid on Algeria and neglected its interests in other regions. This made it vulnerable in North Africa and the Middle East. Since ties with Algeria were sensitive to significant, unpredictable shifts, France's position on its southern flank was made weaker and more precarious. Its moderating role in intra-Arab politics and in the Arab-Israeli conflict was reduced. The French, moreover, were drawn progressively into competition with the Soviets for Algerian favor that the Algerian leadership made little secret of encouraging.[39] The Algerians were aware of their value to the French and traded with increasing skill upon it. The price of Algerian cooperation mounted each year. The French interests embodied in the Evian accords were gradually—and sometimes quite abruptly—redefined to provide greater freedom for the Algerian regime at home to deal with the Muslim and European populations as it chose and to exact even greater material benefits from Paris.

Even as Gaullist France was straining and rupturing its Atlantic and European ties to gain greater freedom of action, it was, not without irony, narrowing its margin of maneuver in the Third World by tying itself closely to Algeria. As the 1960's unfolded, both states would come to the painful conclusion that too close a relationship was suffocating; that each had much to gain from a broader set of foreign relations in the Mediterranean and beyond. But first let us turn to the transition period from dependence to interdependence.

The Sacrifice of Personal Rights

The Evian accords sought to protect the personal safety and property of the European population and of those Algerians who had cooperated with France during the rebellion. They were of little avail. French nationals disappeared or were detained without charges. Thousands of *harkis* (Algerians who had served in French military units) were killed, harassed, or rendered propertyless.[40] The right of French Algerians to participate equal to their number in national and local politics was ignored, and the Court of Guarantees and the Safeguard Association that were to protect French personal rights were never placed into effective operation.[41] Patrimonial rights were often breached;[42] the free circulation of persons and goods was restricted; exchange controls were gradually instituted; and French Algerians were forbidden to leave the country without first securing a certificate attesting to the discharge of their tax obligations.[43] Private property was either placed under tighter Algerian control or nationalized. On May 9, 1963, the Algerian government placed all categories of agricultural, commercial, and industrial private property under state protection. Under this decree the three remaining

40. *L'Année politique, 1963*, p. 195.
41. Jean de Broglie, "Quarante mois de rapports franco-algériens," *Revue de défense nationale*, XXI (Dec. 1965), 1834.
42. *Ibid.*, p. 1835.
43. *L'Année politique, 1963*, pp. 201–202; Zartman, *op. cit.*, p. 1100.

French daily newspapers were nationalized in contravention of the Evian insistence on freedom of expression. Lands or property which were found to be vacant (*biens vacants*)—or forcefully vacated— were transferred to worker committees for disposition. Even this fiction was to give way quickly enough to outright expropriation of all foreign lands in decrees issued in March and October 1963. The crops of many foreign cultivators were seized. In conjunction with these nationalizations, the Algerian government restricted the right of access of French nationals to Algerian courts for indemnification or relief of alleged violations of their rights and status.[44] These actions were taken without the consultation with officials of the French government that had been provided for by the Evian decisions. Nationalizations and increased property controls, through taxation or government regulation, continued through the remaining years of Gaullist rule. All mining activities were nationalized in May 1966. A year and a half later, Algerian banks were granted a monopoly of all financial transactions.

The French government's response to these infractions was timid and circumspect. It succeeded in securing Algerian acceptance of the principle of indemnification, but was unable to derive much practical effect from this concession. There was also some attempt to tie French aid to the payment of Algerian debts, but the Algerians successfully resisted this effort, notwithstanding the close relation indicated by the Evian accords between Algeria's guarantee of private personal and property rights and French assistance. The French government appeared paralyzed by these successive attacks on the personal status of French citizens in Algeria. The Gaullist regime sympathized with the Algerian claim that it had a sovereign right to deal with its nationals as it wished and that treaty obligations were subject to reinterpretation when they conflicted with state interests. De Gaulle was to display the same logic for entirely different purposes in his unilateral revision of French commitments within NATO in 1966.

That Gaullist policy toward Algeria should have moved in counterpoint to its movements in Europe and in the Atlantic was partly explained by the considerations already discussed and by the special interests it wished to advance. The Paris government, as one observer

44. *Ibid.*, p. 1095.

remarked, "did not care to open a grave crisis in its relations with
Algeria and to compromise what for her remained essential: . . .
the atomic experimental centers, the oil interests, the cultural and
technical cooperation, and, in a general way, the role that Algeria
play[ed] in African politics." [45] And foremost among these was oil.

Oil: A Bond and Source of Friction

The larger Third World role that France assigned Algeria rested
critically on oil. Oil touched every important aspect of French-
Algerian conflict and cooperation. The Gaullist government gave impetus to the long-held French aspiration to become a major oil-
producing country, like the United States and Great Britain, and to
develop sources of supply that minimized dependence on other states.
Extensive investments were encouraged in Algerian oil, estimated at
1 percent of the world's reserves. These totaled more than $1 billion
at the signing of the Evian accords,[46] which confirmed France's privileged oil concessions in Algeria. The Saharan oil regulations published under French rule and the property rights of French oil companies were recognized. New concessions were to be granted to
French companies over foreign competitors on bids of equivalent
value. The companies were permitted to dispose of their profits as
they chose and to be exempt from currency regulations and restrictions on the free flow of capital.

These concessions were attacked almost immediately after the
proclamation of Algerian political independence. Making no secret
of its long-term intention to nationalize the oil and gas industry, the
Algerian government obliged French oil companies to keep 50 percent of their receipts in Algeria and place them under tighter exchange control and review. In September 1964, the Algerian government inaugurated the construction of a third pipeline under
contract with a British firm.[47] This action ran counter to previously
observed rules protecting the right of French mining companies to
transport oil without interference or pressure from the Algerian
state.

The 1965 oil agreement attempted to place relations with Algeria

45. *L'Année politique, 1963,* p. 204.
46. *Annuaire, 1965,* p. 69.
47. *L'Année politique, 1964,* pp. 325–326.

on a new and firmer base that would protect French interests and promote French global objectives. From this dual perspective, the pact was more than a simple commercial contract for oil. First, it was signed by two governments. This formula facilitated the extension of greater financial benefits to Algeria than would have been possible under a normal commercial agreement. Still inexperienced in oil dealings and greatly influenced by collectivist thought, the Algerians preferred to deal with a government agency rather than with a private corporation. Second, France underwrote Algeria's sale of oil at prices higher than those prevailing in world markets. The French agreed to buy Algerian oil for fifteen years at a fixed price, which at least one estimate placed as high as 65 percent above that paid by Germany for oil. At the same time, production costs of firms operating in Algeria were higher than those in Middle East countries or in Libya where the wells were near ocean depots. For tax purposes, a reference price of $2.08 a barrel was established as the base upon which Algeria would calculate its revenues. Third, a series of agreements were reached to foster Algerian demands that sought to expand national control over mining, oil, and gas resources and to tie their exploitation to Algerian modernization and industrialization. A joint French-Algerian company was to undertake new exploration. Eighty percent of these efforts were to be paid for by France, but profits deriving from new discoveries were to be equally divided.

France agreed to provide an additional billion francs—about $200 million—in assistance over a five-year period under the terms of the July 1965 accord on oil. This sum was to be made available in annual 200 million franc slices, and was to be divided into a grant of 40 million francs for Algerian industrial development and 160 million francs in soft loans at 3 percent interest and repayable over twenty years. An *Organisme de Coopération Industrielle* (OCI), governed jointly by France and Algeria, was to administer this aid, replacing the *Organisme Saharian* (OS) recognized under the Evian accords.[48] Indigenous cadres of technicians were to be formed under French direction to speed the eventual Algerian takeover of oil production and distribution.[49]

48. Hayter, *op. cit.*, pp. 133–136.
49. See *Annuaire, 1965,* for an extensive discussion of the oil accord.

The accord seemed to advance the French goal to become a major oil state and to assure a constant supply of oil at an established price, critical elements for the expansion of French industry. The agreement also served to improve France's balance-of-payments position since the transactions with Algeria, which retained important ties to the French monetary zone, would be settled in francs. By 1968, 11 percent of France's imports were for petroleum products. In 1969, Algeria supplied France with approximately 24.5 million tons of oil or approximately 30 percent of its total import needs. In decreasing its dependence for oil on the Anglo-American companies, it risked becoming increasingly dependent on its former Algerian charge.

Declining French Military Presence

Like so many of the other clauses of the Evian accords, France's military presence in Algeria was quickly revised after 1962. In April 1963, Ben Bella publicly criticized the Evian military clauses. Under Algerian pressure, France accelerated its troop withdrawals. All French troops, except for those at bases leased under the 1962 agreement, were evacuated by June 1964, approximately eight months ahead of schedule. In January and April 1964, the Algerian government asked that the French military presence be further reduced and, specifically, that the naval base at Mers-el-Kébir be vacated. By declassifying Mers-el-Kébir as strategically vital, a decision based on the importance of atomic weapons and on the decreased need for naval bases,[50] France evacuated the base a decade before its lease was to expire. Meanwhile, the bases used for atomic testing were gradually closed as French sites in the Pacific became available well before the five-year lease was up for renewal. The French continued to operate a school for Algerian pilots at Bou Sfer, and a small contingent of French military were engaged in training activities, largely with the internal security forces, and in advising the ministry of defense.

As the French military presence declined, Russian penetration increased, given impetus by the Six-Day War. In 1970, two to three thousand Russian military personnel were engaged in Algeria. Most of Algeria's military forces, including officer cadets and submarine

50. *Annuaire, 1967,* p. 154.

crews, were receiving Russian training. Some six hundred pilots and air crews were undergoing training in the Soviet Union. Almost all of Algeria's heavy military equipment was Russian-supplied.[51] The Soviets also had access to air bases in Algeria at Laghouat, Ouargla, and Ambuel. The use of the naval facilities at Mers-el-Kébir was still denied them.

The Algerians evidenced considerable sensitivity to French criticism that they were falling under Soviet political influence as a result of the Russian military presence. The Algerians expressed a desire to balance Soviet military aid with French economic predominance. They did not hesitate to criticize openly the Soviet Union for what they believed to be overly cautious support of the Arab cause. The temperate reaction of Algeria to the Czechoslovakian invasion, however, gave some weight to the French view. The question of whether the Algerians were being drawn into the Soviet orbit was complicated by the penchant of the Algerian government, whatever its professed Marxist leanings, to let contracts with American, British, and West German firms for goods and services, despite tensions with the latter over the recognition of East Germany and the rupture of diplomatic relations with the United States over the Six-Day War and with Great Britain over Rhodesia.[52] Some specialists suggested that American influence was in the long run a greater threat than Communism to French interests in Algeria.[53] Algerian behavior defies easy analysis in terms of Russian and Anglo-American spheres of influence. In 1969, Algeria ordered twenty-eight French Fouga-Magister training aircraft and fifteen Puma helicopters. These purchases offset some of its dependence on the Soviet Union for heavy military equipment.

Commerce and Finance

French interest in Algeria was also commercial and financial. In 1969, Algeria stood eighth among France's principal customers and seventh among its suppliers; France held first place in Algerian imports and exports. As Chapter 10 discusses in more detail, these trade patterns grew less important to both sides under the Pompidou

---

51. Richard Booth, *The Armed Forces of the African States: 1970,* Institute for Strategic Studies, Adelphi Paper No. 67, May 1970, p. 6.
52. *Problèmes africains et tiers monde,* No. 517, Oct. 23, 1969.
53. Interviews, Paris, Feb. 1970–May 1971.

administration. Their downtrend in the early 1970's does not change their significance for Franco-Algerian relations during the de Gaulle years. In 1969, Algeria supplied approximately one third of France's oil needs. France's position as Algeria's major supplier offset France's deficits with its former dependency and maintained its delicate balance of payments in equilibrium. Exchange was listed in francs. Moreover, Algeria's then tenuous ties with the franc zone and its accumulating franc holdings contributed to the stabilization of the franc, especially during the crisis of 1968. Although Algeria converted francs into other currencies during the financial panic—half a billion francs were changed into German marks and American dollars in 1968—it continued to hold over 600 million francs in reserve.[54] During de Gaulle's attacks on the dollar, large Algerian holdings in francs also provided additional leeway for the Gaullist campaign against American monetary hegemony.

Two problems of particular importance for French-Algerian relations concerned wine and workers. France agreed in 1964 to purchase eight million hectoliters of wine a year.[55] Pressured by wine growers in the Midi, the French government unilaterally reversed the accord. Initially, one million hectoliters were permitted to enter France. This amount was subsequently increased to four million a year. France also tried unsuccessfully to link the wine problem to the indemnification of French citizens and enterprises for Algeria's expropriations. Sale of Algerian wine to the Soviet Union at half the price paid by France did not improve relations. The Algerians retorted that the vineyards were a legacy of colonialism and that the French had an obligation to buy Algerian wine, whatever their needs.

The entry of Algerian workers into France was particularly crucial from an economic and human perspective. Many arrived without jobs, sick, homeless, and without means of support. In 1970, there were approximately seven hundred thousand Algerian workers and their families in France. Estimates placed the remittances sent by them to Algeria at $200 million a year.[56] Algeria gained in foreign exchange as its serious unemployment problem was ameliorated. The French needed Algerian labor. Algerians did jobs refused by French

54. *Annuaire, 1967*, p. 207.
55. *L'Année politique, 1964*, p. 234.
56. Interviews, Paris, 1970–1971.

workers and accepted lower wages and less desirable living and working conditions.

The growing importance of the Soviet Union in Algerian trade and economic development was a potentially threatening element in Franco-Algerian commercial relations. There were three thousand civilian Soviet technicians in Algeria in 1970 occupying posts ranging from the training of oil technicians to the construction of steel complexes. The value of trade was also steadily increasing. Accords brought trade between the two states to $125 million in 1969. This contrasted with $98 million a year before. The two countries expected trade totals to reach $200 million by 1973. The Soviet Union also contracted for 500,000 tons of oil in 1969 and up to 750,000 in 1970.[57]

The Flow of Aid Continued

Despite Algerian violations of the Evian accords and subsequent strained relations, the French government largely honored its economic, cultural, and technical aid commitments under the Evian accords. French aid in the form of grants totaled in excess of 800 million francs in 1963 and over 700 million in 1964. To these sums may be added grants of 200 and 110 million francs in each year, respectively, to compensate French farmers and enterprises for the loss of property. In these years, Algeria received almost all of French aid for the Maghreb and enjoyed assistance comparable to the entire amount earmarked for Black Africa. As Table 2 indicates, however, the long-run flow of outright grants has steadily declined. The reduction was inevitable for a number of reasons: the stabilization of the Algerian government and administration, the almost total discharge of the personnel contracts signed under the former French administration, and the redefinition and linkage of French aid to the oil accord with Algeria of July 1965.

Cultural and technical assistance also played an important role in the French presence in Algeria. The spread of French culture was an important goal of foreign policy, and support of foreign aid in France partly depended on the widely shared value of the *rayonnement* of French culture. The dissemination of the French way of life

---

57. *Annuaire, 1968*, p. 233; Guy de Carmoy, "France, Algeria, and the Soviet Penetration in the Mediterranean," *Interplay*, Oct. 1968, pp. 24–25. Later statistics are not available.

Table 2. Financial aid to Algeria, 1963–1969 (millions of francs)

Type of aid	1963	1964	1965	1966	1967	1968	1969
Economic							
Tied*	400	400	275	107.5	109	52	50
Untied	400	290	200	120	100	100	90
Support of Saharan							
Development							
Organization	30	47	57	52.5	33.5	25	20
TOTAL	830	737	532	280	242.5	177	160

Sources: Jean de Broglie, "Quarante mois de rapports Franco-Algériens," *Revue de défense nationale*, XXI (April 1965), 1834; *Annuaire de l'Afrique du nord*, 1967, *op. cit.*, pp. 332–333; *ibid.*, 1968, pp. 221–222.
* Tied aid refers to grants that must secure joint Algerian-French approval before disbursment and is usually related to purchases of goods and services in the donor country; untied aid goes directly into the general Algerian treasury and is discretionary.

and language was conceived as an important instrument for enlarging political influence and advancing economic interests abroad, notwithstanding the difficulty of accurately measuring its effects. Expectantly enough, Algeria was especially favored in cultural and technical assistance. Table 3 presents the allocated amounts for cultural

Table 3. French cultural assistance in the Maghreb, 1967–1969 (millions of francs)

	Algeria			Morocco			Tunisia		
	1967	1968	1969	1967	1968	1969	1967	1968	1969
Type of aid									
Teaching	108.0	121.0	136.0	62.0	62.0	72.0	41.0	41.0	47.0
Student assistance	1.7	1.7	1.9	2.3	2.0	1.9	1.2	1.1	1.1
Cultural activities	2.8	2.8	2.7	3.2	3.6	3.4	1.3	1.4	1.3
Artist exchanges	.4	.4	.5	.3	.3	.4	.2	.2	.2
Investment credits	1.4	1.2	–	–	–	–	–	–	–
TOTAL*	114.3	127.0	141.3	67.9	68.2	77.4	44.1	44.2	50.3

Source: Annuaire de l'Afrique du nord, 1968, *op. cit.*, p. 217.
* Distortions in totals due to rounding to nearest hundred thousand.

assistance in major categories for Algeria, Tunisia, and Morocco in the years from 1967–1969. A small but steady rise in the total amounts afforded for this activity can be discerned in contrast with the decline in financial aid. For 1969, Algeria was accorded 22 percent of the entire cultural budget or about half of the total assigned to the Maghreb. The number of French teachers totaled approximately 6,400 as of July 1, 1968.

Technical assistance, while modest, was important since it supported key personnel in the Algerian economy. In 1969, 64 million francs were earmarked for this activity as compared to 46.4 million francs in 1968 and 44 million francs in 1967. The number of technical assistants in Algerian administrative service stood at 2,371 on July 1, 1968, as against 10,000 at the beginning of 1963.

Advances of credit from the French treasury also provided needed liquidity for Algeria. These were especially important in the transition period to independence. In 1962–1963, 550 million francs were accorded Algeria, and the bulk of this credit was reimbursed. Between June and November 1962, before the treasuries of Algeria and France were separated, France continued to pay for Algerian administration. During this transition phase, the Algerians overdrew their accounts in the French treasury at an estimated 2.0 billion francs. The Algerian government permitted massive amounts of capital to be repatriated to France. Between January 1962 and July 1963, 1.3 billion francs from bank accounts and 380 million francs from postal deposits were sent to Europe, mostly to French accounts.[58] The French sought to protect this flow of funds despite its harmful impact on Algerian solvency. The momentum of the Constantine plan, attaining spending levels of two billion francs a year before independence, encouraged French officials to desist from serious reprisals. The French were concerned about protecting these investments and preserving the conditions necessary for the execution of contracts with French industry and contractors already under way.

Gaullist France Confronts Tunisia and Morocco

In contrast to its Algerian policy, France showed much less patience through most of the Gaullist period with Tunisia and Morocco over the problems of decolonization and adjustment to nationhood. The de Gaulle government penalized them for actions it disapproved, while Algeria escaped retribution for more serious incursions against

58. Hayter, *op. cit.*, p. 133.

France and French citizens. Economic assistance to Tunisia and Morocco was considerably less than the millions granted to Algeria although the needs of these two countries were as urgent, and neither had oil. Their combined population exceeded that of Algeria. The number of French citizens residing in both countries was larger after 1963 than the number remaining in Algeria. The moderate foreign policies of Tunisia and Morocco, especially with respect to the Arab-Israeli crisis, and the Western orientation of both states found little encouragement in France until the end of the 1960's.

Tunisia

The Algerian War prevented any real *rapprochement* between France and Tunisia after the declaration of Tunisian independence. The Gaullist government initially attempted, as already noted, to improve relations, and a number of accords bearing on economic relations and military security were signed. With the exception of those at Bizerte, the French agreed in June 1958 to evacuate all their troops within a four-month period, and talks on France's status in Bizerte were announced. Tunisia's request to the Security Council to protect its borders against French violations was withdrawn. An important commercial accord was signed in October 1959, and President Bourguiba expressed support of de Gaulle's self-determination formula for Algeria.

These surface accords could not long hide fundamental differences over the war. Even as Tunisia was reaching agreement on the departure of French troops on June 17, it was meeting at Tunis with FLN and Moroccan representatives to agree on the basic aims of the Algerian revolutionists. On September 20, 1958, Tunisia recognized the provisional government of the Republic of Algeria, and on October 1 joined the Arab League. Relations hit a low point on July 21–22, 1961, when the Tunisian government provoked an armed attack against Bizerte. In response to street demonstrations in Bizerte against French military presence, the de Gaulle government reinforced the naval garrison with paratroops. A bloody clash ensued between French and Tunisian regulars in which more than 700 Tunisians and 27 French troops were killed.

A number of factors help explain the Tunisian decision to create a crisis—desire to improve its stature in the Arab community, to demonstrate a revolutionary zeal equal to the FLN, to assert its Saharan claims, and to reinforce the Bourguiba government's hold on the country.[59] The French government repaired to the accords of June 17, 1958, rejecting Tunisian entreaties over Bizerte and its appeal to the United Nations for help. With the end of the Algerian War, France finally agreed to evacuate Bizerte. On October 15, 1963, France's military presence in Tunisia was fully terminated.

Tunisia would have preferred better relations with France. The commercial accord of 1959 survived the Bizerte incident. Tunisia looked to the end of the Algerian War as the necessary condition for wider cultural, economic, and technical cooperation with France. It had suffered when aid was slowed and then cut off in 1957. In August 1963, accords on financial assistance and payments of Tunisian debts were again reached. These covered the resumption of aid totaling about $40 million a year. Agreement was also reached on the status of Tunisian workers in France, French investments in Tunisia, and procedures for conciliation and arbitration.[60] Additional accords were concluded in February 1964 on financial assistance to Tunisia for economic development at the 1963 figure of $40 million, and amendments favoring Tunisia were made to the 1959 commercial code for wheat and wine.[61]

These understandings were undone, however, in the spring of 1964. Tunisia proposed to seize lands identified as "colonial" and to apply new rules for indemnification of foreigners. The French government condemned these as violating the 1963–1964 accords. Propelled by financial need and Algeria's revolutionary example, the Tunisian government expropriated the foreign properties anyway. On May 11, 1964, 400,000 hectares of land, 270,000 belonging to French citizens, were nationalized, along with stock and equipment. In addition, Tunisia increased controls on the free flow of capital.

France reacted with swift, unexpected severity. Aid was severed on June 11, and the 1959 accord granting preferential commercial treatment to Tunisia was denounced. So also were the February

59. *L'Année politique, 1961*, pp. 486–493. For general reviews, see J. P. Pigasse, "Ombres et lumières sur la tunise," *Politique étrangère*, XXXIV, No. 5–6 (1969), 615–630; Victor Silvera, "L'Etat actuel des rapports franco-tunisiens," *Revue de défense nationale*, XXII (Dec. 1966), 2014–2032.

60. *L'Année politique, 1963*, p. 213.

61. *Ibid., 1964*, p. 259.

1964 amendments on wheat and wine. Some technical assistants were withdrawn. Tunisia replied by blocking French imports, but it was the larger loser since Tunisian exports to France were halved in 1964. By 1970 these had still not returned to 1963 levels which totaled 337 million francs in value.[62] Repeated Tunisian efforts to improve relations met with a cool response. France assumed the pose that it did not recognize the Tunisian expropriations as legitimate and that, consequently, it could not settle the issue simply through the indemnification of French citizens. Unlike Algeria, Tunisia was considered dispensable. Tunisia had no oil. Nor were the Bourguiba government's temperate political ideology, contrasted with the revolutionary zeal of the Algerian leadership, and its moderate stand in Arab politics congenial to Gaullist global stratagems and posturing in the Mediterranean. Deep personal differences between Presidents de Gaulle and Bourguiba, moreover, cannot be discounted as important contributing factors to the rift. After the rupture, all that remained intact of French-Tunisian relations were the cultural and technical accords. As Table 3 reveals, these were honored and have even registered modest increases in French expenditures. France's cultural penetration into Tunisia was great, and in this sector the French were intent on maintaining a foothold while allowing Tunisia to seek relief for economic aid from the United States and commercial benefits within the EEC.

Morocco

Morocco did not fare appreciably better than Tunisia in the 1960's. During the Algerian War there were repeated clashes between Moroccan and French troops. The issue of French military presence was not settled until 1961 when the last remnants of imperial rule were withdrawn. French aid was effectively suspended during the war although it had never been very extensive. Morocco was more reserved in its support of the Algerian rebels than Tunisia, but on key matters, the Moroccan regimes under Mohammed V and, after his death, Hassan II sided with the FLN. Like Tunisia, Morocco joined the Arab League in October 1958, recognized the Algerian provisional government, and opposed France in the United Nations.

62. Ministère de l'Economie et des Finances, *Statistiques du commerce extérieur de la France, 1966*, p. 30. Hereafter cited *Statistiques du commerce*.

It also attempted to mediate the conflict between Algeria and France, but without success. Incidents like the 1956 seizure of FLN leaders traveling under Moroccan auspices strained relations.

Relations continued to be thorny even after the Evian accords. In 1963, Hassan II's trip to France led to accords on a number of disputed points, including the status of Moroccan laborers, loans totaling more than $40 million, technical assistance, and the freeing of French assets blocked in Morocco. The decision of the Moroccan government, following the example of Tunisia and Algeria, to reclaim foreign lands in Morocco undid these attempts at improving relations with France. A partial indemnification for expropriated lands was settled upon in 1964, but farm equipment and stock were not included. Morocco envisioned the end of all foreign land holdings by 1968, a goal that has yet to be achieved.[63] In addition, Morocco limited capital transfers out of the country, imports, French physicians working in Morocco, and the rights of French citizens before Moroccan courts.[64]

Discord on these points was deepened over the Ben Barka affair of 1965. With the assistance of French secret police, the Moroccan revolutionary leader Ben Barka was kidnapped on a Paris street and apparently executed by Moroccan agents. A French court condemned several Moroccan citizens, including the minister of the interior, as having been implicated in the assassination. Relations were broken off between the two states. The French ambassador was recalled, aid to Morocco was suspended, and political and economic relations continued to deteriorate.

Gaullist Global Policy: No Room for Tunisia and Morocco

At least part of the explanation of France's differential treatment toward Algeria, on the one hand, and Tunisia and Morocco, on the other, appeared rooted in Gaullist global designs. In terms of Gaullist calculations, Algeria's value stemmed from its revolutionary internal and external policies. The moderate nature of the Tunisian and Moroccan regimes—the former a one-party republic, the latter a slowly modernizing but absolute monarchy—did not fit the desired image of a progressive France willing to cooperate with any regime, how-

63. Interviews, Paris, Aug. 1970–May 1971.
64. *Annuaire, 1965,* p. 202.

ever revolutionary or Marxist. The moderation of the Tunisian and Moroccan governments that should have facilitated cooperation with France had the opposite effect. More assistance to Tunisia and Morocco would have likely diminished aid to Algeria. Closer alignment with the former French protectorates would have strengthened the suspicion that French cooperation with a socialist regime was of surface value and, once tested, would terminate. It suited Gaullist France, anxious to project the image of a new North-South relation between a developed and an underdeveloped state, to be identified with the seemingly more progressive socialist measures of the Algerian government.

Neither Tunisia nor Morocco adopted Algeria's revolutionary rhetoric. Both appeared to be as much forced by Algeria's initiatives in expropriating foreign lands as persuaded that social reform could be accomplished easily through the seizure of foreign property and capital investments. French *colons* continued to operate freely in Morocco. Both states, and particularly Morocco, were more pragmatic in their approach toward economic development and more disposed to individual foreign and domestic enterprise. This attitude was of limited utility for Gaullist pretensions as a leader of the Third World in the vanguard with revolutionary and ultranationalist regimes. Gaullist France counted on Algeria to improve its East-West and North-South position. Tunisia and Morocco were temporarily less useful on an ideological level to the degree that they aligned their domestic policies on Western models even as they were castigated for having expropriated French property.

Gaullist France had other incentives, too, to permit its relations with Tunisia and Morocco to deteriorate. Rightist criticism in France that attacked the Gaullist regime for its timidity toward Algeria was offset by the forceful stands taken against Tunisia. Leftist criticism was also diluted in the condemnation of the Moroccan minister of the interior for his part in the assassination plot against Ben Barka. In both cases, France could pocket the saving from canceled aid and trade obligations. It could reasonably expect both regimes to temper their retaliation. Neither was disposed to Algerian extremism, and each eagerly sought, especially Tunisia, amicable relations with France despite repeated rebuffs. Gaullist France could draw benefit from the limits that the Tunisian and Moroccan regimes placed on themselves in much the same way that France could take advantage of the limits imposed by United States self-interest in protecting even a recalcitrant France from Soviet aggression. Finally, below the surface of these political rifts, commercial relations with Morocco could continue and the loss suffered in Tunisian trade could be tolerated, at least until the social and economic dislocations of 1968. Technical and cultural assistance, the principal means for the maintenance of the French presence, was largely insulated from these stormy political quarrels by the implicit consent of the Tunisian and Moroccan governments; this permitted France to advance its interests elsewhere while minimizing its losses in the Maghreb.

But it was at the foreign policy level that the utility of Tunisia and Morocco was most clearly discounted in the middle 1960's. In light of France's increasing alignment with the Soviet Union before 1968 and the increasing identification of the United States as the principal global threat to France's independence, the Western-oriented foreign policies of Tunisia and Morocco hindered rather than helped the Gaullist offensive against the Anglo-American powers. The liabilities of too close a relation with Tunisia and Morocco were discernable at three levels: (1) the rival conception of neutralism practiced by each of the states and its relation to Gaullist global policy; (2) the standing of Tunisia and Morocco in intra-Arab politics; and (3) the varying responses of France and its former protectorates to the Six-Day War. In contrast to Algeria, neutralism for Tunisia was more a tactic by which it sought to extract benefits from East and West than an instrument to intervene in the struggle or a measure by which to assign blame or praise to one power or the other. Under Mohammed V, Morocco had assumed a policy of doctrinaire neutralism that found temporary expression in the Casablanca group composed of Morocco, Egypt, Mali, Ghana, Guinea, and Algeria. The group fostered Moroccan designs on Mauritania and, partially in return, Morocco aligned with some of the more militant elements of the Maghreb, Black French Africa, and the Middle East. But with the accession of Hassan II, the Casablanca group lapsed, and Morocco, while not rejecting a policy of nonalignment and neutrality in the East-West struggle, encouraged Western aid and investment. The increasing Anglo-American disposition of Tunisia and Morocco conflicted with the Gaullist search for a new global balance that would offset American power. Tunisian and Moroccan brands of neutralism facilitated Anglo-American penetration of the Maghreb which had already been foreshadowed in the arms purchases made by Tunisia in the late 1950's from the United States. Tunisia's recognition of South Vietnam, furthermore, contradicted France's condemnation of the war and strengthened the American diplomatic position over the conflict.

Tunisia and Morocco also stood to the right on the political scale within the Arab world. Too close an identification with either state threatened to blur the image projected by Gaullist France of its support of Arab nationalism under the leadership of states like Egypt and Algeria and its unreserved opposition to American and British influence in the region. Tunisia had particular difficulty with Egypt and Syria over the issue of internal subversion. Relations between Tunisia and Egypt were broken over the latter's support of Bourguiba's rival, Youssef Ben Salan. They outwardly improved with Egypt's offer to support Tunisia during the Bizerte crisis of 1961. Tunisia attended the Arab summit of 1964 where the Egyptian and Tunisian heads of state met. The principle of polycentrism within the Arab camp was confirmed in yet another meeting of Arab states in 1965. In the pact signed on September 16, the Arab nations agreed to refrain from intervening in the internal affairs of each other and to respect the regimes already constituted.

This accord was, however, short-lived. In 1966, Nasser and his followers unleashed a bitter attack on Bourguiba, who had had the temerity to criticize the Egyptian president for having led the Arab states to an impasse over the questions of Arab-Israeli relations and the Palestine problem. Nasser refused to attend the Arab meeting scheduled for Algeria on July 22. Aiming his barbs at Tunisia, Nasser announced that his country could not sit "at the same table" with "reactionary Arab forces." "However," he said, "if the reactionary Arabs end their policy of alliance with imperialism against the forces of Arab nationalism and demonstrate concretely their good faith in favor of united action for Palestine, we will reconsider our position." [65] Relations between Cairo and Tunis were again broken in October 1966. Relations with Morocco also cooled with its show of

65. *Ibid., 1966*, p. 278.

interest in the scheme of Saudi Arabia's King Faisal to promote a vast Islamic grouping.[66] For tactical reasons, Tunisia evidenced interest in the proposal, which never had much prospect of succeeding.

Tunisia's audacious position on Israel and Palestine, viewed by Arab standards, further estranged it from the uncompromising elements of the Arab League. In opposing Egypt, Syria, and Iraq, President Bourguiba called on the Arab states to recognize the *de facto* existence of Israel and chided the Palestinians to self-help. Morocco proved more guarded on the Israeli-Arab split. But in trying to avoid taking sides, it was held suspect by its Arab confreres. Tunisia condemned the Israeli invasion, but equally charged that Egypt's Nasser had led the Arab states to an ignominious defeat.

Close association with Tunisia and Morocco did not appear to facilitate the Gaullist government's aim to return France to the Middle East as a regional power. The moderation of both regimes in their internal government and foreign policies, relative to the other Arab states, was out of step with the revolutionary rhetoric of self-determination marking Gaullist global doctrine in the aftermath of the Algerian War. Firm ties with either did little to improve France's image as a champion of Arab nationalism. The announced policy of neutralism and nonalignment of both states in the Cold War, but their Western bent in practice, also conflicted with the Gaullist effort to align with Soviet Third World policies even while quietly searching for ways to impede the expansion of Soviet influence in the Maghreb and Middle East. Meanwhile, France's shipment of military equipment to Israel would continue—at a modest but tidy profit.

66. *Ibid., 1966*, p. 279.

10
Reversion to Regional Revisionism: The Mediterranean

The Politics of Weakness

The Six-Day War of June 1967 forced a re-examination of French foreign policy in the Mediterranean. It confronted France with hard choices, avoided since the end of the Algerian War, at three inter-related levels. First, Gaullist France had to choose between Israel and the Arab states. Specifically, the polarization of opinion between Arab and Jew in the area made it impossible for Gaullist France to reconcile a policy of unlimited arms sales to Israel with its claim of support for Arab objectives.

Embarrassing to France was the decisive impact that its weapons had on the conflict. The French Mirage bombers used by Israel quickly achieved air superiority over the Russian-supplied arms of the Arab states and provided the key to the brilliant Israeli military victory. The Arab states, humiliated by their defeat, expected compensation. Retrenchment in Israel was the price for France's standing with the Arab states. Payment was expected not only by those countries directly engaged in the war, like Jordan and Egypt, but also by militant Arab states, like Algeria, whose intransigence often exceeded that of the belligerents themselves.

Previous moral and material commitments to Israel hampered the policy shift. Moreover, French public opinion, strongly favoring the Israeli cause, resisted any notion of abandoning Israel when foreign help was most needed. Had not Israel stood with France against "its" Arabs? Now Israel needed help with "its" Arabs. The task facing the de Gaulle and Pompidou regimes was to mollify domestic opinion, respond to Arab pressures, and still discharge some measure of France's obligations to Israel on which the preservation of its interests and influence in the Jewish state depended, not to mention what mediating role it might wish to play.[1] The recrimination and hate vented by the war hardly afforded an auspicious setting for a successful balancing of these contending forces.

Second, the war imposed choices on France between the Arab states. Insulating the Maghreb from the Middle East was rendered considerably more difficult. The war spilled over the Nile past Libya and engulfed the Maghreb to Morocco at the western outpost of the Arab world. To hold its own in the western Mediterranean and in Black Africa, France needed to develop a policy applicable to the region as a whole, yet sensitive to the enormous internal differences among the states and the rivalries between them. The Franco-Algerian relation was too uncertain a foundation on which to build France's Mediterranean policy and to protect the delicate edifice of France's extensive security, economic, diplomatic, and even cultural interests now shaken by the war. The increasing cost of maintaining France's privileged position in Algeria reinforced the argument for a widening stance among the Arab states.[2] The remedy was not without hazards. Priorities had to be set on France's interests among the Arab states, divided between traditional monarchies like Morocco and Saudi Arabia, moderate regimes like Tunisia and Lebanon, and militant governments like revolutionary Algeria and Libya.

Finally, the war seriously complicated France's relations with the superpowers. Détente in Europe was threatened. The conflict increased the possibility of superpower entry into the Mediterranean and other regions. Egyptian, Syrian, and Iraqi dependence on the Soviet Union was reinforced; Jordanian and especially Israeli reliance on the United States and Great Britain was increased. As the stock of these states rose among their clients, what France had to sell faced being ignored or discounted. The problem was to define a policy that would strike yet another precarious balance and satisfy a number of conflicting demands. It would have to be policy that would (1) maximize France's standing with as many Mediterranean

1. One survey notes that as late as February 1970, 54 percent of the French people disapproved of their government's policy toward Israel and the Middle East war. *Newsweek,* European edition, March 16, 1970, p. 17.

2. See the suggestive article of Jean Teillac, "Le Maghreb en 1968," *Revue de défense nationale,* XXIV (May 1968), 849–857.

states as possible; (2) slow the rate and minimize the magnitude of superpower penetration of the region; (3) draw advantage from the superpower conflict, including a privileged place for France at the Middle East negotiating table; (4) preserve the form and some substance of the growing alignment between France and the Soviet Union in the Mediterranean and in Europe; and (5) retain the security protection of the United States while combating American attempts to promote its competing political and economic interests to those of France's in both areas.

The crises of 1968 did not help French chances of success in achieving these clashing aims. As noted elsewhere, the May upheaval nearly overturned the de Gaulle regime. What could then be made of French claims to great-power status and how serious could Gaullist global hopes be taken? The resulting financial and economic upheaval and the Soviet invasion of Czechoslovakia exposed how much France depended on Anglo-American support for its security, economic well-being, and larger diplomatic goals. None of these unfortunate events could be said to have improved France's position or its maneuverability in the Middle East game. Indeed, the very exposure of weakness strengthened the argument already current in policy circles that something new had to be tried in the Mediterranean—and quickly.

To achieve the Herculean tasks that the de Gaulle and Pompidou governments set for France, three intertwined courses of action were followed: (1) dealignment with Israel and alignment with the Arab position in the Middle East conflict; (2) continued French assertion of a big-power role in settling the conflict and the insulation of the region from superpower contention; and (3) efforts to regroup the western Mediterranean states around French leadership. Despite an impressive number and range of initiatives, as the concluding section suggests, France's position in the Mediterranean remained essentially weak.

Dealignment and Alignment in the Middle East

The first casualty of the Six-Day War was France's tie with Israel, an alliance that had seemed enduring to many until the 1967 clash. President de Gaulle had twice assured Prime Minister David Ben

Gurion that France was Israel's "friend and ally." The pledge was reaffirmed in a private meeting with Levi Eshkol, Ben Gurion's successor.[3] Continued sale of French arms, including Mirage aircraft, gave concrete expression to these assuring words of support for Israel. Growing trade and cooperation in scientific and technological ventures, even encompassing work in nuclear development, appeared to bind the two states together.

French-Israeli cooperation had been forged in their common experience of discord with the Arab states. France had helped to establish the state of Israel. As France struggled to maintain an Arab empire to which many Frenchmen felt their destiny to be bound, so Israel battled to preserve its existence as a state. They found common cause in opposing Arab nationalism. Their cooperation reached its peak in the abortive strike against Egypt in 1956.[4] In attacking Egypt first, Israel became the spearhead of the Anglo-French expedition to topple Egypt's President Nasser from power.[5] Moreover, all through the Algerian War, Israel was one of the few voices that sustained France's beleaguered position.

Until Egypt's closing of the Gulf of Aqaba to Israeli shipping in May 1967, the limits of French-Israeli cooperation had not been fully tested. The end of the Algerian War and the final liquidation of the French empire had effectively, if not perceptibly, eroded much of the marriage of convenience that underlay the initial alignment. The rude shock of the war in the Middle East dissolved most of the remaining bonds between the two states. The possibility of global war arising from the regional conflict was apparently a genuine concern of President de Gaulle. There was evidence to support the view that the de Gaulle government feared, even before the Israeli attack, that an armed clash would promote Russian penetration of the eastern and western Mediterranean even further than they might wish to go; that the moderate Arab states would be undermined; that oil shipments, vital to French and European industry, would be menaced; and that the Palestine issue would be internationalized to the point that other foreign powers, including China, might inter-

3. Interviews, Paris, 1970–1971.
4. For a lengthy discussion of Israeli-French cooperation, see Michel Bar-Zohar, *Suez: Ultra Secret* (Paris: Fayard, 1964).
5. Général André Beaufre, *L'Expédition de suez* (Paris: Grasset, 1967).

vene in the region. The French presence in the Maghreb and in Francophone Africa would inevitably come under seige.[6]

Siding with Israel in a war with the Arab states would snuff emerging French efforts to improve its relations in the Middle East, from which it had been effectively excluded since World War II, partly through British maneuvering.[7] Relations with Algeria, militant in its opposition to any concession to Israel, were tense already on such issues as oil and economic aid; they could only worsen if France irritated Algeria's sensitivities by backing Israel after the attack on Egypt. There were other Arab oil-producing states to consider. If France's identification with Arab nationalism advanced its position among those states, particularly among oil producers, the loss of good relations with Israel would be an acceptable price to pay, especially if the spread of anti-American sentiment, as a consequence of aiding Israel, fostered French interests in the Mediterranean.

France's substantive policy toward the June 1967 war may be roughly divided into two periods, corresponding to the events immediately leading up to the war and those that followed. The French government conceded Egypt's right to request the withdrawal of United Nations troops from its territory in spring 1967, although it discreetly questioned the wisdom of Secretary General U Thant's rapid execution of the Egyptian demand. De Gaulle had always been cool to the UN's peacekeeping functions in the Congo and the Middle East; only a year earlier his government had ordered the withdrawal of all NATO forces from French territory. The French also upheld the principle of free navigation of international waters, including the Gulf of Aqaba, but, like the other Western powers, showed great reluctance forcefully to break the Egyptian embargo encouraged by the Soviet Union. They rejected the Israeli government's view that the blockade represented a serious threat to Israel's territorial integrity and security and was linked to the build-up of Egyptian troops along the Suez Canal, to Syrian border incursions, and to the Palestinian guerrilla raids against Israeli territory and citizens. Following the settlement of the 1956 Suez crisis, France had obligated itself under the 1957 accord to uphold Israel's terri-

6. Paul Balta, "La France et le monde arabe: II—les réalités politiques," *Revue de défense nationale,* XXVI (June 1970), 926–927.

7. Zohar, *op. cit.,* pp. 29–31.

torial integrity. Apprised of the relatively small number of Israeli
ships using the Gulf of Aqaba, the French government saw little
basis for the Israeli contention that its life as a state was being challenged, nor any immediate need to precipitate an armed crisis to
assert its right to use the Gulf for Israeli shipping.[8]

The reported exchange between Israeli Foreign Minister Abba
Eban and President de Gaulle on May 24 summarized the French
position. Eban was to have reminded de Gaulle that "many countries
are committed to sustain our rights and to stand by us if the blockade
of the straits were renewed. The most vigorous and lucid expression
of it was given by the French representative in 1957." [9] De Gaulle's
reply qualified French commitments: "Yes, but that was in 1957.
Today, we live in 1967." [10] For the guarantees sought by Israel,
France offered little more than a procedural formula—big four agreement—rather than a specific pledge of support. It needs hardly to be
said that no other state was offering more.

The Israeli government was both privately and publicly warned,
moreover, that France would neither support nor approve the action
of any government that first used armed force whatever the nature
of the provocation. The Egyptian blockade, however inconvenient,
did not justify war.[11] President de Gaulle revealed in his news conference of November 28, 1967, that on May 24, the French government told the Israeli Foreign Minister Abba Eban "that eventually
it would lay the blame on whomever would first enter into combat.
. . . If Israel is attacked, I told him," de Gaulle went on, "we will
not allow it to be destroyed. But if you attack we will condemn your
initiative." [12] On June 2, two days before the actual outbreak of
hostilities, France publicly reiterated the May 24 warning and informed Israel that further arms shipments would be banned. According to one Israeli source, arms had continued to flow at an
uninterrupted and increasing rate up to the June 2 halt. An order
for $40 million was placed only a month before the war began.

8. A useful account of the background events to the Arab-Israeli War is
found in the informed commentary of Michel Bar-Zohar's *Histoire secrète de
la guerre d'Israël* (Paris: Fayard, 1968).
9. *Ibid.*, p. 115.
10. *Ibid.*
11. *Ibid.*
12. *FFP*, July–Dec. 1967, p. 136.

Meanwhile, however, the French called on the Soviet Union, the United States, and Great Britain to meet on the Middle East crisis and jointly to forbid each of the two parties from starting to fight.[13] France's Western partners hesitated; the Soviet Union demurred although consultations between the two governments were not excluded.[14] The French saw no lasting solution to the Middle East crisis without Soviet cooperation. The Israelis had serious doubts that an agreement protecting their interests could be achieved in negotiations with the Russians.

In responding to the June war, France strove to adopt a neutral position. Interest and circumstances, however, drove it to align with the Arab position enunciated most articulately at the United Nations.[15] French policy was overtaken by events. The Middle East strategic balance was disrupted by the rapid Israeli victory, the humiliation of the Arabs, and the confrontation of the United States and the Soviet Union in the region. The war eroded what middle ground existed between Israel and the Arab states.[16] France moved accordingly to side with the Arabs. It refused to recognize Israeli occupation of Arab territory and remained unmoved by Israeli demands for territorial adjustments to assure its security. With the other members of the Security Council, it rejected Israel's claims to exercise sole control over Jerusalem. France counseled instead some form of internationalization of the city. It also remained attached to the view, shared strongly by the Arab states, that Israeli withdrawal was a precondition to negotiations for a peaceful settlement of the war. It could not accept the notion that Israel could unilaterally settle the status of the peoples living in the territories that it occupied after the Six-Day War.

France's neutrality, tilted in Arab favor, was also suggested in its

13. *Ibid.*
14. *L'Année politique, 1967*, pp. 171–173.
15. The most thorough review of United Nations actions after the outbreak of hostilities is found in Arthur Lall, *The U.N. and the Middle East Crisis, 1967* (New York: Columbia University Press, 1968). The French position is stated throughout. For a generous interpretation of French actions that minimizes a charge of self-interest on the part of France in the Middle East, examine Nasser H. Aruri and Natalie Hevener, "France and the Middle East: 1967–1968," *Middle East Journal*, XXIII (Autumn 1969), 484–502.
16. President de Gaulle reviews this thinking and action on the crises in his news conference of November 28, 1967, *FFP*, July–Dec. 1967.

United Nations votes on key issues. It supported the Yugoslav resolution in the special United Nations General Assembly meeting of June 1967 calling for the immediate withdrawal of Israeli forces without reference to security guarantees for Israel or respect for the international right of any state, including Israel, to use the Gulf of Aqaba. On the other hand, France did not vote for the Latin American counterresolution that linked withdrawal to security guarantees for the belligerents. France joined the Arab states in attacking Israeli reprisal raids against Jordan and Lebanon for their harboring of Palestinian guerrillas.[17] France carefully distinguished between the military actions of a state (like Israel) and the terrorist activities of irregular bands of armed units representing no national state. The Pompidou government was the last of the major Western powers to condemn the seizure and destruction of passenger planes by Palestinian guerrillas in late summer 1970. Its sharpest criticism during the unfolding of the incident was reserved for the United States, which was warned against intervening in the area.[18]

Central to the French position was Security Council Resolution 242, passed on November 22, 1967.[19] The measure sketched the elements of a peace settlement under United Nations auspices. In linking the questions of Israeli withdrawal, establishment of secure and recognized boundaries, freedom of navigation, the Palestine issue, and the creation of regional security arrangements, it went beyond the Yugoslav and Latin American proposals. The French showed a marked preference for dealing with the substantive issues of the Middle East question as a whole under the terms of the November 22 resolution. It insisted, as the discussion below suggests, on the form that the settlement should take: big four agreement within the framework of the Security Council resolution. President de Gaulle summarized the French position in his news conference of November 28. Stiff conditions were defined for Israel's participation in negotiating the conflict: evacuation of all territories taken by force, the end of belligerency, and (something for Israel) "the mutual recognition of each State involved by all the others." "Through

17. *PEF,* Jan.–June 1968, pp. 53–54; *ibid.,* Jan.–June 1969, pp. 20, 45.
18. *Le Monde,* Sept. 26, 1970, p. 1.
19. United Nations, Security Council, *Official Records,* 22d year, 1967, Supplements, Resolutions and Decisions of the Security Council, pp. 8–9. Hereafter cited *Official Records.*

the decision of the United Nations, in the presence and under the guarantee of its forces," said the French president, "it would probably be possible to set the specific outline of the frontiers [a hint of adjustments desired by Israel], the conditions of life and security on both sides, the lot of the refugees and minority groups and the conditions of free navigation for all, notably in the Gulf of Aqaba and the Suez Canal." [20]

Whatever appeal the French view may have had in Arab quarters (they repeatedly praised France),[21] it struck few responsive chords in Israeli circles. Neither the substance of France's proposals, nor the form that they took—big-power guarantee under the United Nations—was held in high esteem even within the UN. The memory of the Aqaba incident was too fresh. The impotence of the UN to prevent the struggle, the mischievous effect of the precipitous withdrawal of international security forces from Egyptian territory, and the vacillation of the Western powers when the straits were closed offered slight encouragement to the Israeli government that the French proposals were a reliable remedy for its security concerns. Indeed, as French policy unfolded in the Middle East, its standing as a possible mediator diminished in the eyes of the Israelis.[22]

The French were skeptical of the American tendency to isolate the specific issues of the Middle East conflict for resolution and to build on these successes in the hope of developing mutual confidence among the regional rivals and of gradually expanding the scope of accord. First, the French wished the United States to be more forceful in persuading Israel to submit to the UN resolution of November 22. The *ad hoc* American approach allegedly freed Israel from its obligation to adhere to the UN and Security Council prescriptions.[23] Second, the pragmatic American negotiating posture was viewed as unresponsive to the range, complexity, and interwoven character of the issues surrounding the Arab-Israeli conflict. Foreign Minister Maurice Schumann wondered aloud, albeit diplomatically and discreetly, before the National Assembly about the American

20. *FFP,* July–Dec. 1967, p. 137.
21. See the discussion below, pp. 523–543.
22. Interview in Paris with Israeli official, Sept. 17, 1970. U.N. sentiment and reaction to French big-power proposals are summarized in Lall, *op. cit., passim.*
23. *PEF,* Jan.–June 1971, p. 200.

initiatives under the rubric of the so-called Rogers plan, named after United States Secretary of State William Rogers. He chided Secretary of State Rogers for having asked too little of Israel. He doubted, too, that the subsequent American proposal that the belligerents agree to the reopening of the Suez Canal, apart from the other points in contest, would succeed. States were reluctant to concede on small points or peripheral issues out of fear that they might compromise their positions on vital matters. "Could a limited arrangement be adopted for the re-opening of the Suez Canal?" he asked. "It is not surprising that the question is posed with a growing anxiety and skepticism. The Security Council resolution forms a whole: there is a link between the first phase of evacuation and the subsequent retreat of occupation forces on the international frontier." [24]

The French expressed particular skepticism about the inclination of American diplomacy to distinguish the Palestine issue from the immediate problems arising from the war, including, most importantly, the Israeli occupation of previously Arab-controlled territory. No final resolution of the Arab-Israeli dispute was seen possible unless the refugee problem was finally addressed. Only then, too, could a diplomatic wall be created that might stem or at least control foreign intrusion into the region—a special concern for a France vulnerable on its southern flank. The analogy with Algeria initially had some currency in government circles. Palestine, like Algeria, was pictured at different times as developing into a separate state out of its exterior struggle. The military setbacks administered by Jordan and Israel to the Palestinian guerrilla bands gradually sapped enthusiasm for the Algerian model as applicable to the refugee question. Nevertheless, there was public intimation that the American peace initiatives of summer 1970, at the time the Rogers plan was first accepted by the belligerents as a basis for negotiations, contributed to upheaval in the Jordanian-Palestinian clash and catalyzed, if it did not directly precipitate, the skyjackings of September 1970 by Palestinian armed units. There was the suggestion that the American proposals took insufficient account of the Palestinian claims and provided inadequate channels for their ventilation, encouraging extralegal means to dramatize their demands.[25]

24. *Ibid.*
25. *Le Monde,* Sept. 26, 1970, p. 1.

Egypt and Jordan appeared willing to distinguish the Palestine problem from the issue of occupied territories. American, more than French, diplomacy was attentive to the use of this wedge in the deadlock to bring some element of peace to the region. Moreover, some Arab states were more exposed than France on the Palestine question. Tunisian President Habib Bourguiba urged, even before the outbreak of hostilities in 1967, that the Palestinians assume more responsibility for their future. Bourguiba won little support and was sharply attacked within the Arab fraternity. He could fear, too, for his own internal security. Partial vindication came only after the bitter experience of the Six-Day War. Tunisia's position received tentative, if only temporary, consent from some of its principal Arab rivals—Egypt in particular—at the Arab summit at Rabat in December 1969. In sometimes appearing to be more Arab than the Arabs, France did not necessarily damage its standing in the Arab world. If Egypt temporized on the Palestine problem, irreconcilables like the Algerians conceived the Palestine and the occupied territories questions as of a piece in the struggle against what they portrayed to be Israeli expansionism as the instrument of Western (and American) imperialism.[26]

France's publicly stated views were not entirely silent on these charges. President de Gaulle drew attention to what he termed the tendency of the Jewish people to dominate others: "The establishment of a Zionist home in Palestine and then, after World War II, the establishment of a State of Israel raised . . . a certain number of apprehensions. . . . Some even feared that the Jews—up to then scattered, but who had remained what they had been down through the ages, that is, *an elite people, sure of itself and dominating*—once they gathered on the site of their former grandeur, might come to change into a fervent and conquering ambition the very touching hopes that they had had for nineteen centuries." [27] The long letter of rebuttal sent by former Israeli Premier David Ben Gurion, a personal friend of de Gaulle's, did little to ease tensions between Paris and Tel Aviv.[28] If de Gaulle's reply softened the charge of "domi-

26. *Maghreb,* No. 37 (Jan.–Feb. 1970), 10–11. Algeria and Syria rejected the Security Council resolution of November 22, 1967, and refused to accept the outcome of the Rabat meeting.
27. *FFP,* July–Dec. 1967, p. 137. Emphasis added.
28. *Ibid.,* pp. 156–165.

nation," [29] it also took occasion to criticize Israeli policy for failing to heed French counsel: "I remain convinced that, by disregarding the warnings given . . . by . . . the French Republic, by opening hostilities, by taking territories and there practicing the repression and expulsions that inevitably are the consequence of an occupation that everything indicates is leading to annexation, by affirming before the world that the settlement of the conflict can be achieved only on the basis of the lands conquered, and not on condition that the latter be evacuated, Israel is exceeding the boundaries of necessary moderation." [30] These themes continued to be struck after de Gaulle's departure. Foreign Minister Maurice Schumann characterized Israeli policy as an " 'inclination to annex,' " which he defined as "a certain inability to define its position on its fundamental problem, the fate of the occupied territories and that of one million Arabs." [31]

France's arms embargo was perhaps the most revealing aspect of its policy toward the Middle East. The June 2, 1967, proscription was initially rationalized as a means of restraining Israel and of offering an example to other Middle East arms suppliers to curtail shipments to the region. Failing in both objectives, France partially lifted the ban in the months that followed. It attempted to retain some influence over the Israeli government by permitting arms to flow to Israel for almost all forms of military equipment except Mirage aircraft. The level of arms trade sent to Israel after the outbreak of the Six-Day War until the imposition of what appeared to be a total embargo on January 3, 1969, was greater than that of any comparable preceding period.[32] The French felt obliged, however, to act vigorously in the wake of the Israeli raid on the Beirut airport in December 1968. Aimed at a traditional client of France, the attack damaged France's image as a defender of Arab rights. Even this embargo proved to be selective.

Israel forced France's hand in late 1969. It launched a campaign to block the sale of Mirages to Libya. Press leaks embarrassed the French government. French officials conspired with Israeli agents to

29. *Ibid.*, pp. 180–181.
30. *Ibid.*, p. 180.
31. *PEF*, Jan.–June 1970, p. 143; these charges are also alluded to by Schumann in *ibid.*, Jan.–June 1971, p. 200.
32. Interview, Paris, Sept.–Dec. 1970. As Table 1 below indicates, exports to Israel rose 50 percent between 1967 and 1968, from $66 million to $99 million.

circumvent the government's ban on arms by transferring five missile-launching coastal craft to Israel in December 1969. The new Pompidou embargo on arms to Israel was finally announced as total to assure protesting Arab states. The government's control over its own policy appeared sufficiently tenuous to justify a reorganization of the arms production services in the military establishment and an increase in the powers of the customs officials to prevent further incidents.

To justify anticipated arms sales to Lebanon, Libya, Algeria, and Iraq, the French distinguished between states on the field of battle and those which were not formally engaged despite the hostile action that they might have taken against the combatants. Iraqi participation in the Six-Day War and the dispatch of Algerian troops to the Suez Canal were conveniently ignored. France also allowed that it would not sell arms to any state that had an aggressive policy or intended to use French weapons for internal suppression. Iraqi attempts to suppress Kurd independence escaped this loosely enforced injunction, as did the sale of military equipment to Portugal and South Africa, where it was used to suppress domestic opposition.[33]

In more candid moments, the French conceded these logical contradictions but justified them as politically necessary for any one of three reasons of state. French arms sales to the Middle East contestants were dwarfed by those made by the superpowers; they were alleged, and not without some justification, to flow at a ratio of one to one hundred of the arms supplied by these powers.[34] Destabilization of the region lay then more with the superpowers than with France. Second, the French attempted to cast their arms policy in the larger context of their aims in the western Mediterranean. This shifted the

<hr/>

33. A useful, if biased, summary of the French embargo policy toward Israel is found in Dan, et al., De Gaulle contre Israel. See also the spirited defense of the Libyan arms sale by Prime Minister Jacques Chaban-Delmas, La Politique de la france en méditerranée. For a probing, if sometimes emotional, critique of French policy toward Israel after the Six-Day War, see Raymond Aron, De Gaulle, Israel, and the Jews, trans. John Sturrock (New York: Praeger, 1969). It contrasts with the interpretation offered by Aruri and Hevener in n. 15, above.

34. Remarks of Michel Debré as Minister of Defense, Le Monde, Jan. 23, 1970, p. 3; ibid., Jan. 24, 1970, p. 3. Some support for Debré's position is found in the statistics on arms sales published in Institute for Strategic Studies, The Military Balance: 1970–71, pp. 116–120. Sales covering the period July 1969 to June 1970 are listed.

terms of the objection from arms sales as such to the validity of French goals. "There is no French policy on arms contracts," argued Foreign Minister Schumann, in defending Mirage sales to Libya. "There is a Mediterranean policy for France which . . . has only one aim: to prevent . . . the western Mediterranean . . . and if possible . . . the whole of the Mediterranean basin, from becoming again, or from remaining a theater for cold war and a supplementary state in the rivalry of the great powers." [35]

Finally, the French confessed that they had little choice but to assume a pro-Arab stance in light of their interests in the area and the modest means at their disposal to realize them. They had to align with these states to advance their interests or face exclusion from the region and forego the profitable opportunities that it afforded. Sale of military equipment in 1969 accounted for 25 percent of France's heavy industrial exports.[36] The difference in attitude toward Israel and the Arab states is suggested in the remarks of Michel Debré during his tenure as foreign minister under the de Gaulle government:

France has a policy towards Israel, she also has a policy towards the Arab world. These two policies are elements of one French policy. Insofar as Israel is concerned . . . this State has the right to exist, it has the right to pursue its internal development, the right of its security and that of benefiting from all the essential guarantees that international law recognizes. . . .

France has similarly a policy towards the Arab and Muslim world. Geography and history, despite its tests, [and] our economic and cultural interests invite us to maintain—and to develop good relations with these States, notably with the closest ones of the Mediterranean. These two attitudes are the expression of one single policy which is French policy. If the French do not think first about their country, who will do it for them? No one. This policy is naturally guided by our interests, because every people has the duty to defend its interests.[37]

France might have had one policy toward the Middle East, but it rested on two sets of criteria of widely different import. Toward the Israelis it was grounded on the formal requirements of international

35. *PEF*, Jan.–June 1970, p. 144.
36. *Le Monde*, Jan. 23, 1970, p. 3.
37. *PEF*, Jan.–June 1968, pp. 47–48.

law and referred to the right of a recognized state to exist and to expect this right to be honored by other states. Toward the Arabs, French policy not only rested on these minimal expectations but was informed by vastly more extensive considerations of mutual national interests.

The French partially banked on their advanced political standing in Arab circles to prepare the ground for the expansion of vitally needed economic ties in the area.[38] This expectation had at least two closely entwined roots. First, the Arab accent on political factors in their economic dealings struck a responsive note in Gaullist diplomacy which tended to link economic and political considerations. The mercantilist cast of French foreign policy had revealed itself in the attack on the American dollar (1964–1968), two vetoes of the British entry into the Common Market (1963 and 1967), and re-sistance to the expansion of the EEC Commission's political authority. The French asserted that the active involvement of their state in arranging economic accords abroad, contrasted with the greater private enterprise of business firms in the Anglo-American states and in Germany, was a positive advantage among the Arab states. The 1965 oil accord with Algeria was cited as a somewhat strained, yet, until 1970, workable model for future Arab-French commercial ties. That the three largest oil suppliers of France—Algeria, Iraq, and Libya—were so-called "progressive" Arab states reinforced the Pompidou government in its statist orientation, until the oil crisis with Algeria in 1971, in reaching commercial accords with the Medi-terranean states.

Second, on grounds of competitive advantage, the French were latecomers in developing Middle East markets and in exploiting the oil resources of the area. They were encouraged to stress the attrac-tiveness of their political views whereas their Western competitors had a contrary incentive to emphasize the desirability of their goods and services and to protect their economic position from the po-litical tempests of the region. The average trade deficit with the

38. An excellent survey of French economic policy toward the Middle East is found in Paul Balta, *Revue de défense nationale*, May 1970, pp. 769–779. See also his analysis of the political dimensions of French Middle East policy, n. 6, above. A more general discussion of Arab-French relations, with a de-cidedly pro-Arab cast, is found in Paul Balta and Claudine Rulleau, *La Poli-tique arabe de la France* (Paris: Sindbad, 1973).

eleven Arab states listed in Table 4 was $541.4 million for 1965–1970. France's negative trade balances with the Arab states, particularly with its oil suppliers, advised alignment on foreign policy for the sake of economic gain, all the more so since its three primary suppliers—Algeria, Iraq, and Libya—were in the militant wing of the Arab states. In 1968, these three states accounted for 61 percent of France's imports from states listed in Table 4 and 53 percent of its exports. As Tables 4 and 5 indicate, France also ran sizable annual deficits with the six Arab states that, until 1971, supplied over 80 percent of France's oil needs. The largest deficits were run in 1967 and 1968 at −$720.7 and −$711.3 million, respectively, for each year. These markets were already dominated by France's principal Western competitors—the United States, Great Britain, and West Germany—and they were increasingly attracted, as was Algeria, to Soviet commercial propositions. Yet it is precisely with these states that France's balance-of-payments deficit was most acute, although they were in the best financial position to buy abroad.

Expected losses in Israeli trade after the June war never materialized despite the embargoes on arms. Except for 1968, French trade with Israel in 1971 exceeded all previous levels. Between 1965 and 1971, French imports from Israel averaged $28.7 million and exports $71.24 million, for an average annual favorable balance of $42.5 million. This volume of trade was overshadowed, however, by France's trade with the eleven Arab states noted in Table 4. Although France continued to run serious trade deficits with its oil suppliers, these states were central to its efforts to improve its trade position and to assure adequate energy resources for its industrial development. The trade structure between Israel and France was heavily influenced by the sale of military equipment; approximately one half of the $90 million of material sent by France to Israel in 1968 was in the form of military supplies.[39] Possibilities for commercial expansion in a state whose population was approximately three million were limited.

The Arab countries, with a total population of one hundred million, promised both larger commercial and arms sales. Exploitation of these markets was much more urgent than close political ties with

39. Ministère de l'Economie et des Finances, *Statistiques du commerce extérieur de la France, année 1969,* pp. 16–23.

Table 4. French trade with selected eastern and western Arab states, 1965–1971 (millions of U.S. dollars)

	1965		1966		1967		1968		1969		1970		1971	
	I	E	I	E	I	E	I	E	I	E	I	E	I	E
Eastern Mediterranean states														
Iraq	184.8	6.8	190.0	13.1	250.9	12.3	270.1	20.1	245.1	18.3	203.9	35.1	308.1	47.1
Libya	110.0	25.6	129.8	22.5	149.3	31.6	175.3	30.4	230.0	40.2	274.1	42.7	321.5	96.7
Kuwait	153.6	9.1	143.3	12.3	146.6	14.0	125.9	12.2	132.1	30.2	177.6	46.0	213.7	49.3
Muscat/Oman	33.4	1.6	53.2	5.1	60.0	5.4	115.0	14.6	107.7	51.6	101.1	78.1	204.1	81.7
Saudi Arabia	49.4	10.7	54.9	22.4	78.8	16.5	76.4	19.2	84.7	36.9	171.6	33.7	369.4	37.3
Qatar	26.1	1.4	32.2	1.2	44.8	1.7	61.1	1.7	33.2	2.6	32.0	2.4	59.5	2.4
Egypt	17.8	54.0	15.0	38.6	16.6	44.1	16.2	64.0	19.6	85.4	32.0	63.5	30.6	70.7
Lebanon	2.8	42.7	7.3	46.2	4.9	46.1	3.6	74.7	3.8	63.6	3.3	89.4	3.7	102.9
Subtotal	577.9	151.9	625.7	161.4	526.9	171.7	843.6	236.9	856.2	328.8	995.6	390.9	1202.5	488.1
Balance of Trade	−426.0		−464.3		−355.2		−606.7		−527.4		−604.7		−714.4	
Western Mediterranean states														
Algeria	569.6	511.7	563.5	437.1	530.9	404.5	557.4	471.3	599.6	460.1	637.0	562.4	233.5	500.7
Morocco	238.4	166.5	227.4	187.5	212.8	189.0	188.9	168.8	205.6	183.0	212.1	214.4	219.7	218.2
Tunisia	34.7	94.7	60.8	88.5	48.7	84.5	40.8	79.8	43.1	98.3	43.2	108.2	45.4	129.5
Subtotal	842.7	772.9	851.7	713.1	792.4	678.0	787.1	719.9	848.3	741.4	892.3	885.0	498.6	848.4
Balance of Trade	−69.8		−138.6		−114.4		−67.2		−106.9		−7.3		349.8	
Total: East and West Mediterranean	1420.6	924.8	1477.4	874.5	1319.3	849.7	1630.7	956.8	1704.5	1070.2	1887.9	1275.9	1701.1	1336.5
Total: Balance of Trade	−495.8		−602.9		−469.6		−673.9		−634.3		−612.0		−364.6	
Israel	12.6	43.3	17.0	47.1	22.1	66.0	29.6	99.1	34.0	68.4	35.4	79.3	50.5	97.5

Source: International Monetary Fund and the International Bank for Reconstruction and Development, Direction of Trade, Annual, 1961–1965, pp. 118–120; ibid, 1966–1970, pp. 121–123; ibid., October 1972, pp. 16–18.

Table 5. Rank and percent of French crude oil imports by country of origin, 1967–1971

	1967*	1968*	1969*	1970*	1971*
Selected Eastern and Western Arab sources (from Table 4)					
Algeria	(1) 29.6	(1) 31.1	(1) 28.6	(1) 26.6	(7) 7.2
Iraq	(2) 19.7	(2) 19.3	(3) 17.2	(3) 12.0	(2) 14.9
Libya	(4) 12.1	(3) 13.6	(2) 17.3	(2) 17.4	(3) 14.3
Kuwait	(3) 12.2	(4) 9.9	(4) 9.1	(4) 11.0	(5) 10.3
Saudi Arabia	(5) 5.6	(5) 5.6	(5) 5.4	(5) 9.3	(1) 16.4
Qatar	3.1	1.5	2.2	1.7	2.6
Egypt	N/R†	‡	(6) 5.2	.6	.6
Muscat/Oman§	N/R	N/R	N/R	N/R	N/R
TOTAL	82.3	81.0	85.0	78.6	66.3
Other significant sources					
Iran	(6) 4.0	(6) 3.9	(7) 4.3	3.7	5.5
Nigeria	N/R	N/R	N/R	(6) 5.1	(4) 11.4
Venezuela	(7) 3.7	(7) 3.1	2.7	2.4	1.9
Soviet Union	2.5	2.0	2.1	1.4	2.4
Abu Dahbi	N/R	N/R	N/R	(7) 4.5	(6) 8.9
All others	7.6	8.2	4.4	4.2	3.8

Source: Calculated from tables compiled by the Oil Committee of the Organization for Economic Cooperation and Development, *Oil Statistics, 1967: Supply and Disposal* (Paris: Organization for Economic Cooperation and Development, 1963), pp. 26–27; *ibid.*, 1968, pp. 26–27; *ibid.*, 1969, pp. 26–27; *ibid.*, 1970, pp. 26–27; *ibid.*, 1971, pp. 26–27.

* Includes only those countries separately reported that ranked in the top seven suppliers during the five-year period, 1967–1971. Numbers in parentheses indicate rankings as oil suppliers to France.

† Not reported.

‡ Less than one-tenth percent.

§ OECD's *Oil Statistics* does not report Muscat/Oman separately, although the total trade statistics in Table 4 indicate that it is a significant supplier of French crude oil.

Israel. In the period between 1965 and 1969, French imports from the eight Arab Middle East states noted in Table 4 increased by almost 60 percent; exports more than doubled. These increases offset the general stagnation in French trade accounts with the Maghreb during the same period. France's Mediterranean policy appeared to be paying in trade and oil dividends with the Middle East, and it was holding its own in the face of increased competition and political differences with the Maghreb states, to be discussed below, on issues other than those concerned with the Middle East war.

But in abandoning Israeli ties as too costly, the de Gaulle and Pompidou governments were equally solicitous to avoid ensnarlment in inter-Arab politics. The French bowed to many of the icons of Arab nationalism that were so reportedly despised a decade before—rectification of the Palestine refugee problem, condemnation of American imperialism, nonalignment and neutrality in the Soviet-American struggle, Arab socialism. Refuge in these shibboleths lessened the urgency to choose between rival Arab forces. These intergroup conflicts were left to the Arabs to resolve, as best they could, or to the superpowers to mediate. Either outcome, while it risked compromising France's interests, held open the prospect of profit from internal Arab quarrels and from Arab ingratitude toward the superpowers for their attempts to restrain family conflicts. France's support of the Arab cause against Israel created some incentive among the Arab states to have France participate in negotiations with the United States and the Soviet Union over the Middle East in order to plead Arab interests. Cultivating Arab support for its great power claim tended to strengthen, however marginally, France's standing before the superpowers in spite of what might otherwise have been their preference to dismiss France, at worst, as a spoiler or, at best, as a nuisance.

Big Power Accord and French Status in the Mediterranean

Since the Six-Day War deepened superpower penetration of the Mediterranean, expansion of France's role and influence in the region after 1967 depended increasingly on its capacity to affect superpower relations in the region. The shift away from Israel toward the Arab view and improving bilateral ties with the western Mediterranean states, as discussed below, was helpful. Neither was conclusive. To keep French views and interests before the superpowers, the de Gaulle and, more extensively, the Pompidou governments initiated a broad range of diplomatic activities that can be conveniently grouped around (1) repeated assertions of France's special role within the Security Council, (2) overtures for European community support, (3) representations to Washington and Moscow, and (4) general appeals for Arab neutrality in the superpower struggle.

Until the Yom Kippur War of October 1973, nothing was more constant nor more subject to change than the French formula for peace in the Mediterranean: four-power accord among the United States, Soviet Union, Great Britain, and France. The French insisted that they had a right to define the terms of accord between the Arab states and Israel and the larger security arrangements for the region. President de Gaulle stressed France's material power, embodied in the *force de frappe,* and his government's pursuit of a global policy to justify France's big-power claim. President Pompidou, more sensitive to France's modest military and material prowess, emphasized its privileged UN status, its geographic position, and its past regional importance and present interests in Europe and in the Mediterranean to underwrite its right to be at any bargaining table that might be set up to make authoritative decisions for the region.[40]

France's self-asserted importance as a regional power, reflected in its ties to the European and Mediterranean states, and its elevated juridical standing in the international community as a permanent member of the UN Security Council reinforced each other.[41] What France might lack in original or derivative power was compensated for by its moral and legal standing. The argument subtly articulated by French diplomacy was as self-serving as it was circular: French regional standing in the hierarchy of European and Middle East powers gave it a special international status; that status, already recognized by its UN role, granted it regional privileges and influence.

The form in which the Middle East crisis might be settled was as important to the French as the substantive terms of agreement between the belligerents. The preferred mechanism, before the October 1973 outbreak of the fourth Arab-Israeli war, was a *concertation*

40. See Chapters 3 and 8 above for additional discussions of this change between the de Gaulle and Pompidou regimes regarding the assumptions underlying French global policy. See also Pompidou's announcement of a Mediterranean policy, *PEF,* July–Dec. 1969, p. 160. Relevant also is Pompidou's outline of those factors prompting his call of October 31, 1973, for regular summit meetings of the Nine (*Le Monde,* Nov. 2, 1973, p. 4).

41. For a discussion of the Pompidou shift to the Mediterranean, see *Journal de Genève,* Feb. 11, 1969, p. 5, and Feb. 14, 1969, pp. 1, 5; *Le Capital,* Feb. 10, 1969, p. 5; *New York Herald Tribune,* International edition, March 20, 1970. See also the three-part article of Louis-Jean Duclos, *La Croix,* July 8–10, 1970; and *Le Monde,* Feb. 25, 1970, p. 1. For a right-of-center Gaullist view, read Philippe de St. Robert, *Le Jeu de la france en méditerranée* (Paris: Julliard, 1970); for a summary review of key points, see André Fontaine, "Pompidou's Mediterranean Policy," *Interplay* (April 1970), pp. 12–14.

à quatre with the respective ambassadors of the four major powers acting as the principal instrument in the search for an accord that would then be duly applied to the conflicting regional states. The United Nations mission, authorized under the Security Council resolution of November 22, 1967, would be instructed by the Security Council under the control of its permanent members. France's four-power formula would be mediated through UN institutions and legal procedures. The Rogers plan of 1970, which sought to create other channels than the UN mission under Gunner Jarring for negotiations between the Arab states and Israel, emphasized direct bilateral talks between the interested parties under superpower sponsorship. In a speech that could not have failed to upset French government sensitivities, President Nixon proposed to the United Nations that the superpowers were in effect capable of deciding not only the Middle East affair, but other conflicts as well.[42] The Rogers approach, in keeping with the preference of the Nixon administration for working directly on the Soviet Union and the regional powers, undermined France's attempts to protect its role as a leading actor in the Mediterranean drama.

The four-power formula was as important to France as an end in itself as it was as a means for finding a lasting solution to the Arab-Israeli conflict. In emphasizing its historical and legal standing rather than its strategic military power and global interests, Pompidou's France implicitly adopted the traditional stance of a weak power. Better to tie stronger states in knots of legal obligations when direct means of influence were wanting or, if applied, counterproductive.

The recognition of France's enfeebled condition, especially after the series of crises in 1968, was not entirely original with President Pompidou. That President de Gaulle was aware both of France's receding power assets vis-à-vis the United States and the Soviet Union in the Middle East and its awkward position as the *demandeur* vis-à-vis the Arab states, particularly those producing oil, was suggested in his about-face on the UN's peacekeeping role. Whereas

---

42. See France's sharp criticism of President Nixon's speech before the United Nations in which he called for Soviet-American accord on global problems, *Le Monde,* Nov. 1–2, 1970, p. 2; a brief review of French policy toward the United Nations as an institution is found in *Le Monde,* Oct. 20, 1970, pp. 6–7.

France heaped scorn on UN activities in the Congo and refused to pay its assessed share of the cost of the operation, the United Nations as resurrected in French policy was the desired international instrument to assert France's national views. The new accent responded to Arab views after the Six-Day War and conformed to then current Soviet policy.[43]

Meanwhile, the United States, less able than before to influence UN opinion or the behavior of its secretary general and more sensitive to Israeli anxieties about the dubious credibility of UN guarantees, downgraded its role in resolving the conflict. The United States trusted to its own initiatives and, not without irony for the French, more traditional channels of diplomacy. The procedural niceties, sketched in Security Council Resolution 242, were scrupulously observed. However, the direct talks envisioned under the Rogers plan included the special representative of the secretary general only in that a report would be sent to him by the Arab states and Israel of the results of their negotiations. Decisions would be initially taken elsewhere than within a UN framework. A courtesy copy of any accord would be duly registered with the United Nations; the other Security Council members, including France, would be informed, but would not participate, in the talks.[44]

French diplomacy was also active in Europe to bolster its sagging Mediterranean posture and its challenged UN position. Shortly before the expansion of the European community, it maneuvered in the councils of the European Six to gain adherents to the substance and form of its Middle East views. In May 1971, following procedures outlined in the Davignon report of autumn 1970, the Six agreed on what appeared to be a common Middle East position. At French suggestion, the report was not published. This did not prevent French Foreign Minister Maurice Schumann from commenting on what he felt was the political significance of the accord. Support was alleged for the French interpretation of Security Council Resolution 242:

I will keep to the main point [of the report] . . . : the ministers of foreign affairs reaffirm their approval of resolution 242 of the Security Coun-

43. *FFP*, July–Dec. 1967, p. 137.
44. *L'Année politique, 1970*, pp. 289–293.

cil of 22 November 1967 and underline the necessity of applying it in all its parts.

Do the countries of the Common Market claim an active role in the Middle East crisis? No. Our interest is not to present ourselves as a new mediator in the conflict, but to support the international community whose will is expressed in the United Nations by the intervention of the General Assembly . . . and of the Security Council whose four permanent members have always recognized the existence of an interest superior to national interests or finally by the secretary general, U Thant, to whom I renew the assurance of our sympathy.[45]

This diplomatic step forward became ensnared shortly thereafter in the tangle of Arab and Israeli politics. Neither side wished to forego EEC support. German Foreign Minister Walter Scheel was submitted to sharp questioning on the Middle East during his visit to Israel in July 1971. His answers contrasted with the picture of harmony painted by Schumann in his remarks of June 1. What was firm for Schumann was provisional for Scheel: "The so-called document of the Six," said Scheel to the *Jerusalem Post,* "is only a working paper which is far from having been approved." [46] On the key question of what interpretation to attach to the Security Council resolution, Scheel observed: "There are differences between the French and West German positions with respect to the Near East. . . . The attitude of Bonn supports the interpretation given by Washington and London to the Security Council resolution of November 1967. There is no necessity that Israel commit itself to a total retreat of its troops as a precondition to the opening of peace negotiations." [47] Part of the controversy turned further on the difference between the French and English translation of the Security Council resolution. The English version spoke of withdrawal "from occupied territories"; the French presentation referred to *"des territoires occupés"* ("from *the* occupied territories"). The more ambiguous English statement provided more latitude in language, if not in fact, for adjustments in the boundaries between Israel and its Arab neighbors prior to, or after, the total or partial withdrawal of Israeli forces.[48]

The publication of the secret May document by *Die Welt* on July 10

45. *PEF,* Jan.–June 1971, pp. 199–200.
46. *Le Monde,* July 10, 1971, p. 24.
47. *Ibid.*
48. *Official Records,* pp. 8–9.

exposed more points of difference between Germany and France.[49] The French did not dispute the authenticity of the report and were accused of having divulged its contents. The publication embarrassed the Bonn government so solicitous to be on good terms with all parties. In trying to please the French, Israelis, and Arabs, it satisfied none.

Besides the withdrawal issue, doubts were raised over the meaning between demilitarized and buffer zones to be established under the Security Council resolution. The creation of neutral zones on both sides of the former frontier was likely to cost more to Israel, given its limited land base, than to the Arabs. Conflict between the assurances given by Scheel to the Israelis and the prescription of the Six appeared, too, on the important questions of defining frontiers. Minimum rectification was to be permitted, according to the account of the document, only with the accord of the interested parties. This largely excluded the Arabs. The awkwardness of the German position was not relieved by the exposure of the outline offered by the Six on the status of the Suez Canal and Jerusalem. The canal would be open to all who wished to use it, but differences of opinion were to be settled by the Security Council. On its face, the formula was unacceptable to Israel whatever its value for the French standing in the United Nations. The possibility of accepting some form of mixed control for Jerusalem was also objectionable to the Israeli government, not to mention the perverse effect its implementation might have had on the German government's own problem with a divided Berlin.

But there were other strings to the French diplomatic bow. In playing them, France attempted to draw on superpower differences and on the fears and expectations of the Arab states which, while anxious for outside support, worried about keeping their independence. The first impulse of the de Gaulle government at the outbreak of hostilities in June 1967 was to castigate the United States. Its involvement in Vietnam was considered to have been a contributing cause to the Middle East conflict. However farfetched the causal link, the interpretation was in step with Arab rationalizations of their defeat. It was in line, too, with Soviet charges of American imperial expansion around the globe.[50]

These posturings did not preclude more attention to NATO security

49. A review of the article is found in *Le Monde*, July 16, 1971, p. 3.
50. *FFP*, Jan.–June 1967, p. 103.

ties. As late as June 1968, the French refused to associate themselves with Point 9 of a NATO Council resolution: "The Ministers of the countries taking part in the Defense Planning Committee, concerned at the recent expansion of Soviet activity in the Mediterranean, decided that their Permanent Representatives, . . . would take under early consideration measures designed to safeguard the security interests of NATO members in the Mediterranean area and to improve the effectiveness of allied forces in the area." [51] But the following November, after the Czech invasion, France accepted an even stronger statement that called attention to the Soviet Mediterranean menace and issued a warning to the Soviets that "any . . . intervention directly or indirectly influencing the situation in Europe or in the Mediterranean would cause an international crisis with serious consequences." [52] French naval units began cooperating with NATO surveillance efforts, and naval ships, stationed in the Atlantic, were redeployed to the Mediterranean. The French Mediterranean fleet compared favorably in conventional striking power with Soviet naval forces in the area and, in combination with NATO elements, completely overshadowed them.[53]

On the other hand, France attempted to satisfy Soviet political and economic objectives in the Mediterranean. President de Gaulle's refusal in 1967 to honor France's obligations to defend Israel's access to the Gulf of Aqaba was rooted in his fear not only of global war stemming from an Arab-Israeli confrontation, but in his determination to protect the progress made toward détente in Europe and to foster France's privileged position with the Soviet Union. France would not pit itself against the Soviet Union and make shambles of its European policy. Moreover, France's preservation of its position in the Maghreb and the expansion of its interests in the Mashreq were seen to be contingent upon Soviet accord or acquiescence. Recognition of the Soviet Union's legitimate presence and interests in the Mediterranean area—what no previous French regime had ever done—created the re-

51. *NATO Handbook* (Brussels: NATO Information Service, 1968), pp. 37–38.

52. Carmoy, *Interplay*, Oct. 1968, p. 25.

53. René Mertens, "The Naval Forces in the Mediterranean," in *Military Forces and Potential Conflicts in the Mediterranean* (Paris: Atlantic Institute, 1970), pp. 41–51

ciprocal expectation that the Soviet Union would acknowledge French claims. The United States and Great Britain would be the obvious losers in the growing alignment of French and Soviet positions. The French could then claim to represent Western interests in the Mediterranean. In the absence of its forceful criticism of Israeli and American policy, the Arab states would presumably have no alternative but reliance on the Soviet Union. In this respect, Pompidou's maneuvering in the Mediterranean was consistent with Gaullist doctrine. It encouraged a Soviet interest to have France at the European and Mediterranean bargaining tables. Four-power talks for both areas became the agreed-upon formula, legitimizing French presence and paying due respect to France's Security Council position.

In its effort to drive a wedge between the Arab states and the superpowers, France applied its well-developed criticism of bloc politics to the Mediterranean. Under this somewhat worn rubric, the United States and the Soviet Union were condemned again with a more or less even hand. The Arab states were warned that their independence would be jeopardized by a major conflict between the superpowers. France offered itself as an alternative, citing its cooperative relations with Algeria as a model for a third course (if not force). Whereas the superpowers were interested and engaged, France, in the words of Foreign Minister Maurice Schumann, was "impartial and neutral." [54] The French worked for a Mediterranean free from superpower military presence (even while cooperating with NATO forces and accommodating the Soviet Union). Phrases characterizing the Mediterranean as the *"Mare Nostrum* of France" or as a "lake of peace" began circulating in journalistic centers in response to the new accent on France's southern flank.[55]

The gospel of nonalignment had much to recommend it for a state of France's modest material capacity. In the absence of some measure of Arab nonalignment, it was difficult to see how France could make its influence felt or maximize what benefits there were to be had at the expense of the superpowers. The split between the United States and the Soviet Union, however deplorable and potentially dangerous, was nevertheless useful to a France bent on penetrating the Arab world

54. *PEF*, Jan.–June 1971, p. 201.
55. See St. Robert, *op. cit.*, pp. 121–124; Fontaine, *Interplay*, April 1970, pp. 12–14.

and holding on to its gains and traditional presence in the Maghreb and Africa. Much of the French diplomatic strategy in the region after the Six-Day War aimed more at minimizing the adverse effects of Middle East conflicts on France than at easing or mediating them. They were not of France's making. On the other hand, its delicately balanced and finely calibrated diplomacy was an admission that it was dependent on forces operating in the region which it could not influence greatly; that it had to rely on the differences and divergencies between the Arab states, between the Arabs and Israel, between the superpowers, and between them and their various and overlapping clients to play a winning regional game; and that it would draw what profit it could from these conflicts without creating new ones or contributing to division of long standing. The Mediterranean policy of the de Gaulle and Pompidou governments provided lessons in the politics of weakness.

The Yom Kippur War of October 1973 cast further doubt on the efficacy of the superpower phase of France's Mediterranean policy by reinforcing, at least temporarily, two trends: superpower concert and Arab cooperation. What the impact of the war would be on France's Mediterranean posture was difficult to assess at the time of Pompidou's death in April 1974. The first shocks, however, were not reassuring for French attempts to establish an independent national posture in the region.

The expectation that France could rely on its permanent seat in the Security Council to influence the behavior of the regional actors proved a mirage. The four-power formula, pursued after the Six-Day War, was lost in the labyrinths of UN diplomacy, a victim of superpower neglect and the attrition of numerous and fruitless meetings between subalterns representing the four powers. It lost credibility, moreover, when Communist China replaced the Taiwan regime on the Security Council. France's failure to make the permanent members of the Security Council the principal instrument in establishing a Middle East cease-fire and in arranging negotiations between the belligerents in the October 1973 hostilities demonstrated the receding utility of the UN as a tool of French policy. The October 22 resolution of the Security Council was largely the product of superpower accord, not the result of bargaining among the permanent members. The antagonists were asked to cease hostilities and to engage immediately in negotiation to end their differences under "appropriate auspices." [56] There was no doubt, as the Geneva talks between Israel and the Arabs indicated in December 1973, that "appropriate auspices" meant the United States and the Soviet Union. Excluded was any major role for the UN secretary general, envisioned under Security Resolution 242 of November 1967, or the other permanent members of the Security Council. French attempts to include the armed forces of the permanent members in the UN peacekeeping force established under the Security Council resolution of October 25 were also foiled, inducing France to abstain from the final vote. (China took no part in any of the votes on the Middle East cease-fire.) The superpowers, and most pointedly the United States, dismissed the French arguments that such a course would not only provide the military means needed to enforce the peace but also harness the combined political will of the major powers to ensure an equitable settlement of the conflict. Drawing on Gaullist logic, Washington and Moscow established their credentials as the cosponsors of the Geneva talks through their massive military and material support of the regional opponents. The superpowers preferred to rest their claims on arms and not on their legal position or charter obligations as members of the Security Council.

Efforts to insinuate France between the United States and the Soviet Union within the Middle East were similarly unavailing in dealing directly with the superpowers during the conflict. Like its EEC partners, France was not consulted before the United States organized an air bridge to replenish Israel's military stocks and to furnish newer, sophisticated equipment to counter Soviet-supplied arms to the Arabs which had scored heavily against Israeli armor and air power in the opening stages of the October war. Nor was France (or its NATO allies) contacted by Washington when President Nixon ordered a world-wide military alert, ostensibly to neutralize the Soviet threat of unilateral intervention in the Middle East to assure Israeli compliance with the superpower-sponsored cease-fire in order to prevent additional damage to Arab forces. The Pompidou government supported the refusal of all NATO states (except Portugal) to provide facilities for United States aircraft to supply arms to Israel—a possibility that France had effectively precluded in withdrawing from NATO in

56. *Le Monde,* Oct. 23, 1973, pp. 1, 3.

1966. Like them, it also resisted Washington's attempt to extend the
Atlantic Alliance to the Middle East conflict in the test of wills with
the Soviet Union and the Arab states. But the more significant fact
was that neither set of actions appreciably influenced United States
behavior and, indeed, may have reinforced American indignation under the Nixon administration to strike a bargain outside of NATO
and the alliance in dealing with the Soviet Union.[57] Meanwhile, as
Chapter 3 suggests, France's dependence on the United States security
guarantee became more pronounced as the SALT and MBFR talks
proceeded. French recognition of their dependency assumed the paradoxical forms during the Middle East crisis of 1973 of renewed
affirmations of fidelity to the Atlantic Alliance while attacking the
United States for having weakened the credibility of its security commitment to Europe in cooperating with the Soviet Union to halt the
Yom Kippur War.[58]

The Soviet Union equally fell short of French expectations. The
Pompidou government lamented the lack of consultations provided
under previous accords and the failure of the Soviet Union to keep
its pledge to strengthen the role of the Security Council. The utility
of Paris as Moscow's favored partner in European détente diminished
as Bonn and Washington became the preferred suitors. Deepening
French reluctance about moving quickly toward agreement within the
context of the European Conference on Security and Cooperation on
questions of borders, human and economic exchange, and rules for
intervention in the domestic affairs of the European states also conflicted with Soviet aims.[59] In the Middle East, France had little to
offer the Soviet Union after the Yom Kippur War that it had not
already earned by its own efforts. Nor did the French have much
incentive to bolster Soviet power in the region. After the Six-Day
War, the United States appeared to be the expanding power; after the
1973 outbreak, the Soviet Union seemed to be in the ascendancy,
pressuring France and Western Europe on their eastern and southern flanks. Containing Soviet, not American, power became the major
French preoccupation of the middle 1970's.

57. See *ibid.*, Oct. 28–29, 1973, pp. 1, 4, for the remarks of President Nixon
and spokesmen from the Departments of State and Defense.
58. *New York Times*, Dec. 11, 1973, pp. 1, 5.
59. *Le Monde*, July 5, 1973, p. 1.

The Yom Kippur War also produced a higher degree of Arab unity in the Arab-Israeli conflict than ever before. This development, whose future course cannot be discerned at this writing, had three immediate adverse effects on French regional strategy. First, appeals to Arab neutrality in the superpower struggle lost force. The Arab states needed the Soviet Union to intercede on their behalf in talks with Israel through pressures on the United States. Symptomatic of the eclipse of neutralist sentiment in the immediate aftermath of the October 1973 war was Libya's isolation in the Arab camp. Prime Minister Qaddafi's attack on the Soviet Union's ambiguous support of the Arab cause received no open avowals from other Arab capitals or from Egypt or Syria, which reportedly did not consult Libya before attacking Israel despite their membership in the Federation of Arab Republics. Second, opportunities to play the Arab states off against each other were reduced as long as war appeared imminent. The west Arab states of Tunisia, Morocco, and Algeria were increasingly drawn to support the east Arab states, nullifying French efforts, as sketched below, to insulate the Mashreq from the Maghreb.[60] Finally, the success of the partial Arab oil embargo against Europe accented France's (and Europe's) dependence on Middle East oil and made them more susceptible to Arab demands.

As France's standing before the superpowers and the Arab states slipped in the wake of the Yom Kippur War, the Pompidou government returned to the European community as a vehicle to magnify French influence. Conditions for forging a united position were riper than two years earlier. The Nine shared a common experience of impotence in the Middle East drama, reduced to spectators by the indigenous regional actors and the superpowers. Yet the impact of the Arab embargo fell harder and more quickly on the European states, which imported 80 percent of their oil from the Middle East, than on the United States, which drew only 15 percent of its oil needs from the Arab states. Decreasing energy sources weakened Europe's industrial power and threatened economic growth, productivity, and employment. Higher oil prices further undermined their efforts to control inflation and protect foreign markets. The security interests of the Nine were hostage to superpower accords (the UN

60. *Ibid.*, Nov. 6, 1973, p. 1, and *ibid.*, Nov. 7, 1973, p. 6, report Tunisian, Moroccan, and Algerian support for the Egyptian-Syrian position.

peacekeeping resolutions of October 1973) and discords (the United States alert) arising unpredictably from the implacable hatreds and vicissitudes of Middle East politics.

The Nine responded first on October 13 in a communiqué requesting the end of hostilities and the opening of peace negotiations under the terms of the Security Council Resolution 242.[61] On October 31, President Pompidou called for an emergency summit conference of EEC heads of government and state to speak with one voice on the crisis and thereby to exercise a European influence on the Middle East and on world politics.[62] The Nine elaborated their position in a joint statement of November 6, affirming the importance of the Security Council and Resolution 242 as the appropriate instruments for peace discussions.[63] Israel was expected to withdraw its troops from all occupied territories although there were discreet hints of possible boundary rectifications, such as the Golan Heights, to assure the security of exposed parts of Israel. The December 15–16 summit, after some reported reluctance of France and Britain to go along, joined in a Dutch-German sponsored declaration. A compendium of large carrots and small sticks, it stated that the oil embargo could have serious repercussions on developed and developing countries, hinted that European public opinion would be more disposed to Arab views if more oil were forthcoming, and tendered the possibility of increased European financial and technical aid to cooperating Arab oil-producing states.[64]

The significance of these early European moves of the Pompidou government was difficult to evaluate. These elements appeared to have emerged. First, the French position adopted in 1967 regarding the substantive items that had to be addressed in reaching a Middle East settlement was largely vindicated in the successive positions taken by the Nine in fall 1973. Second, France won diplomatic points in Nine support for the form of the settlement, namely, that it should be negotiated and guaranteed within the framework of the UN Security Council. Third, the Nine belatedly recognized that they would have to hang together or they would hang separately. The total embargo

61. *Ibid.*, Oct. 16, 1973, p. 7.
62. *Ibid.*, Nov. 2, 1973, p. 1.
63. *Ibid.*, Nov. 17, 1973, pp. 1, 7.
64. *Washington Post,* Dec. 16, 1973, p. 6.

directed at the Netherlands because of its initial support of Israel was a portent of the fate awaiting them. How long the Nine would be able to maintain a common front in the face of energy shortages could not be predicted. It was clear, however, that France's weakness in the Mediterranean was predicable of its EEC partners if they stood alone vis-à-vis the superpowers and the Arab states.

Diplomatic Offensive in the Western Mediterranean

Spain, Tunisia, and Morocco

The third principal element of France's Mediterranean strategy—and the focus of President Pompidou's initial announcement of a new regional policy—[65] was aimed at strengthening bilateral ties with the southern European and Arab states. It was specifically directed at the three Francophone Maghreb states of Tunisia, Morocco, and Algeria and at Libya, which was portrayed as a Maghreb state.[66] In Europe, Spain, Italy, and Greece were objects of Paris's efforts to draw them within a larger policy framework under its leadership to promote its specific interests in the region and also stem superpower penetration. Preaching the virtues of nonalignment, France warned its European and Arab neighbors that failure to adopt these political habits risked infecting the western Mediterranean with the fever of the eastern half.

Among the European states, Spain appeared most attracted to French overtures. Foreign Minister Michel Debré visited Madrid in February 1970. Both states expressed the hope of maintaining the Mediterranean free of superpower control. Debré was sympathetic to the Spanish notion of a neutralized Mediterranean from which would be withdrawn the American and Soviet fleets, but placed the Spanish suggestion within the framework of four-power talks on the Middle East. A year later the French government received the Spanish foreign minister in Paris; it marked the first time that a Madrid official had been formally invited to the French capital since the

65. *PEF*, July–Dec. 1969, p. 160.
66. A subtle sign of the change can be seen in *Maghreb*, the government-sponsored bimonthly review of events in the Maghreb. Until May–June 1969, only Algeria, Morocco, and Tunisia were covered. Thereafter, Libya was included.

Spanish Civil War. The visit led to the purchase of thirty Mirage aircraft, and in June 1970 a French-Spanish military accord was reached that envisioned the exchange of territory between the two states for the use of their armed forces and joint cooperation between military staffs in planning, maneuvers, and arms production;[67] those accords opened the way, in the fall of 1970, to wider talks on Mediterranean security.[68]

The emerging Spanish-French alignment in the Mediterranean responded to a larger commonality of interests. France progressively became Spain's privileged European partner and its interlocutor with Western and Eastern Europe. Under French tutelage, Spain was to move along its chosen course toward the mainstream of European political and economic life. French sponsorship of Spanish association in the EEC appeared to be a major objective.

The hope of drawing Spain into Europe was a continuing theme struck by President de Gaulle during his twelve years of exile under the Fourth Republic.[69] On at least one occasion he characterized Europe as extending from Gibraltar to the Urals.[70] During his presidency, de Gaulle raised the possibility of Spain's adherence to a European political union. In his news conference of September 9, 1965, in the midst of the EEC controversy, he alluded to Spain's conceivable interest in a French plan for European cooperation. The following December, he voiced the hope that several neighboring states, presumably including Spain, would one day join the European economic group. Three weeks after the Luxembourg settlement, he suggested that the Six address themselves to the question of their relations with Spain.[71] President Pompidou viewed the role of France as an intermediary for Spain in Europe in a similar light: "I believe that it is in the interest of Spain," he said in his news conference of January 21, 1971, "to be open to Europe and that geography pushes it to do so through France as go-between." [72]

On a global scale, Spain's election to the UN Security Council

67. *Le Monde,* June 23, 1970, p. 1; *Journal de Genève,* June 27, 1970, p. 7.
68. *Le Monde,* Oct. 26, 1970, p. 7.
69. Jouve, *op. cit.,* I, 171–174.
70. *Ibid.,* I, 171.
71. *Ibid.,* I, 174.
72. *PEF,* Jan.–June 1971, p. 57.

carried obvious benefits for France. Furthermore, greater French-Spanish cooperation bolstered Spain's bargaining position with the United States over bases, security guarantees, and economic assistance. Spain's importance appeared sufficiently critical to American strategists that President Nixon personally visited with General Franco in September 1970 on a swing through the Mediterranean states. (France was conspicuously ignored.) Spain could also hope for tacit French acquiescence in its determined drive to rid Gibraltar of the British.[73]

The *rapprochement* was not without its difficulties. The condemnation to long confinement of fifteen Basque nationalists at Burgos in December 1970 reflected the continued repressiveness of the Franco regime. It complicated France's hope of drawing Spain and its more liberal European neighbors closer together and strained ties between France and Spain. Progress hinged on the continued influence of groups, such as Opus Dei, within the Spanish government to support an opening to Western Europe and on liberalization of personal freedom in Spain. The second was a necessary condition of the first, yet neither was a certainty. General Franco's decision to postpone scheduled talks with French Foreign Minister Maurice Schumann in early 1971, as a result of Spanish charges of interference in the Burgos affair,[74] illustrated the problem of aligning two states with vastly different regimes. By the summer, important officials of both states were again conferring on matters of common concern, but few were optimistic about the rapid pace of Spain's assimilation into Europe or into France's schemes for the Mediterranean. De Gaulle understood a key element of the problem in remarks made in 1948: "It is only down a democratic road that France and Spain will be truly able to meet and walk together." [75] The official Paris visit in October 1973 of Prince Juan Carlos, Franco's designated successor, provided no evidence that Spain was finally prepared to embark on the path marked out by de Gaulle twenty-five years earlier.[76]

73. *PEF,* Jan.–June 1969, pp. 78–80. Also see *l'Express,* Feb. 17, 1969, p. 4; *Le Monde,* Feb. 5, 1969, p. 1.

74. President Pompidou answered these charges in his news conference of January 21, 1971, *PEF,* Jan.–June 1971, p. 57.

75. Jouve, *op. cit.,* I, 172.

76. *Le Monde,* Oct. 23, 1973, pp. 1, 11 and *ibid.,* Oct. 24, 1973, p. 10.

Neither state, however, was able to entice Italy to follow its example of strictly European cooperation in the Mediterranean. The Italian government preferred the protection of NATO and the Sixth Fleet to the yet unrealized benefits of a Mediterranean grouping under French leadership.[77] Similarly, the decision of the Nixon administration to sell heavy arms to the Greek military government undercut French attempts to increase their influence in the Aegean. The French were outbid in their Mirage offer to Greece, but were eventually successful in concluding a more modest arms deal with the Athens government. France still harbored the hope, however, as its abstention within the Council of Europe condemning the Greek military regime suggested, of playing the role of European mediator along the lines being followed with respect to Spain. Timing was not propitious in the early 1970's.

Within the Maghreb, Tunisia and, somewhat less, Morocco were disposed to French overtures. Bourguiba's Tunisia had attempted unsuccessfully since 1964 to improve its standing in Paris. Tunisia's call for a French commonwealth, however flattering to Gaullist nationalism, received no public hearing or acknowledgement. Relations remained arrested until the crises of 1968 exposed the high cost of French intransigence. "Let us forget the past . . . and look forward towards the future," President de Gaulle was quoted as saying to Bahi Ladgham, President Bourguiba's close political ally, during his visit to Paris in October 1968. A month later, Foreign Minister Michel Debré announced the government's intention to "readjust the modalities of our cooperation . . . with the Tunisian government." [78] A loan approximating 100 million francs was negotiated in 1968 with the Bank of France to assist Tunisian economic growth. In February 1969, General de Gaulle received Habib Bourguiba, Jr., son of the Tunisian president. It was the first time since 1961 that a Tunisian minister had come to France on an official visit.

The communiqué issued by the two governments on February 5 exposed a remarkable agreement on major issues affecting both states, including military cooperation, the Middle East, Africa, and economic, cultural, and technical assistance. No longer ignored as dis-

77. Italian reluctance is reported in *Journal de Genève,* Feb. 14, 1969, p. 1.
78. *Perspectives,* Feb. 15, 1969, p. 8; also, *PEF,* July–Dec. 1968, p. 153.

pensable, Tunisia was accorded an important role in maintaining the precarious political and strategic balance which, said the communiqué, "ought to reign in the Mediterranean zone and to which the two countries declared themselves equally and especially attached." [79] Whereas the Gaullist government had before denigrated close French-Tunisian cooperation, it was now apparent "to the two delegations," noted the joint declaration, "that their cooperation . . . constituted a factor of progress and peace in the Mediterranean, and more particularly in the Maghreb, in the development of which the security and stability of Tunisia makes an essential contribution." [80]

President Pompidou continued his predecessor's efforts to tie France and Tunisia more closely together than before. French Foreign Minister Maurice Schumann visited Tunisia in November 1969 and reaffirmed the points covered the previous February.[81] French assistance had already been helpful in facilitating the association of Tunisia and Morocco with the Common Market in March 1969. Out of the renewed commitment to strengthen their bilateral contacts, the two states gradually developed a closer convergence of diplomatic and strategic views in the Mediterranean than had existed for over a decade. They held joint military exercises. France pledged greater financial and technical assistance to help Tunisia reach its planning goals. These took the form largely of loans and credits to the Tunisian government to assist on projects of common interest. French businesses were also encouraged to invest funds through government insurance guarantees against losses.[82]

Major cultural and technical assistance accords, moreover, were signed in February and June 1969, respectively.[83] The February 5 communiqué written by Debré and Bourguiba, Jr., had concluded by recognizing "the importance of close multilateral cooperation between the Francophone states. . . . Tunisia, in this respect," said the declaration, "continues to play a particularly important role." [84] Because of the timing of the communiqué and the signing of a five-year cultural

79. *PEF,* Jan.–June 1969, p. 77.
80. *Ibid.*
81. *Ibid.,* Jan.–July 1969, pp. 126–128.
82. *Le Monde,* Nov. 20, 1969, p. 1; also *ibid.,* Nov. 26, 1969, p. 1, on French-Tunisian military cooperation.
83. *PEF,* Jan.–June 1969, pp. 100, 172.
84. *Ibid.,* p. 78.

accord on February 14, the observation about cultural relations had more than passing interest. On February 17, approximately thirty French-speaking states from four continents sent delegates to Niamey, Niger, to create a multilateral organization for Francophone co-operation.[85] If the effort was in line with the traditional French interest in cultural expansion, it was not without broader and more immediate political ramifications. Culture was a highly valued instrument of French foreign policy. It was being employed where it would be welcomed, in the campaign to prop France's tottering global standing and reinforce its presence in the Mediterranean and in Africa. Bourguiba's Tunisia was a ready and willing tool.

The overtures to Tunisia paralleled those to Morocco although progress was bound to be slower. The de Gaulle government was unable to lift the precondition for better relations—the removal from office of General Oufkir, the Moroccan minister of the interior. During President de Gaulle's last month in office, talks at lower levels, dealing with economic aid, began.[86] In June 1969, two months after de Gaulle's departure, France agreed to assist Moroccan economic planning in selected technical areas. Modest steps like these eased President Pompidou's decision to lift the Oufkir ban since the Moroccan government gave no sign of budging. "I did not accede to de Gaulle," King Hassan II was quoted. "I have no reason to do so before Pompidou." [87] On December 15, President Pompidou announced the reopening of diplomatic relations between France and Morocco. General Oufkir was discreetly away on business when the French ambassador came to present his credentials. He would be very much in evidence a year later when Foreign Minister Maurice Schumann visited Morocco and was seen shaking hands with the General still under the judgment of the French courts.

Contacts quickly multiplied between the two states as groups of legislators, industrialists, and labor representatives visited each other. These were capped by King Hassan II's personal visit to France in February 1970.[88] French Foreign Minister Maurice Schumann re-

85. See *Francophone 1969/70*, No. 2 (March 1970). The entire issue reviews the Francophone effort for the year.
86. *Le Monde*, April 5–6, 1970, p. 3.
87. *Paris presse*, Dec. 19, 1969, p. 1.
88. *PEF*, Jan.–June 1970, pp. 32–33, 52.

turned to Morocco the following December. It was only at this time, almost a year after the French-Tunisian governments had first agreed on a joint communiqué, that France and Morocco were able to draft a common statement of purpose. Unlike the Tunisian announcements of February and November 1970, there were essentially no references to military, technical, economic, or cultural cooperation. The principal accomplishment was the creation of a mixed intergovernmental commission to review French-Moroccan relations on a continuing basis. The commission was a reminder that some institutional mechanism was needed to manage, if not resolve, the points in contest between the two states. Agreement was clearer, expectedly enough, on support for the Arab cause in the Middle East. Morocco also found France's ideas about the Mediterranean in line with its own neutralist course in the Cold War.[89] Both agreed that the Mediterranean should be "a zone of peace, of stability, and of fruitful cooperation between the seaboard states in respect of the independence and of the sovereignty of all partners." [90]

Economic and financial differences, some arising before the Ben Barka affair, helped explain the reserve of the communiqué. The French still pressed the indemnification cases of its nationals as well as demands for their greater personal freedom and for more discretion in transferring funds out of Morocco. Little could be done to slow King Hassan's "moroccanization" campaign of tertiary industries, a favored reformist program among Leftist elements. Foreigners and specifically the French, who composed the largest foreign contingent of ninety thousand nationals, were most adversely affected. The Moroccans wanted more French aid to balance their trade deficits to help realize their economic planning goals and to underwrite more of France's technical and cultural assistance program. They preferred, too, to be less dependent on France and asked, following Algeria's example, that indigenous cadres be developed in various technical areas of expertise.[91]

89. See Ali Skalli, "Les Constants dans la politique extérieur du Maroc," *France-Eurafrique,* No. 208 (July–Aug. 1969). The article is summarized in *Maghreb,* No. 35 (Sept.–Oct. 1969), p. 46.

90. *PEF,* July–Dec. 1970, p. 242.

91. A useful sketch of French-Moroccan relations is found in *Maghreb,* No. 43 (Jan.–Feb. 1971), pp. 13–14.

France did accord increased assistance to Morocco in a protocol signed in April 1970. Approximately 265 million francs were to be devoted to specific economic programs, including 100 million francs to alleviate Morocco's chronic trade imbalances.[92] This envelope doubled a year later. In May 1971, the French government signed three accords totaling 520 million francs in aid or about $100 million. In both cases, the funds were to be spent largely for French products.[93] These points of progress did not mean that France was prepared to fill Morocco's economic and investment needs. It was no more in a position to assume such an obligation with Morocco than with Tunisia. More francs fled Morocco in 1970 than returned in investment. American aid supplied 48 percent of all foreign assistance to Morocco. The accords still represented tangible progress. If the ties between the two states were looser and more detached than might be suggested by the inflated language of diplomatic friendship used by the leadership of both countries, they contrasted favorably with the frigid relations of the immediate post-Ben Barka period between 1965 and 1968.[94]

The considerations underlying France's efforts to improve its relations with Tunisia and Morocco were multiple. Most prominent among them were the general factors, discussed above, bearing on France's regional weakness. Moreover, as turmoil grew in the Middle East and what profit might be drawn from it had long passed the point of marginal return, the moderation of the former protectorates was viewed in a more favorable light. The new look at Tunisia and Morocco corresponded roughly with a heightened perception of the unreliability of the Algerian-French axis. Helping the re-evaluation were the positive strides being made by the Bourguiba and Hassan regimes to draw closer to the eastern Arab states. Both were staunch supporters of the Palestinian cause, yet they avoided the inflammatory language characteristic of Algerian and Libyan pronouncements. Morocco successfully hosted Muslim and Arab summit conferences in September and December 1969, respectively. King Hassan II displayed extraordinary diplomatic skill in keeping the warring delegations together long enough to agree on a joint communiqué,

92. *Ibid.*, No. 39 (May–June 1970), p. 9.
93. *Ibid.*, No. 46 (July–Aug. 1971), p. 27.
94. *Ibid.*, No. 43 (Jan.–Feb. 1971), pp. 13–14.

however vague its outlines and meaningless its impact on Arab politics. Holding the meetings was an accomplishment for Morocco in Arab politics.

Tunisia's moderation was no less valued. Freed from the opprobrium attached to the Moroccan throne, republican Tunisia was able to widen its ties with the eastern Arabs and, specifically, with neighboring Libya to a greater degree than the Hassan government. In the fall of 1970, Tunisia became the focal point of Arab attempts, later proved abortive, to mediate the dispute between the Palestinian guerrillas and Jordan. A more cautious and less ambitious France under President Pompidou could see virtue in moderation. Tunisia was singled out for special attention. Going beyond its predecessor, the Pompidou government expressed its "attachment to the peaceful balance which ought to reign in the Mediterranean and in pursuit of which Tunisia, thanks to its geographic position, its political stability and its international audience, is especially called to play a positive role." [95]

Both states conducted a vigorous foreign policy with the superpowers and their clients while attempting to preserve their own political independence.[96] Their balanced diplomacies, emphasizing bilateral ties of mutual advantage with all states, regardless of regime, were in harmony with France's Mediterranean aims. Having abandoned de Gaulle's inflated ambitions in the immediate post-Evian period, Pompidou's France shunned no state from which benefits could be drawn, nor ignored any which could offer France access to the region. The Bourguiba and Hassan regimes responded to French preachments of insulating the Mediterranean from the superpower struggle while extracting what favors could be had from both sides. For all their Arab chauvinism, neither wished the upheaval of the eastern Mediterranean to upset their delicately balanced internal politics or their opportunistically oriented foreign policies. It was helpful, too, to keep on good terms with France and with its EEC partners. Such a course was a partial alternative to superpower dependence. Both states accordingly were more consistent supporters

95. *PEF*, July–Dec. 1969, p. 127.
96. The bimonthly issues of *Maghreb* detail the contacts between Tunisia and Morocco and the superpowers and their clients. See also the *Annuaire de l'Afrique du Nord* for each appropriate year.

of France's big-power formula for the Middle East than were their immediate Arab neighbors. There were also points of accord on maintaining a barrier to superpower penetration of Black Africa and on extending efforts to develop greater Maghreb economic cooperation.

Algeria and Libya

There was no gainsaying the importance for France's revised Mediterranean policy of closer ties with Tunisia and Morocco. Progress was jeopardized, however, in the absence of similar improvement in Franco-Algerian relations. The vaunted Gaullist praise for the Algiers-Paris axis could not muffle the rising criticism on both sides. The principal source of friction was oil. It bore on every other important relation. The two governments, especially the French, had approved the intermeshing of oil with their other bilateral ties. French technical, cultural, and especially economic aid were integral parts of the oil package accepted by both states in 1965. Algeria exchanged oil concessions for expected help toward its ambitious program of modernization and industrialization. Outlets for Algerian workers and wine were similarly linked to the fate of the joint exploitation of Algeria's oil resources.

However much the Algerians valued French counsel to resist superpower penetration of the Mediterranean or however much they were pleased with France's stand on all-Arab questions (President Boumedienne wrote a personal letter complimenting de Gaulle's embargo on arms to Israel),[97] they were ultimately more interested in concrete questions of oil, aid, and economic advantage. They were also concerned about freeing themselves from the last vestiges of what they perceived as French colonial domination and anxious to avoid trading this dependency for another on one or the other of the superpowers. French Mediterranean policy was of lesser moment to Algeria than the outcome of the specific differences between the two states. Algeria's willingness to follow France's regional lead was, therefore, contingent on lubricating these friction points in the form of French concessions to make the Paris-Algiers axis turn more smoothly.

97. *PEF*, Jan.–June 1969, p. 41.

There was, however, a fundamental conflict between the official French and Algerian perceptions of their relation. Gaullist France ostensibly treated Algeria as an equal partner. The 1965 oil agreement was to be more than a contract of mutual convenience. It was part of a larger French commitment to help Algeria achieve economic independence to complement its political freedom, a demonstration of economic and political cooperation between vastly different regimes and social systems. Algeria was to be the preferred instrument of France's Third World strategy and to be given priority for assistance over the other Francophone states. Cooperation between the two states was pictured as a kind of code of rights and duties of the two partners aimed at achieving supposedly common political goals. Mutual political convenience tended to be raised to the level of legal obligation and privilege; the exchange of economic benefits tended to be treated as matters of perpetual right.[98]

The Algerians viewed the world differently. The 1965 accord was a provisional arrangement. Its vitality depended on Algeria's calculation of its needs and interests. Unable to exploit its oil and gas reserves without French help in 1965, the Algerian state felt obliged to accept an arrangement based on what the "rapport of forces" between the two states permitted. The Algerian leadership had not renounced its pledge, taken before independence, eventually to assume sovereign control over the country's natural resources and to exercise an unrestricted right to dispose of them as it saw fit. The Algerian regime conceded, temporarily, the economic and political capacity of the French oil companies and government to influence the development of Algeria's gas and oil riches, but not their right to do so. Turning France out in 1962 would have meant a loss of production and a decrease of investment that could only have retarded Algeria's economic advance. Nevertheless, for the Algerians, their self-styled revolution could not be completed until they dissolved these restrictions on their sovereign control and until—more

98. Two useful reviews of the Algerian-French oil accord and its larger implications for cooperation are found in the article of P. Valberg, "Cinq ans après: Bilan des accords franco-algériens de coopération industrielle et pétrolière du 29 juillet 1965," *Annuaire, 1969,* pp. 55–92. Also very helpful is Jean-Pierre Sereni's "La Politique algérienne des hydrocarbures," *Maghreb,* No. 45 (May–June 1971), pp. 31–49.

importantly—they acquired the capital, technical skills, and managerial cadres capable of replacing French expertise and economic help.

By 1968, a year before the agreement was due for formal revision, the Algerian government felt sufficiently strong to challenge the 1965 document and place relations on an entirely different basis than that officially sanctioned by the French government. Instead of cooperative relations between privileged partners, the Algerians preferred discrete bilateral accords in specific areas of mutual interest. That was all the 1965 accords and succeeding cultural and technical accords were in their eyes. In place of a confining relation with France, they wished to widen the spectrum of their economic, political, and even security ties with other states. France would be only one element of Algeria's Mediterranean policy, and not necessarily its focal point. The Algerians learned much from French diplomacy, not the least of which was the skill of manipulating announced universal goals for national advantage. Algeria, too, had larger aspirations in the Arab world and the Third World. These pretensions were not to interfere, however, with the task of acquiring material benefits where they could be had.

The assumptions and practice of France's Mediterranean policy suggested a similar orientation. But France had the more difficult task of breaking with the past without seeming to have done so. (There were domestic opinion and previously stated Gaullist designs on Algeria to consider.) At the same time there was some transitional utility, to gain political bargaining leverage over Algeria, to make emotional appeals to traditional Algerian-French friendship or to make outraged, righteous objections to Algeria's unilateral policy moves aimed at erecting a bilateral relation resting less on sentiment than on calculated reciprocal advantage. That is, whatever announced French policy reflected of previous Gaullist rhetoric about Algeria (the French simultaneously believed they had legal rights and that these had political bargaining power), operational policy from the start of the negotiations on oil in November 1969 also evidenced some awareness of the determination of Algerian negotiators to break with the old formulas governing oil and gas and to establish the French presence in Algeria on a basis more suited to Algerian control and preferences. Moreover, even as the French complained of

Algerian violations of solemn commitments that created the privileged relations between the two states, a growing circle of opinion within the government was intent on widening France's stance in the Mediterranean, much as the Algerians were attempting to do in reverse order.[99]

The Algerians demonstrated considerable sophistication in fashioning a brief to justify the recapture of their oil interests. The de Gaulle government could hardly quarrel with Algeria's repeated assertion of sovereignty over its natural resources. The Algerian attack was broad and deep.[100] First, they accused the French oil companies of failing to maintain adequate investment levels consistent with the 1965 commitments. Prospecting by ASCOOP, a joint French-Algerian enterprise, had yielded only twenty million tons of new oil reserves. Some wells were alleged to be overexploited, others underutilized. The French partner in Sonatrach, the Algerian national oil company, had spent 220 million francs since 1965 although the Algerians had hoped for at least 300 million.[101]

The differences between the French companies and the Algerian government were not easily reconciled. The companies made their investment decisions on the basis of prevailing opportunity costs; the Algerians, bent on using oil and gas to run their industrial program, were interested in drilling as many wells as possible regardless of alternative investment opportunities. Concessionaire rights were tantamount to limits on the rate and magnitude of Algeria's pursuit of its extensive industrialization effort.

Second, the Algerians were sensitive about questions of fiscal policy. They wished to increase the requirement that 50 percent of the business receipts of the French oil companies remain in Algeria. They sought, too, some compensation for the revenues earned by France through taxation of oil products. These, they felt, belonged in some way to the Algerian state since they derived from the exploitation of its natural resources. The tax claim made by Algeria was added to its criticism of what it believed to be the French govern-

99. See n. 2 above.
100. The Algerian case appears in the *New York Herald Tribune*, International edition, May 14, 1971, pp. 8–9.
101. *Problèmes africains et tiers monde*, No. 517, Oct. 23, 1969.

ment's policy of favoring French oil companies over its obligations to aid Sonatrach.

Third, and most significantly, the two states differed over the reference price for oil, the artificially stated price on which Algeria's oil revenues were calculated. The 1965 accord set a price of $2.08 a barrel. According to Algerian calculations, inflation had long overtaken that price. They were also dissatisfied with not having received the so-called "Suez premium" of a 5 percent increase in the selling price of Mediterranean oil as a result of the closing of the Suez Canal. They stressed the argument, too, that Algerian oil was closer and better in quality than its competitors.[102] Finally, the percentage of ownership over Algeria's oil and gas resources was a bone of contention. The French were willing to concede 35 percent ownership to the Algerians, who wanted majority control.[103]

The Algerians displayed no less impressive skills in the long, Byzantine negotiations over a settlement on which hung most of the Algerian-French tie. These took place at two distinct levels. The first was direct negotiations between France and Algeria. The second consisted of larger discussions between the international oil companies in which the French companies and their affiliates participated.[104] Each state relied at different times on these more encompassing talks to reinforce its particular position in the hassle over oil. Little progress was made on the major points at issue in 1970. Meanwhile, Algerian pressures mounted. Most foreign oil concerns were nationalized. Temporarily exempted were the French companies and the American firms of El Paso and Getty Oil, which had already accepted contractual arrangements specified by the Algerian government.

In July 1970, the Algerian government unilaterally set the reference price for oil at $2.85 a barrel. The French objected that the decision violated French rights protected by the 1965 accord. Few arguments could have been less persuasive to the Algerians. Algeria also raised the 50 percent requirement to 80 percent. These strains were only

---

102. *Le Monde diplomatique,* Sept. 1970, p. 16.

103. *Le Monde,* March 9, 1971, p. 15.

104. The state-owned ERAP group announced it would not participate in the talks, but the French Petroleum Company, principally in private hands, was an active participant.

partly eased by the French agreement to assist Algeria's construction of a giant gas liquification plant at Skikda and the French oil companies' concession of back royalties of 675 million francs in January 1971.

February was the crisis month. The French, hoping to gain additional bargaining leverage from the outcome of talks between Persian Gulf oil suppliers and the international petroleum cartels, broke off negotiations with the Algerians in early February. The latter countered three weeks later. On February 24, Algeria assumed control of 51 percent of France's oil interests and nationalized all pipeline and gas-producing installations. This dramatic, but not wholly unexpected, action was accompanied by a pattern of coercive tactics employed by both sides. Diplomats were incarcerated; nationals on both sides were harassed, imprisoned on dubious charges, or expelled; threats of a diplomatic break were daily bruited abroad; and French oil technicians were summarily withdrawn to France, crippling oil production operations on which Algeria's economic life depended. At the same time, both sides issued conciliatory statements that neither could profit from a complete rupture. Obscured by the pyrotechnics was the shrewd and calculating measure each side took of the other. Both master and pupil adroitly mixed words of bombast and conciliation with demands and concessions to suit the negotiating requirements of the moment.[105]

The Algerians were no less active on the international level of negotiations. They joined the principal international organization of oil producers in 1969,[106] immediately pressed members to demand higher prices, and took a common stand to compel an increase in oil revenues from the major oil companies. Algeria relished using French pronouncements in favor of higher prices for primary products coming from the Third World as a form of aid to underdeveloped countries.[107] It had a ready partner, too, in revolutionary Libya, led by an inexperienced and impressionable group of young army offi-

---

105. The daily issues of *Le Monde* and *Le Figaro* from January through April 1971 should be consulted for details on the negotiations which can only be summarized here.

106. *Le Monde*, Dec. 12, 1970, p. 35.

107. See communiqué between the French and Algerian foreign ministers, Oct. 1970, *PEF*, July–Dec. 1970, p. 95.

cers. Algeria also led in the formation of a regional bloc, including Libya, Iraq, and Egypt, to press for prices that not only reflected the higher requests of the Persian Gulf group but provided an additional premium from European buyers because of the proximity and quality of the Mediterranean producers.[108] It was able to rely on Libyan support to resist the pressures of the French oil companies. The Libyan government approved a common position to resist, in the words of President Boumedienne, "the plots, threats, and the economic pressures that the French companies are attempting to carry out against Algeria." [109] The Libyans assured the Algerians that they would sell Algerian oil to break the boycott launched by the French firms. Libya's success in April 1971 in securing a reference price of $3.45 a barrel strengthened Algeria's hand to demand $3.60.

The result of these maneuvers was compromise, not rupture. The ties of interest, including oil, were too great to give full vent to diplomatic pique or *amour-propre*. "Oil is probably, at the present time, in a country like France, the most elemental product," said President Pompidou in late June 1971. "To scorn oil is fashionable, but fatal!" [110] President Boumedienne had already indicated willingness to indemnify the Algerian seizures. The French government quietly stopped insisting on tying oil to France's over-all presence in Algeria. Technical and cultural cooperation as well as wine and workers could be treated separately from oil. To meet rising criticism of the government's handling of the Algerian negotiations, Foreign Minister Maurice Schumann also catalogued, in April and June, France's many interests in Algeria: France was still Algeria's first trading partner and its eighth commercial client; achieving France's Mediterranean security and diplomatic objectives were inconceivable without Algerian cooperation; relations with the other Maghreb states hinged critically on preserving France's position in Algeria; France had simply invested too much of its economic and political capital to abandon its work of over 130 years.[111]

The way was opened to a settlement of outstanding differences. On April 15, 1971, Prime Minister Jacques Chaban-Delmas formally

108. *Le Monde,* March 9, 1971, p. 15.
109. *Maghreb,* No. 46 (July–Aug. 1971), p. 7.
110. *PEF,* Jan.–June 1971, p. 244.
111. *Ibid.,* pp. 155–156, and especially 202–207.

broke with the hallowed Gaullist notion that oil negotiations were the province of the Algerian and French states. These were turned over to the French oil companies. The enterprises most concerned were the state-owned ERAP group and the French Petroleum Company, a private firm with strong public backing. ERAP had most at stake in the talks. Most of its investments were in Algeria, and 80 percent of its supplies came from Algerian sources. FPC, with more extensive holdings, counted on Algeria for approximately 20 percent of its needs and, unlike ERAP, was more successful in resisting proposals for joint ventures with Algerian enterprises.[112] President Pompidou summarized the new French orientation. The break with the past was formally made. Algeria was no longer France's privileged Third World partner:

For our part, we hold apart our differences [with Algeria] from human problems either of Algerians in France or of French in Algeria, we pursue cooperation in the critical area of education and culture. We are ready to participate in Algeria's economic development, in proportion to our possibilities, our interests and in relation to the value of the projects undertaken. In other words, *we do not give Algeria a priority in our cooperation,* but we do not exclude it either from the number of States with which we cooperate closely and especially we abstain from any polemic.[113]

The oil controversy was satisfactorily settled in the succeeding months of 1971. FPC signed an accord in June 1971; ERAP followed a few months later. Both the oil companies and Algeria sobered after the initial shock of the partial nationalizations wore off. The oil company boycotts of Algerian oil and their threats to take legal action against foreign agents purchasing it had some effect. More damaging was the 25 percent cutback in production occasioned by the precipitate French pullout. Expected larger sales of Algerian oil to the Soviet Union and the East European states did not materialize.[114] The Algerians learned, too, the hard economic lesson of scarce resources. As foreign financial sources dried up, they were forced to

112. *Le Monde,* July 20, 1971, p. 9. Alain Murcier's article makes clear that the issues were even more complicated than can be explained here.
113. *PEF,* Jan.–June 1971, p. 244.
114. *Le Monde,* June 22, 1971, pp. 1–2; *Le Nouvel observateur,* June 14, 1971, pp. 34–35.

reduce their search for new oil reserves.[115] A more accommodating policy was advised, and the Algerians shifted their course accordingly. For their part, the French still found Algerian oil useful. Under the new agreement with the French oil companies, Algeria assumed control over 75 percent of its oil production and all of its natural gas and pipeline facilities. This contrasted with 30 percent of its oil production resources and 25 percent of its pipeline and natural gas installations before the takeovers.[116]

The break over oil and the passing of the privileged Algerian-French relation was not without its positive aspects for French foreign policy. France was induced to widen its oil supply base in the Mediterranean. In 1971, when tensions with Algeria reached their peak, France had already shifted its oil purchases to other suppliers, including Saudi Arabia, Iraq, Nigeria, and Abu Dahbi. Saudi Arabia, among the most conservative and traditional of the Arab states, replaced Algeria as France's foremost supplier. The latter dropped to seventh. However, no state, as Table 5 above reveals, supplied more than 16 percent of France's oil needs, contrasting with the high of 31 percent provided by Algeria in 1968. French supplies came from a larger number of states, and no one source was permitted to dominate purchases. Freed from commitments to Algeria, the French Petroleum Company also secured important oil concessions from Iraq in June 1972. In gaining greater access to Iraqi oil supplies and exploitation rights, FPC secured a competitive advantage over rival Western firms and recouped some of the momentum and losses suffered in the forced withdrawal from Algeria. French hopes of being a leading world oil power were kept alive while sources of supply were kept open and better protected against abrupt cut-offs by any one state, like Algeria. What could not be foreseen was the Arab unity of the Yom Kippur War which resulted in a partial ban on oil to France from the major oil-producing states.

Differences with Algeria would appear to have helped, not harmed, France's over-all trade position with the Arab Mediterranean states. France maintained its level of exports to Algeria in 1971 while reducing its imports, mostly of oil, by more than half. Until

---

115. *Le Monde,* Aug. 16, 1971, p. 16.
116. *Le Monde diplomatique,* Jan. 1972, p. 27.

1971, France ran a heavy annual deficit in trade with Algeria. The dramatic reversal of 1971 amounted to a $267 million surplus that offset France's deficits with other Arab oil suppliers. France's deficits with these nations, listed in Table 4, were cut in half or by about $250 million. French exports to the eastern Arab states increased by $100 million in one year from 1970 to 1971. In the period 1965 to 1971, French exports to the Middle East Arab states more than tripled.

The Algerians and French were also closer together on regional policy than might have been suggested by the vituperative rhetoric issuing from each capital. Like France, Algeria did not permit its ideological pronouncements to dictate entirely its search for profit at the expense of both superpowers. As noted above, the Algerians had successfully solicited considerable technical, economic, and military aid from the Russians. The seven-year commercial accord signed with the Soviet Union at the close of 1968 widened the future possibilities of Algerian trade in order to reduce over time its dependence on the French market. Economic contacts with Britain and the United States also multiplied. A multimillion dollar, long-term contract was let to supply natural gas to United States firms; technical assistance arrangements were similarly reached with Anglo-American concerns. A request of nearly $300 million in loans from the World Bank reportedly was spurred by the anticipated sale of natural gas to the United States.[117] Algeria's progress in its dealings with the superpowers partly explained its decision to revise the 1965 oil accord.[118]

Broader access to the aid, capital, expertise, and markets of the superpowers and France provided a setting in which the Algerians could better resist pressures from any of the three. France might have less influence over an independent Algeria than it might desire, but the Algerians could be expected to acquit themselves in a test of strength with the superpowers, too.[119] That Algeria could profit from

117. *Maghreb,* No. 46 (July–Aug. 1971), p. 20.
118. See the summary of French-Algerian relations found in Nicole Grimaud, "Algérie-France: décolonisation systématique par le procédé des nationalisations," Centre d'Etudes des Relations Internationales, Feb. 1971, mimeo.
119. Interview with Edward Behr, *Newsweek,* Paris edition, Aug. 18, 1970. Behr has spent a great deal of time in Algeria and has talked extensively with Algerian leaders.

the competition of these states for its favor was suggested in the example offered by the United States. It turned a deaf ear to French hints that Algerian requests for approval of import licenses for natural gas and of a loan from the World Bank be given unsympathetic treatment. As one American diplomat confided to a *Le Monde* correspondent: "We remember the *coup* of Libya [France's sale of Mirages to Libya]. France, when it took our place there, explained to us that it was doing so in order to prevent the Russians from doing it. Amen. We have only to explain today to Paris that if we are talking with Algeria, it is in order to avoid France seeing the USSR replace her. Of course, Paris asked us to be tough. But why should we have been? Did President Pompidou give us a gift when he denounced the invasion of Laos during his trip to Black Africa? Absolutely not. And what was he seeking with his Mediterranean policy if not to chase us out of the region? Right. We don't owe him anything, and, moreover, we need that Algerian gas." [120]

The Algerians also turned to Western and Eastern Europe for help. Accords with all of the Soviet satellites were reached on varied forms of technical, economic, or cultural cooperation.[121] No less than its Maghreb neighbors, it sought associate status in the EEC. Similarly, it favored a détente in Europe, closer ties between the Mediterranean and European states of both blocs as well as the neutral states, and a right to participate in the European Conference on Security and Cooperation. The wider range of bilateral relations with the European states pursued by Algeria was in keeping with French attempts to strike a similar set of gainful ties. The network of bilateral working relations between Mediterranean and European states across bloc divisions was itself perceived as a source of regional stability. Meanwhile, France still enjoyed an advantageous position in Algeria (and the greater Maghreb) relative to its EEC partners.[122]

Algeria also displayed affinity for France's hopes (not fully consistent with the interest in playing off the superpowers) of keeping the Mediterranean insulated from the global conflict between the United

120. *Le Monde,* April 18–19, 1971, p. 6.
121. The bimonthly issues of *Maghreb* detail these accords; summary tables are found in the annual issue of the *Annuaire de l'Afrique du nord.*
122. See the excellent and subtle review of *Maghreb* and EEC economic and political relations in B. Etienne's "Maghreb et C.E.E.," *Annuaire de l'Afrique du nord, 1969,* pp. 169–202.

States and the Soviet Union. Nonalignment was the honored foreign policy principle. The Mediterranean was to be a lake of peace: "The Mediterranean ought to find its vocation under the mark of a union among peoples in order to be a place of peaceful convergence, and not a field of competition for domineering ends. The interest of all is that the Mediterranean return to the Mediterraneans. Under these conditions, any policy of zones of influence ought to be rejected, bases and foreign fleets definitely withdrawn from this part of the world, one of the most exposed to the fluctuations of international politics." [123] Once the oil revision was about to be settled the Algerian government reverted again to the language of conciliation. Algerian Foreign Minister Abdel Aziz Bouteflika observed in July 1971 that French-Algerian cooperation was a valued example for all states of the region. It was the basis for making the Mediterranean region "a lake of cooperation, of stability and of peace." [124] This theme was pursued when Algeria hosted the Third World conference of nonaligned states in September 1973 and clashed with Cuba's Fidel Castro, who pressed to exempt the Soviet Union from attack as a neocolonial power.[125] The Yom Kippur War advised Algeria temporarily to soft pedal its nonalignment strategy.[126] Its renewal largely depended on a final settlement of the Middle East conflict, including not only accord between Israel and its Arab neighbors but also the creation of a Palestinian state.[127]

The Algerians also supported other French foreign policy hopes. They approved of greater economic and political cooperation in the formation of a greater Maghreb. Unlike Libya, Algeria settled in the late 1960's most of its differences with Tunisia and Morocco and learned to live peacefully, if sometimes uneasily, with republican Tunisia and monarchical Morocco. Developing ties with Black Africa was a major French and Algerian policy goal. Not surprisingly, the Algerians sought their own, not France's, advantage. Whatever the difficulties of working with Algeria were, its thirteen million people and vigorous government administration could not be easily ignored.

123. *Le Monde diplomatique,* Jan. 1972, p. 20.
124. *Le Monde,* July 11–12, 1971, p. 1.
125. *Ibid.,* Sept. 9–10, 1973, p. 1.
126. Prime Minister Boumedienne visited Moscow during the crisis to present his views, *ibid.,* Oct. 17, 1973, pp. 1–2.
127. *Le Monde diplomatique,* Nov. 1973, p. 7.

Unique among the Arab states, it had gained the principal share of control over its own oil and gas resources. Algeria, moreover, did not hide its ambition to become an Arab leader and a potential rival to Egypt. Witness its sponsorship in November 1973 of an Arab unity conference to bolster the Egyptian-Syrian position in talks with Israel under the auspices of the superpowers.[128] The continuity of the Algerian government and its strong internal rule, however alien to French democratic sensitivities, was a source of stability in the Maghreb and in the larger, more turbulent Arab world. These qualities came to be more admired in France with the passing of Gaullist illusions. The heightened awareness of the Pompidou government of France's tenuous position in the Mediterranean and its vulnerability to upheaval in the region did nothing to diminish the attractiveness of holding fast in Algeria until the next storm.

The *coup de Libye* of late 1969 appeared to be the most spectacular success of President Pompidou's Mediterranean policy. A month after the declaration of a new posture on France's southern flank, the French government announced its decision to sell 110 Mirage aircraft, including 30 Mirage III's of advanced design, to the revolutionary government of Libya. The regime of Colonel Qaddafi had assumed power in a *coup d'état* the preceding September. A march was stolen on the superpowers which, according to French sources, were prepared to sell arms to the new revolutionary regime. To soften American chagrin, shortly before President Pompidou's trip to the United States, the French argued that the dispatch of French arms buttressed Western interests and blunted Soviet penetration of the Mediterranean basin; better the French than the Russians, though some Americans might have wondered. Moreover, to counter United States objections that the sale had an unsettling effect on the area, both militarily and politically, the French pointed to the long and staggered schedule of delivery of the aircraft (which bought time while awaiting a Middle East agreement), the restrictions placed on the transfer or use of the Mirages by third states, and the absence of an adequate number of pilots and crews to fly and service the sophisticated equipment.[129] To placate the Soviets, the French re-

128. *Le Monde,* Nov. 30, 1973, p. 1.
129. The Libyan sale is defended by Prime Minister Jacques Chaban-Delmas in *La Politique de la France en méditerranée.*

versed themselves; better the French than the Americans, who were less disposed to accede to the Soviet Union's wishes in the Middle East (and Europe). The Libyan sale, adding Mirages to those flying over Spain and Israel, armed the French with a new argument that four, not two, state accords would reflect the power realities of the region.

Since France's penetration occurred in the immediate wake of the Libyan government's decision to expel British and American forces from the territory, it was the obvious beneficiary of the losses suffered by the Anglo-American states after the Six-Day War. The French had cause to be pleased with the Libyan leadership's rhetorical embrace of the nonalignment formula. In December 1969, the Libyan and Algerian governments agreed that all foreign naval forces should leave the region.[130] To be sure the Libyans were disposed to Soviet enticements. In praising France's Middle East stand, the Qaddafi government also singled out the Soviet Union as the best friend of the Arab states.[131] Sympathy for the Soviet Union, however, did not prevent the Libyan regime, filled with the rhetoric of Arab and Islamic nationalism,[132] from supporting Egyptian President Sadat's purge of Communist elements in his government or from intervening in Sudan's civil strife of July 1971. In the latter case, the Libyans were instrumental in reinstating Gafaar Al-Nimeiry, the deposed Sudanese president, who seized the occasion of the abortive coup to crush the Communist forces within his government.[133]

Unrelenting Libyan support for the slogans of Arab and Islamic nationalism strengthened France's Arab credentials by association. The Libyans, like the Algerians, were unyielding in their hostility to Israel and in their announced support of the Palestinian guerrillas against Jordan and Israel. The Federation of Arab Republics approved by Libya, Egypt, and Syria in September 1971 tied Libya formally to its East Arab neighbors. For all its disadvantages, the Federation had the provisional utility of placing France in the vanguard of the Western states in ostensible support for Arab unity. The harm was slight for the goal was distant by any measure. In building

130. *Maghreb,* No. 37 (Jan.–Feb. 1970), p. 23.
131. *Ibid.,* p. 7
132. See the interview with Colonel Qaddafi, *Le Monde,* May 6, 1971, pp 1, 6.
133. *Maghreb,* No. 47 (Sept.–Oct. 1971), p. 24.

Libya's military strength, moreover, France could pose as the defender of Arab solidarity, reinforce its alignment with the progressive (and oil-producing) wing of the Arab states, and still contribute to the division among the Arabs through assistance to Libya as an independent state. The Libyans were publicly enthusiastic about the Federation, but careful to retain control over their oil revenues. The absence of a Syrian representative at the second annual celebration of Libya's rule under the military regime was as conspicuous as Sudan's failure to join the Federation after having been one of the initiators of the scheme.

The economic benefits of the Mirage sale lent material substance to the potential political gains. Libyan economic relations were reportedly to be guided by "the position adopted by interested states with regard to the Israeli-Arab conflict." [134] One informed source reported that "among the number of western states which are interested in the Libyan market, France occupies a special place because the intensification of economic ties between the two states stems from *a political will*. Libya . . . is disposed to a country which, far from constituting a threat on the international plane, has several times shown an understanding of Libyan arguments and its sympathy for the young state." [135] The $400 million in foreign exchange that France was scheduled to earn would partially offset its oil purchases in Libya over the next half decade. The sale of the aircraft opened the way, too, to the sale of supporting military equipment and larger commercial orders. French oil companies already enjoyed some limited prospecting rights in Libya. Increased purchases of Libyan oil broadened France's supply base and somewhat decreased its reliance on Algerian production.[136]

Hazards Facing the French Course in the Mediterranean

France's Mediterranean policy was as much an admission of weakness as a genuine attempt to stem the erosion of its position there. The superpower challenge was bothersome. France's Mediterranean

134. *Ibid.*, No. 39 (May–June 1970), p. 7.
135. *Ibid.*, No. 45 (May–June 1971), p. 12. Emphasis added.
136. Representative comment is found in n. 41, above, and in *Combat*, Jan. 28, 1970, p. 1; *L'Express*, Jan. 20, 1970, p. 22; *Le Monde*, Jan. 28, 1970, p. 3 and Oct. 15, 1970, p. 3.

policy partially hinged on the continued division, mutual suspicion, and ineptitude of the United States and the Soviet Union. But as a strategically weak and dependent power, France had nothing to gain and everything to lose if that rivalry erupted into a military confrontation. The dilemma was sharply posed: neither a Soviet-American regional accord nor such intense strife that armed hostilities flared between them was acceptable. France's moderate behavior in the United Nations during the October 1973 crisis, acceding to superpower leadership yet condemning a condominium for the region, exemplified the search for a middle course between superpower concert and armed conflict.

The greater fear of the early 1970's was superpower agreement at the expense of French interests, an analysis of the conditions for Mediterranean peace which appeared to be essentially correct. What state or group of states could effectively pit themselves against these great powers if they stood together? But in that case, need they take seriously into account French interests or sensitivities? The Rogers plan, the SALT talks, the sale of military equipment to the Greek junta, President Nixon's conspicuous failure in September 1970 to visit Paris during his tour of Mediterranean powers, his remarkable appeal to the Soviet Union for global accord from the United Nations rostrum the following month, and superpower sponsorship of the Middle East peace talks of December 1973—all these actions suggested that the United States was not prepared to give an affirmative answer to this question. Nor was it certain that the Soviet Union would either. The United States, not France, had most to offer the Soviet Union in political accommodation in the Middle East and Europe, in trade credits and technical exchange, and in relief from the arms race. Even in the absence of American compensations, the Soviets had little perceptible incentive—despite French expectations—to forego much of their economic and political gains among the Arab states to satisfy French needs.

Under the best conditions for French diplomacy—intense, but non-military, superpower rivalry—there was reason to question whether France could maintain a viable competitive position against one or the other of the superpowers even as they dissipated the bulk of their energies and resources in their global duel. The allure of France's neutralist and nonalignment preachings to small powers was roughly proportional to the risks of involvement in the struggle between the United States and the Soviet Union. As these risks diminished, the game of extracting benefits from the superpowers, preferably both at the same time, grew in appeal. Everyone—France not excepted—played the game to a greater or lesser degree. Indeed, French diplomacy offered valuable instruction for less experienced states. Tunisia and Morocco became old hands at the balancing act. Algeria, too, could on convenient occasions ignore its blasts at the Anglo-American imperialists long enough to seek beneficial trade concessions and draw on previously condemned capitalist firms for technical help and investments. Growing Soviet sales to Algeria and its increasing dependence on Soviet military assistance also struck at France's preponderant position.

In a bilateral contest with the superpowers, France was at a disadvantage from the start. It heavily depended on Middle East oil and the expansion of exports to the region. As suppliant (*demandeur,* if you will), its bargaining leverage was necessarily circumscribed. France's charge that the superpowers sought their own national advantage in arrangements with small states was not without substance, but France was far less able to allay the national ambitions of the Mediterranean states with arms and economic aid. It did not have the same degree of superpower ability to cajole, compromise, or command. Neither could a militarily vulnerable France assure the security of the regional states to compensate for the tutelage they had to endure under great-power patronage.

The growing competition of its European partners heightened France's difficulty. West Germany's sales to the Middle East approximately doubled those of France. It offered strong inducements, too, to the Maghreb states, particularly Morocco. The German government was not oblivious to the political requirements of Middle East penetration. Its awkward handling of the public exposure of the EEC paper on the Mediterranean in 1971, while hardly an inspiring example of skilled diplomacy, suggested unwillingness to back Israel unconditionally at the expense of access to Arab oil, markets, and capitals. Despite its temporary eclipse in the Middle East, England was an experienced player of the game, and still had a firm foothold among the moderate Arab states on both sides of the Nile. The technical aid supplied by British companies to the Algerians had some role

in the French-Algerian break. No less than France, British firms sali-
vated when Middle East and Maghreb markets were dangled before
them. If the Mediterranean was no longer the lifeline of the British
empire, its geographical position and oil were still factors in the
strategic calculus.

France faced mounting pressure from its European partners and
the Maghreb states to revise gradually its privileged economic and
trading positions in the western Mediterranean. The Rome Treaty
had sanctioned France's position when it commanded the remains of
an empire. The turnabout in France's relations with its former wards
and the gradual Europeanization of Middle East politics and economics placed France on an equal footing with its European partners.
They saw little justification for France's advantaged access to the markets of its former dependencies through trade and investment privileges retained as remains of its colonial past.

Alternatively, France needed the support of its European partners,
as the Yom Kippur War demonstrated, in advancing its regional interests among the Arab states and before the superpowers. But there was
room for skepticism about the vision and will of the Pompidou administration in nudging forward these preliminary gropings toward a
European foreign policy or even in maintaining a façade of European
unity toward the Arab states. Pompidou's France displayed resourcefulness in manipulating the levers of European diplomacy, but these
were not attached to any implementing machinery, partly because of
French resistance to any move to develop institutional mechanisms
until common policy views were defined. That the Geneva talks began without reference to the Nine suggests that neither the superpowers nor the Arabs nor the Israelis were impressed with the closing
of Europe's ranks.

France's bilateral ties with its southern European neighbors in the
Mediterranean, Spain and Italy, also left much room for improvement. Spain's slow internal liberalization limited the de Gaulle and
Pompidou governments in developing closer economic and military
ties with the Franco regime and in coordinating the foreign policies of
the two states. The Burgos affair was symptomatic of a deeper ma-
laise, not an accidental occurrence. It hindered France's bridge-
building efforts between the northern and southern states of Western
Europe. Regime differences counted for more in dividing the two

states than Gaullist doctrine was officially prepared to admit. The Italian government and firms also preferred to seek their fortunes through their own enterprise rather than through bilateral ventures with the French.

Morocco and especially Tunisia offered only slightly brighter prospects. There were no serious domestic impediments to bettering relations; all sides hoped for more exchanges. Much of the barrier was simply France's material weakness. France could not assume the economic burdens of its colonial past, nor did the de Gaulle and Pompidou governments exhibit much wish to do so. For their part, Morocco and Tunisia had learned to adapt to the frustrating experience of the 1950's with France. Their active diplomacies carried them around the globe in search of assistance. The effort was too developed and too beneficial to be abandoned at the first signs of favorable winds blowing from Paris.

Algeria offered less room for optimism. It demonstrated how tenacious a small state could be in resisting the blandishments and pressures of a middle-range power, like France. Resolving its immediate differences with France was more important than dealing with real, but more remote, threats stemming from the spread of Middle East upheaval to the Maghreb. Like Tunisia and Morocco, it could subscribe in the abstract to French pronouncements of Maghreb unity and the military neutralization of the Mediterranean from the superpower conflict, but it could not forego its demands on France or its right to act unilaterally, however adverse the effect on French interests, if retaliation was likely to be weak and ineffectual. Besides, revolutionary ideology could not be fully dismissed as a contributing influence on Algerian behavior regarding Palestine and the Six-Day and Yom Kippur wars. Nor did the two economic systems, different in size, development, and internal controls, mesh as smoothly as the Gaullist government publicly purported to believe during the 1960's. France and Algeria were like two trapeze artists. France's hold on the Mediterranean depended on its partner's grip, yet neither could be fully sure of the other.

Algeria largely destroyed lingering illusions in France's Third World offensive. If it was a means of entry, it led to a different world than that promised by de Gaulle. France was not universally loved and admired, nor did it enjoy necessarily higher esteem than the superpowers. Algeria retaught France a harsh lesson about Third World diplomacy that it might have been spared by closer appreciation of its own acquisitive behavior. France was only one alternative among others for the Mediterranean states, and not always the most attractive. Except for Mirages and military equipment, modest technical, economic, and cultural assistance, and a political stance favoring the Arabs, France was hampered in competing with the superpowers and with its European partners for favor among the regional powers. Algeria offered instruction in how a small state could effectively pit France against one or the other of the superpowers. Moreover, close working relations between the Libyan and Algerian governments tended to dilute Paris' influence on both regimes. The coolness of both to France's four-power solutions for the Middle East and to its reliance on UN Resolution 242 as the key to a settlement weakened its arguments before the superpowers. Its difficulties in dealing with Libya and Algeria—whatever rhetorical and psychic impact its gains, such as the Mirage sale, might have had—inevitably tarnished its big-power image.

Enlisting Libya in France's Mediterranean schemes proved as difficult as with Algeria. Whereas France wished to insulate the Maghreb from the Middle East and draw Libya into a greater Maghreb grouping, Libya moved east and announced its intention to drag the Maghreb behind it: "We belong to the Maghreb," said Libyan Foreign Minister Bouisir, "but the principal problem of the Arab world is situated presently in the Mashreq, it is Palestine. We turn therefore to the Mashreq while attempting to draw the Maghreb behind us." [137] Three months later, Colonel Qaddafi averred: "There is neither an Arab Mashreq nor an Arab Maghreb, but one Arab nation." [138] Any notion of Libya's joining a great Maghreb political or economic organization, a direction toward which the deposed government of King Indris appeared headed, was unambiguously rejected shortly after the installation of the new regime. [139] On the other hand, Libya's initiative in forming the Federation of Arab Republics raised doubts about the effectiveness of the political conditions attached to the Mirage sale. It was not at all clear whether

137. *Maghreb,* No. 37 (Jan.–Feb. 1970), p. 23.
138. *Ibid.,* No. 39 (May–June 1970), p. 22.
139. *Ibid.,* No. 37 (Jan.–Feb. 1970), p. 7.

the Libyan government felt obliged to respect the restrictions placed by France on the use of the planes. Libyan assertions of freedom to dispose of the planes as it wished did little to assure the French government.[140] Added to these concerns was the support given by the Tripoli government to Chad revolutionaries.[141] France's prestige in Black Africa and its policy of sealing the region off from the tumult of Middle East politics and the global competition of the major powers hinged partially on the success of the Black Chad government's capacity, with strong French military and economic assistance, to crush dissident elements, including Arab groups opposed to the regime. Libya, not Algeria, was proving to be a bridge to the Third World, at least in the Middle East and Africa. It was a bridge, however, leading France directly to the problems of the Third World, and not to their solution.

French Mediterranean policy was clever by half. However much France pledged its fidelity to Arab nationalism, it could not fully escape the risk that at any moment it would be tarred with the imperialist brush if it failed to respond adequately to the latest demands from the Arab states. Paradoxically, neither Arab division nor unity held great promise of advancing France's interests or influence or role in the Mediterranean. On the one hand, the question of whose brand of nationalism was to be supported remained a problem in inter-Arab politics, and France faced the same difficulty that other Western powers did in treading a narrow line between the progressive, moderate, and traditionalist regimes. The Gaullist conception of international relations as deriving from states, and not regimes, appeared less compelling to the Libyans and—somewhat less so—to the Algerians as a consequence of their interpretation of their revolutionary experience. No upper limit could be discerned to the future tribute that France might be expected to pay to Arab nationalism in its diverse forms nor the hard choices that such demands might place on French policy in the Mediterranean. On the other hand, Arab unity, especially among the oil-producing states, challenged French economic and political independence. Mortgaged to the amount and price of Arab oil were the rate of France's economic growth, the competitiveness of its products in world markets, the growth and

140. *New York Herald Tribune,* International edition, April 20, 1971, p. 2.
141. *Le Monde,* Sélection hebdomadaire, Jan. 27–Feb. 2, 1972, pp. 1–2.

distribution of national income, employment levels, and social and political stability.

French policy on its southern flank threatened to collapse from the weight of its own stresses. One example is the reaction of the Maghreb states to the Six-Day War. For Tunisia, it marked a violation of international law by Israel, a recognized state; for Morocco, it assumed the character of a holy war; for Algeria, it signified a new phase of a larger struggle against Western imperialism;[142] for Libya, it was an occasion to renew the struggle against Israel under Egyptian leadership and to restore the Arab lands in Palestine. These variable reactions derived from the widely differing political organizations, ambitions, leadership perspectives, and national histories of the four states, as well as from the different rates and stages of their respective economic and social development. There was little to indicate in the historical evolution of the relation between France and these independent states that any single formula could be applied to the establishment of close bilateral ties or that these states could be grouped around a common foreign policy defined by Paris or even by themselves except under stress conditions, like the Yom Kippur War, and then only temporarily and, as the Arab summit of Algiers suggested, ambiguously.[143] General de Gaulle was perhaps a prophet in spite of himself when he observed, shortly before Algerian independence: "A Mediterranean alliance is an idea and a hope, but it is not a reality. In any case, it is not a reality of the moment." [144]

The Pompidou government, while early proclaiming its commitment to Mediterranean unity and to the promotion of an enlarged role for France in the region, acted on the Gaullist prophecy of continued division and discord among the states. After 1971, France broadened its posture, especially in trade and oil relations, among the Arab Mediterranean states. It displayed an acute appreciation of the conflicting regional forces at play—between the Arab states, between Arabs and Jews, between the superpowers, and between the middle-range powers of Europe (with a rising Japan and China in the wings).

142. "Le Maghreb et la crise iraélo-arabe," *Maghreb,* No. 22 (July–Aug. 1967), pp. 8–15. See also Richard A. Roughton, *Middle East Journal,* 1969, pp. 433–434.

143. *Le Monde,* Nov. 30, 1973, pp. 1ff.

144. Quoted in Sulzburger, *Last of the Giants,* p. 65.

The task addressed by the Pompidou government was more one of retaining France's balance in the region in the face of these clashing elements than of imposing or improving a balance among them. In the early 1970's, Pompidou's pragmatic approach proved more effective in promoting French interests, however modest the results or tenuous the influence, than the global posturings of the later de Gaulle years. The Yom Kippur War threatened this progress. The shifting sands of Middle East politics made footing difficult for a power like France, more *demandeur* than determiner of the interstate and internal politics of the region.

PART IV

**FRENCH INTERNATIONAL POLICY
UNDER THE FIFTH REPUBLIC**

11
Conclusions

The preceding chapters have outlined French global policy under the Fifth Republic. Some generalizations, however interim and provisional, are now in order. These may be conveniently divided into two groups. The first concerns the Gaullist critique of the international system arising out of World War II. The second involves attempts under the de Gaulle and Pompidou regimes to define a new international role for France that would not only contribute to a new international order but would also enhance French power and prestige.

The Gaullist Critique and the International System

Stability and the End of the Cold War

The Gaullist critique of the instability of the superpower conflict and of the bipolarity of the international system after World War II could not be easily ignored. The Cold War possessed unstable features, recognized even by the participants, that risked eruption into nuclear war. Undisciplined by the countervailing power of other states, the superpower conflict tended to become globalized, to dominate and absorb most significant components of world politics. As it extended geographically, drawing most states into its field of attraction, it enlarged functionally, encompassing an ever-widening number of state activities—diplomatic, economic, military, scientific, and even cultural. The superpowers were more inclined to treat other states as stakes, providing land, resources, and political and propaganda support for the Cold War battle, than as independent political entities with their own claims and legitimate pursuits. Alternately, the United States and the Soviet Union became progressively ensnared in the multiple local conflicts of these satellites, clients, and petitioners. Neutral and nonaligned states could not be safely left alone as the Cold War heightened in emotional fever and ideological pitch. Any sign that suggested the penetration of a superpower into an area hitherto not covered by the Cold War—say, the Congo, the Middle East, or Southeast Asia—prompted a counterreaction by its rival. Global politics was being progressively transformed into the image projected by the superpower struggle.

What de Gaulle saw as already having developed to an advanced degree was a global grid of conflict points—geographic and functional—that threatened to draw the superpowers into a direct confrontation. Any one point, once activated, could lead to a military clash of potentially disastrous global proportions. Local conflicts in Europe, where the armies of the two military blocs faced one another, in Southeast Asia, or in the Caribbean were linked to the Cold War struggle. Given the vast resources of both states and their global interests, each friction point was a potential test of will between the United States and the Soviet Union.

There was more than a little truth, too, in the Gaullist charge that the Cold War distorted the expected patterns of international politics, based on national differences. The result was a heightening of conflicts already latent in interstate relations. Within the Gaullist view, conflicts were endemic to international affairs. Rather than decentralize and dissipate them to limit their destructive effects, Cold War politics and strategic maneuvering aggregated and aggravated these frictions, making them parts of the superpower struggle.

The Cold War led, ironically, to a reductionism in world politics in the very transformation and amplification of local conflicts into global problems. It frustrated the expression of local differences between states and differences between client states and their superpower sponsors. In a perverse way, the Cold War falsified the conflict of interests between the United States and the Soviet Union. Problems lost their intrinsic worth. Small incidents risked magnification in value as they were invested with Cold War significance and rhetoric. Issues that might otherwise have been isolated and resolved piecemeal and pragmatically were infected with the taint of Cold War politics. Threats over Quemoy and Matsu, for example, were latent causes of global strife. Crises in Berlin, the Gulf of Aqaba, Vietnam, and Cuba provided more grist for the Gaullist mill. Even when a superpower confronted a rival other than its counterpart, such as the United States and China or North Vietnam, the struggle was interpreted, not in its own terms, but as a test of strength between the United States and the Soviet Union; or, more widely still, between the free and Communist worlds.

The functional expansion of the capabilities of national power drawn into global politics was superimposed on the geographic extension of the Cold War. Few if any aspects of foreign policy could escape evaluation in terms of their impact on superpower politics. Trade, monetary relations, cultural exchanges, even the quality of educational instruction and the habits and mores of the individual citizens were factors in the conflict. The horizontal extension and vertical spiraling of the Cold War intensified and destabilized global politics.

Even the domestic politics of states could not be insulated from the Cold War. The French pointed to an unfortunate reciprocal and reinforcing relation between the instability of bipolar global politics and the internal politics of states, particularly among the fragile and delicately balanced regimes of the Third World. The superpower conflict polarized the internal politics of the states of Europe and the underdeveloped world. The temptation was powerful to appeal to a superpower to aid a regime in difficult domestic straits. As cases in point, de Gaulle cited the 1958 landing of the United States marines in Lebanon, a semiclient of France, and the progressive intervention of the United States in Vietnam, a former French dependency. No superpower could tolerate the loss of a state because a hostile faction had assumed government control. The multiple and often ill-fitting pieces of the domestic politics of states, differing in local color, nuance, and significance, were under incessant pressure to conform to the exterior, artificially created forms of the superpower conflict.

The pattern of bipolar international politics and of the diverse forms of domestic struggle for power from state to state tended to merge so that conflicts at either level activated the other and the two reinforced each other to the detriment of efforts to inhibit the outbreak of war across state boundaries. As a consequence, the possibility of peaceful coexistence between divergent regimes, such as those of Algeria and France, were hampered. In Gaullist terms, the Cuban missile crisis partially arose from the refusal of the United States to accept a Communist government on an island less than a hundred miles from its shore. The Cuban government's nominal Communist character was interpreted by Washington as a Soviet triumph in the Cold War and, inversely, as a major strategic threat. Cuba seemed to offer the Soviet Union a chance to outflank the United States politically and to close the strategic gap by placing missiles on the island. A chain of unforeseen circumstances led from domestic upheaval on a small waterlocked country to the threat of global nuclear war. Superpower misperceptions of each other's intentions reciprocally reinforced each other in a devolutionary spiral to the point of a direct military confrontation that neither wished. If in the resulting crisis France stood steadfast with the United States, de Gaulle was quick to utilize the incident to bolster his arguments that the United States could not be trusted to defend Europe and that the European states risked their own security and independence in becoming too entangled in America's Third World relations and in superpower quarrels. Overstated as the arguments were, to maximize their propaganda value in support of France's cold war with its principal Atlantic partner, they were not entirely without foundation.

Conceived in universal moral, political, and military terms, the Cold War hindered the creation of zones of neutral and nonaligned states as buffers between the superpowers. These might have tempered the global conflict and discouraged its horizontal and vertical enlargement. The Arab-Israeli conflict illustrated this point. It progressively assumed global proportions, lost its strictly regional character, and risked absorption into the Cold War. Local states and regimes, searching to improve their situations, searched for superpower sponsors. France's four-power formula, though self-serving, did have some salutary features. Cold War rhetoric was downplayed; efforts were made to localize the conflict in its regional setting. Regional states were encouraged to measure their relations with others by calculations of reciprocal interest, not by those imposed by the superpowers. Similarly, the Vietnam conflict proved increasingly intractable as the political commitments of the superpowers were extended to the contending regimes and as their enormous reservoirs of blood and treasure were engaged in the war. The local issues became hopelessly entwined with the larger issues of the Cold War; combined, the political thicket became all but impassable.

There was something, too, to the Gaullist argument that Cold War politics inhibited the development of new participants in international relations. New centers of international authority and influence were needed as balancing agents to check the United States and the Soviet Union. Two key actors without roles appropriate to their resources, historical experience, and geographic position were Europe (presumably under French leadership) and China. The Gaullist analysis of the conditions for Europe's disengagement from the Cold War, for its return as an independent force in global politics, and for the reduction of East-West tensions was ahead of its time. If imitation is the highest form of flattery, the Gaullist prescriptions for détente in Europe became models for the other European states and even the United States. According to Gaullist thinking, détente could be advanced only if Europe withdrew from the Cold War; or, at a minimum, if the center of the superpower conflict were shifted to other parts of the globe. There was little hope of reaching an accord with the Soviet Union on Europe's future—on its boundaries, security arrangements, and the political relations between its members—unless the two blocs were weakened and militarily disengaged.

The global security requirements of the superpowers conflicted, according to de Gaulle, with the long-run interest of the European states to escape the political and economic constraints and security risks of the Cold War. This was the larger significance of Gaullist France's withdrawal from NATO, but not the Atlantic Alliance. This was the systemic aim of its recognition of the Oder-Neisse line between Germany and Poland in 1959, years before the United States hinted at the same viewpoint and over a decade before the Brandt government accepted the inevitable. This was the meaning, too, of de Gaulle's encouragement of Germany to follow its lead in reaching an accommodation with the Soviet Union. Germany had to assume increased responsibility for the advancement of détente. The notion of negotiating from a position of strength had not yielded its reputed dividends. The formula *"defense cum détente"* had to be reversed. West Germany's ties to NATO would have to be loosened over time, its postwar boundaries accepted, its claims for unification muted, and its right to resort to force, particularly nuclear weapons, renounced in achieving its policy goals. Once these conditions were met, Europe might again emerge as an independent political grouping in world politics, as a balance to the superpowers, as an arbiter of their struggle, and as a pole of attraction for the Third World.

The Cold War also prevented China from playing a role as a stabilizing force appropriate to its geographic position and size in global politics. The expected national antagonisms between Peking and Moscow, signaled early in de Gaulle's administration, could not be given full play as long as China's attention was directed principally at the United States and its coterie of followers. The American intervention in Vietnam warped the politics of Southeast Asia and the conflict lines of world politics. China's diplomacy should logically have been directed, according to the Gaullist analysis, largely against the Soviet Union. Border differences, national competitiveness, and racial antagonisms were believed stronger than common pledges to the principles of Marx and Lenin. That the Sino-Soviet split should have developed and deepened despite the American challenge in Asia—first Korea and then Vietnam—was testimony to the Gaullist analysis. It justified France's recognition of the Peking regime. It lent weight to France's efforts, over American objections, to reintegrate China into the world community and to give China's seat in the United Nations to the Red regime. France counted on Chinese pressures on the Soviet Union to induce the Moscow government to settle its differences with the West European states and to relax its hold on its Eastern satellites in exchange for security assurances from the Western states. France was too small and European unity too underdeveloped to take advantage of this scheme in the early 1970's. Not without irony, the Sino-American *rapprochement* and the more formal creation of a Peking-Moscow-Washington triangle, partly through American emulation of Gaullist policies, opened these possibilities for Western Europe. Not without interest, too, was the choice of Paris as the contact point between Peking and Washington pending the establishment later of formal diplomatic relations.

Legitimacy: The Nation-State and the Representation of State Interests

Gaullist thought and policies linked global stability to legitimacy, understood as the preservation of the nation-state system and the representation of diverse and often conflicting interests of states in international relations. These Gaullist assumptions were consistent with the definition of legitimacy advanced by one celebrated practitioner and student of state behavior: "an agreement about the nature of workable arrangements and about the permissible aims and methods of foreign policy." [1] A superpower condominium might bring stability in the short run as some argued.[2] War might even be provisionally ruled out as an instrument of superpower politics. The two nuclear giants might agree on spheres of influence, or they might agree on nonviolent rules to conduct their struggle, or both. Such accords, de Gaulle concluded, could only be at the expense of the other states; their independence or their self-defined vital interests were likely to be compromised. Failure of international politics to meet the demands of smaller states only mortgaged the future. Their frustrations were long-run sources of global instability. Unless they were accommodated by the superpowers, they threatened regional and global peace. Other states, not just the superpowers, had a right to define "the permissible aims and methods of foreign policy." Following Gaullist assumptions, arrangements suitable only to Washington and Moscow were "unworkable."

Illustrations were plentiful. If the German question had to be settled to the satisfaction of the Soviet Union and the United States, it also had to be accepted by the Germans. Neither the de Gaulle nor the Pompidou regimes lost sight of their aim to balance German, American, and Soviet needs, and not satisfy any one to the exclusive disadvantage of the others. De Gaulle's opposition, for example, to Soviet pressures on Berlin from 1958 to 1962 stiffened the West's negotiating position. Avoided were concessions that might have unsettled allied cohesion more fundamentally than the deviating course later taken by France within NATO; French-German ties were solidified enough to prompt the French-German Friendship Treaty. Furthermore, China, isolated, unable to complete its civil war, had little incentive to conform to more moderate norms of international behavior. So also France's aspirations to be a global power were unrequited due to bipolarity. For the Gaullist government, the objective

1. Henry A. Kissinger, *A World Restored* (Boston: Houghton Mifflin, 1957), p. 1.
2. Kenneth N. Waltz, "The Stability of the Bipolar World," *Daedalus*, XLIII (Summer 1964), 881–909.

merit of these claims was of less import than that they were asserted by recognized states which had the authority to set the agenda for international politics. The Cold War politics of the superpowers infringed on the right of smaller states to pursue their own nationally determined goals.

Gaullist doctrine more readily than American or Soviet ideology accepted differences of geography, history, local circumstance, and interest as primary forces of international relations requiring accommodation. Communist and capitalist notions of interstate relations were, according to the Gaullist critique, imperfect and refracted representations of international politics. Communist dogma could not explain the clashes of the Soviet Union with Albania, Yugoslavia, or China. Nor could the Soviet leadership adequately justify in Marxist ideological terms the suppression of Hungary in 1956 and Czechoslovakia in 1968. American pretense of defending the free world appeared no less suspect. Crowded uneasily under this banner were the liberal states of Western Europe, the military juntas of Greece and Pakistan, the authoritarian regimes of Portugal and Turkey, and a host of military and semimilitary governments stretching from Saigon to Rio de Janeiro. De Gaulle's periodic attacks on these rationalizations, while serving French interests to embarrass the superpowers, injected a refreshing note of candor otherwise conspicuously absent in superpower dealings and pronouncements.

The de Gaulle regime was particularly astute in challenging the sanguine interpretations offered by American officials of United States policies. The Gaullist offensive against the MLF went far to explain its demise. The French were remarkably successful in probing the contradiction between the military policies of the Kennedy-Johnson administrations toward NATO and their advocacy of European economic and political union. A Europe unable to defend itself was not likely to develop into a cohesive force and to assume an independent role in international affairs. The French analysis of the dollar's weakness due to chronic balance-of-payments deficits, while unrecognized for over a decade, was not far from the mark. The Nixon administration's international monetary policies testified belatedly to the logic of the French analysis if not to the feasibility and relevance of the Gaullist prescriptions for reforming the international monetary system.

The French critique of superpower behavior and ideology was not restricted to the United States. The Soviet Union also came under heavy fire for its invasion of Czechoslovakia. If, for tactical reasons, French-announced policies carried more criticism of American than Soviet policies in the Middle East, French operational policies aimed at blunting the selfish drives of both countries in the Mediterranean region. Though the modesty of France's material means made it a poor second choice as a sponsor for a Mediterranean state, it did hold open the possibility of a West European alternative that could one day command more respect than France alone. The rub was France's actual contribution to a unified European foreign policy. Gaullist words, not surprisingly, exceeded French actions, a point to which we will return below.

The Gaullist characterization of international politics made more sense to daily experience than official American or Soviet pronouncements. First, Gaullist ideology more readily incorporated the diversity of international politics and the difficulties of reaching accords involving conflicting interstate interests. These were not easily cut to the procrustean bed of Cold War politics. Second, the Gaullist understanding of foreign affairs drained much of the emotional fervor and excessive moralism from Soviet and American justifications of their behavior. The clash of doctrinal pronouncements itself fired the conflict and hindered its resolution. The interminable bargaining, haggling, and improbable compromises of interstate relations could be explained on simpler grounds than the class struggle or the fight for a peaceful world based on the principle of collective security. The Gaullist conception of international relations admitted to an infinite combination of state relations, bilateral and multilateral, with little more need for their justification than the mutual service of national cupidity of the states involved.

France under the de Gaulle government was among the first of the Western states to exploit the dilemmas of the balance of terror that restrained both superstates from resorting to nuclear war to resolve their differences. This condition created new possibilities for the maneuverability of small and middle states. They could defy a superpower with impunity (whether they had nuclear weapons or not), play one superpower against the other for advantage, and develop profitable ties with states across bloc lines.

The French example under the de Gaulle and Pompidou regimes

provided fresh evidence that predictions of the impending collapse of the nation-state were premature. The French Fifth Republic understood the transformation in power that international relations had undergone. Small states obviously could not challenge a superpower directly in a military confrontation involving nuclear weapons. Even de Gaulle's praise for the *force de frappe* could not hide the vulnerability of French defenses revealed in the Czech incident of 1968. But even in nuclear affairs, the Gaullist insistence on a strategic capacity to defend its citizenry as the ultimate basis of the French state's domestic and international authority was not fully emptied of meaning by the weakness of the French nuclear striking force. The paradox derived from the destructiveness of nuclear weapons. Since the superpowers were constrained in using their nuclear weapons, they were drawn to the level of nonnuclear powers. In their own contest, moreover, one was the hostage of the other; neither state could assert a reliable military capability to assure its own security. As long as nuclear weapons could not be feasibly employed, and as long as the possibility of nuclear war was remote, the tie between nuclear weapons and state authority grew more tenuous. The Gaullist relation between nuclear weapons, state authority, and the capacity of the nation-state system to satisfy human needs for security made sense only if the state's ability to defend its citizens was tested in war. But that contingency was considered only possible, not probable. As long as the state's defenses went untested, nonnuclear and small nuclear powers could claim with different degrees of plausibility that their defense forces could still serve their respective national security needs. They could still retain, in Gaullist terms, a claim to original political authority.

These theoretical considerations had more immediate practical implications for de Gaulle. The de Gaulle government's pronouncements seemed to emphasize old international politics: the concern with military force as the principal instrument of a state's diplomacy. The new politics turned on the use of other forms of national capability to project a state's will abroad. Industrialization, GNP figures, financial credit, and a strong currency provided much of the new coinage of state interchanges of power. A state's scientific progress and its technological achievements—even feats like the Russian Sputnik and the American moon landing—were novel standards for a state's international standing. The quality of its internal government, the degree of its social development, the equity in the distribution of material wealth, and the amount of personal freedom fostered were elements of international influence. The intellectual and moral force of its governing ideology and even the nature of its historical experience were factors in the struggle for power. The French, American, Russian, and Chinese revolutionary experiences competed with each other as models for Third World states to follow. The subtlety and sophistication of a nation's cultural life and its adaptability to the circumstances of peoples abroad were parts of a state's panoply of power to win friends, influence peoples, and manifest its will in world affairs.

The de Gaulle Fifth Republic was not unmindful of these new requirements of international politics. A state had to develop a wider range of national capabilities and apply them over a larger geographic area to participate effectively in the politics of material and milieu competition. Behind the façade of the *force de frappe,* the de Gaulle government encouraged France's industrialization and economic expansion. Defense expenditures aimed, as in the United States, at enlarging the scientific and technological establishment as a motor for economic growth. The military-industrial-academic establishment, condemned in the United States, became an operative ideal for Gaullist technocrats. If agricultural policy was important for France in the EEC, it was a way of finding an outlet for surplus production and for transferring part of the cost of France's industrialization and modernization to its European partners, and, specifically, to Germany whose economic leadership posed the most immediate threat to France's position in Western Europe. In ending the Algerian War, France could also join the rhetoric of its own revolution to the revolution of rising expectations in the Third World. French culture was organized, too, to spread the gospel of France's universal mission.

The larger significance of Gaullist France's critique of superpower behavior, its pointed attack on the United States, and its own development of a wider spectrum of national capabilities to engage itself in the contest with the superpowers was the assertion, made with varying degrees of clarity, that other forms of national power than military force were a reasonable basis for a state's international authority and claims on other states. The Pompidou government was especially attentive to these nonnuclear elements. Corrected were many of the verbal excesses of its predecessor. The superpowers might dominate the military hierarchy of states, but their ability to transform their superiority in organized violence into other forms of national capabilities and influence were limited. There were opportunities for other states to combine as countervailing forces. At other levels of competition than nuclear deterrence, the superpowers could be reduced to equality and even disadvantaged in international competition.

Again, France could illustrate its case with multiple examples. After the Gaullist exposition of the national drives of the United States and the Soviet Union, their claims to a higher morality were of doubtful merit. The Gaullist criticism reduced their respective moral images of themselves to a shabby pursuit of selfish interests. In economic affairs, the United States and the Soviet Union were likewise vulnerable. Lagging Russian productivity and American economic dislocation, inflation, and monetary difficulties exposed them to criticism. The German mark and Japanese yen—even the franc by comparison—stood in higher monetary repute than the American dollar in the early 1970's. The dollar finally succumbed to its own excesses; its weakness gave some leverage, however fleeting, to the franc, evidenced in choosing the meeting between Presidents Nixon and Pompidou as the occasion for the announcement of the United States decision to raise the price of gold and devalue the dollar. The fall of the dollar standard highlighted the potential ascendancy of the West European states in international monetary affairs if a common position could be forged among them.

The diplomatic finesse of France and of smaller states could be used to outmaneuver the United States in the United Nations General Assembly; so much so that the United States enthusiasm for the world organization flagged as its influence declined in that body. Witness, too, the display of bargaining talent of the oil-producing states in the global negotiations of 1971, and thereafter. There were also numerous examples of clever regimes, like Bourguiba's in Tunisia, which could simultaneously secure favors from the United States, the Soviet Union, China, and the West European states. France's trying experience with Algeria attested to the difficulties of dealing with a small, militarily inferior state from a position of economic weakness. On the other hand, France's relations with Algeria contrasted favorably with those between the United States and Cuba. They set a high standard for conduct for North-South relations between developed and underdeveloped states.

The Anglo-French Concorde, whatever its doubtful economic future, suggested that technological feats were not the exclusive property of the superpowers. Chinese explosion of an H-bomb also gave pause to the superpowers—a backward state could challenge the nuclear might of the major industrial powers of the globe. Japan's economic miracle, based on an advanced technology and an energetic populace, presented still another problem to the superstates.

The differentiation of national capabilities was, therefore, the basis for the development of regional and global hierarchies of states, resting on diverse forms of power, that could stand apart from the superpower conflict. Within these geofunctional hierarchies, within and across bloc lines or traditional regional groupings, states had the opportunity to develop a larger number of bilateral and multilateral ties with other states over a wider spectrum of activities. These alignments would presumably be suited to their national strategies aimed at achieving their particular objectives. Leadership roles were not superpower monopolies. Smaller states could aspire to a protagonist role within selected areas where their natural or developed traits and resources could warrant a position of international prominence. Indeed, France's quest for *grandeur* was to be partially found in promoting a more fluid pattern of interstate relations. These would be conditioned more by calculations of reciprocal national advantage than by Cold War pressures and superpower demands. The de Gaulle vision potentially admitted to a larger number of combinations of satisfactory relations for small and middle powers, as they defined their own interests, however misguidedly, than a tight, bipolar international system under Soviet-American direction.

French Global Policy under the Fifth Republic: National and Systemic Dimensions

Gaullist Nationalism and the International System

De Gaulle, as visionary, grasped the revolutionary changes in world politics arising from World War II and the subsequent titanic struggle between the United States and the Soviet Union. The construction of state groupings or *ensembles* capable of contesting the superpowers could alone restore the disrupted multipolar balance of the prewar years. Europe's ascendancy was key to the restoration of a multipolar international system. De Gaulle looked beyond the nation-state as it had developed in Europe. France's *grandeur* was portrayed as a part of a resurgent Europe.

But de Gaulle, as master of statecraft, whose personal glory derived from his achievements as a national leader, recoiled from the implications of his own image of the future of international relations. Like the elders of Plato's *Laws,* he and his followers remained committed to the old order even while they permitted their thoughts to take flight of their actions.[3] His best efforts and those of his government were devoted to the preservation of an international regime that his own critique found gravely wanting. Imagination gave way to worn formulas and tired maxims; the future was mortgaged to the faint and receding memories of a glorious past. De Gaulle could neither extricate himself nor his administration's policies from the past. He could not free himself from the revisionist goal of restoring France to its former rank among nations. He could not commit himself and France to a future that advised smaller states, by his own analysis, to combine their power if they wished to influence the behavior of the superpowers and, concomitantly, global affairs.

De Gaulle's government launched an impressive program to fit France to the new conditions of international politics in developing its national capabilities. The effort was bound to be limited in scope and effect. However total the effort, France's resources remained modest. France's global aims could be plausibly realized only on a European scale. But committing France to Europe potentially spelled its demise as an independent state. The Gaullist cure for the international disease of the Cold War was as bitter to accept as the superpower struggle itself. Thus French global policy under de Gaulle struggled against itself, projecting an ambiguous image in executing its aims. Torn between limited resources and soaring, limitless national aims, French global policy condemned itself to pragmatic tactical adjustments and opportune alignments, waiting for a better day

3. See the author's "French Strategy Emergent: General André Beaufre— A Critique," *World Politics,* XIX (April 1967), 417–442.

when perhaps the weakness of its rivals rather than its own material strength would return it to the first rank among nations. It was a policy of "muddling through," obscured by a Gaullist genius for dramatic posturing and arresting turns of phrase that suggested more substance and coherence in French behavior than close examination could justify.

Gaullist nationalism became a major obstacle to the realization of its own alternative to superpower bipolarity. De Gaulle's call to the colors to end the war in Algeria may have been necessary. But continued assertions of nationalism reduced the weight of France's contribution to a new international politics that would avoid the shortcomings of the bipolar system and the pitfalls of the prewar international order whose unfortunate history of national suspicions, animosities, and destructive wars held out little reason for optimism. De Gaulle's remarkable candor regarding his hopes for France armed French diplomacy with a probing scalpel to expose the flaws of superpower claims. But the drive for national gain hindered the building of *ensembles,* the formation of centers of geographic and functional power, to contest the hegemonic assertions of the United States and the Soviet Union. The nationalist-inspired policies of the Gaullist Fifth Republic alienated more than aggregated the pieces of power scattered among the European states that might have, if assembled, contested superpower rule. There is evidence, too, that the de Gaulle regime unwittingly fostered many of the very features of international politics condemned by the French president.

To the degree that it worked, short of catastrophic wars, the balance-of-power system before World War I, based on a small number of European states of relatively equal size, conformed to a number of key rules and assumptions. First, the participants pursued moderate ends. None sought the overturn of its rival's regimes; none sought the destruction of the international system. Each accepted his relative station in the international hierarchy and joined, almost automatically, with other states to check any that sought a radical transformation of the distribution of power.

Second, each used moderate means to influence the behavior of other states. War was not forbidden, but was usually limited. It was useful not only to support national diplomatic objectives, but also to check any state or coalition seeking to overturn the power relations among the principal states. War was resorted to even to restore a temporarily upset balance among the states. The coalition against Napoleonic France was a classic example of the working of the system. It sought to restrain a revolutionary force bent on pursuing immoderate ends and employing, for its epoch, limitless means.

Third, the domestic politics of the different states and their governing regimes were insulated by and large from the vicissitudes of international politics. The French and Russian revolutions were heresies precisely because they sought to overturn the domestic authority of rival regimes. Each was countered by a hostile coalition that aimed to restore the previous international order and to protect the menaced regimes. The Congress of Vienna proved successful for almost a century; the invasion of the Soviet Union by the Western states after World War I, on the other hand, was a disaster. In Gaullist terms, the Cold War was a clash of not one, but two revolutionary forces in world affairs. Their struggle threatened not only global peace but the integrity of the internal governing arrangements of other states. A cardinal tenet of Gaullist doctrine, although violated by the Fifth Republic in practice, was the restoration of the principle of nonintervention in the domestic affairs of states, including civil wars in the developing states. It was important to the de Gaulle argument that differences in regimes were of little consequence in determining the structure and modalities of international conflict; the latter were dependent on other factors.

These rules could be observed for much of the eighteenth and nineteenth centuries because they rested on at least two implicit assumptions: multipolarity and homogeneity. More than two states of approximately equal capabilities were ranged against each other; and there was in fact a considerable similarity in the internal governing arrangements and values of the competing states. Under these rules and assumptions, the system generated incentives for the states, in pursuing their selfish interests, to support the system simultaneously. The states resisted the temptation to change the rules and assumptions of the international order out of fear of forging an opposing coalition. Excessive national appetite was checked. The ally of today was the enemy of tomorrow. The choice of friends depended on the perceived distribution of power of the moment and the challenge directed against the order by the expanding demands of any state. All states were compensated for their moderation by the lower risks run in maintaining security, status, and internal control.

The de Gaulle regime condemned the immoderate goals of the superpowers. Yet the aim of *grandeur* matched the breadth of ambition of the United States and the Soviet Union. An ideology of self-aggrandizement was not calculated to check the ambitions of nation-states. It provided a rationale for venting the emotions of the nation's populace. *Grandeur* escaped precise definition. It invited inflated rhetoric and expansive claims. There was no reason why other states might not follow the French example. The heterogeneity and diversity of power of the states of the modern system, however, could not assure that the states would interpret their charge of *grandeur* in limited terms. The weak were tempted, like France, to seek international influence beyond their means; the new states of the Third World were encouraged to pursue their national ambitions at the expense of neighbors. If these assertions of independence had the salutary effect of checking superpower expansionism and complicating condominial rule, they also risked breaking down the processes of compromise and conciliation moderating the competing national demands of rival states. The benign nationalism of the Dutch and Danes could be relied upon to be self-disciplined. The same could not be said, for example, of different forms of Arab nationalism. There was also the questionable example being given by France to a politically dissatisfied Germany.

The Gaullist quest for *grandeur* posed, rather than solved, the problem of establishing ordered and equitable relations between states. It is difficult to quarrel with French insistence that all states whose interests were affected by a decisoin should participate in its determination and execution. France's criticism of superpower pretensions to resolve international conflict, disarmingly proclaimed in President Nixon's speech during ceremonies at the twenty-fifth anniversary of the United Nations, was telling. France's critique of the Rogers plan gave point, too, to its denunciation that the superpowers were neither morally nor even physically competent to impose an agreed order on the world or to provide a workable process of decision making through which the claims of smaller states or groups, like the Palestinian refugees, could be articulated and realized without recourse to force. What was disturbing to recognize, however, was that France fell short of its own standards. A yawning gap appeared between its pronouncements in favor of the consensual nature of international relations and its getting and spending in the Mediterranean and in Europe to advance its own interests at the expense of other states.

The French were on firm ground in indicating that the nation-state was still the repository of political authority and meaning for the different peoples of the globe. More questionable was the impression that such a statement exhausted the moral and legal problems of establishing a workable international system or that French behavior was equal to the high standards set for other states in realizing a more stable and legitimate international order. Criticism of France's failings, however, in no way absolved or mitigated the charges that could be raised against the great powers in their management of foreign relations or in the execution of their international responsibilities; it confirmed them.

There was also a logical contradiction between the quest for *grandeur* and the insulation of domestic politics from the turmoil of international politics. *Grandeur* subordinated domestic affairs to foreign policy goals. Were other states to adopt France's foreign policy objectives, there would be a tendency within the international system to break down the barriers between interior and exterior politics. The instabilities of different regimes would then contribute to the destabilizing tendencies of the multipolar system. The internal struggles for power within each regime would become increasingly tied to the turbulent movements of global politics. Regimes indeed mattered in world politics. Pressures would also be reinforced to increase the competition among states. Just as the superpowers attached more value to their own global strategic needs than to those of smaller states, so also a universalized pursuit of *grandeur* by smaller states would reduce all states to means or functions of each other's foreign policy. Mutual intervention in domestic politics would become a strong temptation to assure security at home for a ruling regime and to expand its influence abroad. Gaullist *grandeur,* if accepted by other states, would logically encourage instability in international and domestic politics as prominent features of the Gaullist alternative to superpower rule. The 1968 crisis in France, moreover, suggested the shortcomings of inflating foreign policy rhetoric and objectives beyond the will and capacity of a people to support them.

The vacuity and necessarily unrealizable nature of *grandeur,* however defined by a state, ill-suited it as a guide for the foreign policies of France or of any other state. It was vague enough to justify any policy or shift. Who could gainsay the Libyan revolutionary government's decision to pursue its own brand of *grandeur?* In the name of Arab nationalism, it could justify one transgression after another of international comity as it intervened in the internal politics of its neighbors in Sudan and Morocco. There was no logical reason why *grandeur* should be restricted to France. Gaullism's special pleading remained unconvincing to most foreign governments—if UN debates offer any guide—and to many Frenchmen as well.[4]

Confidence in the Gaullist conception of international relations was further undermined by the practice of French alignment strategy under the de Gaulle administration. Superpower bipolarity inhibited flexibility in interstate alignments. But de Gaulle offered the opposite extreme as an ideal. The permeability of national bilateral ties injected uncertainty and unreliability into international relations. Stability is to some degree a function of mutually shared expectations among states. Military, economic, and diplomatic planning and operations are contingent on some relatively fixed assumptions about the behavior of other states over time. Even their conflicts depended on them. Arms control was impossible without them. In breaking with Western European and, specifically, United States policies, Gaullist France made more of the ideology of France's independence in international relations in theory than its interdependence in fact would appear to have justified. There is, of course, no rigid formula to define clearly those areas where any state should follow a truly national strategy to promote its own interests or when it should concert its efforts with other states for the mutual benefit of all. It was de Gaulle who was most clear on the point that groups of states or *ensembles* had to be constructed to pool their resources to meet the superpower challenge. On the other hand, the overstatement of French independence in word and deed confused and complicated the task of

4. Arthur Lall, *op. cit., passim.*

forming adequate coalitions in different geographic and functional areas to contest superpower demands. The standard for judgment was de Gaulle's, hoisted as he was on his own petard.

Like *grandeur,* the volatility of France's alignment strategy under de Gaulle could be applied to international relations, with minimal damage (and even some benefit) for international order, so long as it did not become the *modus operandi* of other states, too. It placed an enormous burden on traditional modes of diplomacy, taxing the resources and reasonableness of even experienced states. It also assumed a dispassionate ability on the part of leadership elites to take finely calibrated assessments of their state's alignment mix to maximize exterior payoffs and quickly to shift alignment commitments, like capital in economic enterprises, to more profitable outlets. That de Gaulle's skill in international manipulation and maneuver could be found elsewhere was highly doubtful. That he himself was found wanting on more than one occasion was suggested in France's frustrating experiences in the Mediterranean and in Europe. Moreover, the capacity to shift alignments required more control over domestic opinion than many states, particularly the Western liberal democracies, could feasibly command—or even wished to have. The 1968 domestic crisis in France evidenced a lack of control on de Gaulle's part. Furthermore, inflammatory Gaullist rhetoric did not help rival governments in their adjustments to new international combinations desired by France. It may have been de Gaulle's intent to throw American decision making off balance with his verbal barbs and unexpected policy changes. But he also provoked overreactive protective measures, such as the weekly pledging sessions of the United States commitment to NATO or to Germany's foreign policy objectives. De Gaulle undid much of what he ostensibly sought: to loosen American-German ties and reduce the American presence in Europe. He made American public opinion less disposed to his arguments than he might have wished.

Even elite opinion in foreign policy, which should have known better, was blinded often by de Gaulle's intemperate remarks. The problem of controlling the emotions of government personnel grew so great in the United States that President Lyndon Johnson credited his administration with a major accomplishment in resisting an emotional response to Gaullist provocations: "Many people expected me to denounce the French leader's moves and to resist his disruptive tactics, but I had long since decided that the only way to deal with de Gaulle's fervent nationalism was by restraint and patience. . . . To have attacked de Gaulle would only have further enflamed French nationalism and offended French pride. It also would have created strains among the nations of the European Common Market and complicated their domestic politics." [5]

The tenuous character of international commitments stressed by de Gaulle posed serious problems for international stability when combined with his insistence that nuclear weapons were indispensable to discharge the security responsibilities of the nation-state. As France gradually learned, there was more to building a credible nuclear defense force than a determined will. The material requirements of constructing a viable second-strike force were consistently underestimated. The French example, however, was not one to be followed by other states. If one could count on de Gaulle to remain cool-headed during a crisis—for example, the Cuban missile affair—the same could not be predicated with confidence of other state leaders in possession of rudimentary nuclear capabilities and primitive forms of delivery vehicles. The logical tie forged in Gaullist foreign policy practice between an expansionist foreign policy, domestic instability, and global politics, and the reliance on immoderate means in international bargaining did not present a reassuring picture for the future. Under de Gaulle, France might be able to hold these elements in check. That other governments would prove equally successful in curbing their own avarice and the aroused appetites of their citizenry once in possession of nuclear weapons was not beyond question.

The French retort that the superpowers and Britain were equally culpable for proliferation can hardly be denied. But judged by the demanding criteria that de Gaulle applied to France's behavior, French nuclear policies cannot easily escape being faulted for deepening the problem of nuclear proliferation. France's opposition to the test ban and, curiously enough, to the nonproliferation treaty, which served its security interests against the possibility of a resurgent Germany, were difficult to justify on the strained reasoning advanced

5. Johnson, *Vantage Point*, p. 305.

by French strategists. The absence of France's voice at the Geneva disarmament talks robbed it of an opportunity to influence global arms control and disarmament policy and to serve as a voice for smaller states, a role it presumably relished.

Gaullism's oligarchical alternative to superpower bipolarity was plausible only if the counterbalancing force was Western Europe, not France alone. But Gaullist France could not be judged a friend of European union, however defined. French policy was unable to accept the logic of its probing analysis of international relations—the superpower balance of terror, the resources available to Europe to challenge their rule, and the rise of the Third World as an opportunity for the expansion of European influence around the globe. Gaullist France was unable to adopt a policy of fostering supranational values and institutions. Such a commitment would have inevitably weakened the attraction of French nationalism, symbolized by the man of June 18. Merged, too, in a larger European grouping would have been French means and genius.

Whatever the drawbacks of the European Economic Community, and they were admittedly numerous as de Gaulle demonstrated, it rested on the principle of a higher authority than the individual nation-states. De Gaulle may have been correct in rejecting the optimistic assumptions of the Europeanists about the possibility of creating a supranational authority that would be accepted by the peoples of Europe, an authority with means and will to resist American and Soviet blandishments and pressures. The Dutch, the Germans, and the Italians were not above using the EEC for parochial purposes. So did Britain in remaining outside; and in entering, its reasons remained principally national. The French could not equitably be blamed for doing likewise—even though they did it so well and often so much better than their European partners. But Gaullist France offered little alternative to continued superpower rule in the absence of the creation of some effective supranational authority. There was little chance that Europe's resources and skills could be marshaled to play the world role de Gaulle conceived for it and for France. The Monnet conception of union may well have opened Europe to superpower manipulation and installed the United States more firmly than ever on the Continent. But de Gaulle's nationalistic solution offered as bleak a future. Divided, the West European states were lowered to the level of the Balkans before World War I, mere stakes in the struggle among the principal European states. They became the stakes of the larger global struggle of the superpowers. One analyst perceptively concluded that de Gaulle preferred "a small but independent France, using the freedom of maneuver lesser powers derive from the nuclear stalemate, to being 'integrated' in the cage of a larger, more powerful, yet actually neither independent nor coherent European Community in which America's automatic yes-sayers would prevail." [6] The individual European states might have enjoyed a form of relative independence when compared to their postwar importance, but in going their separate ways, their influence on the structure, processes, and rules of international relations was inevitably less. And so also was it the case for France.

If *grandeur* could be realized in Gaullist terms, it was in defining (1) the security arrangements between states and guaranteeing their enforcement; (2) the rules governing access and intervention in the foreign and domestic relations of states; and (3) the goals that should animate international politics. France needed more than rhetoric to accomplish these goals. It needed to join its modest capabilities with those of other states, particularly with the West European partners whose combined resources matched the material strength, economically if not militarily, of the superpowers. The anticipated benefits of a more fluid and flexible international system were threatened by inattention to the practical problem of building adequate checks and balances into international politics and of controlling centrifugal forces by means other than superpower intervention. Incentives for the concerting of small and middle-power resources were eroded in Gaullist France's call for a common response to superpower rule, presumably under French leadership.

Militarily, the French doctrine of multilateral deterrence could be implemented realistically only by a unified European nuclear force. Only Western Europe possessed the resources to create a modest, yet invulnerable, deterrent. The combination of British and French nuclear forces was indispensable, yet the French and (concededly) the British governments showed little tangible interest in constructing a European nuclear defense. France remained cool. French repre-

6. Hoffmann, *New Republic,* April 12, 1969, p. 20. See also the first part of the article, *New Republic,* April 5, 1969.

sentatives abstained from talks with the informally established European group within NATO. Gaullists in the Pompidou government
were still skeptical of joint European defense arrangements, although
they might fear Soviet political penetration if American troops withdrew. A slowdown in French defense spending, following the events
of 1968, further hampered France in overcoming its nuclear disadvantage. As the 1970's unfolded, France was saddled with a costly
defense system of questionable strategic value. Despite its best efforts,
it was still militarily dependent on the United States. The future was
not brighter as the arms race continued. The distance between the
superpowers and the small nuclear powers threatened to grow with
the development of long-range, underwater-launched missiles and
ABM systems and with the improvement of multiple warhead guidance, warning, and detection technologies.

France's global role was no less constrained in economic affairs.
The European states were most effective in influencing United States
economic policies when they stood together. Under de Gaulle, French
monetary diplomacy, even if its perceptive analysis of the dollar's
weakness is conceded, was singularly unsuccessful in inducing the
European states to follow its lead. Its thinly veiled national aims and
its failure to articulate feasible alternatives to the economic and defense roles played by the United States weakened the attractiveness
and credibility of its proposals. The Paris-Bonn tie was key to a
European currency. The refusal of the de Gaulle administration to
contemplate the coordination of joint policies under the surveillance
of extranational bodies impeded a united European approach.

France's contribution to a common European policy toward the
Third World was equally ambiguous. Aid policy remained principally
bilateral. France resisted any loss of political influence or trade privileges among its former dependencies to its European partners. Its
self-seeking in the Mediterranean had little appeal for other members
of the EEC except as a justification for their own national drives.
The Munich talks were perceived as an occasion to harness EEC
support for the French position rather than as an opportunity to
develop a coordinated European approach to the Middle East conflict. If little can be said in favor of Germany's dissembling over the
affair, France was in a poor position to criticize the grasping motives
of its partners. What attraction the European states might have had

as an alternative to the functions discharged by the superpowers was dissipated in the pursuit of their individual national strategies.

De Gaulle could accept these shortcomings in multilateral cooperation with equanimity; it was never a guiding objective of Gaullist diplomacy. Expanding France's independence, influence, and status vis-à-vis the states of the Atlantic community, Europe, and the Third World, however, were critical aims. The failure of the de Gaulle regime to realize its great expectations in these areas opened its policies and de Gaulle's personal brand of diplomacy to more telling criticism on their own terms. The real question facing France was not whether it could be independent of other states, as de Gaulle generally preferred to state the issue although he knew better, but how its dependency on other states could be tolerated at least cost to its security, economic, and diplomatic goals. Left to de Gaulle's successors was the unfinished business, foreshadowed in the Soames affair, of redefining France's alignments in order to project its will more effectively abroad.

President Georges Pompidou: Changes in Substance, Strategy, and Style

The de Gaulle attack on the superpowers was auspiciously launched. It roughly corresponded to six major changes in international relations: (1) the growth of the balance of terror; (2) the full emergence of an expansionist America which, after the Cuban missile crisis, appeared to have become ascendant in the bipolar Cold War struggle; (3) the reappearance of economically strong and politically assertive West European states joined together under the Rome Treaty to cooperate toward the goal of greater economic and political integration; (4) increased stirrings in Eastern Europe for greater independence from the Soviet Union; (5) the rise of the Third World, bent on national self-determination and economic development; and (6) the break-up of Communist cohesion with the schism of Maoist China, opposed to American and Soviet domination of international politics.

These changes provided the conditions for the Gaullist attack on superpower rule and, specifically, on American imperial proclivities. They heralded the impotence of the United States and the Soviet Union, short of self-destructive nuclear war, to arrest the evolution of the international system toward muted multipolarity. They afforded the incentive for France's deviating course and the occasion to propose and test alternative alignment patterns among states than those elicited by rigid bipolar politics. The balance of terror paralyzed both superpowers and hampered them diplomatically in extending their sway around the globe. Demands for greater economic, social, and political freedom in Western and Eastern Europe provided fertile grounds for Gaullist nationalist doctrines. American military intervention in Cuba (1961), Santo Domingo (1965), and Vietnam, and the Soviet invasion of Czechoslovakia (1968), belied superpower claims of support for national movements in Europe and the Third World. These contradictions nourished the Gaullist critique of superpower rule. The decolonization of the underdeveloped world and the creation of a host of new and fragile states, jealous of their recently achieved political independence, reinforced the trend, already in an advanced stage in Europe, of a globally diverse international community of states increasingly resistant to the allures and pressures of the superstates. Even the alleged commitment to a common ideology, as in the case of Russia and China, could not bridge national differences in historical experience, perspective, or interest—or even race. These enlarging East-West and North-South splits provided Gaullist France opportunities, not all of which were fully exploited, for the promotion of its national and systemic objectives.

French deviationism rested, however, on a number of unarticulated expectations that were not fully tested until the late 1960's. Most critical was continued domestic social stability and economic growth. Second was the anticipation that France's EEC partners would resign themselves to Gaullist demands for Britain's exclusion from direct participation in West Europe's economic and political future and would accede to French proposals for a common agricultural policy. Third was the expectation of gradual Soviet (and German) acceptance of France's interlocutory role in developing a *rapprochement* between East and West Europe and in liberalizing Soviet rule of its European satellites. Fourth, Third World states were expected to be receptive to Gaullist France's claims to global leadership and responsive to French national aims and interests.

Finally, Gaullist France acted on the assumption that the encroachments of an imperial America had to be resisted—an imperative of multipolar politics—but that the United States would, nevertheless, continue to act as an imperial power intent on preserving its special international status and, specifically, its privileged protectorate position in Europe. Other great powers, including France, had done the same. Vietnam offered confirming evidence of American expansionist drives. Gaullist accusation that Washington prompted the Israeli preventive attack against the Arab states was more than an emotional and thoughtless outburst. Although it carried such overtones, the charge was but one more illustration offered by Paris to expose the destabilizing effects produced by two revolutionary forces in international relations—the Soviet Union *and* the United States.[7] Indeed, de Gaulle alleged that the United States, given superior resources and a more pronounced inclination to intervene in the interstate relations and domestic politics of other states, was the principal disruptive force in world politics.

By the time of de Gaulle's resignation in April 1969, the implicit expectations underlying Gaullist policy lost much of their plausibility and persuasiveness as a basis for an independent French posture. The May events exposed the fragile social and economic structure and the unstable political consensus supporting French foreign policy. The Soviet Union remained impervious to French probings that sought to relax its control over East Europe or to liberalize its own and its satellites' economic and political institutions.

Western Europe also proved resistant to Gaullist overtures. By the end of the 1960's, West Germany, as the dispute over mark evaluation in fall 1968 suggested, was less responsive to French economic (and political) needs than during the Adenauer or Erhard periods. The Bonn government was disposed, too, to frame and foster its own *Ostpolitik*. France's example encouraged emulation, but not the suspension of Germany's right to act in its own behalf or to use only those diplomatic means that were consistent with Gaullist aims and strictures. The Five were also a match for the French president, holding the common agricultural program hostage to opening discussions on Britain's entry into the Common Market.

The Third World, if events in the Mediterranean provided any guide, manifested little sympathy for France's global or regional leadership or for its special interests. It was paradoxical that the de

7. This view is shared by other than Gaullist supporters in France. See Raymond Aron, *République impérialiste: 1945–1972* (Paris: Calmann-Lévy, 1972).

Gaulle government, so determined to widen France's freedom of maneuver and to assert its independence from superpower control, should have narrowed its stance in the Mediterranean arena to reliance largely on a selected number of so-called "progressive" Arab states. Its political and security interests, economic needs, and even cultural objectives were ill served by fastidious and discriminating standards applied by the Gaullist regime—Tunisia comes quickly to mind—in defining its relations with the states of the region.

Lastly, American zeal in expanding its imperial domain was a spent force by the close of President Johnson's administration. Nor could United States determination to hold on to its European position, the basis for the Gaullist expectation of continued American willingness to defend Europe at minimal cost to France, be automatically assumed and manipulated for French advantage. There were increasing signs of United States desire to bargain with the Soviet Union over their respective European assets and to reach a settlement of their political differences in Europe. Signals included the first SALT and Berlin accords, MBFR and additional SALT discussions, broadening economic ties between the superpowers, cautious American support for Germany's *Ostpolitik,* gradual acceptance of American participation in the Soviet-inspired call for a European Conference on Security and Cooperation, and negotiations to halt the Yom Kippur War and bring peace to the Middle East. France, too, supported many of these moves. But the danger to be avoided in these negotiating arenas was possible collusion between the superpowers at the expense, conceivably, of Europe's (and France's) independence and interests.

The political priorities and the alignment patterns struck by the de Gaulle government appeared increasingly unresponsive to France's national needs. Paradoxically, the rigidity of Gaullist diplomacy in its later years handicapped France from drawing benefit from the more fluid international framework to which its own deviant behavior had given impulse and impetus. On the other hand, the Pompidou administration focused on the exploitation of clear and present opportunities for immediate material advantage even at the expense of announced principles, such as, for example, fixed exchange rates for foreign currencies. President Pompidou's direction of French foreign policy differed in at least three notable respects from that of his predecessor. These shifts appeared to be functionally related to the Pompidou administration's emphasis on extracting maximum national gains from an increasingly multipolar global politics.

First, foreign policy was subordinated to domestic concerns, reversing the priorities of the de Gaulle administration. Second, the security, economic, and diplomatic alignments inherited from the de Gaulle era were significantly altered, particularly in President Pompidou's accent on France's ties with its Atlantic and West European partners. Finally, President Pompidou's style in foreign and domestic policy contrasted sharply with de Gaulle's.

A caveat should be entered against making any invidious comparisons between the de Gaulle and Pompidou stewardships of French foreign policy. De Gaulle's record and the problems he faced were more profound and taxing than those confronted by Pompidou. From 1958 until his resignation in 1969, de Gaulle worked to transform the international system through the resolution of the Cold War and the dissolution of bloc politics. This historic mission was consistent in measure and moment with those that he had previously assumed: in 1940 he rallied a demoralized people after their military defeat and loss of political independence; in 1958 he forestalled incipient civil war and prevented military government; between 1958 and 1962 he settled the Algerian War, liquidated the remains of French empire, and preserved civilian rule—issues that destroyed the Fourth Republic. Except for the events of May 1968, President Pompidou, then prime minister, never had to resolve political crises of such magnitude, gravity, or duration. Finally, de Gaulle wrote more to explain his actions and more has been written about his political thought and behavior than about perhaps any modern statesman except Winston Churchill and Mao Tse-tung. Since the problems with which de Gaulle dealt were more fundamental and more is known about his role in them, his responses in word and deed are intrinsically more significant for statesmen and students of foreign policy. That they have attracted greater attention and exploration comes as no surprise. Pompidou is interesting to the degree that he has departed from the Gaullist legacy. At this point it may be useful to summarize Pompidou's innovations in the substance, strategies, and style of France's conduct of its foreign relations.

Domestic policy and politics were the dominant passions of the

Pompidou regime. De Gaulle subordinated domestic goals to his exterior designs. Under Pompidou, domestic and foreign policy and France's alignments abroad, whatever the policy area, were to reinforce domestic political stability, especially Fifth Republic institutions, and to promote France's economic growth. Accelerated industrialization to create a growth rate of 6 percent a year headed the goals of the French Sixth Plan adopted in May 1971. Increased emphasis was given to scientific and technological development and to its rapid translation into profitable business enterprise. In 1970, for the first time under the Fifth Republic, expenditure for education and research exceeded that for national defense. A slowdown in the realization of France's military atomic programs and the relative stagnation of foreign aid expenditures, despite a steadily rising GNP, was also registered. A renewed accent was placed on attracting foreign investments, including capital from the United States, on strengthening the franc while resisting its re-evaluation upward, and on retaining France's competitive advantage in world markets. These shifts in priority responded to the yearnings of the French people. Foreign policy was to be the instrument, not the end, of the government's program. *Bonheur,* not *grandeur,* was the animating aim.

Paralleling these attempts to improve France's economic well-being and to widen the Gaullist party's stance at home were efforts by the Pompidou regime to broaden France's security, economic, and diplomatic alignments abroad. Shortly before President de Gaulle's resignation, there were signs of a significant widening of France's international posture. First, criticism of the United States, as the major disruptive force in international relations and as the principal, immediate threat to France's policy goals, was moderated. The United States, as the domestic and foreign crises of 1968 revealed, was still a potentially valuable partner in bolstering the shaky institutions of the Fifth Republic through its economic support during the fall monetary upheaval and through its encouragement of Soviet restraint in Europe. De Gaulle's attack on the United States, partly based on an acutely perceptive analysis of expanding United States power in the early and middle 1960's and partly rooted in progressively outdated emotional and psychic experiences of the 1940's, pitted France against the strongest state on the globe. Gaullist France, moreover, foreswore the potential benefits of drawing on American influence that greater accommodation of American power might have yielded. Gaullist France preferred to risk specific national aims and interests for the sake of larger, longer range systemic purposes. By 1969 it had become evident, however, that the United States, particularly in security affairs, had to be coaxed and cajoled to retain, not reduce, its previous commitments to defend Europe. Insulation against adverse American monetary and trade policies had to be sought, too, not only in the countervailing power of a cohesive EEC but also— and contrarily—in covert or open overtures for favored United States consideration. The latter expectation implied a willingness on the part of the French government in dealing with the United States to forego opportunities for developing a common European front when it suited France's interests and to strike a bargain, tacitly or directly, with Washington. There were also American investment possibilities to weigh and encourage. As President Pompidou's trip to the United States, his meeting with President Nixon in the Azores (1971) and Iceland (1973), and France's bargaining position in the Smithsonian monetary talks suggested, the United States was a potentially useful tool in strengthening France's economic position with its European partners. The tricky task was to reconcile increasingly incompatible goals: cooperation in Europe with the solicitations of favored American treatment.

Enlarging ties with its West European neighbors, including Britain, was another important Pompidou change in France's alignment structure. Britain's entry into the Common Market, as discussed in more detail above, served multiple purposes.[8] Relations with the Five immediately improved, setting the stage for final approval of a definitive financial regulation for agriculture. Britain's assumption of EEC obligations raised expectations that its economic and political ties with the United States would gradually loosen in favor of commonly defined European interests within the Brussels grouping. This slow evolutionary development could be expected to generate incentives for multiplying close British-European bonds that might eventually result in closer West European security cooperation. Meanwhile, Britain's entry opened new markets and afforded Europe new economic, scientific, and technological capabilities useful in meeting United

8. See Chapter 8, pp. 412–425.

States pressures and competition. Britain might be enticed to formulate its policies increasingly within a European context while its residual ties with the United States might serve as a hedge against precipitous United States military withdrawal from Europe. American sentiment and interest in foreign policy might still be retained in Europe's (and France's) employ. Britain was also to play a moderating role in Western Europe. Its traditional commitment to democratic government strengthened faltering Fifth Republic institutions. Its skill and weight, if diluting France's leadership possibilities in Western Europe as de Gaulle had feared, offset rising German power and independence. A Europe of the Nine, based on French confederal ideas, which were also congenial to British thinking, traditions, and public opinion, afforded Germany a plausible and attractive alternative for its energies and ambitions relative to the subordinate role assigned to it by the superpowers—either as a knight to their kings or as a dispensable pawn between them.

In playing on the West European chessboard, Pompidou's France chose completion and enlargement of the EEC over its institutional strengthening. Gaullist strategies, based on inflated estimates of France's negotiating leverage, had proven too confining and marginally beneficial. The considerations advising completion and enlargement over strengthening were persuasive. First, the differences among the West European states were too great to attach much weight to the possibility of constructing, in the immediate future, common European security, economic, or diplomatic positions toward third states.[9] Differences turned on the substantive value assigned to each policy area by the European states, the domestic and foreign policy strategies pursued by each to reach its defined objectives, and the amount and duration of domestic support, often subject to rapid and wide oscillation, that each could harness to its foreign policy goals. Second, the West European states, including France, looked in the immediate future to the United States and the Soviet Union for different forms of assistance relative to their divergent aims. Third, Pompidou's France was sensitive to American anxieties and Soviet fears of too cohesive and formidable a Western Europe.

9. These differences are even conceded by some of the most ardent and thoughtful proponents of the thesis of eventual European integration. See Lindberg and Scheingold, *Europe's Would-Be Polity*.

Too much a show of cooperation might prompt a counterproductive superpower reaction; too little cooperation might reduce Europe's potential weight in bargaining with the United States and the Soviet Union. The Pompidou regime tried to tread the line between these poles.

The Pompidou government, while employing a European rhetoric, still tended to follow the Gaullist practice of using Europe for narrow national and personal gain. On the surface, Pompidou's European policy appeared more credible than de Gaulle's. He encouraged speculations about a European minister and a political secretariat; he conceded marginal authority to the EEC Commission and the European Parliament; and he practiced the art of European summitry politics more than his predecessor. Operational French policy under Pompidou, however, did little to build or bolster traditional institutions within the EEC. It reasserted national control over France's diverse relations with other states and prompted the confederal development of the EEC through the Council of Ministers and the permanent representatives. The transnational and supranational solutions of the 1950's and 1960's, calculated to respond to interdependent state relations, were disciplined under the Pompidou administration to national integrative processes centered in the French presidency. The weak "Yes" given by the French in the April 1972 referendum suggested that domestic opinion was not disposed to go much beyond Gaullist reservations in supporting supranational institutions. It would be misleading, too, to suggest that President Pompidou looked with enthusiasm upon such a prospect. In calling for a referendum on the issue of British entry, he risked a negative reply and a halt in progress toward European integration. The European idea was in effect employed, not entirely successfully, as a handmaiden of the French president.

The broadening of France's Mediterranean base paralleled its approach to Western and Eastern Europe. The number of levels of conflicting alignments to be struck and managed were as complex and resistant to manipulation as those in Europe. There were the added problems of a larger number of actors in the region, the absence of multilateral organizations, like NATO and the EEC, to articulate, aggregate, and propose remedies for divergent state claims, and the greater volatility and emotional content of the political attitudes and issues troubling the region. First, the Soviet Union's presence had to be recognized and resisted. It had to be recognized as a Mediterranean power that France (and the West) had to accommodate; it had to be resisted as a potential security threat on France's southern flank and as a competitor for economic privilege and political influence among the Arab states. Second, the United States and France's West European partners appeared alternately as potential props for French policy in the area—recall France's overtures to the United States during the oil crisis with Algeria in 1970–1971 and modest EEC attempts to fashion a common Mediterranean policy—and as competitors for what benefits the region had to offer. Third, relations with the Arab states further complicated France's management of its conflicting relations with the regional actors. Algeria most pointedly exemplified the dilemma facing Paris in developing a coherent approach appropriate to the divisions of the region. Algeria, which was to have been France's gateway to the Third World, became an obstacle to better Third World relations and a handicap in constructing a more profitable network of market outlets for French products and of more assured sources for energy supplies. France's support for the Arab position in the Arab-Israeli dispute helped but did not assure French success in balancing conflicting Arab demands and sensitivities. There was, lastly, the Israeli-Arab conflict itself. Pompidou muted the harsher lines of French policy toward Israel, but as the Yom Kippur War suggested, the threat of violent eruption engulfing all of the interested states in the region, including France, could not be dismissed.

Changes in the diplomatic strategies pursued by the Pompidou administration complemented these shifts in France's alignment structure after de Gaulle's departure. Even before President de Gaulle's resignation, there were signs abroad of a significant reorientation in French policy. The Pompidou government carried forward these shifts, gave them sharper form, while attempting, as in its European and Mediterranean policies, to add new strings to the French bow. The Gaullist conception of international relations—of the incessant competition and conflict between states—was not abandoned. Rejected instead by the Pompidou administration were some of the dramatic strategems that its predecessor had employed to promote French interests.

The Pompidou government, first of all, accented regionalism over globalism. De Gaulle pictured France as a global power with special interests in Europe, the Mediterranean (particularly the Maghreb), and Black Africa. Until 1968, Gaullist France claimed to have global interests and an international role of proportional magnitude. Its regional concerns and its asserted pre-eminence in these areas derived from its world-wide stature. Regionalism followed globalism. Under Pompidou, France relied more on its regional presence and history than its pretended global standing to justify its right to be at any bargaining table that might be empaneled to make authoritative decisions for these areas. Its regional role allegedly placed its global claims on a new and more solid foundation, and not the reverse. France was a global power because it was first of all a regional power whose influence rested more on its skilled diplomacy, economic prowess, cultural superiority, and historical achievements than on its newly constructed and yet untried nuclear striking forces. For the Pompidou regime, globalism followed regionalism.

Within each region, moreover, there was a greater propensity in the Pompidou government to speak for France alone, and not act as the self-appointed spokesman for a region. On his return to Paris after his visit to the United States in March 1970, President Pompidou told the French public that "in Washington, I represented France, I did not represent Europe." [10] And when the French president spoke in Europe's name, as the Pompidou campaign for approval of the April 1972 referendum suggested, it did so on the implied authorization of the French nation. The success of a regional policy depended on the support of the French nation expressed in solemn referenda or in the election of its chief magistrate and legislators.

The Pompidou administration also upgraded French use of multilateral diplomacy. Overestimating France's modest material resources and his own persuasive skills, de Gaulle stressed direct power dealings and identified France's global status with the creation of a nuclear striking force. International authority was considered to have been earned, deriving fundamentally from France's capacity to defend its vital interests. France's permanent membership on the

10. *Le Monde,* March 14, 1970, p. 2.

Security Council ostensibly registered, in de Gaulle's reasoning, its uncontroverted strategic strength, political maturity, diplomatic virtuosity, and economic and social stability. Its authority was original, a product of its own efforts, past and present, and not conferred by the United Nations Charter, nor by its ties with other states.

The Gaullist approach conceded maneuverability to more powerful states to define their relations more as a matter of might than as a consequence of collectively defined right. It played into the hands of the superpowers, France's European partners, especially an economically strong and politically assertive Germany, and even smaller states, like Algeria, which had leverage in selected policy areas, like energy supplies. In a crude bilateral contest of will, France was at a disadvantage. Too great a stress on bilateral diplomacy to the exclusion of multilateral devices tended to magnify the influence of France's principal and more powerful opponents. Underemployed was the talent and experience of the Quai d'Orsay in diplomatic dealings. Multilateral diplomacy also had the virtue of ensnaring stronger states in political, legal, and moral obligations that limited their unilateral capacity to shape the international environment to suit their own views and interests. Decisions reached through multilateral processes hindered superpower capacity to ignore the claims of lesser powers like France. Through the assertion of their legal, if not material, equality, they increased their opportunity to influence big-power diplomacy.

The increased interest of the Pompidou administration in multilateral diplomacy was variously manifested. Initially following Gaullist practice, Pompidou's France stressed four-power accord as the proper instrument to decide Germany's future, including Berlin and intra-German relations. Implicitly reserved was a French demurrer over possible superpower decisions on Germany that might be reached over France's head. The four-power formula for peace in the Middle East was similarly stressed, and, accordingly, the Rogers plan, conceived outside a quadripartite framework, was resisted. Pompidou also tended to group states pragmatically in terms of France's immediate policy needs, as in the areas of civilian nuclear energy, investment, and monetary policy. Going further, the Pompidou government preferred, at least in early negotiations, to risk France's security interests within an elaborately defined and in-

tricately constructed European Conference on Security and Cooperation—including members of rival blocs and neutrals, all ostensibly sitting as independent powers—than to trust to the SALT talks
or to the NATO-Warsaw pact discussions over MBFR to protect its
vital concerns.

Participation in international organizations was also increasingly
emphasized. France under Pompidou discreetly assumed a more
vocal and visible role in NATO and WEU ministerial meetings. Witness its participation in the debates over NATO representation in
MBFR and its repeated affirmation of France's commitment to the
Atlantic Alliance. The Hague compromise of December 1969 and
France's increased participation in EEC policy circles offered additional evidence of a bent toward greater use of international institutions for national gain. Moreover, as the United States backed away
from the IMF, France stressed the utility of the organization as a
mechanism for reaching joint decisions on international monetary
policy.

This same pattern could be seen in French policy toward the
United Nations. Invidious Gaullist comparisons were dropped. "As
the United Nations becomes a scene of disturbance, confusions, and
division," said President de Gaulle in the midst of UN criticism of
the Algerian War, "it acquires the ambition to intervene in all kinds
of matters. . . . The result is that it carries to the local scene its
global incoherence." [11] Contrasting with the de Gaulle administration's low esteem for the world organization, Foreign Minister
Maurice Schumann in September 1970 made a special plea for its
strengthening.[12] In support of this policy line, the French-Soviet
protocol of October 1970, establishing a bilateral procedure for
regularized discussion of problems of mutual interest, called special
attention to the responsibilities of both states for global security under
the United Nations Charter.[13] Bilateral diplomacy was invoked to
support France's position in multilateral diplomatic maneuvering.

The superior status of the Security Council over the General As-

11. *Major Addresses,* p. 121.
12. *Le Figaro,* Sept. 19, 1970, p. 3. For a brief review of the French posture
in the United Nations under President Pompidou, consult *Le Monde,* Oct. 20,
1970, pp. 6–7.
13. *Le Figaro,* Oct. 14, 1970, p. 6.

sembly continued to be emphasized by Pompidou's France, but for different reasons than those advanced by de Gaulle. Whereas under de Gaulle, France's right to make authoritative decisions for the international community stood essentially outside the United Nations, to which was relegated the ceremonial task of sanctifying decisions taken elsewhere, the Pompidou government chided the superpowers, and particularly a reluctant United States, to accept the Security Council's paramount responsibility for world security. De Gaulle assigned such responsibility to those states possessing nuclear weapons. These fortuitously, by historical accident, were the five permanent members of the Security Council (including Communist China). The Pompidou regime, however, increasingly relied on France's possession of a permanent seat on the Security Council, resting on historical and legal credentials, to support France's right to participate in big-power decisions in the Mediterranean, in Europe, and in Africa. France's regional presence, manifested in its daily diplomacy, economic activity, security arrangements, and advanced cultural development, testified to its global status and to its right to a permanent Security Council seat. Regional presence and Security Council membership conspired to underwrite France's privileged international standing.

The widening of France's opportunities in bilateral and multilateral diplomacy necessitated depreciation of the de Gaulle tactic of the "empty chair." The utility of this technique rested on the assumption that France's material power, political importance, and moral stature were so critical that any international accord affecting France's interests was fatally defective unless Paris participated in its framing and execution. De Gaulle repeatedly cited the Yalta agreement to underline his meaning. So long as the major threat to international stability was the superpower conflict in which other states, including France, were stakes, not independent actors, an empty chair policy was nationally and systemically functional. It provided a means, however circumscribed, to limit France's involvement in the superpower struggle. But as the Cold War moderated and the prospects of superpower cooperation grew, the tactic of the open chair lost much of its effectiveness and rationale. By the late 1960's, as the outlines of a muted multipolar international system became clearer, France found itself progressively isolated or ignored in NATO, IMF, WEU, EEC, and UN deliberations. The superpowers and Germany forged ahead in a détente politics that had initially been given impetus by Gaullist France. It became obvious that, unless France modified its empty chair posture, it risked being confronted with *faits accomplis* that were potentially detrimental to its interests. Through greater participation in establishing international processes it could remind the United States, as in NATO ministerial convocations, of its European security interests and its obligations under the Atlantic Alliance to defend Europe. Within the IMF and under the auspices of GATT, France, joined by its European partners, could press the United States to adhere to its international trade obligations and to comply with IMF rules. The European banner was also useful to rally Germany, Britain, and France's other partners in its conception of a European Europe and to its policy views, particularly in developing a common front before the United States or the Soviet Union on terms responsive to French interests. De Gaulle's "empty chair" legacy survived principally in France's security negotiations with other states, including most notably MBFR and the moribund Geneva talks over disarmament. Its application even to these areas, as President Pompidou's pronouncements in Moscow during his January 1973 visit evidenced, were subject to relaxation if France would otherwise find itself isolated and disadvantaged and the Pompidou administration's domestic position weakened. Moreover, as Paris' increasingly pessimistic attitude toward the ECSC talks suggested, France's participation in a given international arena did not imply approval or commitment to the achievement of the announced goals of the gathering.

Changes in France's alignments and in its stratagems to manipulate them for its advantage suited President Pompidou's conception of political authority and his approach to coalition politics in domestic and foreign policy. Lacking de Gaulle's personal prestige and historical credentials, Pompidou explicitly defined his authority in terms of the confidence that the French electorate invested in him through referenda and elections. He claimed no reservoir of authority outside popular rule. President Pompidou also differed from his predecessor in his greater reliance on party and coalition politics to establish his national writ and influence. The cabinets under Jacques Chaban-Delmas and Pierre Messmer, Pompidou's two successive choices as prime minister, grouped Gaullists, Democratic Centrists under Jacques Duhamel, and Independent Republicans under Giscard d'Estaing to maintain a firm presidential hold on the National Assembly. De Gaulle's understanding of the source of his political authority transcended the domestic competition for power; Pompidou's was intrinsically tied to its outcome.

Ruling by factional and party coalitions served also, as Pompidou explained, as a model for his prescriptions about how a European Europe might eventually be constructed.[14] Enlarging the number of possible combinations of France's alignments and broadening the bilateral and multilateral base of French diplomatic strategy, within and outside international organizations, were necessary conditions for the building of coalitions in global politics that would assist French national aims and interests. De Gaulle's diplomacy, especially in its later forms, had constricted the possible groupings that could be feasibly contemplated or formed. On more than one occasion, de Gaulle's pronouncements and behavior, particularly as they affected the Anglo-American states, galvanized opposition to his proposals and initiatives. The Soames affair brought to light all of these unfortunate results of de Gaulle's approach to diplomacy. Pompidou's stance in regional and global politics was guided by the immediate objectives of maximizing the possible benefits of coalition politics, not in multiplying combinations against France, particularly those led or abetted by a superpower. Depending on the issues and stakes, French diplomacy under Pompidou was keyed to encourage that mix of states—in Europe, the Third World, or between the superpowers —that was calculated, pragmatically and opportunistically, to foster French needs of the moment. And, as the referendum on Europe of April 1972 suggested, France's participation in regional and world politics was forged as a tool for domestic welfare whose advancement was conceived as critical to political stability and presidential rule, institutional and personal.

President Pompidou's personal style in politics was also adapted to his notions of how domestic and foreign policy should be properly managed. De Gaulle's desire to command world attention, to create the very structure and terms of world politics, assumed softened form

14. Consult Chapter 8, pp. 425–438.

in President Pompidou. De Gaulle's striving for personal and political independence, the hallmarks of a charismatic leader, were no longer projected as an international screen through the medium of an eternal France. For Pompidou, the deed was as important as the word. For de Gaulle, the word and the heroic gesture, like Rostand's Cyrano de Bergerac, were of intrinsic worth, whether politically fruitful or futile. The tensions within de Gaulle's life, between authority and liberty, between dedication to tradition and to a free, malleable future, became in a way the model for the historic conflicts between rival states.[15] France, in Gaullist garb, was to be the protagonist of an endless human epic. The oracular pronouncements of the Elysée Palace and the contrived periodic news conferences gave verbal expression to the ongoing activity of the state. Personal and national redemption were found in perpetual artistic creativity.

In the Gaullist vision, a free France was both the instrument and embodiment of history. With the great powers, it decided the perennial questions of peace and war. De Gaulle synthesized the role of charismatic leader, calculating prince, and prescient poet in a drama that unfolded in his mind and was expressed in his and France's words, gestures, and actions before a world audience. "I amused them [the French] with flags," de Gaulle told Malraux, "I made them be patient while waiting for what, if not France." [16] Gaullist dramaturgy was the high theater of Strindberg's *A Dream Play,* where the creative poet was the protagonist. There was little room for the vacillation or moral ambiguity of Shakespeare's *Hamlet* or *Macbeth,* and certainly no place for the theater of boredom of Beckett's *Waiting for Godot.* So also did Gaullist France amuse the world while making it wait, too, for what, if not for France?

To Pompidou fell the role of Giraudoux' Hector, tired of battle and skeptical of the possibilities of armed conflict to perfect men and states. Better to conciliate or conform to the clashing views of others than to force an issue to the mutual disadvantage of all. Better to hold to what one has while bargaining for the rest, bidding and biding time to increase one's carefully husbanded store of wealth, status, and influence. Pompidou preferred to dicker than demand; to rule by

15. The most incisive treatment of this tension is found in Paul de la Gorce's biography, *De Gaulle.*
16. Malraux, *Les Chênes,* p. 23.

craft and compromise than by command. He was more sensitive to France's weaknesses than to its opportunities for initiative. To be sure, some of the Gaullist rhetoric of France's universal mission remained. This objective cannot be totally ignored in explaining French foreign policy behavior in the post-de Gaulle era. But the stress on concrete, tangible gains in international dealings was the touchstone for the Pompidou government's approach to foreign affairs. Material economic and political benefits were valued more than the flickering manifestations of national glory through dramatic refusals, psychologically satisfying perhaps, but of questionable political effect.

There was a lessened tendency, too, to strive to impress France's will on events rather than to draw as much profit as possible from the discrete manipulation of conflicts of other states. None of the changes commenced during the years of the Pompidou government suggested that the goals of a more decentralized global system and the reduction, if not the elimination of superpower influence, had been completely renounced. These objectives, however, were subordinated to more urgent domestic priorities and their realization was consigned to a distant future.

Presidents de Gaulle and Pompidou approached foreign policy from polar points. De Gaulle focused largely on systemic concerns, often sacrificing immediate national benefits that might have been drawn from the alignments struck with other states. This is not to say that his stewardship of French foreign policy cannot be criticized, as discussed above,[17] for advancing a conception of international politics that encouraged a volatile, competitive nationalism. De Gaulle's proposals were as potentially destabilizing and self-destructive as continued superpower conflict. However, he never carried his own teachings to their logical, if perversely political, conclusion, partly because of rigidities in his conduct of French diplomacy, partly because his pursuit of France's narrow national interests was informed by a systemic concern of overriding importance. He rarely lost sight of the epic proportions of his statecraft: peace and war.

President Pompidou worked on a smaller scale. He concentrated on exploiting the possibilities for national gain of multipolar politics. He focused his attention and France's resources on the real rewards

17. See above, pp. 567–579.

to be extracted from a better management of an increasing number and broadening range of France's ties with other states. In this sense, he was de Gaulle's *bon elève*. But preliminary evidence of France's policy toward the Atlantic, European, and Mediterranean states suggests that the Pompidou administration slighted the broader, systemic purposes, animating de Gaulle's opportunistic use of France's alignments with other states. De Gaulle's dealings in France's name for national advantage were not reducible solely to self-interested terms. They could not be understood apart from their systemic significance. On the other hand, Pompidou downplayed concern, temporarily at least, for what France might again contribute in the way of diagnostic criticism of the defects of the international system or what initiatives it might take, unilaterally or with others, to correct them. De Gaulle's vocally assertive and rhetorically dramatic nationalism aroused more than assured France's European partners. Pompidou's manipulative nationalism, veiled in the supranational slogans and symbols of a European Europe, attempted, through increased integration at a national level of France's diplomatic relations, to place French public opinion in a state of mind, psychologically and politically, to permit his government to reach and execute accords with its West European partners. Understandings had to be reached, too, with non-Gaullist elements of the Center and Right of the French political spectrum to broaden the regime's domestic power base. De Gaulle apparently had little taste for the accommodations and compromises that internal and external conditions in the late 1960's and 1970's imposed on French diplomacy and on the Paris government in advancing France's national and systemic aims. Pompidou's style was more adaptive than de Gaulle's to these new imperatives.[18]

De Gaulle was pessimistic about what he had accomplished in his rendering of France's *grandeur*. He apparently doubted the commitment of his successors to his vision of France's special responsibilities in the affairs of states. In his conversation with Malraux in December 1969, he already sensed the change: "What we wished—between you and me, why not give it its true name: grandeur—is finished. Oh!

18. Pierre Viansson-Ponté reviews Pompidou's life, careers, and personal style in a long and perceptive analysis published in *Le Monde* after the French president's death on April 2, 1974. See *Le Monde,* Sélection hebdomadaire, April 4–10, 1974, pp. 1–4.

France can still surprise the world; but later. She is going to negotiate everything. With the Americans and even the Russians, with
the Germans and the Communists. It has begun." [19]

De Gaulle's assessment of his regime's achievements may well prove
too pessimistic. The tests he applied were too parochial. Despite his
sense for the monumental in history and his acute consciousness of
his unique talents for statecraft, de Gaulle's personal and national
pride, not unlike Eliot's Thomas à Becket, still drove him to do the
right thing—to challenge superpower rule—for the wrong reasons.

If France's reach under de Gaulle was beyond its grasp, its contribution to our understanding of contemporary international relations and its criticism of the hazards of Cold War politics were not
without merit. De Gaulle's repeated assertions of France's power,
prestige, and privileged status obscured, ironically enough, the true
measure of *grandeur* earned for France under his administration: the
promotion of a safer and saner international order. In the absence
of Charles de Gaulle and his Fifth Republic, what other leader or
state was prepared to play the role of critic and judge of international
stability, legitimacy, and equity? For all the unfortunate omissions
and dubious commissions of French foreign policy in practice, it is
still difficult to resist the conclusion that had there been no Gaullist
France, it would have had to be invented.

19. Malraux, *Les Chênes,* p. 41.

Index of Sources

To assist the reader in checking citations, an index of most of the primary and secondary sources used in the work has been compiled. Newspapers, magazines, and other fugitive materials have not been included. Only works actually cited appear below.

Most of the documents are listed alphabetically by source. The number after an author's name or an official document indicates the page where the full citation appears. Where more than one article or book by an author is cited, a short title indicates the appropriate reference. Two exceptions should be noted. Heavily used serial documents, including *Politique étrangère de la France, L'Année politique,* and *French Foreign Policy,* and the annual political handbooks of the Western European Union, are listed alphabetically by title, not source. The sundry documents issuing irregularly from the Comité Interministériel under the French prime minister are listed alphabetically under these sources. The title of a work is given for an official document or a journal article whose author is unknown.

599

General Index

China, People's Republic of (*cont.*)
452, 492, 515, 550, 559, 592; conflict
with Soviet, 164, 240–241, 269, 345,
465, 560, 562, 579; influence of, 129,
340, 398; and Middle East, 516; recognition of, 51, 323, 560; threat of,
90, 124, 126; *see also* France
China, Republic of, 59, 113, 515
Churchill, Winston, 20, 278, 401, 583
Cold War, 11, 69, 70, 237, 372, 451, 488,
502, 579, 592; effects of, 45, 52, 179,
258, 264, 285, 418, 452; French desire
to end, 88, 239, 252–253, 255, 320,
322, 324, 341, 344, 352, 440, 568;
French on, 353, 555–560, 563, 567,
570; and Third World, 75, 526; U.S.
on, 237
Collective Reserve Units (CRU), 188,
189, 194–195
Colombey les Deux Eglises, 260–261
Colombo (Italian EEC Councilor), 333
Colonialism, 32, 37, 273, 447, 448, 449–
450, 451, 455, 464–465, 466, 477, 480,
580
Colons, Algerian, 453, 454–456, 457, 460,
461, 468, 471, 485
Comecon, 354
Commissariat de l'Enérgie Atomique
(CEA), 275
Commission, EEC, 49, 246–247, 273, 284,
286, 304, 405, 503; agriculture plan,
326, 327, 337, 405–406; authority of,
246, 274, 286, 288, 337, 338, 435;
budgetary policy, 332, 334, 337–338,
410; French on, 274, 284, 331, 334,
587; Pompidou on, 432, 433–434; role
in EEC enlargement, 385–386; tariff
policy, 277; *see also* European Economic Community (EEC)
Common Market, *see* European Economic Community (EEC)
Commonwealth, British, 278, 279, 299,
309, 310–311, 314, 315, 377, 379, 380,
409, 410, 411–412, 414, 421
Commonwealth Sugar Act, 410, 412
Communist parties: Egyptian, 542;
French, 23, 29, 33, 36, 38, 78, 253,
259, 353, 363, 432, 455; Soviet, 165;
Sudanese, 542; Western European, 395
Communities, European, 15, 354; benefits of, 246, 328; and federalists, 248,
250; French and, 241, 242, 261, 262,
292, 293, 304, 315, 340; fusion of executives, 306, 318; Germany and, 261–
262, 342; Netherlands in, 302; policies,
294, 302–303, 304; success, 308; threats
to, 297; *see also* European Coal and
Steel Community, European Defense
Community, European Economic Community, *and* Euratom
Compte de Saxe, Maurice, 98
Confederation, European, 242, 244–247,

262, 291, 303, 304, 321, 328, 331, 332,
336, 337, 347, 399, 427, 586
Conference on Security and Cooperation
in Europe, 155
Congo, 49, 79–80, 163, 449, 458, 466,
493, 510, 556
Connally, John, 217–218, 223
Constantine plan, 480
Coordinating Committee, Group of Ten,
221
Copenhagen, 230, 437
Council of Ministers, EEC: agricultural
policy, 220, 328, 406; on British EEC
entry, 383; Dutch and, 304; French
and, 331, 333, 433, 587; on Greece,
523; monetary policy, 225, 437; plans
for, 294, 295, 297; powers, 246–247,
298, 308, 317, 327, 332, 333, 334, 337,
388, 434–435; trade policy, 273, 282,
283, 284; voting policy, 331–332, 335
Council of Ministers, French, 32, 369
Coup d' état of May 1958, 251
Court of Guarantees, 471
Court of Justice, European, 298
Couve de Murville, Maurice: and de
Gaulle, 19
—policies: agricultural, 330; détente,
344, 353, 370; disarmament, 134; European union, 292; North African,
130; trade, 369
—policy toward: Atlantic Alliance, 132;
EEC, 284, 327, 333, 334; Great Britain, 202, 299–300, 382, 383, 407;
NATO, 92, 112–113; Soviet, 322, 366,
367; West Germany, 271, 293, 359
Credit, international, 179, 190
Cuba, 113, 463, 464, 465, 466, 556, 557–
558, 567, 580
Cuban missile crisis, 86–87, 90, 92, 115–
116, 123, 132, 272, 452, 557–558, 575,
579
Cultural aid, 478, 486, 523, 524–525,
529, 535, 539, 548
Cultural exchange, 321, 364, 369, 399,
557
Customs union, 326
Czechoslovakia, 69, 75, 88, 89, 135, 320,
329, 366, 367, 368, 369, 374, 394; Soviet invasion, 38, 71, 87, 89, 90, 139,
151, 176, 208, 257, 340, 351–352, 362,
375, 393, 394, 399, 442, 476, 491, 513,
562, 563, 564, 580
Czyrankiewicz, Joseph (Polish president),
367

Daddah, Ould, 466
Dairy products, 289, 290, 311, 379, 408,
410, 412, 414
Davignon plan, 443, 510
Debré, Michel, 243; and de Gaulle, 19
—policies: British EEC entry, 407, 431;
defense, 121, 145, 147, 151–152, 173;

**French International Policy
under de Gaulle and Pompidou**

Designed by R. E. Rosenbaum.
Composed by The Colonial Press Inc.
in 10 point linotype Times Roman, 3 points leaded,
with display lines in Optima Semibold.
Printed letterpress from type by The Colonial Press.
Bound by The Colonial Press
in Columbia book cloth
and stamped in All Purpose foil.